Do your students come to class prepared?

How do you hold your students accountable?

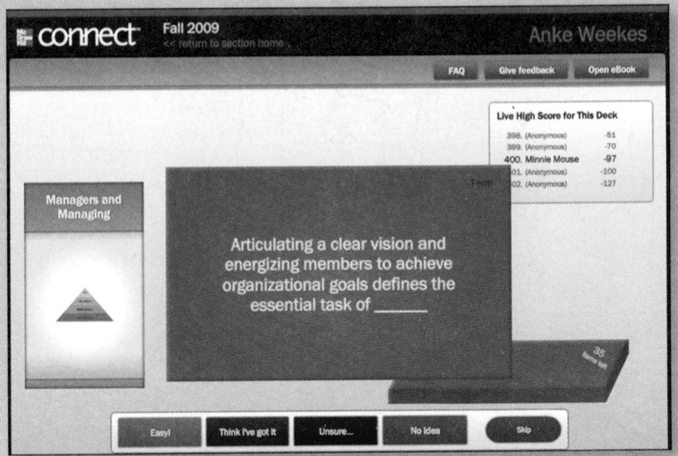

Based on students' self-diagnoses of their proficiency, *LearnSmart* intelligently provides students with a series of adaptive questions. This provides students with a personalized one-on-one tutor experience.

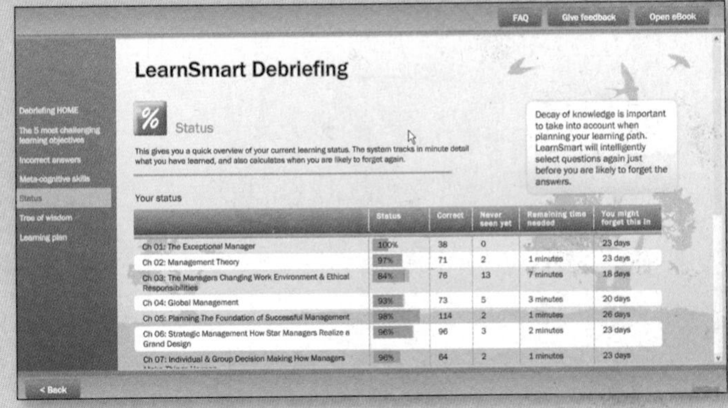

You can incorporate *LearnSmart* into your course in a number of ways to...

- Gauge student knowledge before a lecture
- Reinforce learning after a lecture
- Prepare students for assignments and exams

Connect Management powered by *LearnSmart* provides the following Instructor Benefits

- Holds your students accountable and tracks progress
- Assignments are automatically graded
- Students are better prepared for class
- Materials are directly related to textbook and course
- Improves comprehension

Connect Management powered by *LearnSmart* provides the following Student Benefits

- Fun, motivating, and engaging way to learn
- Saves time: efficient and effective way to study
- Improves student grade
- Reinforces concepts

Discover for yourself how *Connect Management* ensures students will **connect** with the content, learn more effectively, and **succeed** in your course.

Essentials of Contemporary Management

Fourth Edition

Gareth R. Jones
Texas A&M University

Jennifer M. George
Rice University

McGraw-Hill
Irwin

ESSENTIALS OF CONTEMPORARY MANAGEMENT

Published by McGraw-Hill/Irwin, a business unit of The McGraw-Hill Companies, Inc., 1221 Avenue of the Americas, New York, NY, 10020.

Some ancillaries, including electronic and print components, may not be available to customers outside the United States.

This book is printed on acid-free paper.

4 5 6 7 8 9 0 DOW/DOW 1 0 9 8 7 6 5 4 3 2 1

ISBN 978-0-07-813722-8
MHID 0-07-813722-5

Vice president and editor-in-chief: *Brent Gordon*
Publisher: *Paul Ducham*
Executive editor: *Michael Ablassmeir*
Director of development: *Ann Torbert*
Development editor: *Kelly I. Pekelder*
Editorial assistant: *Andrea Heirendt*
Vice president and director of marketing: *Robin J. Zwettler*
Executive marketing manager: *Anke Braun Weekes*
Vice president of editing, design, and production: *Sesha Bolisetty*
Senior project manager: *Bruce Gin*
Lead production supervisor: *Michael R. McCormick*
Designer: *Cara Hawthorne, cara david DESIGN*
Senior photo research coordinator: *Lori Kramer*
Photo researcher: *Teri Stratford*
Media project manager: *Jennifer Lohn*
Typeface: *10.25/12 Baskerville*
Compositor: *Laserwords Private Limited*
Printer: *R. R. Donnelley*

Library of Congress Cataloging-in-Publication Data

Jones, Gareth R.
Essentials of contemporary management / Gareth R. Jones, Jennifer M. George.–4th ed.
p. cm.
Includes bibliographical references and index.
ISBN-13: 978-0-07-813722-8 (alk. paper)
ISBN-10: 0-07-813722-5 (alk. paper)
1. Management. I. George, Jennifer M. II. Title.
HD31.J5974 2011
658–dc22

2009043309

www.mhhe.com

Brief Contents

Contents

Part One Management and Managers

Chapter One

Chapter Two

Management in Action

Management in Action

Contents

Chapter Three

Chapter Four

Contents

Contents

Management in Action

Management in Action

Contents

Management in Action

Management in Action

Contents

Chapter Eleven Effective Team Management 356

Chapter Twelve Building and Managing Human Resources 388

Contents

Preface

In the fourth edition of our book, *Essentials of Contemporary Management,* we keep to our theme of providing students with the most contemporary and up-to-date account of the changing environment of management and management practices. In revising our book, we continue to strive to make our text relevant and interesting to students. And we know from feedback we have received from instructors and students that the text does engage them. It encourages them to make the effort necessary to assimilate the text material because they find it useful and relevant. We continue to mirror the changes taking place in management practices by incorporating recent developments in management theory into our text and by providing vivid, current examples of the way managers of well-known companies–large and small–have responded to the dramatic changes in the economy that have been taking place. Indeed, we have increased our focus on small businesses in the revised edition and have integrated many more examples of the problems these companies face into the text.

Of course, the number and complexity of the strategic, organizational, and human resource challenges facing managers and all employees have continued to increase since the economic recession that started in 2007. In most companies, managers at all levels are playing "catch-up" as they work toward meeting these challenges by implementing new and improved management techniques and practices just as they have been forced to downsize and lay off millions of employees. In today's highly competitive business environment even relatively small differences in performance between companies–for example, in the speed at which they can bring new products or services to market or in the ways they motivate their employees to find ways to reduce costs or improve performance–can combine to give one company a significant competitive advantage over another. Managers and companies that utilize proven management techniques and practices in their decision making and actions increase their effectiveness over time. Companies and managers that are slower to implement new management techniques and practices find themselves at a growing competitive disadvantage that makes it even more difficult to catch up. Thus, in many industries there is a widening gap between the most successful companies whose performance reaches new heights and their weaker competitors, because their managers have made better decisions about how to use a company's resources in the most efficient and effective ways.

The challenges facing managers continue to mount as changes in the global environment such as increasing global outsourcing and rising commodity prices impact organizations, large and small. Moreover, the revolution in information technology has transformed the way managers make decisions across all levels of a company's hierarchy and across all its functions and global divisions. This fourth edition of our book addresses these emerging challenges. For example, we extend our treatment of global outsourcing and examine the many managerial issues that must be addressed when millions of functional jobs in information technology, customer service, and manufacturing are being sent to countries overseas. Similarly, increasing globalization means that managers must respond to the effects of major differences in the legal rules and regulations and ethical values and norms that prevail in countries around the globe.

Other major challenges we continue to expand on in the new fourth edition include the impact of the steadily increasing diversity of the workforce on companies and how this increasing diversity makes it imperative for managers to understand how and why people differ so that they can effectively manage and reap the performance benefits of diversity. Similarly, across all functions and levels, managers and employees must continuously search out ways to "work smarter" and increase performance. Using new information technology to improve all aspects of an organization's operations to enhance efficiency and customer responsiveness is a vital part of this process. So too is the continuing need to innovate and improve the quality of goods and services, and the ways they are produced, to allow an organization to compete effectively. We have significantly revised the fourth edition of *Essentials of Contemporary Management* to address these challenges to managers and their organizations.

Major Content Changes

We have not altered the organization of our chapters in this new edition; they follow the same sequence. Instructors tell us that they like the chapter changes we made last time and that they improved the learning experience. For example, instructors approve of the way we integrated our coverage of entrepreneurship into Chapter 5, "Decision Making, Learning, Creativity, and Entrepreneurship," because it complements the discussion of creativity and allows us to discuss the many different issues involved in effective decision making over time. At the same time, our three-chapter sequence on strategy, structure, and control systems to improve competitive advantage was well received. But once again, encouraged by the increasing number of instructors and students who are using our book with each new edition, and based on the reactions and suggestions of both users and reviewers, we have revised and updated our book in the following ways.

CONTINUALLY UPDATED RESEARCH CONCEPTS First, just as we have included pertinent new research concepts in each chapter, so we have been careful to eliminate outdated or marginal management concepts. As usual, our goal has been to streamline our presentation and keep the focus on the changes that have been taking place that have the most impact on managers and organizations. Our goal is not to have students study too many, too long chapters just for the sake of including all outmoded management theory. In today's world of video downloads, sound bites, and text messaging less is often more–especially when students are often burdened by time pressures stemming from the need to work long hours at paying jobs. Second, we have added significant new management content in most of the chapters and have reinforced their importance by using many new relevant small and large company examples that are described in the all-new chapter opening cases, "Management Snapshots," in the many boxed illustrations inside each chapter, and in the new (mainly from 2009) "*BusinessWeek* Case in the News" closing cases.

We feel confident that the major changes we have made to the fourth edition of *Essentials of Contemporary Management* reflect the changes that are occurring in management and the workplace; we also feel they offer an account of management that will stimulate and challenge students to think about their future in the world of organizations.

EMPHASIS ON APPLIED MANAGEMENT Our contemporary approach also is illustrated by the way we have chosen to organize and discuss contemporary management issues. We have gone to great lengths to bring the manager back into the subject matter of management. That is, we have written our chapters from the perspective of current or future managers to illustrate, in a hands-on way, the problems and opportunities they face and how they can effectively meet them. For example, in Chapter 3 we provide an integrated treatment of ethics and diversity that clearly explains their significance to practicing managers. In Chapter 6, we provide an integrated treatment of planning, strategy, and competitive advantage, highlighting the crucial choices managers face as they go about performing the planning role. Throughout the text, we emphasize important issues managers face and how management theory, research, and practice can help them and their organizations be effective.

This applied approach can also be clearly seen in the last two chapters of the book that cover the topics of managing information systems, technology, and operations management, topics that have tended to be difficult to teach to new management students in an interesting and novel way. Our chapters provide a student-friendly, behavioral approach to understanding the management processes entailed in information systems and operations management. As our reviewers noted, while most books' treatment of these issues is dry and quantitative, ours comes alive with its focus on how managers can manage the people and processes necessary to give an organization a competitive advantage.

FLEXIBLE ORGANIZATION Another factor of interest to instructors is the way we have designed the grouping of chapters to allow instructors to teach the chapter material in the order that best suits their needs. Instructors are not tied to the planning, organizing, leading, controlling framework, even though our presentation remains consistent with this approach.

Acknowledgments

Finding a way to integrate and present the rapidly growing literature on contemporary management and make it interesting and meaningful for students is not an easy task. In writing and revising the several drafts of *Essentials of Contemporary Management,* we have been fortunate to have had the assistance of several people who have contributed greatly to the book's final form. First, we are grateful to Michael Ablassmeir, our executive editor, for his support and commitment to our project, and for always finding ways to provide the resources that we needed to continually improve and refine our book. Second, we are grateful to Kelly Pekelder, our developmental editor, for so ably coordinating the book's progress, and to her and Anke Braun Weekes, our marketing manager, for providing us with concise and timely feedback and information from professors and reviewers that have allowed us to shape the book to the needs of its intended market. We also thank Cara Hawthorne for executing an awe-inspiring design and Bruce Gin for coordinating the production process. We are also grateful to the many colleagues and reviewers who provided us with useful and detailed feedback, perceptive comments, and valuable suggestions for improving the manuscript.

Producing any competitive work is a challenge. Producing a truly market-driven textbook requires tremendous effort beyond simply obtaining reviews on a draft manuscript. Our goal behind the development of *Essentials of Contemporary Management* has been clear-cut: to be the most customer-driven essentials of management text and supplement package ever published! The favorable reception that our book has received from its users suggests that our thorough product development plan did lead to a book that has met the expectations of both faculty and students. For the new edition, we have continued to add new reviewers to the over 200 faculty who originally took part in developmental activities ranging from regional focus groups to manuscript reviews and surveys. Consequently, we're confident that the changes we have made to our book and its excellent support package will even more closely meet your expectations and needs.

Our thanks to these faculty who have contributed greatly to *Essentials of Contemporary Management:*

Garry Adams, *Auburn University*
M. Ruhul Amin, *Bloomsburg University of Pennsylvania*
Fred Anderson, *Indiana University of Pennsylvania*
Jacquelyn Appeldorn, *Dutchess Community College*
Barry Armandi, *SUNY–Old Westbury*
Dave Arnott, *Dallas Baptist University*
Debra Arvanites, *Villanova University*
Douglas E. Ashby, *Lewis & Clark Community College*
Joe Atallah, *Devry University*
Kenneth E. Aupperle, *The University of Akron*
Barry S. Axe, *Florida Atlantic University*
Andrea D. Bailey, *Moraine Valley Community College*
Jeff Bailey, *University of Idaho*
Robert M. Ballinger, *Siena College*
Moshe Banai, *Bernard M, Baruch College*
Frank Barber, *Cuyahoga Community College*
Reuel Barksdale, *Columbus State Community College*
Sandy Jeanquart Barone, *Murray State University*
Lorraine P. Bassette, *Prince George's Community College*
Gene Baten, *Central Connecticut State University*
Myra Jo Bates, *Bellevue University*
Josephine Bazan, *Holyoke Community College*
Hrach Bedrosian, *New York University*
Omar Belkhodja, *Virginia State University, School of Business*
James Bell, *Texas State University–San Marcos*
Ellen A. Benowitz, *Mercer County Community College*
Stephen Betts, *William Paterson University*
Jack C. Blanton, *University of Kentucky*
David E. Blevins, *University of Arkansas at Little Rock*
Mary Jo Boehms, *Jackson State Community College*
Karen Boroff, *Seton Hall University*
Jennifer Bowers, *Florida State University*
Barbara Boyington, *Brookdale Community College*
Dan Bragg, *Bowling Green State University*
Charles Braun, *Marshall University*
Dennis Brode, *Sinclair Community College*
Gil Brookins, *Siena College*
Murray Brunton, *Central Ohio Technical College*
Patricia M. Buhler, *Goldey-Beacom College*
Judith G. Bulin, *Monroe Community College*
David Cadden, *Quinnipiac College*
Thomas Campbell, *University of Texas–Austin*
Thomas Carey, *Western Michigan University*

Barbara Carlin, *University of Houston*
Daniel P. Chamberlin, *Regents University–CRB*
Larry Chasteen, *Stephen F. Austin State University*
Raul Chavez, *Eastern Mennonite University*
Nicolette De Ville Christensen, *Guilford College*
Anthony A. Cioffi, *Lorain County Community College*
Sharon F. Clark, *Lebanon Valley College*
Sharon Clinebell, *University of Northern Colorado*
Dianne Coleman, *Wichita State University*
Elizabeth Cooper, *University of Rhode Island*
Anne Cowden, *California State University–Sacramento*
Thomas D. Craven, *York College of Pennsylvania*
Kent Curran, *University of North Carolina*
Arthur L. Darrow, *Bowling Green State University*
Tom Deckelman, *Walsh College*
D. Anthony DeStadio, *Pittsburgh Technical Institute*
Ron DiBattista, *Bryant College*
Thomas Duening, *University of Houston*
Charles P. Duffy, *Iona College*
Steve Dunphy, *The University of Akron*
Subhash Durlabhji, *Northwestern State University*
Robert A. Eberle, *Iona College*
Karen Eboch, *Bowling Green State University*
Robert R. Edwards, *Arkansas Tech University*
Susan Eisner, *Ramapo College of New Jersey*
William Eldridge, *Kean College*
Pat Ellsberg, *Lower Columbia College*
Stan Elsea, *Kansas State University*
Scott Elston, *Iowa State University*
Judson Faurer, *Metro State College of Denver*
Dale Finn, *University of New Haven*
Charles Flaherty, *University of Minnesota*
Alisa Fleming, *University of Phoenix*
Lucinda Fleming, *Orange County Community College*
Robert Flemming, *Delta State University*
Jeanie M. Forray, *Eastern Connecticut State University*
Marilyn L. Fox, *Minnesota State University, Mankato*
Ellen Frank, *Southern Connecticut State University*
Joseph A. Gemma, *Providence College*
Neal Gersony, *University of New Haven*
Donna H. Giertz, *Parkland College*
Leo Giglio, *Dowling College*
David Glew, *Texas A&M University*
Carol R. Graham, *Western Kentucky University*
Matthew Gross, *Moraine Valley Community College*
John Hall, *University of Florida*
Eric L. Hansen, *California State University–Long Beach*
Justin U. Harris, *Strayer College*
Allison Harrison, *Mississippi State University*
Sandra Hartman, *University of New Orleans*
Brad D. Hays, *North Central State College*
Gary Hensel, *McHenry Community College*
Robert A. Herring III, *Winston-Salem State University*
Eileen Bartels Hewitt, *University of Scranton*
Stephen R. Hiatt, *Catawba College*
Tammy Bunn Hiller, *Bucknell University*
Adrienne Hinds, *Northern Virginia Community College*
Anne Kelly Hoel, *University of Wisconsin–Stout*
Eileen Hogan, *Kutztown University*
Jerry Horgesheiner, *Southern Utah State*
Gordon K. Huddleston, *South Carolina State University*
John Hughes, *Texas Tech University*
Larry W. Hughes, *University of Nebraska at Kearney*
Tammy Hunt, *University of North Carolina–Wilmington*
Gary S. Insch, *West Virginia University*
Charleen Jaeb, *Cuyahoga Community College*
Velma Jesser, *Lane Community College*
Richard E. Johe, *Salem College*
Gwendolyn Jones, *The University of Akron*
Kathy Jones, *University of North Dakota*
Marybeth Kardatzke, *North Harris Montgomery Community College District*
Jim Katzenstein, *California State University–Dominguez Hills*
Jehan G. Kavoosi, *Clarion University of Pennsylvania*
Robert J. Keating, *University of North Carolina at Wilmington*
Frank Khoury, *Berkeley College*
Peggi Koenecke, *California State University–Sacramento*
Donald Kopka, *Towson University*
Dennis Lee Kovach, *Community College of Allegheny County–North Campus*
Mark Kunze, *Virginia State University*
Ken Lehmenn, *Forsyth Technical Community College*
Lianlian Lin, *California State Polytechnic University*
Grand Lindstrom, *University of Wyoming*
John Lipinski, *Robert Morris University*
Mary Lou Lockerby, *College of DuPage*
Esther Long, *University of Florida*
E. Geoffrey Love, *University of Illinois*
George S. Lowry, *Randolph-Macon College*

George E. Macdonald Jr., *Laredo Community College*
Bryan Malcolm, *University of Wisconsin*
Z. A. Malik, *Governors State University*
Mary J. Mallott, *George Washington University*
Christine Marchese, *Nassau Community College*
Jennifer Martin, *York College of Pennsylvania*
Lisa McCormick, *Community College of Allegheny County*
Reuben McDaniel, *University of Texas*
Robert L. McKeage, *The University of Scranton*
John A. Miller, *Bucknell University*
Richard R. J. Morin, *James Madison University*
Don Moseley, *University of South Alabama–Mobile*
Behnam Nakhai, *Millersville University of Pennsylvania*
Robert D. Nale, *Coastal Carolina University*
Daniel F. Nehring, *Morehead State University*
Thomas C. Neil, *Clark Atlanta University*
Brian Niehoff, *Kansas State University*
Judy Nixon, *University of Tennessee*
Cliff Olson, *Southern Adventists University*
Karen Overton, *HCC–Northeast College*
Ralph W. Parrish, *University of Central Oklahoma*
Dane Partridge, *University of Southern Indiana*
Sheila J. Pechinski, *University of Maine*
Marc Pendel, *Ball State University*
Fred Pierce, *Northwood University*
Mary Pisnar, *Baldwin Wallace College*
Laynie Pizzolatto, *Nicholls State University*
Eleanor Polster, *Florida International University*
Paul Preston, *University of Texas–San Antonio*
Samuel Rabinowitz, *Rutgers University–Camden*
Gerald Ramsey, *Indiana University Southeast*
Charles Rarick, *Transylvania University*
Deana K. Ray, *Forsyth Technical Community College*
Robert A. Reber, *Western Kentucky University*
Bob Redick, *Lincoln Land Community College*
Douglas Richardon, *Eastfield College*
Tina L. Robbins, *Clemson University*
Deborah Britt Roebuck, *Kennesaw State University*
Harvey Rothenberg, *Regis University*
Catherine Ruggieri, *St. John's University*
George Ruggiero, *Community College of Rhode Island*
Kathleen Rust, *Elmhurst College*
Robert Rustic, *University of Findlay*
Cyndy Ruszkowski, *Illinois State University*
Nestor St. Charles, *Dutchess Community College*
Lynda St. Clair, *Bryant College*
Michael Santoro, *Rutgers University*
John L. Schmidt Jr., *George Mason University*
Gerald Schoenfeld Jr., *James Madison University*
Don Schreiber, *Baylor University*
Robert Schwartz, *University of Toledo*
Amit Shah, *Frostburg State University*
Michael Shapiro, *Dowling College*
Raymond Shea, *Monroe Community College*
Richard Ray Shreve, *Indiana University Northwest*
Sidney Siegel, *Drexel University*
Thomas D. Sigerstad, *Frostburg State University*
Roy L. Simerly, *East Carolina University*
Randi L. Sims, *Nova Southeastern University*
Sharon Sloan, *Northwood University*
Erika E. Small, *Coastal Carolina University*
Brien Smith, *Ball State University*
Marjorie Smith, *Mountain State University*
Raymond D. Smith, *Towson State University*
William A. Sodeman, *University of Southern Indiana*
Carl J. Sonntag, *Pikes Peak Community College*
Robert W. Sosna, *Menlo College*
William Soukup, *University of San Diego*
Rieann Spence-Gale, *Northern Virginia Community College–Alexandria Campus*
H. T. Stanton Jr., *Barton College*
Jerry Stevens, *Texas Tech University*
William A. Stoever, *Seton Hall University*
Charles I. Stubbart, *Southern Illinois University at Carbondale*
James K. Swenson, *Moorhead State University*
Karen Ann Tarnoff, *East Tennessee State University*
Jerry L. Thomas, *Arapahoe Community College*
Joe Thomas, *Middle Tennessee State University*
Kenneth Thompson, *DePaul University*
John Todd, *University of Arkansas*
Thomas Turk, *Chapman University*
Isaiah Ugboro, *North Carolina A & T University*
Linn Van Dyne, *Michigan State University*
Jaen Vanhoegaerden, *Ashridge Management College*
Barry L. Van Hook, *Arizona State University*
Gloria Walker, *Florida Community College*
Stuart H. Warnock, *University of Southern Colorado*
Toomy Lee Waterson, *Northwood University*
Philip A. Weatherford, *Embry-Riddle Aeronautical University*
Ben Weeks, *St. Xavier University*
Emilia S. Westney, *Texas Tech University*
Donita Whitney-Bammerlin, *Kansas State University*
Robert Williams, *University of North Alabama*

W. J. Williams, *Chicago State University*
Shirley A. Wilson, *Bryant College*
Robert H. Woodhouse, *University of St. Thomas*
Michael A. Yahr, *Robert Morris College*
D. Kent Zimmerman, *James Madison University*

Finally, we are grateful to two incredibly wonderful children, Nicholas and Julia, for being all that they are and for the joy they bring to all who know them.

Gareth R. Jones
Mays College of Business, Texas A&M University

Jennifer M. George
Jesse H. Jones Graduate School of Business, Rice University

Authors

Gareth Jones is a Professor of Management in the Lowry Mays College and Graduate School of Business at Texas A&M University. He received his B.A. in Economics/Psychology and his Ph.D. in Management from the University of Lancaster, U.K. He previously held teaching and research appointments at the University of Warwick, Michigan State University, and the University of Illinois at Urbana-Champaign. He is a frequent visitor and speaker at universities in both the United Kingdom and the United States.

He specializes in strategic management and organizational theory and is well known for his research that applies transaction cost analysis to explain many forms of strategic and organizational behavior. He is currently interested in strategy process, competitive advantage, and information technology issues. He is also investigating the relationships between ethics, trust, and organizational culture and studying the role of affect in the strategic decision-making process.

He has published many articles in leading journals of the field, and his recent work has appeared in the *Academy of Management Review,* the *Journal of International Business Studies,* and *Human Relations.* An article on the role of information technology in many aspects of organizational functioning was published in the *Journal of Management.* One of his articles won the *Academy of Management Journal*'s Best Paper Award, and he is one of the most prolific authors in the *Academy of Management Review.* He is or has served on the editorial boards of the *Academy of Management Review,* the *Journal of Management,* and *Management Inquiry.*

Gareth Jones has taken his academic knowledge and used it to craft leading textbooks in management and three other major areas in the management discipline: organizational behavior, organizational theory, and strategic management. His books are widely recognized for their innovative, contemporary content and for the clarity with which they communicate complex, real-world issues to students.

Jennifer George is the Mary Gibbs Jones Professor of Management and Professor of Psychology in the Jesse H. Jones Graduate School of Business at Rice University. She received her B.A. in Psychology/Sociology from Wesleyan University, her M.B.A. in Finance from New York University, and her Ph.D. in Management and Organizational Behavior from New York University. Prior to joining the faculty at Rice University, she was a Professor in the Department of Management at Texas A&M University.

Professor George specializes in organizational behavior and is well known for her research on mood and emotion in the workplace, their determinants, and their effects on various individual and group-level work outcomes. She is the author of many articles in leading peer-reviewed journals such as the *Academy of Management Journal,* the *Academy of Management Review,* the *Journal of Applied Psychology, Organizational Behavior and Human Decision Processes, Journal of Personality and Social Psychology,* and *Psychological Bulletin.* One of her papers won the Academy of Management's Organizational Behavior Division Outstanding Competitive Paper Award, and another paper won the *Human Relations* Best Paper Award. She is, or has been, on the editorial review boards of the *Journal of Applied Psychology, Academy of Management Journal, Academy of Management Review, Administrative Science Quarterly, Journal of Management, Organizational Behavior and Human Decision Processes, Organizational Science, International Journal of Selection and Assessment,* and *Journal of Managerial Issues;* was a consulting editor for the *Journal of Organizational Behavior;* and was a member of the SIOP *Organizational Frontiers Series* editorial board. She is a Fellow in the American Psychological Association, the American Psychological Society, and the Society for Industrial and Organizational Psychology and a member of the Society for Organizational Behavior. Professor George recently completed a six-year term as an associate editor for the *Journal of Applied Psychology.* She also has coauthored a widely used textbook titled *Understanding and Managing Organizational Behavior.*

Guided Tour

Rich and Relevant Examples An important feature of our book is the way we use real-world examples and stories about managers and companies to drive home the applied lessons to students. Our reviewers were unanimous in their praise of the sheer range and depth of the rich, interesting examples we use to illustrate the chapter material and make it come alive. Moreover, unlike boxed material in other books, our boxes are seamlessly integrated into the text; they are an integral part of the learning experience, and not tacked on or isolated from the text itself. This is central to our pedagogical approach.

A **Management Snapshot** opens each chapter, posing a chapter-related challenge and then discussing how managers in one or more organizations responded to that challenge. These vignettes help demonstrate the uncertainty and excitement surrounding the management process.

Our box features are not traditional boxes; that is, they are not disembodied from the chapter narrative. These thematic applications are fully integrated into the reading. Students will no longer be forced to decide whether or not to read boxed material. These features are interesting and engaging for students while bringing the chapter contents to life.

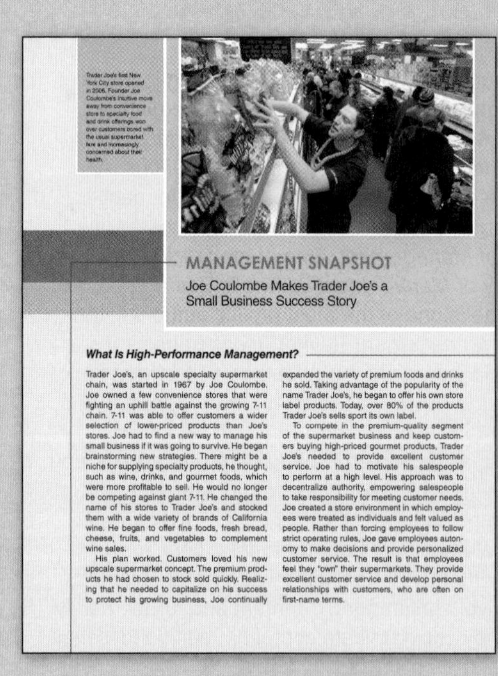

Trader Joe's first New York City store opened in 2006. Founder Joe Coulombe's intuitive move away from convenience store to specialty food and drink offerings won over customers bored with the usual supermarket fare and increasingly concerned about their health.

MANAGEMENT SNAPSHOT

Joe Coulombe Makes Trader Joe's a Small Business Success Story

What Is High-Performance Management?

Trader Joe's, an upscale specialty supermarket chain, was started in 1967 by Joe Coulombe. Joe owned a few convenience stores that were fighting an uphill battle against the growing 7-11 chain. 7-11 was able to offer customers a wider selection of lower-priced products than Joe's stores. Joe had to find a new way to manage his small business if it was going to survive. He began brainstorming new strategies. There might be a niche for supplying specialty products, he thought, such as wine, drinks, and gourmet foods, which were more profitable to sell. He would no longer be competing against giant 7-11. He changed the name of his stores to Trader Joe's and stocked them with a wide variety of brands of California wine. He began to offer fine foods, fresh bread, cheese, fruits, and vegetables to complement wine sales.

His plan worked. Customers loved his new upscale supermarket concept. The premium products he had chosen to stock sold quickly. Realizing that he needed to capitalize on his success to protect his growing business, Joe continually expanded the variety of premium foods and drinks he sold. Taking advantage of the popularity of the name Trader Joe's, he began to offer his own store label products. Today, over 80% of the products Trader Joe's sells sport its own label.

To compete in the premium-quality segment of the supermarket business and keep customers buying high-priced gourmet products, Trader Joe's needed to provide excellent customer service. Joe had to motivate his salespeople to perform at a high level. His approach was to decentralize authority, empowering salespeople to take responsibility for meeting customer needs. Joe created a store environment in which employees were treated as individuals and felt valued as people. Rather than forcing employees to follow strict operating rules, Joe gave employees autonomy to make decisions and provide personalized customer service. The result is that employees feel they "own" their supermarkets. They provide excellent customer service and develop personal relationships with customers, who are often on first-name terms.

MANAGEMENT INSIGHT

Different Ways to Compete in the Soft-Drink Business

"Coke" and "Pepsi" are household names worldwide. Together, Coca-Cola and PepsiCo control over 70% of the global soft-drink market and over 75% of the U.S. soft-drink market. Their success can be attributed to the differentiation strategies they developed to produce and promote their products–strategies that have made them two of the most profitable global organizations. There are several parts to their differentiation strategies. First, both companies built global brands by manufacturing the soft-drink concentrate that gives cola its flavor but then selling the concentrate in a syrup form to bottlers throughout the world. The bottlers are responsible for producing and distributing the actual cola. They add carbonated water to the syrup, package the resulting drink, and distribute it to vending machines, supermarkets, restaurants, and other retail outlets. The bottlers must also sign an exclusive agreement that prohibits them from bottling or distributing the products of competing soft-drink companies. This creates a barrier to entry that helps prevent new companies from entering the industry.

Second, Coca-Cola and PepsiCo charge the bottlers a *premium price* for the syrup; they then invest a large part of the profits in advertising to build and maintain brand awareness. The money they spend on advertising (in 2007 each company spent over $600 million) to

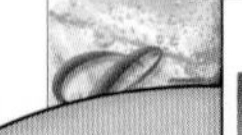

ETHICS IN ACTION

Johnson & Johnson's Ethical Culture

Johnson & Johnson is so well known for its ethical culture that it has been judged as having the best corporate reputation for two years in a row, based on a survey of over 26,000 consumers conducted by Harris Interactive and the Reputation Institute at New York University.[50] Johnson & Johnson grew from a family business led by General Robert Wood Johnson in the 1930s to a major maker of pharmaceutical and medical products. Attesting to the role of managers in creating ethical organizational cultures, Johnson emphasized the importance of ethics and responsibility to stakeholders and wrote the first Johnson & Johnson Credo in 1943.[51]

The credo continues to guide employees at Johnson & Johnson today and outlines the company's commitments to its different stakeholder groups. It emphasizes that the organization's first responsibility is to doctors, nurses, patients, and consumers. Following this group are suppliers and distributors, employees, communities, and, lastly, stockholders.[52] This credo has served managers and employees at Johnson & Johnson well and guided some difficult decision making, such as the decision to recall all Tylenol capsules in the U.S. market after cyanide-laced capsules were responsible for seven deaths in Chicago.

True to its ethical culture and outstanding reputation, Johnson & Johnson always ... well-being before profit. For example, around 20 years ago, John- ... used as a tanning product at a time when the harmful ... known by the public.[53] The product ma...

Additional in-depth examples appear in boxes throughout each chapter. **Management Insight** boxes illustrate the topics of the chapter, while the **Ethics in Action**, **Managing Globally**, **Focus on Diversity**, and **Technology Byte** boxes examine the chapter topics from each of these perspectives.

MANAGER AS A PERSON

How Judy Lewent Became One of the Most Powerful Women in Corporate America

With annual sales of over $45 billion, Merck is one of the largest developers and marketers of advanced pharmaceuticals. In 2000, the company spent more than $3 billion on R&D to develop new drugs–an expensive and difficult process fraught with risk. Most new drug ideas fail to emerge from development. It takes an average of $300 million and 10 years to bring a new drug to market, and 7 out of 10 new drugs fail to make a profit for the developing company.

Given the costs, risks, and uncertainties of new drug development, Judy Lewent, then director of capital analysis at Merck, decided to develop a decision support system that could help managers make more effective R&D investment decisions. Her aim was to give Merck's top managers the information they needed to evaluate proposed R&D projects on a case-by-case basis. The system that Lewent and her staff developed is referred to in Merck as the "Research Planning Model."[70] At the heart of this decision support system is a sophisticated model. The input variables include data on R&D spending, manufacturing costs, selling costs, and demand conditions. The relationships between the input variables are modeled by means of several equations that factor in the probability of a drug's making it through development and to market. The outputs of this modeling process are the revenues, cash flows, and profits that a project might generate.

The Merck model does not use a single value for an input variable, nor does it compute a single value for each output. Rather, a range is specified for each input variable (such as high, medium, and low R&D spending). The computer repeatedly samples at random from the range of values for each input variable and produces a probability distribution of values for each output. So, for example, instead of stating categorically that a proposed R&D project will yield a profit of $500 million, the decision support system produces a probability distribution. It might state that although $500 million is the most likely profit, there is a 25% chance that the profit will be less than $300 million and a 25% chance that it will be greater than $700 million.

Merck now uses Lewent's decision support system to evaluate all proposed R&D investment decisions. In addition, Lewent has developed other decision support system models that Merck's managers can use to help them decide, for example, whether to enter into joint ventures with other companies or how best to hedge foreign exchange risk. As for Lewent, her reward was promotion to the position of chief financial officer of Merck. She became one of the most powerful women in corporate America.

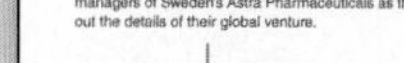

Judy Lewent, chief financial officer of Merck, consults with managers of Sweden's Astra Pharmaceuticals as they work out the details of their global venture.

Further emphasizing the unique content covered in Chapter 2, Values, Attitudes, Emotions, and Culture: The Manager as a Person, the **Manager as a Person** boxes focus on how real managers brought about change within their organizations. These examples allow us to reflect on how individual managers dealt with real-life, on-the-job challenges related to various chapter concepts.

Small Business

NEW! Expanded Use of Small Business Examples To ensure that students see the clear connections between the concepts taught in their Principles of Management course and the application in their future jobs in a medium or small business, Jones and George have expanded the number of examples of the opportunities and challenges facing founders, managers, and employees in small businesses.

Experiential Learning Features We have given considerable time and effort to developing state-of-the-art experiential end-of-chapter learning exercises that drive home the meaning of management to students. These exercises are grouped together at the end of each chapter in a section called "Management in Action." The following activities are included at the end of every chapter:

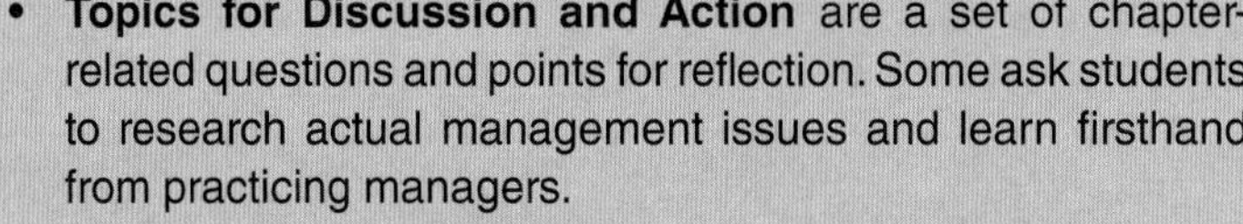

- **Topics for Discussion and Action** are a set of chapter-related questions and points for reflection. Some ask students to research actual management issues and learn firsthand from practicing managers.

- **Building Management Skills** is a self-developed exercise that asks students to apply what they have learned from their own experience in organizations and from managers or from the experiences of others.

- **Managing Ethically** is an exercise that presents students with an ethical scenario or dilemma and asks them to think about the issue from an ethical perspective to better understand the issues facing practicing managers.

- **Small Group Breakout Exercise** is designed to allow instructors in large classes to utilize interactive experiential exercises.

- **Be the Manager** presents a realistic scenario where a manager or organization faces some kind of challenge, problem, or opportunity. These exercises provide students with a hands-on way of solving "real" problems by applying what they've just learned in the chapter.

Each chapter has at least one

BusinessWeek

- **BusinessWeek Case in the News** that is an actual or shortened version of a *BusinessWeek* article. The concluding questions encourage students to think about how real managers deal with problems in the business world.

Assurance of Learning Ready Many educational institutions today are focused on the notion of assurance of learning, an important element of some accreditation standards. *Essentials of Contemporary Management, Fourth Edition*, is designed specifically to support your assurance of learning initiatives with a simple, yet powerful solution.

Each test bank question for *Essentials of Contemporary Management* maps to a specific chapter learning outcome/objective listed in the text. You can use our test bank software, EZ Test and EZ Test Online, or *Connect Management* to easily query for learning outcomes/objectives that directly relate to the learning objectives for your course. You can then use the reporting features of EZ Test to aggregate student results in similar fashion, making the collection and presentation of assurance of learning data simple and easy.

AACSB Statement The McGraw-Hill Companies are a proud corporate member of AACSB International. To support the importance and value of AACSB accreditation, *Essentials of Contemporary Management, Fourth Edition*, recognizes the curricula guidelines detailed in the AACSB standards for business accreditation by connecting selected questions in the text and/or the test bank to the six general knowledge and skill guidelines in the AACSB standards.

The statements contained in *Essentials of Contemporary Management, Fourth Edition,* are provided only as a guide for the users of this textbook. The AACSB leaves content coverage and assessment within the purview of individual schools, the mission of the school, and the faculty. While *Essentials of Contemporary Management* and the teaching package make no claim of any specific AACSB qualification or evaluation, we have within *Essentials of Contemporary Management* labeled selected questions according to the six general knowledge and skill areas.

Integrated Learning System Great care was used in the creation of the supplementary material to accompany *Essentials of Contemporary Management.* Whether you are a seasoned faculty member or a newly minted instructor, you'll find our support materials to be the most thorough and thoughtful ever created.

- **Instructor's Resource CD-ROM** This IRCD allows instructors to easily create their own custom presentations using the following resources: Instructors' Manual, Test Bank, EZ Test, and PowerPoint® presentations.

- **Instructor's Manual (IM)** The IM supporting this text has been completely updated by Kimberly Jaussi of SUNY Binghamton in order to save instructors' time and support them in delivering the most effective course to their students. For each chapter, this manual provides a chapter overview and lecture outline with integrated PowerPoint® slides, lecture enhancers, notes for end-of-chapter materials, video cases and teaching notes, and more.

- **PowerPoint® Presentation** 40 slides per chapter feature reproductions of key tables and figures from the text as well as original content, prepared by Brad Cox of Midlands Tech. Lecture-enhancing additions such as quick polling questions and company or video examples from outside the text can be used to generate discussion and illustrate management concepts.

- **Test Bank and EZ Test** The test bank has been thoroughly reviewed, revised, and improved. There are approximately 100 questions per chapter, including true/false, multiple-choice, and essay. Each question is tagged with learning objective, level of difficulty (corresponding to Bloom's taxonomy of educational objectives), AACSB standards, the correct answer, and page references. The new AACSB tags allow instructors to sort questions by the various standards and create reports to help give assurance that they are including recommended learning experiences in their curricula.

  McGraw-Hill's flexible and easy-to-use electronic testing program **EZ Test** (found on the IRCD) allows instructors to create tests from book-specific items. It accommodates a wide range of question types, and instructors may add their own questions. Multiple versions of the test can be created, and any test can be exported for use with course management systems such as WebCT or BlackBoard. And now **EZ Test Online** (**www.eztestonline.com**) allows you to access the test bank virtually anywhere at any time, without installation, and it's even easier to use. Additionally, it allows you to administer EZ Test–created exams and quizzes online, providing instant feedback for students.

McGraw-Hill *Connect Management*

Less Managing. More Teaching. Greater Learning.

McGraw-Hill *Connect Management* is an online assignment and assessment solution that connects students with the tools and resources they'll need to achieve success.

McGraw-Hill *Connect Management* helps prepare students for their future by enabling faster learning, more efficient studying, and higher retention of knowledge.

McGraw-Hill *Connect Management* Features

Connect Management offers a number of powerful tools and features to make managing assignments easier, so faculty can spend more time teaching. With *Connect Management*, students can engage with their coursework anytime and anywhere, making the learning process more accessible and efficient. *Connect Management* offers you the features described below.

Diagnostic and Adaptive Learning of Concepts: LearnSmart

Students want to make the best use of their study time. The LearnSmart adaptive self-study technology within *Connect Management* provides students with a seamless combination of practice, assessment, and remediation for every concept in the textbook. LearnSmart's intelligent software adapts to every student response and automatically delivers concepts that advance the student's understanding while reducing time devoted to the concepts already mastered. The result for every student is the fastest path to mastery of the chapter concepts. LearnSmart

- Applies an intelligent concept engine to identify the relationships between concepts and to serve new concepts to each student only when he or she is ready.
- Adapts automatically to each student, so students spend less time on the topics they understand and practice more those they have yet to master.
- Provides continual reinforcement and remediation, but gives only as much guidance as students need.
- Integrates diagnostics as part of the learning experience.
- Enables you to assess which concepts students have efficiently learned on their own, thus freeing class time for more applications and discussion.

Online Interactives

Online Interactives are engaging tools that teach students to apply key concepts in practice. These Interactives provide them with immersive, experiential learning opportunities. Students will engage in a variety of interactive scenarios to deepen critical knowledge of key course topics. They receive immediate feedback at intermediate steps throughout each exercise, as well as comprehensive feedback at the end of the assignment. All Interactives are automatically scored and entered into the instructor gradebook.

Student Progress Tracking

Connect Management keeps instructors informed about how each student, section, and class is performing, allowing for more productive use of lecture and office hours. The progress-tracking function enables you to

- View scored work immediately and track individual or group performance with assignment and grade reports.
- Access an instant view of student or class performance relative to learning objectives.
- Collect data and generate reports required by many accreditation organizations, such as AACSB.

Smart Grading

When it comes to studying, time is precious. *Connect Management* helps students learn more efficiently by providing feedback and practice material when they need it, where they need it. When it comes to teaching, your time also is precious. The grading function enables you to

- Have assignments scored automatically, giving students immediate feedback on their work and side-by-side comparisons with correct answers.
- Access and review each response; manually change grades or leave comments for students to review.
- Reinforce classroom concepts with practice tests and instant quizzes.

Simple Assignment Management

With *Connect Management,* creating assignments is easier than ever, so you can spend more time teaching and less time managing. The assignment management function enables you to

- Create and deliver assignments easily with selectable end-of-chapter questions and test bank items.
- Streamline lesson planning, student progress reporting, and assignment grading to make classroom management more efficient than ever.
- Go paperless with the eBook and online submission and grading of student assignments.

Instructor Library

The *Connect Management* Instructor Library is your repository for additional resources to improve student engagement in and out of class. You can select and use any asset that enhances your lecture. The *Connect Management* Instructor Library includes

- Instructor Manual.
- PowerPoint® files.
- TestBank.
- Management Asset Gallery.
- eBook.

Student Study Center

The *Connect Management* Student Study Center is the place for students to access additional resources. The Student Study Center

- Offers students quick access to lectures, practice materials, eBooks, and more.
- Provides instant practice material and study questions, easily accessible on the go.
- Give students access to self-assessments, video materials, Manager's Hot Seat, and more.

Lecture Capture Via Tegrity Campus

Increase the attention paid to lecture discussion by decreasing the attention paid to note taking. For an additional charge, Lecture Capture offers new ways for students to focus on the in-class discussion, knowing they can revisit important topics later. See page xxxviii for further information.

McGraw-Hill *Connect Plus Management*

McGraw-Hill reinvents the textbook-learning experience for the modern student with *Connect Plus Management.* A seamless integration of an eBook and *Management, Connect Plus Management* provides all of the *Connect Management* features plus the following:

- An integrated eBook, allowing for anytime, anywhere access to the textbook.
- Dynamic links between the problems or questions you assign to your students and the location in the eBook where that problem or question is covered.
- A powerful search function to pinpoint and connect key concepts in a snap.

In short, *Connect Management* offers you and your students powerful tools and features that optimize your time and energies, enabling you to focus on course content, teaching, and student learning. *Connect Management* also offers a wealth of content resources for both instructors and students. This state-of-the-art, thoroughly tested system supports you in preparing students for the world that awaits.

For more information about *Connect*, go to **www.mcgrawhillconnect.com,** or contact your local McGraw-Hill sales representative.

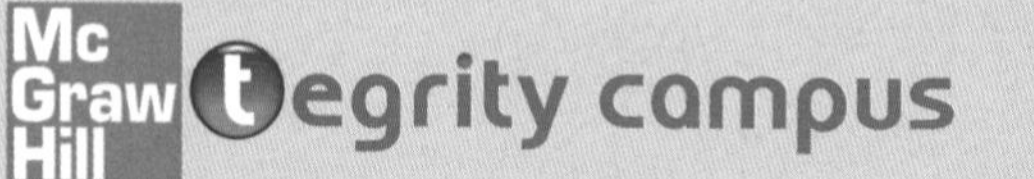

Tegrity Campus: Lectures 24/7

Tegrity Campus is a service that makes class time available 24/7 by automatically capturing every lecture in a searchable format for students to review when they study and complete assignments. With a simple one-click start-and-stop process, you capture all computer screens and corresponding audio. Students can replay any part of any class with easy-to-use browser-based viewing on a PC or Mac.

Educators know that the more students can see, hear, and experience class resources, the better they learn. In fact, studies prove it. With Tegrity Campus, students quickly recall key moments by using Tegrity Campus's unique search feature. This search helps students efficiently find what they need, when they need it, across an entire semester of class recordings. Help turn all your students' study time into learning moments immediately supported by your lecture.

Lecture Capture enables you to

- Record and distribute your lecture with a click of button.
- Record and index PowerPoint® presentations and anything shown on your computer so it is easily searchable, frame by frame.
- Offer access to lectures anytime and anywhere by computer, iPod, or mobile device.
- Increase intent listening and class participation by easing students' concerns about note taking. Lecture Capture will make it more likely you will see students' faces, not the tops of their heads.

To learn more about Tegrity, watch a two-minute Flash demo at **http://tegritycampus.mhhe.com**.

McGraw-Hill Customer Care Contact Information

At McGraw-Hill, we understand that getting the most from new technology can be challenging. That's why our services don't stop after you purchase our products. You can e-mail our product specialists 24 hours a day to get product training online. Or you can search our knowledge bank of Frequently Asked Questions on our support Web site. For customer support, call **800-331-5094**, e-mail **hmsupport@mcgraw-hill.com**, or visit **www.mhhe.com/support**. One of our technical support analysts will be able to assist you in a timely fashion.

Support Materials

McGraw-Hill's New Management Asset Gallery! McGraw-Hill/Irwin Management is excited to now provide a one-stop shop for our wealth of assets, making it super quick and easy for instructors to locate specific materials to enhance their courses.

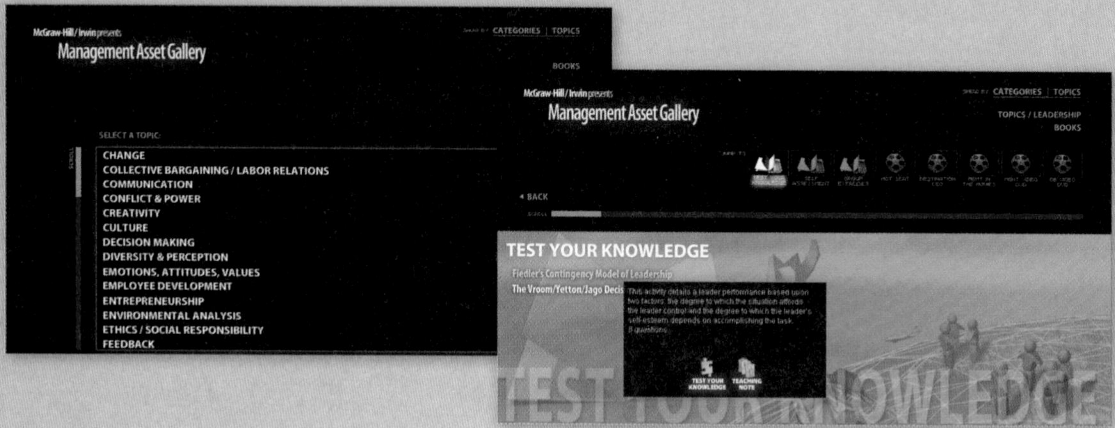

All of the following can be accessed within the Management Asset Gallery:

Manager's Hot Seat

NEW Look And Expanded 6 New Clips! This interactive, video-based application puts students in the manager's hot seat and builds critical thinking and decision-making skills and allows students to apply concepts to real managerial challenges. Students watch as 21 real managers apply their years of experience when confronting unscripted issues such as bullying in the workplace, cyber loafing, globalization, intergenerational work conflicts, workplace violence, and leadership versus management.

Self-Assessment Gallery Unique among publisher-provided self-assessments, our 23 self-assessments provide students with background information to ensure that they understand the purpose of the assessment. Students test their values, beliefs, skills, and interests in a wide variety of areas, allowing them to personally apply chapter content to their own lives and careers.

Every self-assessment is supported with PowerPoints® and an instructor manual in the Management Asset Gallery, making it easy for the instructor to create an engaging classroom discussion surrounding the assessments.

Test Your Knowledge To help reinforce students' understanding of key management concepts, Test Your Knowledge activities give students a review of the conceptual materials followed by application-based questions to work through. Students can choose practice mode, which provides them with detailed feedback after each question, or test mode, which provides feedback after the entire test has been completed. Every Test Your Knowledge activity is supported by instructor notes in the Management Asset Gallery to make it easy for the instructor to create engaging classroom discussions surrounding the materials the students have completed.

Management History Timeline This Web application allows instructors to present and students to learn the history of management in an engaging and interactive way. Management history is presented along an intuitive timeline that can be traveled through sequentially or by selected decade. With the click of a mouse, students learn the important dates, see the people who influenced the field, and understand the general management theories that have molded and shaped management as we know it today.

Video Library DVDs McGraw-Hill/Irwin offers the most comprehensive video support for the Principles of Management classroom through course library video DVDs. This discipline has volume library DVDs tailored to integrate and visually reinforce chapter concepts. The library volume DVDs contain more than 70 clips! The rich video material, organized by topic, comes from sources such as *BusinessWeek* TV, PBS, NBC, BBC, SHRM, and McGraw-Hill. Video cases and video guides are provided for some clips.

Destination CEO Videos

BusinessWeek produced video clips featuring CEOs on a variety of topics. Accompanying each clip are multiple-choice questions and discussion questions to use in the classroom or assign as a quiz.

Online Learning Center (OLC)

www.mhhe.com/jones4e

Find a variety of online teaching and learning tools that are designed to reinforce and build on the text content. Students will have direct access to the learning tools while instructor materials are password protected.

BusinessWeek Subscription

Students can subscribe to *BusinessWeek* for a specially priced rate of $8.25 in addition to the price of this text, when instructors order the *BusinessWeek* Edition.

eBook Options

eBooks are an innovative way for students to save money and to "go green." McGraw-Hill's eBooks are typically 55% off the bookstore price. Students have the choice between an online and a downloadable CourseSmart eBook.

Through CourseSmart, students have the flexibility to access an exact replica of their textbook from any computer that has Internet service without plug-ins or special software via the online version, or to create a library of books on their hard drive via the downloadable version. Access to the CourseSmart eBooks is one year.

Features CourseSmart eBooks allow students to highlight, take notes, organize notes, and share the notes with other CourseSmart users. Students can also search for terms across all eBooks in their purchased *CourseSmart* library. CourseSmart eBooks can be printed (five pages at a time).

More info and purchase Please visit **www.coursesmart.com** for more information and to purchase access to our eBooks. CourseSmart allows students to try one chapter of the eBook, free of charge, before purchase.

Custom Textbook Option Offer your students a textbook that matches your course exactly in four simple steps! McGraw-Hill's Primis Online digital database offers the flexibility to customize your course including material from the largest online collection of textbooks, readings, and cases. Please visit **www.primisonline.com** for more information, or call (800) 962-9342.

Custom eBook Option Primis leads the way in customized eBooks with hundreds of titles available at prices that save students over 55% off the regular print purchase price. Additional information is available at (800) 962-9342 or by visiting **www.ebooks.primisonline.com**.

Essentials of Contemporary Management

The Management Process Today

CHAPTER 1

Learning Objectives

After studying this chapter, you should be able to

1. Describe what management is, why management is important, what managers do, and how managers use organizational resources efficiently and effectively to achieve organizational goals. **[LO1]**
2. Distinguish among planning, organizing, leading, and controlling (the four principal managerial tasks), and explain how managers' ability to handle each one affects organizational performance. **[LO2]**
3. Differentiate among three levels of management, and understand the tasks and responsibilities of managers at different levels in the organizational hierarchy. **[LO3]**
4. Distinguish among three kinds of managerial skill, and explain why managers are divided into different departments. **[LO4]**
5. Discuss some major changes in management practices today that have occurred as a result of globalization and the use of advanced information technology (IT). **[LO5]**
6. Discuss the principal challenges managers face in today's increasingly competitive global environment. **[LO6]**

Trader Joe's first New York City store opened in 2006. Founder Joe Coulombe's intuitive move away from convenience store to specialty food and drink offerings won over customers bored with the usual supermarket fare and increasingly concerned about their health.

MANAGEMENT SNAPSHOT

Joe Coulombe Makes Trader Joe's a Small Business Success Story

What Is High-Performance Management?

Trader Joe's, an upscale specialty supermarket chain, was started in 1967 by Joe Coulombe. Joe owned a few convenience stores that were fighting an uphill battle against the growing 7-11 chain. 7-11 was able to offer customers a wider selection of lower-priced products than Joe's stores. Joe had to find a new way to manage his small business if it was going to survive. He began brainstorming new strategies. There might be a niche for supplying specialty products, he thought, such as wine, drinks, and gourmet foods, which were more profitable to sell. He would no longer be competing against giant 7-11. He changed the name of his stores to Trader Joe's and stocked them with a wide variety of brands of California wine. He began to offer fine foods, fresh bread, cheese, fruits, and vegetables to complement wine sales.

His plan worked. Customers loved his new upscale supermarket concept. The premium products he had chosen to stock sold quickly. Realizing that he needed to capitalize on his success to protect his growing business, Joe continually expanded the variety of premium foods and drinks he sold. Taking advantage of the popularity of the name Trader Joe's, he began to offer his own store label products. Today, over 80% of the products Trader Joe's sells sport its own label.

To compete in the premium-quality segment of the supermarket business and keep customers buying high-priced gourmet products, Trader Joe's needed to provide excellent customer service. Joe had to motivate his salespeople to perform at a high level. His approach was to decentralize authority, empowering salespeople to take responsibility for meeting customer needs. Joe created a store environment in which employees were treated as individuals and felt valued as people. Rather than forcing employees to follow strict operating rules, Joe gave employees autonomy to make decisions and provide personalized customer service. The result is that employees feel they "own" their supermarkets. They provide excellent customer service and develop personal relationships with customers, who are often on first-name terms.

The theme for Trader Joe's stores reinforces this. The design of the stores creates the feeling of a Hawaiian resort. Joe's employees wear loud Hawaiian shirts, store managers are called captains, and the store décor uses lots of wood. Tiki huts provide customers with food and drink samples, for example.

How does Joe Coulombe go about *controlling* salespeople? From the outset he created a policy of promotion from within the company so that the highest-performing salespeople could rise to become store captains and beyond in the organization. He treated employees fairly to encourage them, in turn, to provide personalized customer service. He decided that full-time employees should earn at least the median household income for their communities, which averaged $7,000 a year in the 1960s and is $48,000 today—an astonishingly high amount compared to the pay of employees of regular supermarkets such as Kroger's and Safeway. Store captains, who play a crucial role in reinforcing Trader Joe's culture, are rewarded with salaries and bonuses that can exceed $100,000 a year. Salespeople know that as the store chain expands they may also be promoted to captain.

In 2009, Trader Joe's had over 320 stores in 23 states and is still expanding because Joe's approach to managing his small business created the right foundation for an upscale specialty supermarket to grow and prosper. In 2009, Trader Joe's was ranked the second best supermarket in the United States by *Consumer Reports,* the leading consumer products review magazine.

Overview

The way Joe Coulombe created Trader Joe's illustrates many of the challenges managers face. Managers must possess many kinds of skills, knowledge, and abilities. Management is an unpredictable process. Making the right decision is difficult; even effective managers make mistakes. The most effective managers are the ones, like Joe Coulombe, who continually strive to find ways to improve their companies' performance.

In this chapter, we look at what successful managers do and what skills and abilities they must develop. We also identify the different kinds of managers that organizations need. Finally, we discuss some of the challenges that managers must address if their organizations are to grow and prosper.

What Is Management?

When you think of a manager, what kind of person comes to mind? Do you see someone who, like Joe Coulombe, Andrea Jung, CEO of Avon, or Michael Dell, can determine the future prosperity of a large for-profit company? Or do you see the administrator of a not-for-profit organization, such as a community college, library, or charity? The person in charge of your local Wal-Mart store or McDonald's restaurant? What do all these people have in common? First, they all work in organizations. **Organizations** are collections of people who work together and coordinate their actions to achieve a wide variety of goals and desired future outcomes.[1] Second, managers are the people responsible for supervising and making the most of an organization's human and other resources to achieve its goals.

organizations Collections of people who work together and coordinate their actions to achieve a wide variety of goals or desired future outcomes.

management The planning, organizing, leading, and controlling of human and other resources to achieve organizational goals efficiently and effectively.

Management is the planning, organizing, leading, and controlling of human and other resources to achieve organizational goals efficiently and effectively. An organization's *resources* include assets such as people and their skills, know-how, and experience; machinery; raw materials; computers and information technology; and patents, financial capital, and loyal customers and employees.

Figure 1.1
Efficiency, Effectiveness, and Performance in an Organization

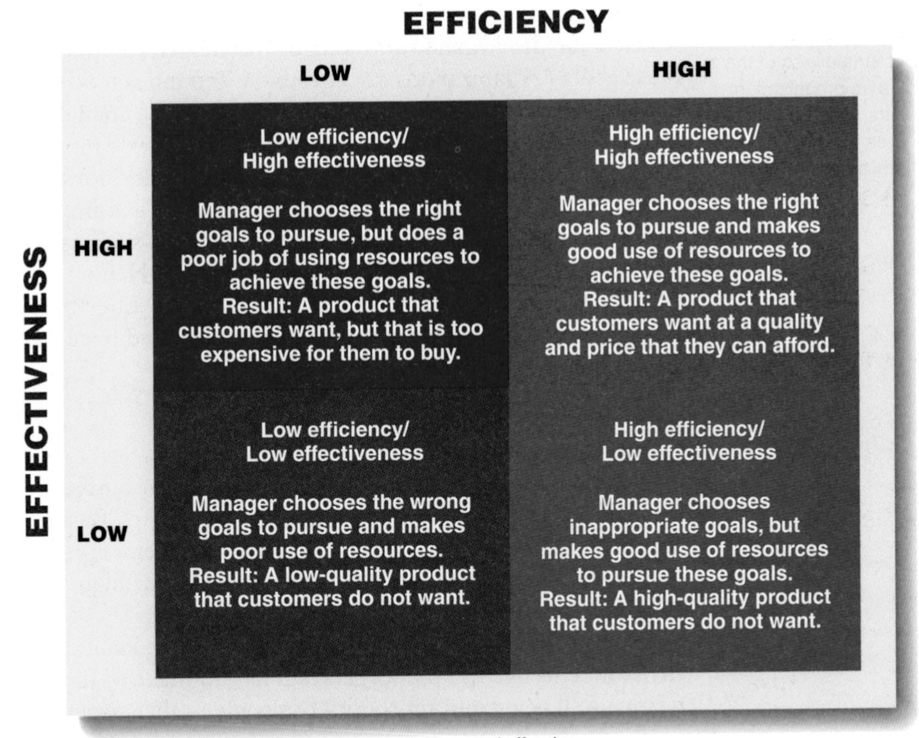

High-performing organizations are efficient *and* effective.

LO1 Describe what management is, why management is important, what managers do, and how managers use organizational resources efficiently and effectively to achieve organizational goals.

Achieving High Performance: A Manager's Goal

One of the most important goals of organizations and their members is to provide goods or services that customers value. The principal goal of CEO Joe Coulombe is to manage Trader Joe's so that it creates desirable fresh grocery items and thus an increasing stream of loyal customers. Similarly, the principal goal of doctors, nurses, and hospital administrators is to increase their hospital's ability to make sick people well and to do so cost-effectively. The principal goal of each McDonald's manager is to produce burgers, salads, fries, and coffees that people want to pay for and eat so that they become loyal return customers.

Organizational performance is a measure of how efficiently and effectively managers use available resources to satisfy customers and achieve organizational goals. Organizational performance increases in direct proportion to increases in efficiency and effectiveness (see Figure 1.1). What are efficiency and effectiveness?

organizational performance A measure of how efficiently and effectively a manager uses resources to satisfy customers and achieve organizational goals.

efficiency A measure of how productively resources are used to achieve a goal.

Efficiency is a measure of how productively resources are used to achieve a goal.[2] Organizations are efficient when managers minimize the amount of input resources (such as labor, raw materials, and component parts) or the amount of time needed to produce a given output of goods or services. For example, McDonald's develops ever more efficient fat fryers that not only reduce the amount of oil used in cooking, but also speed up the cooking of french fries. UPS develops new work routines to reduce delivery time, such as instructing drivers to leave their truck doors open when going short distances. A manager's responsibility is to ensure that an organization and its members perform as efficiently as possible all the activities needed to provide goods and services.

effectiveness A measure of the appropriateness of the goals an organization is pursuing and of the degree to which the organization achieves those goals.

Effectiveness is a measure of the *appropriateness* of the goals that managers have selected for the organization and of the degree to which the organization achieves those goals. Organizations are effective when managers choose appropriate goals and then achieve them. Some years ago, for example, managers at McDonald's decided on the goal of providing breakfast service to attract more customers. The choice of this goal has proved very smart, for breakfast sales now account for more than 30% of McDonald's revenues and are still increasing–an important reason for its record profits in 2009. High-performing organizations, such as Trader Joe's, McDonald's, Wal-Mart, Intel, Home Depot, Accenture, and Habitat for Humanity, are simultaneously efficient and effective (see Figure 1.1). Effective managers are those who choose the right organizational goals to pursue and have the skills to utilize resources efficiently.

Why Study Management?

Today, more students are competing for places in business courses than ever before; the number of people wishing to pursue Master of Business Administration (MBA) degrees–today's passport to an advanced management position–either on campus or from online universities and colleges is at an all-time high. Why is the study of management currently so popular?[3]

First, in any society or culture resources are valuable and scarce, so the more efficient and effective use that organizations can make of those resources, the greater the relative well-being and prosperity of people in that society. Because managers are the people who decide how to use many of a society's most valuable resources–its skilled employees, raw materials like oil and land, computers and information systems, and financial assets–they directly impact the well-being of a society and the people in it. Understanding what managers do and how they do it is of central importance to understanding how a society creates wealth and affluence for its citizens.

Second, although most people are not managers, and many may never intend to become managers, almost all of us encounter managers because most people have jobs and bosses. Moreover, many people today are working in groups and teams and have to deal with coworkers. Studying management helps people to deal with their bosses and their coworkers. It reveals how to understand other people at work and make decisions and take actions that win the attention and support of the boss and coworkers. Management teaches people not yet in positions of authority how to lead coworkers, solve conflicts between them, achieve team goals, and so increase performance.

Third, in any society, people are in competition for a very important resource–a job that pays well and provides an interesting and satisfying career–and understanding management is one important path toward obtaining this objective. In general, jobs become more interesting the more complex or responsible they are. Any person who desires a motivating job that changes over time might therefore do well to develop management skills and become promotable. A person who has been working for several years and then returns to school for an MBA can usually, after earning the degree, find a more interesting, satisfying job and one that pays significantly more than the previous job. Moreover, salaries increase rapidly as people move up the organizational hierarchy, whether it is a school system, a large for-profit business organization, or a not-for-profit charitable or medical institution.

Indeed, the salaries paid to top managers are enormous. For example, the CEOs and other top executives or managers of companies such as Xerox, Avon, Walt Disney, GE, and McDonald's receive millions in actual salary each year. However, even more

Figure 1.2
Four Tasks of Management

staggering is the fact that many top executives also receive stock or shares in the company they manage, as well as stock options that give them the right to sell these shares at a certain time in the future.[4] If the value of the stock goes up, then the managers keep the difference between the price they obtained the stock option for (say, \$10) and what it is worth later (say, \$33). By the time Michael Eisner resigned as CEO of Disney in 2005 he had received over \$1 billion from selling his stock options. When Steve Jobs became CEO of Apple again in 1997 he accepted a salary of only \$1 a year. However, he was also awarded stock options that, with the fast rise in Apple's stock price in the 2000s, were worth several billion dollars by 2008. He was also given the free use of a \$90 million jet.[5] These incredible amounts of money provide some indication of both the responsibilities and the rewards that accompany the achievement of high management positions in major companies–and flow to anybody who successfully creates and manages a small business. What is it that managers actually do to receive such rewards?[6]

Essential Managerial Tasks

LO2 Distinguish among planning, organizing, leading, and controlling (the four principal managerial tasks), and explain how managers' ability to handle each one affects organizational performance.

The job of management is to help an organization make the best use of its resources to achieve its goals. How do managers accomplish this objective? They do so by performing four essential managerial tasks: *planning, organizing, leading,* and *controlling* (see Figure 1.2). The arrows linking these tasks in Figure 1.2 suggest the sequence in which managers typically perform them. French manager Henri Fayol first outlined the nature of these managerial activities around the turn of the 20th century in *General and Industrial Management,* a book that remains the classic statement of what managers must do to create a high-performing organization.[7]

Managers at all levels and in all departments–whether in small or large companies, for-profit or not-for-profit organizations, or organizations that operate in one country or throughout the world–are responsible for performing these four tasks, which we look at next. How well managers perform these tasks determines how efficient and effective their organizations are.

Planning

planning Identifying and selecting appropriate goals; one of the four principal tasks of management.

To perform the **planning** task, managers identify and select appropriate organizational goals and courses of action; they develop strategies for how to achieve high performance. The three steps involved in planning are (1) deciding which goals the organization will pursue, (2) deciding what strategies to adopt to attain those goals, and (3) deciding how to allocate organizational resources to pursue the strategies that attain those goals. How well managers plan and develop strategies determines how effective and efficient the organization is–its performance level.[8]

Michael Dell sits in the dorm room at the University of Texas–Austin, where he launched his personal computer company as a college freshman. When he visited, the room was occupied by freshmen Russell Smith (left) and Jacob Frith, both from Plano, Texas.

As an example of planning in action, consider the situation confronting Michael Dell, founder and CEO of Dell Computer, one of the largest PC makers in the United States. In 1984, the 19-year-old Dell saw an opportunity to enter the PC market by assembling PCs and then selling them directly to customers. Dell began to plan how to put his idea into practice. First, he decided that his goal was to sell an inexpensive PC, to undercut the prices of companies like IBM, Compaq, and Apple. Second, he had to decide on a course of action to achieve this goal. He decided to sell directly to customers by telephone and to bypass expensive computer stores that sold Compaq and Apple PCs. He also had to decide how to obtain low-cost components and how to tell potential customers about his products. Third, he had to decide how to allocate his limited funds (he had only $5,000) to buy labor and other resources. He chose to hire three people and work with them around a table to assemble his PCs.

Thus, to achieve his goal of making and selling low-price PCs, Dell had to plan, and as his organization grew, his plans changed and became progressively more complex. Dell and his managers are continually planning how to help the company maintain its position as the highest-performing PC maker. In 2003, Dell announced it would begin to sell printers and Internet music players, which brought it into direct competition with Hewlett-Packard (HP), the leading printer maker, and Apple, with its new PCs and iPod. It has since expanded the range of products it sells to include LCD screens of all sizes, digital cameras, TVs, and all kinds of broadband and other digital information services.

Dell's new plan has not worked very successfully, however. Apple remains the clear leader in the Internet music download and player business, and HP's printers far outsell Dell's. In fact, Dell's share of the global PC market has fallen sharply, and it was forced to lower prices to compete with HP, which caught up and passed Dell in PC sales.[9] HP has become the largest global PC maker. In addition, Apple is also one of Dell's main competitors today. Also, Taiwan PC maker Acer bought struggling Gateway to become the third largest global PC maker. To reverse Dell's declining performance and meet these challenges, Michael Dell decided to once again become its CEO and has pursued new strategies to better compete. Dell has fought back to once again become the largest U.S. PC maker, and it is locked in a major battle with its competitors in 2009.

strategy A cluster of decisions about what goals to pursue, what actions to take, and how to use resources to achieve goals.

As the battle between Dell, HP, Acer, and Apple suggests, the outcome of planning is a **strategy**, a cluster of decisions concerning what organizational goals to pursue, what actions to take, and how to use resources to achieve these goals. The decisions that were the outcome of Michael Dell's original planning formed a *low-cost strategy*. A low-cost strategy is a way of obtaining customers by making decisions that allow an organization to produce goods or services more cheaply than its competitors so that it can charge lower prices than they do. Throughout its history, Dell has been constantly refining this strategy and exploring new strategies to reduce costs; Dell became the most profitable PC maker as a result of its low-cost strategy, but when HP and Acer also lowered their costs it lost its competitive advantage and its profits fell. By contrast, since its founding Apple's strategy has been to deliver new, exciting, and unique computer and digital products, such as its futuristic PCs, iPods, and iPhones, to customers–a strategy known as *differentiation*.[10] Although this strategy almost ruined Apple in the 1990s when customers bought cheaper Dell PCs rather than Apple's higher-priced PCs, today its sales have increased as customers turn to its stylish PCs and Dell has been forced to offer more exciting, innovative products to fight back.

Planning strategy is complex and difficult, especially because planning is done under uncertainty when the result is unknown. Managers take major risks when they commit organizational resources to pursue a particular strategy. Dell succeeded spectacularly in the past with its low-cost strategy, but presently Apple is succeeding spectacularly with its differentiation strategy. HP, after many problems, has enjoyed a turnaround because by lowering its costs it is now able to offer customers attractive PCs at prices similar to Dell's. Managers at Dell and HP are continually planning how to outperform each other. In 2008 Acer became a major rival as its global market share increased sharply. In Chapter 6 we focus on the planning process and on the strategies organizations can select to respond to opportunities or threats in an industry.

As we saw in the Manager's Snapshot at the beginning of the chapter, the way in which Joe Coulombe went about creating a successful management approach for his small business, a specialty, upscale supermarket, illustrates how important planning and strategy making are to a manager's success.

Organizing

organizing Structuring working relationships so organizational members work together to achieve organizational goals; one of the four principal tasks of management.

organizational structure A formal system of task and reporting relationships that coordinates and motivates organizational members so that they work together to achieve organizational goals.

Organizing is structuring working relationships so organizational members interact and cooperate to achieve organizational goals. Organizing people into departments according to the kinds of job-specific tasks they perform lays out the lines of authority and responsibility among different individuals and groups. Managers must decide how best to organize resources, particularly human resources.

The outcome of organizing is the creation of an **organizational structure**, a formal system of task and reporting relationships that coordinates and motivates members so that they work together to achieve organizational goals. Organizational structure determines how an organization's resources can be best used to create goods and services. As his company grew, for example, Michael Dell, just like Joe Coulombe, faced the issue of how to structure the organization. Early on Dell was hiring 100 new employees a week and deciding how to design his managerial hierarchy to best motivate and coordinate managers' activities. As his organization has grown to become the world's largest PC maker, he and his managers have created progressively more complex kinds of organizational structures to help achieve their goals. We examine the organizing process in detail in Chapter 7.

Ken Chenault, pictured here, is the president and CEO of American Express Company. Promoted in 1997, he climbed the ranks from their Travel Related Services Company, thanks to his "even temper and unrelenting drive." Respected by colleagues for his personality, most will say they can't remember him losing his temper or raising his voice. His open-door policy for subordinates allows him to mentor AmEx managers and encourages all to enter and "speak their minds."

Leading

An organization's *vision* is a short, succinct, and inspiring statement of what the organization intends to become and the goals it is seeking to achieve–its desired future state. In **leading,** managers articulate a clear organizational vision for the organization's members to accomplish, and they energize and enable employees so that everyone understands the part he or she plays in achieving organizational goals. Leadership involves managers using their power, personality, influence, persuasion, and communication skills to coordinate people and groups so that their activities and efforts are in harmony. Leadership revolves around encouraging all employees to perform at a high level to help the organization achieve its vision and goals. Another outcome of leadership is a highly motivated and committed workforce. Employees responded well to Michael Dell's hands-on leadership style, which has resulted in a hardworking, committed workforce. Salespeople at Trader Joe's appreciate how Joe Coulombe's leadership style, which is based on his willingness to delegate authority, give them the autonomy to provide high-quality personalized service. We discuss the issues involved in managing and leading individuals and groups in Chapters 9 through 12.

leading Articulating a clear vision and energizing and enabling organizational members so that they understand the part they play in achieving organizational goals; one of the four principal tasks of management.

controlling Evaluating how well an organization is achieving its goals and taking action to maintain or improve performance; one of the four principal tasks of management.

Controlling

In **controlling,** the task of managers is to evaluate how well an organization has achieved its goals and to take any corrective actions needed to maintain or improve performance. For example, managers monitor the performance of individuals, departments, and the organization as a whole to see whether they are meeting desired performance standards. Michael Dell learned early in his career how important this is. If standards are not being met, managers seek ways to improve performance.

The outcome of the control process is the ability to measure performance accurately and regulate organizational efficiency and effectiveness. To exercise control, managers must decide which goals to measure–perhaps goals pertaining to productivity, quality, or responsiveness to customers–and then they must design control systems that will provide the information necessary to assess performance–that is, to determine to what degree the goals have been met. The controlling task also allows managers to evaluate how well they themselves are performing the other three tasks of management–planning, organizing, and leading–and to take corrective action.

Michael Dell had difficulty establishing effective control systems because his company was growing so rapidly and he lacked experienced managers. In the 1990s Dell's costs soared because no controls were in place to monitor inventory, which had built up rapidly; and in 1994 Dell's new line of laptop computers crashed because poor quality control resulted in a defective product: Some laptops caught fire. To solve these and other control problems, Michael Dell hired hundreds of experienced managers from other companies to put the right control systems in place. As a result, by 1998 Dell was able to make computers for about 10% less than its competitors, which created a major source of competitive advantage it has enjoyed ever since. By 2001 Dell became so efficient it drove its competitors out of the market because it had a 20% cost advantage over them.[11] However, we noted earlier that in the 2000s Dell's rivals, such as HP and Acer, have learned to better control their activities and lower their costs, which has eroded Dell's competitive advantage. Controlling, like the other managerial tasks, is an ongoing, fluid, always-changing process that demands constant attention and action. We cover the most important aspects of the control task in Chapters 13 and 14.

The four managerial tasks–planning, organizing, leading, and controlling–are essential parts of a manager's job. At all levels in the managerial hierarchy, and across all jobs and departments in an organization, effective management means performing these four activities successfully–in ways that increase efficiency and effectiveness.

Levels and Skills of Managers

To perform the four managerial tasks efficiently and effectively, organizations group or differentiate their managers in two main ways–by level in hierarchy and by type of skill. First, they differentiate managers according to their level or rank in the organization's hierarchy of authority. The three levels of managers are first-line managers, middle managers, and top managers–arranged in a hierarchy. Typically, first-line managers report to middle managers, and middle managers report to top managers.

Second, organizations group managers into different departments (or functions) according to their specific set of job-related skills, expertise, and experiences, such as a manager's engineering skills, marketing expertise, or sales experience. A **department**, such as the manufacturing, accounting, engineering, or sales department, is a group of managers and employees who work together because they possess similar skills and experience or use the same kind of knowledge, tools, or techniques to perform their jobs. Within each department are all three levels of management. Next, we examine the reasons why organizations use a hierarchy of managers and group them, by the jobs they perform, into departments.

department A group of people who work together and possess similar skills or use the same knowledge, tools, or techniques to perform their jobs.

LO3 Differentiate among three levels of management, and understand the tasks and responsibilities of managers at different levels in the organizational hierarchy.

Levels of Management

Organizations normally have three levels of management: first-line managers, middle managers, and top managers. (See Figure 1.3.) Managers at each level have different but related responsibilities for utilizing organizational resources to increase efficiency and effectiveness.

At the base of the managerial hierarchy are **first-line managers**, often called *supervisors*. They are responsible for the daily supervision of the nonmanagerial employees who perform many of the specific activities necessary to produce goods and services. First-line managers work in all departments or functions of an organization.

first-line manager A manager who is responsible for the daily supervision of nonmanagerial employees.

Examples of first-line managers include the supervisor of a work team in the manufacturing department of a car plant, the head nurse in the obstetrics department of a hospital, and the chief mechanic overseeing a crew of mechanics in the service function of a new-car dealership. At Dell, first-line managers include the supervisors responsible for controlling the quality of its computers or the level of customer service provided by telephone salespeople. When Michael Dell started his company, he personally controlled the computer assembly process and thus performed as a first-line manager or supervisor.

Figure 1.3
Levels of Managers

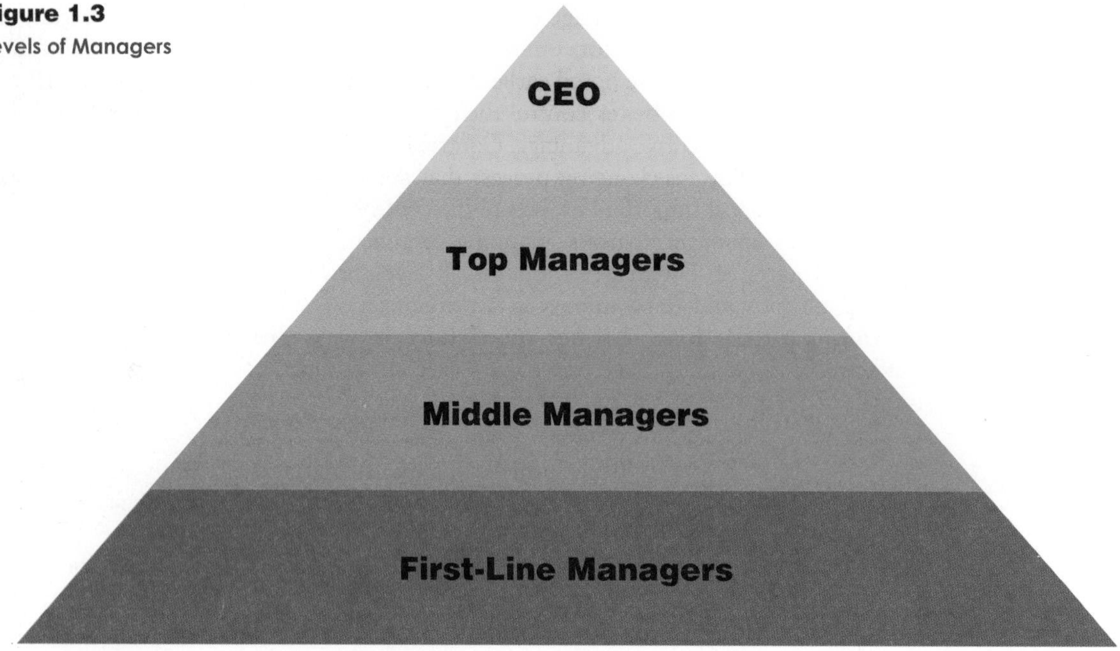

middle manager A manager who supervises first-line managers and is responsible for finding the best way to use resources to achieve organizational goals.

Supervising the first-line managers are **middle managers,** responsible for finding the best way to organize human and other resources to achieve organizational goals. To increase efficiency, middle managers find ways to help first-line managers and nonmanagerial employees better utilize resources to reduce manufacturing costs or improve customer service. To increase effectiveness, middle managers evaluate whether the goals that the organization is pursuing are appropriate and suggest to top managers ways in which goals should be changed. Very often, the suggestions that middle managers make to top managers can dramatically increase organizational performance. A major part of the middle manager's job is developing and fine-tuning skills and know-how, such as manufacturing or marketing expertise, that allow the organization to be efficient and effective. Middle managers make thousands of specific decisions about the production of goods and services: Which first-line supervisors should be chosen for this particular project? Where can we find the highest-quality resources? How should employees be organized to allow them to make the best use of resources?

Behind a first-class sales force, such as Trader Joe's, look for the middle managers responsible for training, motivating, and rewarding the salespeople. Behind a committed staff of high school teachers, look for the principal who energizes them to find ways to obtain the resources they need to do outstanding and innovative jobs in the classroom.

top manager A manager who establishes organizational goals, decides how departments should interact, and monitors the performance of middle managers.

In contrast to middle managers, **top managers** are responsible for the performance of *all* departments.[12] They have *cross-departmental responsibility.* Top managers establish organizational goals, such as which goods and services the company should produce; they decide how the different departments should interact; and they monitor how well middle managers in each department utilize resources to achieve goals.[13] Top managers are ultimately responsible for the success or failure of an organization, and their performance is continually scrutinized by people inside and outside the organization, such as other employees and investors.[14]

Figure 1.4
Relative Amount of Time That Managers Spend on the Four Managerial Tasks

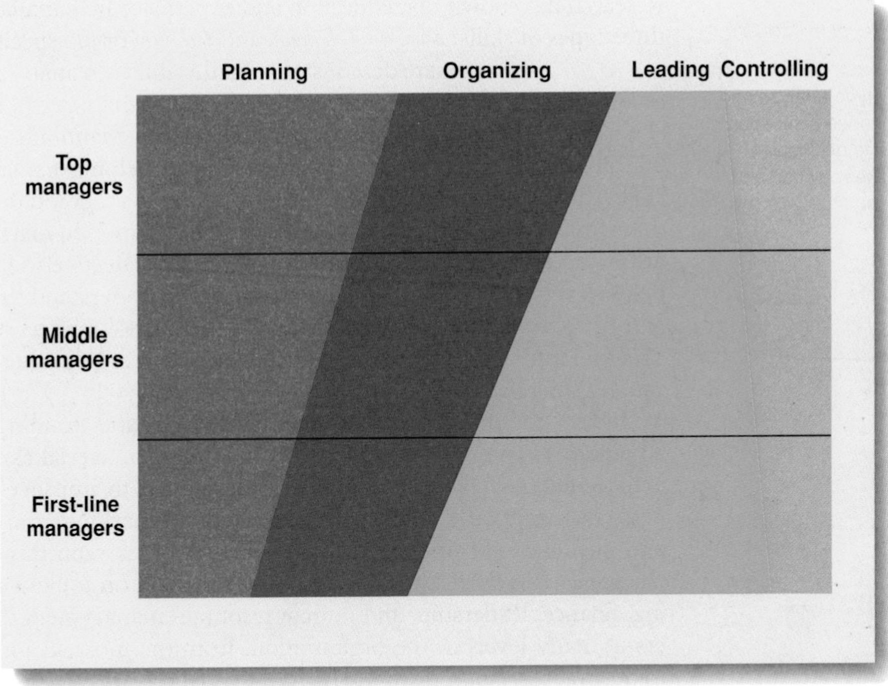

The *chief executive officer (CEO)* is a company's most senior and important manager, the one all other top managers report to. Today, the term *chief operating officer (COO)* is often used to refer to the top manager who is being groomed to take over as CEO when the current CEO retires or leaves the company. Together, the CEO and COO are responsible for developing good working relationships among the top managers of various departments (manufacturing and marketing, for example); usually top managers have the title "vice president." A central concern of the CEO is the creation of a smoothly functioning **top-management team,** a group composed of the CEO, the COO, the president, and the department heads most responsible for helping achieve organizational goals.[15]

top-management team A group composed of the CEO, the COO, the president, and the heads of the most important departments.

The relative importance of planning, organizing, leading, and controlling–the four principal managerial tasks–to any particular manager depends on the manager's position in the managerial hierarchy.[16] The amount of time that managers spend planning and organizing resources to maintain and improve organizational performance increases as they ascend the hierarchy (see Figure 1.4).[17] Top managers devote most of their time to planning and organizing, the tasks so crucial to determining an organization's long-term performance. The lower that managers' positions are in the hierarchy, the more time the managers spend leading and controlling first-line managers or nonmanagerial employees.

LO4 Distinguish among three kinds of managerial skill, and explain why managers are divided into different departments.

Managerial Skills

Both education and experience enable managers to recognize and develop the personal skills they need to put organizational resources to their best use. Michael Dell realized from the start that he lacked sufficient experience and technical expertise in marketing, finance, and planning to guide his company alone. Thus, he recruited experienced managers from other IT companies, such as IBM and HP, to help him build his company.

Research has shown that education and experience help managers acquire and develop three types of skills: *conceptual, human,* and *technical* or job-specific.[18]

conceptual skills The ability to analyze and diagnose a situation and to distinguish between cause and effect.

Conceptual skills are demonstrated in the ability to analyze and diagnose a situation and to distinguish between cause and effect. Top managers require the best conceptual skills because their primary responsibilities are planning and organizing.[19] Formal education and training are very important in helping managers develop conceptual skills. Business training at the undergraduate and graduate (MBA) levels provides many of the conceptual tools (theories and techniques in marketing, finance, and other areas) that managers need to perform their roles effectively. The study of management helps develop the skills that allow managers to understand the big picture confronting an organization. The ability to focus on the big picture lets managers see beyond the situation immediately at hand and consider choices while keeping in mind the organization's long-term goals.

Today, continuing management education and training, including training in advanced IT, are an integral step in building managerial skills because new theories and techniques are constantly being developed to improve organizational effectiveness, such as total quality management, benchmarking, and Web-based organization and business-to-business (B2B) networks. A quick scan through a magazine such as *BusinessWeek* or *Fortune* reveals a host of seminars on topics such as advanced marketing, finance, leadership, and human resources management that are offered to managers at many levels in the organization, from the most senior corporate executives to middle managers. Microsoft, IBM, Motorola, and many other organizations designate a portion of each manager's personal budget to be used at the manager's discretion to attend management development programs.

In addition, organizations may wish to develop a particular manager's abilities in a specific skill area–perhaps to learn an advanced component of departmental skills, such as international bond trading, or to learn the skills necessary to implement total quality management. The organization thus pays for managers to attend specialized programs to develop these skills. Indeed, one signal that a manager is performing well is an organization's willingness to invest in that manager's skill development. Similarly, many nonmanagerial employees who are performing at a high level (because they have studied management) are often sent to intensive management training programs to develop their management skills and to prepare them for promotion to first-level management positions.

human skills The ability to understand, alter, lead, and control the behavior of other individuals and groups.

Human skills include the ability to understand, alter, lead, and control the behavior of other individuals and groups. The ability to communicate, to coordinate, and to motivate people, and to mold individuals into a cohesive team, distinguishes effective from ineffective managers. By all accounts, Andrea Jung, Michael Dell, and Joe Coulombe all possess a high level of these human skills.

Like conceptual skills, human skills can be learned through education and training, as well as be developed through experience.[20] Organizations increasingly utilize advanced programs in leadership skills and team leadership as they seek to capitalize on the advantages of self-managed teams.[21] To manage personal interactions effectively, each person in an organization needs to learn how to empathize with other people–to understand their viewpoints and the problems they face. One way to help managers understand their personal strengths and weaknesses is to have their superiors, peers, and subordinates provide feedback about their job performance. Thorough and direct feedback allows managers to develop their human skills.

technical skills The job-specific knowledge and techniques required to perform an organizational role.

Technical skills are the job-specific skills required to perform a particular type of work or occupation at a high level. Examples include a manager's specific manufacturing,

Figure 1.5
Types and Levels of Managers

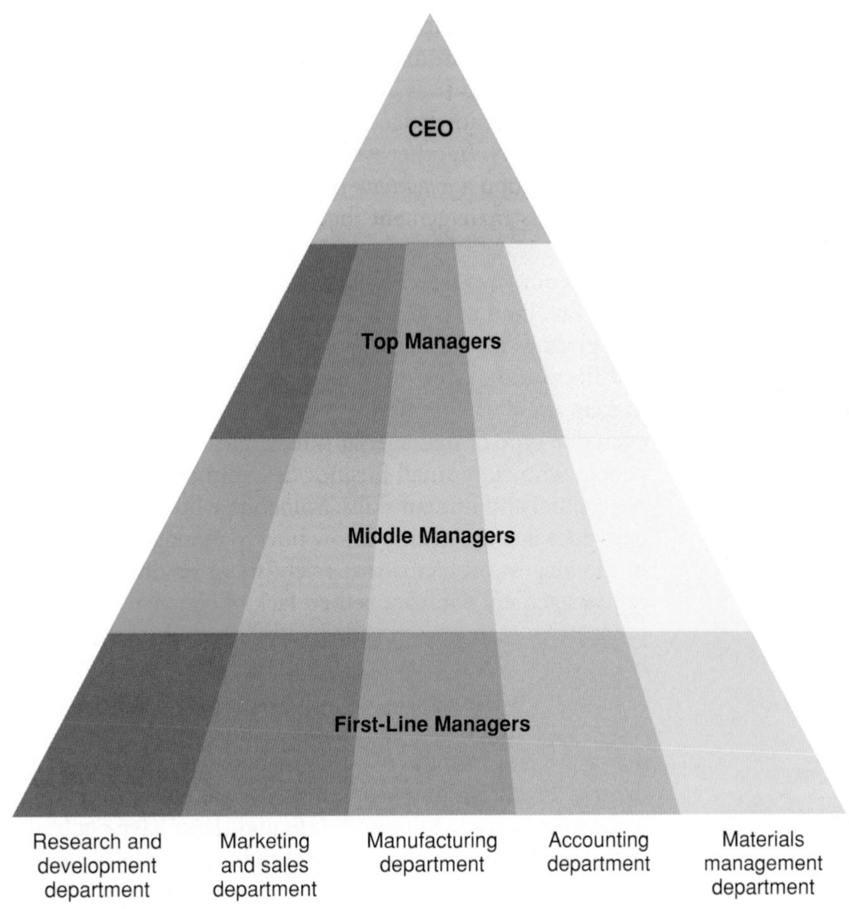

accounting, marketing, and increasingly, IT skills. Managers need a range of technical skills to be effective. The array of technical skills managers need depends on their position in their organizations. The manager of a restaurant, for example, may need cooking skills to fill in for an absent cook, accounting and bookkeeping skills to keep track of receipts and costs and to administer the payroll, and aesthetic skills to keep the restaurant looking attractive for customers.

As noted earlier, managers and employees who possess the same kinds of technical skills typically become members of a specific department and are known as, for example, marketing managers or manufacturing managers.[22] Managers are grouped into different departments because a major part of a manager's responsibility is to monitor, train, and supervise employees so that their job-specific skills and expertise increase. Obviously this is easier to do when employees with similar skills are grouped into the same department because they can learn from one another and become more skilled and productive at their particular jobs.

Figure 1.5 shows how an organization groups managers into departments on the basis of their job-specific skills. It also shows that inside each department, a managerial hierarchy of first-line, middle, and top managers emerges. At Dell, for example, Michael Dell hired experienced top managers to take charge of the marketing, sales, and manufacturing departments and to develop work procedures to help middle and first-line managers control the company's explosive sales growth. When the head of manufacturing found he had no time to supervise computer assembly, he recruited experienced manufacturing middle managers from other companies to assume this responsibility.

core competency The specific set of departmental skills, knowledge, and experience that allows one organization to outperform another.

Today, the term **core competency** is often used to refer to the specific set of departmental skills, knowledge, and experience that allows one organization to outperform its competitors. In other words, departmental skills that create a core competency give an organization a *competitive advantage*. Dell, for example, developed a core competency in materials management that allowed it to make PCs for less than its competitors—a major source of competitive advantage. Similarly, 3M is well known for its core competency in research and development that allows it to innovate new products at a faster rate than its competitors, and Trader Joe's has a competency in customer service that gives its loyal customers an attentive, personalized shopping experience.

Effective managers need all three kinds of skills—conceptual, human, and technical—to help their organizations perform more efficiently and effectively. The absence of even one type of managerial skill can lead to failure. One of the biggest problems that people who start small businesses confront, for example, is their lack of appropriate conceptual and human skills. Someone who has the technical skills to start a new business does not necessarily know how to manage the venture successfully. Similarly, one of the biggest problems that scientists or engineers who switch careers from research to management confront is their lack of effective human skills. Ambitious managers or prospective managers are constantly in search of the latest educational contributions to help them develop the conceptual, human, and technical skills they need to perform at a high level in today's changing and increasingly competitive global environment.

Developing new and improved skills through education and training has become a major priority for both aspiring managers and the organizations they work for. As we discussed earlier, many people are enrolling in advanced management courses; but many companies, such as Microsoft, GE, and IBM, have established their own colleges to train and develop their employees and managers at all levels. Every year these companies put thousands of their employees through management programs designed to identify the employees who the company believes have superior competencies and whom it can develop to become its future top managers. In many organizations promotion is closely tied to a manager's ability to acquire the competencies that a particular company believes are important.[23] At 3M, for example, the ability to successfully lead a new product development team is viewed as a vital requirement for promotion; at IBM, the ability to attract and retain clients is viewed as a skill its consultants must possess. We discuss the various kinds of skills managers need to develop in most of the chapters of this book.

Recent Changes in Management Practices

The tasks and responsibilities of managers have been changing dramatically in recent years. Two major factors that have led to these changes are global competition and advances in new information technology (IT). Stiff competition for resources from organizations both at home and abroad has put increased pressure on all managers to improve efficiency and effectiveness. Increasingly, top managers are encouraging lower-level managers to look beyond the goals of their own departments and take a cross-departmental view to find new opportunities to improve organizational performance. Modern IT gives managers at all levels and in all areas access to more and better information and improves their ability to plan, organize, lead, and control. IT also provides employees with more job-related information and allows them to become more skilled, specialized, and productive.[24]

Restructuring and Outsourcing

To utilize IT to increase efficiency and effectiveness, CEOs and top-management teams have been restructuring organizations and outsourcing specific organizational activities to reduce the number of employees on the payroll and make more productive use of the remaining workforce.

restructuring Downsizing an organization by eliminating the jobs of large numbers of top, middle, and first-line managers and nonmanagerial employees.

Restructuring involves simplifying, shrinking, or downsizing an organization's operations to lower operating costs as many companies have been doing because of the recession that started in 2008. Restructuring can be done by eliminating departments and reducing levels in the hierarchy, both of which result in the loss of large numbers of jobs of top, middle, or first-line managers and nonmanagerial employees. Modern IT's ability to increase efficiency has increased the amount of downsizing in recent years. For example, IT makes it possible for fewer employees to perform a given task because it increases each person's ability to process information and make decisions more quickly and accurately. U.S. companies are spending over $100 billion a year on advanced IT that improves efficiency and effectiveness. We discuss IT's many dramatic effects on management in Chapter 13 and throughout this book.

Restructuring, however, can produce some powerful negative outcomes. It can reduce the morale of the remaining employees who are worried about their own job security. And top managers of many downsized organizations realize that they downsized too far when their employees complain they are overworked and when increasing numbers of customers complain about poor-quality service.[25] Dell faces this charge in the 2000s as it continues to reduce the number of its customer service reps and outsource their jobs to India to lower costs. On the other hand, Trader Joe's has been performing well, and because of its excellent customer service it is still rapidly expanding.

outsourcing Contracting with another company, usually abroad, to have it perform an activity the organization previously performed itself.

Outsourcing involves contracting with another company, usually in a low-cost country abroad, to have it perform a work activity the organization previously performed itself, such as manufacturing, marketing, or customer service. Outsourcing increases efficiency because it lowers operating costs, freeing up money and resources that can be used in more effective ways–for example, to develop new products.

The need to respond to low-cost global competition has speeded outsourcing dramatically in the 2000s. Over 3 million U.S. jobs in the manufacturing sector have been lost since 2000 as companies moved their operations to countries such as China, Taiwan, and Malaysia. Tens of thousands of high-paying jobs in IT have also moved abroad, to countries like India and Russia, where programmers work for one-third the salary of those in the United States. Dell currently employs over 15,000 customer service reps in India, for example.[26]

Large for-profit organizations today typically employ 10% to 20% fewer people than they did 10 years ago because of restructuring and outsourcing. Ford, IBM, AT&T, HP, Dell, and Du Pont are among the thousands of organizations that have streamlined their operations to increase efficiency and effectiveness. The argument is that the managers and employees who have lost their jobs will find employment in new and growing U.S. companies where their skills and experience will be better utilized. For example, the millions of manufacturing jobs that have been sent overseas will be replaced by higher-paying U.S. jobs in the service sector that are made possible because of the growth in global trade.

empowerment The expansion of employees' knowledge, tasks, and decision-making responsibilities.

Empowerment and Self-Managed Teams

The second principal way managers have sought to increase efficiency and effectiveness is by empowering lower-level employees and moving to self-managed teams. **Empowerment** is a management technique that involves giving employees more

John Deer technicians, such as the one working on this tractor, add irreplaceable know-how to help its sales force learn how farmers' specific needs are changing so that they can continually modify its equipment to meet their requirements. Their input has helped John Deere's sales increase significantly—and make its machines more useful to their users.

authority and responsibility over the way they perform their work activities–an approach Joe Coulombe followed at Trader Joe's. The way in which John Deere, the well-known manufacturer of tractors, empowered its employees illustrates how this technique can help raise performance. The employees who assemble Deere's vehicles possess detailed knowledge about how Deere products work. Deere's managers suddenly realized that these employees could become persuasive salespeople if they were given training. So groups of these employees were given intensive sales training and sent to visit Deere's customers and explain to them how to operate and service the company's new products. While speaking with customers, these newly empowered "salespeople" are also able to collect information that helps Deere develop new products that better meet customers' needs. The new sales jobs are only temporary; employees go on assignment but then return to the production line, where they use their new knowledge to find ways to improve efficiency and quality.

LO5 Discuss some major changes in management practices today that have occurred as a result of globalization and the use of advanced information technology (IT).

Often, companies find that empowering employees can lead to so many kinds of performance gains that they use their reward systems to promote empowerment. For example, Deere's moves to empower employees were so successful that the company negotiated a new labor agreement with its employees to promote empowerment. The agreement specifies that pay increases will be based on employees' learning new skills and completing college courses in areas such as computer programming that will help the company increase efficiency and quality. Deere has continued to make greater and greater use of teams throughout the 2000s, and its profits have soared because its competitors simply cannot match its user-friendly machines that are the result of its drive to be responsive to the needs of its customers.

self-managed team A group of employees who assume responsibility for organizing, controlling, and supervising their own activities and monitoring the quality of the goods and services they provide.

Information technology is being increasingly used to empower employees because it expands employees' job knowledge and increases the scope of their job responsibilities. Frequently, IT allows one employee to perform a task that was previously performed by many employees. As a result, the employee has more autonomy and responsibility. IT also facilitates the use of a **self-managed team,** a group of employees who assume collective responsibility for organizing, controlling, and supervising their own work activities.[27] Using IT designed to provide team members with real-time information about each member's performance, a self-managed team can often find ways to accomplish a task more quickly and efficiently. Moreover, self-managed teams assume many of the tasks and responsibilities previously performed by first-line managers, so a company can better utilize its workforce.[28] First-line managers act as coaches or mentors whose job is not to tell employees what to do but to provide advice and guidance and help teams find new ways to perform their tasks more efficiently.[29] Using the same IT, middle managers can easily monitor what is happening in these teams and so make better resource allocation decisions as a result. The way in which IBM developed IT to take advantage of the performance-enhancing benefits of self-managed teams is discussed next.

LO6 Discuss the principal challenges managers face in today's increasingly competitive global environment.

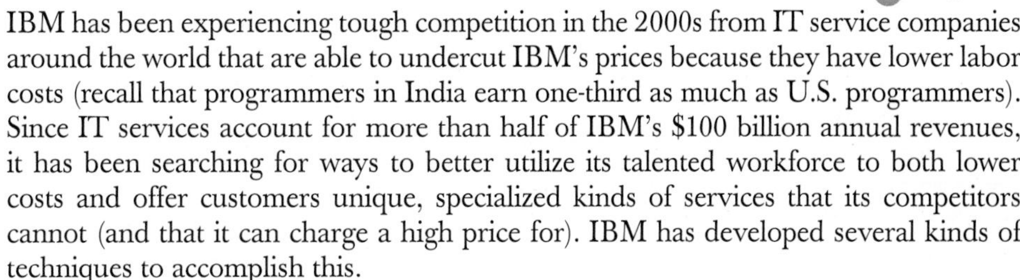

INFORMATION TECHNOLOGY BYTE

IBM Creates Global Self-Managed Teams

IBM has been experiencing tough competition in the 2000s from IT service companies around the world that are able to undercut IBM's prices because they have lower labor costs (recall that programmers in India earn one-third as much as U.S. programmers). Since IT services account for more than half of IBM's $100 billion annual revenues, it has been searching for ways to better utilize its talented workforce to both lower costs and offer customers unique, specialized kinds of services that its competitors cannot (and that it can charge a high price for). IBM has developed several kinds of techniques to accomplish this.

In the 2000s, IBM created "competency centers" around the world that are staffed by employees who share the same specific IT skill. In India, for example, IBM employs over 10,000 IT personnel who specialize in providing technical customer support for large U.S. companies. These employees work in self-managed teams and are responsible for managing all aspects of a particular client's specific needs. By using teams, IBM is now able to offer high-quality personalized service at a low price and compete effectively in the global marketplace.

Most of IBM's employees are concentrated in competency centers located in the countries in which IBM has the most clients and does the most business. These employees have a wide variety of skills, developed from their previous work experience, and the challenge facing IBM is to use these experts efficiently. To accomplish this, IBM used its own IT expertise to develop sophisticated software that allows it to create self-managed teams composed of IBM experts who have the optimum mix of skills to solve a client's particular problems. First, IBM programmers analyze the skills and experience of its 80,000 global consultants and input the results into the software program. Then they analyze and code the nature of a client's specific problem and input that information. IBM's program then matches each specific client problem to the skills of IBM's experts and identifies a list of "best fit" employees. One of IBM's senior managers then narrows down this list and decides on the actual composition of the self-managed team. Once selected, team members, from wherever they happen to be in the world, assemble as quickly as possible and go to work analyzing the client's problem. Together, team members then use their authority to develop the software, hardware, and service package necessary to solve and manage the client's problem.

This new IT allows IBM to create an ever-changing set of global self-managed teams that form to solve the problems of IBM's global clients. At the same time, IBM's IT also optimizes the use of its whole talented workforce because each employee is being placed in his or her "most highly valued use"–that is, in the team where the employee's skills can best increase efficiency and effectiveness. In addition, because each team inputs knowledge about its activities into IBM's internal information system, teams can watch and learn from one another–so their skills increase over time.

Challenges for Management in a Global Environment

Because the world has been changing more rapidly than ever before, managers and other employees throughout an organization must perform at higher and higher levels.[30] In the last 20 years, rivalry between organizations competing domestically (in the same country) and globally (in countries abroad) has increased dramatically. The rise of **global organizations**, organizations that operate and compete in more than one country, has put severe pressure on many organizations to identify better ways to use their resources and improve their performance. The successes of the German chemical companies Schering and Hoechst, Italian furniture manufacturer Natuzzi, Korean electronics companies Samsung and LG, Brazilian plane maker Embraer, and Europe's Airbus Industries are putting pressure on companies in other countries to raise their level of performance to compete successfully against these global organizations.

global organizations Organizations that operate and compete in more than one country.

Even in the not-for-profit sector, global competition is spurring change. Schools, universities, police forces, and government agencies are reexamining their operations because looking at the way activities are performed in other countries often reveals better ways to do them. For example, many curriculum and teaching changes in the United States have resulted from the study of methods that Japanese and European school systems use. Similarly, European and Asian hospital systems have learned much from the U.S. system–which may be the most effective, though not the most efficient, in the world.

Today, managers who make no attempt to learn from and adapt to changes in the global environment find themselves reacting rather than innovating, and their organizations often become uncompetitive and fail.[31] Five major challenges stand out for managers in today's world: building a competitive advantage, maintaining ethical standards, managing a diverse workforce, utilizing new information systems and technologies, and practicing global crisis management.

Building Competitive Advantage

What are the most important lessons for managers and organizations to learn if they are to reach and remain at the top of the competitive environment of business? The answer relates to the use of organizational resources to build a competitive advantage. **Competitive advantage** is the ability of one organization to outperform other organizations because it produces desired goods or services more efficiently and effectively than its competitors. The four building blocks of competitive advantage are superior *efficiency; quality; speed, flexibility,* and *innovation;* and *responsiveness to customers* (see Figure 1.6).

competitive advantage The ability of one organization to outperform other organizations because it produces desired goods or services more efficiently and effectively than they do.

Organizations increase their efficiency when they reduce the quantity of resources (such as people and raw materials) they use to produce goods or services. In today's competitive environment, organizations continually search for new ways to use their resources to improve efficiency. Many organizations are training their workforces in the new skills and techniques needed to operate heavily computerized assembly plants. Similarly, cross-training gives employees the range of skills they need to perform many different tasks, and organizing employees in new ways, such as in self-managed teams, allows them to make good use of their skills. These are important steps in the effort to improve productivity. Japanese and German companies invest far more in training employees than do American or Italian companies.

Managers must improve efficiency if their organizations are to compete successfully with companies operating in Mexico, China, Malaysia, and other countries where

Figure 1.6
Building Blocks of Competitive Advantage

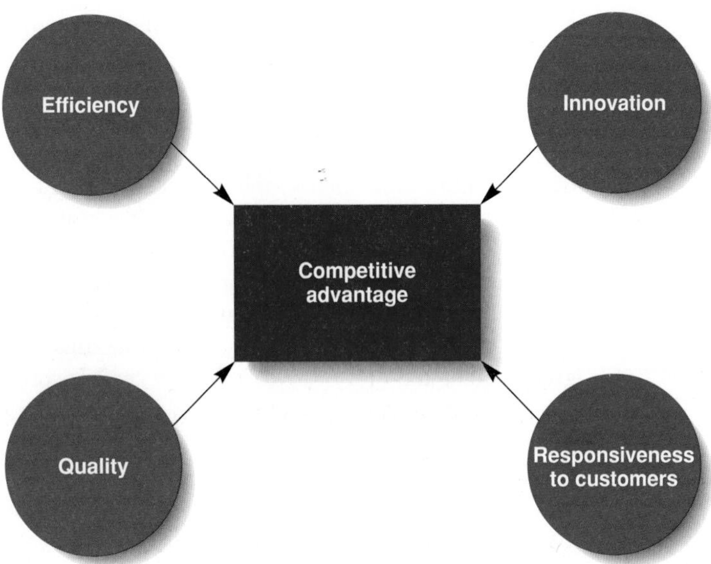

employees are paid comparatively low wages. New methods must be devised either to increase efficiency or to gain some other competitive advantage–higher-quality goods, for example–if outsourcing and the loss of jobs to low-cost countries are to be prevented.

The challenge from global organizations such as Korean electronics manufacturers, Mexican agricultural producers, and European marketing and financial firms also has increased pressure on companies to improve the skills and abilities of their workforces in order to improve the quality of their goods and services. One major thrust to improving quality has been to introduce the quality-enhancing techniques known as *total quality management (TQM)*. Employees involved in TQM are often organized into quality control teams and are responsible for finding new and better ways to perform their jobs; they also must monitor and evaluate the quality of the goods they produce. We discuss ways of managing TQM successfully in Chapter 14.

Today, companies can win or lose the competitive race depending on their *speed*–how fast they can bring new products to market–or their *flexibility*–how easily they can change or alter the way they perform their activities to respond to the actions of their competitors. Companies that have speed and flexibility are *agile competitors:* Their managers have superior planning and organizing abilities; they can think ahead, decide what to do, and then speedily mobilize their resources to respond to a changing environment. We examine how managers can build speed and flexibility in their organizations in later chapters.

innovation The process of creating new or improved goods and services or developing better ways to produce or provide them.

Innovation, the process of creating new or improved goods and services that customers want or developing better ways to produce or provide goods and services, poses a special challenge. Managers must create an organizational setting in which people are encouraged to be innovative. Typically, innovation takes place in small groups or teams; management decentralizes control of work activities to team members and creates an organizational culture that rewards risk taking. For example, Apple and Nike cooperated and formed a team to think about how to link their products. The Apple/Nike team came up with the idea for a new model of iPod that would be able to record and measure the distance its owner had run, among other things, and the companies formed an alliance to make it.[32] Managing innovation and creating a work setting that encourages risk taking are among the most difficult managerial tasks.

Organizations compete for customers with their products and services, so training employees to be responsive to customers' needs is vital for all organizations, but particularly for service organizations. Retail stores, banks, and hospitals, for example, depend entirely on their employees to perform behaviors that result in high-quality service at a reasonable cost.[33] As many countries (the United States, Canada, and Switzerland are just a few) move toward a more service-based economy (in part because of the loss of manufacturing jobs to China, Malaysia, and other countries with low labor costs), managing behavior in service organizations is becoming increasingly important. Many organizations are empowering their customer service employees and giving them the authority to take the lead in providing high-quality customer service. As noted previously, the empowering of nonmanagerial employees changes the role of first-line managers and often leads to the more efficient use of organizational resources.

Because of intense global competition, companies like Kodak, Xerox, Apple, GM, Ford, Levi Strauss, Heinz, and a host of others lost their competitive advantage. For example, technological change and the move toward digital imaging led demand for Kodak's film and light-based Xerox copiers to plunge. Others like GM and Levi Strauss have suffered because low-cost competitors undercut their prices. The managers of these companies face the challenge of turning around the performance of their companies by finding ways to restore competitive advantage.

turnaround management The creation of a new vision for a struggling company based on a new approach to planning and organizing to make better use of a company's resources to allow it to survive and prosper.

Sometimes the best efforts of managers to revitalize their organization's fortunes fail, and faced with bankruptcy, the directors of these companies are forced to appoint a new CEO who has a history of success in rebuilding a company. **Turnaround management** is the creation of a new vision for a struggling company using a new approach to planning and organizing to make better use of a company's resources to allow it to survive, and eventually prosper. It involves developing radical new strategies such as reducing the number of products sold, changing how they are made and sold, and major closings of corporate and manufacturing operations. Organizations that appoint turnaround CEOs are generally experiencing a crisis because they have become inefficient or ineffective; sometimes this is because of poor management over a continuing period, and sometimes it occurs because a competitor introduces a new product or technology that makes their own products unattractive to customers. For example, when Apple introduced the iPhone in 2007, sales of the former best-selling mobile phone, Motorola's Razr, plummeted because customers want state-of-the-art products; Motorola's very survival was in question in 2009 unless it can introduce innovative new cell phones.

Turnaround management is a particularly difficult and complex management task because it is done under conditions of great uncertainty. Customers, employees, and investors are unsure about the future; for example, will customer service be available, will employees retain their jobs, and will investors get their money back? The risk of failure is greater for a troubled company, and usually a more radical restructuring and company reorganization are necessary to turn around its performance. Few companies stay on top all the time–and the only place left is "down"–and this is why it is so important that managers continually monitor how well their company is performing compared to its rivals, as we discuss in Chapter 6.

Achieving a competitive advantage requires that managers use all their skills and expertise, as well as their companies' other resources, to improve efficiency, quality, innovation, and responsiveness to customers. We will revisit this theme often as we examine the ways managers plan strategies, organize resources and activities, and lead and control people and groups to increase efficiency and effectiveness.

Maintaining Ethical and Socially Responsible Standards

Managers at all levels are under considerable pressure to make the best use of resources to increase the level at which their organizations perform.[34] For example, top managers feel pressure from shareholders to increase the performance of the entire organization to boost its stock price, improve profits, or raise dividends. In turn, top managers may then pressure middle managers to find new ways to use organizational resources to increase efficiency or quality and thus attract new customers and earn more revenues–and then middle managers hit on their department's supervisors.

Pressure to increase performance can be healthy for an organization because it leads managers to question the way the organization is working and it encourages them to find new and better ways to plan, organize, lead, and control. However, too much pressure to perform can be harmful.[35] It may induce managers to behave unethically, and even illegally, when dealing with people and groups inside and outside the organization.[36] For example, a purchasing manager for a nationwide retail chain might buy inferior clothing as a cost-cutting measure; or to secure a large foreign contract, a sales manager in a large defense company might offer bribes to foreign officials. These issues faced the managers of companies that make footwear and clothing in the 1990s, when customers learned about the sweatshop conditions in which garment and shoe workers around the world labored. Companies such as Nike and Wal-Mart have made major efforts to stop sweatshop practices and prevent managers abroad from adopting work practices that harm their workers. They now employ hundreds of inspectors who police the factories overseas that make the products they sell and who can terminate contracts with suppliers when they behave in an unethical or illegal way.

The issue of social responsibility, discussed in Chapter 3, centers on deciding what, if any, obligations a company has toward the people and groups affected by its activities–such as employees, customers, or the communities in which it operates. Some companies have strong views about social responsibility; their managers believe they should protect the interests of others. But some managers may decide to act in an unethical way and put their own interests, or their company's, first, hurting others in the process. For example, Metabolife and NVE Pharmaceuticals used to make ephedra, a widely used dietary supplement. To protect their business, they did not reveal serious complaints about ephedra until forced to do so by lawsuits brought by people harmed by the drug. When Metabolife finally released over 16,000 customer reports about its ephedra products, it listed nearly 2,000 adverse reactions, including 3 deaths.[37]

One year later the Food and Drug Administration (FDA) obtained the legal power to demand information from all the makers of ephedra pills. This revealed over 16,000 adverse-report events experienced by users, including at least 36 deaths. As a result, it became illegal to make or sell ephedra in the United States.[38]

The old saying *Caveat emptor,* "Buyer beware," remains true whenever a customer is deciding to buy an unknown product.[39] Another example showing why companies, managers, and customers must always keep the need to act in an ethical and socially responsible way at the forefront of their decision making is profiled in the following "Ethics in Action."

ETHICS IN ACTION

How Not to Run a Meatpacking Plant

By all appearances the Westland/Hallmark Meat Co., owned by its CEO Steven Mendell, was considered to be one of the most efficient, sanitary, and state-of-the-art meatpacking companies in the United States. Based in Chico, California, its meatpacking plant, which regularly passed inspections by the United States Department of Agriculture (USDA), employed over 200 workers who slaughtered and then prepared the beef for shipment to fast-food restaurants such as Burger King and Taco Bell. Most of the millions of pounds of meat the plant prepared yearly, however, was delivered under contract to one of the federal government's most coveted accounts: the National School Lunch Program. In 2005 the plant was named supplier of the year by the National School Lunch Program.[40]

So, when at the end of 2007 the Humane Society turned over a videotape, secretly filmed by one of its investigators who had taken a job as a plant employee, to the San Bernardino County District Attorney that showed major violations of safety procedures, this caused an uproar. The videotape showed two workers dragging sick cows up the ramp that led to the slaughterhouse using metal chains and forklifts, and shocking them with electric prods and shooting streams of water in their noses and faces. Not only did the tape show inhumane treatment of animals, it also provided evidence that the company was flouting the ban on allowing sick animals to enter the food supply chain–something that federal regulations explicitly outlawed for fear of human health and disease issues.

Small Business

By February 2008 the USDA, concerned that contaminated beef had entered the supply chain, especially the one to the nation's schools, issued a notice for the recall of 143 million pounds of beef processed in the plant over the last two years, the largest recall in history. In addition, the plant was shut down as the investigation proceeded. In March 2008, CEO Steven Mendell was subpoenaed to appear before the House Panel on Energy and Commerce Committee. He denied that these violations had taken place and that any diseased cows had entered the food chain. However, when panel members demanded that he view the videotape that he claimed he had not seen even though it was widely available, he was forced to acknowledge that "two cows" had in fact entered the plant and

Westland/Hallmark Meat Company CEO Steven Mendell on the stand before Congress. Behind him plays the secretly taken video of cattle being driven into the meatpacking plant. Mendell's company, putting profits before ethical accountability, is responsible for the largest ground beef recall ever to take place in the United States.

that inhumane treatment of animals had taken place.[41] Moreover, federal investigators turned up evidence that as early as 1996 the plant had been cited for overuse of electric prods to speed cattle through the plant and had been cited for other violations since, suggesting that these abuses had been going on for a long period. This view gained strength when one of the workers shown in the videotape claimed that he had just been "following orders from his supervisor" and that workers were pressured to ensure 500 cows a day were slaughtered and processed so the plant could meet its quota and make the high profits the meatpacking business provides.

These unethical, and often illegal, business practices caused major fears that over the years thousands of sick cows have entered the food chain, and most of the 143 million pounds of beef recalled have already been consumed. Not only consumers and schoolchildren have been harmed by these unethical actions–it seems likely that the plant will be permanently shut down and that all 220 workers will lose their jobs. In addition, the employees directly implicated in the video have already been prosecuted, and one, who pleaded guilty to animal abuse, was convicted and sentenced to six months imprisonment.[42] Whether or not the company's managers will experience the same fate remains to be seen, but clearly all stakeholders have been hurt by the unethical and inhumane practices that, as the Humane Society had suspected for years, were commonplace in the plant.

Managing a Diverse Workforce

A major challenge for managers everywhere is to recognize the ethical need and legal requirement to treat human resources in a fair and equitable manner. Today the age, gender, race, ethnicity, religion, sexual preference, and socioeconomic makeup of the workforce present new challenges for managers. To create a highly trained and motivated workforce, as well as to avoid major class-action lawsuits, managers must establish human resource management (HRM) procedures and practices that are legal, are fair, and do not discriminate against any organizational members.[43]

In the past, white male employees dominated the ranks of management. Today increasing numbers of organizations are realizing that to motivate effectively and take advantage of the talents of a diverse workforce, they must make promotion opportunities available to all employees, including women and minorities.[44] Managers must recognize the performance-enhancing possibilities of a diverse workforce, such as the ability to take advantage of the skills and experiences of different kinds of people.[45] Union Bank of

Union Bank's customer service representatives, such as the employee pictured here, are well known for building relationships with their diverse customer groups to improve the level of customer service. The diverse nature of Union Bank's employees reflects the diverse customer groups the bank serves.

California, one of the 30 largest banks in the United States, is a good example of a company that has utilized the potential of its diverse employees.[46]

Based in San Francisco, Union Bank operates in one of the most diverse states in the nation, California, where more than half the population is Asian, black, Hispanic, or gay. Recognizing this fact, the bank always had a policy of hiring diverse employees. However, the bank did not realize the potential of its diverse employees to create a competitive advantage until 1996 when George Ramirez, a vice president at Union Bank, proposed that the bank create a marketing group to attract Hispanic customers. His idea was so successful that a group of African-American employees, and later Asian-American and gay and lesbian employees, proposed similar marketing campaigns.

After these groups' considerable success in recruiting new customers, it was clear to Union Bank's managers that they could use employee diversity to improve customer service too (e.g., by staffing banks in Latino neighborhoods with Latino employees).[47] Then they realized they could also enhance the quality of decision making inside the organization.[48] The bank's reputation of being a good place for minorities to work has attracted highly skilled and motivated minority job candidates.

As its former CEO Takahiro Moriguchi said when accepting a national diversity award for the company, "By searching for talent from among the disabled, both genders, veterans, gay, all ethnic groups and all nationalities, we gain access to a pool of ideas, energy, and creativity as wide and varied as the human race itself. I expect diversity will become even more important as the world gradually becomes a truly global marketplace."[49] Union Bank's diversity practices have become a model for many other companies seeking to emulate its success.[50]

Managers who value their diverse employees and invest in developing these employees' skills and capabilities succeed best in promoting performance over the long run. Today, more and more organizations are realizing that people are their most important resource. We discuss the many issues surrounding the management of a diverse workforce in Chapter 3.

IT and E-Commerce

As we have discussed, another important challenge for managers is the efficient use of advanced IT.[51] New technologies such as computer-controlled manufacturing and Web-based IT that link and enable employees in new ways are continually being developed. One interesting example of how IT is changing the jobs of people at all organizational levels comes from UPS. UPS drivers used to rely on maps, note cards, and their own experience to plan the fastest way to deliver hundreds of parcels each day. This changed quickly after UPS invested $700 million to develop a computerized route optimization system that each evening plans out each of its 56,000 drivers' routes for the next day. Efficiency is realized, for example, by minimizing the number of left turns, which waste both time and gas. The program has been incredibly successful. UPS drivers now drive millions of fewer miles each month, even as they deliver an increased number of packages at a faster rate.

IT enables not just individual employees but also self-managed teams by providing them with more important information and allowing for virtual interactions around the globe by using the Internet. Increased global coordination helps to improve quality and increase the pace of innovation. Microsoft, Hitachi, IBM, and most companies now search for new IT that can help them to build a competitive advantage. The importance of IT is discussed in detail in Chapter 13, and throughout the text you will find icons that alert you to examples of how IT is transforming the way companies operate.

Practicing Global Crisis Management

Today, another challenge facing managers and organizations is global crisis management. The causes of global crises or disasters fall into three main categories: natural causes, man-made causes, and international terrorism and geopolitical conflicts. Crises that arise because of natural causes include the hurricanes, tsunamis, earthquakes, famines, and diseases that have devastated so many countries in the 2000s; hardly any country has been left untouched by their effects. Java, for example, which was inundated by the huge Pacific tsunami of 2004, experienced a devastating earthquake in 2006 that also killed thousands of people and left tens of thousands more homeless.

Man-made crises are the result of factors such as global warming, pollution, and the destruction of the natural habitat or environment. Pollution, for example, has become an increasingly significant problem for companies and countries to deal with. Companies in heavy industries such as coal and steel have polluted millions of acres of land around major cities in eastern Europe and Asia; billion-dollar cleanups are necessary. The 1986 Chernobyl nuclear power plant meltdown released over 1,540 times as much radiation into the air as occurred at Hiroshima; over 50,000 people died as a result, while hundreds of thousands more have been affected.

Man-made crises, such as global warming due to emissions of carbon dioxide and other gases, may have made the effects of natural disasters more serious. For example, increasing global temperatures and acid rain may have increased the intensity of hurricanes, led to unusually strong rains, and contributed to lengthy droughts. Scientists are convinced that global warming is responsible for the destruction of coral reefs (which are disappearing at a fast rate), forests, animal species, and the natural habitat in many parts of the world. The shrinking polar ice caps are expected to raise the sea level by a few, but vital, inches.

Finally, increasing geopolitical tensions, which are partly the result of the speed of the globalization process itself, have upset the balance of world power as different countries and geographic regions attempt to protect their own economic and political interests. Rising oil prices, for example, have strengthened the bargaining power of major oil-supplying countries. This has led the United States to adopt global political strategies, including its war on terrorism, to secure the supply of oil vital to protect its national interest. In a similar way, countries in Europe have been forming contracts and allying with Russia to obtain its supply of natural gas, and Japan and China have been negotiating with Iran and Saudi Arabia. The rise of global terrorism and terrorist groups is to a large degree the result of changing political, social, and economic conditions that have made it easier for extremists to influence whole countries and cultures.

Management has an important role to play in helping people, organizations, and countries respond to global crises because it provides lessons on how to plan, organize, lead, and control the resources needed to both forestall and respond effectively to a crisis. Crisis management involves making important choices about how to (1) create teams to facilitate rapid decision making and communication, (2) establish the organizational chain of command and reporting relationships necessary to mobilize a fast response, (3) recruit and select the right people to lead and work in such teams, and (4) develop bargaining and negotiating strategies to manage the conflicts that arise whenever people and groups have different interests and objectives. How well managers make such decisions determines how quickly an effective response to a crisis can be implemented, and it sometimes can prevent or reduce the severity of the crisis itself.

Summary and Review

WHAT IS MANAGEMENT? A manager is responsible for supervising the use of an organization's resources to meet its goals. An organization is a collection of people who work together to achieve a wide variety of goals. Management is the process of using organizational resources to achieve organizational goals effectively and efficiently through planning, organizing, leading, and controlling. An efficient organization makes the most productive use of its resources. An effective organization pursues appropriate goals and achieves these goals by using its resources to create the goods or services that customers want. **[LO1]**

ESSENTIAL MANAGERIAL TASKS The four principal managerial tasks are planning, organizing, leading, and controlling. Managers at all levels of the organization and in all departments perform these tasks. Effective management means managing these activities successfully. **[LO2]**

LEVELS AND SKILLS OF MANAGERS Organizations typically have three levels of management. First-line managers are responsible for the day-to-day supervision of nonmanagerial employees. Middle managers are responsible for developing and utilizing organizational resources efficiently and effectively. Top managers have cross-departmental responsibility. Top managers must establish appropriate goals for the entire organization and verify that department managers are utilizing resources to achieve those goals. Three main kinds of managerial skills are conceptual, human, and technical. The need to develop and build technical skills leads organizations to divide managers into departments according to their job-specific responsibilities. **[LO3, 4]**

RECENT CHANGES IN MANAGEMENT PRACTICES To increase efficiency and effectiveness, many organizations have restructured and downsized operations and outsourced activities to reduce costs. Companies are empowering their workforces and utilizing self-managed teams to increase efficiency and effectiveness. Managers are increasingly using IT to achieve competitive advantage. **[LO5]**

CHALLENGES FOR MANAGEMENT IN A GLOBAL ENVIRONMENT Today's competitive global environment presents many challenges to managers. One of the main challenges is building a competitive advantage by increasing efficiency; quality; speed, flexibility, and innovation; and customer responsiveness. Others are behaving in an ethical and socially responsible way toward people inside and outside the organization; managing a diverse workforce; and practicing global crisis management. **[LO6]**

Management in Action

Topics for Discussion and Action

DISCUSSION

1. Describe the difference between efficiency and effectiveness, and identify real organizations that you think are, or are not, efficient and effective. [LO1]
2. In what ways can managers at each of the three levels of management contribute to organizational efficiency and effectiveness? [LO3]
3. Identify an organization that you believe is high-performing and one that you believe is low-performing. Give five reasons why you think the performance levels of the two organizations differ so much. [LO2, 4]
4. What are the building blocks of competitive advantage? Why is obtaining a competitive advantage important to managers? [LO5]
5. In what ways do you think managers' jobs have changed the most over the last 10 years? Why have these changes occurred? [LO6]

ACTION

6. Choose an organization such as a school or a bank; visit it; then list the different organizational resources it uses. How do managers use these resources to maintain and improve its performance? [LO2, 4]
7. Visit an organization, and talk to first-line, middle, and top managers about their respective management roles in the organization and what they do to help the organization be efficient and effective. [LO3, 4]
8. Ask a middle or top manager, perhaps someone you already know, to give examples of how he or she performs the managerial tasks of planning, organizing, leading, and controlling. How much time does he or she spend in performing each task? [LO3]
9. Find a cooperative manager who will allow you to follow him or her around for a day. List the roles the manager plays, and indicate how much time he or she spends performing them. [LO3, 4]

Building Management Skills

Thinking about Managers and Management [LO2, 3, 4]

Think of an organization that has provided you with work experience and of the manager to whom you reported (or talk to someone who has had extensive work experience). Then answer these questions.

1. Think of your direct supervisor. Of what department is he or she a member, and at what level of management is this person?
2. How do you characterize your supervisor's approach to management? For example, which particular management tasks and roles does this person perform most often? What kinds of management skills does this manager have?
3. Do you think the tasks, roles, and skills of your supervisor are appropriate for the particular job he or she performs? How could this manager improve his or her task performance? How can IT affect this?
4. How did your supervisor's approach to management affect your attitudes and behavior? For example, how well did you perform as a subordinate, and how motivated were you?

5. Think of the organization and its resources. Do its managers utilize organizational resources effectively? Which resources contribute most to the organization's performance?
6. Describe the way the organization treats its human resources. How does this treatment affect the attitudes and behaviors of the workforce?
7. If you could give your manager one piece of advice or change one management practice in the organization, what would it be?
8. How attuned are the managers in the organization to the need to increase efficiency, quality, innovation, or responsiveness to customers? How well do you think the organization performs its prime goals of providing the goods or services that customers want or need the most?

Managing Ethically [LO1, 3]

Think about an example of unethical behavior that you observed in the past. The incident could be something you experienced as an employee or a customer or something you observed informally.

1. Either by yourself or in a group, give three reasons why you think the behavior was unethical. For example, what rules or norms were broken? Who benefited or was harmed by what took place? What was the outcome for the people involved?
2. What steps might you take to prevent such unethical behavior and encourage people to behave in an ethical way?

Small Group Breakout Exercise [LO2, 3, 4]

Opening a New Restaurant

Form groups of three or four people, and appoint one group member as the spokesperson who will communicate your findings to the entire class when called on by the instructor. Then discuss the following scenario.

You and your partners have decided to open a large, full-service restaurant in your local community; it will be open from 7 a.m. to 10 p.m. to serve breakfast, lunch, and dinner. Each of you is investing $50,000 in the venture, and together you have secured a bank loan for $300,000 more to begin operations. You and your partners have little experience in managing a restaurant beyond serving meals or eating in restaurants, and you now face the task of deciding how you will manage the restaurant and what your respective roles will be.

1. Decide what each partner's managerial role in the restaurant will be. For example, who will be responsible for the necessary departments and specific activities? Describe your managerial hierarchy.
2. Which building blocks of competitive advantage do you need to establish to help your restaurant succeed? What criteria will you use to evaluate how successfully you are managing the restaurant?
3. Discuss the most important decisions that must be made about (a) planning, (b) organizing, (c) leading, and (d) controlling to allow you and your partners to utilize organizational resources effectively and build a competitive advantage.
4. For each managerial task, list the issues to solve, and decide which roles will contribute the most to your restaurant's success.

Be the Manager [LO2, 5]

Problems at Achieva

You have just been called in to help managers at Achieva, a fast-growing Internet software company that specializes in B2B network software. Your job is to help Achieva solve some management problems that have arisen because of its rapid growth.

Customer demand to license Achieva's software has boomed so much in just two years that more than 50 new software programmers have been added to help develop a new range of software products. Achieva's growth has been so swift that the company still operates informally, its organizational structure is loose and flexible, and programmers are encouraged to find solutions to problems as they go along. Although this structure worked well in the past, you have been told that problems are arising.

There have been increasing complaints from employees that good performance is not being recognized in the organization and that they do not feel equitably treated. Moreover, there have been complaints about getting managers to listen to their new ideas and to act on them. A bad atmosphere is developing in the company, and recently several talented employees left. Your job is to help Achieva's managers solve these problems quickly and keep the company on the fast track.

Questions

1. What kinds of organizing and controlling problems is Achieva suffering from?
2. What kinds of management changes need to be made to solve them?

BusinessWeek Case in the News [LO2, 3, 4]

The Art of CEO Succession

Pulling off a CEO transition is never easy. DuPont's smooth baton passing early this year underscores the importance of having a solid plan. This is not an easy time to nurture a new generation of corporate leaders. Training budgets are being slashed while a depressed housing market has made it harder to move around for better job opportunities. And yet the need for top talent is growing. A record 1,484 U.S.-based chief executives left their jobs in 2008, according to outplacement firm Challenger, Gray & Christmas. Many more could step down this year as losses mount and executive angst runs high. "The CEO job today is more stressful and draining than at any time in history," says Tom Stemberg, the founder and former CEO of Staples. "People have just run out of gas." At a time when corporations worldwide are crying out for new thinking, for a sense of how to plan for the next CEO, look at the seamless CEO transition at DuPont.

CEO Charles Holliday had spotted top lieutenant Ellen J. Kullman as a potential successor more than a decade ago. Holliday, a gregarious Tennessean and DuPont lifer who became CEO in early 1998, had mentored Kullman since they met in the early 1990s in Tokyo. He was running the Asia-Pacific operations, and she was visiting as a senior manager in the electronic imaging unit. He was impressed with Kullman's willingness to learn. "There goes a future leader," Holliday recalls saying to himself. Kullman remembers being peppered with questions. "He scared me," she says. Kullman joined DuPont as a marketing manager in 1988 and was quickly promoted, distinguishing herself by improving troubled units. She was tapped in 1995 to run DuPont's $2 billion titanium technologies business and later turned a newly formed safety-products division into what became the company's highest-earning segment during the time she ran it. "We had to change our business model three times before we found the right one," Kullman recalls. "There were times when I questioned whether we could get there or not." Kullman was executive vice president when Holliday told her in September 2008 that she would soon replace him in running DuPont. Although her appointment came a bit sooner than Wall Street analysts expected, no one was surprised to see her taking over as CEO at the start of 2009.

Holliday himself had a lot of help in getting to the top job. He came to the company on a summer internship and says he was mentored all through his career, even after he got the CEO job. Former DuPont chief Irving Shapiro, who ran the company during the 1970s, critiqued Holliday's performance after shareholder meetings, and outside executive coach Bill Morin taught him to be more up-front with his staff. Holliday says he began talking about succession "immediately" on becoming CEO. In addition to the usual "truck list"—a roster of people who could run the show if he were hit by the proverbial 18-wheeler—he tried to imagine who would be best suited to lead DuPont in the 21st century. In his mind, Kullman was an obvious possibility.

Although the mother of three's gender and marketing background made her an unusual CEO candidate for DuPont, Holliday felt the aggressive and sometimes sharp-tongued Kullman had a keen ability to see around corners. While many colleagues—including Kullman's husband, who also works at DuPont—counseled her against taking over the nascent safety-products unit, Holliday says Kullman "was able to grasp the image of what it could be." For instance, she came up with new uses for Kevlar synthetic fibers, a brand made famous in bulletproof vests. Among the more popular innovations: $7,000 tornado-proof storm rooms. When the time came for Holliday to leave, he knew who was ready to replace him. Along with helping Kullman join the General Motors (GM) board in 2004 to broaden her management perspective, he encouraged her to work with a coach to modify her impatient nature. "If I made a statement before, I was just one of the group. Now, it's law," says Kullman. "I have to make sure I am getting everyone's input." The decisions Kullman makes today may translate into a very different DuPont in the future. With almost one-quarter of sales tied to the auto industry, she'll need to look elsewhere for growth. Kullman knows that her biggest decision, though, is not which businesses to invest in, but which people.

Questions

1. What kind of managerial skills did Holliday sense that Kullman possessed to make him want to appoint her as his successor?
2. What kind of manager do you think that Kullman will be in the future?
3. What skills do you believe you possess that will make you a successful manager?

Source: Matthew Boyle, "The Art of CEO Succession." Reprinted from April 30, 2009 issue of *BusinessWeek* by special permission, copyright © 2009 The McGraw-Hill Companies, Inc.

BusinessWeek Case in the News [LO1, 4, 6]

The Outsider at Ford

Almost 30 months after Alan R. Mulally left Boeing to become chief executive of Ford Motor, it's still easy to peg him as an industry outsider. Talking to Wall Street analysts in November, Mulally described the debut of the tiny, fuel-sipping Ford Ka at the "Paris Air Show" when he meant the "Paris Motor Show." Earlier this year, Mulally showed how he'd tried to stop appending an airplane doodle to his signature, but struggled to ink a car instead. "Rats. I still haven't got the car down," he said, in the "aw shucks" Kansas delivery that has become as familiar in Detroit as his off-the-rack blazers and shirts.

Outsider CEOs have a decidedly varied track record. Some bring in their own people and impose a jarring management philosophy on a corporate culture, as Robert Nardelli did at Home Depot with such mixed results that the board pushed him out. Some are unsuited to running an unfamiliar business. Former S.C. Johnson CEO William Perez's 13-month stint at Nike comes to mind. Others tread more softly and succeed, like Eric Schmidt, the former Novell guy who runs Google. Mulally arguably falls into the latter category. Since arriving he has left most of the team he inherited in place and quieted talk that an aerospace guy couldn't run an automaker.

But the man who chose Mulally, Chairman William Clay Ford Jr., says his CEO's progress in shaking up a calcified culture has thus far kept Ford independent and away from the U.S. Treasury's loan window. Under Mulally, decision making is more transparent, once-fractious divisions are working together, and cars of better quality are moving faster from design studio to showroom. John Casesa, whose Casesa Shapiro consulting firm advises the industry, is impressed, too. "The speed with which Mulally has transformed Ford into a more nimble and healthy operation has been one of the more impressive jobs I've seen," he says. "It probably would have been game over for Ford already but for the changes he has brought."

A History of "Organ Rejection"

When Mulally was tapped as Ford CEO in the spring of 2006, reaction inside the company ranged from suspicion to outrage. What did an airplane guy know about the car business? "There were lots of raised eyebrows," recalls Bill Ford. The management team was particularly rattled, especially those who were hoping to fill the job themselves. One by one they stopped by Ford's office to ask him what the heck he was doing. Ford told them the company needed fresh perspective.

No one understood the travails of running the automaker better than Henry Ford's great-grandson. The company was bureaucratic and hostile to new ideas. And below the C-suite, it hadn't yet sunk in that Ford was fighting for its life. The chairman also knew his company had a history of "organ rejection," or spurning outsiders. He had watched executives from outside arrive at Ford only to be isolated and even hazed. He resolved to give Mulally all the help and advice he needed.

Even before Mulally accepted the job, the two men had candid exchanges about Ford's problems. One time, at Ford's Ann Arbor home, Mulally wanted to know why the company had allowed forays into luxury makes such as Jaguar, Land Rover, and Aston Martin to distract it from the Ford brand. Bill Ford told Mulally it was worse than that: Executives had come to view working on Ford, rather than the luxe brands, as a "career problem." Mulally's biggest challenge, Ford said, would be breaking down silos, specifically the operating regions around the world—Europe, Asia, South America, and Australia—that were more interested in defending their turf than working together. It was a culture, Ford explained, where one's career had come to mean more than the company.

If Ford had one key insight to share, it was this: "Ford," he told Mulally, "is a place where they wait for the leader to tell them what to do." His point was that Ford staffers below the top echelon weren't sufficiently involved in decision making. That resonated with Mulally. At Boeing, he hadn't always been the most inclusive manager—until then-CEO Phil Condit told Mulally he needed to broaden his view to running an entire company rather than just a division and hooked him up with executive coach Marshall Goldsmith.

Goldsmith's team interviewed some 25 of Mulally's subordinates and peers to pinpoint what needed work. Mulally got high marks for coordinating Boeing's global supply chain and hitting production targets. But he was criticized for leaving too much of his team out of the loop. Mulally, they said, needed to check in more often to let his reports know if they were headed in the right direction. Mulally included more people in the decision-making process—and asked that they be coached as well. "It would be far less effective for this process to be just about me," he says. "I wasn't going to succeed if my team didn't succeed."

By the time Mulally took Ford's helm, he had met with every senior staffer and asked a trunkful of questions. "Alan said there was a lot he didn't know, but that he was a quick study," says Ford. But once he settled in, Mulally began providing the answers, meeting with employees in groups ranging from 25 to several hundred. No speeches. Just off-the-cuff remarks followed by 45 minutes or so of Q&A.

Meetings about Meetings

Mulally told employees Ford's existing turnaround blueprint was essentially sound. Besides dramatically reducing head count and closing factories, the "Way Forward Plan" called for Ford to modernize plants so they could handle multiple models rather than just one. A second piece of the plan was more controversial: a switch to vehicles that could be sold in several markets. This required a centralization that was anathema to the divisions around the world—fiefdoms used to developing cars themselves. This was the part of the plan that Mulally wanted to accelerate. Some executives sought meetings with Bill Ford to complain. "I didn't permit it," he says.

Mulally knew that to get his way, he would have to change Ford's culture. In the coming months, Ford employees would hear him say, over and over, "That doesn't work for me." This included Ford's penchant for cycling executives into new jobs every few years. The idea was to groom well-rounded managers. But no one was in a job long enough to make a difference or feel accountable. In the five years before Mulally arrived, executive Mark Fields ran the Mazda Motor affiliate, Ford Europe, the luxury Premier Auto Group, and the North and South American businesses. "I'm going into my fourth year in the same job," says Fields, still president of the Americas. "I've never had such consistency of purpose before."

Another thing that had to change: a culture that "loved to meet," as Bill Ford puts it. Managers commonly held "pre-meetings," where they schemed how to get their stories straight for higher-ups. It was a classic CYA maneuver and antithetical to problem solving. Mulally had seen this kind of thing before when he was running engineering at Boeing's commercial plane division.

In 1997, Boeing took a $2.7 billion charge when commercial suffered a communications breakdown and failed to match production to rising demand; two assembly lines closed down for a month. When Mulally became CEO of the commercial plane division in 1999, he kicked off a new era of radical transparency that made it harder to hide problems.

He took that philosophy to Ford. As at Boeing, Mulally was determined to have a constant stream of data that would give his team a weekly snapshot of Ford's global operations and hold executives' performance up against profit targets. Constantly updated numbers—later validated by pre-earnings quarterly audits—would make it impossible for executives to hide unpleasant truths. But that wasn't the only objective. "Information should never be used as a weapon on a team," says Mulally. Rather, the numbers would help executives anticipate problems and tweak strategy accordingly.

Coherence and Cooperation

Two and a half years after taking the reins at Ford, Mulally certainly can't point to the conventional measure of corporate success: profits. So what has he achieved so far?

Mulally has imposed discipline on a company that veered from one strategy to the next. Brands such as Lincoln and Mercury changed their positioning every year. Today the plan, hashed over with dealers who have been given more say, is locked: Lincoln will focus on premium sedans and SUVs, while Mercury will sell premium small cars and crossovers.

Now that Ford's far-flung fiefdoms are starting to collaborate, a once wasteful and balkanized vehicle development system is beginning to cohere. To make sure it all runs smoothly, Mulally tapped a Ford veteran, Derrick Kuzak, as his global car development chief, a first for Ford. Kuzak has pushed his people to improve interiors, sold management on small gas-sipping engines that won't cost consumers as much as hybrids, and created huge cost savings by making sure SUVs and trucks share more parts. "He has the confidence of management and people working for him, so he gets the right projects through and the wrong ones stopped," says design consultant Jim Hall of 2953 Analytics. Kuzak's big test comes next year, when the U.S. starts getting the same acclaimed Ford vehicles sold in Europe, rather than the dumbed-down versions of the past.

Mulally has staked his reputation on the 2010 Taurus sedan. When he became CEO, the Taurus name had been relegated to the museum of dead brands. Ford had so botched successors to America's best-selling car of the 1980s that it had decided it was a lost cause. Mulally saw things differently. He believed the Taurus name had value and before long challenged his team to deliver a new car in 24 months using the existing platform but with a whole new look. The Taurus rolling into showrooms in summer 2009 looks nothing like the old model, which Mulally compared to "a deflated football." Sleek and chiseled like Ford's European sedans, it already has wowed critics. The question is whether $35,000 for a fully loaded model will fly in a recession. After all, the previous incarnation sold for a discounted 16 grand.

Questions

1. What kinds of skills does Alan Mulally have as a manager?
2. How has he been using these skills to change the way Ford operates?
3. What are the main differences between the way he acts as a manager and Ford's old-time established managers?

Source: David Kiley, "Alan Mulally: The Outsider at Ford." Reprinted from *BusinessWeek* online, March 5, 2009, by special permission, copyright © 2009 by The McGraw-Hill Companies, Inc.

History of Management Thought

APPENDIX

The systematic study of management began in the closing decades of the 19th century, after the Industrial Revolution had swept through Europe and America. In the new economic climate, managers of all types of organizations–political, educational, and economic–were increasingly turning their focus toward finding better ways to satisfy customers' needs. Many major economic, technical, and cultural changes were taking place at this time. With the introduction of steam power and the development of sophisticated machinery and equipment, the Industrial Revolution changed the way goods were produced, particularly in the weaving and clothing industries. Small workshops run by skilled workers who produced hand-manufactured products (a system called *crafts production*) were being replaced by large factories in which sophisticated machines controlled by hundreds or even thousands of unskilled or semiskilled workers made products. For example, raw cotton and wool that in the past families or whole villages working together had spun into yarn were now shipped to factories where workers operated machines that spun and wove large quantities of yarn into cloth.

Owners and managers of the new factories found themselves unprepared for the challenges accompanying the change from small-scale crafts production to large-scale mechanized manufacturing. Moreover, many of the managers and supervisors in these workshops and factories were engineers who had only a technical orientation. They were unprepared for the social problems that occur when people work together in large groups (as in a factory or shop system). Managers began to search for new techniques to manage their organizations' resources, and soon they began to focus on ways to increase the efficiency of the worker–task mix. They found help from Frederick W. Taylor.

F. W. Taylor and Scientific Management

Frederick W. Taylor (1856–1915) is best known for defining the techniques of **scientific management**, the systematic study of relationships between people and tasks for the purpose of redesigning the work process to increase efficiency. Taylor was a manufacturing manager who eventually became a consultant and taught other managers how to apply his scientific management techniques. Taylor believed that if the amount of time and effort that each worker expends to produce a unit of output (a finished good or service) can be reduced by increasing specialization and the division of labor, the production process will become more efficient. Taylor believed the way to create the most efficient division of labor could

Frederick W. Taylor, founder of scientific management, and one of the first people to study the behavior and performance of people in the workplace.

best be determined by using scientific management techniques, rather than intuitive or informal rule-of-thumb knowledge. Based on his experiments and observations as a manufacturing manager in a variety of settings, he developed four principles to increase efficiency in the workplace:[1]

- Principle 1: *Study the way workers perform their tasks, gather all the informal job knowledge that workers possess, and experiment with ways of improving the way tasks are performed.*

  To discover the most efficient method of performing specific tasks, Taylor studied in great detail and measured the ways different workers went about performing their tasks. One of the main tools he used was a time and motion study, which involves the careful timing and recording of the actions taken to perform a particular task. Once Taylor understood the existing method of performing a task, he then experimented to increase specialization; he tried different methods of dividing up and coordinating the various tasks necessary to produce a finished product. Usually this meant simplifying jobs and having each worker perform fewer, more routine tasks. Taylor also sought to find ways to improve each worker's ability to perform a particular task–for example, by reducing the number of motions workers made to complete the task, by changing the layout of the work area or the type of tool workers used, or by experimenting with tools of different sizes.

- Principle 2: *Codify the new methods of performing tasks into written rules and standard operating procedures.*

  Once the best method of performing a particular task was determined, Taylor specified that it should be recorded so that the procedures could be taught to all workers performing the same task. These rules could be used to further standardize and simplify jobs–essentially, to make jobs even more routine. In this way efficiency could be increased throughout an organization.

- Principle 3: *Carefully select workers so that they possess skills and abilities that match the needs of the task, and train them to perform the task according to the established rules and procedures.*

  To increase specialization, Taylor believed workers had to understand the tasks that were required and be thoroughly trained in order to perform a task at the required level. Workers who could not be trained to this level were to be transferred to a job where they were able to reach the minimum required level of proficiency.[2]

- Principle 4: *Establish a fair or acceptable level of performance for a task, and then develop a pay system that provides a reward for performance above the acceptable level.*

  To encourage workers to perform at a high level of efficiency, and to provide them with an incentive to reveal the most efficient techniques for performing a task, Taylor advocated that workers benefit from any gains in performance. They should be paid a bonus and receive some percentage of the performance gains achieved through the more efficient work process.

By 1910, Taylor's system of scientific management had become nationally known and in many instances faithfully and fully practiced.[3] However, managers in many organizations chose to implement the new principles of scientific management selectively. This decision ultimately resulted in problems. For example, some managers using scientific management obtained increases in performance, but rather than sharing performance gains with workers through bonuses as Taylor had advocated, they simply increased the amount of work that each worker was expected to do. Many workers experiencing the reorganized work system found that as their performance increased, managers required them to do more work for the same pay. Workers also learned that increases in performance often meant fewer jobs and a greater threat of layoffs because fewer workers were needed. In addition, the specialized, simplified jobs were often monotonous and repetitive, and many workers became dissatisfied with their jobs.

From a performance perspective, the combination of the two management practices–(1) achieving the right mix of worker–task specialization and (2) linking people and tasks by the speed of the production line–resulted in huge savings in cost and huge increases in output that occur in large, organized work settings. For example, in 1908, managers at the Franklin Motor Company using scientific management principles redesigned the work process, and the output of cars increased from 100 cars a month to 45 cars a day; workers' wages, however, increased by only 90%.[4]

Taylor's work has had an enduring effect on the management of production systems. Managers in every organization, whether it produces goods or services, now carefully analyze the basic tasks that workers must perform and try to create a work environment that will allow their organizations to operate most efficiently. We discuss this important issue in Chapter 7.

Weber's Bureaucratic Theory

Side by side with scientific managers studying the person–task mix to increase efficiency, other researchers were focusing on how to increase the efficiency with which organizations were managed. Max Weber, a German professor of sociology, outlined his famous principles of **bureaucracy**–a formal system of organization and administration designed to ensure efficiency and effectiveness–and created bureaucratic theory. A bureaucratic system of administration is based on five principles:

- Principle 1: *In a bureaucracy, a manager's formal authority derives from the position he or she holds in the organization.*

  Authority is the power to hold people accountable for their actions and to make decisions concerning the use of organizational resources. Authority gives managers the right to direct and control their subordinates' behavior to achieve organizational goals. In a bureaucratic system of administration, obedience is owed to a manager, not because of any personal qualities–such as personality, wealth, or social status–but because the manager occupies a position that is associated with a certain level of authority and responsibility.[5]

- Principle 2: *In a bureaucracy, people should occupy positions because of their performance, not because of their social standing or personal contacts.*

  This principle was not always followed in Weber's time and is often ignored today. Some organizations and industries are still affected by social networks

Max Weber developed the principles of bureaucracy during Germany's burgeoning industrial revolution to help organizations increase their efficiency and effectiveness.

in which personal contacts and relations, not job-related skills, influence hiring and promotion decisions.

- Principle 3: *The extent of each position's formal authority and task responsibilities, and its relationship to other positions in an organization, should be clearly specified.*

When the tasks and authority associated with various positions in the organization are clearly specified, managers and workers know what is expected of them and what to expect from each other. Moreover, an organization can hold all its employees strictly accountable for their actions when they know their exact responsibilities.

- Principle 4: *Authority can be exercised effectively in an organization when positions are arranged hierarchically, so employees know whom to report to and who reports to them.*[6]

Managers must create an organizational hierarchy of authority that makes it clear who reports to whom and to whom managers and workers should go if conflicts or problems arise. This principle is especially important in the armed forces, FBI, CIA, and other organizations that deal with sensitive issues involving possible major repercussions. It is vital that managers at high levels of the hierarchy be able to hold subordinates accountable for their actions.

- Principle 5: *Managers must create a well-defined system of rules, standard operating procedures, and norms so that they can effectively control behavior within an organization.*

Rules are formal written instructions that specify actions to be taken under different circumstances to achieve specific goals (for example, if A happens, do B). **Standard operating procedures (SOPs)** are specific sets of written instructions about how to perform a certain aspect of a task. A rule might state that at the end of the workday employees are to leave their machines in good order, and a set of SOPs specifies exactly how they should do so, itemizing which machine parts must be oiled or replaced. **Norms** are unwritten, informal codes of conduct that prescribe how people should act in particular situations. For example, an organizational norm in a restaurant might be that waiters should help each other if time permits.

Rules, SOPs, and norms provide behavioral guidelines that increase the performance of a bureaucratic system because they specify the best ways to accomplish organizational tasks. Companies such as McDonald's and Wal-Mart have developed extensive rules and procedures to specify the behaviors required of their employees, such as "Always greet the customer with a smile."

Weber believed that organizations that implement all five principles establish a bureaucratic system that improves organizational performance. The specification of positions and the use of rules and SOPs to regulate how tasks are performed make it easier for managers to organize and control the work of subordinates. Similarly, fair and equitable selection and promotion systems improve managers' feelings of security, reduce stress, and encourage organizational members to act ethically and further promote the interests of the organization.[7]

If bureaucracies are not managed well, many problems can result. Sometimes managers allow rules and SOPs, "bureaucratic red tape," to become so cumbersome that decision making becomes slow and inefficient and organizations are unable to change. When managers rely too much on rules to solve problems and not enough on their own skills and judgment, their behavior becomes inflexible. A key challenge for managers is to use bureaucratic principles to benefit, rather than harm, an organization.

The Work of Mary Parker Follett

If F. W. Taylor is considered the father of management thought, Mary Parker Follett (1868–1933) serves as its mother.[8] Much of her writing about management and the way managers should behave toward workers was a response to her concern that Taylor was ignoring the human side of the organization. She pointed out that management often overlooks the multitude of ways in which employees can contribute to the organization when managers allow them to participate and exercise initiative in their everyday work lives.[9] Taylor, for example, never proposed that managers involve workers in analyzing their jobs to identify better ways to perform tasks, or even ask workers how they felt about their jobs. Instead, he used time and motion experts to analyze workers' jobs for them. Follett, in contrast, argued that because workers know the most about their jobs, they should be involved in job analysis and managers should allow them to participate in the work development process.

Mary Parker Follett, an early management thinker who advocated, "Authority should go with knowledge . . . whether it is up the line or down."

Follett proposed, "Authority should go with knowledge . . . whether it is up the line or down." In other words, if workers have the relevant knowledge, then workers, rather than managers, should be in control of the work process itself, and managers should behave as coaches and facilitators–not as monitors and supervisors. In making this statement, Follett anticipated the current interest in self-managed teams and empowerment. She also recognized the importance of having managers in different departments communicate directly with each other to speed decision making. She advocated what she called "cross-functioning": members of different departments working together in cross-departmental teams to accomplish projects–an approach that is increasingly utilized today.[10] She proposed that knowledge and expertise, not managers' formal authority deriving from their position in the hierarchy, should decide who would lead at any particular moment. She believed, as do many management theorists today, that power is fluid and should flow to the person who can best help the organization achieve its goals. Follett took a horizontal view of power and authority, rather than viewing the vertical chain of command as being most essential to effective management. Thus, Follett's approach was very radical for its time.

The Hawthorne Studies and Human Relations

Probably because of its radical nature, Follett's work went unappreciated by managers and researchers until quite recently. Most continued to follow in the footsteps of Taylor, and to increase efficiency, they studied ways to improve various characteristics of the work setting, such as job specialization or the kinds of tools workers used. One series of studies was conducted from 1924 to 1932 at the Hawthorne Works of the Western Electric Company.[11] This research, now known as the Hawthorne studies, was initiated as an attempt to investigate how characteristics of the work setting–specifically the level of lighting or illumination–affect worker fatigue and performance. The researchers conducted an experiment in which they systematically measured worker productivity at various levels of illumination.

Workers in a telephone manufacturing plant, in 1931. Around this time, researchers at the Hawthorne Works of the Western Electric Company began to study the effects of work setting characteristics—such as lighting and rest periods—on productivity. To their surprise, they discovered that workers' productivity was affected more by the attention they received from researchers than by the characteristics of the work setting—a phenomenon that became known as the Hawthorne effect.

The experiment produced some unexpected results. The researchers found that regardless of whether they raised or lowered the level of illumination, productivity increased. In fact, productivity began to fall only when the level of illumination dropped to the level of moonlight, a level at which presumably workers could no longer see well enough to do their work efficiently.

As you can imagine, the researchers found these results very puzzling. They invited a noted Harvard psychologist, Elton Mayo, to help them. Mayo proposed another series of experiments to solve the mystery. These experiments, known as the relay assembly test experiments, were designed to investigate the effects of other aspects of the work context on job performance, such as the effect of the number and length of rest periods and hours of work on fatigue and monotony.[12] The goal was to raise productivity.

During a two-year study of a small group of female workers, the researchers again observed that productivity increased over time, but the increases could not be solely attributed to the effects of changes in the work setting. Gradually, the researchers discovered that, to some degree, the results they were obtaining were influenced by the fact that the researchers themselves had become part of the experiment. In other words, the presence of the researchers was affecting the results because the workers enjoyed receiving attention and being the subject of study and were willing to cooperate with the researchers to produce the results they believed the researchers desired.

Subsequently, it was found that many other factors also influence worker behavior, and it was not clear what was actually influencing the Hawthorne workers' behavior. However, this particular effect–which became known as the **Hawthorne effect**–seemed to suggest that the attitudes of workers toward their managers affect the level of workers' performance. In particular, the significant finding was that a manager's behavior or leadership approach can affect performance. This finding led many researchers to turn their attention to managerial behavior and leadership. If supervisors could be trained to behave in ways that would elicit cooperative behavior from their subordinates, then productivity could be increased. From this view emerged the **human relations movement,** which advocates that supervisors be behaviorally trained to manage subordinates in ways that elicit their cooperation and increase their productivity.

The importance of behavioral or human relations training became even clearer to its supporters after another series of experiments–the bank wiring room experiments. In a study of workers making telephone-switching equipment, researchers Elton Mayo and F. J. Roethlisberger discovered that the workers, as a group, had deliberately adopted a norm of output restriction to protect their jobs. Other group members subjected workers who violated this informal production norm to sanctions. Those who violated group performance norms and performed above the norm were called "ratebusters"; those who performed below the norm were called "chisellers."

The experimenters concluded that both types of workers threatened the group as a whole. Ratebusters threaten group members because they reveal to managers how fast the work can be done. Chisellers are looked down on because they are not doing their share of the work. Work-group members discipline both ratebusters and chisellers in order to create a pace of work that the workers (not the managers) think is fair. Thus, the work group's influence over output can be as great as the supervisors' influence. Since the work group can influence the behavior of its members, some management theorists argue that supervisors should be trained to behave in ways that gain the goodwill and cooperation of workers so that supervisors, not workers, control the level of work-group performance.

One of the main implications of the Hawthorne studies was that the behavior of managers and workers in the work setting is as important in explaining the level of performance as the technical aspects of the task. Managers must understand the workings of the **informal organization,** the system of behavioral rules and norms that emerge in a group, when they try to manage or change behavior in organizations. Many studies have found that, as time passes, groups often develop elaborate procedures and norms that bond members together, allowing unified action either to cooperate with management in order to raise performance or to restrict output and thwart the attainment of organizational goals.[13] The Hawthorne studies demonstrated the importance of understanding how the feelings, thoughts, and behavior of work-group members and managers affect performance. It was becoming increasingly clear to researchers that understanding behavior in organizations is a complex process that is critical to increasing performance.[14] Indeed, the increasing interest in the area of management known as **organizational behavior,** the study of the factors that have an impact on how individuals and groups respond to and act in organizations, dates from these early studies.

Theory X and Theory Y

Several studies after the Second World War revealed how assumptions about workers' attitudes and behavior affect managers' behavior. Douglas McGregor developed the most influential approach. He proposed that two different sets of assumptions about work attitudes and behaviors dominate the way managers think and affect how they behave in organizations. McGregor named these two contrasting sets of assumptions **Theory X** and **Theory Y**.[15]

According to the assumptions of **Theory X,** the average worker is lazy, dislikes work, and will try to do as little as possible. Moreover, workers have little ambition and wish to avoid responsibility. Thus, the manager's task is to counteract workers' natural tendencies to avoid work. To keep workers' performance at a high level, the manager must supervise them closely and control their behavior by means of "the carrot and stick"–rewards and punishments.

Managers who accept the assumptions of Theory X design and shape the work setting to maximize their control over workers' behaviors and minimize workers' control over the pace of work. These managers believe that workers must be made to do what is necessary for the success of the organization, and they focus on developing rules, SOPs, and a well-defined system of rewards and punishments to control behavior. They see little point in giving workers autonomy to solve their own problems because they think that the workforce neither expects nor desires cooperation. Theory X managers see their role as to closely monitor workers to ensure that they contribute to the production process and do not threaten product quality. Henry Ford, who closely supervised and managed his workforce, fits McGregor's description of a manager who holds Theory X assumptions.

In contrast, **Theory Y** assumes that workers are not inherently lazy, do not naturally dislike work, and, if given the opportunity, will do what is good for the organization. According to Theory Y, the characteristics of the work setting determine whether workers consider work to be a source of satisfaction or punishment; and managers do not need to closely control workers' behavior in order to make them perform at a high level, because workers will exercise self-control when they are committed to organizational goals. The implication of Theory Y, according to McGregor, is that "the limits of collaboration in the organizational setting are not limits of human nature but of management's ingenuity in discovering how to realize the potential represented by its human resources."[16] It is the manager's task to create a work setting that encourages commitment to organizational goals and provides opportunities for workers to be imaginative and to exercise initiative and self-direction.

When managers design the organizational setting to reflect the assumptions about attitudes and behavior suggested by Theory Y, the characteristics of the organization are quite different from those of an organizational setting based on Theory X. Managers who believe that workers are motivated to help the organization reach its goals can decentralize authority and give more control over the job to workers, both as individuals and in groups. In this setting, individuals and groups are still accountable for their activities, but the manager's role is not to control employees but to provide support and advice, to make sure workers have the resources they need to perform their jobs, and to evaluate them on their ability to help the organization meet its goals. The same kinds of debates are raging today as managers seek to increase both the efficiency and effectiveness of their organizations.

Values, Attitudes, Emotions, and Culture: The Manager as a Person

CHAPTER 2

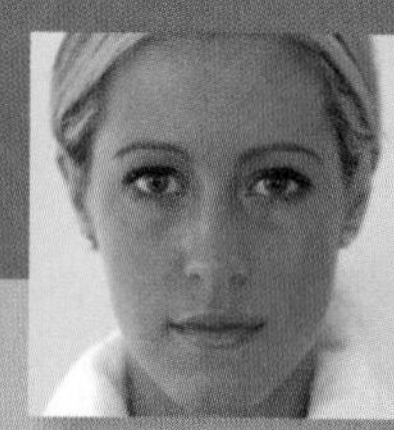

Learning Objectives

After studying this chapter, you should be able to

1. Describe the various personality traits that affect how managers think, feel, and behave. **[LO1]**
2. Explain what values and attitudes are and describe their impact on managerial action. **[LO2]**
3. Appreciate how moods and emotions influence all members of an organization. **[LO3]**
4. Describe the nature of emotional intelligence and its role in management. **[LO4]**
5. Define organizational culture and explain how managers both create and are influenced by organizational culture. **[LO5]**

Mark Wilson, shown here at Ryla's call center headquarters, demonstrates that managing for a productive work environment can also include managing for employees' well-being.

MANAGEMENT SNAPSHOT

Ryla's Caring Culture

How Can Managers Create a Caring Culture and Instill Loyalty in Employees in an Industry Known for Inferior Working Conditions?

Telemarketing and customer-contact organizations are notorious for high levels of turnover and dismal working conditions. Ryla Inc., founded by Mark Wilson in 2001, is a customer-contact and business-process outsourcing firm headquartered in Kennesaw, Georgia.[1] Ryla Inc. has both a caring culture and very loyal employees thanks to Wilson's vision and values. Wilson had years of experience managing call centers at Dun & Bradstreet. His openness to new approaches and ideas led him to recognize a potential opportunity.[2] Wilson imagined a different kind of customer-contact business, one in which his employees would feel "like it's the best job they've ever had."[3]

Having the idea of operating a customer-contact business in a dramatically different way was one thing. Securing the financing to start such a business was another. Wilson hired a consultant to help him approach venture capital firms for financing. Over a dozen of them were unwilling to invest in his idea. Despite this setback, Wilson persisted, and his determination paid off. SJF Ventures, a venture capital firm in Durham, North Carolina, invested $700,000 in return for equity in the company, and Ryla was born.[4]

From the start Wilson has always strived to sustain a work environment and company culture that are true to his own personal values: treating employees with respect, fostering open communication, providing opportunities for training, growth, and development, and demonstrating a real commitment to the well-being of employees and the local community. Ryla has grown and prospered. Today, Ryla has nearly 400 full-time employees, less than 30% turnover in an industry with average turnover rates over 40% and as high as 75%, very high client retention rates, and revenue growth of at least 10% per year.[5]

Call center work tends to be routine and boring. Wilson's emphasis on both creating a caring culture and providing employees with opportunities for training and advancement goes a long way toward building employee loyalty.[6] Wilson maintains an open-door policy and keeps employees informed about how the business is doing. He not only solicits employee suggestions for improvements but also acts on them.[7]

Ryla employees have access to a variety of benefits ranging from medical and life insurance to 401(k) plans, employee assistance programs, and aerobics classes.[8] Employees who remain with Ryla for three years and attain performance and attendance goals become eligible for stock options in the company.[9] Ryla provides employees with the opportunity to advance within the company. Ryla promotes from within, so telemarketing is no longer viewed as a dead-end job. Eighty percent of the managers at Ryla once worked the telephones.[10]

Wilson continually seeks out new ways for his business to better serve customers. Recently, Ryla started focusing on short-term projects requiring quick ramp-up and ramp-down, such as crisis response for product recalls and data breaches.[11] For example, natural emergencies, confidential personal data breaches, and other crisis situations often require organizations to have a response system up and running within a day, and now Ryla provides such services.[12]

Wilson's efforts to create a new and different kind of call center that provides excellent service to clients and a caring and supportive environment for employees have not gone unnoticed in the business community. For example, in 2007, Ryla was one of 35 finalists in *The Wall Street Journal*–Winning Workplace's Top Small Workplaces competition.[13] Loyal employees who never imagined working in telemarketing are satisfied with their jobs and committed to Ryla.[14]

Overview

Like people everywhere, Mark Wilson has his own distinctive personality, values, ways of viewing things, and personal challenges and disappointments. In this chapter, we focus on the manager as a feeling, thinking human being. We start by describing enduring characteristics that influence how managers "manage," as well as how they view other people, their organizations, and the world around them. We discuss as well how managers' values, attitudes, and moods play out in organizations, shaping organizational culture. By the end of this chapter, you will have a good appreciation of how the personal characteristics of managers influence the management process in general, and organizational culture in particular.

Enduring Characteristics: Personality Traits

All people, including managers, have certain enduring characteristics that influence how they think, feel, and behave both on and off the job. These characteristics are **personality traits,** particular tendencies to feel, think, and act in certain ways that can be used to describe the personality of every individual. It is important to understand the personalities of managers because their personalities influence their behavior and their approach to managing people and resources.

personality traits Enduring tendencies to feel, think, and act in certain ways.

Some managers are demanding, difficult to get along with, and highly critical of other people. Other managers may be as concerned about effectiveness and efficiency as highly critical managers but are easier to get along with, are likable, and frequently praise the people around them. Both styles of management may produce excellent results, but their effects on employees are quite different. Do managers deliberately decide to adopt one or the other of these approaches to management? Although they may do so part of the time, in all likelihood their personalities also account for their

different approaches. Indeed, research suggests that the way people react to different conditions depends, in part, on their personalities.[15]

The Big Five Personality Traits

We can think of an individual's personality as being composed of five general traits or characteristics: extraversion, negative affectivity, agreeableness, conscientiousness, and openness to experience.[16] Researchers often consider these the Big Five personality traits.[17] Each of them can be viewed as a continuum along which every individual or, more specifically, every manager falls (see Figure 2.1).

Some managers may be at the high end of one trait continuum, others at the low end, and still others somewhere in between. An easy way to understand how these traits can affect a person's approach to management is to describe what people are like at the high and low ends of each trait continuum. As will become evident as you read about each trait, no single trait is right or wrong for being an effective manager. Rather, effectiveness is determined by a complex interaction between the characteristics of managers (including personality traits) and the nature of the job and organization in which they are working. Moreover, personality traits that enhance managerial effectiveness in one situation may actually impair it in another situation.

extraversion The tendency to experience positive emotions and moods and to feel good about oneself and the rest of the world.

EXTRAVERSION Extraversion is the tendency to experience positive emotions and moods and feel good about oneself and the rest of the world. Managers who are high on extraversion (often called *extraverts*) tend to be sociable, affectionate, outgoing, and friendly. Managers who are low on extraversion (often called *introverts*) tend to be less inclined toward social interactions and to have a less positive outlook. Being high on

Figure 2.1
The Big Five Personality Traits

Managers' personalities can be described by determining where on each of the following continua they fall.

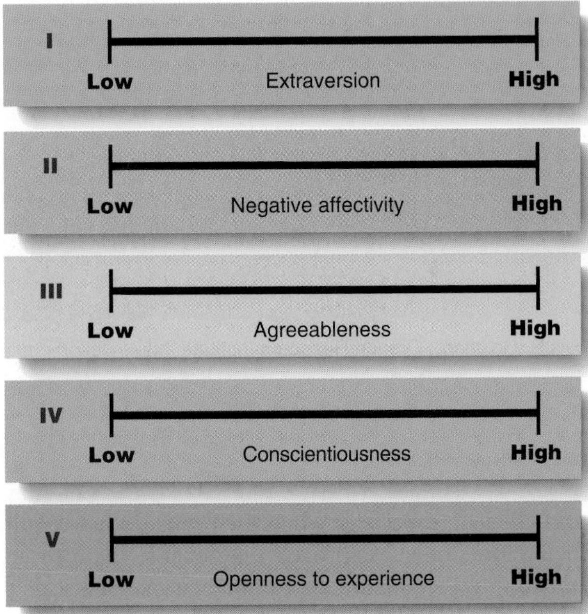

Figure 2.2
Measures of Extraversion, Agreeableness, Conscientiousness, and Openness to Experience

Listed below are phrases describing people's behaviors. Please use the rating scale below to describe how accurately each statement describes *you*. Describe yourself as you generally are now, not as you wish to be in the future. Describe yourself as you honestly see yourself, in relation to other people you know of the same sex as you are and roughly your same age.

1	2	3	4	5
Very inaccurate	Moderately inaccurate	Neither inaccurate nor accurate	Moderately accurate	Very accurate

___ **1.** Am interested in people.
___ **2.** Have a rich vocabulary.
___ **3.** Am always prepared.
___ **4.** Am not really interested in others.*
___ **5.** Leave my belongings around.*
___ **6.** Am the life of the party.
___ **7.** Have difficulty understanding abstract ideas.*
___ **8.** Sympathize with others' feelings.
___ **9.** Don't talk a lot.*
___ **10.** Pay attention to details.
___ **11.** Have a vivid imagination.
___ **12.** Insult people.*
___ **13.** Make a mess of things.*
___ **14.** Feel comfortable around people.
___ **15.** Am not interested in abstract ideas.*
___ **16.** Have a soft heart.
___ **17.** Get chores done right away.
___ **18.** Keep in the background.*
___ **19.** Have excellent ideas.
___ **20.** Start conversations.
___ **21.** Am not interested in other people's problems.*
___ **22.** Often forget to put things back in their proper place.*
___ **23.** Have little to say.*
___ **24.** Do not have a good imagination.*
___ **25.** Take time out for others.
___ **26.** Like order.
___ **27.** Talk to a lot of different people at parties.
___ **28.** Am quick to understand things.
___ **29.** Feel little concern for others.*
___ **30.** Shirk my duties.*
___ **31.** Don't like to draw attention to myself.*
___ **32.** Use difficult words.
___ **33.** Feel others' emotions.
___ **34.** Follow a schedule.
___ **35.** Spend time reflecting on things.
___ **36.** Don't mind being the center of attention.
___ **37.** Make people feel at ease.
___ **38.** Am exacting in my work.
___ **39.** Am quiet around strangers.*
___ **40.** Am full of ideas.

* Item is reverse-scored: 1 = 5, 2 = 4, 4 = 2, 5 = 1
Scoring: Sum responses to items for an overall scale.
Extraversion = sum of items 6, 9, 14, 18, 20, 23, 27, 31, 36, 39
Agreeableness = sum of items 1, 4, 8, 12, 16, 21, 25, 29, 33, 37
Conscientiousness = sum of items 3, 5, 10, 13, 17, 22, 26, 30, 34, 38
Openness to experience = sum of items 2, 7, 11, 15, 19, 24, 28, 32, 35, 40

extraversion may be an asset for managers whose jobs entail especially high levels of social interaction. Managers who are low on extraversion may nevertheless be highly effective and efficient, especially when their jobs do not require excessive social interaction. Their more "quiet" approach may enable them to accomplish quite a bit of work in limited time. See Figure 2.2 for an example of a scale that can be used to measure a person's level of extraversion.

negative affectivity The tendency to experience negative emotions and moods, to feel distressed, and to be critical of oneself and others.

NEGATIVE AFFECTIVITY Negative affectivity is the tendency to experience negative emotions and moods, feel distressed, and be critical of oneself and others. Managers high on this trait may often feel angry and dissatisfied and complain about their own and others' lack of progress. Managers who are low on negative affectivity do not tend to experience many negative emotions and moods and are less pessimistic and critical of themselves and others. On the plus side, the critical approach of a manager high on negative affectivity may sometimes be effective if it spurs both the manager and others to improve their performance. Nevertheless, it is probably more pleasant to work with a manager who is low on negative affectivity; the better working relationships that such a manager is likely to cultivate also can be an important asset. Figure 2.3 is an example of a scale developed to measure a person's level of negative affectivity.

agreeableness The tendency to get along well with other people.

AGREEABLENESS Agreeableness is the tendency to get along well with others. Managers who are high on the agreeableness continuum are likable, tend to be

Figure 2.3
A Measure of Negative Affectivity

Instructions: Listed below are a series of statements a person might use to describe her/his attitudes, opinions, interests, and other characteristics. If a statement is true or largely true, put a "T" in the space next to the item. Or if the statement is false or largely false, mark an "F" in the space.

Please answer every statement, even if you are not completely sure of the answer. Read each statement carefully, but don't spend too much time deciding on the answer.

___ **1.** I worry about things a lot.

___ **2.** My feelings are often hurt.

___ **3.** Small problems often irritate me.

___ **4.** I am often nervous.

___ **5.** My moods often change.

___ **6.** Sometimes I feel bad for no apparent reason.

___ **7.** I often have very strong emotions such as anger or anxiety without really knowing why.

___ **8.** The unexpected can easily startle me.

___ **9.** Sometimes, when I am thinking about the day ahead of me, I feel anxious and tense.

___ **10.** Small setbacks sometimes bother me too much.

___ **11.** My worries often cause me to lose sleep.

___ **12.** Some days I seem to be always "on edge."

___ **13.** I am more sensitive than I should be.

___ **14.** Sometimes I go from feeling happy to sad, and vice versa, for no good reason.

Scoring: Level of negative affectivity is equal to the number of items answered "True."

Source: Auke Tellegen, *Brief Manual for the Differential Personality Questionnaire.* Copyright © 1982. Paraphrased version reproduced by permission of University of Minnesota Press.

affectionate, and care about other people. Managers who are low on agreeableness may be somewhat distrustful of others, unsympathetic, uncooperative, and even at times antagonistic. Being high on agreeableness may be especially important for managers whose responsibilities require that they develop good, close relationships with others. Nevertheless, a low level of agreeableness may be an asset in managerial jobs that actually require that managers be antagonistic, such as drill sergeants. See Figure 2.2 for an example of a scale that measures a person's level of agreeableness.

conscientiousness The tendency to be careful, scrupulous, and persevering.

CONSCIENTIOUSNESS Conscientiousness is the tendency to be careful, scrupulous, and persevering.[18] Managers who are high on the conscientiousness continuum are organized and self-disciplined; those who are low on this trait might sometimes appear to lack direction and self-discipline. Conscientiousness has been found to be a good predictor of performance in many kinds of jobs, including managerial jobs in a variety of organizations.[19] Entrepreneurs who found their own companies, like Mark Wilson profiled in the "Management Snapshot," often are high on conscientiousness. Their persistence and determination help them to overcome obstacles and turn their ideas into successful new ventures. See again Figure 2.2, which also provides an example of a scale that measures conscientiousness.

openness to experience The tendency to be original, have broad interests, be open to a wide range of stimuli, be daring, and take risks.

OPENNESS TO EXPERIENCE Openness to experience is the tendency to be original, have broad interests, be open to a wide range of stimuli, be daring, and take risks.[20] Managers who are high on this trait continuum may be especially likely to take risks and be innovative in their planning and decision making. Entrepreneurs who start their own businesses–like Bill Gates of Microsoft, Jeff Bezos of Amazon.com, and Anita Roddick of The Body Shop–are, in all likelihood, high on openness to experience. This has contributed to their success as entrepreneurs and managers. Mark Wilson, discussed in this chapter's "Management Snapshot," founded his own company and continues to explore new ways for it to grow–a testament to his high level of openness to experience. Managers who are low on openness to experience may be less prone to take risks and more conservative in their planning and decision making. In certain organizations and positions, this tendency might be an asset. The manager of the fiscal office in a public university, for example, must ensure that all university departments and units follow the university's rules and regulations pertaining to budgets, spending accounts, and reimbursements of expenses. Figure 2.2 provides an example of a measure of openness to experience.

Managers who come up with and implement radically new ideas are often high on openness to experience, as is true of Mike Rowe, creator of the hit Discovery Channel TV show *Dirty Jobs*.

MANAGER AS A PERSON

Who Would Have Thought *Dirty Jobs* Would Be a Hit?

Mike Rowe is hardly the person you would have thought would have created a hit TV show like the Discovery Channel's *Dirty Jobs*.[21] Not the most ambitious of types, and as an actor in the business for over two decades who never made it big, his work experiences have ranged from performing with the Baltimore Opera to selling fake diamonds on QVC on TV to appearing in Tylenol commercials.[22] While cohosting a local TV show on CBS-5 in San Francisco, Rowe hit upon the idea behind *Dirty Jobs*. Rowe did a segment on the show called "Somebody's Gotta Do It," viewers

Mike Rowe's openness to experience has given him a real appreciation of all kinds of work and jobs.

liked it, and it really struck a chord with him personally.[23]

His openness to experience led him to try to develop a TV show featuring him working as an apprentice to men and women performing the kinds of hard, dirty work we all depend on and no one wants to do (think bat cave scavenger, worm dung farmer, road-kill cleaner, sewer inspector, pig farmer . . .).[24] As he puts it, his show features "men and women who do the kinds of jobs that make civilized life possible for the rest of us."[25] While he originally had a hard time finding a home for *Dirty Jobs* (the Discovery Channel turned him down twice before agreeing to air a pilot series in 2003), the show has become a bona fide hit, aired 700 times in 2007, and is the Discovery Channel's number-one show, according to David Zaslav, the CEO of Discovery Communications.[26]

Rowe's openness to experience enables him to get down and dirty with the best of them, try his hand at all sorts of dirty jobs, and thoroughly enjoy it. As would be expected, all sorts of mishaps occur and that is part of the fun. And Rowe has come to appreciate the earnestness of the workers he profiles–"the celebration of work, and the mixing of pain and fun."[27] Interestingly enough, although Rowe never had embraced the value of too much hard work in the past, *Dirty Jobs* has instilled in Rowe a healthy respect and admiration for the people who perform all sorts of dirty jobs, work hard at them, and are happy when the work is done.[28]

Successful managers occupy a variety of positions on the Big Five personality trait continua. One highly effective manager may be high on extraversion and negative affectivity, another equally effective manager may be low on both these traits, and still another may be somewhere in between. Members of an organization must understand these differences among managers because they can shed light on how managers behave and on their approach to planning, leading, organizing, or controlling. If subordinates realize, for example, that their manager is low on extraversion, they will not feel slighted when their manager seems to be aloof because they will realize that by nature he or she is simply not outgoing.

Managers themselves also need to be aware of their own personality traits and the traits of others, including their subordinates and fellow managers. A manager who knows that he has a tendency to be highly critical of other people might try to tone down his negative approach. Similarly, a manager who realizes that her chronically complaining subordinate tends to be so negative because of his personality may take all his complaints with a grain of salt and realize that things probably are not as bad as this subordinate says they are.

In order for all members of an organization to work well together and with people outside the organization, such as customers and suppliers, they must understand each other. Such understanding comes, in part, from an appreciation of some of the fundamental ways in which people differ from one another–that is, an appreciation of personality traits.

Other Personality Traits That Affect Managerial Behavior

Many other specific traits in addition to the Big Five describe people's personalities. Here we look at traits that are particularly important for understanding managerial effectiveness: locus of control; self-esteem; and the needs for achievement, affiliation, and power.

internal locus of control The tendency to locate responsibility for one's fate within oneself.

external locus of control The tendency to locate responsibility for one's fate in outside forces and to believe that one's own behavior has little impact on outcomes.

LOCUS OF CONTROL People differ in their views about how much control they have over what happens to and around them. The locus-of-control trait captures these beliefs.[29] People with an **internal locus of control** believe that they themselves are responsible for their own fate; they see their own actions and behaviors as being major and decisive determinants of important outcomes such as attaining levels of job performance, being promoted, or being turned down for a choice job assignment. Some managers with an internal locus of control see the success of a whole organization resting on their shoulders. One example is Mark Wilson in the "Management Snapshot." An internal locus of control also helps to ensure ethical behavior and decision making in an organization because people feel accountable and responsible for their own actions.

People with an **external locus of control** believe that outside forces are responsible for what happens to and around them; they do not think that their own actions make much of a difference. As such, they tend not to intervene to try to change a situation or solve a problem, leaving it to someone else.

Managers need to have an internal locus of control because they *are* responsible for what happens in organizations; they need to believe that they can and do make a difference, as does Mark Wilson at Ryla. Moreover, managers are responsible for ensuring that organizations and their members behave in an ethical fashion, and for this as well they need to have an internal locus of control–they need to know and feel they can make a difference.

self-esteem The degree to which individuals feel good about themselves and their capabilities.

need for achievement The extent to which an individual has a strong desire to perform challenging tasks well and to meet personal standards for excellence.

SELF-ESTEEM **Self-esteem** is the degree to which individuals feel good about themselves and their capabilities. People with high self-esteem believe that they are competent, deserving, and capable of handling most situations, as does Mark Wilson. People with low self-esteem have poor opinions of themselves, are unsure about their capabilities, and question their ability to succeed at different endeavors.[30] Research suggests that people tend to choose activities and goals consistent with their levels of self-esteem. High self-esteem is desirable for managers because it facilitates their setting and keeping high standards for themselves, pushes them ahead on difficult projects, and gives them confidence.

NEEDS FOR ACHIEVEMENT, AFFILIATION, AND POWER Psychologist David McClelland has extensively researched the needs for achievement, affiliation, and power.[31] The **need for achievement** is the extent to which an individual has a strong desire to perform challenging tasks well and to meet personal standards for excellence.

need for affiliation The extent to which an individual is concerned about establishing and maintaining good interpersonal relations, being liked, and having other people get along.

need for power The extent to which an individual desires to control or influence others.

People with a high need for achievement often set clear goals for themselves and like to receive performance feedback. The **need for affiliation** is the extent to which an individual is concerned about establishing and maintaining good interpersonal relations, being liked, and having the people around him or her get along with one another. The **need for power** is the extent to which an individual desires to control or influence others.[32]

Research suggests that high needs for achievement and for power are assets for first-line and middle managers and that a high need for power is especially important for upper-level managers.[33] One study found that U.S. presidents with a relatively high need for power tended to be especially effective during their terms of office.[34] A high need for affiliation may not always be desirable in managers because it might lead them to try too hard to be liked by others (including subordinates) rather than doing all they can to ensure that performance is high. Although most research on these needs has been done in the United States, some studies suggest that these findings may also be applicable to people in other countries such as India and New Zealand.[35]

In summary, desirable personality traits for managers are an internal locus of control, high self-esteem, and high needs for achievement and power. Managers need to be take-charge people who believe that their own actions are decisive in determining their own and their organizations' fates and who believe in their own capabilities. Their personal desire for accomplishment and influence over others helps them to be effective managers.

Values, Attitudes, and Moods and Emotions

What are managers striving to achieve? How do they think they should behave? What do they think about their jobs and organizations? And how do they actually feel at work? Some answers to these questions can be found by exploring managers' values, attitudes, and moods and emotions.

LO2 Explain what values and attitudes are and describe their impact on managerial action.

Values, attitudes, and moods and emotions capture how managers experience their jobs as individuals. *Values* describe what managers are trying to achieve through work and how they think they should behave. *Attitudes* are their thoughts and feelings about their specific jobs and organizations. *Moods and emotions* encompass how managers actually feel when they are managing. These aspects of managers have important implications for understanding how managers behave, how they treat and respond to others, and how they contribute to organizational effectiveness through their style of planning, leading, organizing, and controlling.

Values: Terminal and Instrumental

terminal value A lifelong goal or objective that an individual seeks to achieve.

instrumental value A mode of conduct that an individual seeks to follow.

The two kinds of personal values are *terminal* and *instrumental.* A **terminal value** is a personal conviction about lifelong goals or objectives; an **instrumental value** is a personal conviction about desired modes of conduct or ways of behaving.[36] Terminal values often lead to the formation of **norms,** or unwritten, informal codes of conduct that prescribe how people should act in particular situations and are considered important by most members of a group or organization, such as behaving honestly or courteously.

Milton Rokeach, one of the leading researchers in the area of human values, identified 18 terminal values and 18 instrumental values that describe each person's value system (see Figure 2.4).[37] By rank ordering the terminal values from 1 (most important as a guiding principle in one's life) to 18 (least important as a guiding principle

Figure 2.4
Terminal and Instrumental Values

Terminal Values	Instrumental Values
A comfortable life (a prosperous life)	Ambitious (hardworking, aspiring)
An exciting life (a stimulating, active life)	Broad-minded (open-minded)
A sense of accomplishment (lasting contribution)	Capable (competent, effective)
A world at peace (free of war and conflict)	Cheerful (lighthearted, joyful)
A world of beauty (beauty of nature and the arts)	Clean (neat, tidy)
Equality (brotherhood, equal opportunity for all)	Courageous (standing up for your beliefs)
Family security (taking care of loved ones)	Forgiving (willing to pardon others)
Freedom (independence, free choice)	Helpful (working for the welfare of others)
Happiness (contentedness)	Honest (sincere, truthful)
Inner harmony (freedom from inner conflict)	Imaginative (daring, creative)
Mature love (sexual and spiritual intimacy)	Independent (self-reliant, self-sufficient)
National security (protection from attack)	Intellectual (intelligent, reflective)
Pleasure (an enjoyable, leisurely life)	Logical (consistent, rational)
Salvation (saved, eternal life)	Loving (affectionate, tender)
Self-respect (self-esteem)	Obedient (dutiful, respectful)
Social recognition (respect, admiration)	Polite (courteous, well-mannered)
True friendship (close companionship)	Responsible (dependable, reliable)
Wisdom (a mature understanding of life)	Self-controlled (restrained, self-disciplined)

Source: Milton Rokeach, *The Nature of Human Values.*

norms Unwritten, informal codes of conduct that prescribe how people should act in particular situations and are considered important by most members of a group or organization.

value system The terminal and instrumental values that are guiding principles in an individual's life.

in one's life) and then rank ordering the instrumental values from 1 to 18, people can give good pictures of their **value systems**—what they are striving to achieve in life and how they want to behave.[38] (You can gain a good understanding of your own values by rank ordering first the terminal values and then the instrumental values listed in Figure 2.4.)

Several of the terminal values listed in Figure 2.4 seem to be especially important for managers—such as *a sense of accomplishment (a lasting contribution), equality (brotherhood, equal opportunity for all),* and *self-respect (self-esteem).* A manager who thinks a sense of accomplishment is of paramount importance might focus on making a lasting contribution to an organization by developing a new product that can save or prolong lives, as is true of managers at Medtronic (a company that makes medical devices such as cardiac pacemakers), or by opening a new foreign subsidiary. A manager who places equality at the top of his or her list of terminal values may be at the forefront of an organization's efforts to support, provide equal opportunities to, and capitalize on the many talents of an increasingly diverse workforce.

Other values are likely to be considered important by many managers, such *as a comfortable life (a prosperous life), an exciting life (a stimulating, active life), freedom (independence, free choice)*, and *social recognition (respect, admiration)*. The relative importance that managers place on each terminal value helps explain what they are striving to achieve in their organizations and what they will focus their efforts on.

Several of the instrumental values listed in Figure 2.4 seem to be important modes of conduct for managers, such as being *ambitious (hardworking, aspiring), broad-minded (open-minded), capable (competent, effective), responsible (dependable, reliable),* and *self-controlled (restrained, self-disciplined)*. Moreover, the relative importance a manager places on these and other instrumental values may be a significant determinant of actual behaviors on the job. A manager who considers being *imaginative (daring, creative)* to be highly important, for example, is more likely to be innovative and take risks than is a manager who considers this to be less important (all else being equal). A manager who considers being *honest (sincere, truthful)* to be of paramount importance may be a driving force for taking steps to ensure that all members of a unit or organization behave ethically, as indicated in the following "Ethics in Action."

ETHICS IN ACTION

Telling the Truth at Gentle Giant Moving

Gentle Giant Moving Company, based in Somerville, Massachusetts, was founded by Larry O'Toole in 1980 and now has over $28 million in revenues and offices in multiple states.[39] While moving is undoubtedly hard work and many people would never think about having a career in this industry, Gentle Giant's unique culture and approach to managing people have not only contributed to the company's success but also provided its employees with satisfying careers. For example, when Ryan Libby was in college, he worked for Gentle Giant during one of his summer vacations to make some extra money. Now the assistant manager for the Providence, Rhode Island, Gentle Giant Office, Libby is contemplating opening an office of his own. As he puts it, "First it was just a paycheck, and it kind of turned into a long-term career."[40]

At Gentle Giant Moving Co., employees are given leadership training, access to company outings, and the opportunity to advance to management positions.

Libby is just the kind of employee O'Toole seeks to hire–employees who start out driving moving trucks and eventually move into management positions running offices. While some moving companies hire a lot of temporary help in the summer to meet seasonal demand, 60% of Gentle Giant employees are employed full-time.[41] Since the demand for moving services is lower in the winter, Gentle Giant uses this time to provide employees with training and leadership development activities. Of course, new employees receive training in the basics of moving: packing, lifting, and carrying household goods in a safe manner. However, employees looking to advance in the company receive training in a host of other areas ranging from project management, communication, problem solving, and customer relations to leadership. An overarching goal of Gentle Giant's

Small Business

training efforts is inculcating in employees the importance of honesty. According to O'Toole, "We really emphasize that what matters most to us is telling the truth."[42]

Training benefits Gentle Giant's employees, customers, and the company as a whole. About one-third of the company's office and management employees started out driving moving trucks. Customers are satisfied because employees are capable, honest, and professional. And the company has continued to grow, prosper, and receive recognition in the business press. For example, in 2007, Gentle Giant was named one of the 15 Top Small Workplaces by *The Wall Street Journal* in collaboration with Winning Workplaces (a nonprofit organization that focuses on helping small- and medium-size companies improve their work environments).[43]

Having fun and getting to know each other as people is also important at Gentle Giant.[44] The company holds parties and arranges for outings for employees to sporting events, amusement parks, and other local attractions. Most workdays, O'Toole takes an employee out to lunch. Some college athletes are attracted to work for Gentle Giant because they see moving as a way to keep fit while at the same time having the opportunity to grow and develop on the job and move into a managerial position if they desire.[45]

All in all, managers' value systems signify what managers as individuals are trying to accomplish and become in their personal lives and at work. Thus, managers' value systems are fundamental guides to their behavior and efforts at planning, leading, organizing, and controlling.

Attitudes

attitude A collection of feelings and beliefs.

An **attitude** is a collection of feelings and beliefs. Like everyone else, managers have attitudes about their jobs and organizations, and these attitudes affect how they approach their jobs. Two of the most important attitudes in this context are job satisfaction and organizational commitment.

job satisfaction The collection of feelings and beliefs that managers have about their current jobs.

JOB SATISFACTION **Job satisfaction** is the collection of feelings and beliefs that managers have about their current jobs.[46] Managers who have high levels of job satisfaction generally like their jobs, feel that they are being fairly treated, and believe that their jobs have many desirable features or characteristics (such as interesting work, good pay and job security, autonomy, or nice coworkers). Figure 2.5 shows sample items from two scales that managers can use to measure job satisfaction. Levels of job satisfaction tend to increase as one moves up the hierarchy in an organization. Upper managers, in general, tend to be more satisfied with their jobs than entry-level employees. Managers' levels of job satisfaction can range from very low to very high and anywhere in between.

organizational citizenship behaviors (OCBs) Behaviors that are not required of organizational members but that contribute to and are necessary for organizational efficiency, effectiveness, and competitive advantage.

According to a recent survey, job satisfaction levels in the United States have declined over the past 20 years or so.[47] In particular, some workers report being dissatisfied with opportunities for growth and advancement on their jobs, heavy workloads and work/life balance issues, performance reviews and bonus plans, and communication in their organizations.[48]

In general, it is desirable for managers to be satisfied with their jobs, for at least two reasons. First, satisfied managers may be more likely to go the extra mile for their organization or perform **organizational citizenship behaviors (OCBs)**, behaviors that are not required of organizational members but that contribute to and are necessary

Figure 2.5
Sample Items from Two Measures of Job Satisfaction

Sample items from the Minnesota Satisfaction Questionnaire:
People respond to each of the items in the scale by checking whether they are

[ ] Very dissatisfied
[ ] Dissatisfied
[ ] Can't decide whether satisfied or not
[ ] Satisfied
[ ] Very satisfied

On my present job, this is how I feel about . . .

____ **1.** Being able to do things that don't go against my conscience.

____ **2.** The way my job provides for steady employment.

____ **3.** The chance to do things for other people.

____ **4.** The chance to do something that makes use of my abilities.

____ **5.** The way company policies are put into practice.

____ **6.** My pay and the amount of work I do.

____ **7.** The chances for advancement on this job.

____ **8.** The freedom to use my own judgment.

____ **9.** The working conditions.

____ **10.** The way my coworkers get along with each other.

____ **11.** The praise I get for doing a good job.

____ **12.** The feeling of accomplishment I get from the job.

The Faces Scale
Workers select the face which best expresses how they feel about their job in general.

11 10 9 8 7 6 5 4 3 2 1

Source: D. J. Weiss et al., *Manual for the Minnesota Satisfaction Questionnaire,* 1967, Minnesota Studies in Vocational Rehabilitation: XXII. Copyright © 1975 by the American Psychological Association. Adapted by permission of Randall B. Dunham and J. B. Brett.

for organizational efficiency, effectiveness, and competitive advantage.[49] Managers who are satisfied with their jobs are more likely to perform these "above and beyond the call of duty" behaviors, which can range from putting in extra-long hours when needed to coming up with truly creative ideas and overcoming obstacles to implement them (even when doing so is not part of the manager's job), or to going out of one's way to help a coworker, subordinate, or superior (even when doing so entails considerable personal sacrifice).[50]

A second reason why it is desirable for managers to be satisfied with their jobs is that satisfied managers may be less likely to quit.[51] A manager who is highly satisfied may never even think about looking for another position; a dissatisfied manager may always be on the lookout for new opportunities. Turnover can hurt an organization because it results in the loss of the experience and knowledge that managers have gained about the company, industry, and business environment.

Managers and employees who are very committed to their organizations may be more inclined to go above and beyond the call of duty by, for example, working long hours when need be.

A growing source of dissatisfaction for many lower- and middle-level managers, as well as for nonmanagerial employees, is the threat of unemployment and increased workloads from organizational downsizings and layoffs. Organizations that try to improve their efficiency through restructuring and layoffs often eliminate a sizable number of first-line and middle management positions. This decision obviously hurts the managers who are laid off, and it also can reduce the job satisfaction levels of managers who remain. They might fear that they may be the next to be let go. In addition, the workloads of remaining employees often are dramatically increased as a result of restructuring, and this can contribute to dissatisfaction.

The ways in which managers and organizations handle layoffs is of paramount importance, not only for the layoff victims but also for those employees who survive the layoff and keep their jobs.[52] Showing compassion and empathy for layoff victims, providing them with as much advance notice as possible about the layoff, providing clear information about severance benefits, and also helping layoff victims in their job search efforts are a few of the ways in which managers can humanely manage a layoff.[53] For example, when Ron Thomas, vice president of organizational development for Martha Stewart Living Omnimedia, had to lay off employees as a result of closing the organization's catalog business, he personally called all the catalog businesses he knew to find out about potential positions for laid-off employees.[54] Efforts such as Thomas's to help layoff victims find new jobs can contribute to the job satisfaction of those who survive the layoff. As Thomas puts it, "If you handle a restructuring well, the word gets out that you're a good place to work . . . if we post a job opening today, we'll get 1,500 résumés tomorrow."[55]

organizational commitment The collection of feelings and beliefs that managers have about their organization as a whole.

ORGANIZATIONAL COMMITMENT **Organizational commitment** is the collection of feelings and beliefs that managers have about their organization as a whole.[56] Managers who are committed to their organizations believe in what their organizations are doing, are proud of what these organizations stand for, and feel a high degree of loyalty toward their organizations. Committed managers are more likely to go above and beyond the call of duty to help their company and are less likely to quit.[57] Organizational commitment can be especially strong when employees and managers truly believe in organizational values; it also leads to a strong organizational culture, as found in Ryla.

Organizational commitment is likely to help managers perform some of their figurehead and spokesperson roles. It is much easier for a manager to persuade others both inside and outside the organization of the merits of what the organization has done and is seeking to accomplish if the manager truly believes in and is committed to the organization. Figure 2.6 is an example of a scale that managers can use to measure a person's level of organizational commitment.

Figure 2.6
A Measure of Organizational Commitment

People respond to each of the items in the scale by checking whether they

[ ] Strongly disagree
[ ] Moderately disagree
[ ] Slightly disagree
[ ] Neither disagree nor agree
[ ] Slightly agree
[ ] Moderately agree
[ ] Strongly agree

____ **1.** I am willing to put in a great deal of effort beyond that normally expected in order to help this organization be successful.

____ **2.** I talk up this organization to my friends as a great organization to work for.

____ **3.** I feel very little loyalty to this organization.*

____ **4.** I would accept almost any type of job assignment in order to keep working for this organization.

____ **5.** I find that my values and the organization's values are very similar.

____ **6.** I am proud to tell others that I am part of this organization.

____ **7.** I could just as well be working for a different organization as long as the type of work was similar.*

____ **8.** This organization really inspires the very best in me in the way of job performance.

____ **9.** It would take very little change in my present circumstances to cause me to leave this organization.*

____ **10.** I am extremely glad that I chose this organization to work for over others I was considering at the time I joined.

____ **11.** There's not too much to be gained by sticking with this organization indefinitely.*

____ **12.** Often, I find it difficult to agree with this organization's policies on important matters relating to its employees.*

____ **13.** I really care about the fate of this organization.

____ **14.** For me this is the best of all possible organizations for which to work.

____ **15.** Deciding to work for this organization was a definite mistake on my part.*

Scoring: Responses to items 1, 2, 4, 5, 6, 8, 10, 13, and 14 are scored such that 1 = strongly disagree; 2 = moderately disagree; 3 = slightly disagree; 4 = neither disagree nor agree; 5 = slightly agree; 6 = moderately agree; and 7 = strongly agree. Responses to "*" items 3, 7, 9, 11, 12, and 15 are scored 7 = strongly disagree; 6 = moderately disagree; 5 = slightly disagree; 4 = neither disagree nor agree; 3 = slightly agree; 2 = moderately agree; and 1 = strongly agree. Responses to the 15 items are averaged for an overall score from 1 to 7; the higher the score, the higher the level of organizational commitment.

Source: L. W. Porter and F. J. Smith, "Organizational Commitment Questionnaire," in J. D. Cook, S. J. Hepworth, T. D. Wall, and P. B. Warr, eds., *The Experience of Work: A Compendium and Review of 249 Measures and Their Use,* Academic Press, 1981, pp. 84–86. Reprinted with permission.

Do managers in different countries have similar or different attitudes? Differences in the levels of job satisfaction and organizational commitment among managers in different countries are likely because these managers have different kinds of opportunities and rewards and because they face different economic, political, or sociocultural forces in their organizations' general environments. In countries with relatively high unemployment rates, such as France, levels of job satisfaction may be higher among employed managers because they may be happy simply to have a job.

Levels of organizational commitment from one country to another may depend on the extent to which countries have legislation affecting firings and layoffs and the extent to which citizens of a country are geographically mobile. In both France and Germany legislation protects workers (including managers) from being fired or laid off. U.S. workers, in contrast, have very little protection. In addition, managers in the United States are more willing to relocate than managers in France and Germany. In France citizens have relatively strong family and community ties; and in Germany housing is expensive and difficult to find. For those reasons citizens in both countries tend to be less geographically mobile than Americans.[58] Managers who know that their jobs are secure and who are reluctant to relocate (such as those in Germany and France) may be more committed to their organizations than managers who know that their organizations could lay them off any day and who would not mind geographic relocations.

Moods and Emotions

LO3 Appreciate how moods and emotions influence all members of an organization.

mood A feeling or state of mind.

emotions Intense, relatively short-lived feelings.

Just as you are sometimes in a bad mood and sometimes in a good mood, so too are managers. A **mood** is a feeling or state of mind. When people are in a positive mood, they feel excited, enthusiastic, active, or elated.[59] When people are in a negative mood, they feel distressed, fearful, scornful, hostile, jittery, or nervous.[60] People who are high on extraversion are especially likely to experience positive moods. People who are high on negative affectivity are especially likely to experience negative moods. However, this is not always the case. People's situations or circumstances also determine their moods. Receiving a raise is likely to put most people in a good mood regardless of their personality traits. People who are high on negative affectivity are not always in a bad mood, and people who are low on extraversion experience positive moods.[61]

Emotions are more intense feelings than moods, are often directly linked to whatever caused the emotion, and are more short-lived.[62] However, once whatever has triggered the emotion has been dealt with, the feelings may linger in the form of a less intense mood.[63] For example, a manager who gets very angry when one of his subordinates has engaged in an unethical behavior may find his anger decreasing in intensity once he has decided how to address the problem. Yet he continues to be in a bad mood the rest of the day, even though he is not directly thinking about the unfortunate incident.[64]

Research has found that moods and emotions affect the behavior of managers and all members of an organization. For example, research suggests that the subordinates of managers who experience positive moods at work may perform at somewhat higher levels and be less likely to resign and leave the organization than the subordinates of managers who do not tend to be in a positive mood at work.[65] Other research suggests that under certain conditions creativity might be enhanced by positive moods, whereas under other conditions negative moods might push people to work harder to come up with truly creative ideas.[66] Recognizing that both mood states have the potential to contribute to creativity in different ways, recent research suggests that employees may be especially likely to be creative to the extent that they experience both mood states (at different times) on the job and the work environment is supportive of creativity.[67]

Other research suggests that moods and emotions may play an important role in ethical decision making. Researchers at Princeton University found that when people are trying to solve difficult personal moral dilemmas, the parts of their brains that are responsible for emotions and moods are especially active.[68]

Recognizing the benefits of positive moods, the Northbrook, Illinois, accounting firm Lipschultz, Levin, & Gray[69] has gone to great lengths to promote positive feelings among its employees. Chief executive Steven Siegel claims that positive feelings promote relaxation and alleviate stress, increase revenues and attract clients, and reduce turnover.

Positive moods are promoted in a variety of ways at Lipschultz, Levin, & Gray. Siegel has been known to put on a gorilla mask at especially busy times. Clerks don chicken costumes. A foghorn announces the signing of a new client. Employees take a break and play miniature golf in the office, play darts, or exercise with a hula-hoop (even during tax time). A casual dress code also lightens things up. Positive moods seem to be pay off for this group of accountants, whose good feelings seem to attract new clients.

Patrick Corboy, president and chief executive of Austin Chemical, switched his account from a bigger firm to Lipschultz, Levin, & Gray. He found the people at the old bigger firm to be "too stuffy and dour for us." Of the accountant William Finestone, who now manages the Austin Chemical account, Corboy says the following: "[He] is a barrel of laughs . . . Bill not only solves our problems more quickly but he puts us at ease, too."[70]

Nevertheless, sometimes negative moods can have their advantages. Some studies suggest that critical thinking and productive devil's advocacy may be promoted by a negative mood. Sometimes especially accurate judgments may be made by managers in negative moods.[71]

Managers need to realize that how they feel affects how they treat others and how others respond to them. For example, a subordinate may be more likely to approach a manager with a somewhat far-out but potentially useful idea if the subordinate thinks the manager is in a good mood. Likewise, when managers are in very bad moods, their subordinates might try to avoid them at all costs. Figure 2.7 is an example of a scale that managers can use to measure the extent to which a person experiences positive and negative moods at work.

Figure 2.7

A Measure of Positive and Negative Mood at Work

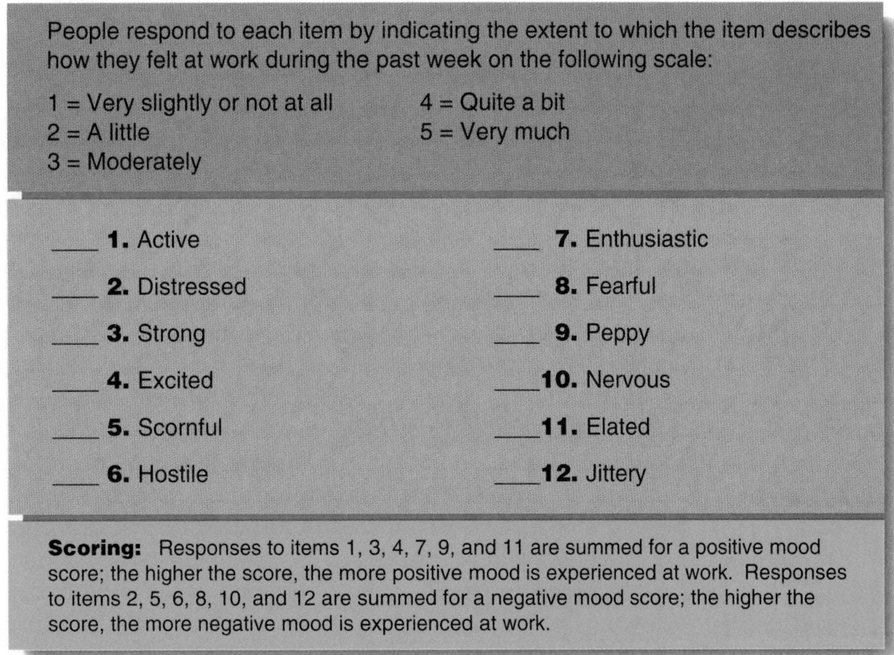

People respond to each item by indicating the extent to which the item describes how they felt at work during the past week on the following scale:

1 = Very slightly or not at all
2 = A little
3 = Moderately
4 = Quite a bit
5 = Very much

____ **1.** Active
____ **2.** Distressed
____ **3.** Strong
____ **4.** Excited
____ **5.** Scornful
____ **6.** Hostile
____ **7.** Enthusiastic
____ **8.** Fearful
____ **9.** Peppy
____ **10.** Nervous
____ **11.** Elated
____ **12.** Jittery

Scoring: Responses to items 1, 3, 4, 7, 9, and 11 are summed for a positive mood score; the higher the score, the more positive mood is experienced at work. Responses to items 2, 5, 6, 8, 10, and 12 are summed for a negative mood score; the higher the score, the more negative mood is experienced at work.

Sources: A. P. Brief, M. J. Burke, J. M. George, B. Robinson, and J. Webster, "Should Negative Affectivity Remain an Unmeasured Variable in the Study of Job Stress?" *Journal of Applied Psychology* 73 (1988), pp. 193–98; M. J. Burke, A. P. Brief, J. M. George, L. Robinson, and J. Webster, "Measuring Affect at Work: Confirmatory Analyses of Competing Mood Structures with Conceptual Linkage in Cortical Regulatory Systems," *Journal of Personality and Social Psychology* 57 (1989), pp. 1091–102.

Emotional Intelligence

In understanding the effects of managers' and all employees' moods and emotions, it is important to take into account their levels of emotional intelligence. **Emotional intelligence** is the ability to understand and manage one's own moods and emotions and the moods and emotions of other people.[72] Managers with a high level of emotional intelligence are more likely to understand how they are feeling and why, and they are more able to effectively manage their feelings. When managers are experiencing stressful feelings and emotions such as fear or anxiety, emotional intelligence enables them to understand why and manage these feelings so that they do not get in the way of effective decision making.[73]

LO4 Describe the nature of emotional intelligence and its role in management.

emotional intelligence The ability to understand and manage one's own moods and emotions and the moods and emotions of other people.

Emotional intelligence also can help managers perform their important roles such as their interpersonal roles (figurehead, leader, and liaison).[74] Understanding how your subordinates feel, why they feel that way, and how to manage these feelings is central to developing strong interpersonal bonds with them.[75] More generally, emotional intelligence has the potential to contribute to effective leadership in multiple ways.[76]

For example, emotional intelligence helps managers understand and relate well to other people.[77] It also helps managers maintain their enthusiasm and confidence and energize subordinates to help the organization attain its goals.[78] Recent theorizing and research suggest that emotional intelligence may be especially important in awakening employee creativity.[79] Managers themselves are increasingly recognizing the importance of emotional intelligence. As Andrea Jung, CEO of Avon Products, states, "Emotional intelligence is in our DNA here at Avon because relationships are critical at every stage of our business."[80] An example of a scale that measures emotional intelligence is provided in Figure 2.8.

Organizational Culture

Personality is a way of understanding why all managers and employees, as individuals, characteristically think and behave in different ways. However, when people belong to the same organization, they often tend to share certain beliefs and values that lead them to act in similar ways.[81] **Organizational culture** comprises the shared set of beliefs, expectations, values, norms, and work routines that influence how members of an organization relate to one another and work together to achieve organizational goals. In essence, organizational culture reflects the distinctive ways organizational members go about performing their jobs and relating to others inside and outside the organization. It may, for example, be a distinctive way in which customers in a particular hotel chain are treated from the time they are greeted at check-in until their stay is completed; or it may be the shared work routines that research teams use to guide new product development. When organizational members share an intense commitment to cultural values, beliefs, and routines and use them to achieve their goals, a *strong* organizational culture exists.[82] When organizational members are not strongly committed to a shared system of values, beliefs, and routines, organizational culture is weak.

LO5 Define organizational culture and explain how managers both create and are influenced by organizational culture.

organizational culture The shared set of beliefs, expectations, values, norms, and work routines that influence the ways in which individuals, groups, and teams interact with one another and cooperate to achieve organizational goals.

The stronger the culture of an organization, the more one can think about it as being the "personality" of an organization because it influences the way its members behave.[83] Organizations that possess strong cultures may differ on a wide variety of dimensions that determine how their members behave toward one another and perform their jobs. For example, organizations differ in terms of how members relate to each other (e.g., formally or informally), how important decisions are made (e.g., top-down or bottom-up), willingness to change (e.g., flexible or unyielding), innovation

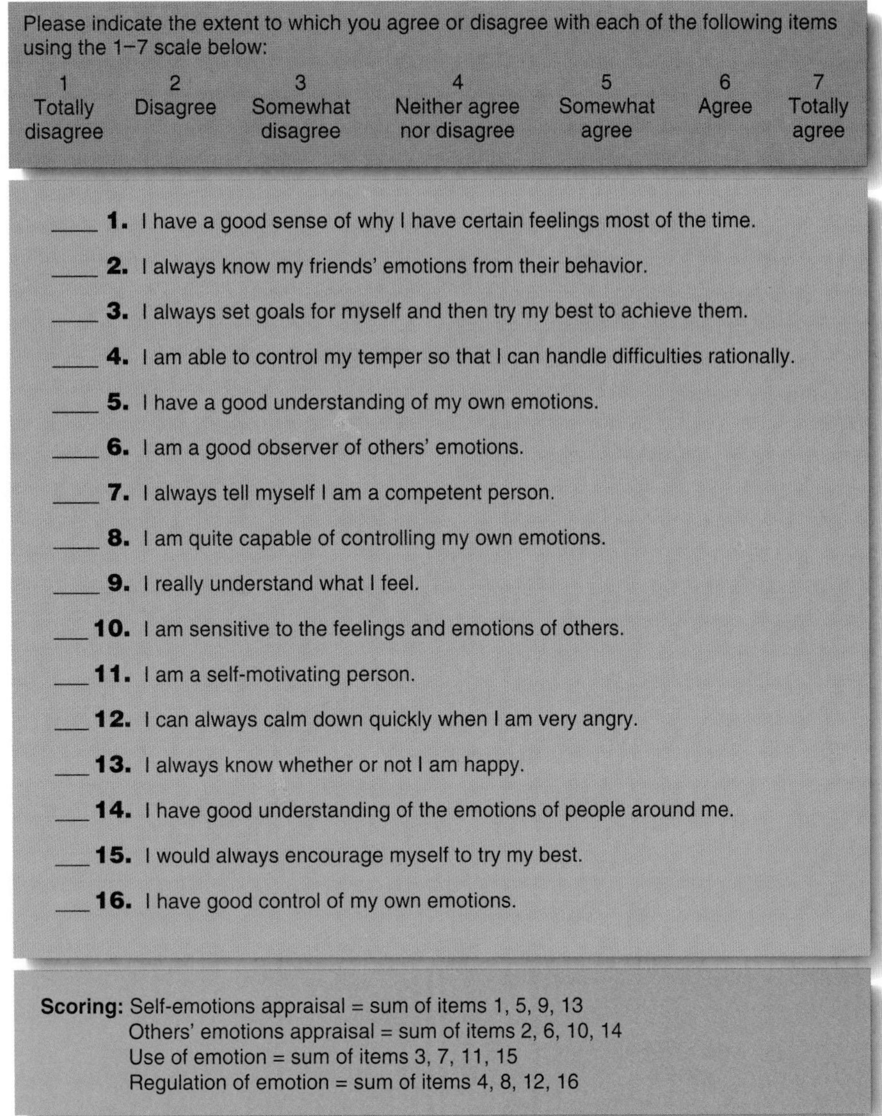
Please indicate the extent to which you agree or disagree with each of the following items using the 1–7 scale below:

1	2	3	4	5	6	7
Totally disagree	Disagree	Somewhat disagree	Neither agree nor disagree	Somewhat agree	Agree	Totally agree

____ **1.** I have a good sense of why I have certain feelings most of the time.

____ **2.** I always know my friends' emotions from their behavior.

____ **3.** I always set goals for myself and then try my best to achieve them.

____ **4.** I am able to control my temper so that I can handle difficulties rationally.

____ **5.** I have a good understanding of my own emotions.

____ **6.** I am a good observer of others' emotions.

____ **7.** I always tell myself I am a competent person.

____ **8.** I am quite capable of controlling my own emotions.

____ **9.** I really understand what I feel.

____ **10.** I am sensitive to the feelings and emotions of others.

____ **11.** I am a self-motivating person.

____ **12.** I can always calm down quickly when I am very angry.

____ **13.** I always know whether or not I am happy.

____ **14.** I have good understanding of the emotions of people around me.

____ **15.** I would always encourage myself to try my best.

____ **16.** I have good control of my own emotions.

Scoring: Self-emotions appraisal = sum of items 1, 5, 9, 13
Others' emotions appraisal = sum of items 2, 6, 10, 14
Use of emotion = sum of items 3, 7, 11, 15
Regulation of emotion = sum of items 4, 8, 12, 16

Figure 2.8
A Measure of Emotional Intelligence

Sources: K. Law, C. Wong, and L. Song, "The Construct and Criterion Validity of Emotional Intelligence and Its Potential Utility for Management Studies," *Journal of Applied Psychology* 89, no. 3 (June 2004), p. 496; C. S. Wong and K. S. Law, "The Effects of Leader and Follower Emotional Intelligence on Performance and Attitude: An Exploratory Study," *Leadership Quarterly* 13 (2002), pp. 243–74.

(e.g., creative or predictable), and playfulness (e.g., serious or serendipitous). In an innovative design firm like IDEO Product Development in Silicon Valley, employees are encouraged to adopt a playful attitude to their work, look outside the organization to find inspiration, and adopt a flexible approach toward product design that uses multiple perspectives.[84] IDEO's culture is vastly different from that of companies such as Citibank and ExxonMobil, in which employees treat each other in a more formal or deferential way, employees are expected to adopt a serious approach to their work, and decision making is constrained by the hierarchy of authority.

Managers and Organizational Culture

Managers play a particularly important part in influencing organizational culture.[85] How managers create culture is most vividly evident in start-ups of new companies. Entrepreneurs who start their own companies are typically also the start-ups' top managers until the companies grow and/or become profitable. They are the firms' founders. These managers literally create their organizations' cultures.

The founders' personal characteristics play an important role. Benjamin Schneider, a well-known management researcher, developed a model that helps to explain the role that founders' personal characteristics play in determining organizational culture.[86] His model, called the **attraction-selection-attrition (ASA) framework**, posits that when founders hire employees for their new ventures, they tend to choose employees whose personalities are similar to their own.[87] These similar employees are more likely to stay with the organization. While employees who are dissimilar in personality might be hired, they are more likely to leave the organization over time.[88] As a result of these attraction, selection, and attrition processes, people in the organization tend to have similar personalities. The typical or dominant personality profile of organizational members determines and shapes organizational culture.[89]

attraction-selection-attrition (ASA) framework A model that explains how personality may influence organizational culture.

For example, when David Kelley became interested in engineering and product design in the late 1970s, he realized that who he was as a person meant that he would not be happy working in the typical corporate environment. Kelley is high on openness to experience, driven to go where his interests take him, and not content to follow others' directives. Kelley knew he needed to start his own business and, with the help of other Stanford-schooled engineers and design experts, IDEO was born.[90]

From the start, IDEO's culture has embodied Kelley's spirited, freewheeling approach to work and design. IDEO features colorful and informal work spaces.

IDEO employees brainstorming—informal communication, casual attire, and flexibility are all hallmarks of this organization.

Kelley emphasizes networking and communicating with as many people as possible to understand a design problem. No project or problem is too big or too small for IDEO. The company designed the Apple Lisa computer and mouse (the precursor of the Mac) and the Palm as well as the Crest Neat Squeeze toothpaste dispenser and the Racer's Edge water bottle.[91] Kelley hates rules, job titles, big corner offices, and all the other trappings of large traditional organizations that stifle creativity. Employees who are attracted to and remain with IDEO value creativity and innovation and embrace one of IDEO's mottos: "Fail often to succeed sooner."[92]

While ASA processes are most evident in small firms such as IDEO, they also can operate in large companies.[93] According to the ASA model, this is a naturally occurring phenomenon to the extent that managers and new hires are free to make the kinds of choices the model specifies. While people tend to get along well with others who are similar to themselves, too much similarity in an organization can actually impair organizational effectiveness. That is, similar people tend to view conditions and events in similar ways and thus can be resistant to change. Moreover, organizations benefit from a diversity of perspectives rather than similarity in perspectives (see Chapter 3). At IDEO, Kelley recognized early on how important it is to take advantage of the diverse talents and perspectives that people with different personalities, backgrounds, experiences, and education can bring to a design team. Hence, IDEO's design teams include not only engineers but others who might have a unique insight into a problem, such as anthropologists, communications experts, doctors, and users of a product. When new employees are hired at IDEO, they meet with many employees who have different backgrounds and characteristics–the focus is not on hiring someone who will "fit in" but, rather, on hiring someone who has something to offer and can "wow" different kinds of people with his or her insights.[94]

In addition to personality, other personal characteristics of managers shape organizational culture; these include managers' values, attitudes, moods and emotions, and emotional intelligence.[95] For example, both terminal and instrumental values of managers play a role in determining organizational culture. Managers who highly value freedom and equality, for example, might be more likely to stress the importance of autonomy and empowerment in their organizations, as well as fair treatment for all. As another example, managers who highly value being helpful and forgiving may not only be tolerant of mistakes but also be prone to emphasize the importance of organizational members' being kind and helpful to one another.

Managers who are satisfied with their jobs, are committed to their organizations, and experience positive moods and emotions might also encourage these attitudes and feelings in others. The result would be an organizational culture emphasizing positive attitudes and feelings. Research suggests that attitudes like job satisfaction and organizational commitment can be affected by the influence of others. Managers are in a particularly strong position to engage in social influence given their multiple roles. Moreover, research suggests that moods and emotions can be "contagious" and that spending time with people who are excited and enthusiastic can increase one's own levels of excitement and enthusiasm.

The Role of Values and Norms in Organizational Culture

Shared terminal and instrumental values play a particularly important role in organizational culture. *Terminal values* signify what an organization and its employees are trying to accomplish, and *instrumental values* guide the ways in which the organization and its members achieve organizational goals. In addition to values, shared norms also are a key aspect of organizational culture. Recall that norms are unwritten, informal rules or guidelines that prescribe appropriate behavior in particular situations. For example, norms at IDEO include not being critical of others' ideas, coming up with multiple ideas before settling on one, and developing prototypes of new products.[96]

Managers determine and shape organizational culture through the kinds of values and norms they promote in an organization. Some managers, like David Kelley of IDEO, cultivate values and norms that encourage risk taking, creative responses to problems and opportunities, experimentation, tolerance of failure in order to succeed, and autonomy.[97] Top managers at organizations such as Microsoft and Google encourage employees to adopt such values to support their commitment to innovation as a source of competitive advantage.

Other managers, however, might cultivate values and norms that indicate to employees that they should always be conservative and cautious in their dealings with others and should try to consult with their superiors before making important decisions or any changes to the status quo. Accountability for actions and decisions is stressed, and detailed records are kept to ensure that policies and procedures are followed. In settings where caution is needed–nuclear power stations, large oil refineries, chemical plants, financial institutions, insurance companies–a conservative, cautious approach to making decisions might be highly appropriate.[98] In a nuclear power plant, for example, the catastrophic consequences of a mistake make a high level of supervision vital. Similarly, in a bank or mutual fund company, the risk of losing investors' money makes a cautious approach to investing highly appropriate.

Managers of different kinds of organizations deliberately cultivate and develop the organizational values and norms that are best suited to their task and general environments, strategy, or technology. Organizational culture is maintained and transmitted to organizational members through the values of the founder, the process of socialization, ceremonies and rites, and stories and language (see Figure 2.9).

VALUES OF THE FOUNDER From the ASA model discussed above, it is clear that founders of an organization can have profound and long-lasting effects on organizational culture. Founders' values inspire the founders to start their own companies in the first place and, in turn, drive the nature of these new companies and their defining characteristics. Thus, an organization's founder and his or her terminal and instrumental values have a substantial influence on the values, norms, and standards of behavior that develop over time within the organization.[99] Founders set the scene for the way cultural values and norms develop because their own values guide the building

Figure 2.9
Factors That Maintain and Transmit Organizational Culture

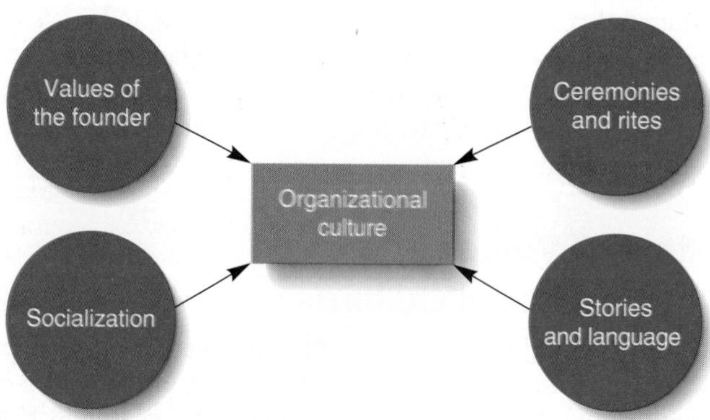

of the company and they hire other managers and employees who they believe will share these values and help the organization to attain them. Moreover, new managers quickly learn from the founder what values and norms are appropriate in the organization and thus what is desired of them. Subordinates imitate the style of the founder and, in turn, transmit their values and norms to their subordinates. Gradually, over time, the founder's values and norms permeate the organization.

A founder who requires a great display of respect from subordinates and insists on proprieties such as formal job titles and formal modes of dress encourages subordinates to act in this way toward their subordinates. Often, a founder's personal values affect an organization's competitive advantage. For example, McDonald's founder Ray Kroc insisted from the beginning on high standards of customer service and cleanliness at McDonald's restaurants. These became core sources of McDonald's competitive advantage. Similarly, Bill Gates, the founder of Microsoft, pioneered certain cultural values at Microsoft. Employees are expected to be creative and to work hard. They are encouraged to dress informally and to personalize their offices. Company events such as cookouts, picnics, and sports events emphasize to employees the importance of being both an individual and a team player.

SOCIALIZATION Socialization is a further means of transmitting organizational culture. Over time, organizational members learn from each other which values are important in an organization and the norms that specify appropriate and inappropriate behaviors. Eventually, organizational members behave in accordance with the organization's values and norms—often without realizing they are doing so. **Organizational socialization** is the process by which newcomers learn an organization's values and norms and acquire the work behaviors necessary to perform jobs effectively.[100] As a result of their socialization experiences, organizational members internalize an organization's values and norms and behave in accordance with them not only because they think they have to but because they think that these values and norms describe the right and proper way to behave.[101]

organizational socialization The process by which newcomers learn an organization's values and norms and acquire the work behaviors necessary to perform their jobs effectively.

At Texas A&M University, for example, all new students are encouraged to go to "Fish Camp" to learn how to be an "Aggie" (the traditional nickname of students at the university). They learn about the ceremonies that have developed over time to commemorate significant events or people in A&M's history. In addition, they learn how to behave at football games and in class and what it means to be an Aggie. As a result of this highly organized socialization program, by the time new students arrive on campus and start their first semester, they have been socialized into what a Texas A&M student is supposed to do, and they have relatively few problems adjusting to the college environment.

The Walt Disney Company sends new "cast members" through Disney University in order to train them in living out and maintaining the Disney culture in whatever their new roles might be, whether that's Pinocchio or Cinderella.

Most organizations have some kind of socialization program to help new employees learn the ropes—the values, norms, and culture of the organization. The military, for example, is well known for the rigorous socialization process it uses to turn raw recruits into trained soldiers. Organizations such as the Walt Disney Company also put new recruits through a rigorous training program to provide them with the knowledge they need not only to perform well in their jobs but also to ensure that each employee plays his or her part in helping visitors to Disneyland have fun in a wholesome theme park. New recruits at Disney are called "cast members" and attend Disney University to learn the Disney culture and their part in it. Disney's culture emphasizes the values of safety, courtesy, entertainment, and efficiency, and these values are brought to life for newcomers at Disney University. Newcomers also learn about the attraction area they will be joining (e.g., Adventureland or Fantasyland) at Disney University and then receive on-the-job socialization in the area itself from experienced cast members.[102] Through organizational socialization, founders and managers of an organization transmit to employees the cultural values and norms that shape the behavior of organizational members. Thus, the values and norms of founder Walt Disney live on today at Disneyland as newcomers are socialized into the Disney way.

CEREMONIES AND RITES Another way in which managers can create or influence organizational culture is by developing organizational ceremonies and rites–formal events that recognize incidents of importance to the organization as a whole and to specific employees.[103] The most common rites that organizations use to transmit cultural norms and values to their members are rites of passage, of integration, and of enhancement (see Table 2.1).[104]

Rites of passage determine how individuals enter, advance within, or leave the organization. The socialization programs developed by military organizations (such as the U.S. Army) or by large accountancy and law firms are rites of passage. Likewise, the ways in which an organization prepares people for promotion or retirement are rites of passage.

Rites of integration might be shared announcements of organizational successes, office parties, and company cookouts. They build and reinforce common bonds among organizational members. IDEO uses many rites of integration to make its employees feel connected to one another and special, such as wild "end-of-year" celebratory bashes. Groups of IDEO employees periodically take time off to go to a sporting event, movie, or meal, or sometimes on a long bike ride or for a sail. These kinds of shared activities can be a source of inspiration on the job. One 35-member design studio at IDEO led by Dennis Boyle has bimonthly lunch fests with no set agenda–anything goes. While enjoying great food, jokes, and camaraderie, studio members often end up sharing ideas for their latest great products, and the freely flowing conversation leads to creative insights.[105]

A company's annual meeting is a rite of integration, offering an opportunity to communicate organizational values to managers, other employees, and shareholders. Wal-Mart makes its annual stockholders' meeting an extravagant ceremony that

Table 2.1
Organizational Rites

Type of Rite	Example of Rite	Purpose of Rite
Rite of passage	Induction and basic training	Learn and internalize norms and values
Rite of integration	Office Christmas party	Build common norms and values
Rite of enhancement	Presentation of annual award	Motivate commitment to norms and values

celebrates the company's success and reinforces the company's high-performance culture. The company often flies thousands of its highest-performing employees to its annual meeting at its Bentonville, Arkansas, headquarters for a huge weekend festival complete with performances by country and western stars. The proceedings are shown live over closed-circuit television in all Wal-Mart stores so that all employees can join in the rites celebrating the company's achievements.[106]

Rites of enhancement, such as awards dinners, newspaper releases, and employee promotions, let organizations publicly recognize and reward employees' contributions and thus strengthen their commitment to organizational values. By bonding members within the organization, rites of enhancement reinforce an organization's values and norms.

STORIES AND LANGUAGE *Stories and language* also communicate organizational culture. Stories (whether fact or fiction) about organizational heroes and villains and their actions provide important clues about values and norms. Such stories can reveal the kinds of behaviors that are valued by the organization and the kinds of practices that are frowned on.[107] At the heart of McDonald's rich culture are hundreds of stories that organizational members tell about founder Ray Kroc. Most of these stories focus on how Kroc established the strict operating values that are at the heart of McDonald's culture. Kroc was dedicated to achieving perfection in McDonald's quality, service, cleanliness, and value for money (QSC&V), and these four central values permeate McDonald's culture. An often retold story describes what happened when Kroc and a group of managers from Houston were touring various restaurants. One of the restaurants was having a bad day operationally. Kroc was incensed about the long lines of customers, and he was furious when he realized that the product customers were receiving that day was not up to his high standards. To address the problem, he jumped up and stood on the front counter and got the attention of all customers and operating crew personnel. He introduced himself, apologized for the long wait and cold food, and told the customers that they could have freshly cooked food or their money back–whichever they wanted. The customers left happy, and when Kroc checked on the restaurant later, he found that his message had gotten through to its managers and crew–performance had improved. Other stories describe Kroc scrubbing dirty toilets and picking up litter inside or outside a restaurant. These and similar stories are spread around the organization by McDonald's employees. They are the stories that have helped establish Kroc as McDonald's "hero."

Because spoken language is a principal medium of communication in organizations, the characteristic slang or jargon–that is, organization-specific words or phrases–that people use to frame and describe events provides important clues about norms and values. "McLanguage," for example, is prevalent at all levels of McDonald's. A McDonald's employee described as having "ketchup in his (or her) blood" is someone who is truly dedicated to the McDonald's way–someone who has been completely socialized to its culture. McDonald's has an extensive training program that teaches new employees "McDonald's speak," and new employees are welcomed into the family with a formal orientation that illustrates Kroc's dedication to QSC&V.

The concept of organizational language encompasses not only spoken language but other clues such as how people dress, the offices they occupy, the cars they drive, and the degree of formality they use when they address one another. Casual dress reflects and reinforces Microsoft's entrepreneurial culture and values. Formal business attire supports the conservative culture found in many banks, which emphasize the importance of conforming to organizational norms such as respect for authority and staying within one's prescribed role. Traders in the Chicago futures and options trading pits frequently wear garish and flamboyant ties and jackets to make their presence known in a sea of faces. The demand for magenta, lime green, and silver lamé jackets featuring bold images such as the Power Rangers–anything that helps the traders stand out and attract customers–is enormous.[108] When employees speak and understand the language of their organization's culture, they know how to behave in the organization and what is expected of them.

At IDEO, language, dress, the physical work environment, and extreme informality all underscore a culture that is adventuresome, playful, risk taking, egalitarian, and innovative. For example, at IDEO, employees refer to taking the consumers' perspective when designing products as "being left-handed." Employees dress in T-shirts and jeans, the physical work environment is continually evolving and changing depending upon how employees wish to personalize their workspace, no one "owns" a fancy office with a window, and rules are nonexistent.[109]

Culture and Managerial Action

While founders and managers play a critical role in the development, maintenance, and communication of organizational culture, this same culture shapes and controls the behavior of all employees, including managers themselves. For example, culture influences the way managers perform their four main functions: planning, organizing, leading, and controlling. As we consider these functions, we continue to distinguish between top managers who create organizational values and norms that encourage creative, innovative behavior and top managers who encourage a conservative, cautious approach by their subordinates. We noted earlier that both kinds of values and norms can be appropriate depending upon the situation and type of organization.

PLANNING Top managers in an organization with an innovative culture are likely to encourage lower-level managers to participate in the planning process and develop a flexible approach to planning. They are likely to be willing to listen to new ideas and to take risks involving the development of new products. In contrast, top managers in an organization with conservative values are likely to emphasize formal top-down planning. Suggestions from lower-level managers are likely to be subjected to a formal review process, which can significantly slow decision making. Although this deliberate approach may improve the quality of decision making in a nuclear power plant, it can have unintended consequences. In the past, at conservative IBM, the planning process became so formalized that managers spent most of their time assembling complex slide shows and overheads to defend their current positions rather than thinking about what they should be doing to keep IBM abreast of the changes taking place in the computer industry. When former CEO Lou Gerstner took over, he used every means at his disposal to abolish this culture, even building a brand-new campus-style headquarters to change managers' mind-sets. IBM's culture is undergoing further changes initiated by its current CEO, Samuel Palmisano.[110]

ORGANIZING What kinds of organizing will managers in innovative and in conservative cultures encourage? Valuing creativity, managers in innovative cultures are likely to try to create an organic structure, one that is flat, with few levels in the hierarchy, and one in which authority is decentralized so that employees are encouraged to work together to find solutions to ongoing problems. A product team structure may be very suitable for an organization with an innovative culture. In contrast, managers in a conservative culture are likely to create a well-defined hierarchy of authority and establish clear reporting relationships so that employees know exactly whom to report to and how to react to any problems that arise.

LEADING In an innovative culture, managers are likely to lead by example, encouraging employees to take risks and experiment. They are supportive regardless of whether employees succeed or fail. In contrast, managers in a conservative culture are likely to use management by objectives and to constantly monitor subordinates' progress toward goals, overseeing their every move. We examine leadership in detail in Chapter 10 when we consider the leadership styles that managers can adopt to influence and shape employee behavior.

CONTROLLING The ways in which managers evaluate, and take actions to improve, performance differ depending upon whether the organizational culture emphasizes formality and caution or innovation and change. Managers who want to encourage risk taking, creativity, and innovation recognize that there are multiple potential paths to success and that failure must be accepted in order for creativity to thrive. Thus, they are less concerned about employees' performing their jobs in a specific, predetermined manner and in strict adherence to preset goals and more concerned about employees' being flexible and taking the initiative to come up with ideas for improving performance. Managers in innovative cultures are also more concerned about long-run performance than short-term targets because they recognize that real innovation entails much uncertainty that necessitates flexibility. In contrast, managers in cultures that emphasize caution and maintenance of the status quo often set specific, difficult goals for employees, frequently monitor progress toward these goals, and develop a clear set of rules that employees are expected to adhere to.

The values and norms of an organization's culture strongly affect the way managers perform their management functions. The extent to which managers buy into the values and norms of their organization shapes their view of the world and their actions and decisions in particular circumstances.[111] In turn, the actions that managers take can have an impact on the performance of the organization. Thus, organizational culture, managerial action, and organizational performance are all linked together.

This linkage is apparent at Hewlett-Packard (HP), a leader in the electronic instrumentation and computer industries. Established in the 1940s, HP developed a culture that is an outgrowth of the strong personal beliefs of the company's founders, William Hewlett and David Packard. Bill and Dave, as they are known within the company, formalized HP's culture in 1957 in a statement of corporate objectives known as the "HP Way." The basic values informing the HP Way stress serving everyone who has a stake in the company with integrity and fairness, including customers, suppliers, employees, stockholders, and society in general. Bill and Dave helped build this culture within HP by hiring like-minded people and by letting the HP Way guide their own actions as managers.

Although the Hewlett-Packard example and our earlier example of IDEO illustrate how organizational culture can give rise to managerial actions that ultimately benefit the organization, this is not always the case. The cultures of some organizations become dysfunctional, encouraging managerial actions that harm the organization and discouraging actions that might lead to an improvement in performance.[112] Recent corporate scandals at large companies like Enron, Tyco, and WorldCom show how damaging a dysfunctional culture can be to an organization and its members. For example, Enron's arrogant, "success-at-all costs" culture led to fraudulent behavior on the part of its top managers.[113] Unfortunately, hundreds of Enron employees have paid a heavy price for the unethical behavior of these top managers and the dysfunctional organizational culture. Not only have these employees lost their jobs, but many also have lost their life savings in Enron stock and pension funds, which became worth just a fraction of their former value before the wrongdoing at Enron came to light. We discuss ethics in depth in the next chapter.

Summary and Review

ENDURING CHARACTERISTICS: PERSONALITY TRAITS Personality traits are enduring tendencies to feel, think, and act in certain ways. The Big Five general traits are extraversion, negative affectivity, agreeableness, conscientiousness, and openness to experience. Other personality traits that affect managerial behavior are locus of control, self-esteem, and the needs for achievement, affiliation, and power. **[LO1]**

VALUES, ATTITUDES, AND MOODS AND EMOTIONS A terminal value is a personal conviction about lifelong goals or objectives; an instrumental value is a personal conviction about modes of conduct. Terminal and instrumental values have an impact on what managers try to achieve in their organizations and the kinds of behaviors they engage in. An attitude is a collection of feelings and beliefs. Two attitudes important for understanding managerial behaviors include job satisfaction (the collection of feelings and beliefs that managers have about their jobs) and organizational commitment (the collection of feelings and beliefs that managers have about their organizations). A mood is a feeling or state of mind; emotions are intense feelings that are short-lived and directly linked to their causes. Managers' moods and emotions, or how they feel at work on a day-to-day basis, have the potential to impact not only their own behavior and effectiveness but also those of their subordinates. Emotional intelligence is the ability to understand and manage one's own and other people's moods and emotions. **[LO2, 3, 4]**

ORGANIZATIONAL CULTURE Organizational culture is the shared set of beliefs, expectations, values, norms, and work routines that influence how members of an organization relate to one another and work together to achieve organizational goals. Founders of new organizations and managers play an important role in creating and maintaining organizational culture. Organizational socialization is the process by which newcomers learn an organization's values and norms and acquire the work behaviors necessary to perform jobs effectively. **[LO5]**

Management in Action

Topics for Discussion and Action

Discussion

1. Discuss why managers who have different types of personalities can be equally effective and successful. [LO1]
2. Can managers be too satisfied with their jobs? Can they be too committed to their organizations? Why or why not? [LO2]
3. Assume that you are a manager of a restaurant. Describe what it is like to work for you when you are in a negative mood. [LO3]
4. Why might managers be disadvantaged by low levels of emotional intelligence? [LO4]

Action

5. Interview a manager in a local organization. Ask the manager to describe situations in which he or she is especially likely to act in accordance with his or her values. Ask the manager to describe situations in which he or she is less likely to act in accordance with his or her values. [LO2]
6. Watch a popular television show, and as you watch it, try to determine the emotional intelligence levels of the characters the actors in the show portray. Rank the characters from highest to lowest in terms of emotional intelligence. As you watched the show, what factors influenced your assessments of emotional intelligence levels? [LO4]
7. Go to an upscale clothing store in your neighborhood, and go to a clothing store that is definitely not upscale. Observe the behavior of employees in each store as well as the store's environment. In what ways are the organizational cultures in each store similar? In what ways are they different? [LO5]

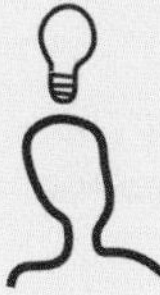

Building Management Skills

Diagnosing Culture [LO5]

Think about the culture of the last organization you worked for, your current university, or another organization or club to which you belong. Then answer the following questions:

1. What values are emphasized in this culture?
2. What norms do members of this organization follow?
3. Who seems to have played an important role in creating the culture?
4. In what ways is the organizational culture communicated to organizational members?

Managing Ethically [LO1, 2]

Some organizations rely on personality and interest inventories to screen potential employees. Other organizations attempt to screen employees by using paper-and-pencil honesty tests.

1. Either individually or in a group, think about the ethical implications of using personality and interest inventories to screen potential employees. How might this practice be

unfair to potential applicants? How might organizational members who are in charge of hiring misuse it?

2. Because of measurement error and validity problems, some relatively trustworthy people may "fail" an honesty test given by an employer. What are the ethical implications of trustworthy people "failing" honesty tests, and what obligations do you think employers should have when relying on honesty tests for screening purposes?

Small Group Breakout Exercise [LO2, 3, 4, 5]

Making Difficult Decisions in Hard Times

Form groups of three or four people, and appoint one member as the spokesperson who will communicate your findings to the whole class when called on by the instructor. Then discuss the following scenario:

You are on the top-management team of a medium-size company that manufactures cardboard boxes, containers, and other cardboard packaging materials. Your company is facing increasing levels of competition for major corporate customer accounts, and profits have declined significantly. You have tried everything you can to cut costs and remain competitive, with the exception of laying off employees. Your company has had a no-layoff policy for the past 20 years, and you believe it is an important part of the organization's culture. However, you are experiencing mounting pressure to increase your firm's performance, and your no-layoff policy has been questioned by shareholders. Even though you haven't decided whether to lay off employees and thus break with a 20-year tradition for your company, rumors are rampant in your organization that something is afoot, and employees are worried. You are meeting today to address this problem.

1. Develop a list of options and potential courses of action to address the heightened competition and decline in profitability that your company has been experiencing.
2. Choose your preferred course of action, and justify why you will take this route.
3. Describe how you will communicate your decision to employees.
4. If your preferred option involves a layoff, justify why. If it doesn't involve a layoff, explain why.

Be the Manager [LO1, 2, 3, 4, 5]

You have recently been hired as the vice president for human resources in an advertising agency. One of the problems that has been brought to your attention is the fact that in the creative departments at the agency, there are dysfunctionally high levels of conflict. You have spoken with members of each of these departments, and in each one it seems that there are a few members of the department who are creating all the problems. All of these individuals are valued contributors who have many creative ad campaigns to their credit. The very high levels of conflict are creating problems in the departments, and negative moods and emotions are much more prevalent than positive feelings. What are you going to do to both retain valued employees and alleviate the excessive conflict and negative feelings in these departments?

BusinessWeek Case in the News [LO1, 2, 5]

Weaving a New Kind of Company

Fabindia, a purveyor of handwoven garments and home furnishings, is one of India's premier retail brands. It has reached that level in part by bringing its suppliers inside the tent. The private company encourages the artisans who make its wares to become shareholders. Selling suppliers a piece of the company is unconventional, especially when most of the partners are illiterate. But if it succeeds, Fabindia could become a model for all kinds of companies, especially in the developing world.

Fabindia was founded in 1960 by John Bissell, an American working for the Ford Foundation in New Delhi, and is now run by his 42-year-old son, William. It has 97 stores in India's big cities and small towns. In 2008, it had revenues of $65 million, an increase of 30% over the previous year. And as Fabindia has grown, it has come to depend entirely on some 22,000 weavers, block printers, woodworkers, and organic farmers to provide the handmade goods it sells. "We're somewhere between the 17th century, with our artisan suppliers, and the 21st century, with our consumers," says Bissell.

Bissell and his staff have worked with the artisans to integrate them into Fabindia and, by extension, the modern economy. At first that meant helping artisans refine their traditional homespun designs to appeal to more chic urban tastes as well as improving the consistency of their wares.

Two years ago, Bissell went even further. He set up 17 centers throughout India, each organized around a particular region's artisanal tradition. These centers, in turn, were incorporated as companies in which artisans collectively own 26%. Fabindia encourages each artisan to buy shares, which cost $2 apiece—a reasonable sum for a weaver who might make a monthly profit of $100 from selling his woven cotton to Fabindia. A wholly owned Fabindia company controls 49% of each subsidiary; the rest is held by other Fabindia employees and private investors. So far, 15,000 artisans have become shareholders. The ownership structure is mutually beneficial for Fabindia and the artisans; the retailer ensures it has the supplies it needs, while the weavers, dyers, and so forth lock in steady income. "We pool our effort and funds, the artisans pool theirs, and we share the risk," says Bissell.

One believer is Mohammad Yaseen Chhipa, who dyes fabric in the dusty village of Pipar in Rajasthan and has been a Fabindia supplier for two decades. Chhipa, 52, is a prosperous man now. His yearly income has grown as Fabindia has, from $8,500 in 1989 to $170,000 today. He owns 560 shares and would like to buy more, but they're in such demand that few people are selling. The artisans can sell their shares to each other only twice a year. Although not many transactions have taken place, there have been enough to triple the share price to $6. Chhipa and other shareholders receive dividends, too, based on how much they produce.

As Bissell makes plans to open 150 more stores in the next four years, he's had to think about how to overcome the natural constraints of his business model. While offering his suppliers a chance to own a piece of the company has helped him lock in suppliers, Bissell won't find it easy to scale up. A yard of *khadi,* the traditional cloth worn by many Indians, takes two hours to weave—and right now Fabindia requires hundreds of thousands of yards a month. Bissell estimates he might need to triple his number of artisans to grow as quickly as he'd like, which would mean setting up several more regional centers. Maintaining the standards of quality would be a challenge. Even if he can solve those two problems, there's still the vexing issue of inventory control. "The whole idea of the Japanese just-in-time inventory is difficult to manage," Bissell says. "Here, it's more like just-in-a-year."

Bissell has been wrestling with possible solutions. One idea is to shift responsibility down the supply chain to the regional centers. His hope is that one day they might be able to do much more in the way of distribution, warehousing, and design. To that end, Bissell has arranged bank credit for these companies so they have access to working capital. And he is bringing some of the centers' employees to Fabindia's New Delhi headquarters for basic business training. The key, says Bissell, is to use what's intrinsic to India. "When you have an appropriate structure," he says, "all the forces flow in your direction and work with you."

Questions

1. How would you describe William Bissell's personality?
2. What terminal and instrumental values are likely to be especially important to him?
3. How would you describe Fabindia's culture?
4. What role do you think John Bissell and William Bissell played in establishing Fabindia's culture?

Source: M. Kripalani, "Weaving a New Kind of Company." Reprinted from March 23 & 30, 2009 issue of *BusinessWeek* by special permission,

BusinessWeek Case in the News [LO2, 4, 5]

A Steely Resolve

Sitting on John J. Ferriola's desk at Nucor's headquarters in Charlotte is a greeting card. Yellow, with bright green, pink, and blue flowers, it's from Diane Williamson, a line worker at Nucor's plant in Darlington, S.C. Inside it says, "Thank you for caring about me and my family." In the past few months, Ferriola, Nucor's chief operating officer, and his boss, CEO Daniel R. DiMicco, have received hundreds of similar cards and e-mails from their staff of 22,000.

It's hard to imagine too many other C-Suite types getting thank-you notes by the basketload these days. But while rivals have laid off thousands, Nucor has shown remarkable loyalty to its people, eschewing layoffs altogether. Despite a dismal fourth quarter, the company paid out a special one-time bonus in January 2009 of $1,000 or $2,000 per worker, reward for a record 2008. Total cost to Nucor: $40 million. In March the company paid an additional $270 million in 2008 profit sharing. "We're making money. We've got jobs," says Michael May, a seven-year veteran of Nucor's Crawfordsville (Ind.) plant. "Financially, Nucor employees are still better off than most."

But not as well off as they once were. After years of record-setting profits, Nucor is struggling just like the automakers, appliance manufacturers, and builders that buy its steel. In the fourth quarter of 2008, its mills went from running at 95% of capacity to 50% practically overnight, as credit-squeezed customers slashed orders. "It was something none of us had ever seen before," says DiMicco.

The pain of the downturn has quickly gone all the way to the shop floor as the drop in output has hit workers' paychecks. Unlike other steelmakers, Nucor pushes as much responsibility for production and efficiency as possible to frontline workers, and ties most of their pay to production. The company, which melts scrap metal and reshapes it into beams and sheets of steel using electric arc furnaces, can ramp up or slow down production more quickly than traditional steelmakers, which need weeks to get a cold mill hot again. So customers are quick to cancel orders, knowing they can get what they need fast enough.

Boosting Morale, Keeping Busy

For many years, Nucor's model has led to superior productivity and growth. That's one reason the company has appeared four times on *BusinessWeek*'s list of top performers. But for workers there's a downside to the model, particularly in tough times. With the line down half the time, bonuses have dwindled, and total pay is down as much as 40%. To keep up morale, management has put a big focus on communication. Ferriola has doubled the time he spends in the plants. Ron Dickerson, general manager of Nucor's Crawfordsville plant, sends weekly notes updating his 750-person staff on order volumes. But the question all managers hear the most is the one they can't answer: "When is this going to end?"

For now, Dickerson is keeping his crews busy rewriting safety manuals, looking for cost savings, and getting ahead on maintenance. Work that used to be done by contractors, such as making special parts, mowing the lawns, and even cleaning the bathrooms, is now handled by Nucor staff. The bathrooms, managers say, were an employee suggestion.

For Nucor's management team, there have been trade-offs. Growth plans are on hold. The company has put off exploring acquisitions. A just-finished galvanizing line is idle. Still, Wall Street is betting the company will take advantage of the turnaround quickly when it comes. It probably won't be this year. But with all the extra efforts in the mills now, DiMicco says he hopes Nucor will be "first out of the box."

Questions

1. What factors likely contribute to employees' job satisfaction and organizational commitment at Nucor?
2. How would you describe Nucor's organizational culture?
3. Which terminal and instrumental values do you think are important in Nucor's culture?
4. How might managers' levels of emotional intelligence influence how they treat employees at Nucor?

Managing Ethics and Diversity

CHAPTER 3

Learning Objectives

After studying this chapter, you should be able to

1. Illustrate how ethics help managers determine the right way to behave when dealing with different stakeholder groups. **[LO1]**
2. Explain why managers should strive to create ethical organizational cultures. **[LO2]**
3. Appreciate the increasing diversity of the workforce and of the organization environment. **[LO3]**
4. Grasp the central role that managers play in the effective management of diversity. **[LO4]**
5. Understand why the effective management of diversity is both an ethical and a business imperative. **[LO5]**
6. Understand the two major forms of sexual harassment and how they can be eliminated. **[LO6]**

Loyal Costco customers like these know that their bargains don't come at the expense of employees' paychecks and benefits.

MANAGEMENT SNAPSHOT

Taking Care of Employees at Costco

What Does Being Ethical Mean When It Comes to Employees?

Managers at Costco, including CEO Jim Senegal, take Costco's Code of Ethics very seriously. Costco Wholesale Corporation is one of the largest wholesale club chains in the United States.[1] One of the principles in Costco's Code of Ethics is "Take Care of Our Employees."[2] Wages at Costco average $17 per hour, over 40% higher than the average hourly wage at Wal-Mart, Costco's major competitor.[3] Costco pays the majority of health insurance costs for its employees (employees pay around 8% of health insurance costs compared to an industry average of around 25%), and part-time employees receive health insurance after they have been with the company six months. Overall, about 85% of Costco employees are covered by health insurance at any point in time, compared with less than 45% of employees at Target and Wal-Mart.[4]

Jim Senegal believes that caring about the well-being of his employees is a win–win proposition. Costco's employees are satisfied, committed, loyal, and motivated. Turnover and employee theft rates at Costco are much lower than industry averages.[5] In the retail industry, turnover tends to be very high and costly. For every employee who quits, a new hire needs to be recruited, tested, interviewed, and trained. Even though pay and benefits are higher at Costco than at rival Wal-Mart, Costco actually has lower labor costs as a percentage of sales and higher sales per square foot of store space than Wal-Mart.[6]

Treating employees well builds customer loyalty at Costco. Surely, customers enjoy the bargains and low prices that come from shopping in a warehouse store, the relatively high quality of the goods Costco stocks, and Costco's policy of not marking up prices by more than 14% or 15% (relatively low markups for retail) even if the goods would sell with higher markups. However, customers are also very loyal to Costco because they know that the company treats its employees well and their bargains are not coming at the expense of employees' paychecks and benefits.[7]

Costco's growth and financial performance have been enviable. Costco started out as a single warehouse store in Seattle, Washington, in 1983.

Now the company has 555 stores (including stores in South Korea, Taiwan, Japan, Canada, and the United Kingdom) and over 54 million members who pay an annual fee to shop at Costco stores.[8]

Like many other companies, Costco felt the effects of the economic downturn in 2008–2009.[9] In the spring of 2009, Costco decided to close its Costco Home stores in Tempe, Arizona, and Kirkland, Washington, because their lease agreements were almost up and demand for home furnishings had lessened during the tough economic times.[10] But while many other companies laid off employees and millions of jobs in the United States and other countries were lost, Costco did its best to avoid laying off employees and instead instituted a freeze on new hiring in its corporate offices.[11] Clearly, "Take Care of Our Employees" is taken very seriously at Costco.[12]

Overview

While a strong code of ethics can influence the way employees behave, what causes people to behave unethically in the first place? Moreover, how do managers and employees determine what is ethical or unethical? In this chapter, we examine the nature of the obligations and responsibilities of managers and the companies they work for toward the people and society that are affected by their actions. First, we examine the nature of ethics and the sources of ethical problems. Second, we discuss the major groups of people, called *stakeholders,* who are affected by the way companies operate. Third, we look at four rules or guidelines that managers can use to decide whether a specific business decision is ethical or unethical and why it is important for people and companies to behave in an ethical way.

We then turn to the issue of the effective management of diversity. This first requires that organizations, their managers, and all employees behave ethically and follow legal rules and regulations in the ways diverse employees are hired, promoted, and treated. Second, effectively managing diversity means learning to appreciate and respond appropriately to the needs, attitudes, beliefs, and values that diverse employees bring to an organization and finding ways to use their skills and talents to benefit them and the company they work for. Finally, we discuss steps managers can take to eradicate sexual harassment in organizations. By the end of this chapter you will understand the central role that the effective management of ethics and diversity plays in shaping the practice of business and the life of a people, society, and nation.

The Nature of Ethics

Suppose you see a person being mugged in the street. How will you behave? Will you help, even though you risk being hurt? Will you walk away? Perhaps you might adopt a "middle way" and not intervene but call the police? Does the way you act depend on whether the person being mugged is a fit male, an elderly person, or even a street person? Does it depend on whether there are other people around, so you can tell yourself, "Oh well, someone else will help or call the police. I don't need to."?

LO1 Illustrate how ethics help managers determine the right way to behave when dealing with different stakeholder groups.

Ethical Dilemmas

The situation described above is an example of an **ethical dilemma,** the quandary people find themselves in when they have to decide if they should act in a way that might help another person or group, and is the "right" thing to do, even though doing

ethical dilemma The quandary people find themselves in when they have to decide if they should act in a way that might help another person or group even though doing so might go against their own self-interest.

ethics The inner guiding moral principles, values, and beliefs that people use to analyze or interpret a situation and then decide what is the "right" or appropriate way to behave.

so might go against their own self-interest.[13] A dilemma may also arise when a person has to decide between two different courses of action, knowing that whichever course he or she chooses will result in harm to one person or group even while it may benefit another. The ethical dilemma here is to decide which course of action is the "lesser of two evils."

People often know they are confronting an ethical dilemma when their moral scruples come into play and cause them to hesitate, debate, and reflect upon the "rightness" or "goodness" of a course of action. Moral scruples are thoughts and feelings that tell a person what is right or wrong; they are a part of a person's ethics. **Ethics** are the inner guiding moral principles, values, and beliefs that people use to analyze or interpret a situation and then decide what is the "right" or appropriate way to behave. At the same time, ethics also indicate what is inappropriate behavior and how a person should behave to avoid doing harm to another person.

The essential problem in dealing with ethical issues, and thus solving moral dilemmas, is that there are no absolute or indisputable rules or principles that can be developed to decide if an action is ethical or unethical. Put simply, different people or groups may dispute which actions are ethical or unethical depending on their own personal self-interest and specific attitudes, beliefs, and values–concepts we discussed in Chapter 2. How, therefore, are we and companies and their managers and employees to decide what is ethical and so act appropriately toward other people and groups?

Ethics and the Law

The first answer to this question is that society as a whole, using the political and legal process, can lobby for and pass laws that specify what people can and cannot do. Many different kinds of laws exist to govern business–for example, laws against fraud and deception and laws governing how companies can treat their employees and customers. Laws also specify what sanctions or punishments will follow if those laws are broken. Different groups in society lobby for which laws should be passed based on their own personal interests and beliefs with regard to what is right or wrong. The group that can summon most support is able to pass the laws that most closely align with its interests and beliefs. Once a law is passed, a decision about what the appropriate behavior is with regard to a person or situation is taken from the personally determined ethical realm to the societally determined legal realm. If you do not conform to the law, you can be prosecuted; and if you are found guilty of breaking the law, you can be punished. You have little say in the matter; your fate is in the hands of the court and its lawyers.

In studying the relationship between ethics and law, it is important to understand that *neither laws nor ethics are fixed principles,* cast in stone, which do not change over time. Ethical beliefs alter and change as time passes, and as they do so, laws change to reflect the changing ethical beliefs of a society. It was seen as ethical, and it was legal, for example, to acquire and possess slaves in ancient Rome and Greece and in the United States until the late 19th century. Ethical views regarding whether slavery was morally right or appropriate changed, however. Slavery was made illegal in the United States when those in power decided that slavery degraded the very meaning of being human. Slavery is a statement about the value or worth of human beings and about their right to life, liberty, and the pursuit of happiness. And if I deny these rights to other people, how then can I claim to have any natural or "god-given" rights to these things myself?

Moreover, what is to stop any person or group that becomes powerful enough to take control of the political and legal process from enslaving me and denying me the right to be free and to own property? In denying freedom to others, we risk losing it ourselves, just as stealing from others opens the door for them to steal from us in return. "Do unto others as you would have them do unto you" is a commonly used ethical or moral rule that people apply in such situations to decide what is the right thing to do. This moral rule is discussed in detail below.

Changes in Ethics over Time

There are many types of behavior–such as murder, theft, slavery, rape, driving while intoxicated–that most, if not all, people currently believe are unacceptable and unethical and should therefore be illegal. There are also, however, many other kinds of actions and behaviors whose ethical nature is open to dispute. Some people might believe that a particular behavior–for example, smoking tobacco or possessing guns–is unethical and so should be made illegal. Others might argue that it is up to the individual or a group to decide if such behaviors are ethical or not and thus whether a particular behavior should remain legal.

As ethical beliefs change over time, some people may begin to question whether existing laws that make specific behaviors illegal are still appropriate today. They might argue that although a specific behavior is deemed illegal, this does not make it unethical and thus the law should be changed. In the United States, for example, it is illegal to possess or use marijuana (cannabis). To justify this law, it is commonly argued that smoking marijuana leads people to try more dangerous drugs. Once the habit of taking drugs has been acquired, people can get hooked on them. More powerful drugs such as the murderous heroin are fearfully addictive, and most people cannot stop using them without help from others. Thus, the use of marijuana, because it might lead to further harm, is an unethical practice.

Coldbath Fields Prison, London, circa 1810. The British criminal justice system around this time was severe: There were over 350 different crimes for which a person could be executed, including sheep stealing. But as ethical beliefs changed over time, so did the laws.

It has been documented, however, that the use of marijuana has many medical benefits for people with certain illnesses. For example, for cancer sufferers who are undergoing chemotherapy and for those with AIDS who are on potent medications, marijuana offers relief from many of the treatment's side effects, such as nausea and lack of appetite. Yet, in the United States, it is illegal in many states for doctors to prescribe marijuana for these patients, so their suffering goes on. Since 1996, however, 35 states have made it legal to prescribe marijuana for medical purposes; nevertheless, the federal government has sought to stop such state legislation. The U.S. Supreme Court ruled in 2005 that only Congress or the states could decide whether the medical use of the drug should be made legal, and people in many states are currently lobbying for a relaxation of state laws against its use for medical purposes.[14] In Canada there has been a widespread movement to decriminalize marijuana. While not making the drug legal, decriminalization removes the threat of prosecution even for uses that are not medically related. An ethical debate is currently raging over this issue in many countries.

The important point to note is that while ethical beliefs lead to the development of laws and regulations to prevent certain behaviors or encourage others, laws themselves can and do change or even disappear as ethical beliefs change. In Britain in 1830 there were over 350 different crimes for which a person could be executed, including sheep stealing. Today there are none; capital punishment and the death penalty are no longer legal in Britain. Thus, both ethical and legal rules are relative: No absolute or unvarying standards exist to determine how we should behave, and people are caught up in moral dilemmas all the time. Because of this we have to make ethical choices.

The previous discussion highlights an important issue in understanding the relationship between ethics, law, and business. Throughout the 2000s many scandals have plagued major companies such as Enron, Arthur Andersen, WorldCom, Tyco, Adelphia, and others. Managers in some of these companies clearly broke the law and used illegal means to defraud investors. At Enron, former chief financial officer Andrew Fastow, and his wife, pleaded guilty to falsifying the company's books so that they could siphon off tens of millions of dollars of Enron's money for their own use.

In other cases, some managers took advantage of loopholes in the law to divert hundreds of millions of dollars of company capital into their own personal fortunes. At WorldCom, for example, former CEO Bernie Ebbers used his position to place six personal, long-time friends on its 13-member board of directors. While this is not illegal, obviously these people would vote in his favor at board meetings. As a result of their support Ebbers received huge stock options and a personal loan of over $150 million from WorldCom. In return, his supporters were well rewarded for being directors; for example, Ebbers allowed them to use WorldCom's corporate jets for a minimal cost–something that saved them hundreds of thousands of dollars a year.[15]

In the light of these events some people said, "Well, what these people did was not illegal," implying that because such behavior was not illegal it was also not unethical. However, not being illegal does *not* make it ethical; such behavior is clearly unethical.[16] In many cases laws are passed *later* to close the loopholes and prevent unethical people, such as Fastow and Ebbers, from taking advantage of them to pursue their own self-interest at the expense of others. Like ordinary people, managers must confront the need to decide what is appropriate and inappropriate as they use a company's resources to produce goods and services for customers.[17]

Stakeholders and Ethics

Just as people have to work out the right and wrong ways to act, so do companies. When the law does not specify how companies should behave, their managers must decide what is the right or ethical way to behave toward the people and groups affected by their actions. Who are the people or groups that are affected by a company's business decisions? If a company behaves in an ethical way, how does this benefit people and society? Conversely, how are people harmed by a company's unethical actions?

stakeholders The people and groups that supply a company with its productive resources and so have a claim on and stake in the company.

The people and groups affected by the way a company and its managers behave are called its stakeholders. **Stakeholders** supply a company with its productive resources; as a result, they have a claim on and stake in the company.[18] Since stakeholders can directly benefit or be harmed by its actions, the ethics of a company and its managers are important to them. Who are a company's major stakeholders? What do they contribute to a company, and what do they claim in return? Below we examine the claims of these stakeholders–stockholders; managers; employees; suppliers and distributors; customers; and community, society, and nation-state (Figure 3.1).

Figure 3.1
Types of Company Stakeholders

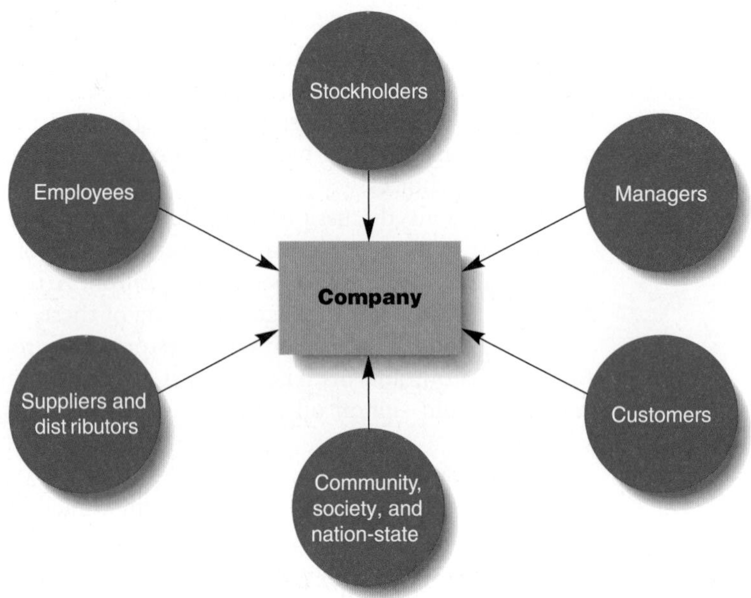

Stockholders

Stockholders have a claim on a company because when they buy its stock or shares they become its owners. Whenever the founder of a company decides to publicly incorporate the business to raise capital, shares of the stock of that company are issued. This stock grants its buyers ownership of a certain percentage of the company and the right to receive any future stock dividends. For example, in December 2004 Microsoft decided to pay the owners of its 5 billion shares a record dividend payout of $32 billion! Bill Gates received $3.3 billion in dividends based on his stockholding, and he donated this money to the Bill and Melinda Gates Foundation, to which he has reportedly donated over $30 billion to date, with the promise of much more to come; so has Warren Buffet, who committed in 2006 to donate at least $30 billion to the Gates Foundation over the next decade. The two richest people in the world have decided to give away a large part of their wealth to serve global ethical causes–in particular to address global health concerns such as malnutrition, malaria, tuberculosis, and AIDS.

Stockholders are interested in the way a company operates because they want to maximize the return on their investment. Thus, they watch the company and its managers closely to ensure that management is working diligently to increase the company's profitability.[19] Stockholders also want to ensure that managers are behaving ethically and not risking investors' capital by engaging in actions that could hurt the company's reputation. Managers of companies such as WorldCom, Brocade Communications, and Enron pursued their own self-interest at the expense of their stakeholders. As a result of their managers' unethical actions, in 2006 WorldCom's ex-CEO Bernie Ebbers was sentenced to a long jail term, as was Enron's former top manager Jeffrey Skilling. And, in 2008, the first of a long line of top managers from many companies who have been accused of backdating stock options to inflate their personal wealth at the expense of stockholders was convicted. Ex-CEO of Brocade Communications Gregory Reyes was found guilty of illegally backdating stock options that resulted in him and his top managers receiving tens of millions of dollars of extra unearned income. He was sentenced to 21 months in jail and fined $15 million.[20]

Managers

Managers are a vital stakeholder group because they are responsible for using a company's financial capital and human resources to increase its performance and thus its stock price.[21] Managers have a claim on an organization because they bring to it their skills, expertise, and experience. They have the right to expect a good return or reward by investing their human capital to improve a company's performance. Such rewards include good salaries and benefits, the prospect of promotion and a career, and stock options and bonuses tied to company performance.

Managers are the stakeholder group that bears the responsibility to decide which goals an organization should pursue to most benefit stakeholders and how to make the most efficient use of resources to achieve those goals. In making such decisions, managers are frequently in the position of having to juggle the interests of different stakeholders, including themselves.[22] These decisions are sometimes very difficult and challenge managers to uphold ethical values because in some cases decisions that benefit some stakeholder groups (managers and stockholders) harm other groups (individual workers and local communities). For example, in economic downturns or when a company experiences performance shortfalls, layoffs may help to cut costs (thus benefiting shareholders) at the expense of the employees laid off. Many U.S. managers have recently been faced with this very difficult decision. On average about 1.6 million employees out of a total labor force of 140 million are affected by mass layoffs each year in the United States;[23] a million jobs from the United States, Europe, and Japan were outsourced to Asia in 2006, and a million since.[24] Layoff decisions are always difficult, as they not only take a heavy toll on workers, their families, and local communities but also mean the loss of the contributions of valued employees to an organization. Whenever decisions such as these are made–benefiting some groups at the expense of others–ethics come into play.

As we discussed in Chapter 1, managers must be motivated and given incentives to work hard in the interests of stockholders. Their behavior must also be scrutinized to ensure they do not behave illegally or unethically, pursuing goals that threaten stockholders' and the company's interests.[25] Unfortunately, we have seen in the 2000s how easy it is for top managers to find ways to ruthlessly pursue their self-interest at the expense of stockholders and employees because laws and regulations were not strong enough to force them to behave ethically.

In a nutshell, the problem has been that in many companies corrupt managers focus not on building the company's capital and stockholders' wealth but on maximizing their own *personal capital and wealth.* In an effort to prevent future scandals the Securities and Exchange Commission (SEC), the government's top business watchdog, has begun to rework the rules governing a company's relationship with its auditor, as well as regulations concerning stock options, and to increase the power of outside directors to scrutinize a CEO. The SEC's goal is to turn many actions that were previously classified as only unethical into illegal behavior in the near future. For example, companies are now forced to reveal to stockholders the value of the stock options they give their top executives and directors, and when they give them these options, and this shows how much such payments reduce company profits. Managers and directors can now be prosecuted if they disguise or try to hide these payments. In 2007, SEC chairman Christopher Cox announced new rules that would require that companies disclose myriad details of executive compensation packages to investors; already the boards of directors of many companies have stopped giving CEOs perks such as free personal jet travel, membership in exclusive country clubs, and luxury accommodations on "business trips."

Indeed, many experts are arguing that the rewards given to top managers, particularly the CEO and COO, have grown out of control in the 2000s. Top managers are today's "aristocrats," and through their ability to influence the board of directors and raise their own pay, they have amassed personal fortunes worth hundreds of millions of dollars. For example, according to a study by the Federal Reserve, U.S. CEOs now get paid about 600 times what the average worker earns, compared to about 40 times in 1980–a staggering increase. Michael Eisner, ex-CEO of Disney, received over $1 billion in Disney stock options. Jack Welch, the former CEO of General Electric and one of the most admired managers in the United States, received more than $500 million in GE stock options as a reward for his services. And Bob Nardelli, ex-CEO of Home Depot, received over $200 million in salary, bonus, stock, stock options, and other perks during the period when Home Depot's stock plunged by 13%. When he was forced out of the company in 2007 he also received a $150 million early-termination payment that had been agreed on in advance.

Is it ethical for top managers to receive such vast amounts of money from their companies? Do they really earn it? Remember, this money could have gone to shareholders in the form of dividends. It could also have gone to reduce the huge salary gap between those at the top and those at the bottom of the hierarchy. Many people argue that the growing disparity between the rewards given to CEOs and to other employees is unethical and should be regulated. CEO pay has become too high because CEOs are the people who set and control one another's salaries and bonuses! They can do this because they sit on the boards of other companies, as outside directors, and thus can control the salaries and stock options paid to other CEOs. As the example of Bernie Ebbers at WorldCom, discussed earlier, suggests, when a CEO can control and select many of the outside directors, the CEO can abuse his or her power. Others argue that because top managers play an important role in building a company's capital and wealth, they deserve a significant share of its profits. Jack Welch, for example, deserved stock options worth $500 million because he created hundreds of billions of dollars in stockholder wealth. Some recent research has suggested that the companies whose CEOs compensation includes a large percentage of stock options tend to experience big share losses more often than big gains, and that on average, company performance improves as stock option use declines![26]

The debate over how much money CEOs and other top managers should be paid is currently raging, especially because the subprime mortgage crisis that began in 2007 showed how much money the CEOs of troubled financial companies earned even as their companies' performance and stock price collapsed. A U.S. House Oversight and Government Reform Committee chaired by Senator Henry Waxman that was convened to examine the issue of high executive pay first noted that *Forbes* magazine estimated the average CEO of the largest 500 companies earned $15.2 million in 2006, an increase of 38 percent over 2005.[27] Then Waxman went on to question the CEOs of financial giants Countrywide Mortgage and Merrill Lynch about how they could justify their high salaries while their companies were losing billions of dollars and their stock values were plunging. He noted, for example, that Countrywide suffered losses of over $1.7 billion in 2007 and that the company's stock had fallen 80%. Yet, during the same period, its CEO Angelo Mozilo received a $1.9 million salary and $20 million more in stock awards contingent upon performance, and sold $121 million in stock he had already been given before the price fell. Similarly, during 2007 Merrill Lynch reported $18 billion in write-downs related to risky subprime mortgages, but its ex-CEO Stanley O'Neal received a retirement package of $161 million when he was forced out of office in 2007. The committee noted that if the company

Top executives, including Angelo Mozilo of Countryside Mortgage and Stanley O'Neal of Merrill Lynch, testify before Senator Henry Waxman in 2008 on the issue of exorbitant CEO compensation packages that remained in full effect even though these companies lost billions of dollars.

had terminated O'Neal for poor performance as a manager, rather than letting him retire, he would not have been entitled to $131 million of the package in unvested stock and options.[28]

Employees

A company's employees are the hundreds of thousands of people who work in its various departments and functions, such as research, sales, and manufacturing. Employees expect that they will receive rewards consistent with their performance. One principal way that a company can act ethically toward employees and meet their expectations is by creating an occupational structure that fairly and equitably rewards employees for their contributions. Companies, for example, need to develop recruitment, training, performance appraisal, and reward systems that do not discriminate against employees and that employees believe are fair.

Suppliers and Distributors

No company operates alone. Every company is in a network of relationships with other companies that supply it with the inputs (e.g., raw materials, components, contract labor, and clients) that it needs to operate. It also depends on intermediaries such as wholesalers and retailers to distribute its products to the final customer. Suppliers expect to be paid fairly and promptly for their inputs; distributors expect to receive quality products at agreed-upon prices.

Once again, many ethical issues arise in the way companies contract and interact with their suppliers and distributors. Important issues concerning how and when payments are to be made or product quality specifications are governed by the terms of the legal contracts a company signs with its suppliers and distributors. Many other issues are dependent on business ethics. For example, numerous products sold in U.S. stores have been outsourced to countries that do not have U.S.-style regulations and laws to protect the workers who make these products. All companies must take an ethical position on the way they obtain and make the products they sell. Commonly this stance is published on a company's Web site.

Customers

Customers are often regarded as the most critical stakeholder group since if a company cannot attract them to buy its products, it cannot stay in business. Thus, managers and employees must work to increase efficiency and effectiveness in order to create loyal customers and attract new ones. They do so by selling customers quality products at a fair price and providing good after-sales service. They can also strive to improve their products over time and provide guarantees to customers about the integrity of their products.

Many laws exist that protect customers from companies that attempt to provide dangerous or shoddy products. Laws exist that allow customers to sue a company whose product causes them injury or harm, such as a defective tire or vehicle. Other laws force companies to clearly disclose the interest rates they charge on purchases–an important hidden cost that customers frequently do not factor into their purchase decisions. Every year thousands of companies are prosecuted for breaking these laws, so "buyer beware" is an important rule customers must follow when buying goods and services.

Community, Society, and Nation

The effects of the decisions made by companies and their managers permeate all aspects of the communities, societies, and nations in which they operate. *Community* refers to physical locations like towns or cities or to social milieus like ethnic neighborhoods in which companies are located. A community provides a company with the physical and social infrastructure that allows it to operate; its utilities and labor force; the homes in which its managers and employees live; the schools, colleges, and hospitals that service their needs; and so on.

Through the salaries, wages, and taxes it pays, a company contributes to the economy of the town or region and often determines whether the community prospers or declines. Similarly, a company affects the prosperity of a society and a nation and, to the degree that a company is involved in global trade, all the countries it operates in and thus the prosperity of the global economy. We have already discussed the many issues surrounding global outsourcing and the loss of jobs in the United States, for example.

Although the individual effects of the way each McDonald's restaurant operates might be small, for instance, the combined effects of the way all McDonald's and other fast-food companies do business are enormous. In the United States alone, over 500,000 people work in the fast-food industry, and many thousands of suppliers like farmers, paper cup manufacturers, builders, and so on depend on it for their livelihood. Small wonder then that the ethics of the fast-food business are scrutinized closely. The industry is the major lobbyer against attempts to raise the national minimum wage (which will be raised to $7.25 an hour by 2009, up from $5.15–a figure that had not changed since 1997), for example, because a higher minimum wage would substantially increase its operating costs. However, responding to protests about chickens raised in cages where they cannot move their wings, McDonald's–the largest egg buyer in the United States–issued new ethical guidelines concerning cage size and related matters that its egg suppliers must abide by if they are to retain its business. What ethical rules does McDonald's use to decide its stance toward minimum pay or minimum cage size?

Business ethics are also important because the failure of companies can have catastrophic effects on a community; a general decline in business activity affects a whole nation. The decision of a large company to pull out of a community, for example, can seriously threaten the community's future. Some companies may attempt to improve their profits by engaging in actions that, although not illegal, can hurt communities and nations. One of these actions is pollution. For example, many U.S. companies reduce costs by trucking their waste to Mexico, where it is legal to dump waste in the Rio Grande. The dumping pollutes the river from the Mexican side, and the effects are increasingly being felt on the U.S. side too.

Rules for Ethical Decision Making

When a stakeholder perspective is taken, questions on company ethics abound.[29] What is the appropriate way to manage the claims of all stakeholders? Company decisions that favor one group of stakeholders, for example, are likely to harm the interests of others.[30] High prices to customers may lead to high returns to shareholders and high salaries for managers in the short run. If in the long run customers turn to companies that offer lower-cost products, however, the result may be declining sales, laid-off employees, and the decline of the communities that support the high-price company's business activity.

When companies act ethically, their stakeholders support them. For example, banks are willing to supply them with new capital, they attract highly qualified job applicants, and new customers are drawn to their products. Thus ethical companies grow and expand over time, and all their stakeholders benefit. The result of unethical behavior is the loss of reputation and resources, shareholders who sell their shares, skilled managers and employees who leave the company, and customers who turn to the products of more reputable companies.

When making business decisions, managers must take the claims of all stakeholders into consideration.[31] To help themselves and employees make ethical decisions and behave in ways that benefit their stakeholders, managers can use four ethical rules or principles to analyze the effects of their business decisions on stakeholders: the *utilitarian, moral rights, justice,* and *practical* rules (Figure 3.2).[32] These rules are useful guidelines that help managers decide on the appropriate way to behave in situations where it is necessary to balance a company's self-interest against the interests of its stakeholders. Remember, the right choices will lead resources to be used where they can create the most value. If all companies make the right choices, all stakeholders will benefit in the long run.[33]

Figure 3.2
Four Ethical Rules

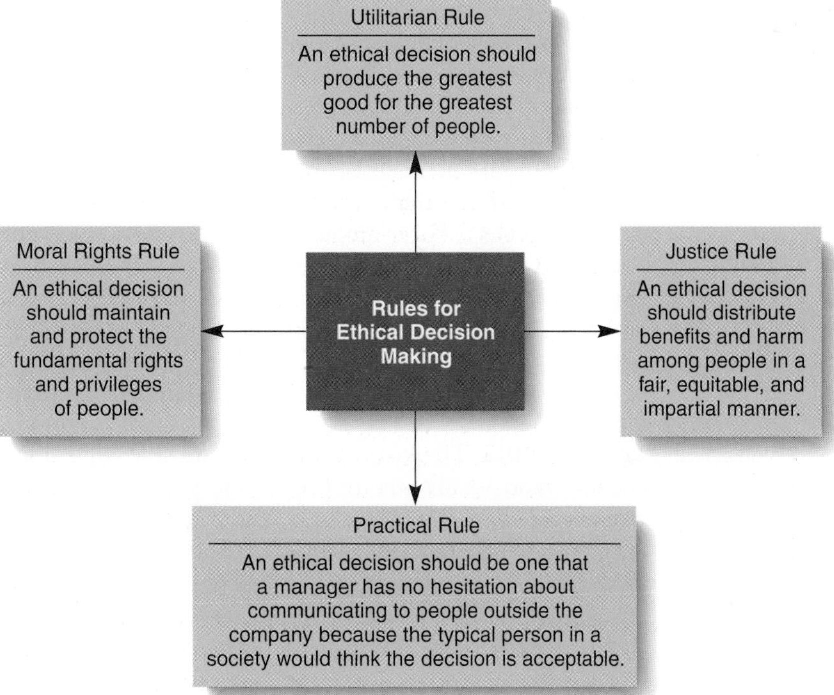

utilitarian rule An ethical decision is a decision that produces the greatest good for the greatest number of people.

UTILITARIAN RULE The **utilitarian rule** is that an ethical decision is a decision that produces the greatest good for the greatest number of people. To decide which is the most ethical course of business action, managers should first consider how different possible courses of business action would benefit or harm different stakeholders. They should then choose the course of action that provides the most benefits, or conversely the one that does the least harm, to stakeholders.[34]

The ethical dilemma for managers is, How do you measure the benefits and harms that will be done to each stakeholder group? Moreover, how do you evaluate the rights of different stakeholder groups, and the relative importance of each group, in coming to a decision? Since stockholders are the owners of the company, shouldn't their claims be held above those of employees? For example, managers might be faced with a choice of using global outsourcing to reduce costs and lower prices to customers or continuing with high-cost production at home. A decision to use global outsourcing benefits shareholders and customers but will result in major layoffs that will harm employees and the communities in which they live. Typically, in a capitalist society such as the United States, the interests of shareholders are put above those of employees, so production will move abroad. This is commonly regarded as being an ethical choice because in the long run the alternative, home production, might cause the business to collapse and go bankrupt, in which case greater harm will be done to all stakeholders.

moral rights rule An ethical decision is one that best maintains and protects the fundamental or inalienable rights and privileges of the people affected by it.

MORAL RIGHTS RULE Under the **moral rights rule,** an ethical decision is a decision that best maintains and protects the fundamental or inalienable rights and privileges of the people affected by it. For example, ethical decisions protect people's rights to freedom, life and safety, property, privacy, free speech, and freedom of conscience. The adage "Do unto others as you would have them do unto you" is a moral rights principle that managers should use to decide which rights to uphold. Customers must also consider the rights of the companies and people who create the products they wish to consume.

From a moral rights perspective, managers should compare and contrast different courses of business action on the basis of how each course will affect the rights of the company's different stakeholders. Managers should then choose the course of action that best protects and upholds the rights of *all* the stakeholders. For example, decisions that might result in significant harm to the safety or health of employees or customers would clearly be unethical choices.

The ethical dilemma for managers is that decisions that will protect the rights of some stakeholders often will hurt the rights of others. How should they choose which group to protect? For example, in deciding whether it is ethical to snoop on employees, or search them when they leave work to prevent theft, does an employee's right to privacy outweigh an organization's right to protect its property? Suppose a coworker is having personal problems and is coming in late and leaving early, placing you in the position of being forced to pick up the person's workload. Do you tell your boss even though you know this will probably get that person fired?

justice rule An ethical decision is a decision that distributes benefits and harms among people and groups in a fair, equitable, or impartial way.

JUSTICE RULE The **justice rule** is that an ethical decision is a decision that distributes benefits and harms among people and groups in a fair, equitable, or impartial way. Managers should compare and contrast alternative courses of action based on the degree to which they will result in a fair or equitable distribution of outcomes for stakeholders. For example, employees who are similar in their level of skill, performance, or responsibility should receive the same kind of pay. The allocation of outcomes should not be based on differences such as gender, race, or religion.

The ethical dilemma for managers is to determine the fair rules and procedures for distributing outcomes to stakeholders. Managers must not give people they like bigger raises than they give to people they do not like, for example, or bend the rules to help their favorites. On the other hand, if employees want managers to act fairly toward them, then employees need to act fairly toward their companies and work hard and be loyal. Similarly, customers need to act fairly toward a company if they expect it to be fair to them–something people who illegally copy digital media should consider.

PRACTICAL RULE Each of the above rules offers a different and complementary way of determining whether a decision or behavior is ethical, and all three rules should be used to sort out the ethics of a particular course of action. Ethical issues, as we just discussed, are seldom clear-cut, however, because the rights, interests, goals, and incentives of different stakeholders often conflict. For this reason many experts on ethics add a fourth rule to determine whether a business decision is ethical: The **practical rule** is that an ethical decision is one that a manager has no hesitation or reluctance about communicating to people outside the company because the typical person in a society would think it is acceptable. A business decision is probably acceptable on ethical grounds if a manager can answer yes to each of these questions:

practical rule An ethical decision is one that a manager has no reluctance about communicating to people outside the company because the typical person in a society would think it is acceptable.

1. Does my decision fall within the accepted *values* or *standards* that typically apply in business activity today?
2. Am I willing to see the decision *communicated* to all people and groups *affected* by it–for example, by having it reported in newspapers or on television?
3. Would the people with whom I have a *significant* personal relationship, such as family members, friends, or even managers in other organizations, *approve* of the decision?

Applying the practical rule to analyze a business decision helps ensure that managers are taking into account the interests of all stakeholders.[35]

Why Should Managers Behave Ethically?

Why is it so important that managers, and people in general, should act ethically and temper their pursuit of self-interest by considering the effects of their actions on others? The answer is that the relentless pursuit of self-interest can lead to a collective disaster when one or more people start to profit from being unethical because this encourages other people to act in the same way.[36] Quickly, more and more people jump onto the bandwagon, and soon everybody is trying to manipulate the situation in the way that best serves their personal ends with no regard for the effects of their action on others.

This situation is sometimes called the "tragedy of the commons." Suppose that in an agricultural community there is common land that everybody has an equal right to use. Pursuing self-interest, each farmer acts to make the maximum use of the free resource by grazing his or her own cattle and sheep. Collectively, all the farmers overgraze the land, which quickly becomes worn out. Then a strong wind blows away the exposed topsoil so that the common land is destroyed. The pursuit of individual self-interest with no consideration for societal interests leads to disaster for each individual and for the whole society because scarce resources are destroyed.[37]

We can look at the effects of unethical behavior on business activity in another way. Suppose companies and their managers operate in an unethical society, meaning one in which stakeholders routinely try to cheat and defraud one another. If stakeholders expect each other to cheat, how long will it take them to negotiate the purchase and shipment of products? When they do not trust each other, stakeholders will probably spend hours

Figure 3.3
Some Effects of Ethical and Unethical Behavior

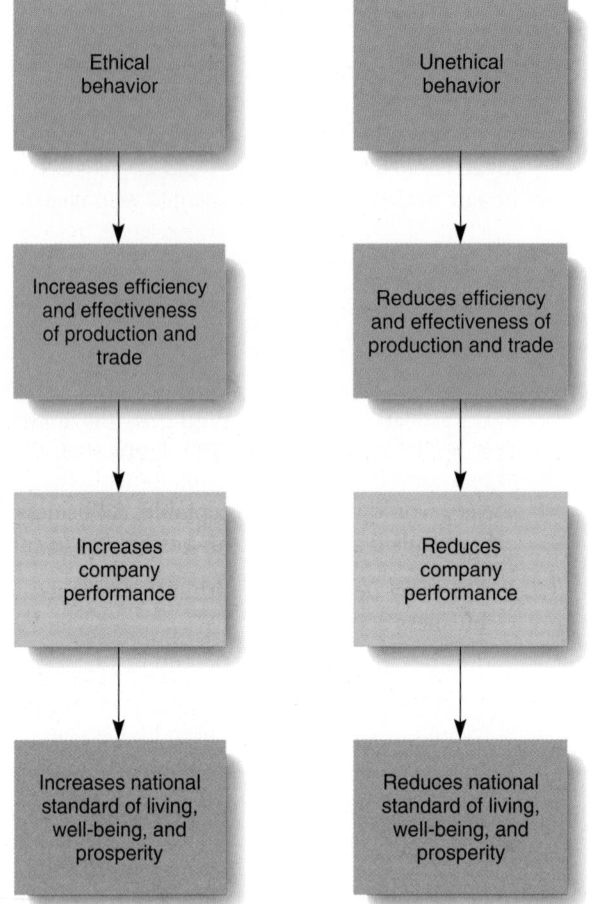

bargaining over fair prices, and this is a largely unproductive activity that reduces efficiency and effectiveness.[38] All the time and effort that could be spent improving product quality or customer service is being lost because it is spent on negotiating and bargaining. Thus, unethical behavior ruins business commerce, and society has a lower standard of living because fewer goods and services are produced, as Figure 3.3 illustrates.

On the other hand, suppose companies and their managers operate in an ethical society, meaning that stakeholders believe they are dealing with others who are basically moral and honest. In this society stakeholders have a greater reason to trust others. **Trust** is the willingness of one person or group to have faith or confidence in the goodwill of another person, even though this puts them at risk (because the other might act in a deceitful way). When trust exists, stakeholders are more likely to signal their good intentions by cooperating and providing information that makes it easier to exchange and price goods and services. When one person acts in a trustworthy way, this encourages others to act in the same way. Over time, as greater trust between stakeholders develops, they can work together more efficiently and effectively, and this raises company performance (see Figure 3.3). As people see the positive results of acting in an honest way, ethical behavior becomes a valued social norm, and society in general becomes increasingly ethical.

trust The willingness of one person or group to have faith or confidence in the goodwill of another person, even though this puts them at risk.

As noted in Chapter 1, a major responsibility of managers is to protect and nurture the resources under their control. Any organizational stakeholders–managers, workers, stockholders, suppliers–who advance their own interests by behaving unethically toward other stakeholders, either by taking resources or by denying resources to others, waste collective resources. If other individuals or groups copy the behavior of the unethical stakeholder ("If he can do it, we can do it, too"), the rate at which collective resources are misused increases, and eventually there are few resources available to produce goods and services. Unethical behavior that goes unpunished creates incentives for people to put their unbridled self-interests above the rights of others.[39] When this happens, the benefits that people reap from joining together in organizations disappear very quickly.

reputation The esteem or high repute that individuals or organizations gain when they behave ethically.

An important safeguard against unethical behavior is the potential for loss of reputation.[40] **Reputation,** the esteem or high repute that people or organizations gain when they behave ethically, is an important asset. Stakeholders have valuable reputations that they must protect because their ability to earn a living and obtain resources in the long run depends on the way they behave on a day-to-day, week-to-week, and month-to-month basis.

If a manager misuses resources and other parties regard that behavior as being at odds with acceptable standards, the manager's reputation will suffer. Behaving unethically in the short run can have serious long-term consequences. A manager who has a poor reputation will have difficulty finding employment with other companies. Stockholders who see managers behaving unethically may refuse to invest in their companies, and this will decrease the stock price, undermine the companies' reputations, and ultimately put the managers' jobs at risk.[41]

All stakeholders have reputations to lose. Suppliers who provide shoddy inputs find that organizations learn over time not to deal with them, and eventually they go out of business. Powerful customers who demand ridiculously low prices find that their suppliers become less willing to deal with them, and resources ultimately become harder for them to obtain. Workers who shirk responsibilities on the job find it hard to get new jobs when they are fired. In general, if a manager or company is known for being unethical, other stakeholders are likely to view that individual or organization with suspicion and hostility, and the reputation of each will be poor. But if a manager or company is known for ethical business practices, each will develop a good reputation.[42]

In summary, in a complex, diverse society, stakeholders, and people in general, need to recognize they are all part of a larger social group. The way in which they make decisions and act not only affects them personally but also affects the lives of many other people. The problem is that for some people their daily struggle to survive and succeed or their total disregard for the rights of others can lead them to lose that "bigger" connection to other people. We can see our relationships to our families and friends, to our school, church, and so on. But we always need to go further and keep in mind the effects of our actions on other people–people who will be judging our actions and whom we might harm by acting unethically. Our moral scruples are like that "other person" but are inside our heads.

Sources of an Organization's Code of Ethics

Codes of ethics are formal standards and rules, based on beliefs about right or wrong, that managers can use to help themselves make appropriate decisions with regard to the interests of their stakeholders.[43] Ethical standards embody views about abstractions such as justice, freedom, equity, and equality. An organization's code of ethics derives from three principal sources in the organizational environment: *societal* ethics, *professional* ethics, and the *individual* ethics of the organization's managers and employees (see Figure 3.4).

societal ethics Standards that govern how members of a society are to deal with each other on issues such as fairness, justice, poverty, and the rights of the individual.

SOCIETAL ETHICS **Societal ethics** are standards that govern how members of a society deal with each other in matters involving issues such as fairness, justice, poverty, and the rights of the individual. Societal ethics emanate from a society's laws, customs,

Figure 3.4
Sources of an Organization's Code of Ethics

and practices, and from the unwritten attitudes, values, and norms that influence how people interact with each other. People in a particular country may automatically behave ethically because they have internalized values and norms that specify how they should behave in certain situations. Not all values and norms are internalized, however. The typical ways of doing business in a society and laws governing the use of bribery and corruption are the result of decisions made and enforced by people with the power to determine what is appropriate.

Societal ethics vary among societies. For example, ethical standards accepted in the United States are not accepted in all other countries. In many economically poor countries bribery is standard practice to get things done, such as getting a telephone installed or a contract awarded. In the United States and many other Western countries, bribery is considered unethical and often illegal.

Societal ethics control self-interested behavior by individuals and organizations–behavior threatening to society's collective interests. Laws spelling out what is good or appropriate business practice provide benefits to everybody. Free and fair competition among organizations is possible only when laws and rules level the playing field and define what behavior is acceptable or unacceptable in certain situations. For example, it is ethical for a manager to compete with managers in other companies by producing a higher-quality or lower-priced product, but it is not ethical (or legal) to do so by spreading false claims about competitors' products, bribing stores to exclude competitors' products, or blowing up competitors' factories.

professional ethics Standards that govern how members of a profession are to make decisions when the way they should behave is not clear-cut.

PROFESSIONAL ETHICS Professional ethics are standards that govern how members of a profession, managers or workers, make decisions when the way in which they should behave is not clear-cut.[44] Medical ethics govern the way doctors and nurses are to treat patients. Doctors are expected to perform only necessary medical procedures and to act in the patient's interest and not in their own. The ethics of scientific research require scientists to conduct their experiments and present their findings in ways that ensure the validity of their conclusions. Like society at large, most professional groups can impose punishments for violations of ethical standards. Doctors and lawyers can be prevented from practicing their professions if they disregard professional ethics and put their own interests first.

Within an organization, professional rules and norms often govern how employees such as lawyers, researchers, and accountants make decisions and act in certain situations, and these rules and norms may become part of the organization's code of ethics. When they do, workers internalize the rules and norms of their profession (just as they do those of society) and often follow them automatically when deciding how to behave.[45] Because most people follow established rules of behavior, people often take ethics for granted. However, when professional ethics are violated, such as when scientists fabricate data to disguise the harmful effects of products, ethical issues rise to the forefront of attention.

individual ethics Personal values and attitudes that govern how individuals interact with other people.

INDIVIDUAL ETHICS Individual ethics are personal values (both terminal and instrumental) and attitudes that govern how individuals interact with other people.[46] Sources of individual ethics include the influence of one's family, peers, and upbringing in general, and an individual's personality and experience. The experiences gained over a lifetime–through membership in significant social institutions such as schools and religions, for example–also contribute to the development of the personal standards and values that a person applies to decide what is right or wrong and whether to perform certain actions or make certain decisions. Many decisions or behaviors that one person finds unethical, such as using animals for cosmetics testing, may be acceptable to another person because of differences in their personalities, values, and attitudes (see Chapter 2).

Ethical Organizational Cultures

LO2 Explain why managers should strive to create ethical organizational cultures.

Managers can emphasize the importance of ethical behavior and social responsibility by ensuring that ethical values and norms are a central component of organizational culture. An organization's code of ethics guides decision making when ethical questions arise, but managers can go one step farther by ensuring that important ethical values and norms are key features of an organization's culture. For example, Herb Kelleher and Southwest Airlines' culture value employee well-being; this emphasis translates into norms dictating that layoffs should be avoided.[47] Ethical values and norms such as these that are part of an organization's culture help organizational members resist self-interested action and recognize that they are part of something bigger than themselves.[48]

Managers' role in developing ethical values and standards in other employees is very important. Employees naturally look to those in authority to provide leadership, and managers become ethical role models whose behavior is scrutinized by their subordinates. If top managers are not ethical, their subordinates are not likely to behave in an ethical manner. Employees may think that if it's all right for a top manager to engage in dubious behavior, it's all right for them, too. The actions of top managers such as CEOs and the president of the United States are scrutinized so closely for ethical improprieties because these actions represent the values of their organizations and, in the case of the president, the values of the nation.

ethics ombudsman An ethics officer who monitors an organization's practices and procedures to be sure they are ethical.

Managers can also provide a visible means of support to develop an ethical culture. Increasingly, organizations are creating the role of ethics officer, or ethics ombudsman, to monitor their ethical practices and procedures. The ethics ombudsman is responsible for communicating ethical standards to all employees, for designing systems to monitor employees' conformity to those standards, and for teaching managers and nonmanagerial employees at all levels of the organization how to respond to ethical dilemmas appropriately.[49] Because the ethics ombudsman has organizationwide authority,

Figure 3.5
Johnson & Johnson's Credo

Our Credo

We believe our first responsibility is to the doctors, nurses and patients,
to mothers and fathers and all others who use our products and services.
In meeting their needs everything we do must be of high quality.
We must constantly strive to reduce our costs
in order to maintain reasonable prices.
Customers' orders must be serviced promptly and accurately.
Our suppliers and distributors must have an opportunity
to make a fair profit.

We are responsible to our employees,
the men and women who work with us throughout the world.
Everyone must be considered as an individual.
We must respect their dignity and recognize their merit.
They must have a sense of security in their jobs.
Compensation must be fair and adequate,
and working conditions clean, orderly and safe.
We must be mindful of ways to help our employees fulfill
their family responsibilities.
Employees must feel free to make suggestions and complaints.
There must be equal opportunity for employment, development
and advancement for those qualified.
We must provide competent management,
and their actions must be just and ethical.

We are responsible to the communities in which we live and work
and to the world community as well.
We must be good citizens—support good works and charities
and bear our fair share of taxes.
We must encourage civic improvements and better health and education.
We must maintain in good order
the property we are privileged to use,
protecting the environment and natural resources.

Our final responsibility is to our stockholders.
Business must make a sound profit.
We must experiment with new ideas.
Research must be carried on, innovative programs developed
and mistakes paid for.
New equipment must be purchased, new facilities provided
and new products launched.
Reserves must be created to provide for adverse times.
When we operate according to these principles,
the stockholders should realize a fair return.

Johnson & Johnson

Source: Johnson & Johnson Annual Report. Copyright © Johnson & Johnson. Reprinted with permission of Johnson & Johnson.

organizational members in any department can communicate instances of unethical behavior by their managers or coworkers without fear of retribution. This arrangement makes it easier for everyone to behave ethically. In addition, ethics ombudsmen can provide guidance when organizational members are uncertain about whether an action is ethical. Some organizations have an organizationwide ethics committee to provide guidance on ethical issues and help write and update the company code of ethics.

Ethical organizational cultures also encourage organizational members to behave in a socially responsible manner. In fact, managers at Johnson & Johnson take social responsibility so seriously that their organization is frequently mentioned as an example of a socially responsible firm. Johnson & Johnson's credo (see Figure 3.5) is one of the many ways in which social responsibility is emphasized at Johnson & Johnson. As discussed in the following "Ethics in Action," Johnson & Johnson's ethical organizational culture provides the company and its various stakeholder groups with numerous benefits.

ETHICS IN ACTION

Johnson & Johnson's Ethical Culture

Johnson & Johnson is so well known for its ethical culture that it has been judged as having the best corporate reputation for two years in a row, based on a survey of over 26,000 consumers conducted by Harris Interactive and the Reputation Institute at New York University.[50] Johnson & Johnson grew from a family business led by General Robert Wood Johnson in the 1930s to a major maker of pharmaceutical and medical products. Attesting to the role of managers in creating ethical organizational cultures, Johnson emphasized the importance of ethics and responsibility to stakeholders and wrote the first Johnson & Johnson Credo in 1943.[51]

The credo continues to guide employees at Johnson & Johnson today and outlines the company's commitments to its different stakeholder groups. It emphasizes that the organization's first responsibility is to doctors, nurses, patients, and consumers. Following this group are suppliers and distributors, employees, communities, and, lastly, stockholders.[52] This credo has served managers and employees at Johnson & Johnson well and guided some difficult decision making, such as the decision to recall all Tylenol capsules in the U.S. market after cyanide-laced capsules were responsible for seven deaths in Chicago.

True to its ethical culture and outstanding reputation, Johnson & Johnson always considers consumer well-being before profit. For example, around 20 years ago, Johnson & Johnson's baby oil was used as a tanning product at a time when the harmful effects of sun exposure were not well known by the public.[53] The product manager for baby oil at the time, Carl Spalding, was making a presentation to top management about marketing plans when the company's president, David Clare, mentioned that tanning might not be healthy.[54] Before launching his planned marketing campaign, Spalding looked into the health-related concerns connected with tanning and discovered some evidence suggesting that health problems could arise from too much exposure to the sun. Even though the evidence was not definitive, Spalding recommended that baby oil no longer be marketed as a tanning aid, a decision that resulted in a 50% decrease in sales of baby oil, to the tune of $5 million.[55]

The ethical values and norms in Johnson & Johnson's culture, along with its credo, guide managers such as Spalding to make the right decision in difficult situations.

Hence, it is understandable why Johnson & Johnson is renowned for its corporate reputation. An ethical culture and outstanding reputation have other benefits in addition to helping employees make the right decisions in questionable situations. Jeanne Hamway, vice president for recruiting, finds that Johnson & Johnson's reputation helps the company recruit and attract a diverse workforce.[56] Moreover, when organizations develop an outstanding reputation, their employees often are less tempted to act in a self-interested or unethical manner. For example, managers at Johnson & Johnson suggest that since employees in the company never accept bribes, the company is known as one in which bribes should not be offered in the first place.[57] All in all, ethical cultures such as Johnson & Johnson's benefit various stakeholder groups in multiple ways.

The Increasing Diversity of the Workforce and the Environment

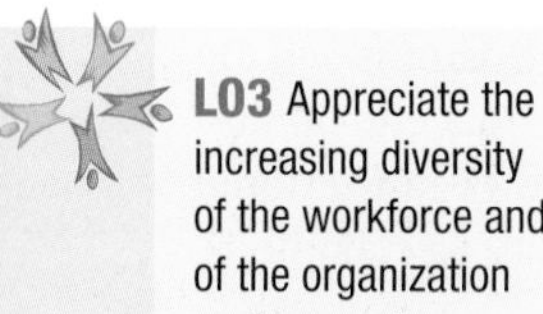

LO3 Appreciate the increasing diversity of the workforce and of the organization environment.

One of the most important management issues to emerge over the last 30 years has been the increasing diversity of the workforce. **Diversity** is dissimilarities among people due to age, gender, race, ethnicity, religion, sexual orientation, socioeconomic background, education, experience, physical appearance, capabilities/disabilities, and other characteristics (see Figure 3.6).

diversity Differences among people in age, gender, race, ethnicity, religion, sexual orientation, socioeconomic background, and capabilities/disabilities.

Diversity raises important ethical and social responsibility issues. It is a critical issue for organizations, one that if not handled well can bring an organization to its knees, especially in our increasingly global environment. There are several reasons why diversity is such a pressing concern:

- There is a strong ethical imperative that diverse people receive equal opportunities and be treated fairly and justly. Unfair treatment is also illegal.

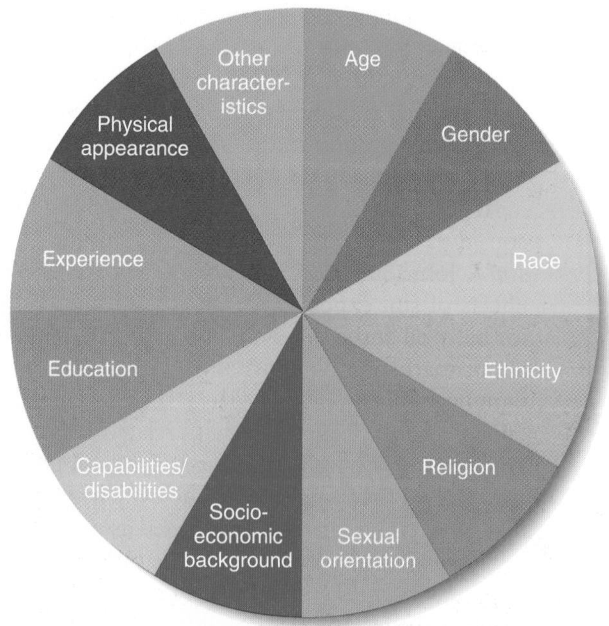

Figure 3.6
Sources of Diversity in the Workplace

- Effectively managing diversity can improve organizational effectiveness.[58] Diversity is an important organizational resource that can help an organization gain a competitive advantage.
- There is substantial evidence that diverse individuals continue to experience unfair treatment in the workplace as a result of biases, stereotypes, and overt discrimination.[59] In one study, résumés of equally qualified men and women were sent to high-priced Philadelphia restaurants (where potential earnings are high). Though equally qualified, men were more than twice as likely as women to be called for a job interview and more than five times as likely to receive a job offer.[60] Findings from another study suggest that both women and men tend to believe that women will accept lower pay than men. This is a possible explanation for the continuing gap in pay between men and women.[61]

Diverse employees may face great barriers. For example, the federal Glass Ceiling Commission Report indicated that African-Americans have the hardest time being promoted and climbing the corporate ladder, that Asians are often stereotyped into technical jobs, and that Hispanics are assumed to be less well educated than other minority groups.[62] (The term **glass ceiling** alludes to the invisible barriers that prevent minorities and women from being promoted to top corporate positions.)[63]

glass ceiling A metaphor for the invisible barriers that prevent minorities and women from being promoted to top corporate positions.

Before we can discuss the multitude of issues surrounding the effective management of diversity, we must document just how diverse the U.S. workforce is becoming.

Age

According to data from the U.S. Census Bureau, the median age of a person in the United States is the highest it has ever been, 36.2 years.[64] Moreover, by 2030, it is projected that 20% of the population will be over 65.[65] Title VII of the Civil Rights Act of 1964 and the Age Discrimination in Employment Act of 1967 are the major federal laws prohibiting age discrimination.[66] We discuss federal employment legislation in more depth in Chapter 12. Major equal employment opportunity legislation that prohibits discrimination among diverse groups is summarized in Table 3.1.

The aging of the population suggests managers need to be vigilant that employees are not discriminated against because of age. Moreover, managers need to ensure that the policies and procedures they have in place treat all workers fairly, regardless of their ages. Effectively managing diversity means that employees of diverse ages are able to learn from each other, work well together, and take advantage of the different perspectives each has to offer.

As the workforce ages, more companies are facing age discrimination lawsuits. Managers need to ensure that all policies and procedures treat workers fairly, regardless of their ages.

Gender

Women and men are almost equally represented in the U.S. workforce (approximately 53.5% of the U.S. workforce is male and 46.5% female),[67] yet women's median weekly earnings are estimated to be $572 compared to $714 for men.[68] Thus, the gender pay gap appears to be as alive and well

Table 3.1

Major Equal Employment Opportunity Laws Affecting Human Resources Management

Year	Law	Description
1963	Equal Pay Act	Requires that men and women be paid equally if they are performing equal work.
1964	Title VII of the Civil Rights Act	Prohibits discrimination in employment decisions on the basis of race, religion, sex, color, or national origin; covers a wide range of employment decisions, including hiring, firing, pay, promotion, and working conditions.
1967	Age Discrimination in Employment Act	Prohibits discrimination against workers over the age of 40 and restricts mandatory retirement.
1978	Pregnancy Discrimination Act	Prohibits discrimination against women in employment decisions on the basis of pregnancy, childbirth, and related medical decisions.
1990	Americans with Disabilities Act	Prohibits discrimination against disabled individuals in employment decisions and requires that employers make accommodations for disabled workers to enable them to perform their jobs.
1991	Civil Rights Act	Prohibits discrimination (as does Title VII) and allows for the awarding of punitive and compensatory damages, in addition to back pay, in cases of intentional discrimination.
1993	Family and Medical Leave Act	Requires that employers provide 12 weeks of unpaid leave for medical and family reasons, including paternity and illness of a family member.

as the glass ceiling. According to the nonprofit organization Catalyst, which studies women in business, while women comprise about 50.5% of the employees in managerial and professional positions, only around 15.4% of corporate officers in the 500 largest U.S. companies (i.e., the *Fortune* 500) are women. Only 6.7% of the top earners are women.[69] These women, such as Andrea Jung, CEO of Avon Products, and Indra Nooyi, CEO of Pepsico, stand out among their male peers and often receive a disparate amount of attention in the media. (We address this issue later, when we discuss the effects of being "salient.") Women are also very underrepresented on boards of directors. They currently hold 14.8% of the board seats of *Fortune* 500 companies.[70] However, as Sheila Wellington, president of Catalyst, indicates, "Women either control or influence nearly all consumer purchases, so it's important to have their perspective represented on boards."[71]

Research conducted by consulting firms suggests that female executives outperform their male colleagues on skills such as motivating others, promoting good communication, turning out high-quality work, and being a good listener.[72] For example, the Hagberg Group performed in-depth evaluations of 425 top executives in a variety of industries, with each executive rated by approximately 25 people. Of the 52 skills assessed, women received higher ratings than men on 42 skills, although at times the differences were small.[73] Results of a recent study conducted by Catalyst found that organizations with higher proportions of women in top-management positions had significantly better financial performance than organizations with lower proportions of female top managers.[74] Another study conducted by Catalyst found that companies with three or more women on their boards of directors performed better in terms of returns on equity, sales, and invested capital than companies with fewer women on their boards or no women.[75] All in all, studies such as these make one wonder why the glass ceiling continues to hamper the progress of women in business.

Race and Ethnicity

The U.S. Census Bureau typically distinguishes between the following races: American Indian or Alaska Native (native Americans of origins in North, Central, or South America), Asian (origins in the Far East, Southeast Asia, or India), African-American (origins in Africa), Native Hawaiian or Pacific Islander (origins in the Pacific Islands such as Hawaii, Guam, and Samoa), and white (origins in Europe, the Middle East, or North Africa). While *ethnicity* refers to a grouping of people based on some shared characteristic such as national origin, language, or culture, the U.S. Census Bureau treats ethnicity in terms of whether a person is Hispanic or not Hispanic. Hispanics, also referred to as Latinos, are people whose origins are in Spanish cultures such as those of Cuba, Mexico, Puerto Rico, and South and Central America. Hispanics can be of different races.[76] According to a recent poll, most Hispanics prefer to be identified by their country of origin (e.g., Mexican, Cuban, or Salvadoran) rather than by the overarching term *Hispanic*.[77]

The racial and ethnic diversity of the U.S. population is increasing at an exponential rate, as is the composition of the workforce.[78] According to the U.S. Census Bureau, approximately one of every three U.S. residents belongs to a minority group (i.e., is not a non-Hispanic white); approximately 67% of the population is white, 13.4% is African-American, 14.4% is Hispanic, and 4.8% is Asian.[79] According to projections released by the U.S. Census Bureau, the composition of the U.S. population in 2050 will be quite different from its composition in 2000. It is estimated that the Hispanic and Asian populations will triple during this 50-year period.[80]

The increasing racial and ethnic diversity of the workforce and the population as a whole underscores the importance of effectively managing diversity. Statistics compiled by the National Urban League suggest that much needs to be done in terms of ensuring that diverse employees are provided with equal opportunities. For example, African-Americans' earnings are approximately 73% of the earnings of whites,[81] and of 10,092 corporate officers in *Fortune* 500 companies, only 106 are African-American women.[82] In the remainder of this chapter, we focus on the fair treatment of diverse employees and explore why this is such an important challenge and what managers can do to meet it. We begin by taking a broader perspective and considering how increasing racial and ethnic diversity in an organization's environment (e.g., customers and suppliers) affects decision making and organizational effectiveness.

At a general level, managers and organizations are increasingly being reminded that stakeholders in the environment are diverse and expect organizational decisions and actions to reflect this diversity. For example, the NAACP (National Association for the Advancement of Colored People) and Children Now (an advocacy group) have lobbied the entertainment industry to increase the diversity in television programming, writing, and producing.[83] The need for such increased diversity is more than apparent.

For example, while Hispanics make up 12.5% of the U.S. population (or 35 million potential TV viewers), only about 2% of the characters in prime-time TV shows are Hispanics (i.e., of the 2,251 characters in prime-time shows, only 47 are Hispanic), according to a study conducted by Children Now.[84] Moreover, only about 1.3% of the evening network TV news stories are reported by Hispanic correspondents, according to the Center for Media and Public Affairs.[85]

Pressure is mounting on networks to increase diversity. Home and automobile buyers are increasingly diverse, reflecting the increasing diversity of the population as a whole.[86] Managers have to be especially sensitive to avoid stereotyping different groups when they communicate with potential customers. For example, Toyota Motor Sales USA made a public apology to the Reverend Jesse Jackson and his Rainbow Coalition for using a print advertisement depicting an African-American man with a Toyota RAV4 sport utility image embossed on his gold front tooth.[87]

Religion

Title VII of the Civil Rights Act prohibits discrimination based on religion (as well as based on race/ethnicity, country of origin, and sex; see Table 3.1.) In addition to enacting Title VII, in 1997 the federal government issued "The White House Guidelines on Religious Exercise and Expression in the Federal Workplace."[88] These guidelines, while technically applicable only in federal offices, also are frequently relied on by large corporations. The guidelines require that employers make reasonable accommodations for religious practices, such as observances of holidays, as long as doing so does not entail major costs or hardships.[89]

A key issue for managers when it comes to religious diversity is recognizing different religions and their beliefs, with particular attention being paid to when religious holidays fall. Critical meetings should not be scheduled during a holy day for members of a certain faith. Managers should be flexible in allowing people to have time off for religious observances. According to Lobna Ismail, director of a diversity training company in Silver Spring, Maryland, when managers acknowledge, respect, and make even small accommodations for religious diversity, employee loyalty is often enhanced. Allowing employees to leave work early on certain days instead of taking a lunch break or posting holidays for different religions on the company calendar can go a long way toward making individuals of diverse religions feel respected and valued as well as enable them to practice their faith.[90] According to research conducted by the Tanenbaum Center for Interreligious Understanding in New York, while only about 23% of employees who feel they are victims of religious discrimination actually file complaints, about 45% of these employees start looking for other jobs.[91]

Capabilities/Disabilities

The Americans with Disabilities Act (ADA) of 1990 prohibits discrimination against persons with disabilities and also requires that employers make reasonable accommodations to enable these people to effectively perform their jobs. In force for more than a decade, the ADA is not uncontroversial. On the surface, few would argue with the intent of this legislation. However, as managers attempt to implement policies and procedures to comply with the ADA, they face a number of interpretation and fairness challenges.

On the one hand, some people with real disabilities warranting workplace accommodations are hesitant to reveal their disabilities to their employers and claim the accommodations they deserve.[92] On the other hand, some employees abuse the ADA by seeking unnecessary accommodations for disabilities that may or may not exist.[93] Thus, it is perhaps not surprising that the passage of the ADA does not appear to have increased employment rates significantly for those with disabilities.[94] A key challenge for managers is to promote an environment in which employees needing accommodations feel comfortable disclosing their need and, at the same time, to ensure that the accommodations not only enable those with disabilities to effectively perform their jobs but also are perceived to be fair by those not disabled.[95]

In addressing this challenge, often managers must educate both themselves and their employees about the disabilities, as well as the very real capabilities, of those who are disabled. For example, during Disability Awareness Week, administrators at the University of Notre Dame sought to increase the public's knowledge of disabilities while also heightening awareness of the abilities of persons who are disabled.[96] The University of Houston conducted a similar program called "Think Ability."[97] According to Cheryl Amoruso, director of the University of Houston's Center for Students with Disabilities, many people are unaware of the prevalence of disabilities and misinformed about their consequences. She suggests, for example, that although students may not be able to see, they can still excel in their coursework and have very successful careers.[98] Accommodations enabling such students to perform up to their capabilities are covered under the ADA.

The ADA also protects employees with acquired immune deficiency syndrome (AIDS) from being discriminated against in the workplace. AIDS is caused by the human immunodeficiency virus (HIV) and is transmitted through sexual contact, infected needles, and contaminated blood products. HIV is not spread through casual, nonsexual contact. Yet, out of ignorance, fear, or prejudice, some people wish to avoid all contact with anyone infected with HIV. Infected individuals may not necessarily develop AIDS. Some individuals with HIV are able to remain effective performers of their jobs, while not putting others at risk.[99]

AIDS awareness training can help people overcome their fears and also provide managers with a tool to prevent illegal discrimination against HIV-infected employees. Such training focuses on educating employees about HIV and AIDS, dispelling myths, communicating relevant organizational policies, and emphasizing the rights of HIV-positive employees to privacy and an environment that allows them to be productive.[100] The need for AIDS awareness training is underscored by some of the problems HIV-positive employees experience once others in their workplace become aware of their condition.[101] Organizations are required to make reasonable accommodations to enable people with AIDS to effectively perform their jobs.

Managers have an obligation to educate employees about HIV and AIDS, dispel myths and the stigma of AIDS, and ensure that HIV-related discrimination is not occurring in the workplace. Home Depot has provided HIV training and education to its store managers. Such training was sorely needed given that over half of the managers indicated it was the first time they had had the opportunity to talk about AIDS.[102] Advances in medication and treatment mean that more infected individuals are able to continue working or are able to return to work after their condition improves.[103] Thus, managers need to ensure that these employees are fairly treated by all members of their organizations. Managers and organizations that do not treat HIV-positive employees in a fair manner, as well as provide reasonable accommodations (e.g., allowing time off for doctor visits or to take medicine), risk costly lawsuits.

Socioeconomic Background

The term *socioeconomic background* typically refers to a combination of social class and income-related factors. From a management perspective, socioeconomic diversity (and, in particular, diversity in income levels) requires that managers be sensitive and responsive to the needs and concerns of individuals who might not be as well off as others. U.S. welfare reform in the middle to late 1990s emphasized the need for single mothers and others receiving public assistance to join or return to the workforce. In conjunction with a strong economy, this led to record declines in the number of families, households, and children living below the poverty level, according to the 2000 U.S. census.[104] However, the economic downturns in the early and late 2000s have reversed past gains, which had lifted families out of poverty. In a very strong economy, it is much easier for poor people with few skills to find jobs. In a weak economy, such as the present, when companies lay off employees, people who need their incomes the most are unfortunately often the first to lose their jobs.[105]

Even with all the gains from the 1990s, the U.S. Census Bureau estimates that 6,825,399 families had incomes below the poverty level in 2000, with 3,581,475 of these families being headed by single women.[106] The Census Bureau relies on predetermined threshold income figures, based on family size and composition, adjusted annually for inflation, to determine the poverty level. Families whose income falls below the threshold level are considered poor.[107] For example, in 2000 a family of four with two children under 18 was considered poor if their annual income fell below $17,463.[108] When workers earn less than $10 or $15 per hour, it is often difficult, if not impossible, for them to meet their families' needs.[109] Moreover, increasing numbers of families are facing the challenge of finding suitable child care arrangements that enable the adults to work long hours and/or through the night to maintain an adequate income level. New information technology has led to more and more businesses operating 24 hours a day, creating real challenges for workers on the night shift, especially those with children.[110]

Hundreds of thousands of parents across the country are scrambling to find someone to care for their children while they are working the night shift, commuting several hours a day, working weekends and holidays, or putting in long hours on one or more jobs. This has led to the opening of day care facilities that operate around the clock. Some managers seek ways to provide care for children of their employees. For example, the Children's Choice Learning Center in Las Vegas, Nevada, operates around the clock to accommodate employees working nights in neighboring casinos, hospitals, and call centers. Randy Donahue, a security guard who works until midnight, picks his children up from the center when he gets off work; his wife is a nurse on the night shift. There currently are five Children's Choice Learning Centers in the United States operating 24 hours a day, and plans are under way to add seven more.[111]

Judy Harden, who focuses on families and child care issues for the United Workers Union, indicates that the demands families are facing necessitate around-the-clock and odd-hour child care options. Many parents simply do not have the choice of working at hours that allow them to take care of their children at night and/or on weekends, never mind when the children are sick.[112] In 1993, Ford Motor Company built an around-the-clock child care facility for 175 children of employees in Livonia, Michigan. Many employees in other locations require such a facility. Some parents and psychologists feel uneasy having children separated from their families for so much time and particularly at night. Unfortunately for many families, this is not a choice but a necessity.[113]

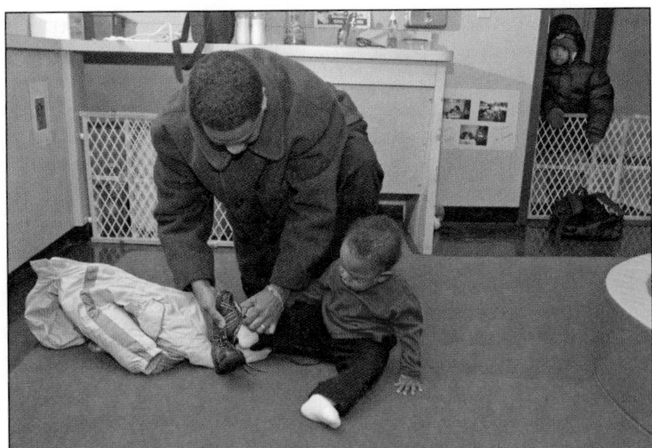

A father drops his children off at a day care facility before going to work. Managers need to be aware that many employees deal with challenging socioeconomic factors such as long commutes and finding suitable child care arrangements.

Socioeconomic diversity means managers need to be sensitive to workers less fortunate in terms of income and financial resources, child care and elder care options, housing opportunities, and existence of sources of social and family support. Managers should try to provide such individuals with opportunities to learn, advance, and make meaningful contributions to their organizations while improving their economic well-being.

Sexual Orientation

Approximately 2% to 10% of the U.S. population is gay or lesbian.[114] While no federal law prohibits discrimination based on sexual orientation, 20 states have such laws, and a 1998 executive order prohibits sexual orientation discrimination in civilian federal offices.[115] An increasing number of organizations recognize the minority status of gay and lesbian employees, affirm their rights to fair and equal treatment, and provide benefits to same-sex partners of gay and lesbian employees.[116] For example, 95% of *Fortune* 500 companies prohibit discrimination based on sexual orientation, and 70% of the *Fortune* 500 provide domestic-partner benefits.[117] As indicated in the "Focus on Diversity," there are many steps that managers can take to ensure that sexual orientation is not used to unfairly discriminate against employees.

FOCUS ON DIVERSITY

Preventing Discrimination Based on Sexual Orientation

While gays and lesbians have made great strides in terms of attaining fair treatment in the workplace, much more needs to be done. In a recent study conducted by Harris Interactive Inc. (a research firm) and Witeck Communications Inc. (a marketing firm), over 40% of gay and lesbian employees indicated that they had been unfairly treated, denied a promotion, or pushed to quit their jobs because of their sexual orientation.[118] Given continued harassment and discrimination despite the progress that has been made,[119] many gay and lesbian employees fear disclosing their sexual orientation in the workplace and thus live a life of secrecy. There are a few openly gay top managers, such as David Geffen, cofounder of DreamWorks SKG, and Allan Gilmour, former vice chairman and CFO of Ford and currently a member of the board of directors of Whirlpool and DTE Energy Company. But many others choose not to disclose or discuss their personal lives, including their long-term partners.[120]

Thus, it is not surprising that many managers are taking active steps to educate and train their employees in regard to issues of sexual orientation. S. C. Johnson & Sons, Inc., maker of Raid insecticide and Glade air fresheners in Racine, Wisconsin, provides mandatory training to its plant managers to overturn stereotypes, and Eastman Kodak, Lehman Brothers Holdings Inc., Merck & Co., Ernst & Young, and Toronto-Dominion Bank all provide training to managers on ways to prevent sexual orientation discrimination.[121] Other organizations such as Lucent Technologies, Microsoft, and Southern California Edison send employees to seminars conducted at prominent business schools. And many companies such as Raytheon, IBM, Eastman Kodak, and Lockheed Martin provide assistance to their gay and lesbian employees through gay and lesbian support groups.[122]

Chubb Corporation takes diversity awareness seriously, as is evidenced by this LGBT sensitivity training session.

The Chubb Group of Insurance Companies, a property and casualty insurance company, provides its managers with a two-hour training session to help create work environments that are safe and welcoming for lesbian, gay, bisexual, and transgender (LGBT) people.[123] The sessions are conducted by two Chubb employees. Usually one of the trainers is straight and the other is gay. The sessions focus on issues that affect a manager's ability to lead diverse teams, such as assessing how safe and welcoming the workplace is for LGBT people, how to refer to gay employees' significant others, and how to respond if employees or customers use inappropriate language or behavior. The idea for the program originated from one of Chubb's employee resource groups. Managers rate the program highly and say that they are better able to respond to the concerns of their LGBT employees while creating a safe and productive work environment for all.[124]

Other Kinds of Diversity

There are other kinds of diversity that are critical for managers to deal with effectively. For example, teams need members with diverse backgrounds and experiences. Cross-functional teams are more and more prevalent in organizations. Members might come from various departments such as marketing, production, finance, and sales (teams are covered in depth in Chapter 11). A team responsible for developing and introducing a new product, for example, often will need the expertise of employees not only from R&D and engineering but also from marketing, sales, production, and finance. Diversity is a plus on such teams.

Other types of diversity abound: For example, employees differ from each other in how attractive they are based on the standards of the culture(s) in which an organization operates and in terms of body weight. Whether individuals are attractive or unattractive, thin or overweight, in most cases has no bearing on their job performance. Yet sometimes physical diversity ends up influencing advancement rates and salaries. A recent study published in the *American Journal of Public Health* found that highly educated obese women earned approximately 30% less per year than women who were not obese and men (regardless of whether or not the men were obese).[125] Clearly, managers need to ensure that all employees are treated fairly, regardless of their physical appearance.

Managers and the Effective Management of Diversity

Managers face many challenges effectively managing diversity. Each kind of diversity presents managers with particular issues they need to appreciate. Understanding these issues is not simple. Research on how different groups are treated and the unconscious biases that might adversely affect them is critical. Studying this research helps managers become aware of the many subtle ways diverse employees come to be treated unfairly. There are many more steps managers can take to become sensitive to diversity, take advantage of all the contributions diverse employees can make, and prevent diverse employees from being unfairly treated.

LO4 Grasp the central role that managers play in the effective management of diversity.

Critical Managerial Roles

In each of their managerial roles (see Table 3.2), managers can either promote the effective management of diversity or derail such efforts. In their interpersonal roles, managers can convey that the effective management of diversity is a valued goal and objective (managers' figurehead role), can serve as role models and institute policies

Table 3.2
Managerial Roles and the Effective Management of Diversity

Type of Role	Specific Role	Example
Interpersonal	Figurehead	Convey that the effective management of diversity is a valued goal and objective.
	Leader	Serve as a role model and institute policies and procedures to ensure that diverse members are treated fairly.
	Liaison	Enable diverse individuals to coordinate their efforts and cooperate with one another.
Informational	Monitor	Evaluate the extent to which diverse employees are being treated fairly.
	Disseminator	Inform employees about diversity policies and initiatives and the intolerance of discrimination.
	Spokesperson	Support diversity initiatives in the wider community and speak to diverse groups to interest them in career opportunities.
Decisional	Entrepreneur	Commit resources to develop new ways to effectively manage diversity and eliminate biases and discrimination.
	Disturbance handler	Take quick action to correct inequalities and curtail discriminatory behavior.
	Resource allocator	Allocate resources to support and encourage the effective management of diversity.
	Negotiator	Work with organizations (e.g., suppliers) and groups (e.g., labor unions) to support and encourage the effective management of diversity.

and procedures to ensure that diverse organizational members are treated fairly (leader role), and can enable diverse individuals and groups to coordinate their efforts and cooperate with each other both inside the organization and at the organization's boundaries (liaison role). In Table 3.2 we summarize some of the ways in which managers can ensure that diversity is effectively managed.

Given the formal authority that managers have in organizations, they typically have more influence than rank-and-file employees. When managers commit to supporting diversity, their authority and positions of power and status influence other members of an organization to make a similar commitment.[126] Research on social influence supports such a link, as people are more likely to be influenced and persuaded by others who have high status.[127]

When managers commit to diversity, their commitment legitimizes the diversity management efforts of others.[128] Resources are devoted to such efforts. All members of an organization believe that their diversity-related efforts are supported and valued. Consistent with this reasoning, top-management commitment and rewards for the support of diversity are often cited as critical ingredients for the success of diversity management initiatives.[129] Seeing managers express confidence in the abilities and talents of diverse employees causes other organizational members to be similarly confident and helps to reduce any misconceived misgivings they may have as a result of ignorance or stereotypes.[130]

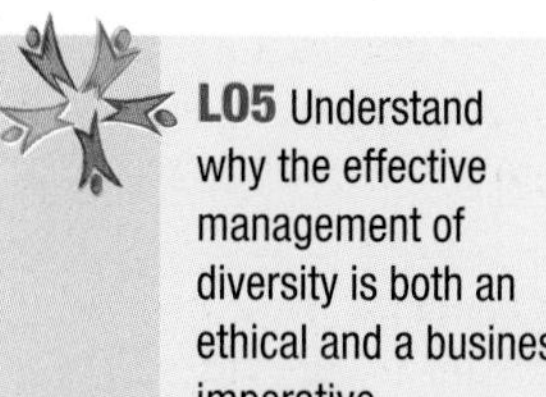

LO5 Understand why the effective management of diversity is both an ethical and a business imperative.

Two other important factors emphasize why managers are so central to the effective management of diversity. The first factor is that women, African-Americans, Hispanics, and other minorities often start out at a slight disadvantage due to the ways in which they are perceived by others in organizations, particularly in work settings where they are a numerical minority. As Virginia Valian, a psychologist at Hunter College who studies gender, indicates, "In most organizations women begin at a slight disadvantage. A woman does not walk into the room with the same status as an equivalent man, because she is less likely than a man to be viewed as a serious professional."[131]

The second factor is that research suggests that slight differences in treatment can cumulate and result in major disparities over time. Even small differences–such as a very slight favorable bias toward men for promotions–can lead to major differences in the number of male and female managers over time.[132] Thus, while women and other minorities are sometimes advised not to make "a mountain out of a molehill" when they perceive they have been unfairly treated, research conducted by Valian and others suggests that molehills (i.e., slight differences in treatment based on irrelevant distinctions such as race, gender, or ethnicity) can turn into mountains over time (i.e., major disparities in important outcomes such as promotions) if they are ignored.[133] Managers have the obligation, from both an ethical and business perspective, to ensure that neither large nor small disparities in treatment and outcomes due to irrelevant distinctions such as race or ethnicity occur in organizations.

Effectively Managing Diversity Makes Good Business Sense

The diversity of organizational members can be a source of competitive advantage, helping an organization provide customers with better goods and services.[134] The variety of points of view and approaches to problems and opportunities that diverse employees provide can improve managerial decision making. Suppose the Budget Gourmet frozen-food company is trying to come up with some creative ideas for new frozen meals that will appeal to health-conscious, time-conscious customers tired of the same old frozen-food fare. Which group do you think is likely to come up with the most creative ideas: a group of white women with master's degrees in marketing from Yale University who grew up in upper-middle-class families in the Northeast or a racially mixed group of men and women who grew up in families with varying income levels in different parts of the country and attended a mix of business schools (New York University, Oklahoma State, University of Michigan, UCLA, Cornell University, Texas A&M University, and Iowa State)? Most people would agree that the diverse group is likely to come up with a wider range of creative ideas. Although this example is simplistic, it underscores one way in which diversity can lead to a competitive advantage.

Just as the workforce is becoming increasingly diverse, so too are the customers who buy an organization's goods or services. In an attempt to suit local customers' needs and tastes, organizations like Target often vary the selection of products available in stores in different cities and regions to appeal to local customers.[135]

Diverse members of an organization are likely to be attuned to what goods and services diverse segments of the market want and do not want. Major car companies, for example, are increasingly assigning women to their design teams to ensure that the needs and desires of female customers (a growing segment of the market) are taken into account in new car design.

For Darden Restaurants, the business case for diversity rests on market share and growth. Darden seeks to satisfy the needs and tastes of diverse customers by providing menus in Spanish in communities with large Hispanic populations.[136] Similarly, market share and growth and the identification of niche markets led Tracey Campbell to cater to travelers with disabilities.[137] She heads InnSeekers, a telephone and online listing resource for bed and breakfasts. Nikki Daruwala works for the Calvert Group in Bethesda, Maryland, a mutual fund that emphasizes social responsibility and diversity. She indicates that profit alone is more than enough of an incentive to effectively manage diversity. As she puts it, "You can look at an automaker. There are more women making decisions about car buying or home buying . . . $3.72 trillion per year are spent by women."[138]

Another way in which the effective management of diversity can positively affect profitability is that it increases retention of valued employees. This decreases the costs of hiring replacements for those who quit. It helps ensure that all employees are highly motivated. Given the current legal environment, more and more organizations are attuned to the need to emphasize the importance of diversity in hiring. Once hired, if diverse employees think they are being unfairly treated, they will be likely to seek opportunities elsewhere. Thus, the recruiting of diverse employees has to be followed up by the ongoing effective management of diversity.

If diversity is not effectively managed and results in turnover rates being higher for members of certain groups who are not treated fairly, profitability will suffer on several counts. Not only are the future contributions of diverse employees lost when they quit, but the organization also has to bear the costs of hiring replacement workers. According to the Employment Management Association, on average it costs more than $10,000 to hire a new employee. Other estimates are significantly higher. For example, Ernst & Young estimates it costs about $1,200,000 to replace

10 professionals, and the diversity consulting firm Hubbard & Hubbard estimates replacement costs average one-and-a-half times an employee's annual salary.[139] Moreover, additional costs from failing to effectively manage diversity stem from time lost due to the barriers diverse members of an organization perceive as thwarting their progress and advancement.[140]

Effectively managing diversity makes good business sense for another reason. More and more, managers and organizations concerned about diversity are insisting that their suppliers also support diversity.[141]

Finally, from both a business and an ethical perspective, the effective management of diversity is necessary to avoid costly lawsuits such as those settled by Advantica (owner of the Denny's chain) and the Coca-Cola Company. In 2000, Coca-Cola settled a class-action suit brought by African-American employees, at a cost of $192 million. The damage such lawsuits cause goes beyond the monetary awards to the injured parties. It can tarnish a company's image. One positive outcome of Coca-Cola's 2000 settlement is the company's recognition of the need to commit additional resources to diversity management initiatives. Coca-Cola is increasing its use of minority suppliers, instituting a formal mentoring program, and instituting days to celebrate diversity with its workforce.[142]

Sexual Harassment

Sexual harassment seriously damages both the people who are harassed and the reputation of the organization in which it occurs. It can cost organizations large amounts of money. In 1995 Chevron Corporation agreed to pay $2.2 million to settle a sexual harassment lawsuit filed by four women who worked at the Chevron Information Technology Company in San Ramon, California. One woman involved in the suit said that she had received violent pornographic material through the company mail. Another, an electrical engineer, said that she had been asked to bring pornographic videos to Chevron workers at an Alaska drill site.[143] More recently, in 2001 TWA settled a lawsuit to the tune of $2.6 million that alleged that female employees were sexually harassed at JFK International Airport in New York. According to the EEOC, not only was sexual harassment tolerated at TWA, but also company officials did little to curtail it when it was brought to their attention.[144]

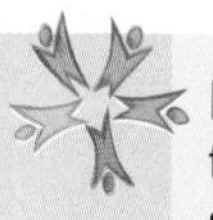

LO6 Understand the two major forms of sexual harassment and how they can be eliminated.

Unfortunately, the events at Chevron and TWA are not isolated incidents.[145] Of the 607 women surveyed by the National Association for Female Executives, 60% indicated that they had experienced some form of sexual harassment.[146] Sexual harassment victims can be women or men, and their harassers do not necessarily have to be of the opposite sex.[147] However, women are the most frequent victims of sexual harassment, particularly those in male-dominated occupations or those who occupy positions stereotypically associated with certain gender relationships, such as a female secretary reporting to a male boss. Though it occurs less frequently, men can also be victims of sexual harassment. Several male employees at Jenny Craig filed a lawsuit claiming that they were subject to lewd and inappropriate comments from female coworkers and managers.[148] Sexual harassment is not only unethical; it is also illegal. Managers have an ethical obligation to ensure that they, their coworkers, and their subordinates never engage in sexual harassment, even unintentionally.

Forms of Sexual Harassment

quid pro quo sexual harassment Asking for or forcing an employee to perform sexual favors in exchange for receiving some reward or avoiding negative consequences.

There are two basic forms of sexual harassment: quid pro quo sexual harassment and hostile work environment sexual harassment. **Quid pro quo sexual harassment** occurs when a harasser asks or forces an employee to perform sexual favors to keep a job, receive a promotion, receive a raise, obtain some other work-related opportunity, or avoid receiving negative consequences such as demotion or dismissal.[149] This "Sleep with me, honey, or you're fired" form of harassment is the more extreme type and leaves no doubt in anyone's mind that sexual harassment has taken place.[150]

hostile work environment sexual harassment Telling lewd jokes, displaying pornography, making sexually oriented remarks about someone's personal appearance, and other sex-related actions that make the work environment unpleasant.

Hostile work environment sexual harassment is more subtle. It occurs when organizational members are faced with an intimidating, hostile, or offensive work environment because of their sex.[151] Lewd jokes, sexually oriented comments or innuendos, vulgar language, displays of pornography, displays or distribution of sexually oriented objects, and sexually oriented remarks about one's physical appearance are examples of hostile work environment sexual harassment.[152] A hostile work environment interferes with organizational members' ability to perform their jobs effectively and has been deemed illegal by the courts. Managers who engage in hostile work environment harassment or allow others to do so risk costly lawsuits for their organizations. For example, in February 2004, a federal jury awarded Marion Schwab $3.24 million after deliberating on her sexual harassment case against Federal Express.[153] Schwab was the only female tractor-trailer driver at the FedEx facility serving the Harrisburg International Airport vicinity in Middletown, Pennsylvania, from 1997 to 2000. During that period, she was the target of sexual innuendos, was given inferior work assignments, and was the brunt of derogatory comments about her appearance and the role of women in society. On five occasions, the brakes on her truck were tampered with. The federal EEOC sued FedEx, and Schwab was part of the suit. FedEx planned to appeal the decision.[154]

The courts have recently recognized other forms of hostile work environment harassment, in addition to sexual harassment. For example, in June 2006, a California jury awarded $61 million in punitive and compensatory damages to two FedEx Ground drivers. The drivers, who are of Lebanese descent, indicated that they faced a hostile work environment and high levels of stress because a manager harassed them with racial slurs for two years.[155] FedEx plans to appeal the decision.[156]

Steps Managers Can Take to Eradicate Sexual Harassment

Managers have an ethical obligation to eradicate sexual harassment in their organizations. There are many ways to accomplish this objective. Here are four initial steps that managers can take to deal with the problem:[157]

- *Develop and clearly communicate a sexual harassment policy endorsed by top management.* This policy should include prohibitions against both quid pro quo and hostile work environment sexual harassment. It should contain (1) examples of types of behavior that are unacceptable, (2) a procedure for employees to use to report instances of harassment, (3) a discussion of the disciplinary actions that will be taken when harassment has taken place, and (4) a commitment to educate and train organizational members about sexual harassment.
- *Use a fair complaint procedure to investigate charges of sexual harassment.* Such a procedure should (1) be managed by a neutral third party, (2) ensure that complaints

are dealt with promptly and thoroughly, (3) protect and fairly treat victims, and (4) ensure that alleged harassers are fairly treated.

- *When it has been determined that sexual harassment has taken place, take corrective actions as soon as possible.* These actions can vary depending on the severity of the harassment. When harassment is extensive, prolonged over a period of time, of a quid pro quo nature, or severely objectionable in some other manner, corrective action may include firing the harasser.
- *Provide sexual harassment education and training to all organizational members, including managers.* The majority of *Fortune* 500 firms currently provide this education and training for their employees. Managers at Du Pont, for example, developed Du Pont's "A Matter of Respect" program to help educate employees about sexual harassment and eliminate its occurrence. The program includes a four-hour workshop in which participants are given information that defines sexual harassment, sets forth the company's policy against it, and explains how to report complaints and access a 24-hour hotline. Participants watch video clips showing actual instances of harassment. One clip shows a saleswoman having dinner with a male client who, after much negotiating, seems about to give her company his business when he suddenly suggests that they continue their conversation in his hotel room. The saleswoman is confused about what to do. Will she be reprimanded if she says no and the deal is lost? After watching a video, participants discuss what they have seen, why the behavior is inappropriate, and what organizations can do to alleviate the problem.[158] Throughout the program, managers stress to employees that they do not have to tolerate sexual harassment or get involved in situations in which harassment is likely to occur.

Barry S. Roberts and Richard A. Mann, experts on business law and authors of several books on the topic, suggest a number of additional factors that managers and all members of an organization need to keep in mind about sexual harassment:[159]

- Every sexual harassment charge should be taken very seriously.
- Employees who go along with unwanted sexual attention in the workplace can be sexual harassment victims.
- Employees sometimes wait before they file complaints of sexual harassment.
- An organization's sexual harassment policy should be communicated to each new employee and reviewed with current employees on a periodic basis.
- Suppliers and customers need to be familiar with an organization's sexual harassment policy.
- Managers should provide employees with alternative ways to report incidents of sexual harassment.
- Employees who report sexual harassment must have their rights protected; this includes being protected from any potential retaliation.
- Allegations of sexual harassment should be kept confidential; those accused of harassment should have their rights protected.
- Investigations of harassment charges and any resultant disciplinary actions need to proceed in a very timely manner.
- Managers must protect employees from sexual harassment from any third-party employees they may interact with in the course of performing their jobs, such as suppliers or customers.[160]

Summary and Review

ETHICS AND STAKEHOLDERS Ethics are moral principles or beliefs about what is right or wrong. These beliefs guide people in their dealings with other individuals and groups (stakeholders) and provide a basis for deciding whether behavior is right and proper. Many organizations have a formal code of ethics derived primarily from societal ethics, professional ethics, and the individual ethics of the organization's top managers. Managers can apply ethical standards to help themselves decide on the proper way to behave toward organizational stakeholders. Ethical organizational cultures are those in which ethical values and norms are emphasized. Ethical organizational cultures can help organizations and their members behave in a socially responsible manner. **[LO1, 2]**

INCREASING DIVERSITY OF WORKFORCE AND ENVIRONMENT Diversity is differences among people due to age, gender, race, ethnicity, religion, sexual orientation, socioeconomic background, and capabilities/disabilities. The workforce and the organizational environment have become increasingly diverse. Effectively managing diversity is an ethical imperative and can improve organizational effectiveness. **[LO3, 5]**

MANAGING DIVERSITY The effective management of diversity is not only an essential responsibility of managers but an ethical and a business imperative. In each of their managerial roles, managers can encourage organizationwide acceptance and valuing of diversity. **[LO4, 5]**

SEXUAL HARASSMENT Two forms of sexual harassment are quid pro quo sexual harassment and hostile work environment sexual harassment. Steps that managers can take to eradicate sexual harassment include development, communication, and enforcement of a sexual harassment policy, use of fair complaint procedures, prompt corrective action when harassment occurs, and sexual harassment training and education. **[LO6]**

Management in Action

Topics for Discussion and Action

Discussion

1. When are ethics and ethical standards especially important in organizations? [LO1]
2. Why might managers do things that conflict with their own ethical values? [LO1]
3. How can managers ensure that they create ethical organizational cultures? [LO2]
4. Why are gay and lesbian workers and workers who test positive for HIV sometimes discriminated against? [LO3]
5. Why might some employees resent workplace accommodations that are dictated by the Americans with Disabilities Act? [LO3]

Action

6. Choose a *Fortune* 500 company not mentioned in the chapter. Conduct research to determine what steps this organization has taken to effectively manage diversity and eliminate sexual harassment. [LO4, 5, 6]

Building Management Skills [LO3, 4, 5, 6]

Solving Diversity-Related Problems

Think about the last time that you (1) were treated unfairly because you differed from a decision maker on a particular dimension of diversity or (2) observed someone else being treated unfairly because that person differed from a decision maker on a particular dimension of diversity. Then answer these questions:

1. Why do you think the decision maker acted unfairly in this situation?
2. In what ways, if any, were biases, stereotypes, or overt discrimination involved in this situation?
3. Was the decision maker aware that he or she was acting unfairly?
4. What could you or the person who was treated unfairly have done to improve matters and rectify the injustice on the spot?
5. Was any sexual harassment involved in this situation? If so, what kind was it?
6. If you had authority over the decision maker (e.g., if you were his or her manager or supervisor), what steps would you take to ensure that the decision maker no longer treated diverse individuals unfairly?

Managing Ethically [LO1]

Some companies require that their employees work very long hours and travel extensively. Employees with young children, employees taking care of elderly relatives, and employees who have interests outside the workplace sometimes find that their careers are jeopardized if they try to work more reasonable hours or limit their work-related travel. Some of these employees feel that it is unethical for their manager to expect so much of them in the workplace and not understand their needs as parents and caregivers.

Questions

1. Either individually or in a group, think about the ethical implications of requiring long hours and extensive amounts of travel for some jobs.
2. What obligations do you think managers and companies have to enable employees to have a balanced life and meet nonwork needs and demands?

Small Group Breakout Exercise [LO3, 4, 5]

Determining If a Problem Exists

Form groups of three or four people, and appoint one member as the spokesperson who will communicate your findings to the whole class when called on by the instructor. Then discuss the following scenario:

You and your partners own and manage a local chain of restaurants, with moderate to expensive prices, that are open for lunch and dinner during the week and for dinner on weekends. Your staff is diverse, and you believe that you are effectively managing diversity. Yet on visits to the different restaurants you have noticed that your African-American employees tend to congregate together and communicate mainly with each other. The same is true for your Hispanic employees and your white employees. You are meeting with your partners today to discuss this observation.

1. Discuss why the patterns of communication that you observed might be occurring in your restaurants.
2. Discuss whether your observation reflects an underlying problem. If so, why? If not, why not?
3. Discuss whether you should address this issue with your staff and in your restaurants. If so, how and why? If not, why not?

Be the Manager [LO3, 4, 5, 6]

You are Maria Herrera and have been recently promoted to the position of director of financial analysis for a medium-size consumer goods firm. During your first few weeks on the job, you took the time to have lunch with each of your subordinates to try to get to know them better. You have 12 direct reports who are junior and senior financial analysts who support different product lines. Susan Epstein, one of the female financial analysts you had lunch with, made the following statement: "I'm so glad we finally have a woman in charge. Now, hopefully things will get better around here." You pressed Epstein to elaborate, but she clammed up. She indicated that she didn't want to unnecessarily bias you and that the problems were pretty self-evident. In fact, Epstein was surprised that you didn't know what she was talking about and jokingly mentioned that perhaps you should spend some time undercover, observing her group and their interactions with others.

You spoke with your supervisor and the former director who had been promoted and had volunteered to be on call if you had any questions. Neither man knew of any diversity-related issues in your group. In fact, your supervisor's response was, "We've got a lot of problems, but fortunately that's not one of them." What are you going to do to address this issue?

BusinessWeek Case in the News [LO1, 2]

As Factories Fail, So Does Business Law

Business had been good, even great. But by early 2008, the lighting manufacturer realized his factory in China was heading for failure. The collapse of the U.S. housing market had devastated demand for his lamps and fixtures sold at American retailers. Costs kept rising in Dongguan, the southern city where he had expanded his operations. So the 43-year-old boss quietly slipped out of China, leaving behind $100,000 to cover the final month's rent and salary for his 400-plus workers. Suppliers were left unpaid.

Lucky he left early. As word spread about the factory's closure, furious employees streamed onto the nearby street, a narrow passage lined with Internet bars and outdoor pool tables. Suppliers drove up in blue moving trucks, blocked the gate, and sent in hired thugs to grab computers, cables, machinery—anything of value. Unable to find the boss, the gang roughed up the company's lawyer and held him hostage for much of the day. "It was a new factory and looked like a gold mine. They were going to take everything out," says the boss, a European who has been in hiding in Taiwan for almost a year.

Order was restored only after the landlord called in five truckloads of police to protect his property. And suppliers who arrived too late were out of luck. Xiao Xiaosan, a maker of metal parts for lamps, says he is owed $76,000. Although he rushed to the factory on the day of the closing, he doubts he'll ever see his money. "It's impossible for me to find the owner outside of China," he says.

As the global recession slams China, bankrupt business owners are shutting factories overnight. Often, they leave the mainland, afraid of angry suppliers and workers and uncertain about legal protections. Dongguan alone last year recorded 673 cases—up 24%—of owners fleeing their factories, leaving behind 113,000 unemployed workers owed $44.1 million. Labor disputes almost doubled, to nearly 80,000.

The problems are spurring everyone to be more cautious. In the past, many deals were made on the basis of trust. But suppliers these days are demanding bigger payments up front. "It's gumming up the normal free flow of goods," says Ben Schwall, an American who heads Aliya Lighting, a Dongguan company that supplies lamps sold at Home Depot, Lowe's, and elsewhere. "A lot of friendly credit is disappearing."

Worried about factories going belly-up, buyers for multinationals are closely monitoring the financial health of their suppliers. "It's a big concern," says William Fung, managing director of Li & Fung, a Hong Kong company that handles purchasing in Asia for retailers worldwide. "The most often-asked question by our buyers is whether the factory . . . will still be around tomorrow." Purchasers who once might have had little contact with suppliers to their suppliers—companies that sell, say, buttons or zippers to a shirtmaker—are now quick to react if they hear those smaller players aren't getting paid, a clear sign of trouble at the factory. "You can only deal with people you have known a long time," says Peter Lau, chairman of Giordano International, a clothing retailer with 2,000 stores across Asia. "And the trust has to be both ways."

In the United States, factory owners could file for bankruptcy, getting some protection from creditors and maybe even court-ordered financing to keep operating. That was supposed to be the case in China, too, under a two-year-old bankruptcy law that was heralded as a key step in market reforms. But few judges have received the necessary training to understand the complex measure, so local officials often discourage hard-pressed owners from filing for bankruptcy. And by compensating creditors before employees, the law undercuts Beijing's desire to minimize labor unrest.

Out of a Job—and Home

In the first 10 months of last year, the bankruptcy law was used in only about 1,000 cases—mostly large state enterprises rather than the thousands of shuttered export-oriented manufacturers. "The bankruptcy law is still at a beginning stage," says John J. Rapisardi, a partner in the New York office of law firm Cadwalader, Wickersham & Taft who advised China on crafting the law.

So instead of orderly liquidation in the courts, workers, suppliers, and creditors take matters into their own hands. When toymaker Smart Union Group collapsed in October, its Hong Kong–based owner closed two sprawling facilities in Dongguan that made toys for Walt Disney and Mattel. He owed $29 million to some 800 suppliers and $3.5 million in pay to 7,600 workers. The local government coughed up the wages after employees staged protests at the town hall. "These workers are migrants who live in the factories," says Huang Huiping, deputy chief of the Dongguan Labor Bureau. "If the boss flees, they have no place to live."

Some authorities are pushing for stronger action. In Guangdong province, labor officials have published the names of deadbeat factory owners in local newspapers to shame them and make it harder for them to open businesses. The labor leaders have developed a blacklist of fugitive bosses and are working with courts to track them down. Others are calling for legislation that would allow criminal prosecution of bosses who flee factories (it's currently a civil violation). "This causes enough social harm that it should be treated as a criminal offense," says Zhu Zhengfu, vice president of the Guangdong Lawyers Association.

While many bankrupt factory owners flee to avoid paying their debts, others worry about their safety. When mobile-phone maker Shenzhen Bandshine Communications Development could no longer pay suppliers or employees last September, boss Zhao Zheng went underground. "I am physically and mentally exhausted and fear for my life," Zhao text-messaged her then-distributor for Southeast Asia. "I have no choice but to go into hiding," the message continued. "She owed money to lots of suppliers," says Jack Zhou, the former distributor, adding she still owes him $90,000. "They came to the factory and broke everything."

Meanwhile, the boss of the Dongguan lighting factory is working to resolve his disputes with suppliers. He hopes to return to China, despite some ambivalence. "I threw away 17 years of business, but sometimes enough is enough," he says while soaking in an outdoor hot spring in the lush mountains near Taipei. "The law in China is something you can hang beside your toilet. In China, [success depends on] whom you know and how much money you have. Anything else is a waste of time."

Questions

1. Why are some factory owners in China going into hiding?
2. Do you think their behavior is ethical or unethical?
3. What ethical obligations do factory owners have toward their employees?
4. What ethical obligations do factory owners have toward suppliers?

Source: D. Roberts, "As Factories Fail, So Does Business Law." Reprinted from April 13, 2009 issue of *BusinessWeek* by special permission, copyright © 2009 by The McGraw-Hill Companies, Inc.

BusinessWeek Case in the News [LO3, 4, 5]

Don't Treat Them Like Baby Boomers

Just prick the surface of Generation Xers' feelings about life Inside large corporations, and you'll likely discover a flood of concerns, as we found in reader responses to the BusinessWeek .com post "Ten Reasons Gen Xers Are Unhappy at Work." This article was originally posted on Harvard Business.org.

What, realistically, can corporations do?

Don't expect that the same approaches that worked well with a boomer workforce will work equally well with Xers. And don't assume that Xers will come to value the same things boomers did "when they grow up." Xers are grown up—and they don't think like boomers.

Teen experiences as latchkey kids and watching adults get laid off from corporations left many in Generation X feeling that one of the most important life priorities is to be able to take care of themselves under any circumstances. So, what Xers want from companies are jobs that offer a variety of career paths and allow them to gain fresh, marketable skills, build a strong network of contacts, and put money in the bank. And that's what corporations should focus on to make themselves more appealing to Xers.

Options First

First, recognize that many classic corporate career paths narrow at the top, making Xers feel that they have fewer options. Articulate career paths that offer multiple possible next steps. For example, position a move with "After this, you will have the experience to take on any one of six jobs." This is different from what a boomer would more likely prefer to hear: "After this, you will be in contention for the top job."

Boomers like to win; Xers like to have options.

Corporations should provide training of all types, support formal education, and ensure a broad set of work experiences to give Xers up-to-date skills and a sense of possibility about their futures. Consider creating lateral career options—the ability to gain additional breadth by moving sideways into other departments. This, too, may seem odd to boomers—a distraction from moving "up"—but Xers view moving "over" as creating options down the road. Since many Xers aspire to run their own entrepreneurial ventures, lateral moves also provide the broad business skills they will need.

Many Xers already maintain strong ties to friends who can be counted on in a crunch. Forming business relationships is valued by many, again with an eye toward future security, and is something corporations should facilitate. Companies that are known as good places to make important contacts, to "see and be seen," have an advantage with Xers. Support reputation- and network-building activities, such as participation in prominent industry or professional forums, learning opportunities, and other external activities. Avoid insularity.

Remember that Xers care about money—a lot. They are probably more money-oriented than boomers, who might be pleased with a promotion (which is equated with "winning"), even if additional financial remuneration is slight or nonexistent. An Xer would almost never find that acceptable.

In addition to self-sufficiency, Xers also place high priority on their children and family relationships. Corporations should be sensitive to the pressures this generation feels to "be there" for their kids more than their parents were for them. For many, this means there is a line they refuse to cross in terms of amount of travel or hours worked. Many would take jobs at lower pay to gain additional flexibility and time with their families. Corporations must offer these options in order to retain members of this generation.

In researching my upcoming book on Gen X, I interviewed a rising Xer corporate star. As we were discussing senior executive assignments, he mused, "I wonder who would want those jobs." I paused. "Well, gee, don't you think your company thinks that you do?" He seemed surprised that his company assumed he would. "Oh, I suppose they do," he said, "but that's not for me."

Organizations that take Xers for granted run the risk of losing key talent. This generation is not enamored with corporate life, so companies have to rethink their approach to appeal to the talent they need to not only attract but retain.

Questions

1. Why is it important for managers to understand what Generation X employees want from their jobs and organizations?
2. How might a lack of understanding between Baby Boom employees and Generation X employees lead to problems in the workplace?
3. Why is it important for Generation X employees to have time to spend with their children and their families?
4. What can managers and organizations do to increase understanding among employees of different generations or age groups?

Source: T. Erickson, "Don't Treat Them Like Baby Boomers." Reprinted from August 25, 2008 issue of *BusinessWeek* by special permission, copyright © 2008 by The McGraw-Hill Companies, Inc.

Managing in the Global Environment

CHAPTER 4

Learning Objectives

After studying this chapter, you should be able to

1. Explain why the ability to perceive, interpret, and respond appropriately to the global environment is crucial for managerial success. **[LO1]**
2. Differentiate between the global task and global general environments. **[LO2]**
3. Identify the main forces in both the global task and general environments and describe the challenges that each force presents to managers. **[LO3]**
4. Explain why the global environment is becoming more open and competitive and identify the forces behind the process of globalization that increase the opportunities, complexities, challenges, and threats that managers face. **[LO4]**
5. Discuss why national cultures differ and why it is important that managers be sensitive to the effects of falling trade barriers and regional trade associations on the political and social systems of nations around the world. **[LO5]**

IKEA's large, modern furniture stores that stock a wide range of affordable, high-quality furniture and accessories have become a favorite with customers around the world—not least because they also offer quality childcare facilities and restaurants.

MANAGEMENT SNAPSHOT

IKEA Is on Top of the Furniture World

Why Is Managing the Global Environment So Complex Today?

IKEA is the largest furniture chain in the world, and in 2009 the Swedish company operated over 265 stores in 24 countries. In 2008 IKEA sales had soared to over $31 billion, or over 20% of the global furniture market, but to its managers and employees this is just the tip of the iceberg. They believe IKEA is poised for massive growth throughout the world in the coming decade because it can provide what the average customer wants: well-designed and well-made contemporary furniture at an affordable price. IKEA's ability to provide customers with affordable furniture is very much the result of its approach to globalization, to the way it treats its global employees and operates its global store empire. In a nutshell, IKEA's global approach revolves around simplicity, attention to detail, cost-consciousness, and responsiveness in every aspect of its operations and behavior.

IKEA's global approach derives from the personal values and beliefs of its founder, Ingvar Kamprad, about how companies should treat their employees and customers. Kamprad, who is in his early 80s, was born in Smaland, a poor Swedish province whose citizens are well known for being entrepreneurial, frugal, and hardworking. Kamprad definitely absorbed these values, for when he entered the furniture business, he made them the core of his management approach. He teaches store managers and employees his values; his beliefs about the need to operate in a no-frills, cost-conscious way; and his view that they are all in business "together," by which he means that every person who works in his global empire plays an essential role and has an obligation to everyone else.

What does Kamprad's approach mean in practice? It means that all IKEA's members fly coach class on business trips, stay in inexpensive hotels, and keep traveling expenses to a minimum. It also means that IKEA stores operate on the simplest set of rules and procedures possible and that employees are expected to cooperate to solve problems and get the job done. Many famous stories exist about the frugal Kamprad, such as that even he always flies coach class and that when he takes a Coke can from the mini-bar in a hotel room, he replaces it with one bought in a store—despite the fact that he is a multibillionaire ranked in the top 20 on the *Forbes* list of the world's richest people!

IKEA's employees see what his global approach means as soon as they are recruited to work in a store in one of the many countries in which the company operates. They start learning about IKEA's global corporate culture by performing jobs at the bottom of the ladder, and they are quickly trained to perform all the various jobs involved in store operations. During this process they internalize IKEA's global values and norms, which center on the importance the company attaches to their taking the initiative and responsibility for solving problems and for focusing on the customer. Employees are rotated between departments and sometimes stores, and rapid promotion is possible for those who demonstrate the enthusiasm and togetherness that signifies they have bought into IKEA's global culture.

Most of IKEA's top managers rose from its ranks, and the company holds "breaking the bureaucracy weeks" in which they are required to work in stores and warehouses for a week each year to make sure they and all employees stay committed to IKEA's global values. No matter which country they operate in, all employees wear informal clothes to work at IKEA—Kamprad has always worn an open-neck shirt—and there are no marks of status such as executive dining rooms or private parking places. Employees believe that if they buy into IKEA's work values, behave in ways that keep its growing global operations streamlined and efficient, and focus on being one step ahead of potential problems, they will share in its success. Promotion, training, above-average pay, a generous store bonus system, and the personal well-being that comes from working in a company where people feel valued are some of the rewards that Kamprad pioneered to build and strengthen IKEA's global approach.

Whenever IKEA enters a new country, it sends its most experienced store managers to establish its global approach in its new stores. When IKEA first entered the United States, the attitude of U.S. employees puzzled its managers. Despite their obvious drive to succeed and good education, employees seemed reluctant to take the initiative and assume responsibility. IKEA's managers discovered that their U.S. employees were afraid mistakes would result in the loss of their jobs, so the managers strove to teach employees the "IKEA way." The approach paid off: The United States has become the company's second-best country market, and IKEA plans to open many more U.S. stores, as well as stores around the world, over the next decade.

Overview

Top managers of a global company like IKEA are always operating in an environment where they are competing with other companies for scarce and valuable resources. Managers of companies large and small have concluded that to survive and prosper in the 21st century, most organizations must become **global organizations,** organizations that operate and compete not only domestically, at home, but also globally, in countries around the world. Operating in the global environment is uncertain and unpredictable because it is complex and constantly changing.

global organization An organization that operates and competes in more than one country.

If organizations are to adapt to this changing environment, their managers must learn to understand the forces that operate in it and how these forces give rise to opportunities and threats. In this chapter, we examine why the environment, both domestically and globally, has become more open, vibrant, and competitive. We examine how forces in the task and general environments affect global organizations and their managers. By the end of this chapter, you will appreciate the changes that have been taking place in the environment and understand why it is important for managers to develop a global perspective as they strive to increase organizational efficiency and effectiveness.

LO1 Explain why the ability to perceive, interpret, and respond appropriately to the global environment is crucial for managerial success.

What Is the Global Environment?

global environment The set of global forces and conditions that operate beyond an organization's boundaries but affect a manager's ability to acquire and utilize resources.

The **global environment** is a set of forces and conditions in the world outside an organization's boundary that affect the way it operates and shape its behavior.[1] These forces change over time and thus present managers with *opportunities* and *threats*. Changes in the global environment, such as the development of efficient new production technology, the availability of lower-cost components, or the opening of new global markets, create opportunities for managers to make and sell more products, obtain more resources and capital, and thereby strengthen their organization. In contrast, the rise of new global competitors, a global economic recession, or an oil shortage poses threats that can devastate an organization if managers are unable to sell its products and revenues and profits plunge. The quality of managers' understanding of forces in the global environment and their ability to respond appropriately to those forces, such as IKEA's managers' ability to make and sell the furniture products customers around the world want to buy, are critical factors affecting organizational performance.

In this chapter we explore the nature of these forces and consider how managers can respond to them. To identify opportunities and threats caused by forces in the environment, it is helpful for managers to distinguish between the *task environment* and the more encompassing *general environment* (see Figure 4.1).

Figure 4.1
Forces in the Global Environment

LO2 Differentiate between the global task and global general environments.

task environment The set of forces and conditions that originate with suppliers, distributors, customers, and competitors and affect an organization's ability to obtain inputs and dispose of its outputs because they influence managers on a daily basis.

The **task environment** is the set of forces and conditions that originate with global suppliers, distributors, customers, and competitors; these forces and conditions affect an organization's ability to obtain inputs and dispose of its outputs. The task environment contains the forces that have the most *immediate* and *direct* effect on managers because they pressure and influence managers on a daily basis. When managers turn on the radio or television, arrive at their offices in the morning, open their mail, or look at their computer screens, they are likely to learn about problems facing them because of changing conditions in their organization's task environment.

The **general environment** includes the wide-ranging global, economic, technological, sociocultural, demographic, political, and legal forces that affect the organization and its task environment. For the individual manager, opportunities and threats resulting from changes in the general environment are often more difficult to identify and respond to than are events in the task environment. However, changes in these forces can have major impacts on managers and their organizations.

The Task Environment

Forces in the task environment result from the actions of suppliers, distributors, customers, and competitors both at home and abroad (see Figure 4.1). These four groups affect a manager's ability to obtain resources and dispose of outputs on a daily, weekly, and monthly basis and thus have a significant impact on short-term decision making.

LO3 Identify the main forces in both the global task and general environments and describe the challenges that each force presents to managers.

general environment The wide-ranging global, economic, technological, sociocultural, demographic, political, and legal forces that affect an organization and its task environment.

suppliers Individuals and organizations that provide an organization with the input resources that it needs to produce goods and services.

Suppliers

Suppliers are the individuals and companies that provide an organization with the input resources (such as raw materials, component parts, or employees) that it needs to produce goods and services. In return, the supplier receives payment for those goods and services. An important aspect of a manager's job is to ensure a reliable supply of input resources.

Take Dell Computer, for example. Dell has many suppliers of component parts such as microprocessors (Intel and AMD) and disk drives (Quantum and Seagate Technologies). It also has suppliers of preinstalled software, including the operating system (Microsoft) and specific applications software (IBM, Oracle, and America Online). Dell's providers of capital, such as banks and financial institutions, are also important suppliers. Cisco Systems and Oracle are important providers of Internet hardware and software for dot-coms.

Dell has several suppliers of labor. One source is the educational institutions that train future Dell employees and therefore provide the company with skilled workers. Another is trade unions, organizations that represent employee interests and can control the supply of labor by exercising the right of unionized workers to strike. Unions also can influence the terms and conditions under which labor is employed. Dell's workers are not unionized; when layoffs became necessary due to an economic slowdown in the early 2000s, Dell had few problems in laying off workers to reduce costs. In organizations and industries where unions are very strong, however, an important part of a manager's job is negotiating and administering agreements with unions and their representatives.

Changes in the nature, number, or type of suppliers result in forces that produce opportunities and threats to which managers must respond if their organizations are to prosper. For example, a major supplier-related threat that confronts managers arises when suppliers' bargaining position is so strong that they can raise the prices of the inputs they supply to the organization. A supplier's bargaining position is especially strong when (1) the supplier is the sole source of an input and (2) the input is vital to the organization.[2] For example, for 17 years G. D. Searle was the sole supplier of NutraSweet, the artificial sweetener used in most diet soft drinks. Not only was NutraSweet an important ingredient in diet soft drinks, but it also was one for which there was no acceptable substitute (saccharin and other artificial sweeteners raised health concerns). Searle earned its privileged position because it invented and held the patent for NutraSweet.[3] Patents prohibit other organizations from introducing competing products for 17 years. When Searle's patent expired, many companies began to produce products similar to NutraSweet, and its price plunged.[4]

In contrast, when an organization has many suppliers for a particular input, it is in a relatively strong bargaining position with those suppliers and can demand low-cost, high-quality inputs from them. Often, an organization can use its power with suppliers to force them to reduce their prices, as Dell frequently does. Dell, for example, is constantly searching for low-cost suppliers abroad to keep its PC prices competitive. At a global level, organizations have the opportunity to buy products from suppliers overseas or to become their own suppliers and manufacture their own products abroad.

It is important that managers recognize the opportunities and threats associated with managing the global supply chain. On the one hand, gaining access to low-cost products made abroad represents an opportunity for U.S. companies to lower their input costs. On the other hand, managers who fail to utilize low-cost overseas suppliers create a threat and put their organizations at a competitive disadvantage.[5] Levi Strauss, for example, was slow to realize that it could not compete with the low-priced jeans sold by Wal-Mart and other retailers, and it was eventually forced to close almost all of its U.S. jean factories and utilize low-cost overseas suppliers to keep the price of its jeans competitive. Now it sells its low-priced jeans in Wal-Mart! The downside to global outsourcing is, of course, the loss of millions of U.S. jobs, an issue we have discussed in previous chapters.

A common problem facing managers of large global companies such as Ford, Procter & Gamble, and IBM is managing the development of a global network of suppliers that will allow their companies to keep costs down and quality high. For example, Boeing's popular 777 jet requires 132,500 engineered parts produced around the world by 545 suppliers.[6] While Boeing makes the majority of these parts, eight Japanese suppliers make parts for the 777's fuselage, doors, and wings; a Singapore supplier makes the doors for the plane's forward landing gear; and three Italian suppliers manufacture wing flaps. Boeing's rationale for buying so many inputs from overseas suppliers is that these suppliers are the best in the world at performing their particular activity and doing business with them helps Boeing to produce a high-quality final product, a vital requirement given the need for aircraft safety and reliability.[7] Its new plane, the Dreamliner, uses even more parts made by overseas suppliers, and Boeing has outsourced some

The purchasing activities of global companies have become increasingly complicated in recent years. More than 500 suppliers around the world produce parts for Boeing's popular 777 and even more will be needed for the new Dreamliner.

of the plane's assembly to companies' abroad–something that has led to the charge that it is giving away the source of its competitive advantage!

The purchasing activities of global companies have become increasingly complicated as a result of the development of a whole range of skills and competencies in different countries around the world. It is clearly in their interests to search out the lowest-cost, best-quality suppliers no matter where they may be. Also, the Internet makes it possible for companies to coordinate complicated, arm's-length exchanges involving the purchasing of inputs and the disposal of outputs.

global outsourcing The purchase of inputs from overseas suppliers or the production of inputs abroad to lower production costs and improve product quality or design.

Global outsourcing is the process by which organizations purchase inputs from other companies or produce inputs themselves throughout the world to lower their production costs and improve the quality or design of their products.[8] To take advantage of national differences in the cost and quality of resources such as labor or raw materials, GM might build its own engines in one country, transmissions in another, and brakes in a third and buy other components from hundreds of global suppliers. Trade expert Robert Reich once calculated that of the $20,000 that customers paid GM for a Pontiac Le Mans, about $6,000 went to South Korea, where the Le Mans was assembled; $3,500 to Japan for advanced components such as engines, transaxles, and electronics; $1,500 to Germany, where the Le Mans was designed; $800 to Taiwan, Singapore, and Japan for small components; $500 to Britain for advertising and marketing services; and about $100 to Ireland for data-processing services. The remaining $7,000 goes to GM–and to the lawyers, bankers, and insurance agents that GM retains in the United States.[9]

Is the Le Mans a U.S. product? Yes, but it is also a Korean product, a Japanese product, and a German product. Today, such global exchanges are becoming so complex that specialized organizations are emerging to help manage global organizations' supply chains–that is, the flow of inputs necessary to produce a product. One example is Li & Fung, profiled here in "Managing Globally."

MANAGING GLOBALLY

Global Supply Chain Management

Finding the overseas suppliers that offer the lowest-priced and highest-quality products is an important task facing the managers of global organizations. Since these suppliers are located in thousands of cities in many countries around the world, finding them is a difficult business. Often, global companies use the services of overseas intermediaries or brokers, located near these suppliers, to find the one that best meets their input requirements. Li & Fung, now run by brothers Victor and William Fung, is one of the brokers that has helped hundreds of global companies to locate suitable overseas suppliers, especially suppliers in mainland China.[10]

In the 2000s, however, managing global companies' supply chains became a more complicated task. To reduce costs, overseas suppliers were increasingly *specializing* in just one part of the task of producing a product. For example, in the past, a company such as Target might have negotiated with an overseas supplier to manufacture 1 million units of some particular shirt at a certain cost per unit. But with specialization, Target might find it can reduce the costs of producing the shirt even further by splitting apart the operations involved in its production and having *different* overseas suppliers, often in *different* countries, perform each operation. For example, to get the lowest cost per unit, rather than negotiating with a single overseas supplier over the price of making a particular shirt, Target might first negotiate with a yarn manufacturer in Vietnam to make the yarn; then ship the yarn to a Chinese supplier to weave it into cloth; and then ship the cloth to several different factories in Malaysia and the Philippines to cut the fabric and sew the shirts. Then, another overseas company might take responsibility for packaging and shipping the shirts to wherever in the world they are required. Because a company such as Target has thousands of different clothing products under production, and they change all the time, the problems of managing such a supply chain to get the full cost savings from global expansion are clearly difficult and costly.

Li & Fung capitalized on this opportunity. Realizing that many global companies do not have the time or expertise to find such specialized low-price suppliers, its founders moved quickly to provide such a service. Li & Fung employs 3,600 agents who travel across 37 countries to locate new suppliers and inspect existing suppliers to find new ways to help its global clients get lower prices or higher-quality products. Global companies are happy to outsource their supply chain management to Li & Fung because they realize significant cost savings. Even though they pay a hefty fee to Li & Fung, they avoid the costs of employing their own agents. As the complexity of supply chain management continues to increase, more and more companies like Li & Fung are appearing.

Distributors

distributors
Organizations that help other organizations sell their goods or services to customers.

Distributors are organizations that help other organizations sell their goods or services to customers. The decisions that managers make about how to distribute products to customers can have important effects on organizational performance. For example, package delivery companies such as FedEx, UPS, and the U.S. Postal Service became vital distributors for the millions of items bought online and shipped to customers by dot-com companies.

The changing nature of distributors and distribution methods can bring opportunities and threats for managers. If distributors become so large and powerful that they can control customers' access to a particular organization's goods and services, they can threaten the organization by demanding that it reduce the prices of its goods and services.[11] For example, the huge retail distributor Wal-Mart controls its suppliers' access to a great number of customers and thus often demands that its suppliers reduce their prices. If an organization such as Procter & Gamble refuses to reduce its prices, Wal-Mart might respond by buying products only from Procter & Gamble's competitors–companies such as Unilever and Dial. In 2004, Wal-Mart announced that by 2006 all its suppliers must adopt a new wireless scanning technology to reduce its cost of distributing products to its stores or it would stop doing business with them.[12]

In contrast, the power of a distributor may be weakened if there are many options. This has been the experience of the four broadcast television networks–ABC, NBC, FOX, and CBS–which "distribute" TV programs. Their ability to demand lower prices from the producers of television programs has been weakened because today hundreds of new cable television channels exist that have reduced the four networks' share of the viewing audience to less than 40%, down from more than 90% a decade ago. Similarly, because there are at least three major package delivery companies–USPS, FedEx, and UPS–dot-coms and other companies would not really be threatened if one delivery firm tried to increase its prices; they could simply switch delivery companies.

It is illegal for distributors to collaborate or collude to keep prices high and thus maintain their power over buyers; however, this frequently happens. In the early 2000s, several European drug companies conspired to keep the price of vitamins artificially high. In 2005 the three largest global makers of flash memory, including Samsung, were also found guilty of price fixing (they collaborated to keep prices high). All these companies paid hundreds of millions of dollars in fines, and many of their top executives were sentenced to jail terms.

Customers

customers Individuals and groups that buy the goods and services that an organization produces.

Customers are the individuals and groups that buy the goods and services that an organization produces. For example, Dell's customers can be segmented into several distinct groups: (1) individuals who purchase PCs for home use, (2) small companies, (3) large companies, (4) government agencies, and (5) educational institutions. Changes in the number and types of customers or in customers' tastes and needs result in opportunities and threats. An organization's success depends on its response to customers.[13] In the PC industry, customers are demanding lower prices and increased multimedia capability, and PC companies must respond to the changing types and needs of customers. A school, too, must adapt to the changing needs of its customers. For example, if more Spanish-speaking students enroll, additional classes in English as a second language may need to be scheduled. A manager's ability to identify an organization's main customers and produce the goods and services they want is a crucial factor affecting organizational and managerial success.

The most obvious opportunity associated with expanding into the global environment is the prospect of selling goods and services to new customers, as Amazon.com's CEO Jeff Bezos discovered when he began to start operating in many countries abroad. Similarly, Accenture and Cap Gemini, two large consulting companies, have established operations throughout the world and recruit and train thousands of overseas consultants to serve the needs of customers in a wide variety of countries.

Today, many products are becoming global products and have gained wide acceptance from customers in countries around the globe. This consolidation is occurring both for consumer goods and for business products and has created enormous opportunities for managers. The global acceptance of Coca-Cola, Apple iPods, McDonald's hamburgers, Doc Martin boots, and Nokia cell phones is a sign that the tastes and preferences of consumers in different countries may not be so different after all.[14] Likewise, large global markets currently exist for business products such as telecommunications equipment, electronic components, computer services, and financial services. Thus, Motorola sells its telecommunications equipment, Intel its microprocessors, and SAP its business systems management software to customers throughout the world.

competitors Organizations that produce goods and services that are similar to a particular organization's goods and services.

Competitors

One of the most important forces that an organization confronts in its task environment is competitors. **Competitors** are organizations that produce goods and services similar to a particular organization's goods and services. In other words, competitors are organizations vying for the same customers. Dell's competitors include other domestic manufacturers of PCs (such as Apple and HP) as well as overseas competitors (such as Sony and Toshiba in Japan and Acer). Dot-com stockbroker E*Trade has other dot-com competitors, like Ameritrade and Scottrade, as well as bricks-and-clicks competitors, such as Bank of America and Wells Fargo.

Rivalry between competitors is potentially the most threatening force that managers must deal with. A high level of rivalry often results in price competition, and falling prices reduce access to resources and lower profits. In the 2000s, competition in the PC industry became intense not only because of an economic slowdown but also because Dell was aggressively cutting costs and prices to increase its global market share.[15] IBM exited the PC business because it was losing millions in its battle against low-cost rivals, and Gateway and HP also suffered, while Dell's profits soared. By 2006, however, HP's fortunes had recovered as it lowered its costs and offered new PCs with AMD's popular chips, while Dell's profit margins had shrunk.

Dell grew quickly to become the biggest global maker of PCs by 2000 as it took advantage of low-cost PC components made abroad and outsourced its PC manufacturing to companies in many Asian countries. In the 2000s, however, it began to experience intense competition from HP, the second-largest PC maker, whose managers were striving to develop a low-cost global network of suppliers and distributors that would allow it to match Dell's low costs. At the same time, PC makers based in Asia, such as Acer, also worked to create a global network that would allow it to sell PCs for prices similar to Dell's, and after Acer bought struggling Gateway Computer in 2006, it became the third-largest PC maker.

Dell's managers, used to being the industry leader, failed to appreciate how fast its global competitors were catching up; they were shocked when HPs new low-cost skills allowed it to overtake Dell to became the biggest global PC maker in 2006, although Dell still retained its lead in the United States. Realizing the growing threat to his company, Michael Dell once again became CEO, and with his top managers he began to develop a new plan to increase Dell's global sales.

The two fastest-growing markets in Asia are China and India, and to regain its position as global leader, Dell had to expand sales in these countries. Since India imposes high tariffs on imported PCs, Dell rushed to open new manufacturing facilities inside the country, where sales in both the consumer and business segments of the PC market are expected to increase 30% each year. It opened a major facility in Chennai, in Southern India, to produce low-price machines tailored for the local market; it expects sales of $500 million from this venture in 2007. However, HP has also been working to expand its presence in India, and opened a second plant in 2007 to help expand its market share, which is already 20%–making it the second-largest PC maker in India.

In China, Dell is competing with domestic market leader Lenovo Group, the Chinese PC maker that bought IBM's PC division and its popular ThinkPad. To compete with Lenovo, which has costs as low as Dell, it has focused on expanding its manufacturing facilities in China to produce PCs customized to the Chinese market. The Dell brand name is popular in China, and in the attempt to reach more Chinese customers and rapidly increase sales of its PCs, in 2007 Dell decided to sell its PCs through Gome, China's largest retail electronics chain. This new strategy worked, and in 2008 Dell doubled to 900 the number of Gome stores that sell its PCs. In 2008 it also decided to sell desktop and notebook computers at Suning, China's second-largest electronics chain; it also plans to increase spending for online marketing and in-store promotions at Gome and Suning to attract the over 1 billion potential Chinese customers.

With these moves, Dell's decision to branch out from its phone and Internet sales strategy and to retail its PCs directly through stores such as Wal-Mart and Best Buy in the United States will put its PCs in more than 12,000 stores worldwide. By 2008 its new global strategy seemed to be working; its attempts to regain the lead in worldwide PC shipments seemed to be paying off as sales in the Asia-Pacific and Japan region rose 28%.[16] But HP, Lenovo, Acer, and all its other global competitors have not been idle. Indeed, HP, which has always retailed its PCs, claims they are available in 81,000 stores around the world, so Dell has much more to do to catch up. The race is on not just to provide low-price PCs to consumers in poorer nations, but to develop new, smaller, sleeker machines, and PCs with state-of-the-art graphics and processing speed for gaming, as well as luxury PCs aimed at capturing market share from Apple, whose high-priced Macs are also attracting increasing numbers of well-heeled customers around the globe.

Because fierce competition drives down prices and profits, unethical companies often try to find ways to collude with competitors to keep prices high. Boeing adopted a different, very unsavory, method to gain market share and beat its rivals. In 2006 Boeing agreed to pay $615 million in fines to end a three-year Justice Department investigation into contracting scandals involving Boeing, thereby avoiding criminal charges or admission of wrongdoing. Boeing had been under investigation for improperly acquiring proprietary competitive information about Lockheed Martin's bidding intentions for government rocket-launching contracts. Once it knew how much Lockheed was willing to bid, it could then simply undercut its price by a few million to win the billion-dollar auction! The government stripped Boeing of $1 billion worth of the contracts it had won through its improper use of the Lockheed documents. Additionally, Boeing illegally recruited senior U.S. Air Force procurement officer Darleen Druyun while she still had authority over billions of dollars in other Boeing contracts. Druyun served nine months in prison for violating federal conflict-of-interest laws. Michael Sears, formerly chief financial officer at Boeing, was fired in 2003 and spent four months in federal prison for illegally recruiting her. The scandals also led to the resignation of Boeing Chairman Phil Condit. Clearly, Boeing went to enormous lengths to beat its rivals, and supposedly it had a strong code of ethics that should have prevented such illegal actions!

Although extensive rivalry between existing competitors is a major threat to profitability, so is the potential for new competitors to enter the task environment. **Potential competitors** are organizations that are not presently in a task environment but could enter if they so choose. Amazon.com, for example, is not currently in the retail furniture or appliance business, but it could enter these businesses if its managers decided it could profitably sell such products online. When new competitors enter an industry, competition increases and prices and profits decrease.

potential competitors Organizations that presently are not in a task environment but could enter if they so choose.

BARRIERS TO ENTRY In general, the potential for new competitors to enter a task environment (and thus increase competition) is a function of barriers to entry.[17] **Barriers to entry** are factors that make it difficult and costly for a company to enter a particular task environment or industry.[18] In other words, the more difficult and costly it is to enter the task environment, the higher are the barriers to entry. The higher the barriers to entry, the fewer the competitors in an organization's task environment and thus the lower the threat of competition. With fewer competitors, it is easier to obtain customers and keep prices high.

barriers to entry Factors that make it difficult and costly for an organization to enter a particular task environment or industry.

Figure 4.2
Barriers to Entry and Competition

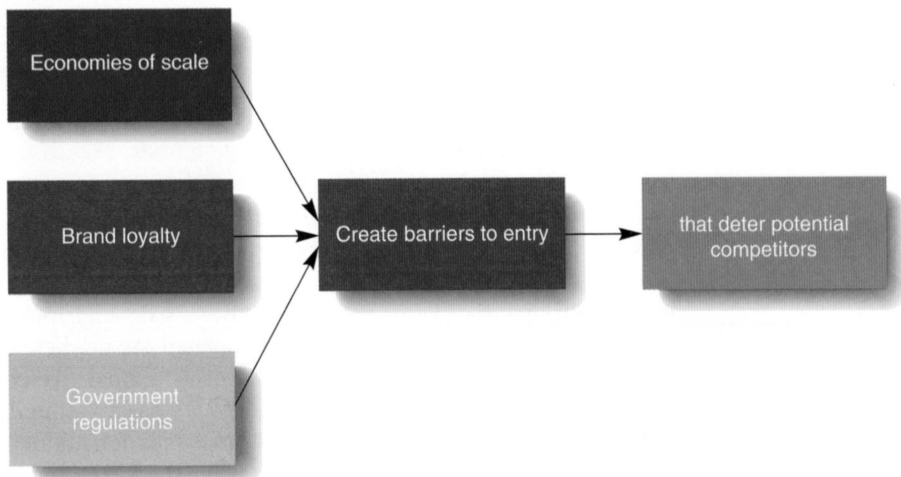

economies of scale Cost advantages associated with large operations.

brand loyalty Customers' preference for the products of organizations currently existing in the task environment.

Barriers to entry result from three main sources: economies of scale, brand loyalty, and government regulations that impede entry (see Figure 4.2). **Economies of scale** are the cost advantages associated with large operations. Economies of scale result from factors such as manufacturing products in very large quantities, buying inputs in bulk, or making more effective use of organizational resources than do competitors by fully utilizing employees' skills and knowledge. If organizations already in the task environment are large and enjoy significant economies of scale, then their costs are lower than the costs that potential entrants will face, and newcomers will find it very expensive to enter the industry. Amazon.com, for example, enjoys significant economies of scale relative to most other dot-com companies.[19]

Brand loyalty is customers' preference for the products of organizations currently existing in the task environment. If established organizations enjoy significant brand loyalty, then a new entrant will find it extremely difficult and costly to obtain a share of the market. Newcomers must bear huge advertising costs to build customer awareness of the goods or services they intend to provide.[20] Both Amazon.com and Yahoo, for example, two of the first dot-coms to go online, enjoy a high level of brand loyalty and have some of the highest Web site hit rates of all dot-coms (the latter also allows them to increase their advertising revenues).

In some cases, *government regulations* function as a barrier to entry at both the industry and the country levels. Many industries that were deregulated, such as air transport, trucking, utilities, and telecommunications, experienced a high level of new entry after deregulation; this forced existing companies in those industries to operate more efficiently or risk being put out of business.

At the national and global level, administrative barriers are government policies that create a barrier to entry and limit imports of goods by overseas companies. Japan is well known for the many ways in which it attempts to restrict the entry of overseas competitors or lessen their impact on Japanese firms. For example, why do Dutch companies export tulip bulbs to almost every country in the world except Japan? Japanese customs inspectors insist on checking every tulip bulb by cutting the stems vertically down the middle, and even Japanese ingenuity cannot put them back together.[21] Japan has come under intense pressure to relax and abolish such regulations, as the following "Managing Globally" suggests.

MANAGING GLOBALLY

American Rice Invades Japan

The Japanese rice market, similar to many other Japanese markets, was closed to overseas competitors until 1993 to protect Japan's thousands of high-cost, low-output rice farmers. Rice cultivation is expensive in Japan because of the country's mountainous terrain, so Japanese consumers have always paid high prices for rice. Under overseas pressure, the Japanese government opened the market, and overseas competitors are now allowed to export to Japan 8% of its annual rice consumption. Despite the still-present hefty overseas tariff on rice–$2.33 per 2.2 pounds–U.S. rice sells for $14 dollars per pound bag, while Japanese rice sells for about $19. With the recession affecting Japan, price-conscious consumers are turning to overseas rice, which has hurt domestic farmers.

The tyranny of the lower price. A Japanese businessman purchases a pre-frozen, U.S.-sourced rice O-bento lunch at a Nippon Tokyo restaurant. Nippon's importing practices have angered Japanese rice farmers.

In the 2000s, however, an alliance between organic rice grower Lundberg Family Farms of California and the Nippon Restaurant Enterprise Co. found a new way to break into the Japanese rice market. Because there is no tariff on rice used in processed foods, Nippon takes the U.S. organic rice and converts it into "O-bento," an organic hot boxed lunch packed with rice, vegetables, chicken, beef, and salmon, all imported from the United States. The new lunches, which cost about $4 compared to a Japanese rice bento that costs about $9, are sold at railway stations and other outlets throughout Japan.[22] They are proving to be very popular and are creating a storm of protest from Japanese rice farmers, who already have been forced to leave 37% of their rice fields idle and grow less profitable crops because of the entry of U.S. rice growers. Japanese and overseas companies are increasingly forming alliances to find new ways to break into the high-price Japanese market, and, little by little, Japan's restrictive trade practices are being whittled away.

In summary, intense rivalry among competitors creates a task environment that is highly threatening and causes difficulty for managers trying to gain access to the resources an organization needs. Conversely, low rivalry results in a task environment where competitive pressures are more moderate and managers have greater opportunities to acquire the resources they need for their organizations to be effective.

The General Environment

Economic, technological, sociocultural, demographic, political, and legal forces in the general environment can have profound effects on forces in the task environment, effects that may not be evident to managers. For example, the sudden, dramatic upheavals in the Internet and dot-com industry environment in the early 2000s were brought about by a combination of changing Internet and digital technology, the softening U.S. stock market and economy, and increasing fears about global recession. These changes triggered intense competition between dot-com companies that further worsened the industry situation.

The implication is clear: Managers must constantly analyze forces in the general environment because these forces affect ongoing decision making and planning. Next, we discuss the major forces in the general environment, and examine their impact on an organization's task environment.

Economic Forces

economic forces Interest rates, inflation, unemployment, economic growth, and other factors that affect the general health and well-being of a nation or the regional economy of an organization.

Economic forces affect the general health and well-being of a country or world region. They include interest rates, inflation, unemployment, and economic growth. Economic forces produce many opportunities and threats for managers. Low levels of unemployment and falling interest rates give more people more money to spend, and as a result organizations have an opportunity to sell more goods and services. Good economic times affect supplies: Resources become easier to acquire, and organizations have an opportunity to flourish, as high-tech companies did throughout the 1990s. The high-techs made record profits as the economy boomed in large part because of advances in information technology and growing global trade.

In contrast, worsening macroeconomic conditions, as in the 2000s, pose a major threat because they limit managers' ability to gain access to the resources their organizations need. Profit-seeking organizations such as retail stores and hotels have fewer customers for their goods and services during economic downturns. Nonprofits such as charities and colleges receive fewer donations during economic downturns. Even a moderate deterioration in national or regional economic conditions can seriously reduce performance. A relatively mild recession was a major factor in the staggering collapse of dot-com companies in the early 2000s; the recession that started in 2008 has caused massive layoffs at most large U.S. companies.

Poor economic conditions make the environment more complex and managers' jobs more difficult and demanding. Managers may need to reduce the number of individuals in their departments and increase the motivation of remaining employees, and managers and workers alike may need to identify ways to acquire and utilize resources more efficiently. Successful managers realize the important effects that economic forces have on their organizations, and they pay close attention to what is occurring in the national and regional economies to respond appropriately.

Technological Forces

technology The combination of skills and equipment that managers use in the design, production, and distribution of goods and services.

technological forces Outcomes of changes in the technology that managers use to design, produce, or distribute goods and services.

Technology is the combination of tools, machines, computers, skills, information, and knowledge that managers use in the design, production, and distribution of goods and services. **Technological forces** are outcomes of changes in the technology that managers use to design, produce, or distribute goods and services. The overall pace of technological change has accelerated greatly in the last decade because of advances in microprocessors and computer hardware and software, and technological forces have increased in magnitude.[23]

Technological forces can have profound implications for managers and organizations. Technological change can make established products obsolete–for example, typewriters, black-and-white televisions, bound sets of encyclopedias–forcing managers to find new ways to satisfy customer needs. Although technological change can threaten an organization, it also can create a host of new opportunities for designing, making, or distributing new and better kinds of goods and services. More powerful microprocessors developed by Intel caused a revolution in IT that spurred demand for PCs, contributed to the success of companies such as Dell and HP, but led to the decline of mainframe computer makers such as IBM.[24] However, IBM responded in the last decade by changing its emphasis from providing computer hardware to providing advanced computer services and consulting, and it has regained its strong global position. Managers must move quickly to respond to such changes if their organizations are to survive and prosper. Today Intel is being pressured by chip maker AMD, which was first to develop a powerful 64-bit PC chip, the Athlon, and has moved quickly to develop its own 64-bit chips.[25] In 2009 both companies competed head to head with their new quad-core chips.

Changes in IT are altering the very nature of work itself within organizations, including that of the manager's job. Telecommuting along the information superhighway, videoconferencing, and text messaging are now everyday activities that provide opportunities for managers to supervise and coordinate geographically dispersed employees. Salespeople in many companies work from home offices and commute electronically to work. They communicate with other employees through companywide electronic mail networks and use video cameras attached to PCs for "face-to-face" meetings with coworkers who may be across the country.

Sociocultural Forces

sociocultural forces Pressures emanating from the social structure of a country or society or from the national culture.

social structure The arrangement of relationships between individuals and groups in a society.

Sociocultural forces are pressures emanating from the social structure of a country or society or from the national culture. Pressures from both sources can either constrain or facilitate the way organizations operate and managers behave. **Social structure** is the arrangement of relationships between individuals and groups in a society. Societies differ substantially in social structure. In societies that have a high degree of social stratification, there are many distinctions among individuals and groups. Caste systems in India and Tibet and the recognition of numerous social classes in Great Britain and France produce a multilayered social structure in each of those countries. In contrast, social stratification is lower in relatively egalitarian New Zealand and in the United States, where the social structure reveals few distinctions among people. Most top managers in France come from the upper classes of French society, but top managers in the United States come from all strata of American society.

national culture The set of values that a society considers important and the norms of behavior that are approved or sanctioned in that society.

Societies also differ in the extent to which they emphasize the individual over the group. For example, the United States emphasizes the primacy of the individual, and Japan emphasizes the primacy of the group. This difference may dictate the methods managers need to use to motivate and lead employees. **National culture** is the set of values that a society considers important and the norms of behavior that are approved or sanctioned in that society. Societies differ substantially in the values and norms that they emphasize. For example, in the United States individualism is highly valued, and in Korea and Japan individuals are expected to conform to group expectations.[26] National culture, discussed at length later in this chapter, also affects the way managers motivate and coordinate employees and the way organizations do business. Ethics, an important aspect of national culture, were discussed in detail in Chapter 3.

Social structure and national culture not only differ across societies but also change within societies over time. In the United States, attitudes toward the roles of women, love, sex, and marriage changed in each past decade. Many people in Asian countries such as Hong Kong, Singapore, Korea, and Japan think that the younger generation

Olive oil gets a boost from today's health trends. Notice the bottle boasting omega-3 content—and the higher price as a result!

is far more individualistic and "American-like" than previous generations. Currently, throughout much of eastern Europe, new values that emphasize individualism and entrepreneurship are replacing communist values based on collectivism and obedience to the state. The pace of change is accelerating.

Individual managers and organizations must be responsive to changes in, and differences among, the social structures and national cultures of all the countries in which they operate. In today's increasingly integrated global economy, managers are likely to interact with people from several countries, and many managers live and work abroad. Effective managers are sensitive to differences between societies and adjust their behaviors accordingly.

Managers and organizations also must respond to social changes within a society. In the last few decades, for example, Americans have become increasingly interested in their personal health and fitness. Managers who recognized this trend early and exploited the opportunities that resulted from it were able to reap significant gains for their organizations. PepsiCo used the opportunity presented by the fitness trend and took market share from archrival Coca-Cola by being the first to introduce diet colas and fruit-based soft drinks. Quaker Oats made Gatorade the most popular sports drink and brought out a whole host of low-fat food products. The health trend, however, did not offer opportunities to all companies; to some it posed a threat. Tobacco companies came under intense pressure due to consumers' greater awareness of negative health impacts from smoking. Hershey Foods and other manufacturers of candy have been threatened by customers' desires for low-fat, healthy foods. The rage for "low-carb" foods in the 2000s led to a huge increase in demand for meat and hurt bread and doughnut companies such as Kraft and Krispy Kreme.

Demographic Forces

demographic forces Outcomes of changes in, or changing attitudes toward, the characteristics of a population, such as age, gender, ethnic origin, race, sexual orientation, and social class.

Demographic forces are outcomes of changes in, or changing attitudes toward, the characteristics of a population, such as age, gender, ethnic origin, race, sexual orientation, and social class. Like the other forces in the general environment, demographic forces present managers with opportunities and threats and can have major implications for organizations. We examined the nature of these challenges in depth in our discussion of diversity in Chapter 3, so we will not discuss these forces again here.

We will note just one important change occurring today: Most industrialized nations are experiencing the aging of their populations as a consequence of falling birth and death rates and the aging of the baby-boom generation. In Germany, for example, the percentage of the population over age 65 is expected to rise to 20.7% by 2010 from 15.4% in 1990. Comparable figures for Canada are 14.4% and 11.4%; for Japan, 19.5% and 11.7%; and for the United States, 13.5% and 12.6%.[27] In the United States the percentage increase is far smaller because of the huge wave of immigration during the 1990s and the large families that new immigrants typically have. However, the absolute number of older people has increased substantially and is increasing opportunities for organizations that cater to older people; the home health care and recreation industries, for example, are seeing an upswing in demand for their services.

The aging of the population also has several implications for the workplace. Most significant are a relative decline in the young people joining the workforce and an increase in the number of active employees willing to postpone retirement past the traditional retirement age of 65. These changes suggest that organizations need to find ways to motivate and utilize the skills and knowledge of older employees, an issue that many Western societies have yet to tackle.

Political and Legal Forces

political and legal forces Outcomes of changes in laws and regulations, such as the deregulation of industries, the privatization of organizations, and the increased emphasis on environmental protection.

Political and legal forces are outcomes of changes in laws and regulations. They result from political and legal developments that take place within a nation, within a world region, or across the world and significantly affect managers and organizations everywhere. Political processes shape a nation's laws and the international laws that govern the relationships among nations. Laws constrain the operations of organizations and managers, and thus create both opportunities and threats.[28] For example, throughout much of the industrialized world there has been a strong trend toward deregulation of industries previously controlled by the state and privatization of organizations once owned by the state.

In the United States, deregulation of the airline industry in 1978 ushered into the task environment of commercial airlines major changes that are still working themselves out. Deregulation allowed 29 new airlines to enter the industry between 1978 and 1993. The increase in airline passenger-carrying capacity after deregulation led to excess capacity on many routes, intense competition, and fare wars. To respond to this more competitive task environment, in the 1980s airlines looked for ways to reduce operating costs. The development of hub-and-spoke systems, the rise of non-union airlines, and the introduction of no-frills discount service are all responses to increased competition in the airlines' task environment. By the 1990s, once again in control of their environments, airlines were making record profits. However, soaring oil prices in the 2000s wiped out these profits, and airlines found themselves once again under pressure. In 2008, for example, Northest Airlines and Delta reported losses that amounted to $10.6 billion due to high fuel costs; they also announced that they wanted to merge to help reduce costs and protect their future. This merger took place in 2008. Clearly, the shape of the airline industry is changing because of economic and political forces.

Another important political and legal force affecting managers and organizations is the political integration of countries that has been taking place during the past decades.[29] Increasingly, nations are joining together into political unions that allow for the free exchange of resources and capital. The growth of the European Union (EU) is one example: Common laws govern trade and commerce between EU member countries, and the European Court has the right to examine the business of global organizations and to approve any proposed mergers between overseas companies that operate inside the EU. For example, Microsoft's anticompetitive business practices have come under scrutiny, and the court refused to approve a proposed merger between GE and Honeywell that had been approved by U.S. regulators. The North American Free Trade Agreement (NAFTA), discussed later in the chapter, has more modest political goals, but as with the EU, it has changed the laws that affect international commerce by lowering the barriers to the free flow of goods and services between member nations.[30]

Indeed, international agreements to abolish laws and regulations that restrict and reduce trade between countries have been having profound effects on global organizations. The fall in legal trade barriers creates enormous opportunities for companies in one country to sell goods and services in other countries. But, by allowing nondomestic companies to compete in a nation's domestic market for customers, falling trade barriers also pose a serious threat because they increase competition in the task environment. Between 1973 and 2006, for example, Japanese competitors increased their share of the U.S. car market from 3% to 30%.[31] This growth would not have been possible without relatively low trade barriers, which allowed producers in Japan to export cars to the United States. However, competition from Toyota, Honda, and other Japanese companies has forced U.S. car companies to improve their operations. Finding new ways to design and make cars is an ongoing process as they fight to protect their market share, which has continued to fall. Japanese carmakers' market share had grown to over 40% by 2008. In essence, the removal of legal restrictions to global trade has the same effect as deregulating industries and removing restrictions against competition: It increases the intensity of competition in the task environment and forces conservative, slow-moving companies to become more efficient, improve product quality, and learn new values and norms to compete in the global environment.

Deregulation, privatization, and the removal of legal barriers to trade are just a few of the many ways in which changing political and legal forces can challenge organizations and managers. Others include increased emphasis on environmental protection and the preservation of endangered species, increased emphasis on safety in the workplace, and legal constraints against discrimination on the basis of race, gender, or age. Managers face major challenges when they seek to take advantage of the opportunities created by changing political, legal, and economic forces.

The Changing Global Environment

In the 21st century, any idea that the world is composed of a set of distinct national countries and markets that are separated physically, economically, and culturally from one another has vanished. Managers now recognize that companies exist and compete in a truly global market. Today, managers regard the global environment as a source of important opportunities and threats that they must respond to. Managers constantly confront the challenges of global competition–establishing operations in a country abroad or obtaining inputs from suppliers abroad–or the challenges of managing in a different national culture.[32] (See Figure 4.3.)

LO4 Explain why the global environment is becoming more open and competitive and identify the forces behind the process of globalization that increase the opportunities, complexities, challenges, and threats that managers face.

In essence, as a result of falling trade barriers, managers view the global environment as open–that is, as an environment in which companies are free to buy goods and services from, and sell goods and services to, whichever companies and countries they choose. They also are free to compete against each other to attract customers around the world. They must establish an international network of operations and subsidiaries to build global competitive advantage. Coca-Cola and PepsiCo, for example, have competed aggressively for 20 years to develop the strongest global soft-drink empire, just as Toyota and Honda have built hundreds of car plants around the world to provide the vehicles that global customers like. This is also becoming increasingly true in the food processing industry, as the following "Managing Globally" suggests.

Figure 4.3
The Global Environment

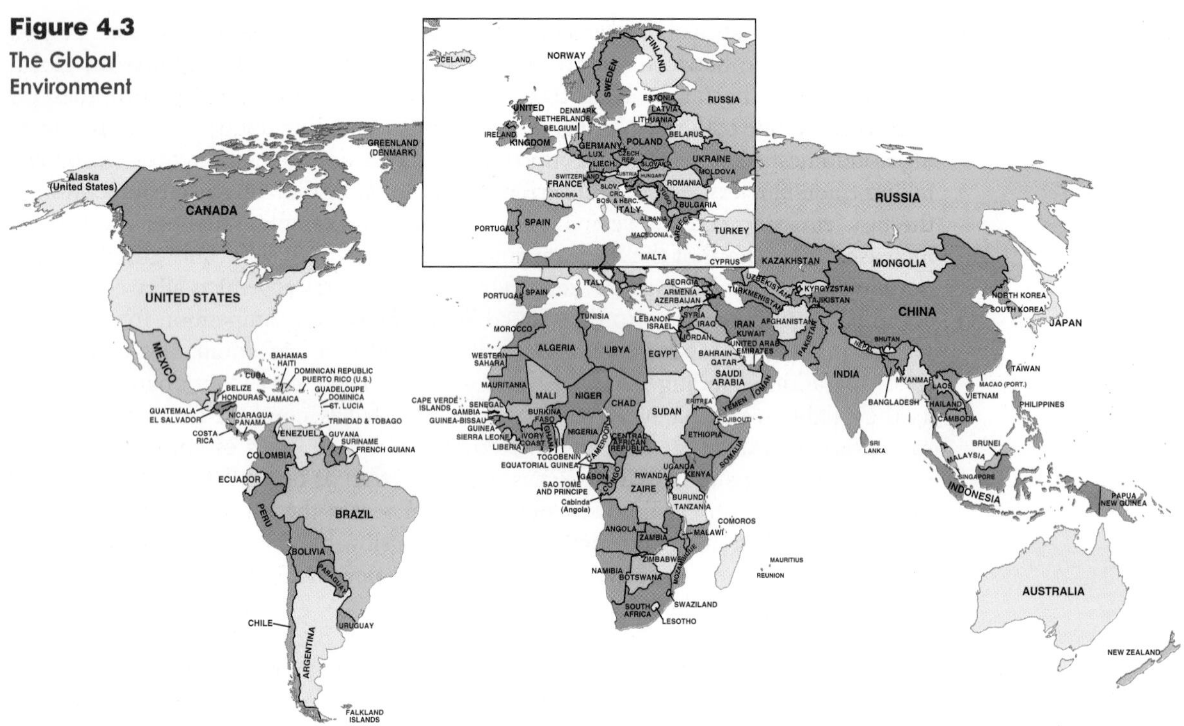

MANAGING GLOBALLY

Customizing Food to the Tastes of Different Cultures

India is a good example of the challenges faced by global food makers, such as Kellogg's and Nestlé, in seeking to expand their global operations and revenues. India's processed food market is worth $90 billion a year and growing. And to compete with domestic food processors, large global food makers have to go to great lengths to make sure their products meet the cultural preferences of Indian consumers. In particular, they have to invest heavily in building food-making plants in the nations in which they do business, often to avoid tariff problems, and they must learn how to customize products extensively to meet the needs of local customers.

Kellogg's in India has learned to offer more than just the standard cornflakes. In recent years, the company has appealed to customers by offering basmati rice and mango-flavored cereal.

When Kellogg's, for example, launched its breakfast cereals in India in the 1990s it failed to understand that most Indians eat cooked breakfasts because milk is normally not pasteurized. Now, with the growing availability of pasteurized or canned milk, it offers exotic cornflakes made from basmati rice and flavored with mango to appeal to customers. Similarly, Nestlé pushed its

Milkmaid condensed milk as being ideal for traditional Indian sweets but with limited success since many local brands are available. Then it took its Maggi noodles brand and once it was given the ethnic "marsala" or mixed curry spice flavor this became a staple in school lunch boxes. It recently launched packaged yogurt.

Today Indian consumers, like those in many Asian nations, are more willing to pay higher prices for convenient packaged foods because of rising incomes and a growing middle class, estimated at some 50 million households. Clearly, given the billions of potential new customers in Asia, as well as in many other developing countries around the world, many challenges remain for global food makers.

In this section, we first explain how this open global environment is the result of globalization and the flow of capital around the world. Next, we examine how specific economic, political, and legal changes, such as the lowering of barriers to trade and investment, have increased globalization and led to greater interaction and exchanges between organizations and countries. Then we discuss how declining barriers of distance and culture have also increased the pace of globalization, and we consider the specific implications of these changes for managers and organizations. Finally, we note that nations still differ widely from each other because they have distinct cultural values and norms and that managers must appreciate these differences if they are to compete successfully across countries.

The Process of Globalization

globalization The set of specific and general forces that work together to integrate and connect economic, political, and social systems across countries, cultures, or geographical regions so that nations become increasingly interdependent and similar.

Perhaps the most important reason why the global environment has become more open and competitive is the increase in globalization. **Globalization** is the set of specific and general forces that work together to integrate and connect economic, political, and social systems *across* countries, cultures, or geographic regions. The result of globalization is that nations and peoples become increasingly *interdependent* because the same forces affect them in similar ways. The fates of peoples in different countries become interlinked as the world's markets and businesses become increasingly interconnected. And, as nations become more interdependent, they become more similar to one another in the sense that people develop a similar liking for products as diverse as cell phones, iPods, blue jeans, Coke, Manchester United, curry, green tea, Japanese cars, and Colombian coffee. One outcome of globalization is that the world is becoming a "global village": Products, services, or people can become well known throughout the world–something IKEA, with its range of furniture designed to appeal to customers around the world, is taking advantage of, as we described at the beginning of the chapter.

But what drives or spurs globalization? What makes people and companies like Nestlé, Toyota, or Microsoft want to venture into an uncertain global environment that puts into motion the complex set of forces that result in globalization? The answer is that the path of globalization is shaped by the ebb and flow of *capital* (valuable wealth-generating assets) as it moves through companies, countries, and world regions seeking its most highly valued use–that is, the investment through which capital can earn the greatest returns (wealth). Managers, employees, and companies like IKEA and Nestlé are motivated to try to profit or benefit by using their skills to make products customers around the world want to buy. Four principal forms of capital flow between countries:

- *Human capital:* the flow of people around the world through immigration, migration, and emigration.

- *Financial capital:* the flow of money capital across world markets through overseas investment, credit, lending, and aid.
- *Resource capital:* the flow of natural resources and semifinished products between companies and countries such as metals, minerals, lumber, energy, food products, microprocessors, and auto parts.
- *Political capital:* the flow of power and influence around the world using diplomacy, persuasion, aggression, and force of arms to protect a country's or world region or political bloc's access to the other forms of capital.

Most of the changes associated with globalization are the result of these four capital flows and the interactions among them, as nations compete on the world stage to protect and increase their standards of living and to further the political goals and social causes that are espoused by their societies' cultures. The next sections look at the factors that have increased the rate at which capital flows between companies and countries. In a positive sense the faster the flow, the more capital is being utilized where it can create the most value, in the sense of people moving to where their skills earn them more money, or investors switching to the stocks or bonds that give them higher dividends or interest, or companies finding lower-cost sources of inputs. In a negative sense, however, a fast flow of capital also means that individual countries or world regions can find themselves in trouble when companies and investors move their capital to invest it in more productive ways in other countries or world regions, often those with lower labor costs or rapidly expanding markets. When capital leaves a country, the result is higher unemployment, recession, and a lower standard of living for its people.

Declining Barriers to Trade and Investment

One of the main factors that has speeded globalization by freeing the movement of capital has been the decline in barriers to trade and investment, discussed earlier. During the 1920s and 1930s, many countries erected formidable barriers to international trade and investment in the belief that this was the best way to promote their economic well-being. Many of these barriers were high tariffs on imports of manufactured goods. A **tariff** is a tax that a government imposes on imported or, occasionally, on exported goods. The aim of import tariffs is to protect domestic industries and jobs, such as those in the auto or steel industry, from overseas competition by raising the price of goods from abroad. In 2001, for example, the U.S. government increased the tariffs on the import of overseas steel to protect U.S. steelmakers; however, under pressure from the European Union, these tariffs were significantly reduced in 2003.

tariff A tax that a government imposes on imported or, occasionally, exported goods.

The reason for removing tariffs is that, very often, when one country imposes an import tariff, others follow suit and the result is a series of retaliatory moves as countries progressively raise tariff barriers against each other. In the 1920s this behavior depressed world demand and helped usher in the Great Depression of the 1930s and massive unemployment. It was to avoid tariffs on U.S. goods entering Europe that the steel tariffs were reduced. In short, rather than protecting jobs and promoting economic well-being, governments of countries that resort to raising high tariff barriers ultimately reduce employment and undermine economic growth.[33]

GATT AND THE RISE OF FREE TRADE After World War II, advanced Western industrial countries, having learned from the Great Depression, committed themselves to the goal of removing barriers to the free flow of resources and capital between countries.

This commitment was reinforced by acceptance of the principle that free trade, rather than tariff barriers, was the best way to foster a healthy domestic economy and low unemployment.[34]

free-trade doctrine The idea that if each country specializes in the production of the goods and services that it can produce most efficiently, this will make the best use of global resources.

The **free-trade doctrine** predicts that if each country agrees to specialize in the production of the goods and services that it can produce most efficiently, this will make the best use of global capital resources and will result in lower prices.[35] For example, if Indian companies are highly efficient in the production of textiles and U.S. companies are highly efficient in the production of computer software, then under a free-trade agreement capital would move to India and be invested there to produce textiles, while capital from around the world would flow to the United States and be invested in its innovative computer software companies. Consequently, prices of both textiles and software should fall because each good is being produced in the location where it can be made at the lowest cost, benefiting consumers and making the best use of scarce capital. This doctrine is, of course, responsible for the increase in global outsourcing and the loss of millions of U.S. jobs in textiles and manufacturing as capital is invested in factories in China and Malaysia. However, millions of jobs have also been created because of new capital investments in high-tech, IT, and the service sector that in theory should offset manufacturing job losses in the long run.

Historically, countries that accepted this free-trade doctrine set as their goal the removal of barriers to the free flow of goods, services, and capital between countries. They attempted to achieve this through an international treaty known as the General Agreement on Tariffs and Trade (GATT). In the half-century since World War II, there have been eight rounds of GATT negotiations aimed at lowering tariff barriers. The last round, the Uruguay Round, involved 117 countries and was completed in December 1993. This round succeeded in lowering tariffs by over 30% from the previous level. It also led to the dissolving of GATT and its replacement by the World Trade Organization (WTO), which today continues the struggle to reduce tariffs and has more power to sanction countries that break global agreements.[36] On average, the tariff barriers among the governments of developed countries declined from over 40% in 1948 to about 3% in 2000, causing a dramatic increase in world trade.[37]

Declining Barriers of Distance and Culture

Historically, barriers of distance and culture also closed the global environment and kept managers focused on their domestic market. The management problems Unilever, the huge British-based, global soap and detergent maker, experienced at the turn of the 20th century illustrate the effect of these barriers.

Founded in London during the 1880s by William Lever, a Quaker, Unilever had a worldwide reach by the early 1900s and operated subsidiaries in most major countries of the British Empire, including India, Canada, and Australia. Lever had a very hands-on, autocratic management style and found his far-flung business empire difficult to control. The reason for Lever's control problems was that communication over great distances was difficult. It took six weeks to reach India by ship from England, and international telephone and telegraph services were very unreliable.

Another problem that Unilever encountered was the difficulty of doing business in societies that were separated from Britain by barriers of language and culture. Different countries have different sets of national beliefs, values, and norms, and Lever found that a management approach that worked in Britain did not necessarily work in India or Persia (now Iran). As a result, management practices had to be tailored to suit each unique national culture. After Lever's death in 1925, top management at Unilever lowered or *decentralized* (see Chapter 7) decision-making authority to the managers of the various national subsidiaries so that they could develop a management approach that suited the country in which they were operating. One result of this strategy was that the subsidiaries grew distant and remote from one another–something that reduced Unilever's performance.[38]

Since the end of World War II, a continuing stream of advances in communications and transportation technology has reduced the barriers of distance and culture that affected Unilever and all global organizations. Over the last 30 years, global communication has been revolutionized by developments in satellites, digital technology, the Internet and global computer networks, and video teleconferencing that allow for the transmission of vast amounts of information and make reliable, secure, and instantaneous communication possible between people and companies anywhere in the world.[39] This revolution has made it possible for a global organization–a tiny garment factory in Li & Fung's network or a huge company such as Nestlé or Unilever–to do business anywhere, anytime, and to search for customers and suppliers around the world.

One of the most important innovations in transportation technology that has made the global environment more open has been the growth of commercial jet travel, which reduced the time it takes to get from one location to another. Because of jet travel, New York is now closer to Tokyo than it was to Philadelphia in the days of the 13 colonies–a fact that makes control of far-flung international businesses much easier today than in William Lever's era. In addition to making travel faster, modern communications and transportation technologies have also helped reduce the cultural distance between countries. The Internet and its millions of Web sites facilitate the development of global communications networks and media that are helping to create a worldwide culture above and beyond unique national cultures. Moreover, television networks such as CNN, MTV, ESPN, BBC, and HBO can now be received in many countries, and Hollywood films are shown throughout the world.

Effects of Free Trade on Managers

The lowering of barriers to trade and investment and the decline of distance and culture barriers has created enormous opportunities for companies to expand the market for their goods and services through exports and investments in overseas countries. Although managers at some organizations, like Barnes & Noble, have shied away from trying to sell their goods and services overseas, the situation of Wal-Mart and Lands' End, which have developed profitable global operations, is more typical. The shift toward a more open global economy has created not only more opportunities to sell goods and services in markets abroad but also the opportunity to buy more from other countries. Indeed, the success in the United States of Lands' End has been based in part on its managers' willingness to import low-cost clothes and bedding from overseas manufacturers. Lands' End purchases clothing from manufacturers in Hong Kong, Malaysia, Taiwan, and China because U.S. textile makers often do not offer the same quality, styling, flexibility, or price.[40] Indeed, most clothing companies, such as Levi Strauss, Wal-Mart, and Target, are major players in the global environment by virtue of their purchasing activities, even if like Target or Dillard's they sell only in the United States.

The manager's job is more challenging in a dynamic global environment because of the increased intensity of competition that goes hand in hand with the lowering of barriers to trade and investment. Thus, as discussed above, the job of the average manager in a U.S. car company became a lot harder from the mid-1970s as a result of the penetration

Mexican workers at CyOptics in Matamoros, Mexico, a high-tech manufacturing facility just across the U.S. border from Brownsville, Texas. CyOptics, a U.S.-owned company, designs, develops, and markets a range of optical chips and components for communications systems. The more competitive environment brought about by NAFTA poses both opportunities and threats for managers.

of the U.S. market by efficient Japanese competitors. Levi Strauss closed its last U.S. clothing factory in 2001 because it could not match the prices of low-cost overseas jeans manufacturers that compete with Levi's to sell to clothing chains such as Wal-Mart, Dillard's, and Target.

REGIONAL TRADE AGREEMENTS The growth of regional trade agreements such as the North American Free Trade Agreement (NAFTA), and most recently the Central American Free Trade Agreement (CAFTA), also presents opportunities and threats for managers and their organizations.

In North America, NAFTA, which became effective on January 1, 1994, had the aim of abolishing the tariffs on 99% of the goods traded between Mexico, Canada, and the United States by 2004. Although it has not achieved this lofty goal, NAFTA has removed most barriers on the cross-border flow of resources, giving, for example, financial institutions and retail businesses in Canada and the United States unrestricted access to the Mexican marketplace. After NAFTA was signed, there was a flood of investment into Mexico from the United States, as well as many other countries such as Japan. Wal-Mart, Costco, Radio Shack, and other major U.S. retail chains have expanded their operations in Mexico; Wal-Mart, for example, is stocking many more products from Mexico in its U.S. stores, and its Mexican store chain is also expanding rapidly.

The establishment of free-trade areas creates an opportunity for manufacturing organizations because it allows them to reduce their costs. They can do this either by shifting production to the lowest-cost location within the free-trade area (for example, U.S. auto and textile companies shifting production to Mexico) or by serving the whole region from one location, rather than establishing separate operations in each country. Some managers, however, view regional free-trade agreements as a threat because they expose a company based in one member country to increased competition from companies based in the other member countries. NAFTA has had this effect; today Mexican managers find themselves facing the threat of head-to-head competition in some industries against efficient U.S. and Canadian companies. But the opposite is true as well: U.S. and Canadian managers are experiencing threats in labor-intensive industries, such as the flooring tile and textile industries, where Mexican businesses have a cost advantage.

In July 2005 the U.S. House of Representatives approved the formation of CAFTA, a regional trade agreement designed to eliminate tariffs on products between the United States and all countries in Central America. By 2006, the Dominican Republic, El Salvador, Guatemala, Nicaragua, and Honduras had also approved and implemented the agreement, but Costa Rica has not. CAFTA is seen as a stepping-stone toward establishing the Free Trade Area of the Americas (FTAA), an ambitious attempt to establish a free-trade agreement that would increase economic prosperity throughout the Americas. FTAA would include all South American and Caribbean nations, except Cuba, as well as those of North and Central America. However, the economic problems many countries have been experiencing, together with major political and ideological differences–such as the political resistance within the United States because of jobs lost to Mexico and Canada–have slowed down the process of integration and globalization. The more competitive environment NAFTA has brought about has increased both the opportunities that managers can take advantage of and the threats they must respond to in performing their jobs effectively.

The Role of National Culture

Despite evidence that countries are becoming more similar to one another because of globalization, and that the world is on the verge of becoming a global village, the cultures of different countries still vary widely because of critical differences in their values, norms, and attitudes. As noted earlier, national culture includes the values, norms, knowledge, beliefs, moral principles, laws, customs, and other practices that unite the citizens of a country.[41] National culture shapes individual behavior by specifying appropriate and inappropriate behavior and interaction with others. People learn national culture in their everyday lives by interacting with those around them. This learning starts at an early age and continues throughout their lives.

Cultural Values and Norms

values Ideas about what a society believes to be good, right, desirable, or beautiful.

The basic building blocks of national culture are values and norms. **Values** are ideas about what a society believes to be good, right, desirable, or beautiful. They provide the basic underpinnings for notions of individual freedom, democracy, truth, justice, honesty, loyalty, social obligation, collective responsibility, the appropriate roles for men and women, love, sex, marriage, and so on. Values are more than merely abstract concepts; they are invested with considerable emotional significance. People argue, fight, and even die over values such as freedom.

Although deeply embedded in society, values are not static; however, change in a country's values is likely to be slow and painful. For example, the value systems of many formerly communist states, such as Russia, are undergoing significant changes as those countries move away from a value system that emphasizes the state and toward one that emphasizes individual freedom. Social turmoil often results when countries undergo major changes in their values.

norms Unwritten, informal codes of conduct that prescribe how people should act in particular situations and are considered important by most members of a group or organization.

folkways The routine social conventions of everyday life.

Norms are unwritten, informal codes of conduct that prescribe appropriate behavior in particular situations and are considered important by most members of a group or organization. They shape the behavior of people toward one another. Two types of norms play a major role in national culture: folkways and mores. **Folkways** are the routine social conventions of everyday life. They concern customs and practices such as dressing appropriately for particular situations, good social manners, eating with the correct utensils, and neighborly behavior. Although folkways define the way people are expected to behave, violation of folkways is not a serious or moral matter. People who violate folkways are often thought to be eccentric or ill-mannered, but they are not usually considered to be evil or bad. In many countries, initially foreigners may be excused for violating folkways because they are unaccustomed to local behavior, but repeated violations are not excused because foreigners are expected to learn appropriate behavior.

mores Norms that are considered to be central to the functioning of society and to social life.

Mores are norms that are considered to be central to the functioning of society and to social life. They have much greater significance than folkways. Accordingly, the violation of mores can be expected to bring serious retribution. Mores include proscriptions against theft, adultery, and incest. In many societies mores have been enacted into law. Thus, all advanced societies have laws against theft and incest. However, there are many differences in mores from one society to another.[42] In the United States, for example, drinking alcohol is widely accepted; but in Saudi Arabia, the consumption of alcohol is viewed as a violation of social norms and is punishable by imprisonment (as many U.S. citizens working in Saudi Arabia have discovered).

Figure 4.4
Hofstede's Model of National Culture

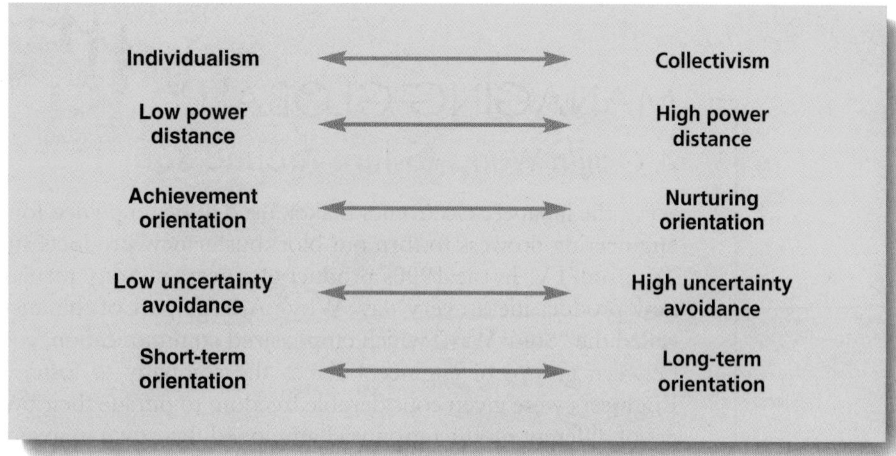

Source: From "Measuring Organizational Cultures: A Qualitative and Quantitative Study across Twenty Cases," by Geert Hofstede, Bram Neuijen, Denise Daval Ohayv, and Geert Sanders, *Administrative Science Quarterly,* Vol. 35, June 1990, pp. 286–316. Reprinted with permission.

LO5 Discuss why national cultures differ and why it is important that managers be sensitive to the effects of falling trade barriers and regional trade associations on the political and social systems of nations around the world.

Hofstede's Model of National Culture

Researchers have spent considerable time and effort identifying similarities and differences in the values and norms of different countries. One model of national culture was developed by Geert Hofstede.[43] As a psychologist for IBM, Hofstede collected data on employee values and norms from more than 100,000 IBM employees in 64 countries. Based on his research, Hofstede developed five dimensions along which national cultures can be placed (see Figure 4.4).[44]

INDIVIDUALISM VERSUS COLLECTIVISM The first dimension, which Hofstede labeled "individualism versus collectivism," has a long history in human thought. **Individualism** is a worldview that values individual freedom and self-expression and adherence to the principle that people should be judged by their individual achievements rather than by their social background. In Western countries, individualism usually includes admiration for personal success, a strong belief in individual rights, and high regard for individual entrepreneurs.[45]

individualism A worldview that values individual freedom and self-expression and adherence to the principle that people should be judged by their individual achievements rather than by their social background.

In contrast, **collectivism** is a worldview that values subordination of the individual to the goals of the group and adherence to the principle that people should be judged by their contribution to the group. Collectivism was widespread in communist countries but has become less prevalent since the collapse of communism in most of those countries. Japan is a noncommunist country where collectivism is highly valued.

collectivism A worldview that values subordination of the individual to the goals of the group and adherence to the principle that people should be judged by their contribution to the group.

Collectivism in Japan traces its roots to the fusion of Confucian, Buddhist, and Shinto thought that occurred during the Tokugawa period in Japanese history (1600–1870s).[46] One of the central values that emerged during this period was strong attachment to the group—whether a village, a work group, or a company. Strong identification with the group is said to create pressures for collective action in Japan, as well as strong pressure for conformity to group norms and a relative lack of individualism.[47]

Managers must realize that organizations and organizational members reflect their national culture's emphasis on individualism or collectivism. Indeed, one of the major reasons why Japanese and American management practices differ is that Japanese culture values collectivism and U.S. culture values individualism, as the following "Managing Globally" suggests.[48]

MANAGING GLOBALLY

A *Gaijin* Works to Turn Around Sony

Sony, the Japanese electronics maker, used to be renowned for using its innovation and engineering prowess to turn out blockbuster new products such as the Walkman and Trinitron TV. In the 1990s product engineers at Sony turned out an average of four new product ideas every day. Why? A large part of the answer was Sony's culture, called the "Sony Way," which emphasized communication, cooperation, and harmony between groups of engineers across the company to foster innovation and change. Engineers were given considerable freedom to pursue their own ideas, and the managers of different product groups championed their own innovations, but problems arose with Sony's approach in the 2000s.

Companies in Korea, Taiwan, and China began to innovate new technologies like digital LCD screens and flash memory that made Sony's technologies obsolete. Companies such as Apple and Nokia came out with the iPod, smartphones, and tablet computers that better fit customer needs than Sony's "old-generation" products such as the Walkman. One reason that Sony experienced major problems responding to these changes was that its culture had changed with its success. The top managers of its many divisions had become used to acting as if they had control of a fiefdom, and, protected by the Japanese tradition of lifetime employment, they worked to promote their own division's interests, not their company's. This competition had increased Sony's bureaucracy and slowed its decision making, making it much harder for Sony to take advantage of its pipeline of new product innovations. At the same time, its research was becoming enormously expensive, as divisions demanded more and more funds to create innovative new products.

Sony's new CEO, Sir Howard Stringer, shakes hands with Sony President and COO Ryoji Chubachi at a news conference in Tokyo in 2006. In his effort to revamp the company, Stringer is confronting difficult, challenging cultural differences while bringing his cost-cutting expertise to bear on Sony's deteriorating situation. Sony is still struggling to regain its former leadership position.

Sensing this was a crucial turning point in their company's history, Sony's Japanese top managers turned to a *gaijin,* or non-Japanese, executive to lead their company. Their choice was Sir Howard Stringer, a Welshman, who headed Sony's North American operations and had been instrumental in cutting costs and increasing the profits of Sony's U.S. division. Stringer cannot speak Japanese, but luckily for him many of Sony's top executives speak English.

Now that he is in command, he faces the problem of reducing costs in Japan, where many Japanese companies have a policy of lifetime employment. He has made it clear that layoffs will be forthcoming, as Sony must reduce its high operating costs. He has also made it clear that the politicking going on between Sony's different product groups must stop and that managers must prioritize new products, investing only in those that have the highest chance of success, for Sony must reduce its huge R&D budget. Indeed, he wants to make engineering, not management, the focus once again at Sony and eliminate the tall, bloated hierarchy that has developed over time–by, for example, downsizing corporate headquarters. In Stringer's own words, the culture or "business of Sony has been management, not making products." However, he has to accomplish this in Japan, which has a national culture known for its collectivist, long-term orientation and for its distrust of *gaijin* or overseas values. And these same values operate inside Sony, so Stringer will have to be hardheaded and push Sony to make the best use of its resources. Stringer demonstrated his hardheaded approach in 2009, when after Sony's losses increased, he replaced his top management team and streamlined the management hierarchy to speed decision making.

power distance The degree to which societies accept the idea that inequalities in the power and well-being of their citizens are due to differences in individuals' physical and intellectual capabilities and heritage.

POWER DISTANCE By **power distance** Hofstede meant the degree to which societies accept the idea that inequalities in the power and well-being of their citizens are due to differences in individuals' physical and intellectual capabilities and heritage. This concept also encompasses the degree to which societies accept the economic and social differences in wealth, status, and well-being that result from differences in individual capabilities.

Societies in which inequalities are allowed to persist or grow over time have *high power distance*. In high-power-distance societies, workers who are professionally successful amass wealth and pass it on to their children, and, as a result, inequalities may grow over time. In such societies, the gap between rich and poor, with all the attendant political and social consequences, grows very large. In contrast, in societies with *low power distance,* large inequalities between citizens are not allowed to develop. In low-power-distance countries, the government uses taxation and social welfare programs to reduce inequality and improve the welfare of the least fortunate. These societies are more attuned to preventing a large gap between rich and poor and minimizing discord between different classes of citizens.

Advanced Western countries such as the United States, Germany, the Netherlands, and the United Kingdom have relatively low power distance and high individualism. Economically poor Latin American countries such as Guatemala and Panama, and Asian countries such as Malaysia and the Philippines, have high power distance and low individualism.[49] These findings suggest that the cultural values of richer countries emphasize protecting the rights of individuals and, at the same time, provide a fair chance of success to every member of society.

achievement orientation A worldview that values assertiveness, performance, success, and competition.

nurturing orientation A worldview that values the quality of life, warm personal friendships, and services and care for the weak.

ACHIEVEMENT VERSUS NURTURING ORIENTATION Societies that have an **achievement orientation** value assertiveness, performance, success, competition, and results. Societies that have a **nurturing orientation** value the quality of life, warm personal relationships, and services and care for the weak. Japan and the United States tend to be achievement-oriented; the Netherlands, Sweden, and Denmark are more nurturing-oriented.

uncertainty avoidance The degree to which societies are willing to tolerate uncertainty and risk.

UNCERTAINTY AVOIDANCE Societies as well as individuals differ in their tolerance for uncertainty and risk. Societies low on **uncertainty avoidance** (such as the United States and Hong Kong) are easygoing, value diversity, and tolerate differences in personal beliefs and actions. Societies high on uncertainty avoidance (such as Japan and France) are more rigid and skeptical about people whose behaviors or beliefs differ from the norm. In these societies, conformity to the values of the social and work groups to which a person belongs is the norm, and structured situations are preferred because they provide a sense of security.

LONG-TERM VERSUS SHORT-TERM ORIENTATION The last dimension that Hofstede described is orientation toward life and work.[50] A national culture with a

long-term orientation A worldview that values thrift and persistence in achieving goals.

short-term orientation A worldview that values personal stability or happiness and living for the present.

long-term orientation rests on values such as thrift (saving) and persistence in achieving goals. A national culture with a **short-term orientation** is concerned with maintaining personal stability or happiness and living for the present. Societies with a long-term orientation include Taiwan and Hong Kong, well known for their high rate of per capita savings. The United States and France have a short-term orientation, and their citizens tend to spend more and save less.

National Culture and Global Management

Differences among national cultures have important implications for managers. First, because of cultural differences, management practices that are effective in one country might be troublesome in another. General Electric's managers learned this while trying to manage Tungsram, a Hungarian lighting products company GE acquired for $150 million. GE was attracted to Tungsram, widely regarded as one of Hungary's best companies, because of Hungary's low wage rates and the possibility of using the company as a base from which to export lighting products to western Europe. GE transferred some of its best managers to Tungsram and hoped it would soon become a leader in Europe. Unfortunately, many problems arose.

One of the problems resulted from major misunderstandings between the American managers and the Hungarian workers. The Americans complained that the Hungarians were lazy; the Hungarians thought the Americans were pushy. The Americans wanted strong sales and marketing functions that would pamper customers. In the prior command economy, sales and marketing activities were unnecessary. In addition, Hungarians expected GE to deliver Western-style wages, but GE came to Hungary to take advantage of the country's low wage structure.[51] As Tungsram's losses mounted, GE managers had to admit that, because of differences in basic attitudes between countries, they had underestimated the difficulties they would face in turning Tungsram around. Nevertheless, by 2001, these problems had been solved, and the increased efficiency of GE's Hungarian operations made General Electric a major player in the European lighting market, causing it to invest another $1 billion.[52]

Often, management practices must be tailored to suit the cultural contexts within which an organization operates. An approach effective in the United States might not work in Japan, Hungary, or Mexico because of differences in national culture. For example, U.S.-style pay-for-performance systems that emphasize the performance of individuals alone might not work well in Japan, where individual performance in pursuit of group goals is the value that receives emphasis.

Managers doing business with individuals from another country must be sensitive to the value systems and norms of that country and behave accordingly. For example, Friday is the Islamic Sabbath. Thus, it would be impolite and inappropriate for a U.S. manager to schedule a busy day of activities for Saudi Arabian managers on a Friday.

A culturally diverse management team can be a source of strength for an organization participating in the global marketplace. Compared to organizations with culturally homogeneous management teams, organizations that employ managers from a variety of cultures have a better appreciation of how national cultures differ, and they tailor their management systems and behaviors to the differences. Indeed, one of the advantages that many Western companies have over their Japanese competitors is greater willingness to build an international team of senior managers.[53]

Summary and Review

WHAT IS THE GLOBAL ENVIRONMENT? The global environment is the set of forces and conditions that operate beyond an organization's boundaries but affect a manager's ability to acquire and utilize resources. The global environment has two components, the task environment and the general environment. **[LO1]**

THE TASK ENVIRONMENT The task environment is the set of forces and conditions that originate with global suppliers, distributors, customers, and competitors that influence managers on a daily basis. The opportunities and threats associated with forces in the task environment become more and more complex as a company expands globally. **[LO2, 3]**

THE GENERAL ENVIRONMENT The general environment comprises wider-ranging global economic, technological, sociocultural, demographic, political, and legal forces that affect an organization and its task environment. **[LO2, 3]**

THE CHANGING GLOBAL ENVIRONMENT In recent years there has been a marked shift toward a more open global environment in which capital flows more freely as people and companies search for new opportunities to create profit and wealth. This has hastened the process of globalization. Globalization is the set of specific and general forces that work together to integrate and connect economic, political, and social systems across countries, cultures, or geographic regions so that nations become increasingly interdependent and similar. The process of globalization has been furthered by declining barriers to international trade and investment and declining barriers of distance and culture. **[LO4, 5]**

Management in Action

Topics for Discussion and Action

Discussion

1. Why is it important for managers to understand the nature of the forces in the global environment that are acting on them and their organizations? [LO1]
2. Which organization is likely to face the most complex task environment, a biotechnology company trying to develop a new cure for cancer or a large retailer like The Gap or Macy's? Why? [LO2, 3]
3. The population is aging because of declining birth rates, declining death rates, and the aging of the baby-boom generation. What might some of the implications of this demographic trend be for (a) a pharmaceutical company and (b) the home construction industry? [LO1, 2, 3]
4. How do political, legal, and economic forces shape national culture? What characteristics of national culture do you think have the most important effect on how successful a country is in doing business abroad? [LO3, 5]
5. After the passage of NAFTA, many U.S. companies shifted production operations to Mexico to take advantage of lower labor costs and lower standards for environmental and worker protection. As a result, they cut their costs and were better able to survive in an increasingly competitive global environment. Was their behavior ethical—that is, did the ends justify the means? [LO4]

Action

6. Choose an organization, and ask a manager in that organization to list the number and strengths of forces in the organization's task environment. Ask the manager to pay particular attention to identifying opportunities and threats that result from pressures and changes in customers, competitors, and suppliers. [LO1, 2, 3]

Building Management Skills

Analyzing an Organization's Environment [LO1, 2, 3]

Pick an organization with which you are familiar. It can be an organization in which you have worked or currently work or one that you interact with regularly as a customer (such as the college that you are currently attending). For this organization do the following:

1. Describe the main forces in the global task environment that are affecting the organization.
2. Describe the main forces in the global general environment that are affecting the organization.
3. Explain how environmental forces affect the job of an individual manager within this organization. How do they determine the opportunities and threats that its managers must confront?

Managing Ethically [LO4, 5]

In recent years, the number of U.S. companies that buy their inputs from low-cost overseas suppliers has been growing, and concern about the ethics associated with employing young children in factories has been increasing. In Pakistan and India, children as young as six years old work long hours to make rugs and carpets for export to Western countries or clay bricks for local use. In countries like Malaysia and in Central America, children and teenagers routinely work long hours in factories and sweatshops to produce the clothing that is found in most U.S. discount and department stores.

Questions

1. Either by yourself or in a group, discuss whether it is ethical to employ children in factories and whether U.S. companies should buy and sell products made by these children. What are some arguments for and against child labor?
2. If child labor is an economic necessity, what ways could be employed to make it as ethical a practice as possible? Or is it simply unethical?

Small Group Breakout Exercise

How to Enter the Copying Business [LO1, 2]

Form groups of three to five people, and appoint one group member as the spokesperson who will communicate your findings to the whole class when called on by the instructor. Then discuss the following scenario:

You and your partners have decided to open a small printing and copying business in a college town of 100,000 people. Your business will compete with companies like FedEx Kinko's. You know that over 50% of small businesses fail in their first year, so to increase your chances of success, you have decided to do a detailed analysis of the task environment of the copying business to discover what opportunities and threats you will encounter. As a group,

1. Decide what you must know about (a) your future customers, (b) your future competitors, and (c) other critical forces in the task environment if you are to be successful.
2. Evaluate the main barriers to entry into the copying business.
3. Based on this analysis, list some of the steps you would take to help your new copying business succeed.

Be the Manager [LO1, 2]

The Changing Environment of Retailing

You are the new manager of a major clothing store that is facing a crisis. This clothing store has been the leader in its market for the last 15 years. In the last three years, however, two other major clothing store chains have opened up, and they have steadily been attracting customers away from your store—your sales are down 30%. To find out why, your store surveyed former customers and learned that they perceive the store as not keeping up with changing fashion trends and new forms of customer service. In examining the way the store operates, you found out that the 10 purchasing managers who buy the clothing and accessories for the store have been buying increasingly from the same clothing suppliers and have become reluctant to try new ones. Moreover, salespeople rarely, if ever, make suggestions for changing the way the store operates, they don't respond to customer requests, and the culture of the store has become conservative and risk-averse.

Questions

1. Analyze the major forces in the task environment of a retail clothing store.
2. Devise a program that will help other managers and employees to better understand and respond to their store's task environment.

BusinessWeek Case in the News [LO1, 3, 4]

Can Outsourcing Save Sony?

Outsourcing isn't a word that executives in Japan like to toss around. Japan Inc. prefers to tie its fortunes to state-of-the-art factories that churn out chips, cars, and flat-screen TVs for the global market. But when Sony Chief Executive Howard Stringer announced on January 22, 2009, that he was considering drastic cost-cutting steps for the company's core electronics division, outsourcing topped his to-do list.

The shift marks a minor victory for Stringer. After more than three years at the helm, Stringer finally appears to be breaking the company's addiction to manufacturing, and to be channeling ever more resources into developing and designing products that users crave. To show he now really means business, the Welsh-born American CEO has said he will close five or six of the company's 57 plants globally and slash the company's budget for factories and chipmaking equipment by a third over the next fiscal year, ending March 2010. "There is no aspect of Sony that isn't being examined right now," Stringer told journalists in Tokyo last week. "We have to move very, very quickly and control our costs."

Sony will spend the next couple of months drawing up a detailed plan. But Stringer appears to have made up his mind about outsourcing one product: TVs. The TV division accounts for 10% of Sony's overall sales but hasn't made a profit since it launched the Bravia brand of flat-panel TVs in 2005.

An In-House Tradition

The shift toward outsourcing is the clearest sign yet that Stringer wants Sony to act more like Apple or Cisco. They consistently earn fatter profit margins by designing their own products and leaving manufacturing to others and have made serious inroads into portable music players and home entertainment systems, where Sony was once king. In contrast, Sony, like many Japanese tech manufacturers, still makes many of its own products in-house, a process known as vertical integration, which "tends to lead to higher overall costs because you need extra layers of management to coordinate all the activities," says Robert Kennedy, a professor at the University of Michigan's Ross School of Business and author of *The Services Shift.*

Before the global financial crisis wiped out consumer spending, Sony seemed confident the TV unit would soon be profitable. The company's LCD TV sales had risen over the past three years, from a little over 1 million units to as many as 15 million expected this fiscal year. Last year, Sony was second in global LCD TV sales, behind Korea's Samsung Electronics.

But the TV unit's problems are now confounding Stringer's efforts to fix what ails Japan's best-known tech brand. Sony officials say they are rushing to centralize TV development and design and consolidate production in Japan after closing one of two domestic plants. "Before the electronics division can be healthy, TVs must be profitable," Ryoji Chubachi, who heads the electronics unit, said last week.

Keeping Secrets

What will Stringer's outsourcing strategy look like? So far, he isn't saying, but experts predict Sony will continue to make ultra-thin high-end TVs on its own. That's where the company can command a premium and earn higher margins. Keeping cutting-edge technology in-house also prevents innovations from being leaked to rivals.

For the small and midsize sets, however, Sony might hire one or more manufacturers in Taiwan or Hong Kong. Wistron, Qisda, AmTRAN Technology, TPV Technology, and Foxconn International, a subsidiary of Taiwan's Hon Hai Precision Industry, have all made LCD TVs for Sony in the past but only in small volumes—less than 8% of Sony's overall TV production last year, according to estimates from market researcher iSuppli. "You might want to keep the premium product, but the commodity product you don't need to be manufacturing yourself," says Macquarie Securities' David Gibson. "It's a simple principle of globalization."

In practice, though, it's anything but simple. To be sure, Sony already relies on contract manufacturers to make some of its point-and-shoot Cybershot digital cameras, Vaio laptops, and PlayStation video game consoles, but Sony's TV unit has always jealously protected its secrets, and outsourcing would mark a serious departure from traditional practice. Currently the company buys the specialized sheets of glass from its joint venture with Samsung and ships them to high-security plants in Asia, North and South America, and Europe for assembly. Most of its suppliers get design specifications for specific parts but know little about the entire assembly process.

Outsourcing doesn't work that way. It involves more collaboration and information sharing. Gartner analyst Yuko Adachi says many U.S. companies begin discussions with contract manufacturers as early as the conceptual or design phase. "It's more of an alliance," she says. Many tech giants have tried to outsource manufacturing to tech companies in Asia, only to end up repeatedly sending teams of designers and engineers to help those companies get up to speed, says iSuppli analyst Adam Pick. Still, says Pick, "If managed properly, [outsourcing products] can be a phenomenal bonus."

Questions

1. What problems is Sony currently experiencing in the global environment?
2. Why is Sony's CEO Howard Stringer considering outsourcing TV production? What potential benefits and costs of outsourcing must Stringer evaluate to make his decision?

Source: Kenji Hall, "Can Outsourcing Save Sony?" Reprinted from *BusinessWeek* online, January 30, 2009, by special permission,

BusinessWeek Case in the News [LO1, 2, 4, 5]

The Other Mexico: A Wave of Investment

K. Alan Russell has spent 23 years clearing bureaucratic and logistical hurdles for U.S. companies running low-cost plants in Ciudad Juárez. Never has he had to do as much hand-holding as now. Each time the Mexican city makes headlines—for kidnappings, murders, or police battles with drug cartels—Russell does damage control. He calls the headquarters of the 28 tenants at his company's industrial parks to tell executives their staff and property are safe. "They need to hear from Ground Zero that there [were] no disruptions and the violence is not affecting their people," he says.

Manufacturers have good reason to hang tough. The 41% drop in the peso against the dollar since August has made Mexico an even cheaper place to manufacture: Factory workers in Juárez can be hired for $1.50 an hour.

Meanwhile, a quiet transformation has begun south of the border. For much of the decade, Mexican officials watched with dismay as multinationals crated up *maquiladora* operations and moved to lower-cost havens in Asia. Mexico's schools, roads, and bureaucracy still rate poorly in international competitiveness rankings, making it hard to graduate to more sophisticated industries.

National statistics obscure the progress several Mexican states and cities have made in boosting their ability to compete. Studying successful models in Asia, the United States, and Europe, local governments collaborate with universities and private industry to upgrade their workforces, parts supply networks, research and development programs, and infrastructure. They have become magnets for factories that go well beyond assembly work. Mexican exports of aerospace products, for example, have nearly tripled, to $3 billion, since 2003. In March, French President Nicolas Sarkozy announced that Eurocopter would invest $550 million to make helicopters in Querétaro, a rising production and engineering base for General Electric and Bombardier.

Mexico also stands to benefit from a subtle but steady shift in strategic thinking by U.S. manufacturers, who are reassessing their reliance on Asia and focusing more on "near-shore" options. Rising Chinese costs and fears of higher trans-Pacific shipping prices if oil spikes again are part of it. With capital scarce and markets hard to forecast, companies don't want to tie up cash in inventory as they wait for their cargo to arrive. Such reasons are driving precision manufacturers like GKN Aerospace, a maker of aircraft engine components, to cluster close to the border in cities like Mexicali. "If you have to reduce costs, China is too far away. Our products can cost $80,000, so we can't afford mistakes," says GKN Mexicali plant manager Ardy Najafian.

Other big factors are China's rampant piracy, quality failures, and communication problems. In Mexico, U.S. companies can better control their operations than in China, where they often must work with government-linked partners. When Fusion Specialties, the number-one maker of mannequins, moved some work offshore in 2007 to cut costs, it chose Juárez over China because goods can reach such U.S. retailers as Nike, Gap, and J. Crew in two days rather than five weeks. Also, "it was a definite risk that we would lose our intellectual property in China," says Richard Moran, vice president for operations at Fusion, which holds patents for its polyurethane molding process.

Some sectors that were devastated by China are already reviving. In February, Beijing's Lenovo opened a plant in Monterrey to make up to 5 million ThinkPad notebook PCs a year. Since October electronics contract manufacturer Jabil Circuit of St. Petersburg, Florida, has more than doubled to 8,000 the staff at its Guadalajara plant, where it shifted some assembly of BlackBerry smartphones from China. Electronics manufacturers Foxconn Electronics of Taiwan and Flextronics have expanded their huge Mexican campuses as well.

Factory jobs are moving from the United States, too. In Mexicali, Skyworks Solutions, a Woburn, Massachusetts, maker of semiconductors for mobile phones and PDAs, is adding 100 jobs to a factory to produce items that had been made in Maryland. Skyworks also has built a 300-strong engineering team. J.C. Nam, the plant's general manager, says two years ago Skyworks considered relocating some work to China, but decided Mexico is actually cheaper because its skilled workforce is more efficient. With engineers' pay averaging around $25,000, including benefits, Nam contends Mexicali's high-tech industry can take off. "We believe there is opportunity in crisis," he says.

With engineering salaries in Mexico starting at around $12,000, the cost gap with India isn't huge. In terms of hourly rates, India is 25% to 30% cheaper than Mexico, says Jagmohan S. Nanaware, general manager of the Monterrey development center of Sasken Communication Technologies, an Indian maker of cell-phone software. But add the indirect costs of travel, high Indian staff turnover, and collaboration at odd hours on complex jobs with colleagues half a world away, and the real gap is closer to 15% to 20%. For many U.S. companies within just an hour or two by air, Monterrey makes more sense. Quality is good, too. "At first we didn't know what kind of engineers we would get, so we brought over six from India," says Nanaware, who doubled his Monterrey staff, to 120, in two years. Within six months, "Mexican engineers were contributing beyond our expectations."

Questions

1. What kinds of advantages can U.S. companies obtain if they move production to Mexico?
2. What are some possible disadvantages and threats of moving production to Mexico?
3. Why are more companies making investments in Mexico as opposed to China?

Source: Pete Engardio and Geri Smith, "The Other Mexico: A Wave of Investment," Reprinted from *BusinessWeek* online, April 9, 2009, by special permission, copyright © 2009 by The McGraw-Hill Companies, Inc.

Decision Making, Learning, Creativity, and Entrepreneurship

CHAPTER 5

Learning Objectives

After studying this chapter, you should be able to

1. Understand the nature of managerial decision making, differentiate between programmed and nonprogrammed decisions, and explain why nonprogrammed decision making is a complex, uncertain process. **[LO1]**
2. Describe the six steps that managers should take to make the best decisions. **[LO2]**
3. Identify the advantages and disadvantages of group decision making, and describe techniques that can improve it. **[LO3]**
4. Explain the role that organizational learning and creativity play in helping managers to improve their decisions. **[LO4]**
5. Describe how managers can encourage and promote entrepreneurship to create a learning organization, and differentiate between entrepreneurs and intrapreneurs. **[LO5]**

The decisions CEO Jochen Zeitz has made at PUMA and the decisions he and other managers continue to make on a day-to-day basis are key contributors to PUMA's success today.

MANAGEMENT SNAPSHOT

Good Decision Making at PUMA

Why Is Decision Making of Paramount Importance in Organizations?

When Jochen Zeitz took over as CEO of PUMA AG in 1993 at the age of 30, the company was facing major threats.[1] PUMA AG, based in the small German sneaker-producing town of Herzogenaurach,[2] had lost money for the past eight years and PUMA North America was facing imminent bankruptcy.[3]

Facing tough decisions about how to turn around the company's fortunes, Zeitz decided that rather than trying to compete based on the performance capabilities of its athletic shoes and equipment, PUMA would focus more on style, colors, and lines of shoes. Essentially, Zeitz saw a potential opportunity in trying to start up a new division focus on experimental fashion and sport as lifestyle. Of course, Zeitz also made difficult decisions to respond to the threats the company was facing by, for example, dramatically reducing costs of production and taking back control over distribution of PUMA products in the United States.[4] And PUMA continues to produce high-performance athletic shoes and gear for serious sport.[5]

Nonetheless, Zeitz's bold decision to pursue the world of fashion and style was a major contributor to PUMA becoming the fourth biggest athletic apparel company worldwide. Recognizing the importance of coming up with creative designs and products, he decided to create a new division called "sport lifestyle" led by Antonio Bertone, then a 21-year-old skateboarder.[6] The division was tasked to create experimental fashion products. In 1998, Bertone partnered with German fashion designer Jil Sander to turn PUMA's traditional 1960s-style cleated soccer shoe into a trendy fashion sneaker using funky colors and suede. At first, this new experimental product line received a lot of skepticism from industry experts and retailers alike; famed soccer player Pelé had worn PUMA cleats, and it was unthinkable to many that PUMA would succeed in the world of fashion. As Zeitz indicates, "It took a while—and from my perspective, a lot of energy—to protect this new little child [the lifestyle group] of PUMA from getting killed . . . Eventually, it became the entire company."[7]

Customers loved the retro look and edgy colors of the new line of sneakers, which are now sold in a variety of venues ranging from the Foot Locker to high-end stores like Barneys to upscale department stores. PUMA has its own showcase boutique in the meatpacking district of Manhattan and 74 stores around the world.[8]

Zeitz continues to pursue new opportunities at PUMA—reinventing traditional products to combine performance with style—and continues to partner with creative thinkers such as Zuly Bet, born in Mali and now a Paris fashion designer, and Yasuhiro Mihara of Japan to create new products.[9]

Former skateboarder Bertone is now based in Boston as PUMA's global director of brand management. Now a top manager, Bertone continues to make decisions to seize opportunities for creative and innovative product lines such as the limited-edition line called Thrift (products made from vintage clothing) and Mongolian Shoe BBQ (shoes that can be customized online).[10]

Zeitz continues to make decisions in response to opportunities and, in the process, has expanded PUMA's range of products in far-reaching directions.[11] Clearly, the decisions Zeitz and other managers make at PUMA are key contributors to the success of PUMA today.[12] And while much uncertainty and ambiguity surrounded these decisions at the time they were made, and they were sometimes met with skepticism, they have propelled PUMA to be a powerhouse of innovation.[13]

Overview

The "Management Snapshot" illustrates how decision making can have a profound influence on organizational effectiveness. The decisions that managers make at all levels in companies large and small can have a dramatic impact on the growth and prosperity of these companies and the well-being of their employees, customers, and other stakeholders. Yet such decisions can be very difficult to make because they are fraught with uncertainty.

In this chapter, we examine how managers make decisions, and we explore how individual, group, and organizational factors affect the quality of the decisions they make and ultimately determine organizational performance. We discuss the nature of managerial decision making and examine some models of the decision-making process that help reveal the complexities of successful decision making. Then we outline the main steps of the decision-making process. Next, we examine how managers can promote organizational learning and creativity and improve the quality of decision making throughout an organization. Finally, we discuss the important role of entrepreneurship in promoting organizational creativity, and we differentiate between entrepreneurs and intrapreneurs. By the end of this chapter, you will appreciate the critical role of management decision making in creating a high-performing organization.

The Nature of Managerial Decision Making

Every time managers act to plan, organize, direct, or control organizational activities, they make a stream of decisions. In opening a new restaurant, for example, managers have to decide where to locate it, what kinds of food to provide to customers, which people to employ, and so on. Decision making is a basic part of every task managers perform.

LO1 Understand the nature of managerial decision making, differentiate between programmed and nonprogrammed decisions, and explain why nonprogrammed decision making is a complex, uncertain process.

As we discussed in the last chapter, one of the main tasks facing a manager is to manage the organizational environment. Forces in the external environment give rise to many opportunities and threats for managers and their organizations. In addition, inside an organization managers must address many opportunities and threats that may arise during the course of utilizing organizational resources. To deal with these opportunities and threats, managers must make decisions–that is, they must select one solution from a set of alternatives. **Decision making** is the process by which managers respond to the opportunities and threats that confront them by analyzing the options and making determinations, or *decisions,* about specific organizational goals and courses of action. Good decisions result in the selection of appropriate goals and courses of action that increase organizational performance; bad decisions result in lower performance.

decision making The process by which managers respond to opportunities and threats by analyzing options and making determinations about specific organizational goals and courses of action.

Decision making in response to opportunities occurs when managers search for ways to improve organizational performance to benefit customers, employees, and other stakeholder groups. In the "Management Snapshot," Jochen Zeitz turned around PUMA's fortunes by the decisions he made in response to opportunities, and he continues to engage in decision making in response to opportunities to this day. *Decision making in response to threats* occurs when events inside or outside the organization are adversely affecting organizational performance and managers are searching for ways to increase performance.[14] When Zeitz become CEO of PUMA, high production costs and an ineffective distribution system were threats that prompted Zeitz to make a number of decisions to improve the performance and viability of the company.[15] Decision making is central to being a manager, and whenever managers engage in planning, organizing, leading, and controlling–their four principal tasks–they are constantly making decisions.

Managers are always searching for ways to make better decisions to improve organizational performance. At the same time, they do their best to avoid costly mistakes that will hurt organizational performance. Examples of spectacularly good decisions include Liz Claiborne's decision in the 1980s to focus on producing clothes for the growing number of women entering the workforce–a decision that contributed to making her company one of the largest clothing manufacturers. Also, Bill Gates's decision to buy a computer operating system for $50,000 from a small company in Seattle and sell it to IBM for the new IBM personal computer turned Gates and Microsoft, respectively, into the richest man and richest software company in the United States. Examples of spectacularly bad decisions include the decision by managers at NASA and Morton Thiokol to launch the *Challenger* space shuttle–a decision that resulted in the deaths of six astronauts in 1986. Also, the decision of Ken Olsen, founder of Digital Equipment Corporation, to stay with mainframe computers in the 1980s and not allow his engineers to spend the company's resources on creating new kinds of personal computers because of his belief that "personal computers are just toys" was a decision that cost Olsen his job as CEO and almost ruined his company.

Programmed and Nonprogrammed Decision Making

Regardless of the specific decisions that a manager makes, the decision-making process is either programmed or nonprogrammed.[16]

An employee takes inventory of office supplies. The decision-making process involved in such a routine, repetitive task is an example of programmed decision making.

PROGRAMMED DECISION MAKING **Programmed decision making** is a *routine,* virtually automatic process. Programmed decisions are decisions that have been made so many times in the past that managers have developed rules or guidelines to be applied when certain situations inevitably occur. Programmed decision making takes place when a school principal asks the school board to hire a new teacher whenever student enrollment increases by 40 students; when a manufacturing supervisor hires new workers whenever existing workers' overtime increases by more than 10%; and when an office manager orders basic office supplies, such as paper and pens, whenever the inventory of supplies on hand drops below a certain level. Furthermore, in the last example, the office manager probably orders the same amount of supplies each time.

programmed decision making Routine, virtually automatic decision making that follows established rules or guidelines.

This decision making is called *programmed* because office managers, for example, do not need to repeatedly make new judgments about what should be done. They can rely on long-established decision rules such as these:

- *Rule 1:* When the storage shelves are three-quarters empty, order more copy paper.
- *Rule 2:* When ordering paper, order enough to fill the shelves.

Managers can develop rules and guidelines to regulate all routine organizational activities. For example, rules can specify how a worker should perform a certain task, and rules can specify the quality standards that raw materials must meet to be acceptable. Most decision making that relates to the day-to-day running of an organization is programmed decision making. Examples include decision making about how much inventory to hold, when to pay bills, when to bill customers, and when to order materials and supplies. Programmed decision making occurs when managers have the information they need to create rules that will guide decision making. There is little ambiguity involved in assessing when the stockroom is empty or counting the number of new students in class.

As profiled in the following "Focus on Diversity," effectively training new employees is essential to reap the benefits of programmed decision making.

NONPROGRAMMED DECISION MAKING Suppose, however, managers are not at all certain that a course of action will lead to a desired outcome. Or, in even more

FOCUS ON DIVERSITY

Programmed Decision Making at UPS

UPS is unrivaled in its use of programmed decision making. Practically all the motions, behaviors, and actions that its drivers perform day in and day out have been carefully honed to maximize efficiency and minimize strain and injuries while delivering high-quality customer service. For example, a 12-step process prescribes how drivers should park their trucks, locate the package they are about to deliver, and step off the truck in 15.5 seconds (a process called "selection" at UPS).[17] Rules and routines such as these are carefully detailed in UPS's "340 Methods" manual (UPS actually has far more than 340 methods). Programmed decision making dictates where drivers should stop to get gas, how they should hold their keys in their hands, and how to lift and lower packages.[18]

When programmed decision making is so heavily relied on, ensuring that new employees learn tried-and-true routines is essential. UPS has traditionally taught new employees with a two-week period of lectures followed by practice.[19] In the 2000s, however, managers began to wonder if they needed to alter their training methods to suit their new Generation Y (Generation Y typically refers to people born after 1980) trainees not so keen on memorization and drills.[20] Generation Y trainees seemed to require more training time to become effective drivers (90–180 days compared to a typical average of 30–45 days), and quit rates for new drivers had increased.[21]

Given the fundamental importance of performance programs for UPS operations, managers decided to try to alter the training new hires receive so it would be better received by Generation Y trainees. In September 2007, UPS opened a new pilot training center called Integrad in Landover, Maryland, which is over 11,000 square feet and cost over $30 million to build and equip. Integrad was developed over a three-year time period through a collaborative effort of over 170 people, including UPS top managers (many of whom started out their careers with UPS as drivers), teams from Virginia Tech and MIT, animators from the Indian company Brainvisa, and forecasters from the Institute for the Future with the support of a grant from the Department of Labor for $1.8 million.[22]

Training at Integrad emphasizes hands-on learning.[23] For example, in Integrad, a UPS truck with transparent sides is used to teach trainees selection so they can actually see the instructor performing the steps and then practice the steps themselves rather than trying to absorb the material in a lecture. Trainees can try out different movements and see, with the help of computer diagrams and simulations, how following UPS routines will help to protect them from injury and how debilitating work as a driver could be to their bodies if they do not follow routines. Video recorders track and document what trainees do correctly and incorrectly so they can see it for themselves rather relying on feedback from an instructor, which they might question. As Stephen Jones, who is in charge of training for UPS and manages Integrad, indicates, "Tell them what they did incorrectly, and they'll tell you, 'I didn't do that. You saw wrong.' This way we've got it on tape and they can see it for themselves."[24]

At Integrad, trainees get practice driving in a pseudo town that has been constructed in a parking lot.[25] And they also watch animated demonstrations on computer screens, participate in simulations, take electronic quizzes, and receive scores on various components that are retained in a database to track learning and performance. Recognizing that Generation Y trainees have a lot of respect for expertise and reputation, older employees also are brought in to facilitate learning at Integrad. Long-time UPS employee Don Petersik, who is about to retire, for example, trains facilitators at Integrad and shares stories with them to reinforce the UPS culture, such as the time he was just starting out as a preloader and, unbeknownst to him, the founder of UPS, Jim Casey, approached him and said, "Hi, I'm Jim. I work for UPS."[26] As Petersik indicates, "What's new about the company now is that our teaching style matches your learning styles."[27] Clearly, when learning programmed decision making is of utmost importance, as it is at UPS, it is essential to take into account diversity in learning styles and approaches.

ambiguous terms, suppose managers are not even clear about what they are really trying to achieve. Obviously, rules cannot be developed to predict uncertain events.

nonprogrammed decision making Nonroutine decision making that occurs in response to unusual, unpredictable opportunities and threats.

Nonprogrammed decision making is required for these *nonroutine* decisions. Nonprogrammed decisions are made in response to unusual or novel opportunities and threats. Nonprogrammed decision making occurs when there are no ready-made decision rules that managers can apply to a situation. Rules do not exist because the situation is unexpected or uncertain and managers lack the information they would need to develop rules to cover it. Examples of nonprogrammed decision making include decisions to invest in a new kind of technology, develop a new kind of product, as did Jochen Zeitz in the "Management Snapshot," launch a new promotional campaign, enter a new market, expand internationally, or start a new business.

intuition Feelings, beliefs, and hunches that come readily to mind, require little effort and information gathering, and result in on-the-spot decisions.

reasoned judgment A decision that takes time and effort to make and results from careful information gathering, generation of alternatives, and evaluation of alternatives.

How do managers make decisions in the absence of decision rules? They may rely on their **intuition**–feelings, beliefs, and hunches that come readily to mind, require little effort and information gathering, and result in on-the-spot decisions.[28] Or they may make **reasoned judgments**–decisions that take time and effort to make and result from careful information gathering, generation of alternatives, and evaluation of alternatives. "Exercising" one's judgment is a more rational process than "going with" one's intuition. For reasons that we examine later in this chapter, both intuition and judgment often are flawed and can result in poor decision making. Thus, the likelihood of error is much greater in nonprogrammed decision making than in programmed decision making.[29] In the remainder of this chapter, when we talk about decision making, we are referring to *nonprogrammed* decision making because it causes the most problems for managers and is inherently challenging.

Sometimes managers have to make rapid decisions and don't have the time for careful consideration of the issues involved. They must rely on their intuition to quickly respond to a pressing concern. For example, when fire chiefs, captains, and lieutenants manage firefighters battling dangerous, out-of-control fires, they often need to rely on their expert intuition to make on-the-spot decisions that will protect the lives of the firefighters and save the lives of others, contain the fires, and preserve property–decisions made in emergency situations entailing high uncertainty, high risk, and rapidly changing conditions.[30] Other times, managers do have the time available to make reasoned judgments but there are no established rules to guide their decisions, such as when deciding whether or not to proceed with a proposed merger. Regardless of the circumstances, making nonprogrammed decisions can result in effective or ineffective decision making.

The *classical* and the *administrative* decision-making models reveal many of the assumptions, complexities, and pitfalls that affect decision making. These models help reveal the factors that managers and other decision makers must be aware of to improve the quality of their decision making. Keep in mind, however, that the classical and administrative models are just guides that can help managers understand the decision-making process. In real life, the process is typically not cut-and-dried, but these models can help guide a manager through it.

classical decision-making model A prescriptive approach to decision making based on the assumption that the decision maker can identify and evaluate all possible alternatives and their consequences and rationally choose the most appropriate course of action.

optimum decision The most appropriate decision in light of what managers believe to be the most desirable future consequences for the organization.

administrative model An approach to decision making that explains why decision making is inherently uncertain and risky and why managers usually make satisfactory rather than optimum decisions.

The Classical Model

One of the earliest models of decision making, the **classical model,** is *prescriptive,* which means that it specifies how decisions *should* be made. Managers using the classical model make a series of simplifying assumptions about the nature of the decision-making process (see Figure 5.1). The premise of the classical model is that once managers recognize the need to make a decision, they should be able to generate a complete list of *all* alternatives and consequences and make the best choice. In other words, the classical model assumes that managers have access to *all* the information they need to make the **optimum decision,** which is the most appropriate decision possible in light of what they believe to be the most desirable future consequences for the organization. Furthermore, the classical model assumes that managers can easily list their own preferences for each alternative and rank them from least to most preferred to make the optimum decision.

The Administrative Model

James March and Herbert Simon disagreed with the underlying assumptions of the classical model of decision making. In contrast, they proposed that managers in the real world do *not* have access to all the information they need to make a decision. Moreover, they pointed out that even if all information were readily available, many managers would lack the mental or psychological ability to absorb and evaluate it correctly. As a result, March and Simon developed the **administrative model** of decision making to explain why decision making is always an inherently uncertain and risky process–and why managers can rarely make decisions in the manner prescribed by the classical model. The administrative model is based on three important concepts: *bounded rationality, incomplete information,* and *satisficing.*

Figure 5.1
The Classical Model of Decision Making

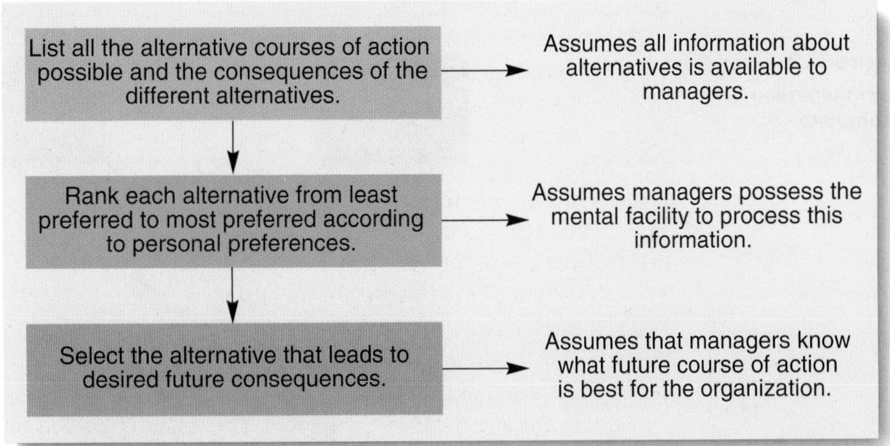

BOUNDED RATIONALITY March and Simon pointed out that human decision-making capabilities are bounded by people's cognitive limitations–that is, limitations in their ability to interpret, process, and act on information.[31] They argued that the limitations of human intelligence constrain the ability of decision makers to determine the optimum decision. March and Simon coined the term **bounded rationality** to describe the situation in which the number of alternatives a manager must identify is so great and the amount of information so vast that it is difficult for the manager to even come close to evaluating it all before making a decision.[32]

bounded rationality Cognitive limitations that constrain one's ability to interpret, process, and act on information.

INCOMPLETE INFORMATION Even if managers did have an unlimited ability to evaluate information, they still would not be able to arrive at the optimum decision because they would have incomplete information. Information is incomplete because the full range of decision-making alternatives is unknowable in most situations and the consequences associated with known alternatives are uncertain.[33] In other words, information is incomplete because of risk and uncertainty, ambiguity, and time constraints (see Figure 5.2).

RISK AND UNCERTAINTY As we saw in Chapter 4, forces in the organizational environment are constantly changing. **Risk** is present when managers know the possible outcomes of a particular course of action and can assign probabilities to them. For example, managers in the biotechnology industry know that new drugs have a 10% probability of successfully passing advanced clinical trials and a 90% probability of failing. These probabilities reflect the experiences of thousands of drugs that have gone through advanced clinical trials. Thus, when managers in the biotechnology industry decide to submit a drug for testing, they know that there is only a 10% chance that the drug will succeed, but at least they have some information on which to base their decision.

risk The degree of probability that the possible outcomes of a particular course of action will occur.

When **uncertainty** exists, the probabilities of alternative outcomes *cannot* be determined and future outcomes are *unknown*. Managers are working blind. Since the probability of a given outcome occurring is *not* known, managers have little information to use in making a decision. For example, in 1993, when Apple Computer introduced the Newton, its personal digital assistant (PDA), managers had no idea what the probability of a successful product launch for a PDA might be. Because Apple was the first to market this totally new product, there was no body of well-known data that Apple's managers could draw on to calculate the probability of a successful launch.

uncertainty Unpredictability.

Figure 5.2
Why Information Is Incomplete

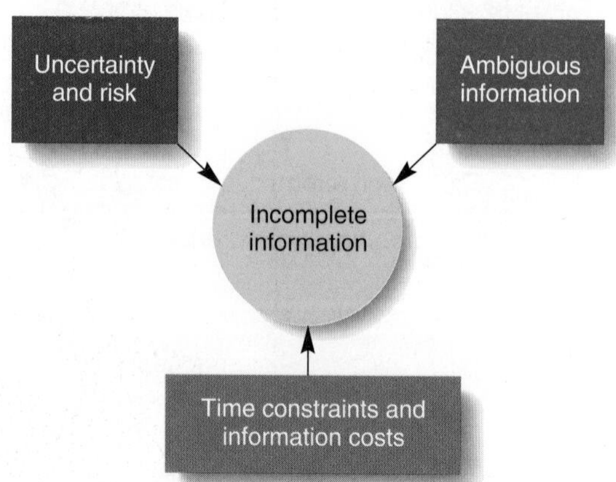

Uncertainty plagues most managerial decision making.[34] Although Apple's initial launch of its PDA was a disaster due to technical problems, an improved version was more successful. In fact, Apple created the PDA market that has boomed during the 2000s as new and different wireless products have been introduced.

ambiguous information Information that can be interpreted in multiple and often conflicting ways.

AMBIGUOUS INFORMATION A second reason information is incomplete is that much of the information managers have at their disposal is ambiguous information. Its meaning is not clear–it can be interpreted in multiple and often conflicting ways.[35] Take a look at Figure 5.3. Do you see a young woman or an old woman? In a similar fashion, managers often interpret the same piece of information differently and make decisions based on their own interpretations.

TIME CONSTRAINTS AND INFORMATION COSTS The third reason information is incomplete is that managers have neither the time nor the money to search for all possible alternative solutions and evaluate all the potential consequences of those alternatives. Consider the situation confronting a Ford Motor Company purchasing manager who has one month to choose a supplier for a small engine part. Of the thousands of potential suppliers for this part, there are 20,000 in the United States alone. Given the time available, the purchasing manager cannot contact all potential suppliers and ask each for its terms (price, delivery schedules, and so on). Moreover, even if the time were available, the costs of obtaining the information, including the manager's own time, would be prohibitive.

satisficing Searching for and choosing an acceptable, or satisfactory, response to problems and opportunities, rather than trying to make the best decision.

SATISFICING March and Simon argue that managers do not attempt to discover every alternative when faced with bounded rationality, an uncertain future, unquantifiable risks, considerable ambiguity, time constraints, and high information costs. Rather, they use a strategy known as satisficing, exploring a limited sample of all potential alternatives.[36] When managers satisfice, they search for and choose acceptable, or satisfactory, ways to respond to problems and opportunities rather than trying to make the optimal decision.[37] In the case of the Ford purchasing manager's search, for example, satisficing may involve asking a limited number of suppliers for their terms, trusting that they are representative of suppliers in general, and making a choice

Figure 5.3 Ambiguous Information: Young Woman or Old Woman?

from that set. Although this course of action is reasonable from the perspective of the purchasing manager, it may mean that a potentially superior supplier is overlooked.

March and Simon pointed out that managerial decision making is often more art than science. In the real world, managers must rely on their intuition and judgment to make what seems to them to be the best decision in the face of uncertainty and ambiguity.[38] Moreover, managerial decision making is often fast-paced, as managers use their experience and judgment to make crucial decisions under conditions of incomplete information. Although there is nothing wrong with this approach, decision makers should be aware that human judgment is often flawed. As a result, even the best managers sometimes end up making very poor decisions.[39]

Steps in the Decision-Making Process

Using the work of March and Simon as a basis, researchers have developed a step-by-step model of the decision-making process and the issues and problems that managers confront at each step. Perhaps the best way to introduce this model is to examine the real-world nonprogrammed decision making that Scott McNealy had to engage in at a crucial point in Sun Microsystems' history.

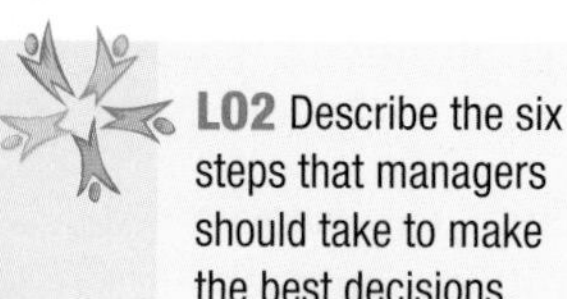

LO2 Describe the six steps that managers should take to make the best decisions.

In early August 1985, Scott McNealy, CEO of Sun Microsystems[40] (a hardware and software computer workstation manufacturer focused on network solutions), had to decide whether to go ahead with the launch of the new Carrera workstation computer, scheduled for September 10. Sun's managers had chosen the date nine months earlier when the development plan for the Carrera was first proposed. McNealy knew that it would take at least a month to prepare for the September 10 launch and that the decision could not be put off.

Customers were waiting for the new machine, and McNealy wanted to be the first to provide a workstation that took advantage of Motorola's powerful 16-megahertz 68020 microprocessor. Capitalizing on this opportunity would give Sun a significant edge over Apollo, its main competitor in the workstation market. McNealy knew, however, that committing to the September 10 launch date was risky. Motorola was having production problems with the 16-megahertz 68020 microprocessor and could not guarantee Sun a steady supply of these chips. Moreover, the operating system software was not completely free of bugs.

If Sun launched the Carrera on September 10, the company might have to ship some machines with software that was not fully operational, was prone to crash the system, and utilized Motorola's less powerful 12-megahertz 68020 microprocessor instead of the 16-megahertz version.[41] Of course, Sun could later upgrade the microprocessor and operating system software in any machines purchased by early customers, but the company's reputation would suffer as a result. If Sun did not go ahead with the September launch, the company would miss an important opportunity.[42] Rumors were circulating in the industry that Apollo would be launching a new machine of its own in December.

Scott McNealy clearly had a difficult decision to make. He had to decide quickly whether to launch the Carrera, but he was not in possession of all the facts. He did not know, for example, whether the microprocessor or operating system problems could be resolved by September 10; nor did he know whether Apollo was going to launch a competing machine in December. But he could not wait to find these things out–he had to make a decision. We'll see what he decided later in the chapter.

Many managers who must make important decisions with incomplete information face dilemmas similar to McNealy's. There are six steps that managers should

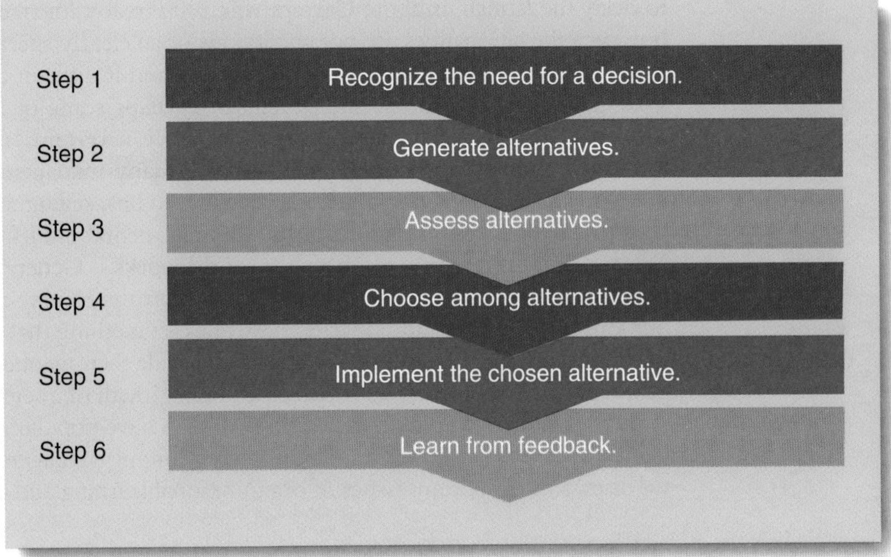

Figure 5.4
Six Steps in Decision Making

consciously follow to make a good decision (see Figure 5.4).[43] We review them in the remainder of this section.

Recognize the Need for a Decision

The first step in the decision-making process is to recognize the need for a decision. Scott McNealy recognized this need, and he realized that a decision had to be made quickly.

Some stimuli usually spark the realization that there is a need to make a decision. These stimuli often become apparent because changes in the organizational environment result in new kinds of opportunities and threats. This happened at Sun Microsystems. The September 10 launch date had been set when it seemed that Motorola chips would be readily available. Later, with the supply of chips in doubt and bugs remaining in the system software, Sun was in danger of failing to meet its launch date.

The stimuli that spark decision making are as likely to result from the actions of managers inside an organization as they are from changes in the external environment.[44] An organization possesses a set of skills, competencies, and resources in its employees and in departments such as marketing, manufacturing, and research and development. Managers who actively pursue opportunities to use these competencies create the need to make decisions. Managers thus can be proactive or reactive in recognizing the need to make a decision, but the important issue is that they must recognize this need and respond in a timely and appropriate way.[45]

Generate Alternatives

Having recognized the need to make a decision, a manager must generate a set of feasible alternative courses of action to take in response to the opportunity or threat. Management experts cite failure to properly generate and consider different alternatives as one reason why managers sometimes make bad decisions.[46] In the Sun Microsystems decision, the alternatives seemed clear: to go ahead with the September 10 launch or to delay the launch until the Carrera was 100% ready for market introduction. Often, however, the alternatives are not so obvious or so clearly specified.

One major problem is that managers may find it difficult to come up with creative alternative solutions to specific problems. Perhaps some of them are used to seeing the world from a single perspective–they have a certain "managerial mind-set." In a manner similar to that of Digital's Olsen, many managers find it difficult to view problems from a fresh perspective. According to best-selling management author Peter Senge, we all are trapped within our personal mental models of the world–our ideas about what is important and how the world works.[47] Generating creative alternatives to solve problems and take advantage of opportunities may require that we abandon our existing mind-sets and develop new ones–something that usually is difficult to do.

The importance of getting managers to set aside their mental models of the world and generate creative alternatives is reflected in the growth of interest in the work of authors such as Peter Senge and Edward de Bono, who have popularized techniques for stimulating problem solving and creative thinking among managers.[48] Later in this chapter, we discuss the important issues of organizational learning and creativity in detail.

Assess Alternatives

Once managers have generated a set of alternatives, they must evaluate the advantages and disadvantages of each one.[49] The key to a good assessment of the alternatives is to define the opportunity or threat exactly and then specify the criteria that *should* influence the selection of alternatives for responding to the problem or opportunity. One reason for bad decisions is that managers often fail to specify the criteria that are important in reaching a decision.[50] In general, successful managers use four criteria to evaluate the pros and cons of alternative courses of action (see Figure 5.5):

1. *Legality:* Managers must ensure that a possible course of action is legal and will not violate any domestic and international laws or government regulations.

Figure 5.5
General Criteria for Evaluating Possible Courses of Action

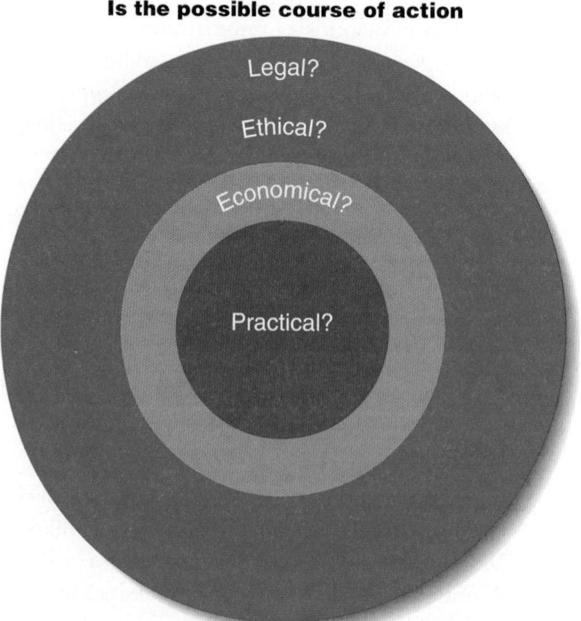

2. *Ethicalness:* Managers must ensure that a possible course of action is ethical and will not unnecessarily harm any stakeholder group. Many of the decisions that managers make may help some organizational stakeholders and harm others (see Chapter 3). When examining alternative courses of action, managers need to be very clear about the potential effects of their decisions.
3. *Economic feasibility:* Managers must decide whether the alternatives are economically feasible–that is, whether they can be accomplished given the organization's performance goals. Typically, managers perform a cost–benefit analysis of the various alternatives to determine which one will have the best net financial payoff.
4. *Practicality:* Managers must decide whether they have the capabilities and resources required to implement the alternative, and they must be sure that the alternative will not threaten the attainment of other organizational goals. At first glance, an alternative might seem to be economically superior to other alternatives, but if managers realize that it is likely to threaten other important projects, they might decide that it is not practical after all.

Very often, a manager must consider these four criteria simultaneously. Scott McNealy framed the problem at hand at Sun Microsystems quite well. The key question was whether to go ahead with the September 10 launch date. Two main criteria were influencing McNealy's choice: the need to ship a machine that was as "complete" as possible (the *practicality* criterion) and the need to beat Apollo to market with a new workstation (the *economic feasibility* criterion). These two criteria conflicted. The first suggested that the launch should be delayed; the second, that the launch should go ahead. McNealy's actual choice was based on the relative importance that he assigned to these two criteria. In fact, Sun Microsystems went ahead with the September 10 launch, which suggests that McNealy thought the need to beat Apollo to market was the more important criterion.

Some of the worst managerial decisions can be traced to poor assessment of the alternatives, such as the decision to launch the *Challenger* space shuttle, mentioned earlier. In that case, the desire of NASA and Morton Thiokol managers to demonstrate to the public the success of the U.S. space program in order to ensure future funding (*economic feasibility*) conflicted with the need to ensure the safety of the astronauts (*ethicalness*). Managers deemed the economic criterion more important and decided to launch the space shuttle even though there were unanswered questions about safety. Tragically, some of the same decision-making problems that resulted in the *Challenger* tragedy led to the demise of the *Columbia* space shuttle in 2003, 17 years later, killing all seven astronauts on board.[51] In both the *Challenger* and the *Columbia* disasters, safety questions were raised before the shuttles were launched; safety concerns took second place to budgets, economic feasibility, and schedules; top decision makers seemed to ignore or downplay the inputs of those with relevant technical expertise; and speaking up was discouraged.[52] Rather than making safety a top priority, decision makers seemed overly concerned with keeping on schedule and within budget.[53]

Choose among Alternatives

Once the set of alternative solutions has been carefully evaluated, the next task is to rank the various alternatives (using the criteria discussed in the previous section) and make a decision. When ranking alternatives, managers must be sure *all* the information available is brought to bear on the problem or issue at hand. As the Sun Microsystems case indicates, however, identifying all *relevant* information for a decision does not mean that the manager has *complete* information; in most instances, information is incomplete.

Perhaps more serious than the existence of incomplete information is the often-documented tendency of managers to ignore critical information, even when it is available. We discuss this tendency in detail below when we examine the operation of cognitive biases and groupthink.

Implement the Chosen Alternative

Once a decision has been made and an alternative has been selected, it must be implemented, and many subsequent and related decisions must be made. After a course of action has been decided–say, to develop a new line of women's clothing–thousands of subsequent decisions are necessary to implement it. These decisions would involve recruiting dress designers, obtaining fabrics, finding high-quality manufacturers, and signing contracts with clothing stores to sell the new line.

Although the need to make subsequent decisions to implement the chosen course of action may seem obvious, many managers make a decision and then fail to act on it. This is the same as not making a decision at all. To ensure that a decision is implemented, top managers must assign to middle managers the responsibility for making the follow-up decisions necessary to achieve the goal. They must give middle managers sufficient resources to achieve the goal, and they must hold the middle managers accountable for their performance. If the middle managers are successful at implementing the decision, they should be rewarded; if they fail, they should be subject to sanctions.

Learn from Feedback

The final step in the decision-making process is learning from feedback. Effective managers always conduct a retrospective analysis to see what they can learn from past successes or failures.[54] Managers who do not evaluate the results of their decisions do not learn from experience; instead, they stagnate and are likely to make the same mistakes again and again.[55] To avoid this problem, managers must establish a formal procedure with which they can learn from the results of past decisions. The procedure should include these steps:

1. Compare what actually happened to what was expected to happen as a result of the decision.
2. Explore why any expectations for the decision were not met.
3. Derive guidelines that will help in future decision making.

Managers who always strive to learn from past mistakes and successes are likely to continuously improve the decisions they make. A significant amount of learning can take place when the outcomes of decisions are evaluated, and this assessment can produce enormous benefits.

Group Decision Making

Many, perhaps most, important organizational decisions are made by groups or teams of managers rather than by individuals. Group decision making is superior to individual decision making in several respects. When managers work as a team to make decisions and solve problems, their choices of alternatives are less likely to fall victim to the biases and errors discussed previously. They are able to draw on the combined skills, competencies, and accumulated knowledge of group

LO3 Identify the advantages and disadvantages of group decision making, and describe techniques that can improve it.

members and thereby improve their ability to generate feasible alternatives and make good decisions. Group decision making also allows managers to process more information and to correct one another's errors. And in the implementation phase, all managers affected by the decisions agree to cooperate. When a group of managers makes a decision (as opposed to one top manager making a decision and imposing it on subordinate managers), the probability that the decision will be implemented successfully increases.

There are some potential disadvantages associated with group decision making. Groups often take much longer than individuals to make decisions. Getting two or more managers to agree to the same solution can be difficult because managers' interests and preferences are often different. In addition, just like decision making by individual managers, group decision making can be undermined by biases. A major source of group bias is *groupthink*.

The Perils of Groupthink

groupthink A pattern of faulty and biased decision making that occurs in groups whose members strive for agreement among themselves at the expense of accurately assessing information relevant to a decision.

Groupthink is a pattern of faulty and biased decision making that occurs in groups whose members strive for agreement among themselves at the expense of accurately assessing information relevant to a decision.[56] When managers are subject to groupthink, they collectively embark on a course of action without developing appropriate criteria to evaluate alternatives. Typically, a group rallies around one central manager, such as the CEO, and the course of action that manager supports. Group members become blindly committed to that course of action without evaluating its merits. Commitment is often based on an emotional, rather than an objective, assessment of the optimal course of action.

The decision President Kennedy and his advisers made to launch the unfortunate Bay of Pigs invasion in Cuba in 1962, the decisions made by President Johnson and his advisers from 1964 to 1967 to escalate the war in Vietnam, the decision made by President Nixon and his advisers in 1972 to cover up the Watergate break-in, and the decision made by NASA and Morton Thiokol in 1986 to launch the ill-fated *Challenger* shuttle all were likely influenced by groupthink. After the fact, decision makers such as these who may fall victim to groupthink are often surprised that their decision-making process and outcomes were so flawed.

The 1986 disastrous take-off of the space shuttle *Challenger.*

When groupthink occurs, pressures for agreement and harmony within a group have the unintended effect of discouraging individuals from raising issues that run counter to majority opinion. For example, when managers at NASA and Morton Thiokol fell victim to groupthink, they convinced each other that all was well and that there was no need to delay the launch of the *Challenger* space shuttle.

Devil's Advocacy

The existence of groupthink raises the question of how to improve the quality of group and individual decision making so that managers make decisions that are realistic and are based on a thorough evaluation of alternatives. One technique known to counteract groupthink is devil's advocacy.[57]

devil's advocacy Critical analysis of a preferred alternative, made in response to challenges raised by a group member who, playing the role of devil's advocate, defends unpopular or opposing alternatives for the sake of argument.

Devil's advocacy is a critical analysis of a preferred alternative to ascertain its strengths and weaknesses before it is implemented.[58] Typically, one member of the decision-making group plays the role of devil's advocate. The devil's advocate critiques and challenges the way the group evaluated alternatives and chose one over the others. The purpose of devil's advocacy is to identify all the reasons that might make the preferred alternative unacceptable after all. In this way, decision makers can be made aware of the possible perils of recommended courses of action.

Devil's advocacy can thus help counter the effects of groupthink.[59] In practice, devil's advocacy is a fairly easy method to implement because it does not involve excessive amounts of managers' time and effort.

Diversity among Decision Makers

Another way to improve group decision making is to promote diversity in decision-making groups (see Chapter 3).[60] Bringing together managers of both genders from various ethnic, national, and functional backgrounds broadens the range of life experiences and opinions that group members can draw on as they generate, assess, and choose among alternatives. Moreover, diverse groups are sometimes less prone to groupthink because group members already differ from each other and thus are less subject to pressures for uniformity.

Organizational Learning and Creativity

The quality of managerial decision making ultimately depends on innovative responses to opportunities and threats. How can managers increase their ability to make nonprogrammed decisions, decisions that will allow them to adapt to, modify, and even drastically alter their task environments so that they can continually increase organizational performance? The answer is by encouraging organizational learning.[61]

LO4 Explain the role that organizational learning and creativity play in helping managers to improve their decisions.

Organizational learning is the process through which managers seek to improve employees' desire and ability to understand and manage the organization and its task environment so that employees can make decisions that continuously raise organizational effectiveness.[62] A **learning organization** is one in which managers do everything possible to maximize the ability of individuals and groups to think and behave creatively and thus maximize the potential for organizational learning to take place. At the heart of organizational learning is **creativity**, the ability of a decision maker to discover original and novel ideas that lead to feasible alternative courses of action. When new and useful ideas are implemented in an organization, **innovation** takes place. Encouraging creativity among managers is such a pressing organizational concern that many organizations hire outside experts to help them develop programs to train their managers in the art of creative thinking and problem solving.

organizational learning The process through which managers seek to improve employees' desire and ability to understand and manage the organization and its task environment.

Creating a Learning Organization

How do managers go about creating a learning organization? Learning theorist Peter Senge identified five principles for creating a learning organization (see Figure 5.6):[63]

1. For organizational learning to occur, top managers must allow every person in the organization to develop a sense of *personal mastery*. Managers must empower employees and allow them to experiment and create and explore what they want.

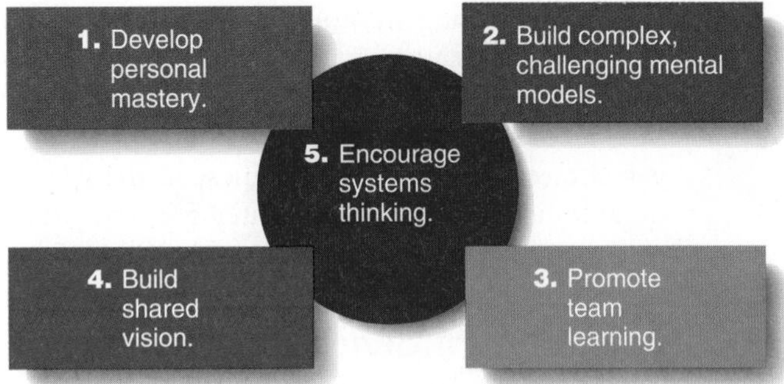

Figure 5.6
Senge's Principles for Creating a Learning Organization

learning organization An organization in which managers try to maximize the ability of individuals and groups to think and behave creatively and thus maximize the potential for organizational learning to take place.

creativity A decision maker's ability to discover original and novel ideas that lead to feasible alternative courses of action.

innovation The implementation of creative ideas in an organization.

2. As part of attaining personal mastery, organizations need to encourage employees to develop and use *complex mental models*–sophisticated ways of thinking that challenge them to find new or better ways of performing a task–to deepen their understanding of what is involved in a particular activity. Here Senge is arguing that managers must encourage employees to develop a taste for experimenting and risk taking.[64]
3. Managers must do everything they can to promote group creativity. Senge thinks that *team learning* (learning that takes place in a group or team) is more important than individual learning in increasing organizational learning. He points out that most important decisions are made in subunits such as groups, functions, and divisions.
4. Managers must emphasize the importance of *building a shared vision*–a common mental model that all organizational members use to frame problems or opportunities.
5. Managers must encourage *systems thinking*. Senge emphasizes that to create a learning organization, managers must recognize the effects of one level of learning on another. Thus, for example, there is little point in creating teams to facilitate team learning if managers do not also take steps to give employees the freedom to develop a sense of personal mastery.

Building a learning organization requires that managers change their management assumptions radically. Developing a learning organization is neither a quick nor an easy process. Senge has been working with Ford Motor Company to help managers make Ford a learning organization. Why does Ford want this? Top management believes that to compete successfully, Ford must improve its members' ability to be creative and make the right decisions.

Increasingly, managers are being called on to promote global organizational learning. For example, managers at Wal-Mart use the lessons derived from its failures and successes in one country to promote global organizational learning across the many countries in which it now operates. For instance, when Wal-Mart entered Malaysia, it was convinced customers there would respond to its one-stop shopping format. It found, however, that Malaysians enjoy the social experience of shopping in a lively market or bazaar and thus did not like the impersonal efficiency of the typical Wal-Mart store. As a result, Wal-Mart has learned the importance of designing store layouts to appeal specifically to the customers of each country in which it operates.

When purchasing and operating a chain of stores in another country, such as the British ASDA chain, Wal-Mart now strives to retain what customers value in the local market while taking advantage of all of its own accumulated organizational learning. For example, Wal-Mart improved ASDA's information technology used for inventory and sales tracking in stores and enrolled ASDA in Wal-Mart's global purchasing operations, which has enabled the chain to pay less for certain products, sell them for less, and, overall, significantly increase sales. At the same time, Wal-Mart empowered local ASDA managers to run the stores; as the president of ASDA indicates, "This is still essentially a British business in the way it's run day to day."[65] Clearly, global organizational learning is essential for companies such as Wal-Mart that have significant operations in multiple countries.

Promoting Individual Creativity

Research suggests that when certain conditions are met, managers are more likely to be creative. People must be given the opportunity and freedom to generate new ideas.[66] Creativity declines when managers look over the shoulders of talented employees and try to "hurry up" a creative solution. How would you feel if your boss said you had one week to come up with a new product idea to beat the competition? Creativity results when employees have an opportunity to experiment, to take risks, and to make mistakes and learn from them. And employees must not fear that they will be looked down on or penalized for ideas that might at first seem outlandish, as it is sometimes those ideas that yield truly innovative products and services.[67] Highly innovative companies such as Google, Apple, and Facebook are well known for the wide degree of freedom they give their managers and employees to experiment and develop innovative goods and services.[68]

Once managers have generated alternatives, creativity can be fostered by providing them with constructive feedback so that they know how well they are doing. Ideas that seem to be going nowhere can be eliminated and creative energies refocused in other directions. Ideas that seem promising can be promoted, and help from other managers can be obtained as well.[69]

Top managers must stress the importance of looking for alternative solutions and should visibly reward employees who come up with creative ideas. Being creative can be demanding and stressful. Employees who believe that they are working on important, vital issues are motivated to put forth the high levels of effort that creativity demands. Creative people like to receive the acclaim of others, and innovative organizations have many kinds of ceremonies and rewards to recognize creative employees.

Promoting Group Creativity

To encourage creativity at the group level, organizations can make use of group problem-solving techniques that promote creative ideas and innovative solutions. These techniques can also be used to prevent groupthink and to help managers uncover biases. Here, we look at three group decision-making techniques: *brainstorming,* the *nominal group technique,* and the *Delphi technique.*

BRAINSTORMING *Brainstorming* is a group problem-solving technique in which managers meet face-to-face to generate and debate a wide variety of alternatives from which to make a decision.[70] Generally, from 5 to 15 managers meet in a closed-door session and proceed like this:

- One manager describes in broad outline the problem the group is to address.
- Group members then share their ideas and generate alternative courses of action.
- As each alternative is described, group members are not allowed to criticize it; everyone withholds judgment until all alternatives have been heard. One member of the group records the alternatives on a flip chart.

These ad agency employees are conducting a brainstorming session. Brainstorming can be used to generate multiple ideas and solutions for problems.

- Group members are encouraged to be as innovative and radical as possible. Anything goes; and the greater the number of ideas put forth, the better. Moreover, group members are encouraged to "piggyback" or build on each other's suggestions.
- When all alternatives have been generated, group members debate the pros and cons of each and develop a short list of the best alternatives.

Brainstorming is very useful in some problem-solving situations–for example, when managers are trying to find a new name for a perfume or for a model of car. But sometimes individuals working alone can generate more alternatives. The main reason for the loss of productivity in brainstorming appears to be **production blocking,** which occurs because group members cannot always simultaneously make sense of all the alternatives being generated, think up additional alternatives, and remember what they were thinking.[71]

production blocking A loss of productivity in brainstorming sessions due to the unstructured nature of brainstorming.

NOMINAL GROUP TECHNIQUE To avoid production blocking, the **nominal group technique** is often used. It provides a more structured way of generating alternatives in writing and gives each manager more time and opportunity to come up with potential solutions. The nominal group technique is especially useful when an issue is controversial and when different managers might be expected to champion different courses of action. Generally, a small group of managers meet in a closed-door session and adopt the following procedures:

nominal group technique A decision-making technique in which group members write down ideas and solutions, read their suggestions to the whole group, and discuss and then rank the alternatives.

- One manager outlines the problem to be addressed, and 30 or 40 minutes are allocated for group members, working individually, to write down their ideas and solutions. Group members are encouraged to be innovative.
- Managers take turns reading their suggestions to the group. One manager writes all the alternatives on a flip chart. No criticism or evaluation of alternatives is allowed until all alternatives have been read.
- The alternatives are then discussed, one by one, in the sequence in which they were first proposed. Group members can ask for clarifying information and critique each alternative to identify its pros and cons.
- When all alternatives have been discussed, each group member ranks all the alternatives from most preferred to least preferred, and the alternative that receives the highest ranking is chosen.[72]

DELPHI TECHNIQUE Both the nominal group technique and brainstorming require that managers meet together to generate creative ideas and engage in joint problem solving. What happens if managers are in different cities or in different parts of the world and cannot meet face-to-face? Videoconferencing is one way to bring distant managers together to brainstorm. Another way is to use the **Delphi technique,** a written approach to creative problem solving.[73] The Delphi technique works like this:

Delphi technique A decision-making technique in which group members do not meet face-to-face but respond in writing to questions posed by the group leader.

- The group leader writes a statement of the problem and a series of questions to which participating managers are to respond.

entrepreneur An individual who notices opportunities and decides how to mobilize the resources necessary to produce new and improved goods and services.

- The questionnaire is sent to the managers and departmental experts who are most knowledgeable about the problem. They are asked to generate solutions and mail the questionnaire back to the group leader.
- A team of top managers records and summarizes the responses. The results are then sent back to the participants, with additional questions to be answered before a decision can be made.
- The process is repeated until a consensus is reached and the most suitable course of action is apparent.

Entrepreneurship and Creativity

LO5 Describe how managers can encourage and promote entrepreneurship to create a learning organization, and differentiate between entrepreneurs and intrapreneurs.

Entrepreneurs are individuals who notice opportunities and decide how to mobilize the resources necessary to produce new and improved goods and services. Entrepreneurs make all of the planning, organizing, leading, and controlling decisions necessary to start new business ventures. Thus, entrepreneurs are an important source of creativity in the organizational world. These people are the David Filo's and Jerry Yang's (founders of Yahoo!) of the world, who make vast fortunes when their businesses succeed. Or they are among the millions of people who start new business ventures only to lose their money when they fail. Despite the fact that an estimated 80% of small businesses fail in the first three to five years, by some estimates 38% of men and 50% of women in today's workforce want to start their own companies.[74]

social entrepreneur An individual who pursues initiatives and opportunities and mobilizes resources to address social problems and needs in order to improve society and well-being through creative solutions.

Social entrepreneurs are individuals who pursue initiatives and opportunities to address social problems and needs in order to improve society and well-being, such as reducing poverty, increasing literacy, protecting the natural environment, or reducing substance abuse.[75] Social entrepreneurs seek to mobilize resources to solve social problems through creative solutions.[76]

As indicated in the following "Ethics in Action," while social entrepreneurs often face challenges in raising funds to support their initiatives, their options are increasing.

Small Business

ETHICS IN ACTION

Finding Funding to Do Good

Typically, venture capitalists who provide funding for entrepreneurs to start their businesses are concerned with getting a good return on their investment and not having to wait a long time to do so, and banks expect entrepreneurs to have a prior track record of success. For social entrepreneurs, this can make raising funds to support their new ventures a real challenge as achieving their social goals are of paramount importance. Fortunately, an increasing number of social venture funds seek to invest in companies that are focused on social goals.[77]

World of Good is a San Francisco Bay Area start-up that creates opportunities for thousands of producers in the developing world by bringing their products to the mainstream consumer market. Through their network of more than 1,200 retail outlets, their signature product line (Original Good), and their new online marketplace for People-Positive and Eco-Positive products (www.worldofgood.com), they seek to create a global network of entrepreneurs in the informal sector, uplifted by their direct access to large-scale markets and empowered through the use of ethical wage standards.

Priya Haji, founder of World of Good, Inc.,

When Priya Haji, the company's cofounder and CEO, initially sought funding for her venture, she had to look beyond traditional banks, who weren't interested because she didn't have a three-year track record.[78] "For them, it didn't make sense," Haji says. "There is a consumer-driven demand for this kind of ethical consumption, but the debt markets don't understand that." Instead, Haji turned to social lenders, and in 2006, reached a deal with three of them: RSF Social Finance, Root Capital, and Shared Interest, each of whom insist that portfolio companies maintain their social missions as they grow.[79] Their investment paid off–the company has doubled revenues every year since.

When Charlie Crystle sought funding for Mission Research, the new social enterprise he cofounded, which provides nonprofits with fundraising software, traditional investors questioned some of Mission's practices, such as giving the software away for free to nonprofits with annual budgets less than $25,000 and even the fact that he was starting a business focused on selling to nonprofits in the first place.[80] Crystle was able to secure $300,000 in funding from Underdog Ventures in return for a 5% share in the company. Unlike other venture capital firms that aim to sell their stake in new ventures within 5–7 years, Underdog is willing to wait 7–8 years and also requires that companies it invests in get prior approval from Underdog if they want to change their social mission.[81]

World of Good and Mission Research have both experienced substantial revenue growth since receiving funding from social investors.[82] Of equal importance, they also are achieving their social goals, which is a prime reason they were founded in the first place. As Crystle indicates, "I focus on building my business and building revenues. . . . But it's not the reason I get up every morning and go to work."[83]

Many managers, scientists, and researchers employed by companies engage in entrepreneurial activity, and they are an important source of organizational creativity. They are involved in innovation, developing new and improved products and ways to make them. Such employees notice opportunities for either quantum or incremental product improvements and are responsible for managing the product development process. These individuals are known as **intrapreneurs**, to distinguish them from entrepreneurs who start their own businesses. But, in general, entrepreneurship involves creative decision making that provides customers with new or improved goods and services.

intrapreneur A manager, scientist, or researcher who works inside an organization and notices opportunities to develop new or improved products and better ways to make them.

There is an interesting relationship between entrepreneurs and intrapreneurs. Many managers with intrapreneurial talents become dissatisfied if their superiors decide neither to support nor to fund new product ideas and development efforts that the managers think will succeed. What do intrapreneurial managers who feel that they are getting nowhere do? Very often they decide to leave their current organizations and start their own companies to take advantage of their new product ideas! In other words, intrapreneurs become entrepreneurs and found companies that often compete with the companies they left. To avoid losing these individuals, top managers must find ways to facilitate the entrepreneurial spirit of their most creative employees. In the remainder of this section we consider issues involved in promoting successful entrepreneurship in both new and existing organizations.

Entrepreneurship and New Ventures

The fact that a significant number of entrepreneurs were frustrated intrapreneurs provides a clue about the personal characteristics of people who are likely to start a new venture and bear all the uncertainty and risk associated with being an entrepreneur.

CHARACTERISTICS OF ENTREPRENEURS Entrepreneurs are likely to possess a particular set of the personality characteristics we discussed in Chapter 2. First, they are likely to be high on the personality trait of *openness to experience,* meaning that they are predisposed to be original, to be open to a wide range of stimuli, to be daring, and to take risks. Entrepreneurs also are likely to have an *internal locus of control,* believing that they are responsible for what happens to them and that their own actions determine important outcomes such as the success or failure of a new business. People with an external locus of control, in contrast, would be very unlikely to leave a secure job in an organization and assume the risk associated with a new venture.

Entrepreneurs are likely to have a high level of *self-esteem* and feel competent and capable of handling most situations–including the stress and uncertainty surrounding a plunge into a risky new venture. Entrepreneurs are also likely to have a high *need for achievement* and have a strong desire to perform challenging tasks and meet high personal standards of excellence.

entrepreneurship The mobilization of resources to take advantage of an opportunity to provide customers with new or improved goods and services.

ENTREPRENEURSHIP AND MANAGEMENT Given that entrepreneurs are predisposed to activities that are somewhat adventurous and risky, in what ways can people become involved in entrepreneurial ventures? One way is to start a business from scratch. Taking advantage of modern IT, many people are starting solo ventures. The total number of small-office and home-office workers is more than 40 million, and each year more than a million new solo entrepreneurs join the ranks of the more than 29 million self-employed.

Intrapreneurs are an important source of organizational creativity.

When people who go it alone succeed, they frequently need to hire other people to help them run the business. Michael Dell, for example, began his computer business as a college student and within weeks had hired several people to help him to assemble computers from the component parts he bought from suppliers. From his solo venture grew Dell Computer, one of the largest PC makers in the world today.

Some entrepreneurs who found a new business often have difficulty deciding how to manage the organization as it grows; **entrepreneurship** is *not* the same as management. Management encompasses all the decisions involved in planning, organizing, leading, and controlling resources. Entrepreneurship is noticing an opportunity to satisfy a customer need and then deciding how to find and use resources to make a product that satisfies that need. When an entrepreneur has produced something that customers want, entrepreneurship gives way to management, as the pressing need becomes providing the product both efficiently and effectively. Frequently, a founding entrepreneur lacks the skills, patience, and experience to engage in the difficult and challenging work of management. Some entrepreneurs find it very hard to delegate authority because they are afraid to risk their company by letting others manage it. As a result, they become overloaded, and the quality of their decision making declines. Other entrepreneurs lack the detailed knowledge necessary to establish state-of-the-art information systems and technology or to create the operations management procedures that are vital to increase the efficiency of their organizations' production systems. Thus, to succeed, it is necessary to do more than create a new product; an entrepreneur must hire managers who can create an operating system that will let a new venture survive and prosper.

Intrapreneurship and Organizational Learning

The intensity of competition today, particularly from agile, small companies, has made it increasingly important for large, established organizations to promote and encourage intrapreneurship to raise the level of innovation and organizational learning. As we discussed earlier, a learning organization encourages all employees to identify opportunities and solve problems, thus enabling the organization to continuously experiment, improve, and increase its ability to provide customers with new and improved goods and services. The higher the level of intrapreneurship, the higher will be the level of learning and innovation. How can organizations promote organizational learning and intrapreneurship?

product champion A manager who takes "ownership" of a project and provides the leadership and vision that take a product from the idea stage to the final customer.

PRODUCT CHAMPIONS One way to promote intrapreneurship is to encourage individuals to assume the role of **product champion,** a manager who takes "ownership" of a project and provides the leadership and vision that take a product from the idea stage to the final customer. 3M, a company well known for its attempts to promote intrapreneurship, encourages all its managers to become product champions and identify new product ideas. A product champion becomes responsible for developing a business plan for the product. Armed with this business plan, the champion appears before 3M's product development committee, a team of senior 3M managers who probe the strengths and weaknesses of the plan to decide whether it should be funded. If the plan is accepted, the product champion assumes responsibility for product development.

skunkworks A group of intrapreneurs who are deliberately separated from the normal operation of an organization to encourage them to devote all their attention to developing new products.

SKUNKWORKS The idea behind the product champion role is that employees who feel ownership for a project are inclined to act like outside entrepreneurs and go to great lengths to make the project succeed. Using skunkworks and new venture divisions can also strengthen this feeling of ownership. A **skunkworks** is a group of intrapreneurs who are deliberately separated from the normal operation of an organization–for example, from the normal chain of command–to encourage them to devote all their attention to developing new products. The idea is that if these people are isolated, they will become so intensely involved in a project that development time will be relatively brief and the quality of the final product will be enhanced. The term *skunkworks* was coined at the Lockheed Corporation, which formed a team of design engineers to develop special aircraft such as the U2 spy plane. The secrecy with which this unit functioned and speculation about its goals led others to refer to it as "the skunkworks."

REWARDS FOR INNOVATION To encourage managers to bear the uncertainty and risk associated with the hard work of entrepreneurship, it is necessary to link performance to rewards. Increasingly, companies are rewarding intrapreneurs on the basis of the outcome of the product development process. Intrapreneurs are granted large bonuses if their projects succeed, or they are granted stock options that can make them millionaires if the product sells well. Both Microsoft and Google, for example, have made hundreds of their employees multimillionaires as a result of the stock options they were granted as part of their reward packages. In addition to receiving money, successful intrapreneurs can expect to receive promotion to the ranks of top management. Most of 3M's top managers, for example, reached the executive suite because they had a track record of successful entrepreneurship. Organizations must reward intrapreneurs equitably if they wish to prevent them from leaving and becoming outside entrepreneurs who might form a competitive new venture. Nevertheless, intrapreneurs frequently do so.

Summary and Review

THE NATURE OF MANAGERIAL DECISION MAKING Programmed decisions are routine decisions made so often that managers have developed decision rules to be followed automatically. Nonprogrammed decisions are made in response to situations that are unusual or novel; they are nonroutine decisions. The classical model of decision making assumes that decision makers have complete information, are able to process that information in an objective, rational manner, and make optimum decisions. March and Simon argue that managers are boundedly rational, rarely have access to all the information they need to make optimum decisions, and consequently satisfice and rely on their intuition and judgment when making decisions. **[LO1]**

STEPS IN THE DECISION-MAKING PROCESS When making decisions, managers should take these six steps: recognize the need for a decision, generate alternatives, assess alternatives, choose among alternatives, implement the chosen alternative, and learn from feedback. **[LO2]**

GROUP DECISION MAKING Many advantages are associated with group decision making, but there are also several disadvantages. One major source of poor decision making is groupthink. Afflicted decision makers collectively embark on a dubious course of action without questioning the assumptions that underlie their decision. Managers can improve the quality of group decision making by using techniques such as devil's advocacy and by increasing diversity in the decision-making group. **[LO3]**

ORGANIZATIONAL LEARNING AND CREATIVITY Organizational learning is the process through which managers seek to improve employees' desire and ability to understand and manage the organization and its task environment so that employees can make decisions that continuously raise organizational effectiveness. Managers must take steps to promote organizational learning and creativity at the individual and group levels to improve the quality of decision making. **[LO4]**

ENTREPRENEURSHIP Entrepreneurship is the mobilization of resources to take advantage of an opportunity to provide customers with new or improved goods and services. Entrepreneurs found new ventures of their own. Intrapreneurs work inside organizations and manage the product development process. Organizations need to encourage intrapreneurship because it leads to organizational learning and innovation. **[LO5]**

Management in Action

Topics for Discussion and Action

Discussion

1. What are the main differences between programmed decision making and nonprogrammed decision making? [LO1]
2. In what ways do the classical and administrative models of decision making help managers appreciate the complexities of real-world decision making? [LO1]
3. Why do capable managers sometimes make bad decisions? What can individual managers do to improve their decision-making skills? [LO1, 2]
4. In what kinds of groups is groupthink most likely to be a problem? When is it least likely to be a problem? What steps can group members take to ward off groupthink? [LO3]
5. What is organizational learning, and how can managers promote it? [LO4]
6. What is the difference between entrepreneurship and intrapreneurship? [LO5]

Action

7. Ask a manager to recall the best and the worst decisions he or she ever made. Try to determine why these decisions were so good or so bad. [LO1, 2, 3]
8. Think about an organization in your local community, your university, or an organization that you are familiar with that is doing poorly. Now think of questions managers in the organization should ask stakeholders to elicit creative ideas for turning around the organization's fortunes. [LO4]

Building Management Skills [LO1, 2, 4]

How Do You Make Decisions?

Pick a decision that you made recently and that has had important consequences for you. It may be your decision about which college to attend, which major to select, whether to take a part-time job, or which part-time job to take. Using the material in this chapter, analyze the way in which you made the decision.

1. Identify the criteria you used, either consciously or unconsciously, to guide your decision making.
2. List the alternatives you considered. Were they all possible alternatives? Did you unconsciously (or consciously) ignore some important alternatives?
3. How much information did you have about each alternative? Were you making the decision on the basis of complete or incomplete information?
4. Try to remember how you reached the decision. Did you sit down and consciously think through the implications of each alternative, or did you make the decision on the basis of intuition? Did you use any rules of thumb to help you make the decision?
5. Having answered the previous four questions, do you think in retrospect that you made a reasonable decision? What, if anything, might you do to improve your ability to make good decisions in the future?

Managing Ethically [LO3]

Sometimes groups make extreme decisions—decisions that are either more risky or more conservative than they would have been if individuals acting alone had made them. One explanation for the tendency of groups to make extreme decisions is diffusion of responsibility. In a group, responsibility for the outcomes of a decision is spread among group members, so each person feels less than fully accountable. The group's decision is extreme because no individual has taken full responsibility for it.

Questions

1. Either alone or in a group, think about the ethical implications of extreme decision making by groups.
2. When group decision making takes place, should members of a group each feel fully accountable for outcomes of the decision? Why or why not?

Small Group Breakout Exercise [LO3, 4]

Brainstorming

Form groups of three or four people, and appoint one member as the spokesperson who will communicate your findings to the class when called on by the instructor. Then discuss the following scenario:

You and your partners are trying to decide which kind of restaurant to open in a centrally located shopping center that has just been built in your city. The problem confronting you is that the city already has many restaurants that provide different kinds of food at all price ranges. You have the resources to open any type of restaurant. Your challenge is to decide which type is most likely to succeed.

Use the brainstorming technique to decide which type of restaurant to open. Follow these steps:

1. As a group, spend 5 or 10 minutes generating ideas about the alternative restaurants that the members think will be most likely to succeed. Each group member should be as innovative and creative as possible, and no suggestions should be criticized.
2. Appoint one group member to write down the alternatives as they are identified.
3. Spend the next 10 or 15 minutes debating the pros and cons of the alternatives. As a group, try to reach a consensus on which alternative is most likely to succeed.

After making your decision, discuss the pros and cons of the brainstorming method, and decide whether any production blocking occurred.

When called on by the instructor, the spokesperson should be prepared to share your group's decision with the class, as well as the reasons the group made its decision.

Be the Manager [LO1, 2, 3, 4, 5]

You are a top manager who was recently hired by an oil field services company in Oklahoma to help it respond more quickly and proactively to potential opportunities in its market. You report to the chief operating officer (COO), who reports to the CEO, and you have been on the job for eight months. Thus far, you have come up with three initiatives you carefully studied, thought were noteworthy, and proposed and justified to the COO. The COO seemed cautiously interested when you presented the proposals, and each time he indicated he would think about them and discuss them with the CEO as considerable resources were involved. Each time, you never heard back from the COO, and after a few weeks elapsed, you casually asked the COO if there was any news on the proposal in question. For the first proposal, the COO said, "We think it's a good idea but the timing is off. Let's shelve it for the time being and reconsider it next year." For the second proposal, the COO said, "Mike [the CEO] reminded me that we tried that two years ago and it wasn't well received in the market. I am surprised I didn't remember it myself when you first described the proposal but it came right back to me once Mike mentioned it." For the third proposal, the COO simply said, "We're not convinced it will work."

You believe that your three proposed initiatives are viable ways to seize opportunities in the marketplace, yet you cannot proceed with any of them. Moreover, for each proposal, you invested considerable amounts of time and have even worked to bring others on board to support the proposal, only to have it shot down by the CEO. When you interviewed for the position, both the COO and the CEO claimed they wanted "an outsider to help them step out of the box and innovate." Yet your experience to date has been just the opposite. What are you going to do?

BusinessWeek Case in the News [LO1, 2, 3, 4, 5]

Real Life Imitates *Real World*

It sounds more like reality TV than a reasoned strategy. Last year, Best Buy picked four groups of salespeople in their 20s and early 30s and asked the strangers to room together for 10 weeks in a Los Angeles apartment complex. On the agenda, besides hanging out at the beach: coming up with businesses the electronics retailer could roll out quickly and cheaply.

Believe it or not, the arrangement worked. Today, in a dozen stores in greater Los Angeles, Best Buy offers a service called Best Buy Studio, which provides Web-design consulting for small businesses. Jeremy Sevush, a former sales-floor department supervisor in West Hollywood, came up with the idea and then worked with executives to launch the venture only a couple of weeks after he moved out of the company apartment last May.

"My friends joked and said I was joining 'Real World: Best Buy Edition,'" says Sevush, 29, referring to the MTV television series that features a youthful cast sharing a home. "Living together and knowing we only had 10 weeks sped up our team-building process. We voluntarily worked longer hours, talking about business models while making spaghetti."

Extreme brainstorming sessions like Best Buy's may be common in the tech sector, where programmers and engineers are sequestered so they can better focus on the next breakthrough. Now other companies are turning employees into temporary housemates, too. Whirlpool, for example, packs eight sales reps off to a house in Benton Harbor, Michigan, to cook and clean together for seven weeks under a program called Real Whirled. By thoroughly familiarizing themselves with Whirlpool appliances, the company hopes, salespeople will become sharper marketers of the goods.

A Pressure Cooker for Ideas

Best Buy retained former IBM manager John Wolpert to create and oversee its innovation project. Wolpert, who runs Team upStart, a consultancy in Sunnyvale, California, had used a similar real-life approach at IBM's Extreme Blue incubator in Austin, but never before at a retailer. He charges up to $75,000 for each 10-week immersive session, including room and board for employees, who are assured they'll get their old jobs back. "There's something magical about taking smart people out of their safety zones and making them spend night and day together," he says. "You have to prioritize on steroids and be absolutely ruthless to prove what you want to do can be done."

With consumers cutting down on electronics purchases these days—Best Buy's same-store sales have been declining since last fall—the Minneapolis company is reevaluating outlays. Best Buy executives won't say whether the real-world version of *The Real World* will be renewed for 2009.

But they say they're keeping Best Buy Studio going to see if it should be expanded. They also want frontline employees to continue to offer up business ideas. "Employees don't need permission to create or innovate," says Brian Dunn, Best Buy's president and chief operating officer, who will succeed Chief Executive Brad Anderson in June. Dunn admits to having a soft spot for store clerks. He started as one 23 years ago.

Questions

1. What kind of decision making takes place at the extreme brainstorming sessions companies like Best Buy are using?
2. For which steps in the decision-making process might these kinds of sessions be especially important?
3. Why might more creative ideas be generated in these kinds of sessions?
4. Why does Best Buy encourage frontline employees to generate new ideas?

Source: Reena Jana, "Real Life Imitates *Real World*." Reprinted from March 23 & 30, 2009 issue of *BusinessWeek* by special permission, copyright © 2009 by The McGraw-Hill Companies, Inc.

BusinessWeek Case in the News [LO1, 4, 5]

Tata Taps a Vast R&D Shop—Its Own

India's Tata vaulted into the global spotlight a few years ago when it began making a series of high-profile acquisitions, from the four-star Pierre hotel in New York to Anglo-Dutch steelmaker Corus to, more recently, luxury carmaker Jaguar Land Rover. But then the world economy swooned, and the $85 billion conglomerate found itself losing customers and buried under a pile of debt.

Time to put innovation initiatives on ice, it might seem. The company's chairman, 72-year-old Ratan Tata, doesn't see it that way. In his 2009 message to Tata's 320,000 employees, he urged them on: "Cut costs. Think out of the box. Even if the world around you is collapsing, be bold, be daring, think big."

Labs around the World

The boss is getting his way. Tata Motors has turned itself into the talk of the global automotive industry with its $2,000 minicar, the Nano, which goes on sale in India this month, and is far along in developing a follow-up, a low-priced electric vehicle. Meanwhile, Tata Chemicals is working on a low-cost antimicrobial water system that uses no electricity, and a UV-blocking nanomaterial that keeps paint from getting bleached by sunlight. And Tata Power is planning to unveil soon an advance in a smart electricity grid.

The companies all share a powerful ally—Tata Consultancy Services (TCS). With 20 labs around the world, TCS for decades has been advising outside clients as varied as British Airways, U.S. engine maker Cummins, and Dutch bank ABN Amro. It was behind a new mobile-phone technology, for instance, that provides Indian farmers with valuable agricultural data. But as its business softened, the outfit two years ago became an in-house consultancy, too. It now shares revenue from the new products or services it and its siblings jointly create.

"We did it with clients. Now we do it with group companies," says TCS chief Subramanian Ramadorai. "It keeps the money and intellectual property rights in the family."

Tata has a long history of innovation in India. During its 117 years in business, the company built the country's first steel mill, power plant, airline, Indian-owned hotel chain, and made-in-India car, as well as the fastest supercomputer outside the United States and Germany.

What separates Mumbai-based Tata from typical U.S. or European companies is its approach to new products and services, says R. Gopalakrishnan, Tata's executive director. He's leading an effort to promote intragroup cross-pollination and get more from the conglomerate's $1.5 billion research and development budget.

While other carmakers spend much of their energy updating existing models, Tata engineered the Nano for a brand-new market. The company also is trying new sales channels. Rather than selling the Nano only in dealerships, the car will be offered in Tata-owned retail chains in India, too, such as department store Westside and electronics outlet Croma.

To keep this string going, some executives, such as Sunil Sinha, chief operating officer of Tata Quality Management Services, would like to develop an all-encompassing complex modeled on General Electric's R&D campus in upstate New York. "Innovation has yet to be strongly embedded across the group," he says.

Nonetheless, ideas are bubbling up. Tata now sponsors annual awards for the best innovations, as well as a prize for entrepreneurial employees who tried but failed, an unusual form of recognition in India. Two years ago just 100 entered the competition; this year, Sinha expects 1,000. Says Murali Sastry, Tata Chemicals' chief scientist, "The innovation bug has hit Tata—and India."

Questions

1. What kind of decision making does Ratan Tata engage in?
2. Do you think Tata is a learning organization? Why or why not?
3. How does Tata encourage its employees to be intrapreneurs?
4. Why does Tata have annual employee awards for the most outstanding innovations as well as for employees who tried to develop a promising new idea and failed?

Source: Manjeet Kripalani, "Tata Taps a Vast R&D Shop—Its Own." Reprinted from April 20, 2009 issue of *BusinessWeek* by special permission, copyright © 2009 by The McGraw-Hill Companies, Inc.

Planning, Strategy, and Competitive Advantage

CHAPTER 6

Learning Objectives

After studying this chapter, you should be able to

1. Identify the three main steps of the planning process and explain the relationship between planning and strategy. **[LO1]**

2. Differentiate between the main types of business-level strategies and explain how they give an organization a competitive advantage that may lead to superior performance. **[LO2]**

3. Differentiate between the main types of corporate-level strategies and explain how they are used to strengthen a company's business-level strategy and competitive advantage. **[LO3]**

4. Describe the vital role managers play in implementing strategies to achieve an organization's mission and goals. **[LO4]**

Planning in and of itself does not always pay off—it must be realistic. With its diversion into buying a game company, Mattel failed to anticipate the rise of such competitors as these Bratz dolls, which have taken a big chunk out of Barbie's profitability.

MANAGEMENT SNAPSHOT

How Mattel's Barbie Knocked Out the Bratz Doll

What Makes It So Hard to Compete in an Industry?

The rapid pace at which the world is changing is forcing the managers of all kinds of companies to develop new strategies to protect their competitive advantage. If they don't, they will be overtaken by agile competitors that respond faster to changing customer fads and fashions. Nowhere is this truer than in the global toy industry, where in the doll business, worth over $10 billion a year in sales, vicious combat is raging. The largest global toy company, Mattel, has earned tens of billions of dollars from the world's best-selling doll, Barbie, since it introduced her almost 50 years ago. Mothers who played with the original dolls bought them for their daughters, and then granddaughters, and Barbie became an American icon. Barbie and all Barbie accessories accounted for almost 50% of Mattel's toy sales by 2000, so protecting its star product was crucial. However, Barbie's continuing success as the best-selling global doll led Bob Eckert, Mattel's CEO, and his top managers to underestimate how much the world had changed, and Mattel began to pursue the wrong strategies in the 2000s.

The Barbie doll was created in the 1960s when most women were homemakers. Her voluptuous shape was a response to a dated view of what the "ideal" woman should look like. Changing cultural views about the roles of girls, women, marriage, and working women in recent decades shifted the tastes of doll buyers. But Mattel's managers did not recognize the threats this change in the environment posed. They continued to bet on Barbie's eternal appeal. In addition, given that Barbie was the best-selling doll, they thought it might be dangerous to make major changes to her appearance. Customers might not like these changes, and so stop buying her. Mattel's top managers decided not to rock the boat, continued to pursue the same strategies, and left the Barbie brand unchanged. Instead, they focused their new strategies on developing new kinds of digital toys and games, given the exploding interest in electronic products.

Mattel was therefore unprepared when a challenge came along in the form of a new kind of doll, the Bratz doll, introduced by MGA Entertainment. Many competitors to Barbie had emerged over the years. The doll business is highly profitable. But no other doll had matched Barbie's appeal to young girls (or their mothers). The marketers and designers behind the Bratz line of dolls had spent a lot of time finding out what the new generation of girls, especially those aged 7–11, wanted from a doll. And it turned out that the Bratz dolls they designed met the desires of these girls. Bratz dolls have larger heads and oversized eyes, wear lots of makeup and short dresses, and are multicultural to give each doll "personality and attitude." The dolls were designed to appeal to a new generation of girls brought up in a fast-changing fashion and music world and in the digital age. The Bratz dolls met the untapped needs of "tween" girls and the new line took off. MGA licensed the rights to make and sell the doll to toy companies overseas, and Bratz quickly became a serious competitor to Barbie.

Mattel was in trouble, and its managers had to change its strategy and bring Barbie up to date. Mattel's designers decided to change Barbie's "extreme" vital statistics. They killed off her old-time boyfriend Ken and replaced him with Blaine, an Aussie surfer. They also recognized they had waited much too long to introduce their own new lines of doll to meet the changed needs of "tween" and other girls in the 2000s. So they rushed out the "My Scene" line of dolls in 2002 that were obvious imitations of Bratz dolls. This new line never matched the popularity of Bratz dolls, however. Mattel also introduced a new line called Flava in 2003 to appeal to even younger girls, but this line flopped completely. At the same time, the decisions that they made to change Barbie and her figure, looks, clothing, and boyfriends came too late, and sales of Barbie dolls continued to fall.

By 2006 sales of the Barbie collection had dropped by 30%—serious stuff because Mattel's profits and stock price hinge on Barbie's success, and so they both plunged. Analysts argued that Mattel had not paid enough attention to its customers' changing needs to be able to move quickly to introduce the new and improved products necessary to keep the company on top of its market. Mattel brought back Ken in 2006. A sign of its mounting problems: In November 2006 Mattel's lawyers filed suit against MGA Entertainment, arguing that the Bratz dolls' copyright rightfully belong to them. Mattel complained that the head designer of Bratz was a Mattel employee when he made the initial drawings for the dolls and that they had applied for copyright protection on a number of early Bratz drawings. Mattel claimed that MGA hired key Mattel employees away from the firm and these employees "stole" sensitive sales information and transferred it to MGA.

In 2008, a judge ruled in Mattel's favor and ordered MGA to stop using the Bratz name, and a jury awarded Mattel $100 million in damages. After an appeal, in 2009 a federal judge upheld this verdict and ruled that the Bratz doll is Mattel property and MGA must stop selling the doll by the end of 2009. So, in a reversal of fortune, Mattel has eliminated its major competitor, which it needed to do—because after it reported one more major decline in sales in the spring of 2009, its stock plunged again.

Overview

As the opening case suggests, in a fast-changing competitive environment such as designing and selling toys, managers must continually evaluate how well products are meeting customer needs, and they must engage in thorough, systematic planning to find new strategies to better meet those needs. This chapter explores the manager's role both as planner and as strategist. First, we discuss the nature and importance of planning, the kinds of plans managers develop, and the levels at which planning takes place. Second, we discuss the three major steps in the planning process: (1) determining an organization's mission and major goals, (2) choosing or formulating strategies to realize the mission and goals, and (3) selecting the most effective ways to implement and put these strategies into action. We also examine several techniques, such as scenario planning

planning Identifying and selecting appropriate goals and courses of action; one of the four principal tasks of management.

and SWOT analysis, that can help managers improve the quality of their planning; and we discuss a range of strategies that managers can use to give their companies a competitive advantage over their rivals. By the end of this chapter, you will understand the vital role managers carry out when they plan, develop, and implement strategies to create a high-performing organization.

Planning and Strategy

Planning, as we noted in Chapter 1, is a process that managers use to identify and select appropriate goals and courses of action for an organization.[1] The organizational plan that results from the planning process details the goals of the organization and the specific set of strategies that managers will implement to attain those goals. Recall, from Chapter 1, that a **strategy** is a cluster of related managerial decisions and actions to help an organization attain one of its goals. Thus, planning is both a goal-making and a strategy-making process.

LO1 Identify the three main steps of the planning process and explain the relationship between planning and strategy.

strategy A cluster of decisions about what goals to pursue, what actions to take, and how to use resources to achieve goals.

mission statement A broad declaration of an organization's purpose that identifies the organization's products and customers and distinguishes the organization from its competitors.

In most organizations, planning is a three-step activity (see Figure 6.1). The first step is determining the organization's mission and goals. A **mission statement** is a broad declaration of an organization's overriding purpose, what it is seeking to achieve from its activities; this statement is also intended to identify what is *unique or important* about its products to its employees and customers as well as to *distinguish or differentiate* the organization in some ways from its competitors. (Three examples of mission statements, those created by Cisco Systems, Wal-Mart, and AT&T, are illustrated later in the chapter, in Figure 6.4.)

The second step is formulating strategy. Managers analyze the organization's current situation and then conceive and develop the strategies necessary to attain the organization's mission and goals. The third step is implementing strategy. Managers decide how to allocate the resources and responsibilities required to implement the strategies among people and groups within the organization.[2] In subsequent sections of this chapter we look in detail at the specifics of each of these steps. But first we examine the general nature and purpose of planning.

Figure 6.1
Three Steps in Planning

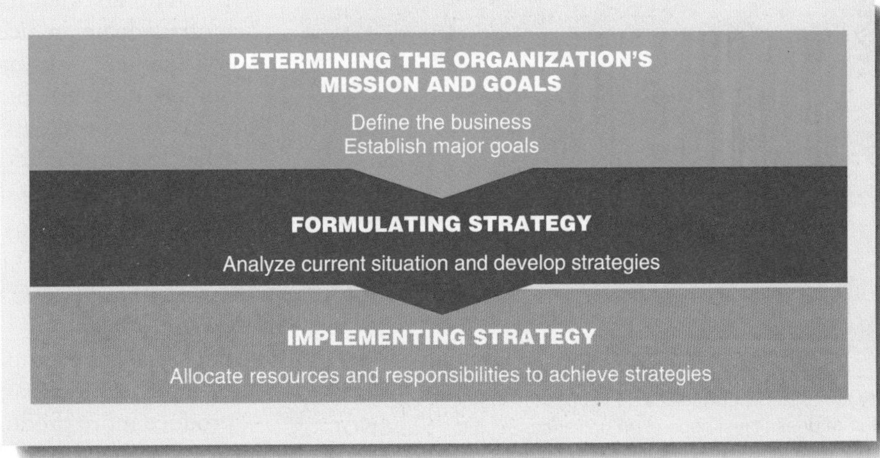

The Nature of the Planning Process

Essentially, to perform the planning task, managers (1) establish and discover where an organization is at the *present time;* (2) determine where it should be in the future, its *desired future state;* and (3) decide how to *move it forward* to reach that future state. When managers plan, they must forecast what may happen in the future in order to decide what to do in the present. The better their predictions, the more effective will be the strategies they formulate to take advantage of future opportunities and counter emerging competitive threats in the environment. As previous chapters noted, however, the external environment is uncertain and complex, and managers typically must deal with incomplete information and bounded rationality. This is why planning and strategy making is such a difficult and risky activity, and if managers' predictions are wrong and strategies fail, organizational performance falls.

Why Planning Is Important

Almost all managers participate in some kind of planning because they must try to predict future opportunities and threats and develop a plan and strategies that will result in a high-performing organization. Moreover, the absence of a plan often results in hesitations, false steps, and mistaken changes of direction that can hurt an organization or even lead to disaster. Planning is important for four main reasons:

1. *Planning is necessary to give the organization a sense of direction and purpose.*[3] A plan states what goals an organization is trying to achieve and what strategies it intends to use to achieve them. Without the sense of direction and purpose that a formal plan provides, managers may interpret their own specific tasks and jobs in ways that best suit themselves. The result will be an organization that is pursuing multiple and often conflicting goals and a set of managers who do not cooperate and work well together. By stating which organizational goals and strategies are important, a plan keeps managers on track so that they use the resources under their control efficiently and effectively.

A group of managers meets to plot their company's strategy. Their ability to assess opportunities and challenges and to forecast the future doesn't just depend on brilliance. Such tools as SWOT analysis can significantly bolster the accuracy of their predictions.

2. *Planning is a useful way of getting managers to participate in decision making about the appropriate goals and strategies for an organization.* Effective planning gives all managers the opportunity to participate in decision making. At Intel, for example, top managers, as part of their annual planning process, regularly request input from lower-level managers to determine what the organization's goals and strategies should be.
3. *A plan helps coordinate managers of the different functions and divisions of an organization to ensure that they all pull in the same direction and work to achieve its desired future state.* Without a well-thought-out plan, for example, it is possible that the members of the manufacturing function will produce more products than the members of the sales function can sell, resulting in a mass

of unsold inventory. This happened to high-flying Internet router supplier Cisco Systems in the early 2000s when manufacturing, which previously had been able to sell all the routers it produced, found it had over $2 billion of inventory that the sales force could not sell; customers now wanted new kinds of optical routers that Cisco had not planned to develop–even though sales had told manufacturing that customer needs were changing.

4. *A plan can be used as a device for controlling managers within an organization.* A good plan specifies not only which goals and strategies the organization is committed to but also *who* bears the responsibility for putting the strategies into action to attain the goals. When managers know that they will be held accountable for attaining a goal, they are motivated to do their best to make sure the goal is achieved.

Henri Fayol, the originator of the model of management we discussed in Chapter 1, said that effective plans should have four qualities: unity, continuity, accuracy, and flexibility.[4] *Unity* means that at any one time only one central, guiding plan is put into operation to achieve an organizational goal; more than one plan to achieve a goal would cause confusion and disorder. *Continuity* means that planning is an ongoing process in which managers build and refine previous plans and continually modify plans at all levels–corporate, business, and functional–so that they fit together into one broad framework. *Accuracy* means that managers need to make every attempt to collect and utilize all available information at their disposal in the planning process. Of course, managers must recognize the fact that uncertainty exists and that information is almost always incomplete (for reasons we discussed in Chapter 5). Despite the need for continuity and accuracy, however, Fayol emphasized that the planning process should be *flexible* enough so that plans can be altered and changed if the situation changes. Managers must not be bound to a static plan.

Levels of Planning

In large organizations planning usually takes place at three levels of management: corporate, business or division, and department or functional. Consider how General Electric (GE) operates. One of the world's largest global organizations, GE competes in over 150 different businesses or industries.[5] GE has three main levels of management: corporate level, business or divisional level, and functional level (see Figure 6.2). At the corporate level are CEO and chairman Jeffrey Immelt, his top management team, and their corporate support staff. Together, they are responsible for planning and strategy making for the organization as a whole.

Below the corporate level is the business level. At the business level are the different *divisions* or *business units* of the company that compete in distinct industries; GE has over 150 divisions, including GE Aircraft Engines, GE Financial Services, GE Lighting, GE Motors, GE Plastics, and NBC. Each division or business unit has its own set of *divisional managers* who control planning and strategy for their particular division or unit. So, for example, GE Lighting's divisional managers plan how to operate globally to reduce costs while meeting the needs of customers in different countries.

Going down one more level, each division has its own set of *functions* or *departments,* such as manufacturing, marketing, human resource management (HRM), and research and development (R&D). For example, GE Aircraft has its own marketing function, as do GE Lighting, GE Motors, and NBC. Each division's *functional managers* are responsible for the planning and strategy making necessary to increase the efficiency and effectiveness of their particular function. So, for example, GE Lighting's marketing

Figure 6.2
Levels of Planning at General Electric

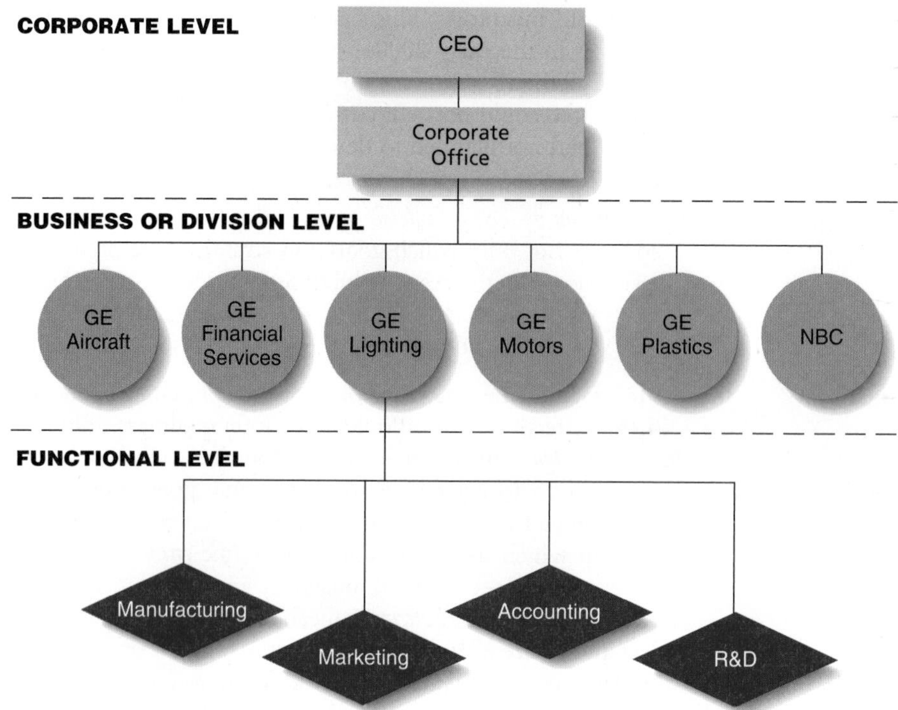

managers are responsible for increasing the effectiveness of its advertising and sales campaigns in different countries to improve lightbulb sales.

Levels and Types of Planning

As just discussed, planning at GE, as at all other large organizations, takes place at each level. Figure 6.3 shows the links among these three levels and the three steps in the planning and strategy-making process illustrated in Figure 6.1.

corporate-level plan Top management's decisions pertaining to the organization's mission, overall strategy, and structure.

corporate-level strategy A plan that indicates in which industries and national markets an organization intends to compete.

The **corporate-level plan** contains top management's decisions concerning the organization's mission and goals, overall (corporate-level) strategy, and structure (see Figure 6.3). **Corporate-level strategy** specifies in which industries and national markets an organization intends to compete and why. One of the goals stated in GE's corporate-level plan is that GE should be first or second in market share in every industry in which it competes. A division that cannot attain this goal may be sold to another company. GE Medical Systems was sold to Thompson of France for this reason. Another GE goal is to acquire other companies that can help a division build its market share to reach its corporate goal of being first or second in an industry. Over the last decade, GE acquired several large financial services companies to meet this goal and has transformed the GE Financial Services Division into one of the largest financial services operations in the world.

In general, corporate-level planning and strategy are the primary responsibility of top or corporate managers.[6] The corporate-level goal that GE should be first or second in every industry in which it competes was first articulated by former CEO Jack Welch. Now, Welch's handpicked successor, Jeffrey Immelt, and his top-management team decide which industries GE should compete in.

business-level plan Divisional managers' decisions pertaining to divisions' long-term goals, overall strategy, and structure.

The corporate-level plan provides the framework within which divisional managers create their business-level plans. At the business level, the managers of each division create a **business-level plan** that details (1) the long-term divisional goals

Figure 6.3
Levels and Types of Planning

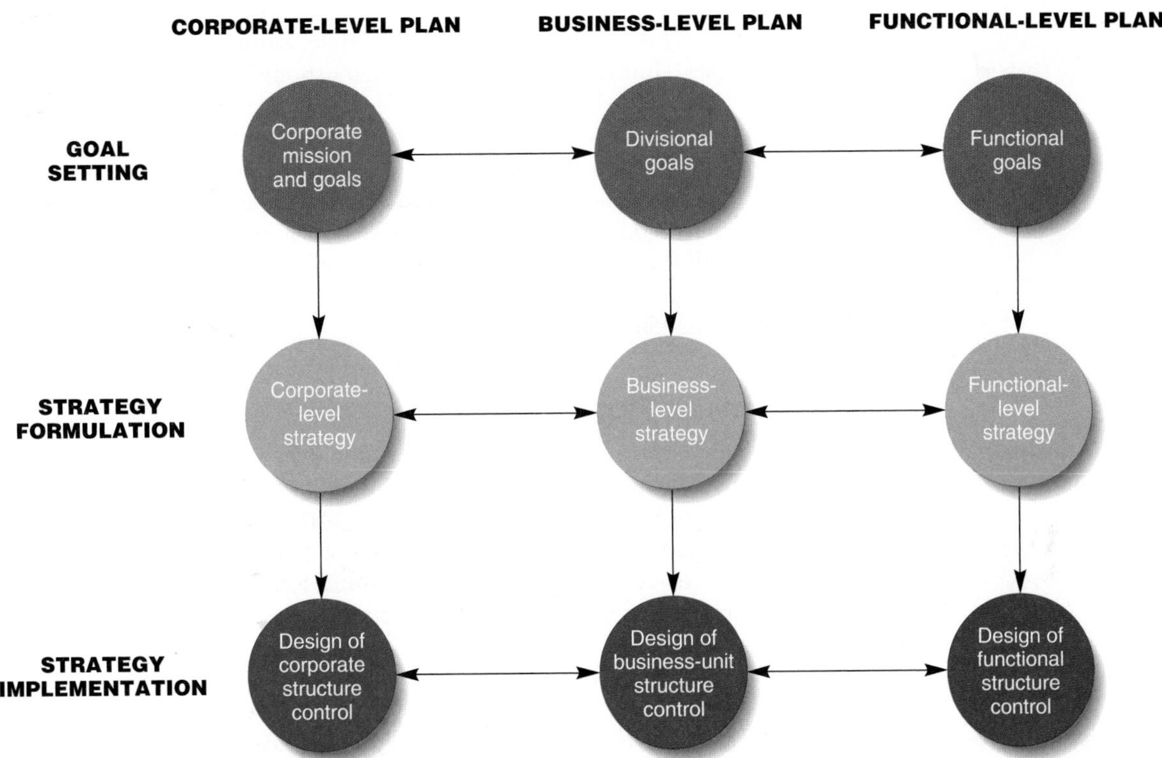

business-level strategy A plan that indicates how a division intends to compete against its rivals in an industry.

functional-level plan Functional managers' decisions pertaining to the goals that they propose to pursue to help the division attain its business-level goals.

functional-level strategy A plan of action to improve the ability of each of an organization's functions to perform its task-specific activities in ways that add value to an organization's goods and services.

that will allow the division to meet corporate goals and (2) the division's business-level strategy and structure necessary to achieve divisional goals. **Business-level strategy** outlines the specific methods a division, business unit, or organization will use to compete effectively against its rivals in an industry. Managers at GE's lighting division (currently number two in the global lighting industry, behind the Dutch company Philips NV) develop strategies designed to help their division take over the number-one spot and better contribute to GE's corporate goals. The lighting division's specific strategies might focus on ways to reduce costs in all departments to lower prices and so gain market share from Philips. For example, GE is currently expanding its European lighting operations in Hungary, which is a low-cost location.[7]

At the functional level, the business-level plan provides the framework within which functional managers devise their plans. A **functional-level plan** states the goals that the managers of each function will pursue to help their division attain its business-level goals, which, in turn, will allow the entire company to achieve its corporate goals. **Functional-level strategy** is a plan of action that managers of individual functions (such as manufacturing or marketing) can take to improve the ability of each function to perform its task-specific activities in ways that add value to an organization's goods and services and thereby increase the value customers receive. Thus, for example, consistent with the lighting division's strategy of driving down costs, its manufacturing function might adopt the goal "To reduce production costs by 20% over the next three years," and functional strategies to achieve this goal might include (1) investing in state-of-the-art European production facilities and (2) developing an electronic global business-to-business network to reduce the costs of inputs and inventory holding.

In the planning process, it is important to ensure that planning across the three different levels is *consistent*–functional goals and strategies should be consistent with divisional goals and strategies, which, in turn, should be consistent with corporate goals and strategies, and vice versa. When consistency is achieved, the whole company operates in harmony; activities at one level reinforce and strengthen those at the other levels, increasing efficiency and effectiveness. To help accomplish this, each function's plan is linked to its division's business-level plan, which, in turn, is linked to the corporate plan. Although few organizations are as large and complex as GE, most plan in the same way as GE and have written plans, which are frequently updated, to guide managerial decision making.

Time Horizons of Plans

time horizon The intended duration of a plan.

Plans differ in their **time horizon**, the period of time over which they are intended to apply or endure. Managers usually distinguish among *long-term plans,* with a time horizon of five years or more; *intermediate-term plans,* with a horizon between one and five years; and *short-term plans,* with a horizon of one year or less.[8] Typically, corporate- and business-level goals and strategies require long- and intermediate-term plans, and functional-level goals and strategies require intermediate- and short-term plans.

Although most companies operate with planning horizons of five years or more, this does not mean that managers undertake major planning exercises only once every five years and then "lock in" a specific set of goals and strategies for that time period. Most organizations have an annual planning cycle that is usually linked to the annual financial budget (although a major planning effort may be undertaken only every few years). So, a corporate- or business-level plan that extends over several years is typically treated as a *rolling plan,* a plan that is updated and amended every year to take account of changing conditions in the external environment. Thus, the time horizon for an organization's 2009 corporate-level plan might be 2014; for the 2010 plan it might be 2015; and so on. The use of rolling plans is essential because of the high rate of change in the environment and the difficulty of predicting competitive conditions five years in the future. Rolling plans enable managers to make midcourse corrections if environmental changes warrant or to change the thrust of the plan altogether if it no longer seems appropriate. The use of rolling plans allows managers to plan flexibly, without losing sight of the need to plan for the long term.

Standing Plans and Single-Use Plans

Another distinction often made between plans is whether they are standing plans or single-use plans. Managers create standing and single-use plans to help achieve an organization's specific goals. *Standing plans* are used in situations in which programmed decision making is appropriate. When the same situations occur repeatedly, managers develop policies, rules, and standard operating procedures (SOPs) to control the way employees perform their tasks. A policy is a general guide to action; a rule is a formal, written guide to action; and a standing operating procedure is a written instruction describing the exact series of actions that should be followed in a specific situation. For example, an organization may have a standing plan about ethical behavior by employees. This plan includes a policy that all employees are expected to behave ethically in their dealings with suppliers and customers; a rule that requires any employee who receives from a supplier or customer a gift worth more than $10 to report the gift; and an SOP that obliges the recipient of the gift to make the disclosure in writing within 30 days.

In contrast, *single-use plans* are developed to handle nonprogrammed decision making in unusual or one-of-a-kind situations. Examples of single-use plans include *programs,* which are integrated sets of plans for achieving certain goals, and *projects,* which are specific action plans created to complete various aspects of a program. One of NASA's major programs was to reach the moon, and one project in this program was to develop a lunar module capable of landing on the moon and returning to the earth.

Because the future is unpredictable, the best way to improve planning is first to generate "multiple futures," or scenarios of the future, based on different assumptions about conditions that *might prevail* in the future and then to develop different plans that detail what a company *should do* in the event that one of these scenarios actually occurs. *Scenario planning* is a learning tool that raises the quality of the planning process and can bring real benefits to an organization.[9] By 1990, more than 50% of *Fortune* 500 companies were using some version of scenario planning, and the number has increased since then.

The great strength of scenario planning is its ability not only to anticipate the challenges of an uncertain future but also to educate managers to think about the future—*to think strategically.*[10]

Determining the Organization's Mission and Goals

As we discussed earlier, determining the organization's mission and goals is the first step of the planning process. Once the mission and goals are agreed upon and formally stated in the corporate plan, they guide the next steps by defining which strategies are appropriate and which are inappropriate.[11] Figure 6.4 presents managers' vision of the mission and goals of three companies, Cisco, Wal-Mart, and AT&T.

Figure 6.4
Three Mission Statements

COMPANY	MISSION STATEMENT
Cisco	Cisco solutions provide competitive advantage to our customers through more efficient and timely exchange of information, which in turn leads to cost savings, process efficiencies, and closer relationships with our customers, prospects, business partners, suppliers, and employees.
Wal-Mart	We work for you. We think of ourselves as buyers for our customers, and we apply our considerable strengths to get the best value for you. We've built Wal-Mart by acting on behalf of our customers, and that concept continues to propel us. We're working hard to make our customers' shopping easy.
AT&T	We are dedicated to being the world's best at bringing people together–giving them easy access to each other and to the information and services they want and need–anytime, anywhere.

Defining the Business

To determine an organization's *mission*–the overriding reason it exists to provide customers with goods or services they value–managers must first *define its business* so that they can identify what kind of value customers are receiving. To define the business, managers must ask three related questions about a company's products: (1) *Who* are our customers? (2) *What* customer needs are being satisfied? (3) *How* are we satisfying customer needs?[12] Managers ask these questions to identify the customer needs that the organization satisfies and the way the organization satisfies those needs. Answering these questions helps managers to identify not only the customer needs they are satisfying now, but the needs they should try to satisfy in the future and who their true competitors are. All of this information helps managers plan and establish appropriate goals.

Establishing Major Goals

Once the business is defined, managers must establish a set of primary goals to which the organization is committed. Developing these goals gives the organization a sense of direction or purpose. In most organizations, articulating major goals is the job of the CEO, although other managers have input into the process. Thus, as we showed in this chapter's opening case, at Mattel, CEO Bob Eckert's primary goal is still to be the leader in every segment of the toy market in which the company competes, even though this is very challenging at present. However, the best statements of organizational goals are ambitious–that is, they stretch the organization and require that all its members work to improve its performance.[13] The role of **strategic leadership**, the ability of the CEO and top managers to convey a compelling vision of what they want to achieve to their subordinates, is important here. If subordinates buy into the vision, and model their behaviors on the leader, they develop a willingness to undertake the hard, stressful work that is necessary for creative, risk-taking strategy making.[14] Many popular books such as *Built to Last* provide lucid accounts of strategic leaders establishing "big, hairy, audacious goals (BHAGs)" that serve as rallying points for their subordinates.[15]

strategic leadership The ability of the CEO and top managers to convey a compelling vision of what they want the organization to achieve to their subordinates.

Although goals should be challenging, they should also be realistic. Challenging goals give managers at all levels an incentive to look for ways to improve organizational performance, but a goal that is clearly unrealistic and impossible to attain may prompt managers to give up.[16] Bob Eckert and his managers must be careful not to discourage Mattel's doll designers by setting unrealistic sales targets, for example.

Finally, the time period in which a goal is expected to be achieved should be stated. Time constraints are important because they emphasize that a goal must be attained within a reasonable period; they inject a sense of urgency into goal attainment and act as a motivator.

Formulating Strategy

In **strategy formulation** managers work to develop the set of strategies (corporate, divisional, and functional) that will allow an organization to accomplish its mission and achieve its goals.[17] Strategy formulation begins with managers systematically analyzing the factors or forces inside an organization and outside in the global environment that affect the organization's ability to meet its goals now and in the future. SWOT analysis and

strategy formulation The development of a set of corporate-, business-, and functional-level strategies that allow an organization to accomplish its mission and achieve its goals.

SWOT analysis A planning exercise in which managers identify organizational strengths (S) and weaknesses (W) and environmental opportunities (O) and threats (T).

the five forces model are two useful techniques managers can use to analyze these factors.

SWOT Analysis

SWOT analysis is a planning exercise in which managers identify *internal* organizational strengths (S) and weaknesses (W) and *external* environmental opportunities (O) and threats (T). Based on a SWOT analysis, managers at the different levels of the organization select the corporate-, business-, and functional-level strategies to best position the organization to achieve its mission and goals (see Figure 6.5). In Chapter 4 we discussed forces in the task and general environments that have the potential to affect an organization. We noted that changes in these forces can produce opportunities that an organization might take advantage of and threats that may harm its current situation.

The first step in SWOT analysis is to identify an organization's strengths and weaknesses. Table 6.1 lists many important strengths (such as high-quality skills in marketing and in research and development) and weaknesses (such as rising manufacturing costs and outdated technology). The task facing managers is to identify the strengths and weaknesses that characterize the present state of their organization.

The second step in SWOT analysis begins when managers embark on a full-scale SWOT planning exercise to identify potential opportunities and threats in the environment that affect the organization at the present or may affect it in the future. Examples of possible opportunities and threats that must be anticipated (many of which were discussed in Chapter 4) are listed in Table 6.1. Scenario planning is often used to strengthen this analysis.

With the SWOT analysis completed, and strengths, weaknesses, opportunities, and threats identified, managers can continue the planning process and determine specific strategies for achieving the organization's mission and goals. The resulting strategies should enable the organization to attain its goals by taking advantage of opportunities, countering threats, building strengths, and correcting organizational weaknesses. To appreciate how managers use SWOT analysis to formulate strategy, consider how Douglas Conant, CEO of Campbell Soup, has used it to find strategies to turn around the performance of the troubled food products maker in the 2000s.

Figure 6.5
Planning and Strategy Formulation

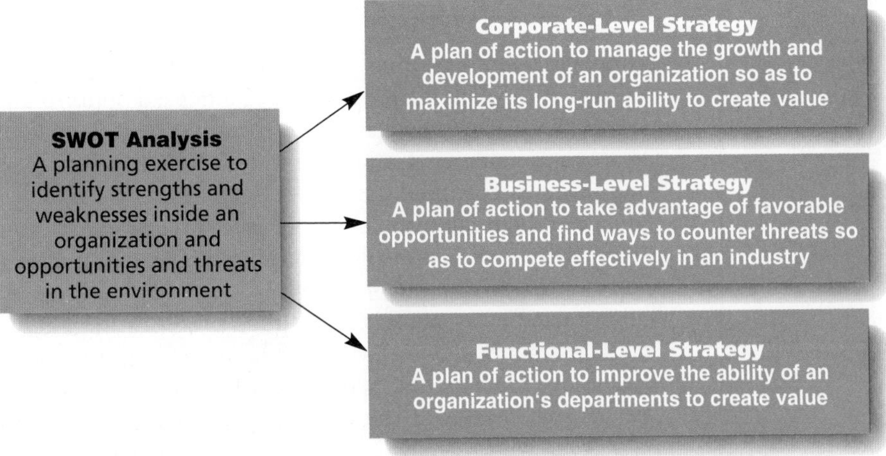

Table 6.1
Questions for SWOT Analysis

Potential Strengths	Potential Opportunities	Potential Weaknesses	Potential Threats
Well-developed strategy?	Expand core business(es)?	Poorly developed strategy?	Attacks on core business(es)?
Strong product lines?	Exploit new market segments?	Obsolete, narrow product lines?	Increase in domestic competition?
Broad market coverage?	Widen product range?	Rising manufacturing costs?	Increase in foreign competition?
Manufacturing competence?	Extend cost or differentiation advantage?	Decline in R&D innovations?	Change in consumer tastes?
Good marketing skills?	Diversify into new growth businesses?	Poor marketing plan?	Fall in barriers to entry?
Good materials management systems?	Expand into foreign markets?	Poor materials management systems?	Rise in new or substitute products?
R&D skills and leadership?	Apply R&D skills in new areas?	Loss of customer goodwill?	Increase in industry rivalry?
Human resource competencies?	Enter new related businesses?	Inadequate human resources?	New forms of industry competition?
Brand-name reputation?	Vertically integrate forward?	Loss of brand name?	Potential for takeover?
Cost of differentiation advantage?	Vertically integrate backward?	Growth without direction?	Changes in demographic factors?
Appropriate management style?	Overcome barriers to entry?	Loss of corporate direction?	Changes in economic factors?
Appropriate organizational structure?	Reduce rivalry among competitors?	Infighting among divisions?	Downturn in economy?
Appropriate control systems?	Apply brand-name capital in new areas?	Loss of corporate control?	Rising labor costs?
Ability to manage strategic change?	Seek fast market growth?	Inappropriate organizational structure and control systems?	Slower market growth?
Others?	Others?	High conflict and politics?	Others?
		Others?	

MANAGER AS A PERSON

Douglas Conant Keeps Stirring Up Campbell Soup

Campbell Soup Co., one of the oldest and best-known global food companies, saw demand for its major product, condensed soup, plummet by 30% during the early 2000s as customers switched from high-salt, processed soups to healthier low-fat, low-salt varieties. Campbell's profits and stock price plunged as its condensed soup business collapsed, and in 2001 its directors brought in a new CEO, Douglas Conant, to help the troubled company. Conant decided it was necessary to develop a three-year turnaround plan to help the company strengthen its market position against aggressive competitors such as General Mills, whose Progresso Soup division had attracted away many of Campbell's customers with its innovative new lines of healthier soup.

One of Conant's first actions was to initiate a thorough SWOT planning exercise. *External analysis* of the environment identified the growth of the organic- and

Douglas Conant, CEO of Campbell's, has revitalized the company through SWOT analysis. From SWOT analysis he has learned how to innovate successful new food products, and Campbell's has emerged as a leader in the low-carb, health-conscious, and luxury-food market segments.

health-food segment of the food market and the increasing number of other kinds of convenience foods as a threat to Campbell's core soup business. It also revealed three growth opportunities: (1) the growing market for health and sports drinks, in which Campbell already was a competitor with its V8 juice; (2) the growing market for quality bread and cookies, in which Campbell competed with its Pepperidge Farm brand; and (3) chocolate products, where Campbell's Godiva brand had enjoyed increasing sales throughout the 1990s.

With the analysis of the environment complete, Conant turned his attention to his organization's resources and capabilities. His *internal analysis* of Campbell identified a number of major weaknesses. These included staffing levels that were too high relative to its competitors and high costs associated with manufacturing its soups because of the use of outdated machinery.

Also, Conant noted that Campbell had a very conservative culture in which people seemed to be afraid to take risks–something that was a real problem in an industry where customer tastes are always changing and new products must be developed constantly. At the same time, the SWOT analysis identified an enormous strength: Campbell enjoyed huge economies of scale because of the enormous quantity of food products that it makes, and it also had a first-rate R&D division capable of developing exciting new food products.

Using the information gained from this SWOT analysis, Conant and his managers decided that Campbell needed to use its product development skills to revitalize its core products and modify or reinvent them in ways that would appeal to increasingly health-conscious and busy consumers. Moreover, it needed to expand its franchise in the health- and sports-, snack-, and luxury-food segments of the market. Also, to increase sales, Campbell's needed to tap into new food outlets, such as corporate cafeterias, college dining halls, and other mass eateries, to expand consumers' access to its foods. Finally, Conant decided to decentralize authority to managers at lower levels in the organization and make them responsible for developing new soup, bread, and chocolate products that met customers' changing needs. In this way he hoped to revitalize Campbell's slow-moving culture and speed the flow of improved and new products to the market.

Conant put his new plan into action, sales of new soup products increased, and he began to put more emphasis on sales of soup at outlets such as 7-11 and Subway and less on supermarket sales.[18] By 2004, analysts felt that he had made a significant difference in Campbell's performance but that there was still a lot to do, as Campbell's operating margins were still shrinking. Carrying on the SWOT analysis, Conant decided Campbell should produce more products to meet the needs of the "low-carb diet," such as new kinds of low-carb bread and cookies. He also decided to shrink the company's operations to lower costs. His goal was to raise profit margins to the level of his major competitors Kraft and General Mills by 2007 using a new three-year plan based on this SWOT analysis.[19]

By 2006 Conant had substantially achieved his goals: Sales of soup had recovered and the Pepperidge Farm and Godiva divisions were earning record sales and profits (sales of Goldfish crackers had increased by 100%!).[20] Campbell's stock price soared, and Conant and employees at all levels received bonuses that rewarded their intense efforts to turn around the company. However, Conant immediately set in motion a new round of SWOT analysis to find new opportunities for developing new kinds of products for new customers.[21]

On the threat side, it was clear that customers wanted more nutritious food and snack products, so he set into motion research to make Campbell's food products more appealing to health-conscious customers. One major opportunity was to reformulate a number of its soups to reduce sodium content, and it introduced new kinds of low-salt soup in 2007. Another opportunity was to develop nutritious luxury soups that would command premium prices.[22] Both these initiatives worked well. On the other hand, pursuing his new goal of making Campbell's foods more nutritious led Conant to question if its highly profitable Godiva chocolate brand was still a good fit for the company. He decided it had become a weakness, and in 2008 he sold it for $850 million.[23] He then used some of the proceeds of this sale to build new company strengths. For example, he invested in R&D to develop the skills needed to customize Campbell's brands to the needs of customers in countries such as India and China, a move that spearheaded global expansion. Under Conant, Campbell's shares in the last five years have posted a total return of 11%, and it has raised its dividend each year. With a culture of innovation permeating the organization, its future looks bright indeed.

The Five Forces Model

A well-known model that helps managers focus on the five most important competitive forces, or potential threats, in the external environment is Michael Porter's five forces model. We discussed the first four forces in the following list in Chapter 4. Porter identified these five factors as major threats because they affect how much profit organizations competing within the same industry can expect to make:

- *The level of rivalry among organizations in an industry:* The more that companies compete against one another for customers–for example, by lowering the prices of their products or by increasing advertising–the lower is the level of industry profits (low prices mean less profit).
- *The potential for entry into an industry:* The easier it is for companies to enter an industry–because, for example, barriers to entry, such as brand loyalty, are low–the more likely it is for industry prices and therefore industry profits to be low.
- *The power of large suppliers:* If there are only a few large suppliers of an important input, then suppliers can drive up the price of that input, and expensive inputs result in lower profits for companies in an industry.
- *The power of large customers:* If only a few large customers are available to buy an industry's output, they can bargain to drive down the price of that output. As a result, industry producers make lower profits.

- *The threat of substitute products:* Often, the output of one industry is a substitute for the output of another industry (plastic may be a substitute for steel in some applications, for example; similarly, bottled water is a substitute for cola). When a substitute for their product exists, companies cannot demand very high prices for it or customers will switch to the substitute, and this constraint keeps their profits low.

Porter argued that when managers analyze opportunities and threats, they should pay particular attention to these five forces because they are the major threats that an organization will encounter. It is the job of managers at the corporate, business, and functional levels to formulate strategies to counter these threats so that an organization can manage its task and general environments, perform at a high level, and generate high profits. At Campbell, Conant performs such an analysis to identify the opportunities and threats stemming from the actions of food industry rivals. For example, as noted earlier, General Mill's Progresso Soups division developed healthier kinds of soups, and this resulted in increased rivalry that lowered Campbell's sales and profits until Campbell succeeded at making new lines of healthy soups itself. Today, both companies are being affected by the threat of rising global food prices as the price of wheat, corn, rice, and dairy products soars. Both companies are striving to reduce operating costs to limit food price increases since the company with the lowest prices will attract the most customers and gain a competitive advantage.

hypercompetition Permanent, ongoing, intense competition brought about in an industry by advancing technology or changing customer tastes.

Today, competition is tough in most industries, whether companies make cars, soup, computers, or dolls. The term **hypercompetition** applies to industries that are characterized by permanent, ongoing, intense competition brought about by advancing technology or changing customer tastes and fads and fashions.[24] Clearly, planning and strategy formulation are much more difficult and risky when hypercompetition prevails in an industry.

Formulating Business-Level Strategies

Michael Porter, the researcher who developed the five forces model, also developed a theory of how managers can select a business-level strategy, a plan to gain a competitive advantage in a particular market or industry.[25] Indeed, Porter argued that business-level strategy creates a competitive advantage because it allows an organization (or a division of a company) to *counter and reduce* the threat of the five industry forces. That is, successful business-level strategy reduces rivalry, prevents new competitors from entering the industry, reduces the power of suppliers or buyers, and lowers the threat of substitutes–and this raises prices and profits.

LO2 Differentiate between the main types of business-level strategies and explain how they give an organization a competitive advantage that may lead to superior performance.

According to Porter, to obtain these higher profits managers must choose between two basic ways of increasing the value of an organization's products: *differentiating the product* to increase its value to customers or *lowering the costs* of making the product. Porter also argues that managers must choose between serving the whole market or serving just one segment or part of a market. Based on those choices, managers choose to pursue one of four business-level strategies: low cost, differentiation, focused low cost, or focused differentiation (see Table 6.2).

low-cost strategy Driving the organization's costs down below the costs of its rivals.

Low-Cost Strategy

With a **low-cost strategy**, managers try to gain a competitive advantage by focusing the energy of all the organization's departments or functions on driving the company's

Table 6.2
Porter's Business-Level Strategies

	Number of Market Segments Served	
Strategy	Many	Few
Low cost	✓	
Focused low cost		✓
Differentiation	✓	
Focused differentiation		✓

costs down below the costs of its industry rivals. This strategy, for example, would require that manufacturing managers search for new ways to reduce production costs, R&D managers focus on developing new products that can be manufactured more cheaply, and marketing managers find ways to lower the costs of attracting customers. According to Porter, companies pursuing a low-cost strategy can sell a product for less than their rivals sell it and yet still make a good profit because of their lower costs. Thus, such organizations enjoy a competitive advantage based on their low prices. For example, BIC pursues a low-cost strategy; it offers customers razor blades priced lower than Gillette's and ballpoint pens less expensive than those offered by Cross or Waterman. Also, when existing companies have low costs and can charge low prices, it is difficult for new companies to enter the industry because entering is always an expensive process.

Differentiation Strategy

differentiation strategy Distinguishing an organization's products from the products of competitors on dimensions such as product design, quality, or after-sales service.

With a **differentiation strategy**, managers try to gain a competitive advantage by focusing all the energies of the organization's departments or functions on *distinguishing* the organization's products from those of competitors on one or more important dimensions, such as product design, quality, or after-sales service and support. Often, the process of making products unique and different is expensive. This strategy, for example, often requires that managers increase spending on product design or R&D to differentiate the product, and costs rise as a result. Organizations that successfully pursue a differentiation strategy may be able to charge a *premium price* for their products, a price usually much higher than the price charged by a low-cost organization. The premium price allows organizations pursuing a differentiation strategy to recoup their higher costs. Coca-Cola, PepsiCo, and Procter & Gamble are some of the many well-known companies that pursue a strategy of differentiation. They spend enormous amounts of money on advertising to differentiate, and create a unique image for, their products. Also, differentiation makes industry entry difficult because new companies have no brand name to help them compete and customers don't perceive other products to be close substitutes, so this also allows for premium pricing and results in high profits.

"Stuck in the Middle"

According to Porter's theory, managers cannot simultaneously pursue both a low-cost strategy and a differentiation strategy. Porter identified a simple correlation:

Differentiation raises costs and thus necessitates premium pricing to recoup those high costs. For example, if BIC suddenly began to advertise heavily to try to build a strong global brand image for its products, BIC's costs would rise. BIC then could no longer make a profit simply by pricing its blades or pens lower than Gillette or Cross. According to Porter, managers must choose between a low-cost strategy and a differentiation strategy. He refers to managers and organizations that have not made this choice as being "stuck in the middle."

Organizations stuck in the middle tend to have lower levels of performance than do those that pursue a low-cost or a differentiation strategy. To avoid being stuck in the middle, top managers must instruct departmental managers to take actions that will result in either low cost or differentiation.

However, exceptions to this rule can be found. In many organizations managers have been able to drive costs below those of rivals and simultaneously differentiate their products from those offered by rivals.[26] For example, Toyota's production system is the most efficient in the world. This efficiency gives Toyota a low-cost strategy vis-à-vis its rivals in the global car industry. At the same time, Toyota has differentiated its cars from those of rivals on the basis of superior design and quality. This superiority allows the company to charge a premium price for many of its popular models.[27] Thus, Toyota seems to be simultaneously pursuing both a low-cost and a differentiated business-level strategy. This example suggests that although Porter's ideas may be valid in most cases, very well-managed companies such as Campbell, Toyota, McDonald's, and Dell may have both low costs and differentiated products–and so make the highest profits of any company in an industry.

Focused Low-Cost and Focused Differentiation Strategies

focused low-cost strategy Serving only one segment of the overall market and trying to be the lowest-cost organization serving that segment.

focused differentiation strategy Serving only one segment of the overall market and trying to be the most differentiated organization serving that segment.

Both the differentiation strategy and the low-cost strategy are aimed at serving many or most segments of a particular market, such as for cars or computers. Porter identified two other business-level strategies that aim to serve the needs of customers in only one or a few market segments.[28] Managers pursuing a **focused low-cost strategy** serve one or a few segments of the overall market and aim to make their organization the lowest-cost company serving that segment. By contrast, managers pursuing a **focused differentiation strategy** serve just one or a few segments of the market and aim to make their organization the most differentiated company serving that segment.

Companies pursuing either of these strategies have chosen to *specialize* in some way by directing their efforts at a particular kind of customer (such as serving the needs of babies or affluent customers) or even the needs of customers in a specific geographic region (customers on the East or West Coast). BMW, for example, pursues a focused differentiation strategy, producing cars exclusively for higher-income customers. By contrast, Toyota pursues a differentiation strategy and produces cars that appeal to consumers in almost *all* segments of the car market, from basic transportation (Toyota Corolla) through the middle of the market (Toyota Camry) to the high-income end of the market (Lexus). An interesting example of how a company pursuing a focused low-cost strategy, by specializing in one market segment, can compete with powerful differentiators is profiled in the following "Management Insight."

MANAGEMENT INSIGHT

Different Ways to Compete in the Soft-Drink Business

"Coke" and "Pepsi" are household names worldwide. Together, Coca-Cola and PepsiCo control over 70% of the global soft-drink market and over 75% of the U.S. soft-drink market. Their success can be attributed to the differentiation strategies they developed to produce and promote their products–strategies that have made them two of the most profitable global organizations. There are several parts to their differentiation strategies. First, both companies built global brands by manufacturing the soft-drink concentrate that gives cola its flavor but then selling the concentrate in a syrup form to bottlers throughout the world. The bottlers are responsible for producing and distributing the actual cola. They add carbonated water to the syrup, package the resulting drink, and distribute it to vending machines, supermarkets, restaurants, and other retail outlets. The bottlers must also sign an exclusive agreement that prohibits them from bottling or distributing the products of competing soft-drink companies. This creates a barrier to entry that helps prevent new companies from entering the industry.

Second, Coca-Cola and PepsiCo charge the bottlers a *premium price* for the syrup; they then invest a large part of the profits in advertising to build and maintain brand awareness. The money they spend on advertising (in 2007 each company spent over $600 million) to develop a global brand name helps Coca-Cola and PepsiCo differentiate their products so that consumers are more likely to buy a Coke or a Pepsi than a lesser-known cola. Moreover, brand loyalty allows both companies to charge a premium or comparatively high price for what is, after all, merely colored water and flavoring.

Cott advertises the fact that any retailer can put its own company name (for example, "Sam's Cola") on its generic Cola.

In the last decade the global soft-drink environment has undergone a major change, however, because of Gerald Pencer, a Canadian entrepreneur who came up with a new strategy for competing against these powerful differentiators. Pencer's strategy was to produce a high-quality, low-priced cola, manufactured and bottled by the Cott Corporation, of which he was CEO at the time, but to sell it as the private-label house brand of major retail stores such as Wal-Mart (Sam's Cola brand) and supermarket chains such as Kroger's (Big K brand), thus bypassing the bottlers. Pencer could implement his *focused low-cost* strategy and charge a low price for his soft drinks because he did not need to spend any money on advertising (the retail stores did that) and because Cott's soft drinks are distributed by the store chains and retailers using their efficient national distribution systems, such as the nationwide trucking system developed by giant retailer Wal-Mart. Retailers are willing to do this because Cott's low-cost soft drinks allow them to make much more profit than they receive from selling Coke or Pepsi. At the same time, the products build their store-brand image.

Pencer implemented this plan first in Canada and then quickly expanded into the United States as retailers' demand for his products grew. He then went on to supply the international market by offering to sell soft-drink concentrate to global retailers at prices lower than Coca-Cola and PepsiCo. By 2004 Cott was the world's largest supplier of retailer-branded carbonated soft drinks.[29] It has manufacturing facilities in Canada, the United States, and the United Kingdom, and a syrup concentrate production plant in Columbus, Georgia, which supply most of the private-label grocery store, drugstore, mass-merchandising, and convenience store chains in these countries. However, note that while Cott is the leading supplier of retailer-branded sodas, it is still focusing on its low-cost strategy. It makes no attempt to compete with Coke and Pepsi, which pursue differentiation strategies and whose brand-name sodas dominate the global soda market.

Increasingly, smaller companies are finding it easier to pursue a focused strategy and compete successfully against large, powerful, low-cost and differentiated companies because of advances in IT that lower costs and enable them to reach and attract customers. By establishing a storefront on the Web, thousands of small, specialized companies have been able to carve out a profitable niche against large bricks-and-mortar competitors. Zara, a Spanish manufacturer of fashionable clothing whose sales have soared in recent years, provides an excellent example of the way even a small bricks-and mortar company can use IT to pursue a focused strategy and compete globally.[30] Zara has managed to position itself as the low-price, low-cost leader in the fashion segment of the clothing market, against differentiators like Gucci, Dior, and Armani, because it has applied IT to its specific needs. Zara has created IT that allows it to manage its design and manufacturing process in a way that minimizes the inventory it has to carry–the major cost borne by a clothing retailer. However, its IT also gives its designers instantaneous feedback on which clothes are selling well and in which countries, and this gives Zara a competitive advantage from differentiation. Specifically, Zara can manufacture more of a particular kind of dress or suit to meet high customer demand, decide which clothing should be sold in its rapidly expanding network of global stores, and constantly change the mix of clothes it offers customers to keep up with fashion–at low cost.

Zara's IT also allows it to manage the interface between its design and manufacturing operations more efficiently. Zara takes only five weeks to design a new collection and then a week to make it. Fashion houses like Chanel and Armani, by contrast, can take six or more months to design the collection and then three more months before it is available in stores.[31] This short time to market gives Zara great flexibility and allows the company to respond quickly to the rapidly changing fashion market, in which fashions can change several times a year. Because of the quick manufacturing-to-sales cycle and just-in-time fashion, Zara offers its clothes collections at relatively low prices and still makes profits that are the envy of the fashion clothing industry.[32]

Zara has been able to pursue a focused strategy that is simultaneously low-cost and differentiated because it has developed many kinds of strengths in functions such as clothing design, marketing, and IT that have given it a competitive advantage. Developing functional-level strategies that strengthen business-level strategy and increase competitive advantage is a vital managerial task. Discussion of this important issue is left until the next chapter. First, we need to go up one planning level and examine how corporate strategy helps an organization achieve its mission and goals.

Formulating Corporate-Level Strategies

Once managers have formulated the business-level strategies that will best position a company, or a division of a company, to compete in an industry and outperform its rivals, they must look to the future. If their planning has been successful the company will be generating high profits, and their task now is to plan how to invest these profits to increase performance over time.

LO3 Differentiate between the main types of corporate-level strategies and explain how they are used to strengthen a company's business-level strategy and competitive advantage.

Recall that *corporate-level strategy* is a plan of action that involves choosing in which industries and countries a company should invest its resources to achieve its mission and goals. In choosing a corporate-level strategy, managers ask, How should the growth and development of our company be managed to increase its ability to create value for customers (and thus increase its performance) over the long run? Managers of effective organizations actively seek out new opportunities to use a company's resources to create new and improved goods and services for customers. Examples of organizations whose product lines are growing rapidly are Google, chipmaker AMD, Apple, and Toyota, whose managers pursue any feasible opportunity to use their companies' skills to provide customers with new products.

In addition, some managers must help their organizations respond to threats due to changing forces in the task or general environment that have made their business-level strategies less effective and have reduced profits. For example, customers may no longer be buying the kinds of goods and services a company is producing (high-salt soup, bulky computer monitors or televisions), or other organizations may have entered the market and attracted away customers (this happened to Intel in the 2000s after AMD began to produce more powerful chips). Top managers aim to find corporate strategies that can help the organization strengthen its business-level strategies and thus respond to these changes and improve performance.

The principal corporate-level strategies that managers use to help a company grow and keep it at the top of its industry, or to help it retrench and reorganize to stop its decline, are (1) concentration on a single industry, (2) vertical integration, (3) diversification, and (4) international expansion. An organization will benefit from pursuing any one or more of these strategies only when the strategy helps further increase the value of the organization's goods and services so that more customers buy them. Specifically, to increase the value of goods and services, a corporate-level strategy must help a company, or one of its divisions, either (1) lower the costs of developing and making products or (2) increase product differentiation so that more customers want to buy the products even at high or premium prices. Both of these outcomes strengthen a company's competitive advantage and increase its performance.

Concentration on a Single Industry

Most growing companies reinvest their profits to strengthen their competitive position in the industry in which they are currently operating; in doing so, they pursue the corporate-level strategy of **concentration on a single industry**. Most commonly, an organization uses its functional skills to develop new kinds of products or it expands the number of locations in which it uses those skills. For example, Apple is expanding the range of its iPods and mobile wireless devices such as the iPhone, while McDonald's, which began as one restaurant in California, focused all its efforts on using its resources to quickly expand across the United States to become the biggest and most profitable U.S. fast-food company.

concentration on a single industry Reinvesting a company's profits to strengthen its competitive position in its current industry.

On the other hand, concentration on a single industry becomes an appropriate corporate-level strategy when managers see the need to *reduce* the size of their organizations to increase performance. Managers may decide to get out of certain industries when, for example, the business-level strategy pursued by a particular division no longer works and the division has lost its competitive advantage. To improve performance, managers now sell off low-performing divisions, concentrate remaining organizational resources in one industry, and try to develop new products customers want to buy. This happened to electronics maker Hitachi when customers were increasingly switching from bulky CRT monitors to newer, flat LCD monitors. Hitachi announced it would close its three CRT factories in Japan, Singapore, and Malaysia and would use its resources to invest in the new LCD technology.[33]

By contrast, when organizations are performing effectively, they often decide to enter new industries in which they can use their resources to create more valuable products. Thus, they begin to pursue vertical integration or diversification.

Vertical Integration

When an organization is performing well in its industry, managers often see new opportunities to create value by either producing the inputs it uses to make its products or distributing and selling its products to customers. Managers at E. & J. Gallo Winery, for example, realized that they could lower Gallo's costs if the company produced its own wine bottles rather than buying bottles from a glass company that was earning good profits from its bottle sales to Gallo. So Gallo established a new division to produce glass bottles more cheaply than buying them; it quickly found that it could also produce new-shaped bottles to help differentiate its wines. **Vertical integration** is a corporate-level strategy in which a company expands its business operations either backward into a new industry that produces inputs for the company's products *(backward vertical integration)* or forward into a new industry that uses, distributes, or sells the company's products *(forward vertical integration)*.[34] A steel company that buys iron ore mines and enters the raw materials industry to supply the ore needed to make steel is engaging in backward vertical integration. A PC maker that decides to enter the retail industry and open a chain of company-owned retail outlets to sell its PCs is engaging in forward integration. For example, in 2001 Apple Computer entered the retail industry when it decided to set up a chain of Apple Stores to sell its computers.

vertical integration Expanding a company's operations either backward into an industry that produces inputs for its products or forward into an industry that uses, distributes, or sells its products.

Figure 6.6 illustrates the four main stages in a typical raw material-to-customer value chain; value is added to the product at each stage by the activities involved

Figure 6.6
Stages in a Vertical Value Chain

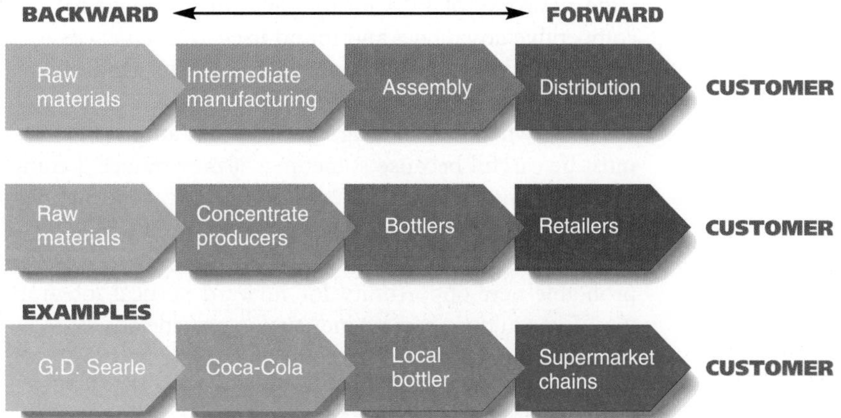

in each industry. For a company based in the assembly stage, backward integration would involve establishing a new division in the intermediate manufacturing or raw material production industries; and forward integration would involve establishing a new division to distribute its products to wholesalers or a retail division to sell directly to customers. A division at one stage or one industry receives the product produced by the division in the previous stage or industry, transforms it in some way–adding value–and then transfers the output at a higher price to the division at the next stage in the chain.

As an example of how this industry value chain works, consider the cola segment of the soft-drink industry. In the raw material industry, suppliers include sugar companies and manufacturers of artificial sweeteners such as NutraSweet and Splenda, which are used in diet colas. These companies sell their products to companies in the soft-drink industry that make concentrate–such as Coca-Cola and PepsiCo, which mix these inputs with others to produce the cola concentrate. In the process, they add value to these inputs. The concentrate producers then sell the concentrate to companies in the bottling and distribution industry, which add carbonated water to the concentrate and package the resulting drink–again adding value to the concentrate. Next, the bottlers distribute and sell the soft drinks to retailers, including stores such as Costco and Wal-Mart and fast-food chains such as McDonald's. Companies in the retail industry add value by making the product accessible to customers, and they profit from direct sales to customers. Thus, value is added by companies at each stage in the raw material-to-consumer chain.

The reason managers pursue vertical integration is that it allows them either to add value to their products by making them special or unique or to lower the costs of making and selling them. An example of using forward vertical integration to increase differentiation is Apple's decision to open its own stores to make its unique products more accessible to customers who could try them out before they bought them. An example of using forward vertical integration to lower costs is Matsushita's decision to open company-owned stores to sell its Panasonic and JVC products and thus keep the profit that otherwise would be earned by independent retailers.[35]

Although vertical integration can strengthen an organization's competitive advantage and increase its performance, it can also reduce an organization's flexibility to respond to changing environmental conditions and create threats that must be countered by changing the organization's strategy. For example, IBM used to produce most of the components it used to make its own mainframe computers. While this made sense in the 1970s when IBM enjoyed a major competitive advantage, it became a major handicap for the company in the 1990s when the increasing use of organization-wide networks of PCs meant slumping demand for mainframes. IBM had lost its competitive advantage and found itself with an excess-capacity problem in its component operations. Closing down this capacity, and exiting the computer components industry, cost IBM over $5 billion.[36]

Thus, when considering vertical integration as a strategy to add value, managers must be careful because sometimes it may reduce a company's ability to create value when the environment changes. This is why so many companies now outsource the production of component parts to other companies and, like IBM, have exited the components industry–by vertically *disintegrating* backward. IBM, however, found a profitable new opportunity for forward vertical integration in the 1990s: It entered the IT consulting services industry to provide advice to large companies about how to install and manage their computer hardware and software.[37] Providing IT services has been a major source of IBM's profitability in the 2000s.

Diversification

diversification Expanding a company's business operations into a new industry in order to produce new kinds of valuable goods or services.

Diversification is the corporate-level strategy of expanding a company's business operations into a new industry in order to produce new kinds of valuable goods or services.[38] Examples include PepsiCo's diversification into the snack-food business with the purchase of Frito Lay, tobacco giant Philip Morris's diversification into the brewing industry with the acquisition of Miller Beer, and GE's move into broadcasting with its acquisition of NBC. There are two main kinds of diversification: related and unrelated.

related diversification Entering a new business or industry to create a competitive advantage in one or more of an organization's existing divisions or businesses.

synergy Performance gains that result when individuals and departments coordinate their actions.

RELATED DIVERSIFICATION **Related diversification** is the strategy of entering a new business or industry to create a competitive advantage in one or more of an organization's existing divisions or businesses. Related diversification can add value to an organization's products if managers can find ways for its various divisions or business units to share their valuable skills or resources so that synergy is created.[39] **Synergy** is obtained when the value created by two divisions cooperating is greater than the value that would be created if the two divisions operated separately and independently. For example, suppose two or more of the divisions of a diversified company can utilize the same manufacturing facilities, distribution channels, or advertising campaigns–that is, share functional activities. Each division has to invest fewer resources in a shared functional activity than it would have to invest if it performed the functional activity by itself. Related diversification can be a major source of cost savings when divisions share the costs of performing a functional activity.[40] Similarly, if one division's R&D skills can be used to improve another division's products and increase their differentiated appeal, this synergy can give the second division an important competitive advantage over its industry rivals–so the company as a whole benefits from diversification.

The way Procter & Gamble's disposable diaper and paper towel divisions cooperate is a good example of the successful production of synergies. These divisions share the costs of procuring inputs such as paper and packaging, a joint sales force sells both products to retail outlets, and both products are shipped using the same distribution system. This resource sharing has enabled both divisions to reduce their costs, and as a result, they can charge lower prices than their competitors and so attract more customers.[41] In addition, the divisions can share the research costs involved in developing new and improved products, such as finding more absorbent material, that increase both products' differentiated appeal. This is something that is also at the heart of 3M's corporate strategy, which is discussed in the following "Management Insight."

MANAGEMENT INSIGHT

How to Make Related Diversification Work

3M is a 100-year-old industrial giant that in 2008 generated almost $25 billion in revenues and over $6 billion in profits from its more than 50,000 individual products, ranging from sandpaper and sticky tape to medical devices, office supplies, and electronic components.[42] From the beginning, 3M has pursued related diversification and created new businesses by leveraging its skills in research and development. Today, the company is composed of more than 40 separate divisions positioned in six major business groups: transportation, health care, industrial, consumer and office, electronics and communications, and specialty materials. The

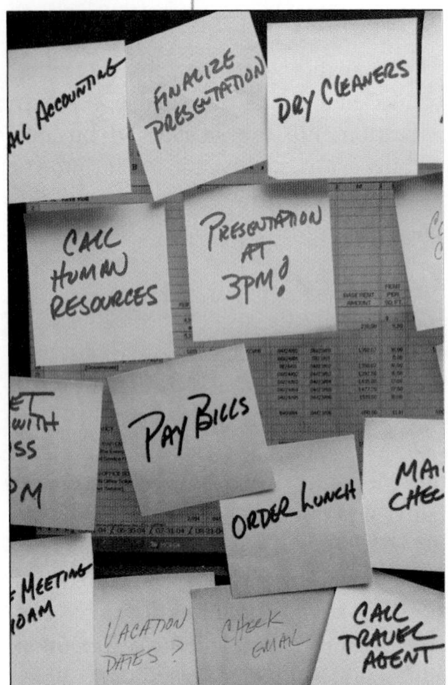

How did we ever survive without Post-it Notes? 3M's intense focus on solving customer problems results in new products that sell very well, including countless variations of the original sticky note.

company currently operates with the goal of producing 40% of sales revenues from products introduced within the previous four years.[43] Its CEO George Buckley has "been on a mission to kick-start growth," and he plans to increase spending on R&D to $1.4 billion or almost 6% of sales to keep achieving this goal.

How does 3M do it? First, the company is a science-based enterprise with a strong tradition of innovation and risk taking. Risk taking is encouraged, and failure is not punished but seen as a natural part of the process of creating new products and business.[44] Second, 3M's management is relentlessly focused on the company's customers and the problems they face. Many of 3M's products have come from helping customers to solve difficult problems. Third, managers set stretch goals that require the company to create new products and businesses at a rapid rate. Fourth, employees are given considerable autonomy to pursue their own ideas; indeed, 15% of employees' time can be spent working on projects of their own choosing without management approval. Many products have resulted from this autonomy, including the ubiquitous Post-it Notes. Fifth, while products belong to business units and it is business units that are responsible for generating profits, the technologies belong to every unit within the company. Anyone at 3M is free to try to develop new applications for a technology developed by its business units. Finally, 3M organizes many companywide meetings where researchers from its different divisions are brought together to share the results of their work. It also implemented an IT system that promotes the sharing of technological knowledge between researchers so that new opportunities can be identified.

In sum, to pursue related diversification successfully, managers search for new businesses where they can use the existing skills and resources in their departments and divisions to create synergies, add value to new products and businesses, and improve their competitive position and that of the entire company. In addition, managers may try to acquire a company in a new industry because they believe it possesses skills and resources that will improve the performance of one or more of their existing divisions. If successful, such skill transfers can help an organization to lower its costs or better differentiate its products because they create synergies between divisions.

unrelated diversification Entering a new industry or buying a company in a new industry that is not related in any way to an organization's current businesses or industries.

UNRELATED DIVERSIFICATION Managers pursue **unrelated diversification** when they establish divisions or buy companies in new industries that are *not* linked in any way to their current businesses or industries. One main reason for pursuing unrelated diversification is that, sometimes, managers can buy a poorly performing company, transfer their management skills to that company, turn around its business, and increase its performance–all of which creates value.

Another reason for pursuing unrelated diversification is that purchasing businesses in different industries lets managers engage in *portfolio strategy,* which is apportioning financial resources among divisions to increase financial returns or spread risks among different businesses, much as individual investors do with their own portfolios. For example, managers may transfer funds from a rich division (a "cash cow") to a new and promising division (a "star") and, by appropriately allocating money between divisions, create value. Though used as a popular explanation in the 1980s for unrelated diversification, portfolio strategy ran into increasing criticism in the 1990s because it simply does not work.[45] Why? As managers expand the scope of their organization's operations and enter more and more industries, it becomes increasingly difficult for top managers to be knowledgeable about all of the organization's diverse businesses. Managers do not have the time to process all of the information required to adequately assess the strategy and performance of each division, and so the performance of the entire company often falls.

This problem arose at GE in the 1970s, as its former CEO Reg Jones commented: "I tried to review each business unit plan in great detail. This effort took untold hours and placed a tremendous burden on the corporate executive office. After a while I began to realize that no matter how hard we would work, we could not achieve the necessary in-depth understanding of the 40-odd business unit plans."[46] Unable to handle so much information, top managers are overwhelmed and eventually make important resource allocation decisions on the basis of only a superficial analysis of the competitive position of each division. This usually results in value being lost rather than created.[47]

Thus, although unrelated diversification can potentially create value for a company, research evidence suggests that *too much* diversification can cause managers to lose control of their organization's core business. As a result, diversification can reduce value rather than create it.[48] Because of this, during the last decade there has been an increasing trend for diversified companies to divest many of their unrelated, and sometimes related, divisions. Managers in companies like Tyco, Dial, and Textron sold off many or most of their divisions and focused on increasing the performance of the core division that remained–in other words, they went back to a strategy of concentrating on a single industry.[49] For example, in 2007 Tyco split into three different companies when it spun off its health care and electronics businesses and focused its activities on engineered and fire and security products, such as its ADT home security business.[50] By 2008, each of the different companies was performing at a higher level under its own team of top managers.[51]

International Expansion

As if planning whether or not to vertically integrate, diversify, or concentrate on the core business was not a difficult enough task, corporate-level managers also must decide on the appropriate way to compete internationally. A basic question confronts the managers of any organization that needs to sell its products abroad and compete in more than one national market: To what extent should the organization customize features of its products and marketing campaign to different national conditions?[52]

global strategy Selling the same standardized product and using the same basic marketing approach in each national market.

multidomestic strategy Customizing products and marketing strategies to specific national conditions.

If managers decide that their organization should sell the same standardized product in each national market in which it competes, and use the same basic marketing approach, they adopt a **global strategy**.[53] Such companies undertake very little, if any, customization to suit the specific needs of customers in different countries. But if managers decide to customize products and marketing strategies to specific national conditions, they adopt a **multidomestic strategy**. Matsushita, with its Panasonic brand, has traditionally pursued a global strategy, selling the same basic TVs, camcorders, and DVD and MP3 players in every country in which it does business and often using the same basic marketing approach. Unilever, the European food and household products company, has pursued a multidomestic strategy. Thus, to appeal to German customers, Unilever's German division sells a different range of food products and uses a different marketing approach than its North American division.

Both global and multidomestic strategies have advantages and disadvantages. The major advantage of a global strategy is the significant cost savings associated with not having to customize products and marketing approaches to different national conditions. For example, Rolex watches, Ralph Lauren or Tommy Hilfiger clothing, Chanel or Armani clothing or accessories or perfume, Dell computers, Chinese-made plastic toys and buckets, and U.S.-grown rice and wheat are all products that can be sold using the same marketing across many countries by simply changing the language. Thus, companies can save a significant amount of money. The major disadvantage of pursuing a global strategy is that, by ignoring national differences, managers may leave themselves vulnerable to local competitors that do differentiate their products to suit local tastes. This occurred in the British consumer electronics industry. Amstrad, a British computer and electronics company, got its start by recognizing and responding to local consumer needs. Amstrad captured a major share of the British audio market by ignoring the standardized inexpensive music centers marketed by companies pursuing a global strategy, such as Sony and Matsushita. Instead, Amstrad's product was encased in teak rather than metal and featured a control panel tailor-made to appeal to British consumers' preferences. To remain competitive in this market, Matsushita had to place more emphasis on local customization of its Panasonic and JVC brands.

A study in contrasts. Matsushita, with its Panasonic brand (shown on the top), has largely pursued a global strategy, selling the same basic TVs and DVD players in every market and using a similar marketing message. Unilever, on the other hand, has pursued a multidomestic strategy, tailoring its product line and marketing approach to specific locations. On the bottom, the CEO of Hindustan Unilever, Keki Dadiseth, holds a box of Surf detergent designed for local customers.

The advantages and disadvantages of a multidomestic strategy are the opposite of those of a global strategy. The major advantage of a multidomestic strategy is that by customizing product offerings and marketing approaches to local conditions, managers may be able to gain market share or charge higher prices for their products. The major disadvantage is that customization raises production costs and puts the multidomestic company at a price disadvantage because it often has to charge prices higher than the prices charged by competitors pursuing a global strategy. Obviously, the choice between these two strategies calls for trade-offs.

Managers at Gillette, the well-known razor blade maker now part of Procter & Gamble, created a strategy that combined the best features of both international strategies. Like Procter & Gamble, Gillette has always been a global organization because its managers quickly saw the advantages of selling its core product, razor blades, in as many countries as possible. Gillette's strategy over the years has been pretty constant: Find a new country with a growing market for razor blades, form a strategic alliance with a local razor blade company and take a majority stake in it, invest in a large marketing campaign, and then build a modern factory to make razor blades and other products for the local market. For example, when Gillette entered Russia after the breakup of the Soviet Union, it saw a huge opportunity to increase sales. It formed a joint venture with a local company called Leninets Concern, which made a razor known as the Sputnik, and then with this base began to import its own brands into Russia. When sales growth rose sharply, Gillette decided to offer more products in the market and built a new plant in St. Petersburg.[54]

In establishing factories in countries where labor and other costs are low and then distributing and marketing its products to countries in that region of the world, Gillette pursued a global strategy. However, all of Gillette's research and development and design activities are located in the United States. As it develops new kinds of razors, it equips its foreign factories to manufacture them when it decides that local customers are ready to trade up to the new product. So, for example, Gillette's latest razor may be introduced in a country abroad years later than in the United States. Thus, Gillette is customizing its product offering to the needs of different countries and so also pursues a multidomestic strategy.

By pursuing this kind of international strategy, Gillette achieves low costs and still differentiates and customizes its product range to suit the needs of each country or world region.[55] Procter & Gamble (P&G) pursues a similar international strategy, and the merger between them to create the world's largest consumer products company came about because of the value that could be realized by pursuing related diversification at a global level. For example, P&G's corporate managers realized that substantial global synergies could be obtained by combining their global manufacturing, distribution, and sales operations across countries and world regions. These synergies have resulted in billions of dollars in cost savings.[56] At the same time, by pooling its knowledge of the needs of customers in different countries, the combined company can better differentiate and position its products throughout the world. P&G's strategy is working; its principal competitors Colgate and Unilever have not performed well in the 2000s, and P&G is developing a commanding global position.

CHOOSING A WAY TO EXPAND INTERNATIONALLY As we have discussed, a more competitive global environment has proved to be both an opportunity and a threat for organizations and managers. The opportunity is that organizations that expand globally are able to open new markets, reach more customers, and gain access to new sources of raw materials and to low-cost suppliers of inputs. The threat is that organizations that expand globally are likely to encounter new competitors in the foreign countries they enter and must respond to new political, economic, and cultural conditions.

Before setting up foreign operations, managers of companies such as Amazon.com, Lands' End, GE, P&G, Dell, and Boeing needed to analyze the forces in the environment of a particular country (such as Korea or Brazil) in order to choose the right method to expand and respond to those forces in the most appropriate way. In general, four basic ways to operate in the global environment are importing and exporting, licensing and franchising, strategic alliances, and wholly owned foreign subsidiaries, Gillette's preferred approach. We briefly discuss each one, moving from the lowest level of foreign involvement and investment required of a global organization and its managers, and the least amount of risk, to the high end of the spectrum (see Figure 6.7).[57]

exporting Making products at home and selling them abroad.

IMPORTING AND EXPORTING The least complex global operations are exporting and importing. A company engaged in **exporting** makes products at home and

Figure 6.7
Four Ways to Expand Internationally

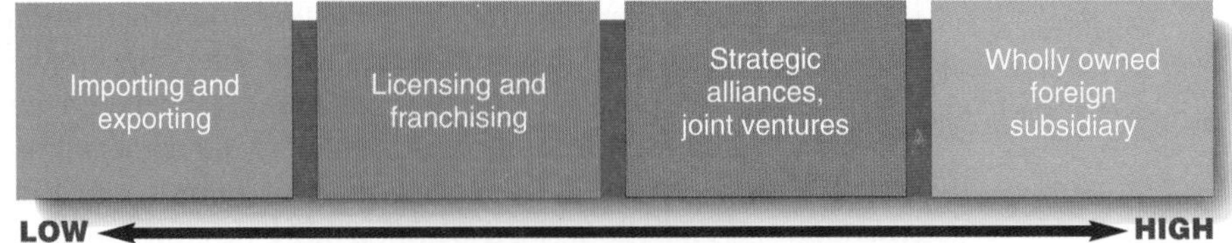

sells them abroad. An organization might sell its own products abroad or allow a local organization in the foreign country to distribute its products. Few risks are associated with exporting because a company does not have to invest in developing manufacturing facilities abroad. It can further reduce its investment abroad if it allows a local company to distribute its products.

importing Selling products at home that are made abroad.

A company engaged in **importing** sells products at home that are made abroad (products it makes itself or buys from other companies). For example, most of the products that Pier 1 Imports and The Limited sell to their customers are made abroad. In many cases the appeal of a product–Irish glass, French wine, Italian furniture, or Indian silk–is that it is made abroad. The Internet has made it much easier for companies to inform potential foreign buyers about their products; detailed product specifications and features are available online, and informed buyers can communicate easily with prospective sellers.

licensing Allowing a foreign organization to take charge of manufacturing and distributing a product in its country or world region in return for a negotiated fee.

LICENSING AND FRANCHISING In **licensing**, a company (the licenser) allows a foreign organization (the licensee) to take charge of both manufacturing and distributing one or more of its products in the licensee's country or world region in return for a negotiated fee. Chemical maker DuPont might license a local factory in India to produce nylon or Teflon. The advantage of licensing is that the licenser does not have to bear the development costs associated with opening up in a foreign country; the licensee bears the costs. A risk associated with this strategy is that the company granting the license has to give its foreign partner access to its technological know-how and so risks losing control over its secrets.

franchising Selling to a foreign organization the rights to use a brand name and operating know-how in return for a lump-sum payment and a share of the profits.

Whereas licensing is pursued primarily by manufacturing companies, franchising is pursued primarily by service organizations. In **franchising**, a company (the franchiser) sells to a foreign organization (the franchisee) the rights to use its brand name and operating know-how in return for a lump-sum payment and a share of the franchiser's profits. Hilton Hotels might sell a franchise to a local company in Chile to operate hotels under the Hilton name in return for a franchise payment. The advantage of franchising is that the franchiser does not have to bear the development costs of overseas expansion and avoids the many problems associated with setting up foreign operations. The downside is that the organization that grants the franchise may lose control over the way in which the franchisee operates and product quality may fall. In this way, franchisers, such as Hilton, Avis, and McDonald's, risk losing their good names. American customers who buy McDonald's hamburgers in Korea may reasonably expect those burgers to be as good as the ones they get at home. If they are not, McDonald's reputation will suffer over time. Once again, the Internet facilitates communication between partners and allows them to better meet each other's expectations.

strategic alliance An agreement in which managers pool or share their organization's resources and know-how with a foreign company, and the two organizations share the rewards and risks of starting a new venture.

STRATEGIC ALLIANCES One way to overcome the loss-of-control problems associated with exporting, licensing, and franchising is to expand globally by means of a strategic alliance. In a **strategic alliance**, managers pool or share their organization's resources and know-how with those of a foreign company, and the two organizations share the rewards or risks of starting a new venture in a foreign country. Sharing resources allows a U.S. company, for example, to take advantage of the high-quality skills of foreign manufacturers and the specialized knowledge of foreign managers about the needs of local customers and to reduce the risks involved in a venture. At the same time, the terms of the alliance give the U.S. company more control over how the good or service is produced or sold in the foreign country than it would have as a franchiser or licenser.

joint venture A strategic alliance among two or more companies that agree to jointly establish and share the ownership of a new business.

A strategic alliance can take the form of a written contract between two or more companies to exchange resources, or it can result in the creation of a new organization. A **joint venture** is a strategic alliance among two or more companies that agree to jointly establish and share the ownership of a new business.[58] An organization's level of involvement abroad increases in a joint venture because the alliance normally involves a capital investment in production facilities abroad in order to produce goods or services outside the home country. Risk, however, is reduced. The Internet and global teleconferencing provide the increased communication and coordination necessary for partners to work together on a global basis. For example, Coca-Cola and Nestlé formed a joint venture to market their teas, coffees, and health-oriented beverages in more than 50 countries.[59] Similarly, BP Amoco and Italy's ENI formed a joint venture to build a $2.5 billion gas-liquefaction plant in Egypt.[60]

wholly owned foreign subsidiary Production operations established in a foreign country independent of any local direct involvement.

WHOLLY OWNED FOREIGN SUBSIDIARIES When managers decide to establish a **wholly owned foreign subsidiary**, they invest in establishing production operations in a foreign country independent of any local direct involvement. Many Japanese car component companies, for example, have established their own operations in the United States to supply U.S.-based Japanese carmakers such as Toyota and Honda with high-quality car components.

Operating alone, without any direct involvement from foreign companies, an organization receives all of the rewards and bears all of the risks associated with operating abroad.[61] This method of international expansion is much more expensive than the others because it requires a higher level of foreign investment and presents managers with many more threats. However, investment in a foreign subsidiary or division offers significant advantages: It gives an organization high potential returns because the organization does not have to share its profits with a foreign organization, and it reduces the level of risk because the organization's managers have full control over all aspects of their foreign subsidiary's operations. Moreover, this type of investment allows managers to protect their technology and know-how from foreign organizations. Large, well-known companies like DuPont, General Motors, and P&G, which have plenty of resources, make extensive use of wholly owned subsidiaries.

Obviously, global companies can use many of these different corporate strategies simultaneously to create the most value and strengthen their competitive position. We have discussed how P&G pursues related diversification at the global level, while it also pursues an international strategy that is a mixture of global and multidomestic. P&G also pursues vertical integration: It operates factories that make many of the specialized chemicals used in its products; it operates in the container industry and makes the thousands of different glass and plastic bottles and jars that contain its products; it prints its own product labels; and it distributes its products using its own fleet of trucks. Although P&G is highly diversified, it still puts the focus on its core individual product lines because it is famous for pursuing brand management–it concentrates resources around each brand, which in effect is managed as a "separate company."

So P&G is trying to add value in every way it can from its corporate- and business-level strategies. At the business level, for example, P&G aggressively pursues differentiation and charges premium prices for its products. However, it also strives to lower its costs and pursues the corporate-level strategies just discussed to achieve this.

Planning and Implementing Strategy

After identifying appropriate business and corporate strategies to attain an organization's mission and goals, managers confront the challenge of putting those strategies into action. Strategy implementation is a five-step process:

LO4 Describe the vital role managers play in implementing strategies to achieve an organization's mission and goals.

1. Allocating responsibility for implementation to the appropriate individuals or groups.
2. Drafting detailed action plans that specify how a strategy is to be implemented.
3. Establishing a timetable for implementation that includes precise, measurable goals linked to the attainment of the action plan.
4. Allocating appropriate resources to the responsible individuals or groups.
5. Holding specific individuals or groups responsible for the attainment of corporate, divisional, and functional goals.

The planning process goes beyond just identifying effective strategies; it also includes plans to ensure that these strategies are put into action. Normally, the plan for implementing a new strategy requires the development of new functional strategies, the redesign of an organization's structure, and the development of new control systems; it might also require a new program to change an organization's culture. These are issues we address in the next two chapters.

Summary and Review

PLANNING Planning is a three-step process: (1) determining an organization's mission and goals; (2) formulating strategy; and (3) implementing strategy. Managers use planning to identify and select appropriate goals and courses of action for an organization and to decide how to allocate the resources they need to attain those goals and carry out those actions. A good plan builds commitment for the organization's goals, gives the organization a sense of direction and purpose, coordinates the different functions and divisions of the organization, and controls managers by making them accountable for specific goals. In large organizations planning takes place at three levels: corporate, business or divisional, and functional or departmental. Long-term plans have a time horizon of five years or more; intermediate-term plans, between one and five years; and short-term plans, one year or less. **[LO1]**

DETERMINING MISSION AND GOALS AND FORMULATING STRATEGY Determining the organization's mission requires that managers define the business of the organization and establish major goals. Strategy formulation requires that managers perform a SWOT analysis and then choose appropriate strategies at the corporate, business, and functional levels. At the business level, managers are responsible for developing a successful low-cost and/or differentiation strategy, either for the whole market or a particular segment of it. At the functional level, departmental managers develop strategies to help the organization either to add value to its products by differentiating them or to lower the costs of value creation. At the corporate level, organizations use strategies such as concentration on a single industry, vertical integration, related and unrelated diversification, and international expansion to strengthen their competitive advantage by increasing the value of the goods and services provided to customers. **[LO1, 2, 3]**

IMPLEMENTING STRATEGY Strategy implementation requires that managers allocate responsibilities to appropriate individuals or groups; draft detailed action plans that specify how a strategy is to be implemented; establish a timetable for implementation that includes precise, measurable goals linked to the attainment of the action plan; allocate appropriate resources to the responsible individuals or groups; and hold individuals or groups accountable for the attainment of goals. **[LO4]**

Management in Action

Topics for Discussion and Action

Discussion

1. Describe the three steps of planning. Explain how they are related. [LO1]
2. What is the relationship among corporate-, business-, and functional-level strategies, and how do they create value for an organization? [LO2, 3]
3. Pick an industry and identify four companies in the industry that pursue one of the four main business-level strategies (low-cost, focused low-cost, etc.). [LO1, 2]
4. What is the difference between vertical integration and related diversification? [LO3]

Action

5. Ask a manager about the kinds of planning exercises he or she regularly uses. What are the purposes of these exercises, and what are their advantages or disadvantages? [LO1]
6. Ask a manager to identify the corporate- and business-level strategies used by his or her organization. [LO2, 3]

Building Management Skills

How to Analyze a Company's Strategy [LO2, 3]

Pick a well-known business organization that has received recent press coverage and that provides its annual reports at its Web site. From the information in the articles and annual reports, answer these questions:

1. What is (are) the main industry(ies) in which the company competes?
2. What business-level strategy does the company seem to be pursuing in this industry? Why?
3. What corporate-level strategies is the company pursuing? Why?
4. Have there been any major changes in its strategy recently? Why?

Managing Ethically [LO1, 4]

A few years ago, IBM announced that it had fired the three top managers of its Argentine division because of their involvement in a scheme to secure a $250 million contract for IBM to provide and service the computers of one of Argentina's largest state-owned banks. The three executives paid $14 million of the contract money to a third company, CCR, which paid nearly $6 million to phantom companies. This $6 million was then used to bribe the bank executives who agreed to give IBM the contract.

These bribes are not necessarily illegal under Argentine law. Moreover, the three managers argued that all companies have to pay bribes to get new business contracts and they were not doing anything that managers in other companies were not.

Questions

1. Either by yourself or in a group, decide if the business practice of paying bribes is ethical or unethical.
2. Should IBM allow its foreign divisions to pay bribes if all other companies are doing so?
3. If bribery is common in a particular country, what effect would this likely have on the nation's economy and culture?

Small Group Breakout Exercise

Low Cost or Differentiation? [LO1, 2]

Form groups of three or four people, and appoint one member as the spokesperson who will communicate your findings to the class when called on by the instructor. Then discuss the following scenario:

You are a team of managers of a major national clothing chain, and you have been charged with finding a way to restore your organization's competitive advantage. Recently, your organization has been experiencing increasing competition from two sources. First, discount stores such as Wal-Mart and Target have been undercutting your prices because they buy their clothes from low-cost foreign manufacturers while you buy most of yours from high-quality domestic suppliers. Discount stores have been attracting your customers who buy at the low end of the price range. Second, small boutiques opening in malls provide high-price designer clothing and are attracting your customers at the high end of the market. Your company has become stuck in the middle, and you have to decide what to do: Should you start to buy abroad so that you can lower your prices and begin to pursue a low-cost strategy? Should you focus on the high end of the market and become more of a differentiator? Or should you try to pursue both a low-cost strategy and a differentiation strategy?

1. Using scenario planning, analyze the pros and cons of each alternative.
2. Think about the various clothing retailers in your local malls and city, and analyze the choices they have made about how to compete with one another along the low-cost and differentiation dimensions.

Be the Manager [LO1, 2]

A group of investors in your city is considering opening a new upscale supermarket to compete with the major supermarket chains that are currently dominating the city's marketplace. They have called you in to help them determine what kind of upscale supermarket they should open. In other words, how can they best develop a competitive advantage against existing supermarket chains?

Questions

1. List the supermarket chains in your city, and identify their strengths and weaknesses.
2. What business-level strategies are these supermarkets currently pursuing?
3. What kind of supermarket would do best against the competition? What kind of business-level strategy should it pursue?

BusinessWeek Case in the News [LO2, 4]

How Acer Is Burning Its PC Rivals

In the personal computer business everybody knows Michael Dell, who changed the industry when he started selling computers out of his college dorm. Mark Hurd has won accolades for reviving Hewlett-Packard. But the most influential force in PCs these days may well be Gianfranco Lanci, the little-known Italian chief executive of Taiwan's Acer. Under his watch, the long-time also-ran has been gobbling up market share and gaining ground on its American rivals. If Lanci can keep the current momentum, Acer could pass second-place Dell in number of computers shipped this year—and close in on

HP. Acer "has a strong chance of overtaking HP," wrote analyst Gokul Hariharan of JPMorgan Chase in a report earlier this month.

Lanci's strategy? He has used Acer's barebones cost structure to get extremely aggressive on price. He moved faster than HP and Dell in marketing a broad selection of the inexpensive portable computers known as netbooks. By selling basic machines for $300 to $600, Acer swiped chunks of market share while the rest of the PC business tanked. In the process, Lanci has driven down prices across the board, torching profits for everyone. "To run a business with lower costs is good when the market is growing," he says. "It's even better when the market is not growing."

Now Lanci is taking this Sherman's March into new territories. On April 7 he unveiled a range of low-priced gizmos that will push Acer into the heart of the PC business and beyond. The company will offer more advanced netbooks at bargain prices, an ultrathin laptop, and the first new machines bearing the Gateway and Packard Bell brands since it acquired those companies in 2007. There's also a new gaming console and, with an eye on Apple, a line of Acer smartphones.

This may be good news for penny-pinching shoppers, but it will create new challenges for Lanci's competitors. HP and Dell will have to face down Acer not just at the low end of the portable market but for higher-end products too. Acer's new ultrathin laptop will have a starting price of $650, compared with $1,800 for a similar HP Voodoo Envy and $2,000 for a Dell Adamo. "They're changing customers' perception of what you should pay for a computer," says Richard Shim, an analyst with the research firm IDC.

Lanci, a 54-year-old Turin-born engineer, has spent most of his career on portable PCs. He was a senior manager at chipmaker Texas Instruments in Italy when Acer bought TI's laptop business in 1997. He made a name for himself by turning Acer into a leading player in Europe, becoming Acer's president in 2005 and CEO last year.

Lanci says his current strategy is simply passing on to customers the savings from Acer's lean operations. Unlike major rivals, Acer sells only through retailers and other outlets, and it outsources all manufacturing and assembly to reduce costs. That has helped cut overhead—research and development, as well as marketing and general and administrative expenses—to 8% of sales, well below the 14% overhead at Dell and 15% at HP.

While many in tech struggle, Acer has boosted profits and seen its stock rise 33% this year. Lanci dismisses critics who say he's too aggressive. "[Prices] have always been going down," he says. "It's the natural evolution of the market."

Questions

1. What kind of business-level strategy is Acer pursuing?
2. What kinds of skills and competences does it possess that allow it to pursue this strategy?
3. In what ways does this strategy allow the company to outperform its rivals Dell and HP?

Source: Bruce Einhorn, "How Acer Is Burning Its PC Rivals." Reprinted from *BusinessWeek* online, April 7, 2009, by special permission, copyright © 2009 by The McGraw-Hill Companies, Inc.

BusinessWeek Case in the News [LO1, 2, 3]

How Procter & Gamble Plans to Clean Up

Since becoming chief executive of Procter & Gamble in 2000, A.G. Lafley has never had it tougher. Shares of the world's biggest consumer-products company have lost a third of their value since last fall. U.S. shoppers are trading down to private-label products from premium-priced brands such as P&G's Tide, Gillette, and Pampers. And the economic downturn is spilling into developing nations where P&G has notched its best growth. Lafley, nonetheless, seems undaunted. The 61-year-old sat down in his Cincinnati office with *BusinessWeek's* Roger O. Crockett to talk about managing through the recession. Here are edited excerpts:

On Spending Priorities

We continue to invest in our core strengths. First, we don't skimp in understanding the consumer. Second is innovation. Our capital spending will go up in 2009 for new engineering and manufacturing technology. And third is branding. Although we actually are spending fewer dollars on advertising because the price of media has gone down, we're delivering more messages to our consumers.

On Product Failures

In our industry only 15% to 20% of new products succeed. P&G's success rate is a little over 50%. But we were at that industry average in the 1990s. We improved our batting average by clarifying and simplifying the innovation process. We set checkpoints with clear measures for each phase of the process from ideation through development and commercialization. If a project looks like it will not make it, we drop it. You learn more from failure than you do from success but the key is to fail early, fail cheaply, and don't make the same mistake twice.

On Premium Pricing

The key thing to understand is that we're not in the commodity business. We're not selling items that fluctuate based on the price of the input materials. We're selling a brand. We can create better value for $1 with a new Downy dishwashing product in Mexico. Or we can do it for $5 or $10 with a household cleaning product like Tide, or for $40 to $50 with a personal-care product like some Olay facial creams. It's all about who is the consumer and what represents value for her.

On Innovation

You need creativity and invention, but until you can connect that creativity to the customer in the form of a product or a service that meaningfully changes their lives, I would argue you don't yet have innovation. We invented a material back in the 1960s that would absorb a lot of water. Until we converted it into a Pampers disposable baby diaper, it was just a new kind of material. We created this entirely new product category, and that created an industry. We'd like to have these kinds of discontinuous innovations be 20% to 25% of what we do. For us to sustain sales and profit growth, we have to innovate.

On P&G's Relationship with Retailers

Virtually every retailer we work with likes the fact that we lead innovation. It creates sales growth in existing categories. It creates new categories that are a source of sales and profit growth in the future. It brings consumers into their stores to try new products, and it brings consumers back to their stores, where they can get products they trust.

On the Rise of Private Labels

Private label is less than 1% of the U.S. retail market, and where it gains traction is in segments that lack innovation. It is difficult to innovate in commodity food categories, which is where private label is winning the most. Private labels are imitators. P&G brands and products are innovators.

On Growth Opportunities

Today we reach a little more than half of the world's 6.7 billion consumers. We want to reach another billion in the next several years, and much of that growth is going to be in the emerging markets, where most babies are being born and where most families are being formed. We see growth across our entire portfolio.

On Acquisitions

Our focus is on long-term, sustainable growth. Acquisitions and divestitures have always been part of that strategy and will continue to be in the future.

On Business Partnerships

Back in 2000 we set a goal of having partners for half of all new products. We hit that goal in 2007–2008. That obviously saves us a lot of money. We can take a P&G dollar and turn it into a dollar and a half to two dollars. Virtually all the work you don't see—taking an order from a retailer or wholesaler, processing orders, scientists working in research centers—is all run collaboratively in back rooms with partners. So our operating margin increases, even though we're still spending on R&D and branding and capital to support innovation.

On Retirement

C'mon, I'm not even 62. I've got some runway left. Right now I'm focused like a laser on P&G and P&G stakeholders. It will probably be something a lot different at 65 and beyond. But this is a seven-day-a-week job, and I still feel young.

Questions

1. What kind of business-level strategy is Procter & Gamble pursuing?
2. What kind of competences does it possess that allow it to pursue this strategy?
3. In what ways is it using other kinds of strategies, such as acquisitions and business partnerships, to build its competitive advantage?

Source: Roger O. Crockett, "How Procter & Gamble Plans to Clean Up." Reprinted from *BusinessWeek* online, April 2, 2009, by special permission, copyright © 2009 by The McGraw-Hill Companies, Inc.

Designing Organizational Structure

CHAPTER 7

Learning Objectives

After studying this chapter, you should be able to

1. Identify the factors that influence managers' choice of an organizational structure. **[LO1]**
2. Explain how managers group tasks into jobs that are motivating and satisfying for employees. **[LO2]**
3. Describe the types of organizational structures managers can design, and explain why they choose one structure over another. **[LO3]**
4. Explain why managers must coordinate jobs, functions, and divisions using the hierarchy of authority and integrating mechanisms. **[LO4]**

Andrea Jung of Avon faced significant challenges in 2006, when the company woke up to the problems engendered by its extremely decentralized structure. Jung's changes mean that regional managers still supervise their own reps, but that the power to develop new products has shifted back to a leaner, more alert corporate headquarters.

MANAGEMENT SNAPSHOT

Avon Is Calling for a New Structure

How Should Managers Organize to Improve Performance?

After a decade of profitable growth under its CEO Andrea Jung, Avon suddenly began to experience falling global sales in the mid-2000s in developing markets in Central Europe, Russia, and China, a major source of its rising sales, as well as in the United States and Mexico. Avon's stock price plunged in 2006, and Jung was shocked by this turn of events; for the first time as CEO she found herself in the position of having to find strategies to solve its problems—rather than new ways to add to its success.[1]

After several months jetting around the globe to visit the managers of its worldwide divisions, she came to a surprising conclusion: Avon's rapid global expansion had given these managers too much autonomy. They had gained so much authority to control operations in their respective countries and world regions that they had made decisions to benefit their own divisions, and these decisions had hurt the performance of the whole company. Avon's country-level managers from Poland to Mexico ran their own factories, made their own product development decisions, and developed their own advertising campaigns. And these decisions were often based on poor marketing knowledge and with little concern for operating costs—their goal was to increase sales as fast as possible. Also, when too much authority is decentralized to managers lower in an organization's hierarchy, these managers often recruit more and more managers to help them build their country "empires." The result was that Avon's global organizational hierarchy had exploded—it had risen from 7 levels to 15 levels of managers in a decade as tens of thousands of extra managers were hired around the globe![2] Because Avon's profits were rising fast, Jung and her top management team had not paid enough attention to the way Avon's organizational structure was becoming taller and taller—just as it was getting wider and wider as it entered more and more countries to expand cosmetics sales.

In 2006, Jung woke up from this nightmare; she had to confront the need to lay off thousands of managers and restructure the organizational hierarchy to reduce costs while maintaining profitability. She embarked on a program to take away the authority of Avon's country-level managers and to transfer authority to regional and corporate headquarters managers to streamline decision making and reduce costs. She cut out seven levels of management and laid off 25% of its global managers in its 114 worldwide markets. Then, using teams of expert managers from corporate headquarters, she embarked on a detailed examination of all Avon's functional activities, country by country, to find out why its costs had risen so quickly and what could be done to bring them under control. The duplication of marketing efforts in countries around the world was one source of these high costs. In Mexico, one team found that country managers' desire to expand their empires led to the development of a staggering 13,000 different products! Not only had this caused product development costs to soar, it had led to major marketing problems, for how could Avon's Mexican sales reps learn about the differences between 13,000 products—and then find an easy way to tell customers about them?

In Avon's new structure the focus was on centralizing all new major product development. Avon develops over 1,000 new products a year, but in the future, while the input from different country managers would be used to customize products to country needs in terms of fragrance, packaging and so on, R&D would be performed in the United States. Similarly, in the future the goal was to develop marketing campaigns targeted toward the average "global" customer, but which could be easily customized to a country or world region by using the appropriate language or the nationality of the models to market the product, for example. Other initiatives have been to increase the money spent on global marketing, which had not kept pace with Avon's rapid global expansion, and a major push to increase the number of Avon ladies in developing nations to attract more customers. In the last two years Avon has recruited another 399,000 reps in China alone![3]

Country-level managers now are responsible for managing this army of Avon reps, and for making sure that marketing dollars are being directed toward the right channels for maximum impact. However, they no longer have any authority to engage in major product development or build new manufacturing capacity—or to hire new managers without the agreement of regional or corporate level managers. The balance of control has changed at Avon, and Jung and all her managers are now firmly focused on making operational decisions in the best interests of the whole company and not just the country in which its cosmetics are sold.

Overview

As the "Management Snapshot" suggests, the challenge facing Andrea Jung of Avon was to identify the best way to organize and control her managers in a new, expanded environment. In this chapter, we examine how managers can organize and control human and other resources to create high-performing organizations.

By the end of this chapter, you will be familiar not only with various organizational structures but also with various factors that determine the organizational design choices that managers make. Then, in Chapter 8, we examine issues surrounding the design of an organization's control systems.

Designing Organizational Structure

Organizing is the process by which managers establish the structure of working relationships among employees to allow them to achieve organizational goals efficiently and effectively. **Organizational structure** is the formal system of task and job reporting relationships that determines how employees use resources to achieve organizational goals.[4] **Organizational design** is the process by which managers

LO1 Identify the factors that influence managers' choice of an organizational structure.

organizational structure A formal system of task and reporting relationships that coordinates and motivates organizational members so that they work together to achieve organizational goals.

organizational design The process by which managers make specific organizing choices that result in a particular kind of organizational structure.

make specific organizing choices about tasks and job relationships that result in the construction of a particular organizational structure.[5]

According to *contingency theory,* managers design organizational structures to fit the factors or circumstances that are affecting the company the most and causing them the most uncertainty.[6] Thus, there is no one best way to design an organization: Design reflects each organization's specific situation, and researchers have argued that in some situations stable, mechanistic structures may be most appropriate while in others flexible, organic structures might be the most effective. Four factors are important determinants of the type of organizational structure or organizing method managers select: the nature of the organizational environment, the type of strategy the organization pursues, the technology (and particularly *information technology*) the organization uses, and the characteristics of the organization's human resources (see Figure 7.1).[7]

The Organizational Environment

In general, the more quickly the external environment is changing and the greater the uncertainty within it, the greater are the problems facing managers in trying to gain access to scarce resources. In this situation, to speed decision making and communication and make it easier to obtain resources, managers typically make organizing choices that result in more flexible structures and entrepreneurial cultures.[8] They are likely to decentralize authority, empower lower-level employees to make important operating decisions, and encourage values and norms that emphasize change and innovation–a more organic form of organizing.

In contrast, if the external environment is stable, resources are readily available, and uncertainty is low, then less coordination and communication among people and functions are needed to obtain resources. Managers can make organizing choices that bring more stability or formality to the organizational structure and can establish values and norms that emphasize obedience and being a team player. Managers in this situation prefer to make decisions within a clearly defined hierarchy of authority and to use detailed rules, standard operating procedures (SOPs), and restrictive norms to guide and govern employees' activities–a more mechanistic form of organizing.

As we discussed in Chapter 4, change is rapid in today's marketplace, and increasing competition both at home and abroad is putting greater pressure on managers to attract

Figure 7.1
Factors Affecting Organizational Structure

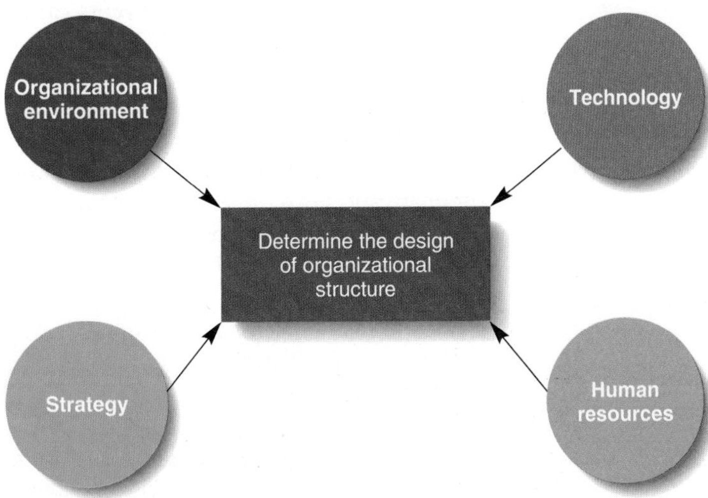

customers and increase efficiency and effectiveness. Consequently, interest in finding ways to structure organizations–such as through empowerment and self-managed teams–to allow people and departments to behave flexibly has been increasing.

Strategy

Chapter 6 suggested that once managers decide on a strategy, they must choose the right means to implement it. Different strategies often call for the use of different organizational structures and cultures. For example, a differentiation strategy aimed at increasing the value customers perceive in an organization's goods and services usually succeeds best in a flexible structure with a culture that values innovation; flexibility facilitates a differentiation strategy because managers can develop new or innovative products quickly–an activity that requires extensive cooperation among functions or departments. In contrast, a low-cost strategy that is aimed at driving down costs in all functions usually fares best in a more formal structure with more conservative norms, which gives managers greater control over the activities of an organization's various departments.[9]

In addition, at the corporate level, when managers decide to expand the scope of organizational activities by vertical integration or diversification, for example, they need to design a flexible structure to provide sufficient coordination among the different business divisions.[10] As discussed in Chapter 6, many companies have been divesting businesses because managers have been unable to create a competitive advantage to keep them up to speed in fast-changing industries. By moving to a more flexible structure, managers gain more control over their different businesses. Finally, expanding internationally and operating in many different countries challenges managers to create organizational structures that allow organizations to be flexible on a global level.[11] As we discuss later, managers can group their departments or divisions in several ways to allow them to effectively pursue an international strategy.

Technology

Recall that technology is the combination of skills, knowledge, machines, and computers that are used to design, make, and distribute goods and services. As a rule, the more complicated the technology that an organization uses, the more difficult it is to regulate or control it because more unexpected events can arise. Thus, the more complicated the technology, the greater is the need for a flexible structure and progressive culture to enhance managers' ability to respond to unexpected situations–and give them the freedom and desire to work out new solutions to the problems they encounter. In contrast, the more routine the technology, the more appropriate is a formal structure, because tasks are simple and the steps needed to produce goods and services have been worked out in advance.

What makes a technology routine or complicated? One researcher who investigated this issue, Charles Perrow, argued that two factors determine how complicated or nonroutine technology is: task variety and task analyzability.[12] *Task variety* is the number of new or unexpected problems or situations that a person or function encounters in performing tasks or jobs. *Task analyzability* is the degree to which programmed solutions are available to people or functions to solve the problems they encounter. Nonroutine or complicated technologies are characterized by high task variety and low task analyzability; this means that many varied problems occur and that solving these problems requires significant nonprogrammed decision making. In contrast, routine technologies are characterized by low task variety and high task analyzability; this means that the problems encountered do not vary much and are easily resolved through programmed decision making.

Examples of nonroutine technology are found in the work of scientists in an R&D laboratory who develop new products or discover new drugs, and they are seen in the planning exercises an organization's top-management team uses to chart the organization's future strategy. Examples of routine technology include typical mass-production or assembly operations, where workers perform the same task repeatedly and where managers have already identified the programmed solutions necessary to perform a task efficiently. Similarly, in service organizations such as fast-food restaurants, the tasks that crew members perform in making and serving fast food are very routine.

Human Resources

A final important factor affecting an organization's choice of structure and culture is the characteristics of the human resources it employs. In general, the more highly skilled its workforce, and the greater the number of employees who work together in groups or teams, the more likely an organization is to use a flexible, decentralized structure and a professional culture based on values and norms that foster employee autonomy and self-control. Highly skilled employees, or employees who have internalized strong professional values and norms of behavior as part of their training, usually desire greater freedom and autonomy and dislike close supervision.

Flexible structures, characterized by decentralized authority and empowered employees, are well suited to the needs of highly skilled people. Similarly, when people work in teams, they must be allowed to interact freely and develop norms to guide their own work interactions, which also is possible in a flexible organizational structure. Thus, when designing organizational structure and culture, managers must pay close attention to the needs of the workforce and to the complexity and kind of work employees perform.

In summary, an organization's external environment, strategy, technology, and human resources are the factors to be considered by managers in seeking to design the best structure and culture for an organization. The greater the level of uncertainty in the organization's environment, the more complex its strategy and technologies, and the more highly qualified and skilled its workforce, the more likely managers are to design a structure and a culture that are flexible, can change quickly, and allow employees to be innovative in their responses to problems, customer needs, and so on. The more stable the organization's environment, the less complex and more well understood its strategy or technology, and the less skilled its workforce, the more likely managers are to design an organizational structure that is formal and controlling and a culture whose values and norms prescribe how employees should act in particular situations.

Later in the chapter we discuss how managers can create different kinds of organizational cultures. First, however, we discuss how managers can design flexible or formal organizational structures. The way an organization's structure works depends on the organizing choices managers make about three issues:

- How to group tasks into individual jobs.
- How to group jobs into functions and divisions.
- How to allocate authority and coordinate or integrate functions and divisions.

Grouping Tasks into Jobs: Job Design

LO2 Explain how managers group tasks into jobs that are motivating and satisfying for employees.

job design The process by which managers decide how to divide tasks into specific jobs.

The first step in organizational design is **job design**, the process by which managers decide how to divide into specific jobs the tasks that have to be performed to provide customers with goods and services. Managers at McDonald's, for example, have decided how best to divide the tasks required to provide customers with fast, cheap food in each McDonald's restaurant. After experimenting with different job arrangements, McDonald's managers decided on a basic division of labor among chefs and food servers. Managers allocated all the tasks involved in actually cooking the food (putting oil in the fat fryers, opening packages of frozen french fries, putting beef patties on the grill, making salads, and so on) to the job of chef. They allocated all the tasks involved in giving the food to customers (such as greeting customers, taking orders, putting fries and burgers into bags, adding salt, pepper, and napkins, and taking money) to food servers. In addition, they created other jobs–the job of dealing with drive-through customers, the job of keeping the restaurant clean, and the job of overseeing employees and responding to unexpected events. The result of the job design process is a *division of labor* among employees, one that McDonald's managers have discovered through experience is most efficient.

At Subway, the roles of chef and server are combined into one, making the job "larger" than the jobs of McDonald's more specialized food servers. The idea behind job enlargement is that increasing the range of tasks performed by the worker will reduce boredom.

Establishing an appropriate division of labor among employees is a critical part of the organizing process, one that is vital to increasing efficiency and effectiveness. At McDonald's, the tasks associated with chef and food server were split into different jobs because managers found that, for the kind of food McDonald's serves, this approach was most efficient. It is efficient because when each employee is given fewer tasks to perform (so that each job becomes more specialized), employees become more productive at performing the tasks that constitute each job.

At Subway sandwich shops, however, managers chose a different kind of job design. At Subway, there is no division of labor among the people who make the sandwiches, wrap the sandwiches, give them to customers, and take the money. The roles of chef and food server are combined into one. This different division of tasks and jobs is efficient for Subway and not for McDonald's because Subway serves a limited menu of mostly submarine-style sandwiches that are prepared to order. Subway's production system is far simpler than McDonald's, because McDonald's menu is much more varied and its chefs must cook many different kinds of foods.

Managers of every organization must analyze the range of tasks to be performed and then create jobs that best allow the organization to give customers the goods and services they want. In deciding how to assign tasks to individual jobs, however, managers must be careful not to take **job simplification**, the process of reducing the number of tasks that each worker performs, too far.[13] Too much job simplification may reduce efficiency rather than increase it if workers find their simplified jobs boring and monotonous, become demotivated and unhappy, and, as a result, perform at a low level.

job simplification The process of reducing the number of tasks that each worker performs.

Job Enlargement and Job Enrichment

In an attempt to create a division of labor and design individual jobs to encourage workers to perform at a higher level and be more satisfied with their work, several researchers have proposed ways other than job simplification to group tasks into jobs: job enlargement and job enrichment.

job enlargement Increasing the number of different tasks in a given job by changing the division of labor.

Job enlargement is increasing the number of different tasks in a given job by changing the division of labor.[14] For example, because Subway food servers make the food as well as serve it, their jobs are "larger" than the jobs of McDonald's food servers. The idea behind job enlargement is that increasing the range of tasks performed by a worker will reduce boredom and fatigue and may increase motivation to perform at a high level–increasing both the quantity and the quality of goods and services provided.

job enrichment Increasing the degree of responsibility a worker has over his or her job.

Job enrichment is increasing the degree of responsibility a worker has over a job by, for example, (1) empowering workers to experiment to find new or better ways of doing the job, (2) encouraging workers to develop new skills, (3) allowing workers to decide how to do the work and giving them the responsibility for deciding how to respond to unexpected situations, and (4) allowing workers to monitor and measure their own performance.[15] The idea behind job enrichment is that increasing workers' responsibility increases their involvement in their jobs and thus increases their interest in the quality of the goods they make or the services they provide.

In general, managers who make design choices that increase job enrichment and job enlargement are likely to increase the degree to which people behave flexibly rather than rigidly or mechanically. Narrow, specialized jobs are likely to lead people to behave in predictable ways; workers who perform a variety of tasks and who are allowed and encouraged to discover new and better ways to perform their jobs are likely to act flexibly and creatively. Thus, managers who enlarge and enrich jobs create a flexible organizational structure, and those who simplify jobs create a more formal structure. If workers are grouped into self-managed work teams, the organization is likely to be flexible because team members provide support for each other and can learn from one another.

The Job Characteristics Model

J. R. Hackman and G. R. Oldham's job characteristics model is an influential model of job design that explains in detail how managers can make jobs more interesting and motivating.[16] Hackman and Oldham's model (see Figure 7.2) also describes the likely

Figure 7.2
The Job Characteristics Model

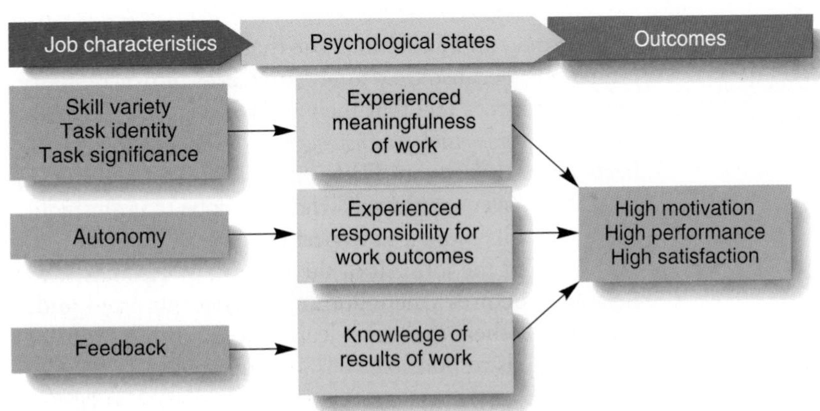

Source: Adapted from J. R. Hackman and G. R. Oldham, *Work Redesign,* Figure 4.2, page 77, © 1980. Reprinted with permission of Pearson Education, Upper Saddle River, NJ.

personal and organizational outcomes that will result from enriched and enlarged jobs.

According to Hackman and Oldham, every job has five characteristics that determine how motivating the job is. These characteristics determine how employees react to their work and lead to outcomes such as high performance and satisfaction and low absenteeism and turnover:

- *Skill variety:* The extent to which a job requires that an employee use a wide range of different skills, abilities, or knowledge. Example: The skill variety required by the job of a research scientist is higher than that called for by the job of a McDonald's food server.
- *Task identity:* The extent to which a job requires that a worker perform all the tasks necessary to complete the job, from the beginning to the end of the production process. Example: A craftsworker who takes a piece of wood and transforms it into a custom-made desk has higher task identity than does a worker who performs only one of the numerous operations required to assemble a flat screen TV.
- *Task significance:* The degree to which a worker feels his or her job is meaningful because of its effect on people inside the organization, such as coworkers, or on people outside the organization, such as customers. Example: A teacher who sees the effect of his or her efforts in a well-educated and well-adjusted student enjoys high task significance compared to a dishwasher who monotonously washes dishes as they come to the kitchen.
- *Autonomy:* The degree to which a job gives an employee the freedom and discretion needed to schedule different tasks and decide how to carry them out. Example: Salespeople who have to plan their schedules and decide how to allocate their time among different customers have relatively high autonomy compared to assembly-line workers, whose actions are determined by the speed of the production line.
- *Feedback:* The extent to which actually doing a job provides a worker with clear and direct information about how well he or she has performed the job. Example: An air traffic controller whose mistakes may result in a midair collision receives immediate feedback on job performance; a person who compiles statistics for a business magazine often has little idea of when he or she makes a mistake or does a particularly good job.

Hackman and Oldham argue that these five job characteristics affect an employee's motivation because they affect three critical psychological states (see Figure 7.2). The more employees feel that their work is *meaningful* and that they are *responsible for work outcomes and responsible for knowing how those outcomes affect others,* the more motivating work becomes and the more likely employees are to be satisfied and to perform at a high level. Moreover, employees who have jobs that are highly motivating are called on to use their skills more and to perform more tasks, and they are given more responsibility for doing the job. All of the foregoing are characteristic of jobs and employees in flexible structures where authority is decentralized and where employees commonly work with others and must learn new skills to complete the range of tasks for which their group is responsible.

Grouping Jobs into Functions and Divisions: Designing Organizational Structure

Once managers have decided which tasks to allocate to which jobs, they face the next organizing decision: how to group jobs together to best match the needs of the organization's environment, strategy, technology, and human resources. Typically, managers first decide to group jobs into departments and they design a *functional structure* to use organizational resources effectively. As an organization grows and becomes more difficult to control, managers must choose a more complex organizational design, such as a divisional structure or a matrix or product team structure. The different ways in which managers can design organizational structure are discussed next. Selecting and designing an organizational structure to increase efficiency and effectiveness is a significant challenge. As noted in Chapter 6, managers reap the rewards of a well-thought-out strategy only if they choose the right type of structure to implement the strategy. The ability to make the right kinds of organizing choices is often what differentiates effective from ineffective managers and creates a high-performing organization.

LO3 Describe the types of organizational structures managers can design, and explain why they choose one structure over another.

Functional Structure

A *function* is a group of people, working together, who possess similar skills or use the same kind of knowledge, tools, or techniques to perform their jobs. Manufacturing, sales, and research and development are often organized into functional departments. A **functional structure** is an organizational structure composed of all the departments that an organization requires to produce its goods or services. Figure 7.3 shows the functional structure that Pier 1 Imports, the home furnishings company, uses to supply its customers with a range of goods from around the world to satisfy their desires for new and innovative products.

functional structure An organizational structure composed of all the departments that an organization requires to produce its goods or services.

Pier 1's main functions are finance and administration, merchandising (purchasing the goods), stores (managing the retail outlets), planning and allocations (managing marketing, credit, and product distribution), and human resources. Each job inside a function exists because it helps the function perform the activities necessary for high organizational performance. Thus, within the planning and allocations function are all the jobs necessary to efficiently advertise Pier 1's products to increase their appeal to customers (such as promotion, photography, and visual communication) and then to distribute and transport the products to stores.

There are several advantages to grouping jobs according to function. First, when people who perform similar jobs are grouped together, they can learn from observing one another and thus become more specialized and can perform at a higher level. The tasks associated with one job often are related to the tasks associated with another job, which encourages cooperation within a function. In Pier 1's planning department, for example, the person designing the photography program for an ad campaign works closely with the person responsible for designing store layouts and with visual communication experts. As a result, Pier 1 is able to develop a strong, focused marketing campaign to differentiate its products.

Second, when people who perform similar jobs are grouped together, it is easier for managers to monitor and evaluate their performance.[17] Imagine if marketing experts, purchasing experts, and real-estate experts were grouped together in one function and supervised by a manager from merchandising. Obviously, the merchandising manager

Figure 7.3
The Functional Structure of Pier 1 Imports

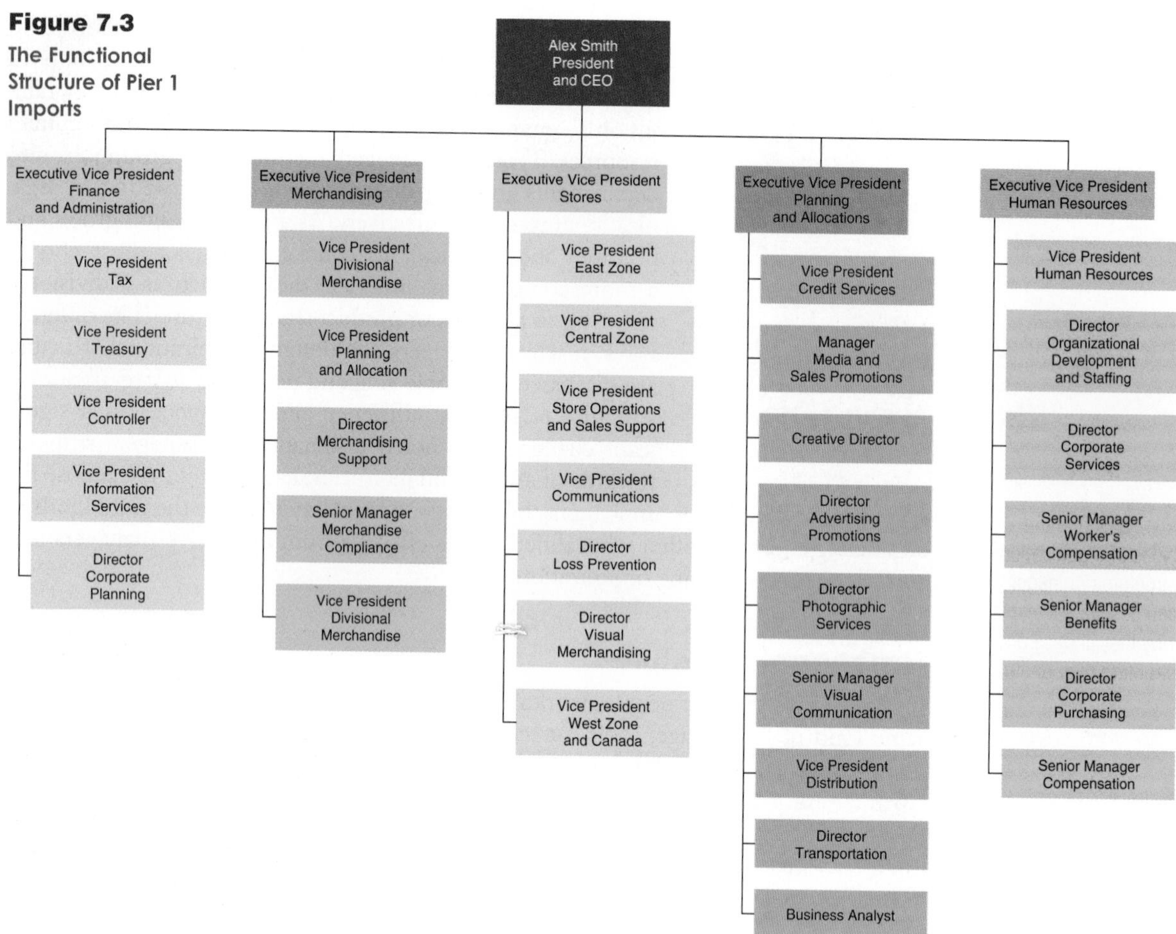

would not have the expertise to evaluate all these different people appropriately. However a functional structure allows workers to evaluate how well coworkers are performing their jobs, and if some workers are performing poorly, more experienced workers can help them develop new skills.

Finally, managers appreciate functional structure because it allows them to create the set of functions they need in order to scan and monitor the competitive environment and obtain information about the way it is changing.[18] With the right set of functions in place, managers are then in a good position to develop a strategy that allows the organization to respond to its changing situation. Employees in the marketing group can specialize in monitoring new marketing developments that will allow Pier 1 to better target its customers. Employees in merchandising can monitor all potential suppliers of home furnishings both at home and abroad to find the goods most likely to appeal to Pier 1's customers and manage Pier 1's global outsourcing supply chain.

As an organization grows, and particularly as its task environment and strategy change because it is beginning to produce a wider range of goods and services for different kinds of customers, several problems can make a functional structure less efficient and effective.[19] First, managers in different functions may find it more difficult to communicate and coordinate with one another when they are responsible for several different kinds of products, especially as the organization grows both domestically

Pier 1 organizes its operations by function, which means that employees can more easily learn from one another and improve the service they provide to its customers.

and internationally. Second, functional managers may become so preoccupied with supervising their own specific departments and achieving their departmental goals that they lose sight of organizational goals. If that happens, organizational effectiveness will suffer because managers will be viewing issues and problems facing the organization only from their own, relatively narrow, departmental perspectives.[20] Both of these problems can reduce efficiency and effectiveness.

Divisional Structures: Product, Market, and Geographic

divisional structure An organizational structure composed of separate business units within which are the functions that work together to produce a specific product for a specific customer.

As the problems associated with growth and diversification increase over time, managers must search for new ways to organize their activities to overcome the problems associated with a functional structure. Most managers of large organizations choose a **divisional structure** and create a series of business units to produce a specific kind of product for a specific kind of customer. Each *division* is a collection of functions or departments that work together to produce the product. The goal behind the change to a divisional structure is to create smaller, more manageable units within the organization. There are three forms of divisional structure (see Figure 7.4).[21] When managers organize divisions according to the *type of good or service* they provide, they adopt a product structure. When managers organize divisions according to the *area of the country or world* they operate in, they adopt a geographic structure. When managers organize divisions according to *the type of customer* they focus on, they adopt a market structure.

PRODUCT STRUCTURE Imagine the problems that managers at Pier 1 would encounter if they decided to diversify into producing and selling cars, fast food, and health insurance–in addition to home furnishings–and tried to use their existing set of functional managers to oversee the production of all four kinds of products. No manager would have the necessary skills or abilities to oversee those four products. No individual marketing manager, for example, could effectively market cars, fast food,

Figure 7.4
Product, Market, and Geographic Structures

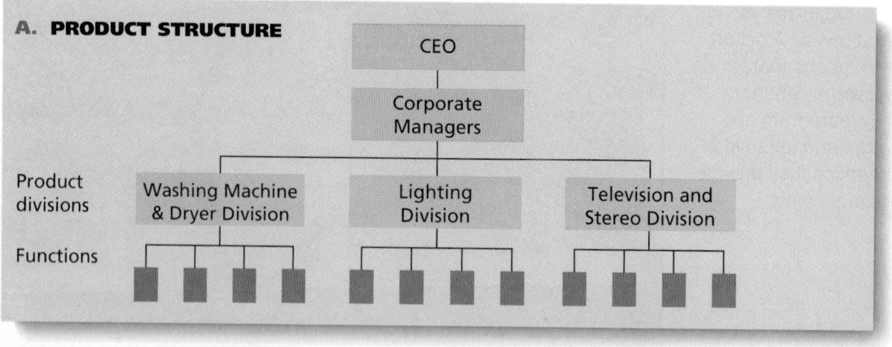

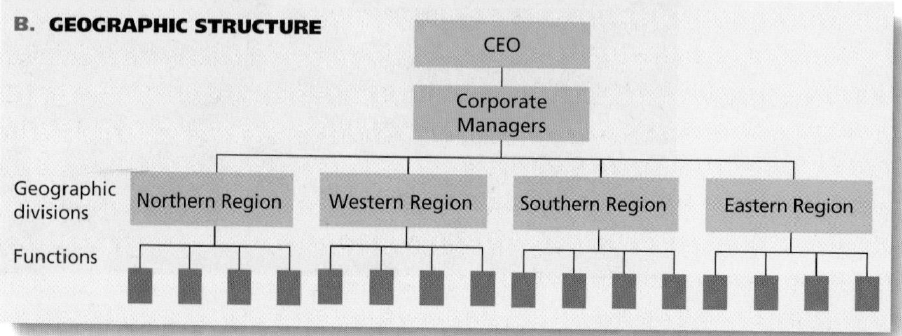

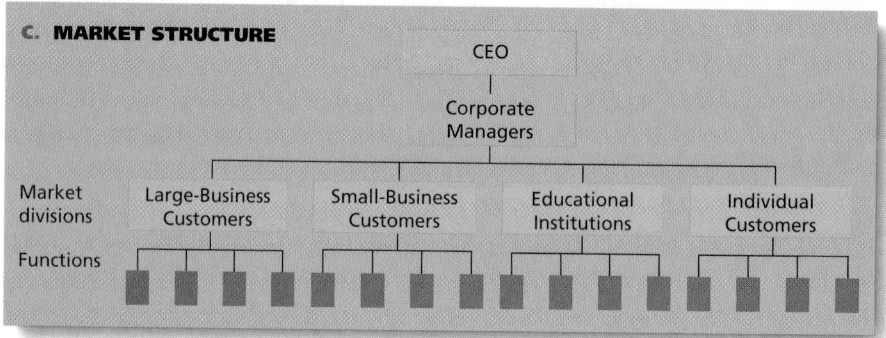

health insurance, and home furnishings at the same time. To perform a functional activity successfully, managers must have experience in specific markets or industries. Consequently, if managers decide to diversify into new industries or to expand their range of products, they commonly design a product structure to organize their operations (see Figure 7.4A).

product structure An organizational structure in which each product line or business is handled by a self-contained division.

Using a **product structure**, managers place each distinct product line or business in its own self-contained division and give divisional managers the responsibility for devising an appropriate business-level strategy to allow the division to compete effectively in its industry or market.[22] Each division is self-contained because it has a complete set of all the functions–marketing, R&D, finance, and so on–that it needs to produce or provide goods or services efficiently and effectively. Functional managers report to divisional managers, and divisional managers report to top or corporate managers.

Grouping functions into divisions focused on particular products has several advantages for managers at all levels in the organization. First, a product structure allows

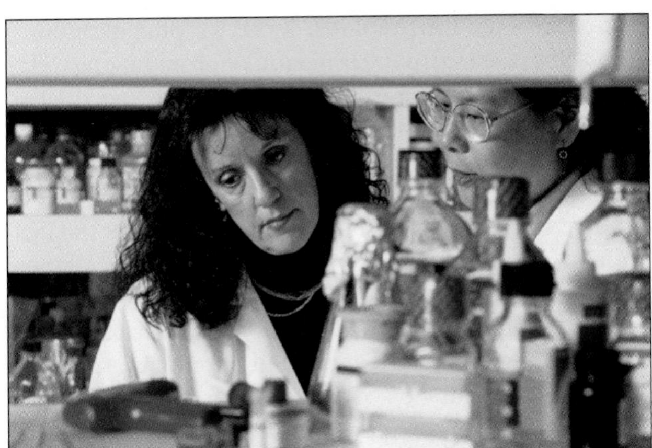

When Glaxo Wellcome and SmithKline Beecham merged, managers resolved the problem of how to coordinate the activities of thousands of research scientists by organizing them into product divisions focusing on clusters of diseases.

functional managers to specialize in only one product area, so they are able to build expertise and fine-tune their skills in this particular area. Second, each division's managers can become experts in their industry; this expertise helps them choose and develop a business-level strategy to differentiate their products or lower their costs while meeting the needs of customers. Third, a product structure frees corporate managers from the need to supervise directly each division's day-to-day operations; this latitude allows corporate managers to create the best corporate-level strategy to maximize the organization's future growth and ability to create value. Corporate managers are likely to make fewer mistakes about which businesses to diversify into or how to best expand internationally, for example, because they are able to take an organizationwide view.[23] Corporate managers also are likely to evaluate better how well divisional managers are doing, and they can intervene and take corrective action as needed.

The extra layer of management, the divisional management layer, can improve the use of organizational resources. Moreover, a product structure puts divisional managers close to their customers and lets them respond quickly and appropriately to the changing task environment. One pharmaceutical company that has recently adopted a new product structure to better organize its activities with great success is GlaxoSmithKline. The need to innovate new kinds of prescription drugs in order to boost performance is a continual battle for pharmaceutical companies. In the 2000s many of these companies have been merging to try to increase their research productivity, and one of them, GlaxoSmithKline, was created from the merger between Glaxo Wellcome and SmithKline Beecham.[24] Prior to the merger, both companies experienced a steep decline in the number of new prescription drugs their scientists were able to invent. The problem facing the new company's top managers was how to best use and combine the talents of the scientists and researchers from both of the former companies to allow them to quickly innovate exciting new drugs.

Top managers realized that after the merger there would be enormous problems associated with coordinating the activities of the thousands of research scientists who were working on hundreds of different kinds of drug research programs. Understanding the problems associated with large size, the top managers decided to group the researchers into eight smaller product divisions to allow them to focus on particular clusters of diseases such as heart disease or viral infections. The members of each product division were told that they would be rewarded based on the number of new prescription drugs they were able to invent and the speed with which they could bring these new drugs to the market. To date, GlaxoSmithKline's new product structure has worked well. By 2008 research productivity had more than doubled since the reorganization, and today a record number of new drugs are moving into clinical trials.[25]

GEOGRAPHIC STRUCTURE When organizations expand rapidly both at home and abroad, functional structures can create special problems because managers in one central location may find it increasingly difficult to deal with the different problems and issues that may arise in each region of a country or area of the world. In these cases, a

geographic structure An organizational structure in which each region of a country or area of the world is served by a self-contained division.

geographic structure, in which divisions are broken down by geographic location, is often chosen (see Figure 7.4B). To achieve the corporate mission of providing next-day mail service, Fred Smith, CEO of FedEx, chose a geographic structure and divided up operations by creating a division in each region. Large retailers such as Macy's, Neiman Marcus, and Brooks Brothers also use a geographic structure. Since the needs of retail customers differ by region–for example, surfboards in California and down parkas in the Midwest–a geographic structure gives retail regional managers the flexibility they need to choose the range of products that best meets the needs of regional customers.

In adopting a *global geographic structure,* such as shown in Figure 7.5A, managers locate different divisions in each of the world regions where the organization operates. Managers are most likely to do this when they pursue a multidomestic strategy, because customer needs vary widely by country or world region. For example, if products that appeal to U.S. customers do not sell in Europe, the Pacific Rim, or South America, then managers must customize the products to meet the needs of customers in those different world regions; a global geographic structure with global divisions will allow them to do this.

In contrast, to the degree that customers abroad are willing to buy the same kind of product, or slight variations thereof, managers are more likely to pursue a global strategy. In this case they are more likely to use a global product structure. In a *global product structure,* each product division, not the country and regional managers, takes responsibility for deciding where to manufacture its products and how to market them in countries worldwide (see Figure 7.5B). Product division managers manage their

Figure 7.5
Global Geographic and Global Product Structures

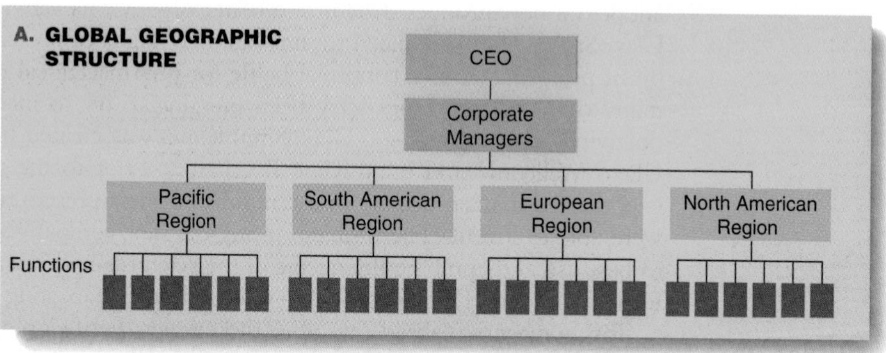

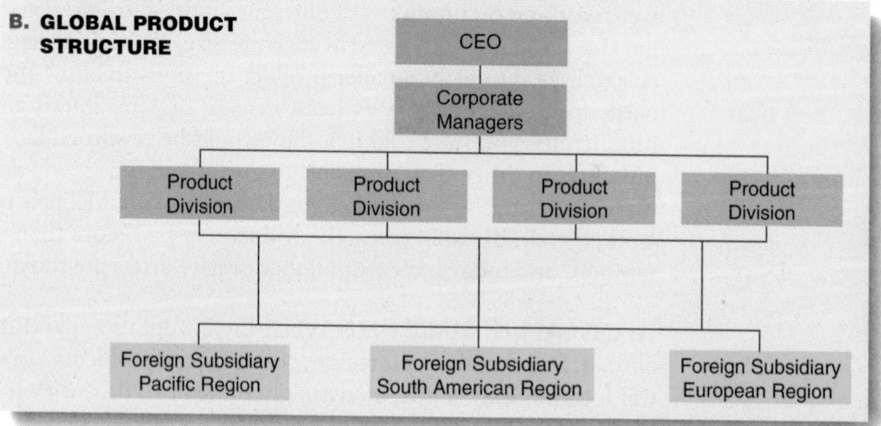

own global value chains and decide where to establish foreign subsidiaries to distribute and sell their products to customers in foreign countries. As we noted at the beginning of this chapter, an organization's strategy is a major determinant of its structure both at home and abroad. The way Nokia uses a global geographic structure to organize its worldwide operations is profiled in the following "Managing Globally."

MANAGING GLOBALLY

Nokia's Geographic Structure Helps It Conquer the World

Nokia took a commanding lead in global cell phone sales over archrival Motorola as a result of its strategy of customizing phones to the needs of local users and assembling the phones in a factory located in a country within the world region where the phones are to be sold. Nokia's most important function is its design and engineering function, which spearheads its global new product development efforts. And to allow this function, and so the company, to perform most effectively, Nokia adopted a global structure to organize its design activities.

Nokia was the first cell phone manufacturer to recognize that the needs of customers differ markedly in different countries of the world. In Western countries, for example, the style of the phone is paramount, as is its ability to offer users services like e-mail and video downloading–hence the popularity of Apple's iPhone, which Nokia was rushing to copy in 2008. In India, customers also value style, and they buy a cell phone as a status symbol and so are willing to pay a premium price for it. But in China customers want a bargain–the phone has to be at the right price point if customers are to buy the entry-level version or be enticed to spend more for premium features. How did Nokia discover how much customer needs diverge among customers in different countries?

Nokia maintains its central design studio in Finland, shown here, where its designers receive the ideas generated by its nine regional design centers scattered across the globe and use them to better customize its phones to the needs of global customers.

Its top managers decided that the engineers in its vast central design studio in Finland should be in charge of basic cell phone R&D, and for monitoring changing global forces in technology and changing customer demand for services such as video downloads, touch screens, colors, and so forth. However, to get close to customers in different countries top managers decided to open nine different geographic design studios in various world regions and countries, such as India and China, where Nokia hopes to generate the most sales revenues. Engineers in these geographical studios, aided by marketing experts, determine the most important country-specific customer preferences.[26] These preferences are then transmitted back to Nokia's Finnish design headquarters, where they are incorporated into the studio's knowledge about changing global preferences for faster Internet service, touch screens, and so on. The result is a range of phones that share much in common but that are also highly customized to the needs of customers in different regions and countries. So, for example, in 2008 Nokia brought out eight different versions of a new entry-level cell phone to better meet global customer needs. One version of this phone is directed specifically at the poorest developing nations, where it is common for a cell phone to be shared among the members of a family—or even by a village.[27] Nokia made this version especially sturdy, and created several different phone directories, so each member of a family, for example, could have his or her own separate list.[28]

So both in design and manufacturing Nokia has adopted a global divisional structure to spearhead its attempts to remain on top in the fiercely competitive global cell phone market; its success so far has been demonstrated by the increasing amounts of its revenues that come from global sales.

MARKET STRUCTURE Sometimes the pressing issue facing managers is to group functions according to the type of customer buying the product, in order to tailor the products the organization offers to each customer's unique demands. A PC maker such as Dell, for example, has several kinds of customers, including large businesses (which might demand networks of computers linked to a mainframe computer), small companies (which may need just a few PCs linked together), educational users in schools and universities (which might want thousands of independent PCs for their students), and individual users (who may want high-quality multimedia PCs so that they can play the latest video games).

market structure An organizational structure in which each kind of customer is served by a self-contained division; also called *customer structure.*

To satisfy the needs of diverse customers, a company might adopt a **market structure,** which groups divisions according to the particular kinds of customers they serve (refer back to Figure 7.4C). A market structure allows managers to be responsive to the needs of their customers and allows them to act flexibly in making decisions in response to customers' changing needs. Dell, for example, moved from a functional to a market structure when it created four market divisions that are each focused on being responsive to a particular type of customer: corporate, small business, home computer users, and government and state agencies. Its new structure worked spectacularly well, as its sales soared through the 1990s.

Matrix and Product Team Designs

Moving to a product, market, or geographic divisional structure allows managers to respond more quickly and flexibly to the particular set of circumstances they confront. However, when information technology or customer needs are changing rapidly and the environment is very uncertain, even a divisional structure may not provide managers with enough flexibility to respond to the environment quickly. To operate effectively under these conditions, managers must design the most flexible kind of organizational structure available: a matrix structure or a product team structure (see Figure 7.6).

matrix structure An organizational structure that simultaneously groups people and resources by function and by product.

MATRIX STRUCTURE In a **matrix structure,** managers group people and resources in two ways simultaneously: by function and by product.[29] Employees are grouped by *functions* to allow them to learn from one another and become more skilled and productive. In addition, employees are grouped into *product teams* in which members of different functions work together to develop a specific product. The result is a complex

Figure 7.6
Matrix and Product Team Structures

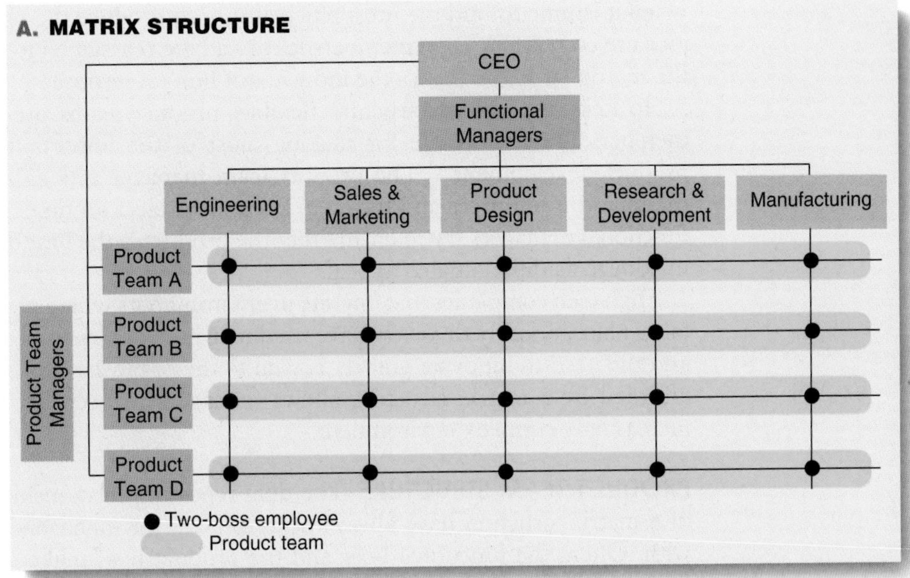

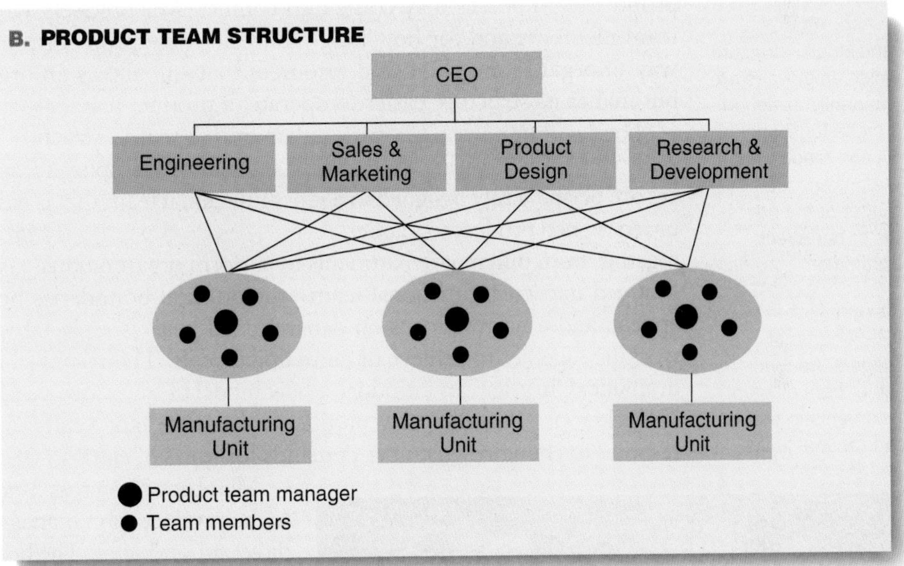

network of reporting relationships among product teams and functions that makes the matrix structure very flexible (see Figure 7.6A). Each person in a product team reports to two managers: (1) a functional boss, who assigns individuals to a team and evaluates their performance from a functional perspective, and (2) the boss of the product team, who evaluates their performance on the team. Thus, team members are known as *two-boss employees*. The functional employees assigned to product teams change over time as the specific skills that the team needs change. At the beginning of the product development process, for example, engineers and R&D specialists are assigned to a product team because their skills are needed to develop new products. When a provisional design has been established, marketing experts are assigned to the team to gauge how customers will respond to the new product. Manufacturing personnel join when it is time to find the most efficient way to produce the product. As their specific jobs are completed, team members leave and are reassigned to new teams. In this way the matrix structure makes the most use of human resources.

To keep the matrix structure flexible, product teams are empowered and team members are responsible for making most of the important decisions involved in product development.[30] The product team manager acts as a facilitator, controlling the financial resources and trying to keep the project on time and within budget. The functional managers try to ensure that the product is the best that it can be in order to maximize its differentiated appeal.

High-tech companies that operate in environments where new product development takes place monthly or yearly have used matrix structures successfully for many years, and the need to innovate quickly is vital to the organization's survival. The flexibility afforded by a matrix structure allows managers to keep pace with a changing and increasingly complex environment.[31]

PRODUCT TEAM STRUCTURE The dual reporting relationships that are at the heart of a matrix structure have always been difficult for managers and employees to deal with. Often, the functional boss and the product boss make conflicting demands on team members, who do not know which boss to satisfy first. Also, functional and product team bosses may come into conflict over precisely who is in charge of which team members and for how long. To avoid these problems, managers have devised a way of organizing people and resources that still allows an organization to be flexible but makes its structure easier to operate: a product team structure.

product team structure An organizational structure in which employees are permanently assigned to a cross-functional team and report only to the product team manager or to one of his or her direct subordinates.

cross-functional team A group of managers brought together from different departments to perform organizational tasks.

The **product team structure** differs from a matrix structure in two ways: (1) It does away with dual reporting relationships and two-boss employees, and (2) functional employees are permanently assigned to a cross-functional team that is empowered to bring a new or redesigned product to market. A **cross-functional team** is a group of managers brought together from different departments to perform organizational tasks. When managers are grouped into cross-functional teams, the artificial boundaries between departments disappear, and a narrow focus on departmental goals is replaced with a general interest in working together to achieve organizational goals. The results of such changes have been dramatic: Chrysler can introduce a new model of car in two years, down from five; Black & Decker can innovate new products in months, not years; and Hallmark Cards can respond to changing customer demands for types of cards in weeks, not months.

A committee looks over an artist's work during a meeting at Hallmark in Kansas City. At Hallmark, cross-functional teams like this one can respond quickly to changing customer demands.

Members of a cross-functional team report only to the product team manager or to one of his or her direct subordinates. The heads of the functions have only an informal, advisory relationship with members of the product teams–the role of functional managers is only to counsel and help team members, share knowledge among teams, and provide new technological developments that can help improve each team's performance (see Figure 7.6B).[32]

Increasingly, organizations are making empowered cross-functional teams an essential part of their organizational architecture to help them gain a competitive advantage in fast-changing organizational environments. For example, Newell Rubbermaid, the well-known maker of more than 5,000 household products, moved to a product team structure because its managers wanted to speed up the rate of product innovation. Managers created 20 cross-functional teams composed of five to seven people from marketing, manufacturing, R&D, and other functions.[33] Each team focuses its energies on a particular product line, such as garden products, bathroom products, or kitchen products. These teams develop more than 365 new products a year.

Hybrid Structure

hybrid structure The structure of a large organization that has many divisions and simultaneously uses many different organizational structures.

A large organization that has many divisions and simultaneously uses many different structures has a **hybrid structure.** Most large organizations use product division structures and create self-contained divisions; then each division's managers select the structure that best meets the needs of the particular environment, strategy, and so on. Thus, one product division may choose to operate with a functional structure, a second may choose a geographic structure, and a third may choose a product team structure because of the nature of the division's products or the desire to be more responsive to customers' needs. Macy's, the largest U.S. department store company, uses a hybrid structure based on grouping by customer and by geography.

As shown in Figure 7.7, in 2008 Macy's organized its four main merchandising divisions, its bricks-and-mortar Bloomingdale's and Macy's store chains, and its online Bloomingdales.com and Macys.com storefronts, as independent divisions in a product division structure. Beneath this organizational layer is another layer of structure because its flagship Macy's store chain operates with a geographic structure that groups stores by region. Macy's, for example, has several different regional divisions that handle its over 800 stores. Each regional office is responsible for coordinating the market needs of the stores in its region and for responding to regional customer needs. The regional office feeds information back to divisional headquarters, where centralized merchandising functions make decisions for all stores.

Organizational structure may thus be likened to the layers of an onion. The outer layer provides the overarching organizational framework–most commonly a product or market division structure–and each inner layer is the structure that each division selects for itself in response to the contingencies it faces–such as a geographic or product team structure. The ability to break a large organization into smaller units or divisions makes it much easier for managers to change structure when the need arises–for example, when a change in technology or an increase in competition in the environment necessitates a change from a functional to a product team structure.

Figure 7.7
Macy's Hybrid Structure

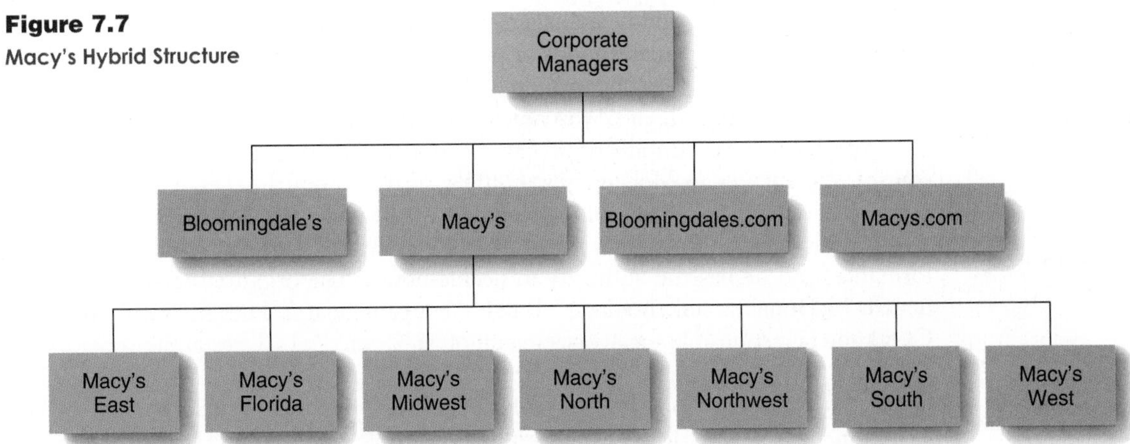

Coordinating Functions and Divisions

The more complex the structure a company uses to group its activities, the greater are the problems of *linking and coordinating* its different functions and divisions. Coordination becomes a problem because each function or division develops a different orientation toward the other groups that affects the way it interacts with them. Each function or division comes to view the problems facing the company from its own particular perspective; for example, they may develop different views about the major goals, problems, or issues facing a company.

LO4 Explain why managers must coordinate jobs, functions, and divisions using the hierarchy of authority and integrating mechanisms.

At the functional level, the manufacturing function typically has a very short-term view; its major goal is to keep costs under control and get the product out the factory door on time. By contrast, the product development function has a long-term viewpoint because developing a new product is a relatively slow process and high product quality is seen as more important than low costs. Such differences in viewpoint may make manufacturing and product development managers reluctant to cooperate and coordinate their activities to meet company goals. At the divisional level, in a company with a product structure, employees may become concerned more with making *their* division's products a success than with the profitability of the entire company. They may refuse, or simply not see the need, to cooperate and share information or knowledge with other divisions.

The problem of linking and coordinating the activities of different functions and divisions becomes more and more acute as the number of functions and divisions increases. We look first at how managers design the hierarchy of authority to coordinate functions and divisions so that they work together effectively. Then we focus on integration and examine the different integrating mechanisms that managers can use to coordinate functions and divisions.

authority The power to hold people accountable for their actions and to make decisions concerning the use of organizational resources.

hierarchy of authority An organization's chain of command, specifying the relative authority of each manager.

span of control The number of subordinates who report directly to a manager.

line manager Someone in the direct line or chain of command who has formal authority over people and resources at lower levels.

staff manager Someone responsible for managing a specialist function, such as finance or marketing.

Allocating Authority

As organizations grow and produce a wider range of goods and services, the size and number of their functions and divisions increase. To coordinate the activities of people, functions, and divisions and to allow them to work together effectively, managers must develop a clear hierarchy of authority.[34] **Authority** is the power vested in a manager to make decisions and use resources to achieve organizational goals by virtue of his or her position in an organization. The **hierarchy of authority** is an organization's *chain of command*–the relative authority that each manager has–extending from the CEO at the top, down through the middle managers and first-line managers, to the nonmanagerial employees who actually make goods or provide services. Every manager, at every level of the hierarchy, supervises one or more subordinates. The term **span of control** refers to the number of subordinates who report directly to a manager.

Figure 7.8 shows a simplified picture of the hierarchy of authority and the span of control of managers in McDonald's in 2008. At the top of the hierarchy is Jim Skinner, CEO and vice chairman of McDonald's board of directors, who took control in 2004.[35] Skinner is the manager who has ultimate responsibility for McDonald's performance, and he has the authority to decide how to use organizational resources to benefit McDonald's stakeholders.[36] Ralph Alvarez is next in line; he is president and COO and is responsible for overseeing all of McDonald's U.S. restaurant operations. Alvarez reports directly to Skinner, as does chief financial officer Peter Bensen. Unlike the other managers, Bensen is not a **line manager,** someone in the direct line or chain of command who has formal authority over people and resources. Rather, Bensen is a **staff manager,** responsible for one of McDonald's specialist functions, finance.

Figure 7.8
The Hierarchy of Authority and Span of Control at McDonald's Corporation

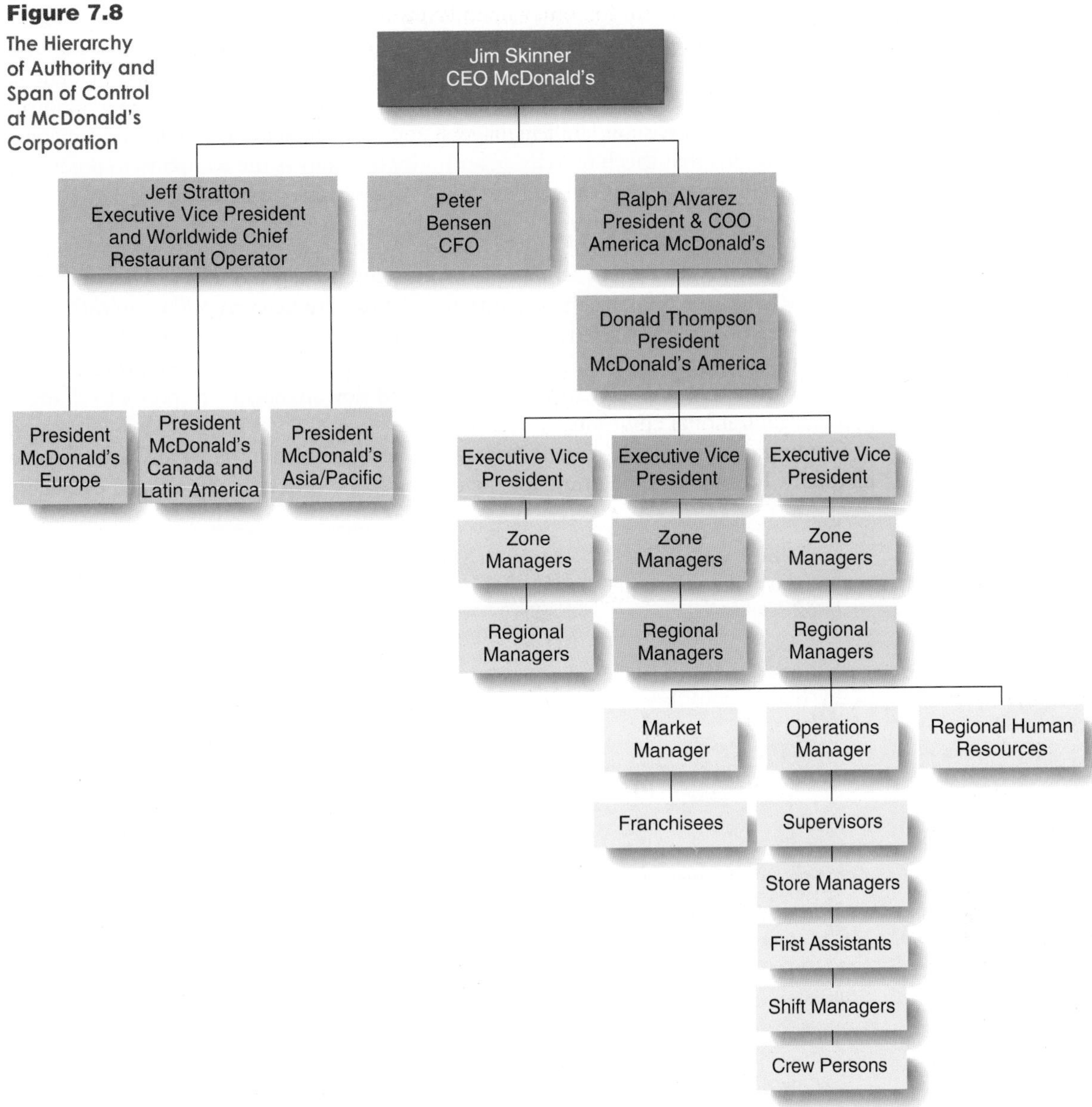

Worldwide chief operations officer Jeff Stratton is responsible for overseeing all functional aspects of McDonald's overseas operations, which are headed by the presidents of world regions: Europe; Canada and Latin America; and Asia/Pacific, Middle East, and Africa. Of special mention is Donald Thompson, who is president of McDonald's U.S. operations and reports to Alvarez.

Managers at each level of the hierarchy confer on managers at the next level down the authority to make decisions about how to use organizational resources. Accepting this authority, those lower-level managers then become responsible for their decisions and are accountable for how well they make those decisions. Managers who make the right decisions are typically promoted, and organizations motivate managers with the prospects of promotion and increased responsibility within the chain of command.

Below Thompson are the other main levels or layers in the McDonald's domestic chain of command–executive vice presidents of its West, Central, and East regions, zone managers, regional managers, and supervisors. A hierarchy is also evident in each company-owned McDonald's restaurant. At the top is the store manager; at lower levels are the first assistant, shift managers, and crew personnel. McDonald's managers have decided that this hierarchy of authority best allows the company to pursue its business-level strategy of providing fast food at reasonable prices.

TALL AND FLAT ORGANIZATIONS As an organization grows in size (normally measured by the number of its managers and employees), its hierarchy of authority normally lengthens, making the organizational structure taller. A *tall* organization has many levels of authority relative to company size; a *flat* organization has fewer levels relative to company size (see Figure 7.9).[37] As a hierarchy becomes taller, problems that make the organization's structure less flexible and slow managers' response to changes in the organizational environment may result.

Communication problems may arise when an organization has many levels in the hierarchy. It can take a long time for the decisions and orders of upper-level managers

Figure 7.9
Tall and Flat Organizations

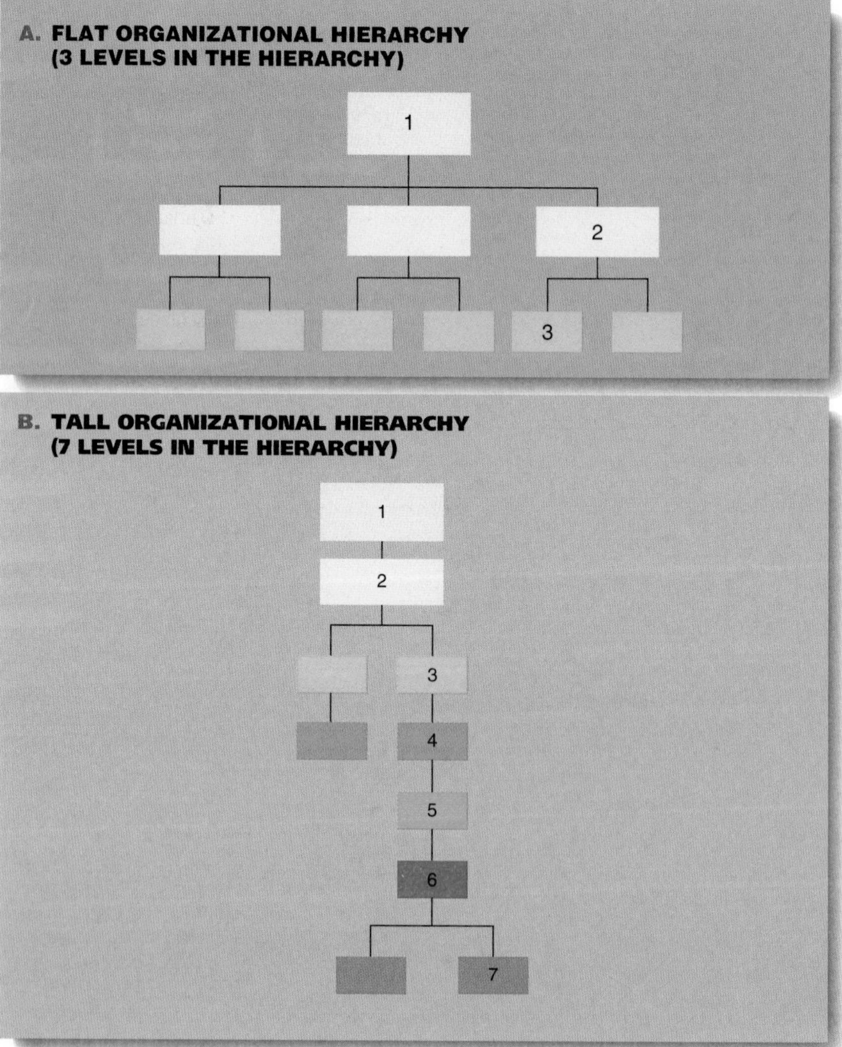

to reach managers further down in the hierarchy, and it can take a long time for top managers to learn how well their decisions worked. Feeling out of touch, top managers may want to verify that lower-level managers are following orders and may require written confirmation from them. Middle managers, who know they will be held strictly accountable for their actions, start devoting too much time to the process of making decisions to improve their chances of being right. They might even try to avoid responsibility by making top managers decide what actions to take.

Another communication problem that can result is the distortion of commands and messages being transmitted up and down the hierarchy, which causes managers at different levels to interpret what is happening differently. Distortion of orders and messages can be accidental, occurring because different managers interpret messages from their own narrow, functional perspectives. Or distortion can be intentional, occurring because managers low in the hierarchy decide to interpret information in a way that increases their own personal advantage.

Another problem with tall hierarchies is that they usually indicate that an organization is employing many managers, and managers are expensive. Managerial salaries, benefits, offices, and secretaries are a huge expense for organizations. Large companies such as IBM and General Motors pay their managers billions of dollars a year. In the early 2000s, hundreds of thousands of middle managers were laid off as dot-coms collapsed and high-tech companies attempted to reduce costs by restructuring and downsizing their workforces. In 2008, as an economic downturn occurred, hundreds of companies also began to announce layoffs to reduce operating costs and to help them make better use of their resources in the future.

THE MINIMUM CHAIN OF COMMAND To ward off the problems that result when an organization becomes too tall and employs too many managers, top managers need to ascertain whether they are employing the right number of middle and first-line managers and whether they can redesign their organizational architecture to reduce the number of managers. Top managers might well follow a basic organizing principle–the principle of the minimum chain of command–which states that top managers should always construct a hierarchy with the fewest levels of authority necessary to efficiently and effectively use organizational resources.

Effective managers constantly scrutinize their hierarchies to see whether the number of levels can be reduced–for example, by eliminating one level and giving the responsibilities of managers at that level to managers above and by empowering employees below. One manager who is constantly trying to empower employees and keep the hierarchy flat is Colleen C. Barrett, the number-two executive of Southwest Airlines.[38] Barrett is the highest-ranking woman in the airline industry. At Southwest, she is well known for continually reaffirming Southwest's message that employees should feel free to go above and beyond their prescribed roles to provide better customer service. Her central message is that Southwest values and trusts its employees, who are empowered to take responsibility. Southwest employees are encouraged not to look to their superiors for guidance but, rather, to find ways on their own to do the job better. As a result, Southwest keeps the number of its middle managers to a minimum. The need to empower workers is increasing as companies battle low-cost foreign competitors by searching for new ways to reduce costs, as the following "Managing Globally" suggests.

decentralizing authority Giving lower-level managers and nonmanagerial employees the right to make important decisions about how to use organizational resources.

CENTRALIZATION AND DECENTRALIZATION OF AUTHORITY Another way in which managers can keep the organizational hierarchy flat is by **decentralizing authority**–that is, by giving lower-level managers and nonmanagerial employees the right to make important decisions about how to use organizational resources.[41]

MANAGING GLOBALLY

How to Use Empowered Self-Managed Teams

In the United States, over 5 million manufacturing jobs were lost to factories in low-cost countries abroad in the early 2000s. While many large U.S. manufacturing companies have given up the battle, some companies such as electronics maker Plexus Corp., based in Neenah, Wisconsin, have been able to find ways of organizing that allow them to survive and prosper in a low-cost manufacturing world. How have they done this? By creating empowered work teams.

Small Business

In the late 1990s, Plexus saw the writing on the wall as more and more of its customers began to outsource the production of electronic components or even the whole product itself to manufacturers abroad. U.S. companies cannot match the efficiency of manufacturers abroad in producing high volumes of a single product, such as millions of a particular circuit board used in a laptop computer. So Plexus's managers decided to focus their efforts on developing a manufacturing technology called "low-high" that could efficiently produce low volumes of many different kinds of products.

Plexus's managers formed a team to design an organizational structure based on creating four "focused factories" in which control over production decisions is given to the workers, who perform all the operations involved in making a product. The managers cross-trained workers so that they can perform any particular operation in their "factory." With this approach, when work slows down at any point in the production of a particular product, a worker further along the production process can move back to help solve the problem that has arisen at the earlier stage.[39]

These two employees monitoring the progress of a circuit board production line embody cross-functional empowerment. If problems occur, they have the authority and expertise to make any changes necessary to keep the production line at full speed.

Furthermore, managers organized workers into self-managed teams that are empowered to make all the decisions necessary to make a particular product in one of the four factories. Since each product is different, these teams have to make their decisions quickly if they are to assemble the product in a cost-effective way. The ability of the teams to make rapid decisions and respond to unexpected contingencies is vital on a production line, where time is money–every minute a production line is not moving adds hundreds or thousands of dollars to production costs. Also, a second reason for empowering teams is that when a changeover takes place from making one product to making another, nothing is being produced, so it is vital that changeover time be kept to a minimum. At Plexus, managers, by allowing teams to experiment and by providing guidance, have reduced changeover time from hours to as little as 30 minutes, so the line is making products over 80% of the time.[40] This incredible flexibility, brought about by the way employees are organized, is the reason why Plexus is so efficient and can compete against low-cost manufacturers abroad.

If managers at higher levels give lower-level employees the responsibility of making important decisions and only *manage by exception,* then the problems of slow and distorted communication noted previously are kept to a minimum. Moreover, fewer managers are needed because their role is not to make decisions but to act as coach and facilitator and to help other employees make the best decisions. In addition, when decision-making authority is low in the organization and near the customer, employees are better able to recognize and respond to customer needs.

Decentralizing authority allows an organization and its employees to behave in a flexible way even as the organization grows and becomes taller. This is why managers are so interested in empowering employees, creating self-managed work teams, establishing cross-functional teams, and even moving to a product team structure. These design innovations help keep the organizational architecture flexible and responsive to complex task and general environments, complex technologies, and complex strategies.

Although more and more organizations are taking steps to decentralize authority, *too much* decentralization has certain disadvantages. If divisions, functions, or teams are given too much decision-making authority, they may begin to pursue their own goals at the expense of organizational goals. Managers in engineering design or R&D, for example, may become so focused on making the best possible product that they fail to realize that the best product may be so expensive that few people will be willing or able to buy it. Also, too much decentralization can result in a lack of communication among functions or divisions; this prevents the synergies that result from cooperation from ever materializing, and organizational performance suffers.

Top managers must seek the balance between centralization and decentralization of authority that best meets the four major contingencies an organization faces (see again Figure 7.1). If managers are in a stable environment, are using well-understood technology, and are producing stable kinds of products (such as cereal, canned soup, or books), then there is no pressing need to decentralize authority, and managers at the top can maintain control of much of organizational decision making.[42] However, in uncertain, changing environments where high-tech companies are producing state-of-the-art products, top managers must often empower employees and allow teams to make important strategic decisions so that the organization can keep up with the changes taking place. No matter what its environment, a company that fails to control the balance between centralization and decentralization will find its performance suffering, as the example of Avon in the "Management Snapshot" at the beginning of the chapter suggested.

Integrating and Coordinating Mechanisms

Much coordination takes place through the hierarchy of authority. However, several problems are associated with establishing contact among managers in different functions or divisions. As discussed earlier, managers from different functions and divisions may have different views about what must be done to achieve organizational goals. But if the managers have equal authority (as functional managers typically do), the only manager who can tell them what to do is the CEO, who has the ultimate authority to resolve conflicts. The need to solve everyday conflicts, however, wastes top-management time and slows strategic decision making; indeed, one sign of a poorly performing structure is the number of problems sent up the hierarchy for top managers to solve.

integrating mechanisms Organizing tools that managers can use to increase communication and coordination among functions and divisions.

To increase communication and coordination among functions or between divisions and to prevent these problems from emerging, top managers incorporate various **integrating mechanisms** into their organizational architecture. The greater the complexity of an organization's structure, the greater is the need for coordination among people, functions, and divisions to make the organizational structure work

Figure 7.10
Types and Examples of Integrating Mechanisms

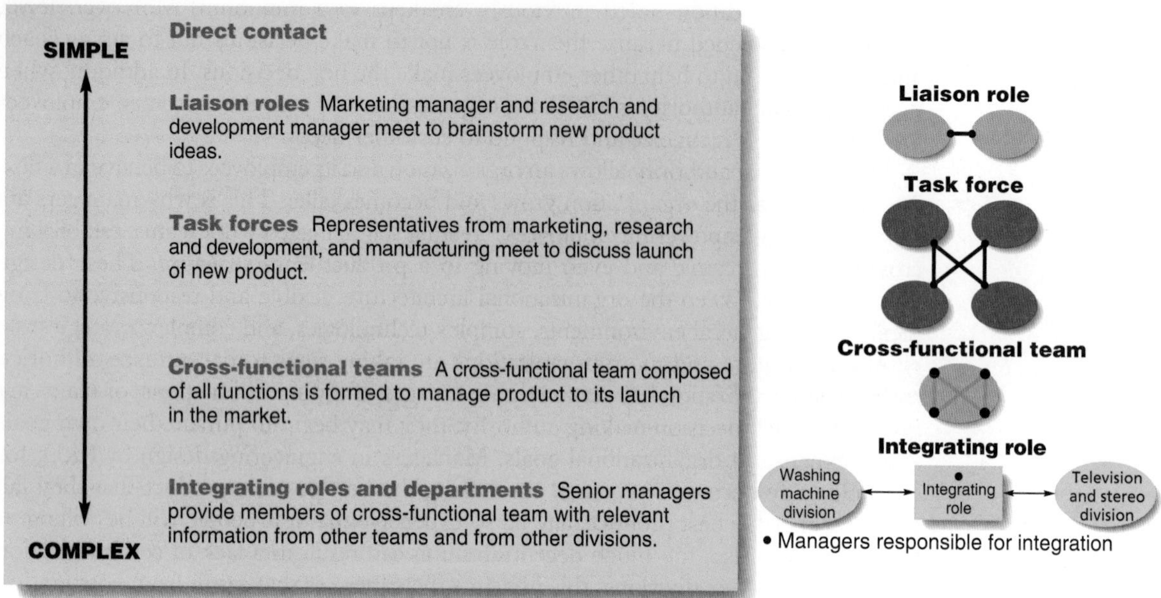

efficiently and effectively.[43] Thus, when managers choose to adopt a divisional, matrix, or product team structure, they must use complex integrating mechanisms to achieve organizational goals. Several integrating mechanisms are available to managers to increase communication and coordination.[44] Figure 7.10 lists these mechanisms, as well as examples of the individuals or groups that might use them.

LIAISON ROLES Managers can increase coordination among functions and divisions by establishing liaison roles. When the volume of contacts between two functions increases, one way to improve coordination is to give one manager in each function or division the responsibility for coordinating with the other. These managers may meet daily, weekly, monthly, or as needed. A liaison role is illustrated in Figure 7.10; the small dot represents the person within a function who has responsibility for coordinating with the other function. Coordinating is part of the liaison's full-time job, and usually an informal relationship develops between the people involved, greatly easing strains between functions. Furthermore, liaison roles provide a way of transmitting information across an organization, which is important in large organizations whose employees may know no one outside their immediate function or division.

TASK FORCES When more than two functions or divisions share many common problems, direct contact and liaison roles may not provide sufficient coordination. In these cases, a more complex integrating mechanism, a **task force**, may be appropriate (see Figure 7.10). One manager from each relevant function or division is assigned to a task force that meets to solve a specific, mutual problem; members are responsible for reporting to their departments on the issues addressed and the solutions recommended. Task forces are often called *ad hoc committees* because they are temporary; they may meet on a regular basis or only a few times. When the problem or issue is solved, the task force is no longer needed; members return to their normal roles in their departments or are assigned to other task forces. Typically, task force members also perform many of their normal duties while serving on the task force.

task force A committee of managers from various functions or divisions who meet to solve a specific, mutual problem; also called *ad hoc committee.*

CROSS-FUNCTIONAL TEAMS In many cases, the issues addressed by a task force are recurring problems, such as the need to develop new products or find new kinds of customers. To address recurring problems effectively, managers are increasingly using permanent integrating mechanisms such as cross-functional teams. An example of a cross-functional team is a new product development committee that is responsible for the choice, design, manufacturing, and marketing of a new product. Such an activity obviously requires a great deal of integration among functions if new products are to be successfully introduced, and using a complex integrating mechanism such as a cross-functional team accomplishes this. As discussed earlier, in a product team structure people and resources are grouped into permanent cross-functional teams to speed products to market. These teams assume long-term responsibility for all aspects of development and making the product.

INTEGRATING ROLES An integrating role is a role whose only function is to increase coordination and integration among functions or divisions to achieve performance gains from synergies. Usually, managers who perform integrating roles are experienced senior managers who can envisage how to use the resources of the functions or divisions to obtain new synergies. One study found that DuPont, the giant chemical company, had created 160 integrating roles to provide coordination among the different divisions of the company and improve corporate performance.[45] The more complex an organization and the greater the number of its divisions, the more important integrating roles are.

MATRIX STRUCTURE When managers must be able to respond quickly to the task and general environments, they often use a matrix structure. The reason for choosing a matrix structure is clear. It contains many of the integrating mechanisms already discussed: The two-boss employees integrate between functions and product teams; the matrix is built on the basis of temporary teams or task forces; and each member of a team performs a liaison role. The matrix structure is flexible precisely because it is formed from complex integrating mechanisms.

strategic alliance An agreement in which managers pool or share their organization's resources and know-how with a foreign company and the two organizations share the rewards and risks of starting a new venture.

In summary, to keep an organization responsive to changes in its task and general environments as the organization grows and becomes more complex, managers must increase coordination among functions and divisions by using complex integrating mechanisms. Managers must decide on the best way to organize their structures to create an organizational architecture that allows them to make the best use of organizational resources.

Strategic Alliances, B2B Network Structures, and IT

Recently, increasing globalization and the use of new IT have brought about two innovations in organizational architecture that are sweeping through U.S. and European companies: strategic alliances and business-to-business (B2B) network structures. A **strategic alliance** is a formal agreement that commits two or more companies to exchange or share their resources in order to produce and market a product.[46] Most commonly strategic alliances are formed because the companies share similar interests and believe they can benefit from cooperating. For example, Japanese car companies such as Toyota and Honda have formed many strategic alliances with particular suppliers of inputs such as car axles, gearboxes, and air-conditioning systems. Over time, these car companies work closely with their suppliers to improve the efficiency and effectiveness of the inputs so that the final product–the car produced–is of higher quality and very often can be produced at lower cost. Toyota and Honda have also established alliances with suppliers throughout the United States and Mexico because both companies now build several models of cars in these countries.

The growing sophistication of IT with global intranets and teleconferencing has made it much easier to manage strategic alliances and allow managers to share information and cooperate. One outcome of this has been the growth of strategic alliances into a network structure. A **network structure** is a series of global strategic alliances that one or several organizations create with suppliers, manufacturers, and/or distributors to produce and market a product. Network structures allow an organization to manage its global value chain in order to find new ways to reduce costs and increase the quality of products–without incurring the high costs of operating a complex organizational structure (such as the costs of employing many managers). More and more U.S. and European companies are relying on global network structures to gain access to low-cost foreign sources of inputs, as discussed in Chapter 6. Shoemakers such as Nike and Adidas are two companies that have used this approach extensively.

network structure A series of strategic alliances that an organization creates with suppliers, manufacturers, and/or distributors to produce and market a product.

Nike is the largest and most profitable sports shoe manufacturer in the world. The key to Nike's success is the network structure that Nike founder and CEO Philip Knight created to allow his company to produce and market shoes. As noted in Chapter 6, the most successful companies today are trying to pursue simultaneously a low-cost and a differentiation strategy. Knight decided early that to do this at Nike he needed organizational architecture that would allow his company to focus on some functions, such as design, and leave others, such as manufacturing, to other organizations.

By far the largest function at Nike's Oregon headquarters is the design function, composed of talented designers who pioneered innovations in sports shoe design such as the air pump and Air Jordans that Nike introduced so successfully. Designers use computer-aided design (CAD) to design Nike shoes, and they electronically store all new product information, including manufacturing instructions. When the designers have finished their work, they electronically transmit all the blueprints for the new products to a network of Southeast Asian suppliers and manufacturers with which Nike has formed strategic alliances.[47] Instructions for the design of a new sole may be sent to a supplier in Taiwan; instructions for the leather uppers, to a supplier in Malaysia. The suppliers produce the shoe parts and send them for final assembly to a manufacturer in China with which Nike has established another strategic alliance. From China the shoes are shipped to distributors throughout the world. Ninety-nine percent of the 120 million pairs of shoes that Nike makes each year are made in Southeast Asia.

This network structure gives Nike two important advantages. First, Nike is able to respond to changes in sports shoe fashion very quickly. Using its global IT system, Nike literally can change the instructions it gives each of its suppliers overnight, so that within a few weeks its foreign manufacturers are producing new kinds of shoes.[48] Any alliance partners that fail to perform up to Nike's standards are replaced with new partners.

outsource To use outside suppliers and manufacturers to produce goods and services.

Second, Nike's costs are very low because wages in Southeast Asia are a fraction of what they are in the United States, and this difference gives Nike a low-cost advantage. Also, Nike's ability to **outsource** and use foreign manufacturers to produce all its shoes abroad allows Knight to keep the organization's U.S. structure flat and flexible. Nike is able to use a relatively inexpensive functional structure to organize its activities. However, sports shoe manufacturers' attempts to keep their costs low have led to many charges that Nike and others are supporting sweatshops that harm foreign workers, as the following "Ethics in Action" suggests.

boundaryless organization An organization whose members are linked by computers, faxes, computer-aided design systems, and video teleconferencing and who rarely, if ever, see one another face-to-face.

The ability of managers to develop a network structure to produce or provide the goods and services customers want, rather than create a complex organizational structure to do so, has led many researchers and consultants to popularize the idea of a **boundaryless organization.** Such an organization is composed of people linked by IT–computers, faxes, computer-aided design systems, and video teleconferencing–who may rarely, if ever, see one another face-to-face. People are utilized when their services are needed, much as in a matrix structure, but they are not formal members of an organization; they are functional experts who form an alliance with an organization, fulfill their contractual obligations, and then move on to the next project.

knowledge management system A company-specific virtual information system that allows workers to share their knowledge and expertise and find others to help solve ongoing problems.

Large consulting companies, such as Accenture and McKinsey & Co., utilize their global consultants in this way. Consultants are connected by laptops to an organization's **knowledge management system,** its company-specific information system that systematizes the knowledge of its employees and provides them with access to other employees who have the expertise to solve the problems that they encounter as they perform their jobs.

The use of outsourcing and the development of network structures is increasing rapidly as organizations recognize the many opportunities they offer to reduce

ETHICS IN ACTION

Of Shoes and Sweatshops

As the production of all kinds of goods and services is being increasingly outsourced to poor regions and countries of the world, the behavior of companies that outsource production to subcontractors in these countries has come under increasing scrutiny. Nike, the giant sports shoe maker with sales of more than $9 billion a year, was one of the first to experience a backlash when critics revealed how workers in these countries were being treated. Indonesian workers were stitching together shoes in hot, noisy factories for only 80 cents a day or about $18 a month.[49] Workers in Vietnam and China fared better; they could earn $1.60 a day. In all cases, however, critics charged that at least $3 a day was needed to maintain an adequate living standard.

These facts generated an outcry in the United States, where Nike was roundly attacked for its labor practices; a backlash against sales of Nike products forced Phil Knight, Nike's billionaire owner, to reevaluate Nike's labor practices. Nike announced that henceforth all the factories producing its shoes and clothes would be independently monitored and inspected. After its competitor Reebok, which also had been criticized for similar labor practices, announced that it was raising wages in Indonesia by 20%, Nike raised them by 25% to $23 a month.[50] Small though this may seem, it was a huge increase to workers in these countries.

Members of United Students against Nike unfurl a banner at the Niketown store in New York accusing Nike of using sweatshop labor to produce its athletic apparel. Nike and other athletic apparel companies have since taken steps to ensure better working conditions for foreign workers.

In Europe, another sportswear company, Adidas, had largely escaped such criticism. But in 1999 it was reported that in El Salvador, a Taiwan-based Adidas subcontractor was employing girls as young as 14 in its factories and making them work for more than 70 hours a week. They were allowed to go to the restroom only twice a day, and if they stayed longer than three minutes, they lost a day's wages.[51] Adidas moved swiftly to avoid the public relations nightmare that Nike had experienced. Adidas announced that henceforth its subcontractors would be required to abide by more strict labor standards.

What happened in the sports shoe industry has happened throughout the clothing industry as well as other industries like electronics and toys in the 2000s. Companies such as Wal-Mart, Target, The Gap, Sony, and Mattel have all been forced to reevaluate the ethics of their labor practices and to promise to keep a constant watch on subcontractors in the future. A statement to this effect can be found on many of these companies' Web pages–for example, Nike's (www.nikebiz.com) and The Gap's (www.thegap.com).

costs and increase organizational flexibility. This push to lower costs has led to the development of electronic **business-to-business (B2B) networks** in which most or all of the companies in an industry (for example, carmakers) use the same software platform to link to each other and establish industry specifications and standards. Then, these companies jointly list the quantity and specifications of the inputs they require and invite bids from the thousands of potential suppliers around the world. Suppliers also use the same software platform, so electronic bidding, auctions, and transactions are possible between buyers and sellers around the world. The idea is that high-volume standardized transactions can help drive down costs at the industry level.

business-to-business (B2B) network A group of organizations that join together and use IT to link themselves to potential global suppliers to increase efficiency and effectiveness.

Today, with advances in IT, designing organizational architecture is becoming an increasingly complex management function. To maximize efficiency and effectiveness, managers must assess carefully the relative benefits of having their own organization perform a functional activity versus forming an alliance with another organization to perform the activity. It is still not clear how B2B networks and other forms of electronic alliances between companies will develop in the future.

Summary and Review

DESIGNING ORGANIZATIONAL STRUCTURE The four main determinants of organizational structure are the external environment, strategy, technology, and human resources. In general, the higher the level of uncertainty associated with these factors, the more appropriate is a flexible, adaptable structure as opposed to a formal, rigid one. **[LO1]**

GROUPING TASKS INTO JOBS Job design is the process by which managers group tasks into jobs. To create more interesting jobs, and to get workers to act flexibly, managers can enlarge and enrich jobs. The job characteristics model provides a tool managers can use to measure how motivating or satisfying a particular job is. **[LO2]**

GROUPING JOBS INTO FUNCTIONS AND DIVISIONS Managers can choose from many kinds of organizational structures to make the best use of organizational resources. Depending on the specific organizing problems they face, managers can choose from functional, product, geographic, market, matrix, product team, and hybrid structures. **[LO3]**

COORDINATING FUNCTIONS AND DIVISIONS No matter which structure managers choose, they must decide how to distribute authority in the organization, how many levels to have in the hierarchy of authority, and what balance to strike between centralization and decentralization to keep the number of levels in the hierarchy to a minimum. As organizations grow, managers must increase integration and coordination among functions and divisions. Six integrating mechanisms are available to facilitate this: direct contact, liaison roles, task forces, cross-functional teams, integrating roles, and the matrix structure. **[LO3, 4]**

STRATEGIC ALLIANCES, B2B NETWORK STRUCTURES, AND IT To avoid many of the communication and coordination problems that emerge as organizations grow, managers are attempting to use IT to develop new ways of organizing. In a strategic alliance, managers enter into an agreement with another organization to provide inputs or to perform a functional activity. If managers enter into a series of these agreements, they create a network structure. A network structure, most commonly based on some shared form of IT, can be formed around one company, or a number of companies can join together to create an industry B2B network. **[LO4]**

Management in Action

Topics for Discussion and Action

Discussion

1. Would a flexible or a more formal structure be appropriate for these organizations: (a) a large department store, (b) a Big Five accountancy firm, (c) a biotechnology company? Explain your reasoning. [LO1, 2]
2. Using the job characteristics model as a guide, discuss how a manager can enrich or enlarge subordinates' jobs. [LO2]
3. How might a salesperson's job or a secretary's job be enlarged or enriched to make it more motivating? [LO2, 3]
4. When and under what conditions might managers change from a functional to (a) a product, (b) a geographic, or (c) a market structure? [LO1, 3]
5. How do matrix structures and product team structures differ? Why is the product team structure more widely used? [LO1, 3, 4]

Action

6. Find and interview a manager, and identify the kind of organizational structure that his or her organization uses to coordinate its people and resources. Why is the organization using that structure? Do you think a different structure would be more appropriate? Which one? [LO1, 3, 4]
7. With the same or another manager, discuss the distribution of authority in the organization. Does the manager think that decentralizing authority and empowering employees is appropriate? [LO1, 3]
8. Interview some employees of an organization, and ask them about the organization's values and norms, the typical characteristics of employees, and the organization's ethical values and socialization practices. Using this information, try to describe the organization's culture and the way it affects the way people and groups behave. [LO1, 5]

Building Management Skills

Understanding Organizing [LO1, 2, 3]

Think of an organization with which you are familiar, perhaps one you have worked for—such as a store, restaurant, office, church, or school. Then answer the following questions:

1. Which contingencies are most important in explaining how the organization is organized? Do you think it is organized in the best way?
2. Using the job characteristics model, how motivating do you think the job of a typical employee in this organization is?
3. Can you think of any ways in which a typical job could be enlarged or enriched?
4. What kind of organizational structure does the organization use? If it is part of a chain, what kind of structure does the entire organization use? What other structures discussed in the chapter might allow the organization to operate more effectively? For example, would the move to a product team structure lead to greater efficiency or effectiveness? Why or why not?
5. How many levels are there in the organization's hierarchy? Is authority centralized or decentralized? Describe the

span of control of the top manager and of middle or first-line managers.

6. Is the distribution of authority appropriate for the organization and its activities? Would it be possible to flatten the hierarchy by decentralizing authority and empowering employees?

7. What are the principal integrating mechanisms used in the organization? Do they provide sufficient coordination among individuals and functions? How might they be improved?

8. Now that you have analyzed the way this organization is structured, what advice would you give its managers to help them improve the way it operates?

Managing Ethically [LO1, 3, 5]

Suppose an organization is downsizing and laying off many of its middle managers. Some top managers charged with deciding whom to terminate might decide to keep the subordinates they like, and who are obedient to them, rather than the ones who are difficult or the best performers. They might also decide to lay off the most highly paid subordinates even if they are high performers. Think of the ethical issues involved in designing a hierarchy, and discuss the following issues.

Questions

1. What ethical rules (see Chapter 3) should managers use to decide which employees to terminate when redesigning their hierarchy?
2. Some people argue that employees who have worked for an organization for many years have a claim on the organization at least as strong as that of its shareholders. What do you think of the ethics of this position—can employees claim to "own" their jobs if they have contributed significantly to the organization's past success? How does a socially responsible organization behave in this situation?

Small Group Breakout Exercise

Bob's Appliances [LO1, 3]

Form groups of three or four people, and appoint one member as the spokesperson who will communicate your findings to the class when called on by the instructor. Then discuss the following scenario:

Bob's Appliances sells and services household appliances such as washing machines, dishwashers, ranges, and refrigerators. Over the years, the company has developed a good reputation for the quality of its customer service, and many local builders patronize the store. Recently, some new appliance retailers, including Best Buy, have opened stores that also provide numerous appliances. To attract more customers, however, these stores also carry a complete range of consumer electronics products—televisions, stereos, and computers. Bob Lange, the owner of Bob's Appliances, has decided that if he is to stay in business, he must widen his product range and compete directly with the chains.

In 2007, he decided to build a 20,000-square-foot store and service center, and he is now hiring new employees to sell and service the new line of consumer electronics. Because of his company's increased size, Lange is not sure of the best way to organize the employees. Currently, he uses a functional structure; employees are divided into sales, purchasing and accounting, and repair. Bob is wondering whether selling and servicing consumer electronics is so different from selling and servicing appliances that he should move to a product structure (see the figure) and create separate sets of functions for each of his two lines of business.[52]

You are a team of local consultants whom Bob has called in to advise him as he makes this crucial choice. Which structure do you recommend? Why?

FUNCTIONAL STRUCTURE

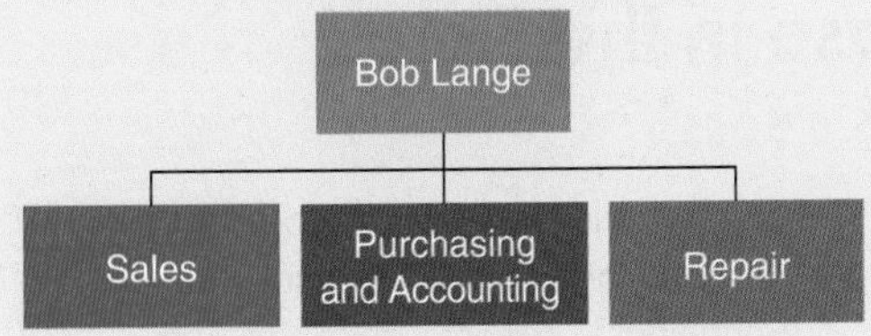

PRODUCT STRUCTURE

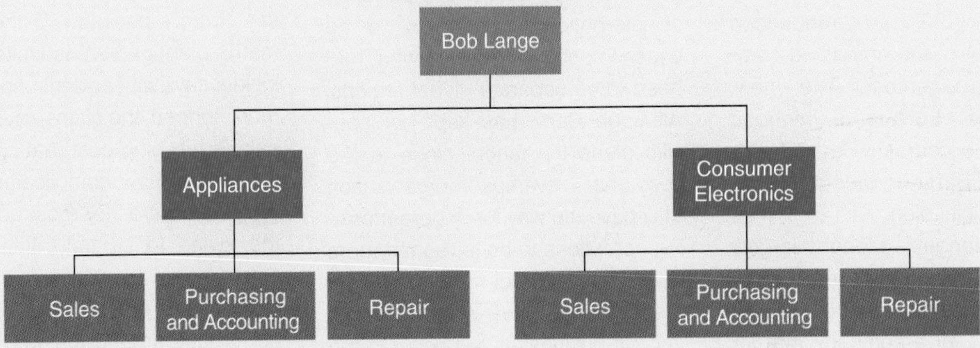

Be the Manager [LO1, 3, 5]

Speeding Up Web Site Design

You have been hired by a Web site design, production, and hosting company whose new animated Web site designs are attracting a lot of attention and a lot of customers. Currently, employees are organized into different functions such as hardware, software design, graphic art, and Web site hosting, as well as functions such as marketing and human resources. Each function takes its turn to work on a new project from initial customer request to final online Web site hosting.

The problem the company is experiencing is that it typically takes one year from the initial idea stage to the time that the Web site is up and running; the company wants to shorten this time by half to protect and expand its market niche. In talking to other managers, you discover that they believe the company's current functional structure is the source of the problem—it is not allowing employees to develop Web sites fast enough to satisfy customers' demands. They want you to design a better one.

Questions

1. Discuss ways in which you can improve how the current functional structure operates so that it speeds Web site development.
2. Discuss the pros and cons of moving to a (a) multidivisional, (b) matrix, or (c) product team structure to reduce Web site development time.
3. Which of these structures do you think is most appropriate, and why?

BusinessWeek Case in the News [LO1, 3, 4]

Yahoo's Bartz Shows Who's Boss

Just six weeks after taking over as chief executive of Yahoo! from cofounder Jerry Yang, Carol Bartz has now made it quite clear who's in charge and what demands she'll place on her executive team. On February 26, Bartz announced an overhaul of the embattled company's management. The new, streamlined structure is intended to make the company "a lot faster on its feet," Bartz wrote in a post on Yahoo's official blog.

The changes, though largely expected after recent reports in the blog BoomTown, are no less momentous for a company that for years has been hobbled by slow decision making and ineffective execution of those decisions. As far back as 2006, one executive who has since left, Brad Garlinghouse, penned a now-famous "Peanut Butter Manifesto" that outlined those management problems. The new management organization has all major executives reporting directly to Bartz, who lamented in her blog post that there's "plenty that has bogged this company down." "It looks like she isn't afraid to go in with a chain saw," says Kevin Lee, CEO of search marketing firm Didit.

Divestitures of Businesses Expected

In the most important leadership picks, current Chief Technology Officer Aristotle "Ari" Balogh will be head of all products and Hilary Schneider, current chief of ad, publishing, and audience groups in the United States, will head North American operations. A new chief of international operations, to be chosen soon, will oversee what had been three separate global regions. Although Bartz has kept her specific plans for Yahoo! close to the vest, her revamped organization may pave the way for underperforming operations to be jettisoned more quickly. "We expect more significant restructurings and divestitures of various businesses will occur in the future as the simpler org chart leads to more of a focus on the company's core businesses," UBS Securities (UBS) analyst Ben Schachter wrote in a report after the announcement.

The more centralized management structure doesn't guarantee Yahoo! will find its footing. Indeed, some observers fret that centralizing too much can hobble innovation. "We tend not to like that much concentration in product development," says Sanford Bernstein analyst Jeffrey Lindsay, who would prefer a structure that focuses on key strategic products such as search ads.

Trying to Speed Decision Making

Still, he and others note that the new organization is a vast improvement over the previous "matrix management" system that handed multiple executives oversight over many products and new projects. That led to slow decision making and little accountability, Yahoo! insiders say. "Carol's patience for the whole matrix management is limited," one insider says with evident understatement. Indeed, the plainspoken Bartz said in her blog post that "you'd be amazed at how complicated some things are here." By most accounts, the swing to centralization is the right move for Yahoo! after so many years of decentralized product groups around the world, each with its own engineering and other functions.

Questions

1. In what specific ways has Yahoo's new CEO, Carol Bartz, changed the company's organizational structure?
2. Why did she make these changes? In what ways does she expect the new structure to benefit Yahoo's strategy and performance?

Source: Robert D. Hof, "Yahoo's Bartz Shows Who's Boss." Reprinted from *BusinessWeek* online, February 26, 2009, by special permission,

BusinessWeek Case in the News [LO3, 4]

GSK and Pfizer Create New HIV Company

The ink is barely dry on its $68 billion merger with Wyeth, but that hasn't stopped Pfizer from launching yet another deal. On April 16, Pfizer announced it will join forces with Britain's GlaxoSmithKline to pool their HIV operations to create a new company devoted to marketing the two companies' existing HIV medicines and developing new ones. The new venture, which will be 85% owned by GSK, will have a 19% share of the HIV market.

"This creates the focus of a specialist company with the support of two big parents," GSK CEO Andrew Witty said in a conference call. "It gives us a huge portfolio—11 medicines on market and 6 in the clinic."

The news comes just a day after Pfizer's head of worldwide research Rod MacKenzie told a conference in New York that "the big research organization model really doesn't work particularly well," calling the "old model" (of which Pfizer was the industry's biggest proponent) too unwieldy, lacking accountability, and overly bureaucratic.

After years of endless mergers and acquisitions to get bigger, now big pharma is intent on getting smaller. The new venture is an attempt by the world's two biggest drug companies to replicate the energy and drive of a small biotech. Witty calls it an opportunity to "create a specialist company . . . with real independence that will have the flexibility to do other deals and license in other products just as a specialist biotech would."

While the new company will centralize sales, marketing, and administration from a new headquarters in London, research and development teams will remain within each parent's organization. They will be contracted out to the new company. This seems at odds with the stated goal of creating the culture of a biotech. It will, however, lead to cost savings of $89 million, most of which will be delivered in 2010, Witty said.

For GSK, which created some of the world's first and best-selling HIV drugs such as AZT and Epivir, many of which are set to lose patent protection in the coming years, the deal offers access to Pfizer's portfolio of new medicines in clinical development, while Pfizer gets the benefit of GSK's strong marketing and distribution in HIV.

Witty, who has repeatedly said he is not interested in mega-mergers, says the new company "is a good example of the way in which we want to create value and generate efficiency in our business." He noted that GSK is looking at various parts of its businesses where it might be possible to create similar alliances. After years of mega-deals, will hiving off research areas to create smaller stand-alone businesses become the new template for pharma? The jury is out. It's clearly a way for both companies to reduce risks and costs.

Questions

1. Why are GSK and Pfizer creating a new "specialist" organization to manage the sale and development of their HIV drugs?
2. How will the new company be organized? In what ways will it help speed the development of new drugs and reduce costs?

Source: Kerry Capell, "GSK and Pfizer Create New HIV Company." Reprinted from *BusinessWeek* online, April 16, 2009, by special permission,

Control, Change, and Entrepreneurship

CHAPTER 8

Learning Objectives

After studying this chapter, you should be able to

1. Define organizational control, and identify the main output and behavior controls managers use to coordinate and motivate employees. **[LO1]**
2. Explain the role of clan control or organizational culture in creating an effective organizational architecture. **[LO2]**
3. Discuss the relationship between organizational control and change, and explain why managing change is a vital management task. **[LO3]**
4. Understand the role of entrepreneurship in the control and change process. **[LO4]**

New Ford CEO Alan Mulally (left), with former CEO Bill Ford (right), who realized the company needed an outsider at the helm to turn around Ford's insular, self-protective culture.

MANAGEMENT SNAPSHOT

A New Approach to Control at Ford

How Should Managers Use Control to Improve Performance?

Ford posted a record loss of $13.3 billion in 2006, after which William Ford III, who had been CEO for the last five years, decided he was not the right person to turn around the company's fortunes.[1] In fact, he was a part of the problem because it turned out that over the years Ford had developed a corporate culture based on empire-building, in which top managers had emulated Ford; they strived to build their own empires, and to protect those empires they would never admit that mistakes had occurred. Finally, Ford's board of directors realized they needed an outsider to change Ford's culture—and the way it was being controlled—and they recruited Alan Mulally, CEO of Boeing in 2006, to become Ford's new CEO.

After arriving Mulally went to hundreds of meetings to meet his new managers, and at one executive meeting he became confused why one top division manager, who obviously did not know the answer to one of Mulally's questions concerning the performance of his car division, had rambled on for several minutes trying to disguise his ignorance. Mulally turned around to his second-in-command Mark Fields and asked him why the manager had done that. Fields explained that "at Ford you never admit when you don't know something."[2]

It turned out that over the years Ford had develop a tall hierarchy composed of managers whose main goal was to protect their turf and avoid any direct blame for its plunging car sales. So, when asked why car sales were falling, they did not admit to bad design and poor quality issues in their divisions; instead, they hid in the details. They brought thick notebooks and binders to meetings, listing the high prices of components and high labor costs to explain why their own particular car models were not selling well or even why they had to be sold at a loss. Mulally wanted to know why Ford's top executives had this inward-looking, destructive mind-set.

He soon realized that the problem was the values and norms in Ford's culture that had created a situation in which the managers of its different divisions and functions thought that the best way to maintain their jobs, salaries, and status was to hoard information and not share it. Thus, values and norms of secrecy and ambiguity, and of emphasizing status and rank to protect information, had developed. The reason only the boss could ask a subordinate to lunch was to enable superiors to hoard information and protect their positions. Ford's culture allowed managers to hide the extent of the problems they were facing and how badly they were performing. What could Mulally do?

He issued a direct order that the managers of every division should share with every other Ford division a detailed statement of the costs they incurred to build each of its vehicles. He insisted that each of Ford's divisional presidents should attend a weekly—rather than a monthly—meeting to discuss openly and share the problems all the company's divisions faced. He also told them that they should bring a different subordinate with them to each meeting so that every manager in the hierarchy would learn of the problems that had been kept hidden.[3] Essentially, Mulally's goal was to demolish the dysfunctional inbred values and norms of Ford's culture that had focused managers' attention on their own empires at the expense of the whole company. No longer would they be allowed to protect their own careers at the expense of customers.

Mulally's goal is to create new values and norms that it is all right to admit mistakes, share information about all aspects of model design and costs, and of course find ways to speed development and reduce costs. He also wants to emphasize norms of cooperation within and across divisions to improve performance. When Mulally arrived he found that no two models shared even the most basic components, such as side mirrors or the hinges that hold up the hood—something that drives up costs. Now, all these kinds of problems are to be addressed through interdivisional openness and cooperation.

How could this situation have gone unchanged in a major car company that has been experiencing increased competition since the mid-1970s? The answer is that the norms and values of an organization's culture are very hard to change; and despite Ford's major problems, no CEO had been able to change the mind-set of the top managers in the company. Ford had even become more hierarchical and bureaucratic over time as its problems increased because poor performance led managers to become even more defensive and concerned to defend their fiefdoms or empires. Can outsider Mulally succeed?[4]

Overview

As the history of Ford suggests, the ways in which managers decide to control the behavior of their employees can have very different effects on the way employees behave. When managers make choices about how to influence and regulate their employees' behavior and performance, they establish the second foundation of organizational architecture, organizational control. And control is the essential ingredient that is needed to bring about and manage organizational change efficiently and effectively, as Alan Mulally is attempting to do at Ford.

As discussed in Chapter 7, the first task facing managers is to establish the structure of task and job reporting relationships that allows organizational members to use resources most efficiently and effectively. Structure alone, however, does not provide the incentive or motivation for people to behave in ways that help achieve organizational goals. The purpose of organizational control is to provide managers with a means of directing and motivating subordinates to work toward achieving organizational goals and to provide managers with specific feedback on how well an organization and its members are performing.

Organizational structure provides an organization with a skeleton, and control and culture give it the muscles, sinews, nerves, and sensations that allow managers to regulate and govern its activities. The managerial functions of organizing and controlling are inseparable, and effective managers must learn to make them work together in a harmonious way.

In this chapter, we look in detail at the nature of organizational control and describe the steps in the control process. We discuss three types of control available to managers to control and influence organizational members–output control, behavior control, and clan control (which operates through the values and norms of an organization's culture).[5] Then we discuss the important issue of organizational change, change that is possible only when managers have put in place a control system that allows them to alter the way people and groups behave. Finally, we look at the role of entrepreneurs and entrepreneurship in changing the way a company operates. By the end of this chapter, you will appreciate the rich variety of control systems available to managers and understand why developing an appropriate control system is vital to increasing the performance of an organization and its members.

What Is Organizational Control?

As noted in Chapter 1, *controlling* is the process whereby managers monitor and regulate how efficiently and effectively an organization and its members are performing the activities necessary to achieve organizational goals. As discussed in previous chapters, when planning and organizing, managers develop the organizational strategy and structure that they hope will allow the organization to use resources most effectively to create value for customers. In controlling, managers monitor and evaluate whether the organization's strategy and structure are working as intended, how they could be improved, and how they might be changed if they are not working.

LO1 Define organizational control, and identify the main output and behavior controls managers use to coordinate and motivate employees.

Control, however, does not mean just reacting to events after they have occurred. It also means keeping an organization on track, anticipating events that might occur, and then changing the organization to respond to whatever opportunities or threats have been identified. Control is concerned with keeping employees motivated, focused on the important problems confronting the organization, and working together to make the changes that will help an organization perform better over time.

The Importance of Organizational Control

To understand the importance of organizational control, consider how it helps managers obtain superior efficiency, quality, responsiveness to customers, and innovation–the four building blocks of competitive advantage.

To determine how efficiently they are using their resources, managers must be able to accurately measure how many units of inputs (raw materials, human resources, and so on) are being used to produce a unit of output. Managers also must be able to measure how many units of outputs (goods and services) are being produced. A control system contains the measures or yardsticks that allow managers to assess how efficiently the organization is producing goods and services. Moreover, if managers experiment with changing the way the organization produces goods and services to find a more efficient way of producing them, these measures tell managers how successful they have been. For example, when managers at Ford decided to adopt a product team structure to design, engineer, and manufacture new car models, they used measures such as time taken to design a new car and cost savings per car produced to evaluate how well the new structure worked in comparison with the old structure. They found that the

A Ford salesperson talks with a prospective car buyer. In the car industry, managers need to control not only the quality of their products but also the quality of their customer service. To improve its customer service, Ford implemented a control system that consists of regularly surveying customers about their experience with particular dealers. If a dealership receives too many complaints, Ford's managers investigate and propose solutions.

new one performed better. Without a control system in place, managers have no idea how well their organization is performing and how its performance can be improved–information that is becoming increasingly important in today's highly competitive environment.

Today, much of the competition among organizations revolves around increasing the quality of goods and services. In the car industry, for example, cars within each price range compete against one another in features, design, and reliability. Thus, whether a customer will buy a Ford Taurus, GM Grand Prix, Chrysler Sebring, Toyota Camry, or Honda Accord depends significantly on the quality of each product. Organizational control is important in determining the quality of goods and services because it gives managers feedback on product quality. If the managers of carmakers consistently measure the number of customer complaints and the number of new cars returned for repairs, or if school principals measure how many students drop out of school or how achievement scores on nationally based tests vary over time, they have a good indication of how much quality they have built into their product–be it an educated student or a car that does not break down. Effective managers create a control system that consistently monitors the quality of goods and services so that they can make continuous improvements to quality–an approach to change that gives them a competitive advantage.

Managers can also help make their organizations more responsive to customers if they develop a control system that allows them to evaluate how well customer-contact employees are performing their jobs. Monitoring employee behavior can help managers find ways to increase employees' performance levels, perhaps by revealing areas in which skill training can help employees or by finding new procedures that allow employees to perform their jobs better. When employees know that their behaviors are being monitored, they may also have more incentive to be helpful and consistent in how they act toward customers. To improve customer service, for example, Ford regularly surveys customers about their experiences with particular Ford dealers. If a dealership receives too many customer complaints, Ford's managers investigate the dealership to uncover the sources of the problems and suggest solutions; if necessary, they might even threaten to reduce the number of cars a dealership receives to force the dealer to improve the quality of its customer service.

Finally, controlling can raise the level of innovation in an organization. Successful innovation takes place when managers create an organizational setting in which employees feel empowered to be creative and in which authority is decentralized to employees so that they feel free to experiment and take risks. Deciding on the appropriate control systems to encourage risk taking is an important management challenge; organizational culture (discussed later in this chapter) becomes important in this regard. To encourage product teams at Ford to perform highly, top managers monitored the performance of each team separately–by examining how each team reduced costs or increased quality, for example–and used a bonus system related to performance to pay each team. The product team manager then evaluated each team member's individual performance, and the most innovative employees received promotions and rewards based on their superior performance.

Control Systems and IT

control systems Formal target-setting, monitoring, evaluation, and feedback systems that provide managers with information about how well the organization's strategy and structure are working.

Control systems are formal target-setting, monitoring, evaluation, and feedback systems that provide managers with information about whether the organization's strategy and structure are working efficiently and effectively.[6] Effective control systems alert managers when something is going wrong and give them time to respond to opportunities and threats. An effective control system has three characteristics: It is flexible enough to allow managers to respond as necessary to unexpected events; it provides accurate information and gives managers a true picture of organizational performance; and it provides managers with the information in a timely manner because making decisions on the basis of outdated information is a recipe for failure.

New forms of IT have revolutionized control systems because they facilitate the flow of accurate and timely information up and down the organizational hierarchy and between functions and divisions. Today, employees at all levels of the organization routinely feed information into a company's information system or network and start the chain of events that affect decision making at some other part of the organization. This could be the department store clerk whose scanning of purchased clothing tells merchandise managers what kinds of clothing need to be reordered or the salesperson in the field who feeds into a wireless laptop information about customers' changing needs or problems.

feedforward control Control that allows managers to anticipate problems before they arise.

Control and information systems are developed to measure performance at each stage in the process of transforming inputs into finished goods and services (see Figure 8.1). At the input stage, managers use **feedforward control** to anticipate problems before they arise so that problems do not occur later, during the conversion process.[7] For example, by giving stringent product specifications to suppliers in advance (a form of performance target), an organization can control the quality of the inputs it receives from its suppliers and thus avoid potential problems during the conversion process. Also, IT can be used to keep in contact with suppliers and to monitor their progress. Similarly, by screening job applicants, often by viewing their résumés electronically, and using several interviews to select the most highly skilled people, managers can lessen the chance that they will hire people who lack the necessary skills or experience to perform effectively. In general, the development of management information systems promotes feedforward control that provides managers with timely information about changes in the task and general environments that may impact their organization later on. Effective managers always monitor trends and changes in the external environment to try to anticipate problems. (We discuss management information systems in detail in Chapter 13.)

Scanning devices, such as the one shown here, are becoming common in all types of work processes, as more companies require real-time information about their products and customers.

Figure 8.1
Three Types of Control

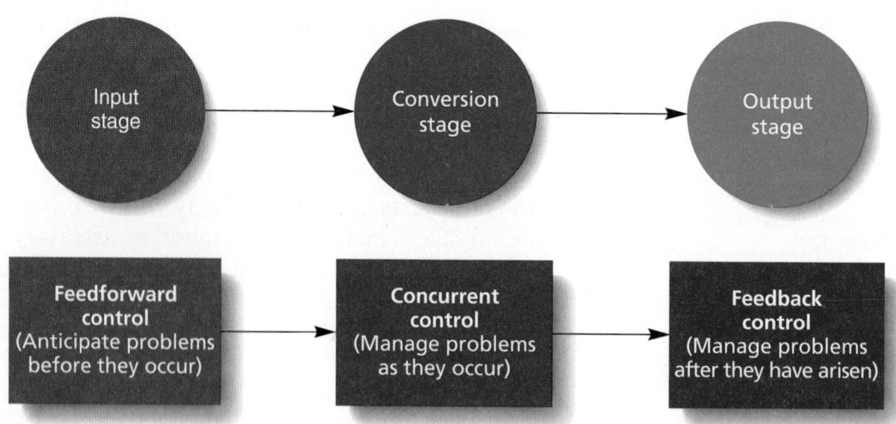

At the conversion stage, concurrent control gives managers immediate feedback on how efficiently inputs are being transformed into outputs so that managers can correct problems as they arise. **Concurrent control** through IT alerts managers to the need to react quickly to whatever is the source of the problem, be it a defective batch of inputs, a machine that is out of alignment, or a worker who lacks the skills necessary to perform a task efficiently. Concurrent control is at the heart of programs to increase quality, in which workers are expected to constantly monitor the quality of the goods or services they provide at every step of the production process and inform managers as soon as they discover problems. One of the strengths of Toyota's production system, for example, is that individual workers are given the authority to push a button to stop the assembly line whenever they discover a quality problem. When all problems have been corrected, the result is a finished product that is much more reliable.

concurrent control Control that gives managers immediate feedback on how efficiently inputs are being transformed into outputs so that managers can correct problems as they arise.

At the output stage, managers use **feedback control** to provide information about customers' reactions to goods and services so that corrective action can be taken if necessary. For example, a feedback control system that monitors the number of customer returns alerts managers when defective products are being produced, and a management information system that measures increases or decreases in relative sales of different products alerts managers to changes in customer tastes so that they can increase or reduce the production of specific products.

feedback control Control that gives managers information about customers' reactions to goods and services so that corrective action can be taken if necessary.

The Control Process

The control process, whether at the input, conversion, or output stage, can be broken down into four steps: establishing standards of performance, and then measuring, comparing, and evaluating actual performance (see Figure 8.2).[8]

- Step 1: *Establish the standards of performance, goals, or targets against which performance is to be evaluated.*

At step 1 in the control process managers decide on the standards of performance, goals, or targets that they will use in the future to evaluate the performance of the entire organization or part of it (such as a division, a function, or an individual). The standards of performance that managers select measure efficiency, quality, responsiveness to customers, and innovation.[9] If managers decide to pursue a low-cost strategy, for example, then they need to measure efficiency at all levels in the organization.

Figure 8.2
Four Steps in Organizational Control

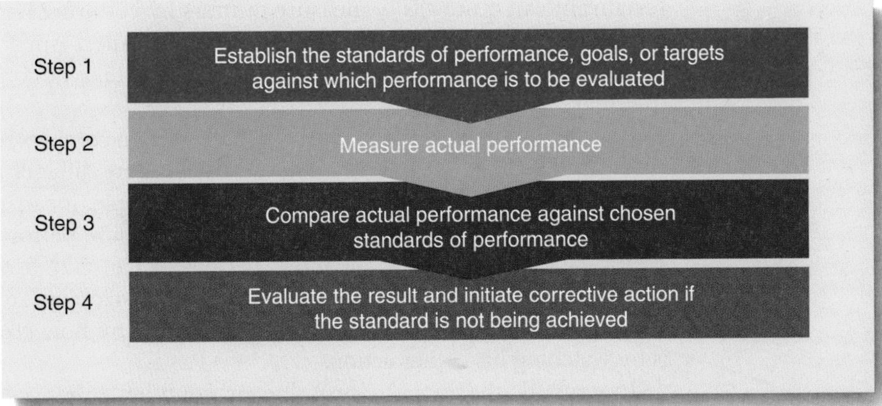

At the corporate level, a standard of performance that measures efficiency is operating costs, the actual costs associated with producing goods and services, including all employee-related costs. Top managers might set a corporate goal of "reducing operating costs by 10% for the next three years" to increase efficiency. Corporate managers might then evaluate divisional managers for their ability to reduce operating costs within their respective divisions, and divisional managers might set cost-savings targets for functional managers. Thus, performance standards selected at one level affect those at the other levels, and ultimately the performance of individual managers is evaluated in terms of their ability to reduce costs. For example, in 2001, struggling Xerox Corp. named Anne Mulcahy as CEO and gave her the challenging task of turning around the company's fortunes. She was selected because of her 25-year reputation as a person who had been highly successful in reducing costs and increasing efficiency in Xerox's general markets division.[10] By 2004, Mulcahy had succeeded; Xerox began to make a profit again as it now could make the products customers wanted and by 2007 was a industry leader again.

The number of standards of performance that an organization's managers use to evaluate efficiency, quality, and so on can run into the thousands or hundreds of thousands. Managers at each level are responsible for selecting those standards that will best allow them to evaluate how well the part of the organization they are responsible for is performing.[11] Managers must be careful to choose the standards of performance that allow them to assess how well they are doing with all four of the building blocks of competitive advantage. If managers focus on just one (such as efficiency) and ignore others (such as determining what customers really want and innovating a new line of products to satisfy them), managers may end up hurting their organization's performance.

- Step 2: *Measure actual performance.*

Once managers have decided which standards or targets they will use to evaluate performance, the next step in the control process is to measure actual performance. In practice, managers can measure or evaluate two things: (1) the actual *outputs* that result from the behavior of their members and (2) the *behaviors* themselves (hence the terms *output control* and *behavior control* used in this chapter).[12]

Sometimes both outputs and behaviors can be easily measured. Measuring outputs and evaluating behavior is relatively easy in a fast-food restaurant, for example, because employees are performing routine tasks. Managers of a fast-food restaurant can quite easily measure outputs by counting how many customers their employees serve and how much money customers spend. Managers can easily observe each employee's behavior and quickly take action to solve any problems that may arise.

When an organization and its members perform complex, nonroutine activities that are intrinsically difficult to measure, it is much more difficult for managers to measure outputs or behavior.[13] It is very difficult, for example, for managers in charge of R&D departments at Merck, Intel, or Microsoft to measure performance or to evaluate the performance of individual members because it can take 5 or 10 years to determine whether the new products that scientists are developing are going to be profitable. Moreover, it is impossible for a manager to measure how creative a research scientist is by watching his or her actions.

In general, the more nonroutine or complex organizational activities are, the harder it is for managers to measure outputs or behaviors.[14] Outputs, however, are usually easier to measure than behaviors because they are more tangible and objective. Therefore, the first kind of performance measures that managers tend to use are those that measure outputs. Then managers develop performance measures or standards that allow them to evaluate behaviors to determine whether employees at all levels are working toward organizational goals. Some simple behavior measures are (1) do employees come to work on time? and (2) do employees consistently follow the established rules for greeting and serving customers? Each type of output and behavior control and the way it is used at the different organizational levels–corporate, divisional, functional, and individual–is discussed in detail subsequently.

- Step 3: *Compare actual performance against chosen standards of performance.*

During step 3, managers evaluate whether–and to what extent–performance deviates from the standards of performance chosen in step 1. If performance is higher than expected, managers might decide that they set performance standards too low and may raise them for the next time period to challenge their subordinates.[15] Managers at Japanese companies are well known for the way they try to raise performance in manufacturing settings by constantly raising performance standards to motivate managers and workers to find new ways to reduce costs or increase quality.

However, if performance is too low and standards were not reached, or if standards were set so high that employees could not achieve them, managers must decide whether to take corrective action.[16] It is easy to take corrective action when the reasons for poor performance can be identified–for instance, high labor costs. To reduce costs, managers can search for low-cost foreign sources of supply, invest more in technology, or implement cross-functional teams. More often, however, the reasons for poor performance are hard to identify. Changes in the environment, such as the emergence of a new global competitor, a recession, or an increase in interest rates, might be the source of the problem. Within an organization, perhaps the R&D function underestimated the problems it would encounter in developing a new product or the extra costs of doing unforeseen research. If managers are to take any form of corrective action, step 4 is necessary.

- Step 4: *Evaluate the result and initiate corrective action (that is, make changes) if the standard is not being achieved.*

The final step in the control process is to evaluate the results and bring about change as appropriate. Whether performance standards have been met or not, managers can learn a great deal during this step. If managers decide that the level of performance is unacceptable, they must try to change the way work activities are performed to solve the problem. Sometimes, performance problems occur because the work standard was too high–for example, a sales target was too optimistic and impossible to achieve. In this case, adopting more realistic standards can reduce the gap between actual performance and desired performance.

However, if managers determine that something in the situation is causing the problem, then to raise performance they will need to change the way resources are being utilized.[17] Perhaps the latest technology is not being used; perhaps workers lack the advanced training needed to perform at a higher level; perhaps the organization needs to buy its inputs or assemble its products abroad to compete against low-cost rivals; perhaps it needs to restructure itself or reengineer its work processes to increase efficiency.

The simplest example of a control system is the thermostat in a home. By setting the thermostat, you establish the standard of performance with which actual temperature is to be compared. The thermostat contains a sensing or monitoring device, which measures the actual temperature against the desired temperature. Whenever there is a difference between them, the furnace or air-conditioning unit is activated to bring the temperature back to the standard. In other words, corrective action is initiated. This is a simple control system, for it is entirely self-contained and the target (temperature) is easy to measure.

Establishing targets and designing measurement systems is much more difficult for managers because the high level of uncertainty in the organizational environment causes managers to rarely know what might happen. Thus, it is vital for managers to design control systems to alert them to problems so that they can be dealt with before they become threatening. Another issue is that managers are not just concerned about bringing the organization's performance up to some predetermined standard; they want to push that standard forward, to encourage employees at all levels to find new ways to raise performance.

In the following sections, we consider the three most important types of control that managers use to coordinate and motivate employees to ensure they pursue superior efficiency, quality, innovation, and responsiveness to customers: output control, behavior control, and organizational culture or clan control (see Figure 8.3). Managers use all three to govern and regulate organizational activities, no matter what specific organizational structure is in place.

Figure 8.3
Three Organizational Control Systems

Type of control	Mechanisms of control
Output control	Financial measures of performance Organizational goals Operating budgets
Behavior control	Direct supervision Management by objectives Rules and standard operating procedures
Organizational culture/clan control	Values Norms Socialization

Output Control

All managers develop a system of output control for their organizations. First, they choose the goals or output performance standards or targets that they think will best measure efficiency, quality, innovation, and responsiveness to customers. Then they measure to see whether the performance goals and standards are being achieved at the corporate, divisional or functional, and individual levels of the organization. The three main mechanisms that managers use to assess output or performance are financial measures, organizational goals, and operating budgets.

Financial Measures of Performance

Top managers are most concerned with overall organizational performance and use various financial measures to evaluate performance. The most common are profit ratios, liquidity ratios, leverage ratios, and activity ratios. They are discussed here and summarized in Table 8.1.[18]

- *Profit ratios* measure how efficiently managers are using the organization's resources to generate profits. *Return on investment (ROI),* an organization's net income before taxes divided by its total assets, is the most commonly used financial performance measure because it allows managers of one organization to compare performance with that of other organizations. ROI allows managers to assess an organization's competitive advantage. *Gross profit margin* is the difference between the amount of revenue generated by a product and the resources used to produce the product. This measure provides managers with information about how efficiently an organization is utilizing its resources and about how attractive customers find the product. It also provides managers with a way to assess how well an organization is building a competitive advantage.
- *Liquidity ratios* measure how well managers have protected organizational resources to be able to meet short-term obligations. The *current ratio* (current assets divided by current liabilities) tells managers whether they have the resources available to meet the claims of short-term creditors. The *quick ratio* tells whether they can pay these claims without selling inventory.
- *Leverage ratios* such as the *debt-to-assets ratio* and the *times-covered ratio* measure the degree to which managers use debt (borrow money) or equity (issue new shares) to finance ongoing operations. An organization is highly leveraged if it uses more debt than equity, and debt can be very risky when profits fail to cover the interest on the debt.
- *Activity ratios* provide measures of how well managers are creating value from organizational assets. *Inventory turnover* measures how efficiently managers are turning inventory over so that excess inventory is not carried. *Days sales outstanding* provides information on how efficiently managers are collecting revenue from customers to pay expenses.

The objectivity of financial measures of performance is the reason so many managers use them to assess the efficiency and effectiveness of their organizations. When an organization fails to meet performance standards such as ROI, revenue, or stock price targets, managers know that they must take corrective action. Thus, financial controls tell managers when a corporate reorganization might be necessary, when they should sell off divisions and exit from businesses, or when they should rethink their corporate-level strategies.[19] Today, financial controls are being taught to all organizational employees, as the following "Management Insight" describes.

Table 8.1
Four Measures of Financial Performance

Profit Ratios		
Return on investment	$= \dfrac{\text{net profit before taxes}}{\text{total assets}}$	Measures how well managers are using the organization's resources to generate profits.
Gross profit margin	$= \dfrac{\text{sales revenues} - \text{cost of goods sold}}{\text{sales revenues}}$	The difference between the amount of revenue generated from the product and the resources used to produce the product.
Liquidity Ratios		
Current ratio	$= \dfrac{\text{current assets}}{\text{current liabilities}}$	Do managers have resources available to meet claims of short-term creditors?
Quick ratio	$= \dfrac{\text{current assets} - \text{inventory}}{\text{current liabilities}}$	Can managers pay off claims of short-term creditors without selling inventory?
Leverage Ratios		
Debt-to-assets ratio	$= \dfrac{\text{total debt}}{\text{total assets}}$	To what extent have managers used borrowed funds to finance investments?
Times-covered ratio	$= \dfrac{\text{profit before interest and taxes}}{\text{total interest charges}}$	Measures how far profits can decline before managers cannot meet interest changes. If ratio declines to less than 1, the organization is technically insolvent.
Activity Ratios		
Inventory turnover	$= \dfrac{\text{cost of goods sold}}{\text{inventory}}$	Measures how efficiently managers are turning inventory over so that excess inventory is not carried.
Days sales outstanding	$= \dfrac{\text{current accounts receivable}}{\text{sales for period divided by days in period}}$	Measures how efficiently managers are collecting revenues from customers to pay expenses.

MANAGEMENT INSIGHT

Making the Financial Figures Come Alive

You might think that financial control is the province of top managers and that employees lower in the organization don't need to worry about the numbers or about how their specific activities affect those numbers. However, some top managers make a point of showing employees exactly how their activities affect financial ratios, and they do so because employees' activities directly affect a company's costs and its sales revenues. One of those managers is Michael Dell.

Dell goes to enormous lengths to convince employees that they need to watch every dime spent in making the PCs that have made his company so prosperous, as well as in saying every word or making every phone call or service call that is needed to

Michael Dell prepares to work the phone lines at Dell's U.S. customer service call center. Dell's emphasis on productivity everywhere means he has no qualms about sitting in an entry-level position for a day both to learn what his employees face and to better teach them.

sell or repair them. Dell believes that all his managers need to have at their fingertips detailed information about Dell's cost structure, including assembly costs, selling costs, and after-sales costs, in order to squeeze out every cent of operating costs. And one good reason for this is that Dell puts a heavy emphasis on the operating-margin financial ratio in measuring his company's performance. Dell doesn't care about how much profits or sales are growing individually; he cares about how these two figures work together, because only if profits are growing faster than sales is the company increasing its long-run profitability by operating more efficiently and effectively.

So he insists that his managers search for every way possible to reduce costs or make customers happier and then help employees learn the new procedures to achieve these goals. At Dell's boot camp for new employees, in Austin, Texas, he has been known to bring financial charts that show employees how each minute spent on performing some job activity, or how each mistake made in assembling or packing a PC, affects bottom-line profitability. In the 2000s Dell's repeated efforts to slice costs while building customer loyalty have boosted efficiency and operating margins; it is much more efficient than HP or Gateway. However, these companies are applying Dell's principles and closing the performance gap, and in the 2000s all kinds of companies have begun training sessions in which employees at all levels are taught how their specific job activities, and the way their functions operate, affect the financial ratios used to judge how well an organization is performing.

Although financial information is an important output control, financial information by itself does not provide managers with all the information they need about the four building blocks of competitive advantage. Financial results inform managers about the results of decisions they have already made; they do not tell managers how to find new opportunities to build competitive advantage in the future. To encourage a future-oriented approach, top managers must establish organizational goals that encourage middle and first-line managers to achieve superior efficiency, quality, innovation, and responsiveness to customers.

Organizational Goals

Once top managers consult with lower-level managers and set the organization's overall goals, they establish performance standards for the divisions and functions. These standards specify for divisional and functional managers the level at which their units must perform if the organization is to achieve its overall goals.[20] Each division is given a set of specific goals to achieve (see Figure 8.4). For example, at General Electric the goal of each division is to be first or second in its industry in profit. Divisional managers then develop a business-level strategy (based on achieving superior efficiency or innovation) that they hope will allow them to achieve that goal.[21] In consultation with functional

Figure 8.4
Organizationwide Goal Setting

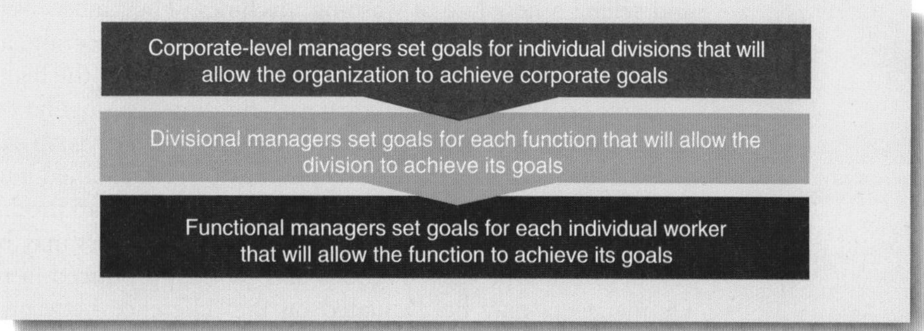

managers, they specify the functional goals that the managers of different functions need to achieve to allow the division to achieve its goals. For example, sales managers might be evaluated for their ability to increase sales; materials management managers, for their ability to increase the quality of inputs or lower their costs; R&D managers, for the number of products they innovate or the number of patents they receive. In turn, functional managers establish goals that first-line managers and nonmanagerial employees need to achieve to allow the function to achieve its goals.

Output control is used at every level of the organization, and it is vital that the goals set at each level harmonize with the goals set at other levels so that managers and other employees throughout the organization work together to attain the corporate goals that top managers have set.[22] It is also important that goals be set appropriately so that managers are motivated to accomplish them. If goals are set at an impossibly high level, managers might work only halfheartedly to achieve them because they are certain they will fail. In contrast, if goals are set so low that they are too easy to achieve, managers will not be motivated to use all their resources as efficiently and effectively as possible. Research suggests that the best goals are *specific, difficult goals*–goals that challenge and stretch managers' ability but are not out of reach and do not require an impossibly high expenditure of managerial time and energy. Such goals are often called *stretch goals*.

Deciding what is a specific, difficult goal and what is a goal that is too difficult or too easy is a skill that managers must develop. Based on their own judgment and work experience, managers at all levels must assess how difficult a certain task is, and they must assess the ability of a particular subordinate manager to achieve the goal. If they do so successfully, challenging, interrelated goals–goals that reinforce one another and focus on achieving overall corporate objectives–will energize the organization.

Operating Budgets

operating budget A budget that states how managers intend to use organizational resources to achieve organizational goals.

Once managers at each level have been given a goal or target to achieve, the next step in developing an output control system is to establish operating budgets that regulate how managers and workers attain their goals. An **operating budget** is a blueprint that states how managers intend to use organizational resources to achieve organizational goals efficiently. Typically, managers at one level allocate to subordinate managers a specific amount of resources to use to produce goods and services. Once they have been given a budget, these lower-level managers must decide how to allocate money for different organizational activities. They are then evaluated for their ability to stay within the budget and to make the best use of available resources. For example, managers at GE's washing machine division might have a budget of $50 million to spend on developing and selling a new line of washing machines. They must decide how much money to allocate to the various functions such as R&D, engineering, and sales so that the division generates the most customer revenue and makes the biggest profit.

Large organizations often treat each division as a singular or stand-alone responsibility center. Corporate managers then evaluate each division's contribution to corporate performance. Managers of a division may be given a fixed budget for resources and be evaluated on the amount of goods or services they can produce using those resources (this is a *cost* or *expense* budget approach). Or managers may be asked to maximize the revenues from the sales of goods and services produced (a *revenue* budget approach). Or managers may be evaluated on the difference between the revenues generated by the sales of goods and services and the budgeted cost of making those goods and services (a *profit* budget approach). Japanese companies' use of operating budgets and challenging goals to increase efficiency is instructive in this context.

In summary, three components–objective financial measures, challenging goals and performance standards, and appropriate operating budgets–are the essence of effective output control. Most organizations develop sophisticated output control systems to allow managers at all levels to keep an accurate account of the organization so that they can move quickly to take corrective action as needed.[23] Output control is an essential part of management.

Problems with Output Control

When designing an output control system, managers must be careful to avoid some pitfalls. For example, they must be sure that the output standards they create motivate managers at all levels and do not cause managers to behave in inappropriate ways to achieve organizational goals.

Suppose top managers give divisional managers the goal of doubling profits over a three-year period. This goal seems challenging and reachable when it is jointly agreed upon, and in the first two years profits go up by 70%. In the third year, however, an economic recession hits and sales plummet. Divisional managers think it is increasingly unlikely that they will meet their profit goal. Failure will mean losing the substantial monetary bonus tied to achieving the goal. How might managers behave to try to preserve their bonuses?

One course of action they might take is to find ways to reduce costs, since profit can be increased either by raising revenues or by reducing costs. Thus, divisional managers might cut back on expensive research and development activities, delay maintenance on machinery, reduce marketing expenditures, and lay off middle managers and workers to reduce costs so that at the end of the year they will make their target of doubling profits and receive their bonuses. This tactic might help them achieve a short-run goal–doubling profits–but such actions could hurt long-term profitability or ROI (because a cutback in R&D can reduce the rate of product innovation, a cutback in marketing will lead to the loss of customers, and so on).

Problems of this sort occurred at Gillette (now owned by Procter & Gamble), whose then-CEO James Kilts attributed a large part of Gillette's problems to the overly ambitious sales and profit goals that his predecessor had set for managers of its divisions (razors and toiletries, Braun appliances, and Duracell batteries). To achieve these ambitious sales targets, divisional managers had slashed advertising budgets and loaded up on inventory, hoping to sell it quickly and generate large revenues. However, this had backfired when customer demand dropped and a recession occurred.

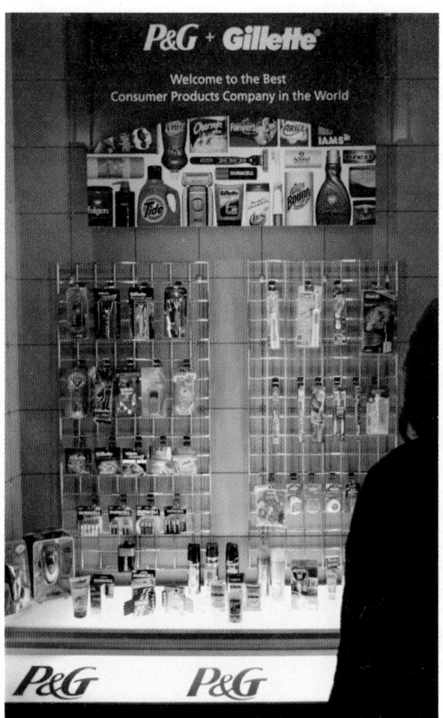

Gillette CEO James M. Kilts, overlooking razors and toiletries, set long-term goals that would lead to long-term sales growth.

Kilts saw that Gillette's managers had not been focusing on the right way to reduce costs. Because managers' salaries and bonuses were based on their ability to meet the ambitious goals that had been set for them, they had acted with a short-term mind-set. Managers had not been thinking about the long-term goal of trying to find the best balance between keeping costs under control, keeping customers happy, and keeping the pipeline of new products full.

Kilts announced that henceforth Gillette would no longer provide specific and unrealistic sales and earning targets that created a "circle of doom" and led managers to behave in just the ways that would prevent them from achieving company goals–by reducing advertising to reduce costs, for example. Kilts decided that Gillette would set long-term goals based on carefully drawn marketing plans that targeted products customers wanted and would lead to long-term sales growth.[24]

As Gillette's experience suggests, long-run effectiveness is what managers should be most concerned about. Thus, managers must consider carefully how flexible they should be when using output control. If conditions change (as they will because of uncertainty in the task and general environments), it is probably better for top managers to communicate to managers lower in the hierarchy that they are aware of the changes taking place and are willing to revise and lower goals and standards. Indeed, many organizations schedule yearly revisions of their five-year plan and goals and use scenario planning to avoid the problems Gillette experienced.

The message is clear: Although output control is a useful tool for keeping managers and employees at all levels motivated and the organization on track, it is only a guide to appropriate action. Managers must be sensitive to how they use output control and must constantly monitor its effects at all levels in the organization.

Behavior Control

Organizational structure by itself does not provide any mechanism that motivates managers and nonmanagerial employees to behave in ways that make the structure work, to say nothing of improving the way it works–hence the need for control. Put another way, managers can develop an elegant organizational structure with highly appropriate task and reporting relationships, but it will work as designed only if managers also establish control systems that allow them to motivate and shape employee behavior.[25] Output control is one method of motivating employees; behavior control is another method. This section examines three mechanisms of behavior control that managers can use to keep subordinates on track and make organizational structures work as they are designed to work: direct supervision, management by objectives, and rules and standard operating procedures (see again Figure 8.3).

Direct Supervision

The most immediate and potent form of behavior control is direct supervision by managers who actively monitor and observe the behavior of their subordinates, teach subordinates the behaviors that are appropriate and inappropriate, and intervene to take corrective action as needed. Moreover, when managers personally supervise subordinates, they lead by example and in this way can help subordinates develop and increase their own skill levels. (Leadership is the subject of Chapter 10.) Thus, control through personal supervision can be a very effective way of motivating employees and promoting behaviors that increase efficiency and effectiveness.[26]

Nevertheless, certain problems are associated with direct supervision. First, it is very expensive because a manager can personally manage only a small number of subordinates effectively. Therefore, if direct supervision is the main kind of control being used in an organization, a lot of managers will be needed and costs will increase. For this reason, output control is usually preferred to behavior control; indeed, output control tends to be the first type of control that managers at all levels use to evaluate performance.

Second, direct supervision can demotivate subordinates if they feel that they are under such close scrutiny that they are not free to make their own decisions. Moreover, subordinates may start to pass the buck and avoid responsibility if they feel that their manager is waiting in the wings ready to reprimand anyone who makes the slightest error.

Third, as noted previously, for many jobs direct supervision is simply not feasible. The more complex a job is, the more difficult it is for a manager to evaluate how well a subordinate is performing. The performance of divisional and functional managers, for example, can be evaluated only over relatively long time periods (this is why an output control system is developed), so it makes little sense for top managers to continually monitor their performance.

Management by Objectives

management by objectives (MBO) A goal-setting process in which a manager and each of his or her subordinates negotiate specific goals and objectives for the subordinate to achieve and then periodically evaluate the extent to which the subordinate is achieving those goals.

To provide a framework within which to evaluate subordinates' behavior and, in particular, to allow managers to monitor progress toward achieving goals, many organizations implement some version of management by objectives. **Management by objectives (MBO)** is a system of evaluating subordinates for their ability to achieve specific organizational goals or performance standards and to meet operating budgets.[27] Most organizations make some use of management by objectives because it is pointless to establish goals and then fail to evaluate whether or not they are being achieved. Management by objectives involves three specific steps:

- Step 1: *Specific goals and objectives are established at each level of the organization.*

Management by objective starts when top managers establish overall organizational objectives, such as specific financial performance targets. Then objective setting cascades down throughout the organization as managers at the divisional and functional levels set their objectives to achieve corporate objectives.[28] Finally, first-level managers and workers jointly set objectives that will contribute to achieving functional goals.

- Step 2: *Managers and their subordinates together determine the subordinates' goals.*

An important characteristic of management by objectives is its participatory nature. Managers at every level sit down with each of the subordinate managers who report directly to them, and together they determine appropriate and feasible goals for the subordinate and bargain over the budget that the subordinate will need to achieve his or her goals. The participation of subordinates in the objective-setting process is a way of strengthening their commitment to achieving their goals and meeting their budgets.[29] Another reason why it is so important for subordinates (both individuals and teams) to participate in goal setting is that doing so enables them to tell managers what they think they can realistically achieve.[30]

- Step 3: *Managers and their subordinates periodically review the subordinates' progress toward meeting goals.*

Once specific objectives have been agreed on for managers at each level, managers are accountable for meeting those objectives. Periodically, they sit down with their subordinates to evaluate their progress. Normally, salary raises and promotions are linked to the goal-setting process, and managers who achieve their goals receive greater rewards than those who fall short. (The issue of how to design reward systems to motivate managers and other organizational employees is discussed in Chapter 9.)

In the companies that have decentralized responsibility for the production of goods and services to empowered teams and cross-functional teams, management by objectives works somewhat differently. Managers ask each team to develop a set of goals and performance targets that the team hopes to achieve–goals that are consistent with organizational objectives. Managers then negotiate with each team to establish its final goals and the budget the team will need to achieve them. The reward system is linked to team performance, not to the performance of any one team member.

Cypress Semiconductor offers an interesting example of how IT can be used to manage the MBO process quickly and effectively. In the fast-moving semiconductor business a premium is placed on organizational adaptability. At Cypress, CEO T. J. Rodgers was facing a problem. How could he control his growing, 1,500-employee organization without developing a bureaucratic management hierarchy? Rodgers believed that a tall hierarchy hinders the ability of an organization to adapt to changing conditions. He was committed to maintaining a flat and decentralized organizational structure with a minimum of management layers. At the same time, he needed to control his employees to ensure that they perform in a manner consistent with the goals of the company.[31] How could he achieve this without resorting to direct supervision and the management hierarchy that it implies?

To solve this problem, Rodgers implemented an online information system through which he can manage what every employee and team is doing in his fast-moving and decentralized organization. Each employee maintains a list of 10 to 15 goals, such as "Meet with marketing for new product launch" or "Make sure to check with customer X." Noted next to each goal are when it was agreed upon, when it is due to be finished, and whether it has been finished. All of this information is stored on a central computer. Rodgers claims that he can review the goals of all employees in about four hours and that he does so each week.[32] How is this possible? He manages by exception and looks only for employees who are falling behind. He then calls them, not to scold but to ask whether there is anything he can do to help them get the job done. It takes only about half an hour each week for employees to review and update their lists. This system allows Rodgers to exercise control over his organization without resorting to the expensive layers of a management hierarchy and direct supervision.

Bureaucratic Control

bureaucratic control Control of behavior by means of a comprehensive system of rules and standard operating procedures.

When direct supervision is too expensive and management by objectives is inappropriate, managers might turn to another mechanism to shape and motivate employee behavior: bureaucratic control. **Bureaucratic control** is control by means of a comprehensive system of rules and standard operating procedures (SOPs) that shapes and regulates the behavior of divisions, functions, and individuals. In the appendix to Chapter 1, we discussed Weber's theory of bureaucracy and noted that all organizations use bureaucratic rules and procedures but some use them more than others.[33]

Rules and SOPs guide behavior and specify what employees are to do when they confront a problem that needs a solution. It is the responsibility of a manager to develop rules that allow employees to perform their activities efficiently and effectively. When employees follow the rules that managers have developed, their behavior is standardized–actions are performed the same way time and time again–and the outcomes of their work are predictable. And, to the degree that managers can make employees' behavior predictable, there is no need to monitor the outputs of behavior because standardized behavior leads to standardized outputs.

Suppose a worker at Toyota comes up with a way to attach exhaust pipes that reduces the number of steps in the assembly process and increases efficiency. Always on the lookout for ways to standardize procedures, managers make this idea the basis of a new rule that says, "From now on, the procedure for attaching the exhaust pipe to the car is as follows." If all workers followed the rule to the letter, every car would come off the assembly line with its exhaust pipe attached in the new way and there would be no need to check exhaust pipes at the end of the line. In practice, mistakes and lapses of attention do happen, so output control is used at the end of the line, and each car's exhaust system is given a routine inspection. However, the number of quality problems with the exhaust system is minimized because the rule (bureaucratic control) is being followed.

Service organizations such as retail stores, fast-food restaurants, and home-improvement stores attempt to standardize the behavior of employees by instructing them on the correct way to greet customers or the appropriate way to serve and bag food. Employees are trained to follow the rules that have proved to be most effective in a particular situation, and the better trained the employees are, the more standardized is their behavior and the more trust managers can have that outputs (such as food quality) will be consistent.[34]

Problems with Bureaucratic Control

All organizations make extensive use of bureaucratic control because rules and SOPs effectively control routine organizational activities. With a bureaucratic control system in place, managers can manage by exception and intervene and take corrective action only when necessary. However, managers need to be aware of a number of problems associated with bureaucratic control, because such problems can reduce organizational effectiveness.[35]

First, establishing rules is always easier than discarding them. Organizations tend to become overly bureaucratic over time as managers do everything according to the rule book. If the amount of red tape becomes too great, decision making slows and managers react slowly to changing conditions. This sluggishness can imperil an organization's survival if agile new competitors emerge.

Second, because rules constrain and standardize behavior and lead people to behave in predictable ways, there is a danger that people become so used to automatically following rules that they stop thinking for themselves. Thus, too much standardization can actually reduce the level of learning taking place in an organization and get the organization off track if managers and workers focus on the wrong issues. An organization thrives when its members are constantly thinking of new ways to increase efficiency, quality, and customer responsiveness. By definition, new ideas do not come from blindly following standardized procedures. Similarly, the pursuit of innovation implies a commitment by managers to discover new ways of doing things; innovation, however, is incompatible with the use of extensive bureaucratic control.

Managers must therefore be sensitive about the way they use bureaucratic control. It is most useful when organizational activities are routine and well understood and when employees are making programmed decisions–for example, in mass-production settings such as Ford or in routine service settings such as stores like Target or Midas Muffler. Bureaucratic control is much less useful in situations where nonprogrammed decisions have to be made and managers have to react quickly to changes in the organizational environment.

To use output control and behavior control, managers must be able to identify the outcomes they want to achieve and the behaviors they want employees to perform to achieve those outcomes. For many of the most important and significant organizational activities, however, output control and behavior control are inappropriate for several reasons:

- A manager cannot evaluate the performance of workers such as doctors, research scientists, or engineers by observing their behavior on a day-to-day basis.
- Rules and SOPs are of little use in telling a doctor how to respond to an emergency situation or a scientist how to discover something new.
- Output controls such as the amount of time a surgeon takes for each operation or the costs of making a discovery are very crude measures of the quality of performance.

organizational culture The set of values, norms, standards of behavior, and common expectations that controls the ways in which individuals and groups in an organization interact with one another and work to achieve organizational goals.

How can managers attempt to control and regulate the behavior of their subordinates when personal supervision is of little use, when rules cannot be developed to tell employees what to do, and when outputs and goals cannot be measured at all or can be measured usefully only over long periods? One source of control increasingly being used by organizations is a strong organizational culture.

Organizational Culture and Clan Control

Organizational culture is another important control system that regulates and governs employee attitudes and behavior. As we discussed in Chapter 2, **organizational culture** is the shared set of beliefs, expectations, values, norms, and work routines that influences how members of an organization relate to one another and work together to achieve organizational goals. **Clan control** is the control exerted on individuals and groups in an organization by shared values, norms, standards of behavior, and expectations. Organizational culture is not an externally imposed system of constraints, such as direct supervision or rules and procedures. Rather, employees internalize organizational values and norms and then let these values and norms guide their decisions and actions. Just as people in society at large generally behave in accordance with socially acceptable values and norms–such as the norm that people should line up at the checkout counters in supermarkets–so are individuals in an organizational setting mindful of the force of organizational values and norms.

clan control The control exerted on individuals and groups in an organization by shared values, norms, standards of behavior, and expectations.

LO2 Explain the role of clan control or organizational culture in creating an effective organizational architecture.

Organizational culture is an important source of control for two reasons. First, it makes control possible in situations where managers cannot use output or behavior control. Second, and more important, when a strong and cohesive set of organizational values and norms is in place, employees focus on thinking about what is best for the organization in the long run–all their decisions and actions become oriented toward helping the organization perform well. For example, a teacher spends personal time after school coaching and counseling students; an R&D scientist works

80 hours a week, evenings, and weekends to help speed up a late project; a salesclerk at a department store runs after a customer who left a credit card at the cash register. An interesting example of a company that has built a strong culture based on close attention to developing the right set of output and behavior controls is UPS, profiled in the following "Manager as a Person."

MANAGER AS A PERSON

James Casey Creates a Culture for UPS

United Parcel Service (UPS) controls more than three-fourths of the ground and air parcel service in the United States, delivering over 10 million packages a day in its fleet of 150,000 trucks.[36] It is also the most profitable company in its industry. UPS employs over 250,000 people, and since its founding as a bicycle-messenger service in 1907 by James E. Casey, UPS has developed a culture that has been a model for competitors such as FedEx and the U.S. Postal Service.

From the beginning, Casey made efficiency and economy the company's driving values and loyalty, humility, discipline, dependability, and intense effort the key norms and standards UPS employees should adopt. UPS has always gone to extraordinary lengths to develop and maintain these values and norms in its workforce.

First, its operating systems from the top of the company down to its trucking operations are the subject of intense scrutiny by the company's 3,000 industrial engineers. These engineers are constantly on the lookout for ways to measure outputs and behaviors to improve efficiency. They time every part of an employee's job. Truck drivers, for example, are instructed in extraordinary detail on how to perform their tasks: They must step from their truck with their right foot first, fold their money face-up, carry packages under their left arm, walk at a pace of 3 feet per second, and slip the key ring holding their truck keys over their third finger.[37] Employees are not allowed to have beards, must be carefully groomed, and are instructed in how to deal with customers. Drivers who perform below average receive visits from training supervisors who accompany them on their delivery routes and instruct them on how to raise their performance level. Not surprisingly, as a result of this intensive training and close behavior control, UPS employees internalize the company's strong norms about the appropriate ways to behave to help the organization achieve its values of economy and efficiency.

UPS drivers must follow strict guidelines regarding appearance, job performance, and customer interactions.

Its search to find the best set of output controls leads UPS to constantly develop and introduce the latest in IT into the company's operations, particularly its materials management operations. In fact, today UPS offers a consulting service to other companies in the area of global supply chain management. Its goal is to teach other companies how to pursue its values of efficiency and economy, values that the company has been pursuing for the last hundred years as a result of the values of its founder.

Adaptive Cultures versus Inert Cultures

Many researchers and managers believe that employees of some organizations go out of their way to help the organization because it has a strong and cohesive organizational culture–an *adaptive culture* that controls employee attitudes and behaviors. Adaptive cultures, such as that at UPS, are cultures whose values and norms help an organization to build momentum and to grow and change as needed to achieve its goals and be effective. By contrast, *inert cultures* are those that lead to values and norms that fail to motivate or inspire employees; they lead to stagnation and often failure over time. What leads to an adaptive or inert culture?

Researchers have found that organizations with strong adaptive cultures, like 3M, UPS, Microsoft, and IBM, invest in their employees. They demonstrate their commitment to their members by, for example, emphasizing the long-term nature of the employment relationship and trying to avoid layoffs. These companies develop long-term career paths for their employees and invest heavily in training and development to increase employees' value to the organization. In these ways, terminal and instrumental values pertaining to the worth of human resources encourage the development of supportive work attitudes and behaviors.

In adaptive cultures employees often receive rewards linked directly to their performance and to the performance of the company as a whole. Sometimes, employee stock ownership plans (ESOPs) are developed in which workers as a group are allowed to buy a significant percentage of their company's stock. Workers who are owners of the company have additional incentive to develop skills that allow them to perform highly and search actively for ways to improve quality, efficiency, and performance. At Dell, for example, employees are able to buy Dell stock at a steep (15%) discount; this allows them to build a sizable stake in the company over time.

Some organizations, however, develop cultures with values that do not include protecting and increasing the worth of their human resources as a major goal. Their employment practices are based on short-term employment according to the needs of the organization and on minimal investment in employees who perform simple, routine tasks. Moreover, employees are not often rewarded based on their performance and thus have little incentive to improve their skills or otherwise invest in the organization to help it to achieve goals. If a company has an inert culture, poor working relationships frequently develop between the organization and its employees, and instrumental values of noncooperation, laziness, and loafing and work norms of output restriction are common.

Moreover, an adaptive culture develops an emphasis on entrepreneurship and respect for the employee and allows the use of organizational structures, such as the cross-functional team structure, that empower employees to make decisions and motivate them to succeed. By contrast, in an inert culture, employees are content to be told what to do and have little incentive or motivation to perform beyond minimum work requirements. As you might expect, the emphasis is on close supervision and hierarchical authority, which result in a culture that makes it difficult to adapt to a changing environment.

Nokia, the world's largest wireless phone maker, headquartered in Finland, is a good example of a company in which managers strived to create an adaptive culture.[38] Nokia's president, Matti Alahuhta, believes that Nokia's cultural values are based on the Finnish character: Finns are down-to-earth, rational, straightforward people. They are also very friendly and democratic people who do not believe in a rigid hierarchy based either on a person's authority or on social class. Nokia's culture reflects these values because innovation and decision making are pushed right down to the bottom line, to teams of employees who take up the challenge of developing the ever-smaller and more sophisticated phones for which the company is known. Bureaucracy is kept to a minimum at Nokia; its adaptive culture is based on informal and personal relationships and norms of cooperation and teamwork.

To help strengthen its culture, Nokia has built a futuristic open-plan steel and glass building just outside Helsinki. Here, in an open environment, its research and development people can work together to innovate new kinds of wireless phones. More than one out of every three of Nokia's 60,000 employees work in research; what keeps these people together and focused is Nokia's company mission to produce phones that are better, cheaper, smaller, and easier to use than competitor's phones.[39] This is the "Nokia Way," a system of cultural values and norms that can't be written down but is always present in the values that cement people together and in the language and stories that its members use to orient themselves to the company.

Another company with an adaptive culture is Merck & Co., one of the largest producers of prescription drugs in the world. Much of Merck's success can be attributed to its ability to attract the very best research scientists, who come because its adaptive culture nurtures scientists and emphasizes values and norms of innovation. Scientists are given great freedom to pursue intriguing ideas even if the commercial payoff is questionable. Moreover, researchers are inspired to think of their work as a quest to alleviate human disease and suffering worldwide, and Merck has a reputation as an ethical company whose values put people above profits.

Although the experience of Nokia and Merck suggests that organizational culture can give rise to managerial actions that ultimately benefit the organization, this is not always the case. The cultures of some organizations become dysfunctional, encouraging managerial actions that harm the organization and discouraging actions that might lead to an improvement in performance.[40] For example, Sunflower Electric Power Corporation, a generation and transmission cooperative, almost went bankrupt in the early 2000s. A state committee of inquiry that was set up to find the source of the problem put the blame on Sunflower's CEO. The committee decided that he had

An aerial view of the cafeteria at Nokia's headquarters in Espoo, Finland. The open architecture of the building reflects the company's culture, which is based on informal and personal relationships and norms of cooperation and teamwork.

created an abusive culture based on fear and blame that encouraged managers to fight over and protect their turf–an inert culture. Managers were afraid to rock the boat or make suggestions since they could not predict what would happen to them.

The CEO was fired and a new CEO, Chris Hauck, was appointed to change the cooperative's culture. He found it very hard to do so as his senior managers were so used to the old values and norms. One top manager, for example, engaged so frequently in the practice of berating one supervisor that the man became physically sick.[41] Hauck fired this manager and other managers as a signal that such behavior would no longer be tolerated. With the help of consultants, he went about the slow process of changing values and norms to emphasize cooperation, teamwork, and respect for others. Clearly, managers can influence the way their organizational culture develops over time, often in a short period of time.

Organizational Change

LO3 Discuss the relationship between organizational control and change, and explain why managing change is a vital management task.

As we have discussed, many problems can arise if an organization's control systems are not designed correctly. One of these problems is that an organization cannot change or adapt in response to a changing environment unless it has effective control over its activities. Companies can lose this control over time, as happened to Ford and Dell, or they can change in ways that make them more effective, as happened to UPS and Wal-Mart.

Interestingly enough, there is a fundamental tension or need to balance two opposing forces in the control process that influences the way organizations change. As just noted, organizations and their managers need to be able to control their activities and make their operations routine and predictable. At the same time, however, organizations have to be responsive to the need to change, and managers and employees have to "think on their feet" and realize when they need to depart from routines to be responsive to unpredictable events. In other words, even though adopting the right set of output and behavior controls is essential for improving efficiency, because the environment is dynamic and uncertain, employees also need to feel that they have the autonomy to depart from routines as necessary to increase effectiveness. (See Figure 8.5.)

Figure 8.5
Organizational Control and Change

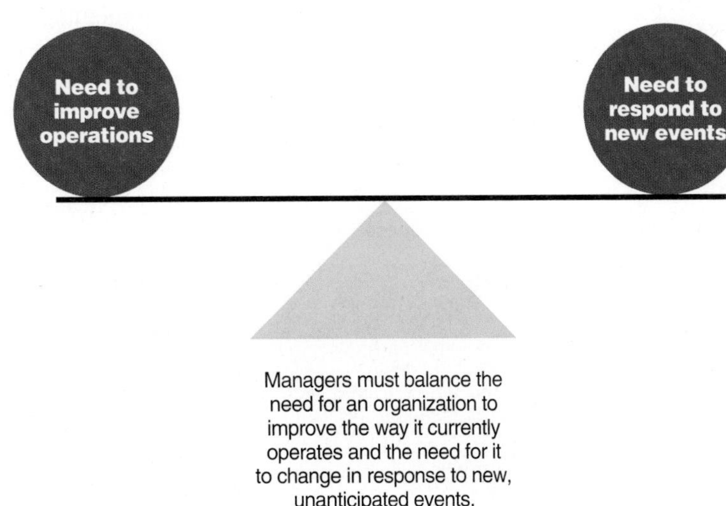

It is for this reason that many researchers believe that the highest-performing organizations are those that are constantly changing–and thus become experienced at doing so–in their search to become more efficient and effective. And companies like UPS, and more recently Ford, are constantly changing the mix of their activities to move forward even as they are seeking to make their existing operations more efficient. For example, UPS entered the air express parcel market, bought a chain of mailbox stores, and began offering a consulting service. At the same time, it has been increasing the efficiency of its ground transport network.

The need to constantly search for ways to improve efficiency and effectiveness makes it vital that managers develop the skills necessary to manage change effectively. Several experts have proposed a model that managers can follow to implement change successfully.[42] **Organization change** is the movement of an organization away from its present state and toward some desired future state to increase its efficiency and effectiveness. Figure 8.6 outlines the steps that managers must take to manage change effectively. In the rest of this section we examine each one.

organization change The movement of an organization away from its present state and toward some desired future state to increase its efficiency and effectiveness.

Assessing the Need for Change

Organizational change can affect practically all aspects of organizational functioning, including organizational structure, culture, strategies, control systems, and groups and teams, as well as the human resource management system and critical organizational processes such as communication, motivation, and leadership. Organizational change can bring alterations in the ways managers carry out the critical tasks of planning, organizing, leading, and controlling and the ways they perform their managerial roles.

Deciding how to change an organization is a complex matter because change disrupts the status quo and poses a threat, prompting employees to resist attempts to alter work relationships and procedures. *Organizational learning,* the process through which managers try to increase organizational members' abilities to understand and appropriately respond to changing conditions, can be an important impetus for change and can help all members of an organization, including managers, effectively make decisions about needed changes.

Assessing the need for change calls for two important activities: recognizing that there is a problem and identifying its source. Sometimes the need for change is obvious, such as when an organization's performance is suffering. Often, however, managers have trouble determining that something is going wrong because problems develop gradually; organizational performance may slip for a number of years before a problem becomes obvious. Thus, during the first step in the change process, managers need to recognize that there is a problem that requires change.

Figure 8.6
Four Steps in the Organizational Change Process

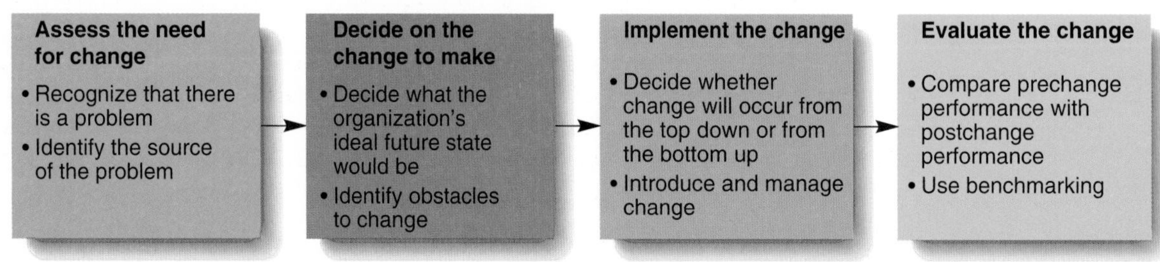

Often the problems that managers detect have produced a gap between desired performance and actual performance. To detect such a gap, managers need to look at performance measures–such as falling market share or profits, rising costs, or employees' failure to meet their established goals or stay within budgets–which indicate whether change is needed. These measures are provided by organizational control systems, discussed earlier in the chapter.

To discover the source of the problem, managers need to look both inside and outside the organization. Outside the organization, they must examine how changes in environmental forces may be creating opportunities and threats that are affecting internal work relationships. Perhaps the emergence of low-cost competitors abroad has led to conflict among different departments that are trying to find new ways to gain a competitive advantage. Managers also need to look within the organization to see whether its structure is causing problems between departments. Perhaps a company does not have integrating mechanisms in place to allow different departments to respond to low-cost competition.

Deciding on the Change to Make

Once managers have identified the source of the problem, they must decide what they think the organization's ideal future state would be. In other words, they must decide where they would like their organization to be in the future–what kinds of goods and services it should be making, what its business-level strategy should be, how the organizational structure should be changed, and so on. During this step, managers also must engage in planning how they are going to attain the organization's ideal future state.

This step in the change process also includes identifying obstacles or sources of resistance to change. Managers must analyze the factors that may prevent the company from reaching its ideal future state. Obstacles to change are found at the corporate, divisional, departmental, and individual levels of the organization.

Corporate-level changes in an organization's strategy or structure, even seemingly trivial changes, may significantly affect how divisional and departmental managers behave. Suppose that to compete with low-cost foreign competitors, top managers decide to increase the resources spent on state-of-the-art machinery and reduce the resources spent on marketing or R&D. The power of manufacturing managers would increase, and the power of marketing and R&D managers would fall. This decision would alter the balance of power among departments and might lead to increased conflict as departments start fighting to retain their status in the organization. An organization's present strategy and structure are powerful obstacles to change.

Whether a company's culture is adaptive or inert facilitates or obstructs change. Organizations with entrepreneurial, flexible cultures, such as high-tech companies, are much easier to change than are organizations with more rigid cultures, such as those sometimes found in large, bureaucratic organizations like the military or GM.

The same obstacles to change exist at the divisional and departmental levels as well. Division managers may differ in their attitudes toward the changes that top managers propose and, if their interests and power seem threatened, will resist those changes. Managers at all levels usually fight to protect their power and control over resources. Given that departments have different goals and time horizons, they may also react differently to the changes that other managers propose. When top managers are trying to reduce costs, for example, sales managers may resist attempts to cut back on sales expenditures if they believe that problems stem from manufacturing managers' inefficiencies.

At the individual level, too, people are often resistant to change because change brings uncertainty and uncertainty brings stress. For example, individuals may resist the introduction of a new technology because they are uncertain about their abilities to learn it and effectively use it.

These obstacles make organizational change a slow process. Managers must recognize the potential obstacles to change and take them into consideration. Some obstacles can be overcome by improving communication so that all organizational members are aware of the need for change and of the nature of the changes being made. Empowering employees and inviting them to participate in the planning for change also can help overcome resistance and allay employees' fears. In addition, managers can sometimes overcome resistance by emphasizing group or shared goals such as increased organizational efficiency and effectiveness. The larger and more complex an organization is, the more complex is the change process.

Implementing the Change

top-down change A fast, revolutionary approach to change in which top managers identify what needs to be changed and then move quickly to implement the changes throughout the organization.

Generally, managers implement–that is, introduce and manage–change from the top down or from the bottom up.[43] **Top-down change** is implemented quickly: Top managers identify the need for change, decide what to do, and then move quickly to implement the changes throughout the organization. For example, top managers may decide to restructure and downsize the organization and then give divisional and departmental managers specific goals to achieve. With top-down change, the emphasis is on making the changes quickly and dealing with problems as they arise; it is revolutionary in nature. Consider how Bob Iger made a major change in Walt Disney's decision making in the following "Manager as a Person."

Bob Iger, Disney's CEO since 2006, breathed new life into Disney by removing a layer of management and returning creative power to its employees.

MANAGER AS A PERSON

Bob Iger's Big Changes at Walt Disney

In 2006, Bob Iger, who had been COO of Disney under its then-CEO Michael Eisner, took control of the troubled company. For several years Disney had been plagued by slow decision making, and analysts claimed it had made many mistakes in putting its new strategies into action. Its Disney stores were losing money, for example; its Internet properties were not getting many "hits"; and even its theme parks seemed to have lost their luster as few new rides or attractions had been introduced.

Iger believed that one of the main reasons for Disney's declining performance was that it had become too tall and bureaucratic and its top managers were following financial rules that did not lead to innovative strategies. So one of Iger's first moves to turn around the performance of the poorly performing company was to dismantle Disney's central strategic planning office. In this office several levels of managers were responsible for sifting through all the new ideas and innovations sent up by Disney's different business divisions, such as theme parks, movies, and gaming, and then deciding which ones to present to the CEO. Iger saw the strategic planning office as a bureaucratic bottleneck that actually reduced the number of ideas coming from below. So he dissolved the office and reassigned its managers back to the different business units.[44]

The result of cutting out an unnecessary layer in Disney's hierarchy has been that more new ideas are being generated by its different business units. The level of innovation has increased because managers are more willing to speak out and champion their ideas when they know they are dealing directly with the CEO and a top management team searching for innovative new ways to improve performance–rather than a layer of strategic planning "bureaucrats" concerned only with the bottom line.[45]

bottom-up change A gradual or evolutionary approach to change in which managers at all levels work together to develop a detailed plan for change.

Bottom-up change is typically more gradual or evolutionary. Top managers consult with middle and first-line managers about the need for change. Then, over time, managers at all levels work to develop a detailed plan for change. A major advantage of bottom-up change is that it can co-opt resistance to change from employees. Because the emphasis in bottom-up change is on participation and on keeping people informed about what is going on, uncertainty and resistance are minimized.

Evaluating the Change

benchmarking The process of comparing one company's performance on specific dimensions with the performance of other, high-performing organizations.

The last step in the change process is to evaluate how successful the change effort has been in improving organizational performance.[46] Using measures such as changes in market share, in profits, or in the ability of managers to meet their goals, managers compare how well an organization is performing after the change with how well it was performing before. Managers also can use **benchmarking**, comparing their performance on specific dimensions with the performance of high-performing organizations, to decide how successful a change effort has been. For example, when Xerox was doing poorly in the 1980s, it benchmarked the efficiency of its distribution operations against that of L. L. Bean, the efficiency of its central computer operations against that of John Deere, and the efficiency of its marketing abilities against that of Procter & Gamble. Those three companies are renowned for their skills in these different areas, and by studying how they performed, Xerox was able to dramatically increase its own performance. Benchmarking is a key tool in total quality management, an important change program discussed in Chapter 14.

In summary, organizational control and change are closely linked because organizations operate in environments that are constantly changing and so managers must be alert to the need to change their strategies and structures. High-performing organizations are those whose managers are attuned to the need to continually modify the way they operate and adopt techniques like empowered work groups and teams, benchmarking, and global outsourcing to remain competitive in a global world.

Entrepreneurship, Control, and Change

As we discussed in Chapter 1, managers are responsible for supervising the use of human and other resources to achieve effective and efficient organizational goals. **Entrepreneurs**, by contrast, are the people who notice opportunities and take responsibility for mobilizing the resources necessary to produce new and improved goods and services. Essentially, entrepreneurs bring about change to companies and industries because they see new and improved ways to use resources to create products customers will want to buy. At the same time, entrepreneurs who start new business ventures are responsible for all the initial planning, organizing, leading, and controlling necessary to make their idea a reality. If their idea is viable and entrepreneurs do attract customers, then their business grows and then they need to hire managers who will take responsibility for organizing and controlling all the specific functional activities such as marketing, accounting, and manufacturing necessary for a growing organization to be successful.

entrepreneurs People who notice opportunities and take responsibility for mobilizing the resources necessary to produce new and improved goods and services.

LO4 Understand the role of entrepreneurship in the control and change process.

Typically, entrepreneurs assume the substantial risk associated with starting new businesses (many new businesses fail), and they receive all the returns or profits associated with the new business venture. These people are the Bill Gateses, Larry Ellisons, or Liz Claibornes of the world who make vast fortunes when their businesses succeed. Or they are among the millions of people who start new business ventures only to lose their money when their businesses fail. Despite the fact that an estimated 80% of small businesses fail in the first three to five years, by some estimates 38% of men and 50% of women in today's workforce want to start their own companies.

Entrepreneurship does not just end once a new business is founded. Entrepreneurship carries on inside an organization over time, and many people throughout an organization take responsibility for developing innovative goods and services. For example, managers, scientists, or researchers employed by existing companies engage in entrepreneurial activity when they develop new or improved products. To distinguish these individuals from entrepreneurs who found their own businesses, employees of existing organizations who notice opportunities for product or service improvements and are responsible for managing the development process are known as **intrapreneurs**. In general, then, **entrepreneurship** is the mobilization of resources to take advantage of an opportunity to provide customers with new or improved goods and services; intrapreneurs engage in entrepreneurship within an existing company.

intrapreneurs Employees of existing organizations who notice opportunities for product or service improvements and are responsible for managing the development process.

entrepreneurship The mobilization of resources to take advantage of an opportunity to provide customers with new or improved goods and services.

An interesting relationship exists between entrepreneurs and intrapreneurs. Many intrapreneurs become dissatisfied when their superiors decide not to support or to fund new product ideas and development efforts that the intrapreneurs think will succeed. What do intrapreneurs do who feel that they are getting nowhere? Very often intrapreneurs decide to leave their employers and start their own organizations to take advantage of their new product ideas. In other words, intrapreneurs become entrepreneurs and found companies that may compete with the companies they left.

Many of the world's most successful organizations have been started by frustrated intrapreneurs who became entrepreneurs. William Hewlett and David Packard left Fairchild Semiconductor, an early industry leader, when managers of that company would not support Hewlett and Packard's ideas; their company soon outperformed Fairchild. Compaq Computer was founded by Rod Canion and some of his colleagues, who left Texas Instruments (TI) when managers there would not support Canion's idea that TI should develop its own personal computer. To prevent the departure of talented people, organizations need to take steps to promote internal entrepreneurship.

There is also an interesting dynamic between entrepreneurship and management. Very often, it turns out that the entrepreneur who initially founded the business does not have the management skills to successfully control and change the business over time. Entrepreneurs may, for example, lack an understanding of how to create the control structure necessary to manage a successful long-term strategy. Entrepreneurs also may not recognize the need to change their companies because they are so close to them; in other words, they "cannot see the forest for the trees."

Frequently a founding entrepreneur lacks the skills, patience, or experience to engage in the difficult and challenging work of management. Some entrepreneurs find it difficult to delegate authority because they are afraid to risk letting others manage their company. As a result, founding entrepreneurs can become overloaded, and the quality of their decision making declines. Other entrepreneurs lack the detailed knowledge necessary to establish state-of-the-art control systems or to create the operations management procedures that are vital to increase the efficiency of their organizations' production systems (discussed in Chapter 14).

In summary, it is necessary to do more than create a new product to succeed; an entrepreneur must hire managers who can create an operating and control system that will allow a new venture to survive and prosper. Very often, venture capitalists, the people who provide the capital to fund a new venture, will lend entrepreneurs the money only if they agree from the outset to let a professional manager become the CEO of the new company. The entrepreneur then holds a senior planning and advisory role in the company, often chairing its board of directors.

Summary and Review

WHAT IS ORGANIZATIONAL CONTROL? Controlling is the process whereby managers monitor and regulate how efficiently and effectively an organization and its members are performing the activities necessary to achieve organizational goals. Controlling is a four-step process: (1) establishing performance standards, (2) measuring actual performance, (3) comparing actual performance against performance standards, and (4) evaluating the results and initiating corrective action if needed. **[LO1]**

OUTPUT CONTROL To monitor output or performance, managers choose goals or performance standards that they think will best measure efficiency, quality, innovation, and responsiveness to customers at the corporate, divisional, departmental or functional, and individual levels. The main mechanisms that managers use to monitor output are financial measures of performance, organizational goals, and operating budgets. **[LO2]**

BEHAVIOR CONTROL In an attempt to shape behavior and induce employees to work toward achieving organizational goals, managers utilize direct supervision, management by objectives, and bureaucratic control by means of rules and standard operating procedures. **[LO2]**

ORGANIZATIONAL CULTURE AND CLAN CONTROL Organizational culture is the set of values, norms, standards of behavior, and common expectations that control the ways individuals and groups in an organization interact with one another and work to achieve organizational goals. Clan control is the control exerted on individuals and groups by shared values, norms, standards of behavior, and expectations. Organizational culture is transmitted to employees through the values of the founder, the process of socialization, organizational ceremonies and rites, and stories and language. The way managers perform their management functions influences the kind of culture that develops in an organization. **[LO2]**

ORGANIZATIONAL CONTROL AND CHANGE There is a need to balance two opposing forces in the control process that influences the way organizations change. On the one hand, managers need to be able to control organizational activities and make their operations routine and predictable. On the other hand, organizations have to be responsive to the need to change, and managers must understand when they need to depart from routines to be responsive to unpredictable events. The four steps in managing change are (1) assessing the need for change, (2) deciding on the changes to make, (3) implementing change, and (4) evaluating the results of change. **[LO3]**

ENTREPRENEURSHIP, CONTROL, AND CHANGE Entrepreneurs are people who notice opportunities and collect and mobilize the resources necessary to produce new and improved goods and services. Intrapreneurs are employees in existing companies who notice opportunities to improve the companies' products and become responsible for managing the change process necessary to bring them to market. Both entrepreneurs and intrapreneurs play important roles in the control and change process. **[LO4]**

Management in Action

Topics for Discussion and Action

Discussion

1. What is the relationship between organizing and controlling? [LO1]
2. How do output control and behavior control differ? [LO1]
3. Why is it important for managers to involve subordinates in the control process? [LO3, 4]
4. What is organizational culture, and how does it affect the way employees behave? [LO2]
5. What kind of controls would you expect to find most used in (a) a hospital, (b) the Navy, (c) a city police force? Why? [LO1]

Action

6. Ask a manager to list the main performance measures that he or she uses to evaluate how well the organization is achieving its goals. [LO1, 2]
7. Interview some employees of an organization, and ask them about the organization's values, norms, socialization practices, ceremonies and rites, and special language and stories. Referring to this information, describe the organization's culture. [LO2, 3]

Building Management Skills [LO1, 2]

Understanding Controlling

For this exercise you will analyze the control systems used by a real organization such as a department store, restaurant, hospital, police department, or small business. Your objective is to uncover all the different ways in which managers monitor and evaluate the performance of the organization and employees.

1. At what levels does control take place in this organization?
2. Which output performance standards (such as financial measures and organizational goals) do managers use most often to evaluate performance at each level?
3. Does the organization have a management-by-objectives system in place? If it does, describe it. If it does not, speculate about why not.
4. How important is behavior control in this organization? For example, how much of managers' time is spent directly supervising employees? How formalized is the organization? Do employees receive a book of rules to instruct them about how to perform their jobs?
5. What kind of culture does the organization have? What are the values and norms? What effect does the organizational culture have on the way employees behave or treat customers?
6. Based on this analysis, do you think there is a fit between the organization's control systems and its culture? What is the nature of this fit? How could it be improved?

Managing Ethically [LO2]

Some managers and organizations go to great lengths to monitor their employees' behavior, and they keep extensive records about employees' behavior and performance. Some organizations also seem to possess norms and values that cause their employees to behave in certain ways.

Questions

1. Either by yourself or in a group, think about the ethical implications of organizations' monitoring and collecting information about their employees. What kind of information is it ethical to collect or unethical to collect? Why? Should managers and organizations inform subordinates they are collecting such information?
2. Similarly, some organizations' cultures, like those of Arthur Andersen, the accounting firm, and of Enron, seemed to have developed norms and values that caused their members to behave in unethical ways. When and why does a strong norm that encourages high performance become one that can cause people to act unethically? How can organizations keep their values and norms from becoming "too strong"?

Small Group Breakout Exercise [LO2, 3]

How Best to Control the Sales Force?

Form groups of three or four people, and appoint one member as the spokesperson who will communicate your findings to the whole class when called on by the instructor. Then discuss the following scenario:

You are the regional sales managers of an organization that supplies high-quality windows and doors to building supply centers nationwide. Over the last three years, the rate of sales growth has slackened. There is increasing evidence that, to make their jobs easier, salespeople are primarily servicing large customer accounts and ignoring small accounts. In addition, the salespeople are not dealing promptly with customer questions and complaints, and this inattention has resulted in a drop in after-sales service. You have talked about these problems, and you are meeting to design a control system to increase both the amount of sales and the quality of customer service.

1. Design a control system that you think will best motivate salespeople to achieve these goals.
2. What relative importance do you put on (a) output control, (b) behavior control, and (c) organizational culture in this design?

Be the Manager [LO1, 3]

You have been asked by your company's CEO to find a way to improve the performance of its teams of Web-design and Web-hosting specialists and programmers. Each team works on a different aspect of Web site production, and while each is responsible for the quality of its own performance, its performance also depends on how well the other teams perform. Your task is to create a control system that will help to increase the performance of each team separately and facilitate cooperation among the teams. This is necessary because the various projects are interlinked and affect one another just as the different parts of a car must fit together. Since competition in the Web-site production market is intense, it is imperative that each Web site be up and running as quickly as possible and incorporate all the latest advances in Web site software technology.

Questions

1. What kind of output controls will best facilitate positive interactions both within the teams and among the teams?
2. What kind of behavior controls will best facilitate positive interactions both within the teams and among the teams?
3. How would you go about helping managers develop a culture to promote high team performance?

BusinessWeek Case in the News [LO1, 3, 4]

How Amazon Aims to Keep You Clicking

Amazon.com has earned a reputation for strong service by letting customers get what they want without ever talking to an employee. Sales clerks are nonexistent. Orders ship with a few mouse clicks. Packages arrive on doorsteps quickly. It all happens with monotonous regularity even as the number of customers has doubled in the past five years to 88 million. But when things go wrong at Amazon—and they occasionally do—the company's employees get involved. That may be where Amazon stands out most markedly from other companies, and helps explain how the company earned the No. 1 spot on *BusinessWeek*'s customer service ranking this year.

One recent February day in Manhattan, Jeff Bezos, Amazon's excitable 45-year-old founder and chief executive, sat still long enough to explain the ideas behind his company's approach. He talked about the distinctions Amazon makes between customer experience and customer service. The latter is only when customers deal with Amazon employees—and Bezos wants that to be the exception rather than the rule. "Internally, customer service is a component of customer experience," he says. "Customer experience includes having the lowest price, having the fastest delivery, having it reliable enough so that you don't need to contact [anyone]. Then you save customer service for those truly unusual situations. You know, I got my book and it's missing pages 47 through 58," he says, breaking into a booming laugh.

Fixing customers' problems builds loyalty with people, says Bezos. But it's also a good way to spot recurring issues that need to be addressed more systematically. Outside merchants are a prime example. For years, Amazon has allowed other retailers to sell through its Web site to broaden the selection of products it offers. But these companies can be an Achilles' heel. At eBay, which also lets merchants sell through its site, there have been complaints about poor service and fraud.

Quality Controls

So Bezos is trying something that no other retailer has been able to pull off: He wants to bring the quality of service from Amazon's outside merchants up to the same level as its own. The company has long let customers rate their experience with merchants, as they can on eBay. But Amazon also has instituted many internal safeguards to track the behavior of merchants. For instance, retailers have to use an e-mail service on the Amazon site to communicate with customers so Amazon can monitor conversations. The company also uses metrics such as how frequently customers complain about a merchant and how often a merchant cancels an order because the product isn't in stock. Partners who have problems with more than 1% of their orders can get booted off the site.

To refine the experience with outside merchants, Amazon in 2006 launched an initiative called Fulfillment by Amazon. Merchants simply send boxes of their products to Amazon's warehouses, and Amazon does the rest. It takes the orders online, packs the box, answers questions, and processes returns. Last quarter, Amazon shipped 3 million units for Fulfillment by Amazon partners, up from 500,000 a year earlier.

Though Amazon charges the merchants, Bezos says that's not why it launched the service. "It's important because it improves the consumer experience so much," he says. "It doesn't make us more money; it's heavy lifting. If you think long-term, I think it's very important for us." It might seem counterintuitive to help small merchants, including ones that undercut you, be more competitive. But for Amazon, the ultimate goal is to gain more control over the shopping experience, making it more consistent and reliable. The idea is that more people will use the online retailer and spend more. To make sure that everyone at Amazon understands how customer service works, each employee, even Bezos, spends two days on the service desk every two years. "It's both fun and useful," says Bezos. "One call I took many years ago was from a customer who had bought 11 things from 11 sellers—and typed in the wrong shipping address."

Taking the Wheel

Amazon has gotten many ideas from trying to address customer complaints. One gripe from years past was that popular items—think Tickle Me Elmo or Crocs Mammoth clog shoes—were at times out of stock. The last thing Amazon wants is for a frustrated shopper to then head to another site or the mall.

During the past two years. Amazon developed new programs to keep hot items in stock and ready for quick delivery. One initiative is something Amazon calls the Milk Run. Instead of waiting for suppliers to deliver to Amazon's warehouses, Amazon sends its own trucks out to pick up top-selling goods. That reduces the number of late or incomplete orders the company receives. The program is "very forward-thinking," says Simon Fleming-Wood, vice president for marketing at Pure Digital Technologies, whose Flip camcorder has been included in weekly Milk Runs.

One of the drawbacks to shopping online, of course, is that people don't feel the instant gratification of getting their purchases right when they buy them. Albert Ko, an online marketer in Irvine, California, always wants his packages as fast as possible. "I'm always pushing them," he says. That's one reason Bezos is expanding Amazon Prime, the program for which customers pay $79 a year to get free two-day shipping on many in-stock products. During the past two years, Bezos has taken it international and increased the number of products that qualify for Prime. "Our vision is to have every item made anywhere in the world in stock and available for free two-day delivery," he says.

Questions

1. Why is customer service or "customer experience" so important to Amazon.com?
2. In what ways does Amazon try to increase the level of customer service over time?
3. In what ways has studying customer complaints helped Amazon to increase the quality of the customer experience and boost sales?

Source: Heather Green, "How Amazon Aims to Keep You Clicking." Reprinted from *BusinessWeek* online, February 19, 2009, by special permission, copyright © 2009 by The McGraw-Hill Companies, Inc.

Motivation

CHAPTER 9

Learning Objectives

After studying this chapter, you should be able to

1. Explain what motivation is and why managers need to be concerned about it. **[LO1]**
2. Describe from the perspectives of expectancy theory and equity theory what managers should do to have a highly motivated workforce. **[LO2]**
3. Explain how goals and needs motivate people and what kinds of goals are especially likely to result in high performance. **[LO3]**
4. Identify the motivation lessons that managers can learn from operant conditioning theory and social learning theory. **[LO4]**
5. Explain why and how managers can use pay as a major motivation tool. **[LO5]**

Enterprise Rent-A-Car is one of the biggest employers of new college graduates in the United States.

MANAGEMENT SNAPSHOT

Motivation at Enterprise Rent-A-Car

How Can Managers Motivate Employees at All Levels to Provide Excellent Customer Service?

Enterprise Rent-A-Car was founded by Jack Taylor in 1957 in St. Louis, Missouri, as a very small auto leasing business.[1] Today, Enterprise is the biggest car rental company in North America with over $9 billion in revenues and over 64,000 employees.[2] One of the biggest employers of new college graduates in the United States, Enterprise typically hires over 7,000 entry-level employees each year.[3] While starting salaries tend to be on the low end and the work can be hard (e.g., a few years back, four assistant managers sued the company claiming that they should receive overtime pay), Enterprise has been ranked among the top 50 best companies for new college graduates to launch their careers by *BusinessWeek* magazine.[4]

A privately held company, Enterprise is very much a family business. In its entire history, Enterprise has had only two CEOs, founder Jack Taylor, who is now retired but still quite involved in the company, and his son Andrew Taylor, who became president in 1980 and CEO in 1994.[5] Nonetheless, Enterprise's policy of promoting from within ensures that all employees who perform well have the opportunity to advance in the company.[6]

One of the keys to Enterprise's success is the way it motivates its employees to provide excellent customer service.[7] Practically all entry-level hires participate in Enterprise's Management Training Program.[8] As part of the program, new hires learn all aspects of the company's business and how to provide excellent customer service. Management trainees first have a four-day training session focused primarily on Enterprise's culture. They are then assigned to a branch office for around 8–12 months where they learn all aspects of the business from negotiating with body shops to helping customers to washing cars. As part of this training, they learn how important high-quality customer service is to Enterprise and how they can personally provide great service, increasing their confidence levels.[9]

All those who do well in the program are promoted after about a year to the position of management assistant. Management assistants who do well are promoted to become assistant branch managers with responsibility for mentoring and supervising employees. Assistant managers who do well can be promoted to become branch managers who are responsible for managing a branch's employees and provision of customer service, rental car fleet, and financial performance. Branch managers with about five years of experience in the position often move on to take up management positions at headquarters or assume the position of area manager overseeing all the branches in a certain geographic region.[10] By training all new hires in all aspects of the business including the provision of excellent customer service, by providing them with valuable experience with increasing levels of responsibility and empowerment, and by providing all new hires who perform well with the opportunity to advance in the company, Enterprise has a highly motivated workforce. As Patrick Farrell, vice president of corporate communications, indicated, "What's unique about our company is that everyone came up through the same system, from the CEOs on down . . . 100% of our operations personnel started as management trainees."[11]

In addition to motivating high performance and excellent customer service through training and promotional opportunities, Enterprise also uses financial incentives to motivate employees. Essentially, each branch is considered a profit center and the managers overseeing the branch and in charge of all aspects of its functioning have the autonomy and responsibility for the branch's profitability almost as if the branch was their own small business or franchise.[12] All branch employees at the rank of assistant manager and higher earn incentive compensation whereby their monthly pay depends upon the profitability of their branch. Managers at higher levels, such as area managers, have their monthly pay linked to the profitability of the region they oversee. Thus, managers at all levels know that their pay is linked to the profitability of the parts of Enterprise for which they are responsible. And they have the autonomy to make decisions ranging from buying and selling cars to even opening new branches.[13]

Another way in which Enterprise motivates its employees is through its philanthropic activities and initiatives to protect the natural environment.[14] For example, the Enterprise Rent-A-Car Foundation has committed $50 million to plant 50 million trees over a 50-year period in public forests. The Foundation also focuses on supporting and giving back to the communities in which Enterprise operates.[15] Of all rental car companies, Enterprise has the biggest fleet of fuel-efficient cars.[16] All in all, the multiple ways in which Enterprise motivates its employees and satisfies its customers have contributed to its ongoing success story.[17]

Overview

Even with the best strategy in place and an appropriate organizational architecture, an organization will be effective only if its members are motivated to perform at a high level. Jack and Andrew Taylor of Enterprise Rent-A-Car clearly realize this. One reason why leading is such an important managerial activity is that it entails ensuring that each member of an organization is motivated to perform highly and help the organization achieve its goals. When managers are effective, the outcome of the leading process is a highly motivated workforce. A key challenge for managers of organizations both large and small is to encourage employees to perform at a high level.

In this chapter we describe what motivation is, where it comes from, and why managers need to promote high levels of it for an organization to be effective and achieve its goals. We examine important theories of motivation: expectancy theory, need theories, equity theory, goal-setting theory, and learning theories. Each provides managers with important insights about how to motivate organizational members.

The theories are complementary in that each focuses on a somewhat different aspect of motivation. Considering all of the theories together helps managers gain a rich understanding of the many issues and problems involved in encouraging high levels of motivation throughout an organization. Last, we consider the use of pay as a motivation tool. By the end of this chapter, you will understand what it takes to have a highly motivated workforce.

The Nature of Motivation

motivation Psychological forces that determine the direction of a person's behavior in an organization, a person's level of effort, and a person's level of persistence.

Motivation may be defined as psychological forces that determine the direction of a person's behavior in an organization, a person's level of effort, and a person's level of persistence in the face of obstacles.[18] The *direction of a person's behavior* refers to the many possible behaviors that a person could engage in. For example, employees at Enterprise Rent-A-Car know that they should do whatever is required to provide high-quality customer service such as giving customers rides to pick up and drop off rental cars. *Effort* refers to how hard people work. Employees at Enterprise Rent-A-Car exert high levels of effort to provide superior customer service. *Persistence* refers to whether, when faced with roadblocks and obstacles, people keep trying or give up. Branch managers at Enterprise Rent-A-Car persistently seek to improve the profitability of their branches while maintaining very high levels of customer service.

LO1 Explain what motivation is and why managers need to be concerned about it.

Motivation is central to management because it explains *why* people behave the way they do in organizations[19]–why employees at Enterprise Rent-A-Car provide excellent customer service. Motivation also explains why a waiter is polite or rude and why a kindergarten teacher really tries to get children to enjoy learning or just goes through the motions. It explains why some managers truly put their organizations' best interests first whereas others are more concerned with maximizing their salaries and why–more generally–some workers put forth twice as much effort as others.

intrinsically motivated behavior Behavior that is performed for its own sake.

Motivation can come from *intrinsic* or *extrinsic* sources. **Intrinsically motivated behavior** is behavior that is performed for its own sake; the source of motivation is actually performing the behavior, and motivation comes from doing the work itself. Many managers are intrinsically motivated; they derive a sense of accomplishment and achievement from helping the organization to achieve its goals and gain competitive advantages. Jobs that are interesting and challenging are more likely to lead to intrinsic motivation than are jobs that are boring or do not make use of a person's skills and abilities. An elementary school teacher who really enjoys teaching children, a computer programmer who loves solving programming problems, and a commercial photographer who relishes taking creative photographs are all intrinsically motivated. For these individuals, motivation comes from performing their jobs whether it be teaching children, finding bugs in computer programs, or taking pictures.

extrinsically motivated behavior Behavior that is performed to acquire material or social rewards or to avoid punishment.

Extrinsically motivated behavior is behavior that is performed to acquire material or social rewards or to avoid punishment; the source of motivation is the consequences of the behavior, not the behavior itself. A car salesperson who is motivated by receiving a commission on all cars sold, a lawyer who is motivated by the high salary and status that go along with the job, and a factory worker who is motivated by the opportunity to earn a secure income are all extrinsically motivated. Their motivation comes from the consequences they receive as a result of their work behaviors.

People can be intrinsically motivated, extrinsically motivated, or both intrinsically and extrinsically motivated.[20] A top manager who derives a sense of accomplishment and achievement from managing a large corporation and strives to reach year-end targets to obtain a hefty bonus is both intrinsically and extrinsically motivated. Similarly, a nurse who enjoys helping and taking care of patients and is motivated by having a secure job with good benefits is both intrinsically and extrinsically motivated. At Enterprise Rent-A-Car, employees are both extrinsically motivated, because of opportunities for promotions and having their pay linked to the performance of their branches or units, and intrinsically motivated, because they get a sense of satisfaction out of serving customers and learning new things. Whether workers are intrinsically motivated, extrinsically motivated, or both depends on a wide variety of factors: (1) workers' own personal characteristics (such as their personalities, abilities, values, attitudes, and needs), (2) the nature of their jobs (such as whether they are interesting and challenging), and (3) the nature of the organization (such as its structure, its culture, its control systems, its human resource management system, and the ways in which rewards such as pay are distributed to employees).

prosocially motivated behavior Behavior that is performed to benefit or help others.

In addition to being intrinsically or extrinsically motivated, some people are prosocially motivated by their work.[21] **Prosocially motivated behavior** is behavior that is performed to benefit or help others.[22] Behavior can be prosocially motivated in addition to being extrinsically and/or intrinsically motivated. An elementary school teacher who not only enjoys the process of teaching young children (has high intrinsic motivation) but also has a strong desire to give children the best learning experience possible, help those with learning disabilities overcome their challenges, and keeps up with the latest research on child development and teaching methods in an effort to continually improve the effectiveness of his teaching has high prosocial motivation in addition to high intrinsic motivation. A surgeon who specializes in organ transplants and enjoys the challenge of performing complex operations, has a strong desire to help her patients regain their health and extend their lives through successful organ transplants, and also is motivated by the relatively high income she earns has high intrinsic, prosocial, and extrinsic motivation. Recent preliminary research suggests that when workers have high prosocial motivation, also having high intrinsic motivation can be especially beneficial for job performance.[23]

outcome Anything a person gets from a job or organization.

Regardless of whether people are intrinsically, extrinsically, or prosocially motivated, they join and are motivated to work in organizations to obtain certain outcomes. An **outcome** is anything a person gets from a job or organization. Some outcomes, such as autonomy, responsibility, a feeling of accomplishment, and the pleasure of doing interesting or enjoyable work, result in intrinsically motivated behavior. Outcomes such as improving the lives or well-being of other people and doing good by helping others result in prosocially motivated behavior. Other outcomes, such as pay, job security, benefits, and vacation time, result in extrinsically motivated behavior.

input Anything a person contributes to his or her job or organization.

Organizations hire people to obtain important inputs. An **input** is anything a person contributes to the job or organization, such as time, effort, education, experience, skills, knowledge, and actual work behaviors. Inputs such as these are necessary for an organization to achieve its goals. Managers strive to motivate members of an organization to contribute inputs–through their behavior, effort, and persistence–that help the organization achieve its goals. How do managers do this? They ensure that members of an organization obtain the outcomes they desire when they make valuable contributions to the organization. Managers use outcomes to motivate people to contribute their inputs to the organization. Giving people outcomes when they contribute inputs and perform well aligns the interests of employees with the goals of the organization as a whole because when employees do what is good for the organization, they personally benefit.

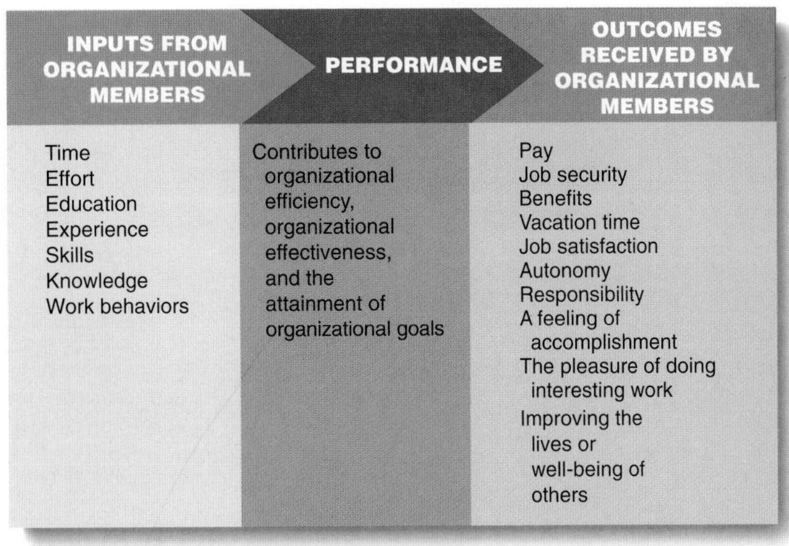

Figure 9.1
The Motivation Equation

This alignment between employees and organizational goals as a whole can be described by the motivation equation depicted in Figure 9.1. Managers seek to ensure that people are motivated to contribute important inputs to the organization, that these inputs are put to good use or focused in the direction of high performance, and that high performance results in workers' obtaining the outcomes they desire.

expectancy theory The theory that motivation will be high when workers believe that high levels of effort lead to high performance and high performance leads to the attainment of desired outcomes.

Each of the theories of motivation discussed in this chapter focuses on one or more aspects of this equation. Each theory focuses on a different set of issues that managers need to address to have a highly motivated workforce. Together, the theories provide a comprehensive set of guidelines for managers to follow to promote high levels of employee motivation. Effective managers, such as Jack and Andrew Taylor in the "Management Snapshot," tend to follow many of these guidelines, whereas ineffective managers often fail to follow them and seem to have trouble motivating organizational members.

Expectancy Theory

LO2 Describe from the perspectives of expectancy theory and equity theory what managers should do to have a highly motivated workforce.

Expectancy theory, formulated by Victor H. Vroom in the 1960s, posits that motivation is high when workers believe that high levels of effort lead to high performance and high performance leads to the attainment of desired outcomes. Expectancy theory is one of the most popular theories of work motivation because it focuses on all three parts of the motivation equation: inputs, performance, and outcomes. Expectancy theory identifies three major factors that determine a person's motivation: *expectancy, instrumentality,* and *valence* (see Figure 9.2).[24]

Expectancy

expectancy In expectancy theory, a perception about the extent to which effort results in a certain level of performance.

Expectancy is a person's perception about the extent to which effort (an input) results in a certain level of performance. A person's level of expectancy determines whether he or she believes that a high level of effort results in a high level of performance. People are motivated to put forth a lot of effort on their jobs only if they think that their effort will pay off in high performance–that is, if they have high expectancy. Think about how motivated you would be to study for a test if you thought that no matter how hard you tried, you would get a D. Think about how motivated a marketing manager

Figure 9.2
Expectancy, Instrumentality, and Valence

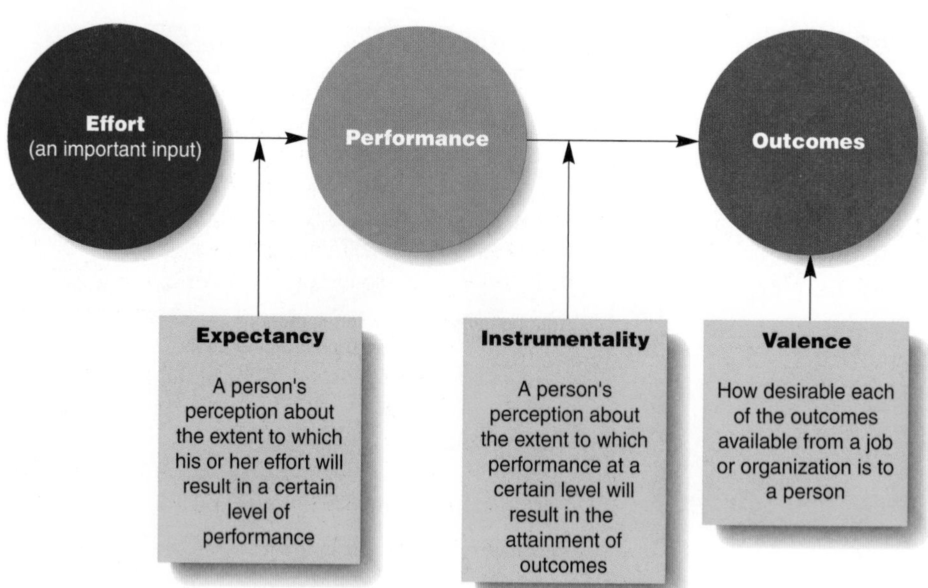

would be who thought that no matter how hard he or she worked, there was no way to increase sales of an unpopular product. In these cases, expectancy is low, so overall motivation is also low.

Members of an organization are motivated to put forth a high level of effort only if they think that doing so leads to high performance.[25] In other words, in order for people's motivation to be high, expectancy must be high. Thus, in attempting to influence motivation, managers need to make sure that their subordinates believe that if they do try hard, they can actually succeed. One way managers can boost expectancies is through expressing confidence in their subordinates' capabilities. Managers at the Container Store, for example, express high levels of confidence in their subordinates. As Container Store cofounder Garrett Boone put it, "Everybody we hire, we hire as a leader. Anybody in our store can take an action that you might think of typically being a manager's action."[26]

In addition to expressing confidence in subordinates, other ways for managers to boost subordinates' expectancy levels and motivation is by providing training so that people have all the expertise needed for high performance and increasing their levels of autonomy and responsibility as they gain experience so that they have the freedom to do what it takes to perform at a high level. For example, the Best Buy chain of over 629 stores selling electronics, computers, music and movies, and gadgets of all sorts boosts salespeople's expectancies by providing them with extensive training in on-site meetings and online. Electronic learning terminals in each department not only help salespeople learn how different systems work and can be sold as an integrated package but also enable them to keep up to date with the latest advances in technology and products. Salespeople also receive extensive training in how to determine customers' needs.[27] At Enterprise Rent-A-Car in the "Management Snapshot," the Management Training Program helps new hires develop high levels of expectancy, and these high levels of expectancy are maintained as experienced employees are given more responsibility and autonomy to ensure that their branches are profitable and provide excellent customer service.

Instrumentality

instrumentality In expectancy theory, a perception about the extent to which performance results in the attainment of outcomes.

Expectancy captures a person's perceptions about the relationship between effort and performance. **Instrumentality**, the second major concept in expectancy theory, is a person's perception about the extent to which performance at a certain level results in the attainment of outcomes (see Figure 9.2). According to expectancy theory, employees are motivated to perform at a high level only if they think that high performance will lead to (or is *instrumental* for attaining) outcomes such as pay, job security, interesting job assignments, bonuses, or a feeling of accomplishment. In other words, instrumentalities must be high for motivation to be high–people must perceive that because of their high performance they will receive outcomes.[28]

Managers promote high levels of instrumentality when they clearly link performance to desired outcomes. In addition, managers must clearly communicate this linkage to subordinates. By making sure that outcomes available in an organization are distributed to organizational members on the basis of their performance, managers promote high instrumentality and motivation. When outcomes are linked to performance in this way, high performers receive more outcomes than low performers. In the "Management Snapshot," Andrew Taylor raises levels of instrumentality and motivation for Enterprise Rent-A-Car employees by linking opportunities for promotion and pay to performance.

Valence

valence In expectancy theory, how desirable each of the outcomes available from a job or organization is to a person.

Although all members of an organization must have high expectancies and instrumentalities, expectancy theory acknowledges that people differ in their preferences for outcomes. For many people, pay is the most important outcome of working. For others, a feeling of accomplishment or enjoying one's work is more important than pay. The term **valence** refers to how desirable each of the outcomes available from a job or organization is to a person. To motivate organizational members, managers need to determine which outcomes have high valence for them–are highly desired–and make sure that those outcomes are provided when members perform at a high level. From the "Management Snapshot," it appears that not only pay but also autonomy, responsibility, and opportunities for promotions are highly valent outcomes for many employees at Enterprise Rent-A-Car.

Providing employees with highly valent outcomes can not only contribute to high levels of motivation, but also has the potential to reduce turnover, as indicated in the following "Management Insight."

MANAGEMENT INSIGHT

Motivating and Retaining Employees at the Container Store

Kip Tindell and Garrett Boone founded the Container Store in Dallas, Texas, in 1978 and Tindell currently serves as CEO and chairman (Boone is chairman emeritus).[29] When they opened their first store, they were out on the floor trying to sell customers their storage and organization products that would economize on space and time and make purchasers' lives a little less complicated. The Container Store has grown to include 42 stores in 20 U.S. markets from coast to coast; although the original store in Dallas had only 1,600 square feet, the stores today average around 25,000 square feet.[30]

The Container Store's motivational approach means that each employee works as a leader—and that those in managerial positions still walk the floor to tidy up displays. Results are extremely positive, with the retail chain boasting significantly lower turnover rates than other chains in the industry.

The phenomenal growth in the size of the stores has been matched by impressive growth rates in sales and profits.[31] Surprisingly enough, Tindell and Boone can still be found on the shop floor tidying shelves and helping customers carry out their purchases.[32] And that, perhaps, is an important clue to the secret of their success. The Container Store has been consistently ranked among *Fortune* magazine's "100 Best Companies to Work For" for 10 years running.[33] In 2009, the Container Store was 32nd on this list.[34]

Early on, Tindell and Boone recognized that people are the Container Store's most valuable asset and that after hiring great people, one of the most important managerial tasks is motivating them. One would think that motivating employees might be especially challenging in the retail industry, which has an average annual turnover rate for full-time salespeople of more than 70% and an annual turnover rate for store managers of over 30%. The Container Store's comparable figures are fractions of these industry statistics, a testament to Tindell and Boone's ability to motivate.[35]

Tindell and Boone have long recognized the importance of rewarding employees for a job well done with highly valent outcomes. For example, starting salaries for salespeople are around $40,000, which is significantly higher than retail averages, and merit pay increases for superior sales performance are about 8% per year. To encourage high individual performance as well as teamwork and cooperation, both individual and team-based rewards are utilized at the Container Store. Some high-performing salespeople earn more than their store managers, which suits the store managers fine as long as equitable procedures are used and rewards are distributed fairly.[36]

Professional development is another valent outcome employees obtain from working at the Container Store. Full-time salespeople receive over 240 hours of training their first year, and all employees have opportunities for additional training and development on an ongoing basis.[37] Employees also have flexible work options and flexible benefits; medical, dental, and 401(k) retirement plans; job security; a casual dress code; and access to a variety of wellness programs ranging from yoga classes and chair massages to a personalized, Web-based nutrition and exercise planner.[38] Another valent outcome is the opportunity to work with other highly motivated individuals in an environment that exudes enthusiasm and excitement. Not only are the Container Store's employees motivated, but they also look forward to coming to work and feel as if their coworkers and managers are part of their family. Employees feel pride in what they do–helping customers organize their lives, save space and time, and have a better sense of well-being. Hence, they not only personally benefit from high performance by receiving highly valent outcomes but also feel good about the products they sell and the help they give customers.[39] Tindell and Boone evidently have never lost sight of the importance of motivation for both organizations and their members.

Figure 9.3
Expectancy Theory

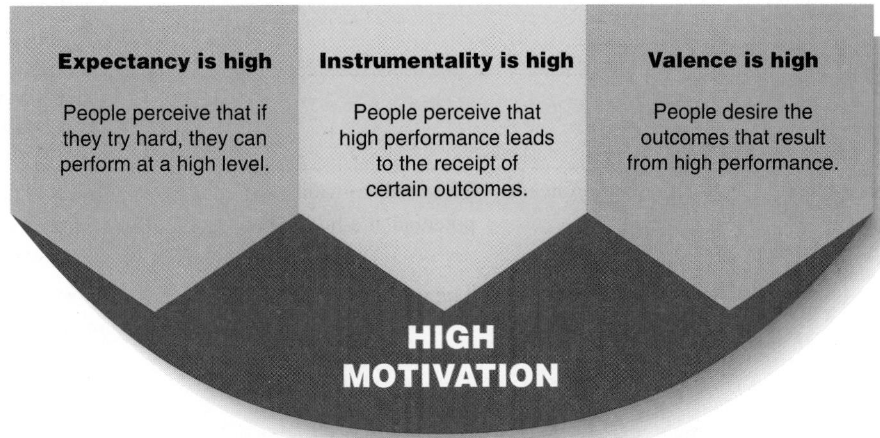

Bringing It All Together

According to expectancy theory, high motivation results from high levels of expectancy, instrumentality, and valence (see Figure 9.3). If any one of these factors is low, motivation is likely to be low. No matter how tightly desired outcomes are linked to performance, if a person thinks it is practically impossible to perform at a high level, then motivation to perform at a high level is exceedingly low. Similarly, if a person does not think that outcomes are linked to high performance, or if a person does not desire the outcomes that are linked to high performance, then motivation to perform at a high level is low.

Need Theories

A **need** is a requirement or necessity for survival and well-being. The basic premise of **need theories** is that people are motivated to obtain outcomes at work that will satisfy their needs. Need theory complements expectancy theory by exploring in depth which outcomes motivate people to perform at a high level. Need theories suggest that to motivate a person to contribute valuable inputs to a job and perform at a high level, a manager must determine what needs the person is trying to satisfy at work and ensure that the person receives outcomes that help to satisfy those needs when the person performs at a high level and helps the organization achieve its goals.

need A requirement or necessity for survival and well-being.

LO3 Explain how goals and needs motivate people and what kinds of goals are especially likely to result in high performance.

There are several need theories. Here we discuss Abraham Maslow's hierarchy of needs, Frederick Herzberg's motivator-hygiene theory, and David McClelland's needs for achievement, affiliation, and power. These theories describe needs that people try to satisfy at work. In doing so, they provide managers with insights about what outcomes motivate members of an organization to perform at a high level and contribute inputs to help the organization achieve its goals.

need theories Theories of motivation that focus on what needs people are trying to satisfy at work and what outcomes will satisfy those needs.

Maslow's Hierarchy of Needs

Psychologist Abraham Maslow proposed that all people seek to satisfy five basic kinds of needs: physiological needs, safety needs, belongingness needs, esteem needs, and self-actualization needs (see Table 9.1).[40] He suggested that these needs constitute a

Table 9.1
Maslow's Hierarchy of Needs

	Needs	Description	Examples of How Managers Can Help People Satisfy These Needs at Work
Highest-level needs ↑	**Self-actualization needs**	The needs to realize one's full potential as a human being	By giving people the opportunity to use their skills and abilities to the fullest extent possible
	Esteem needs	The needs to feel good about oneself and one's capabilities, to be respected by others, and to receive recognition and appreciation	By granting promotions and recognizing accomplishments
	Belongingness needs	Needs for social interaction, friendship, affection, and love	By promoting good interpersonal relations and organizing social functions such as company picnics and holiday parties
	Safety needs	Needs for security, stability, and a safe environment	By providing job security, adequate medical benefits, and safe working conditions
↓ **Lowest-level needs (most basic or compelling)**	**Physiological needs**	Basic needs for things such as food, water, and shelter that must be met in order for a person to survive	By providing a level of pay that enables a person to buy food and clothing and have adequate housing

The lowest level of unsatisfied needs motivates behavior; once this level of needs is satisfied, a person tries to satisfy the needs at the next level.

Maslow's hierarchy of needs An arrangement of five basic needs that, according to Maslow, motivate behavior. Maslow proposed that the lowest level of unmet needs is the prime motivator and that only one level of needs is motivational at a time.

hierarchy of needs, with the most basic or compelling needs–physiological and safety needs–at the bottom. Maslow argued that these lowest-level needs must be met before a person strives to satisfy needs higher up in the hierarchy, such as self-esteem needs. Once a need is satisfied, Maslow proposed, it ceases to operate as a source of motivation. The lowest level of *unmet* needs in the hierarchy is the prime motivator of behavior; if and when this level is satisfied, needs at the next-highest level in the hierarchy motivate behavior.

Although this theory identifies needs that are likely to be important sources of motivation for many people, research does not support Maslow's contention that there is a need hierarchy or his notion that only one level of needs is motivational at a time.[41] Nevertheless, a key conclusion can be drawn from Maslow's theory: People try to satisfy different needs at work. To have a motivated workforce, managers must determine which needs employees are trying to satisfy in organizations and then make sure that individuals receive outcomes that satisfy their needs when they perform at a high level and contribute to organizational effectiveness. By doing this, managers align the interests of individual members with the interests of the organization as a whole. By doing what is good for the organization (that is, performing at a high level), employees receive outcomes that satisfy their needs.

In our increasingly global economy, managers must realize that citizens of different countries might differ in the needs they seek to satisfy through work.[42] Some research suggests, for example, that people in Greece and Japan are especially motivated by

Jobs that involve artistic expression, such as dancing, can help people fulfill higher-level needs.

safety needs and that people in Sweden, Norway, and Denmark are motivated by belongingness needs.[43] In less developed countries with low standards of living, physiological and safety needs are likely to be the prime motivators of behavior. As countries become wealthier and have higher standards of living, needs related to personal growth and accomplishment (such as esteem and self-actualization) become important as motivators of behavior.

Herzberg's Motivator-Hygiene Theory

Adopting an approach different from Maslow's, Frederick Herzberg focuses on two factors: (1) outcomes that can lead to high levels of motivation and job satisfaction and (2) outcomes that can prevent people from being dissatisfied. According to **Herzberg's motivator-hygiene theory**, people have two sets of needs or requirements: motivator needs and hygiene needs.[44] *Motivator needs* are related to the nature of the work itself and how challenging it is. Outcomes, such as interesting work, autonomy, responsibility, being able to grow and develop on the job, and a sense of accomplishment and achievement, help to satisfy motivator needs. To have a highly motivated and satisfied workforce, Herzberg suggested, managers should take steps to ensure that employees' motivator needs are being met.

Herzberg's motivator-hygiene theory A need theory that distinguishes between motivator needs (related to the nature of the work itself) and hygiene needs (related to the physical and psychological context in which the work is performed) and proposes that motivator needs must be met for motivation and job satisfaction to be high.

Hygiene needs are related to the physical and psychological context in which the work is performed. Hygiene needs are satisfied by outcomes such as pleasant and comfortable working conditions, pay, job security, good relationships with coworkers, and effective supervision. According to Herzberg, when hygiene needs are not met, workers are dissatisfied, and when hygiene needs are met, workers are not dissatisfied. Satisfying hygiene needs, however, does not result in high levels of motivation or even high levels of job satisfaction. For motivation and job satisfaction to be high, motivator needs must be met.

Many research studies have tested Herzberg's propositions, and, by and large, the theory fails to receive support.[45] Nevertheless, Herzberg's formulations have contributed to our understanding of motivation in at least two ways. First, Herzberg helped to focus researchers' and managers' attention on the important distinction between intrinsic motivation (related to motivator needs) and extrinsic motivation (related to hygiene needs), covered earlier in the chapter. Second, his theory prompted researchers and managers to study how jobs could be designed or redesigned so that they are intrinsically motivating.

McClelland's Needs for Achievement, Affiliation, and Power

need for achievement The extent to which an individual has a strong desire to perform challenging tasks well and to meet personal standards for excellence.

Psychologist David McClelland has extensively researched the needs for achievement, affiliation, and power.[46] The **need for achievement** is the extent to which an individual has a strong desire to perform challenging tasks well and to meet personal standards for excellence. People with a high need for achievement often set clear goals for themselves and like to receive performance feedback. The **need for affiliation** is the

need for affiliation The extent to which an individual is concerned about establishing and maintaining good interpersonal relations, being liked, and having the people around him or her get along with each other.

need for power The extent to which an individual desires to control or influence others.

extent to which an individual is concerned about establishing and maintaining good interpersonal relations, being liked, and having the people around him or her get along with each other. The **need for power** is the extent to which an individual desires to control or influence others.[47]

While each of these needs is present in each of us to some degree, their importance in the workplace depends upon the position one occupies. For example, research suggests that high needs for achievement and for power are assets for first-line and middle managers and that a high need for power is especially important for upper managers.[48] One study found that U.S. presidents with a relatively high need for power tended to be especially effective during their terms of office.[49] A high need for affiliation may not always be desirable in managers and other leaders because it might lead them to try too hard to be liked by others (including subordinates) rather than doing all they can to ensure that performance is as high as it can and should be. Although most research on these needs has been done in the United States, some studies suggest that the findings may be applicable to people in other countries as well, such as India and New Zealand.[50]

Other Needs

Clearly more needs motivate workers than the needs described by the above three theories. For example, more and more workers are feeling the need for work–life balance and time to take care of their loved ones while simultaneously being highly motivated at work. Interestingly enough, recent research suggests that being exposed to nature (even just being able to see some trees from your office window) has many salutary effects, and a lack of such exposure can actually impair well-being and performance.[51] Thus, having some time during the day when one can at least see nature may be another important need.

Managers of successful companies often strive to ensure that as many of their valued employees' needs as possible are satisfied in the workplace. This is illustrated by the following "Information Technology Byte" on the SAS Institute.

INFORMATION TECHNOLOGY BYTE

High Motivation Rules at the SAS Institute

The SAS Institute is in the enviable position of being listed on *Fortune* magazine's annual ranking of the "100 Best Companies to Work For" for 12 years in a row; in 2009 the SAS Institute was ranked 20th.[52] The SAS Institute is the world's largest privately owned software company, with over 11,000 employees worldwide and approximately $2.6 billion in revenues.[53] Every indicator suggests that SAS employees are highly motivated and perform well while also working 35-hour weeks. How do managers at SAS do it? In large part, by ensuring that employees are highly motivated and the variety of needs they bring to the workplace are satisfied by doing a good job at SAS.[54]

Satisfying the need for intrinsically motivating work has also been a key priority at SAS. Managers strive to make sure that each employee is motivated by the work he or she performs, and employees are encouraged to change jobs to prevent becoming bored with their work (even if the job changes require that SAS provide additional

Many employees at the SAS Institute's headquarters in Cary, North Carolina, take advantage of an on-site recreation and fitness center.

training). Moreover, in contrast to the approach at some of the company's competitors, all new product development work at SAS is performed in-house, so employees have the opportunity to experience the excitement of developing a new product and seeing it succeed.[55]

The SAS Institute satisfies employees' needs for economic security by paying them fairly and providing them with secure jobs. Employees have their own offices, and the work environment is rich in pleasant vistas, whether they be artwork on the walls or views of the rolling hills of Cary, North Carolina, at company headquarters. Managers at SAS realize that needs for work–life balance are a top priority for many of their employees and seek to satisfy these needs in a variety of ways, including 35-hour workweeks, on-site day care and medical care, unlimited sick days, and high chairs in the company cafeteria so that employees can dine with their kids. Moreover, employees and their families are encouraged to use the 200 acres that surround company headquarters for family walks and picnics.[56]

Since the company was founded, CEO Jim Goodnight has been committed to motivating employees to develop creative and high-quality products that meet customers' needs. Today, 91% of the top 100 companies in the *Fortune* 500 list use SAS products for a wide variety of purposes including risk management, monitoring and measuring performance, managing relations with suppliers and customers, and detecting fraud.[57] SAS also provides educational software for schools and teachers through SAS in School.[58] Clearly, motivating employees and helping to satisfy their needs is a win–win situation for SAS.

Equity Theory

Equity theory is a theory of motivation that concentrates on people's perceptions of the fairness of their work *outcomes* relative to, or in proportion to, their work *inputs*. Equity theory complements expectancy and need theories by focusing on how people perceive the relationship between the outcomes they receive from their jobs and organizations and the inputs they contribute. Equity theory was formulated in the

LO2 Describe from the perspectives of expectancy theory and equity theory what managers should do to have a highly motivated workforce.

1960s by J. Stacy Adams, who stressed that what is important in determining motivation is the *relative* rather than the *absolute* levels of outcomes a person receives and inputs a person contributes. Specifically, motivation is influenced by the comparison of one's own outcome–input ratio with the outcome–input ratio of a referent.[59] The *referent* could be another person or a group of people who are perceived to be similar to oneself; the referent also could be oneself in a previous job or one's expectations about what outcome–input ratios should be. In a comparison of one's own outcome–input ratio to a referent's ratio, one's *perceptions* of outcomes and inputs (not any objective indicator of them) are key.

Equity

equity theory A theory of motivation that focuses on people's perceptions of the fairness of their work outcomes relative to their work inputs.

equity The justice, impartiality, and fairness to which all organizational members are entitled.

Equity exists when a person perceives his or her own outcome–input ratio to be equal to a referent's outcome–input ratio. Under conditions of equity (see Table 9.2), if a referent receives more outcomes than you receive, the referent contributes proportionally more inputs to the organization, so his or her outcome–input ratio still equals your ratio. Maria Sanchez and Claudia King, for example, both work in a shoe store in a large mall. Sanchez is paid more per hour than King but also contributes more inputs, including being responsible for some of the store's bookkeeping, closing the store, and periodically depositing cash in the bank. When King compares her outcome–input ratio to Sanchez's (her referent's), she perceives the ratios to be equitable because Sanchez's higher level of pay (an outcome) is proportional to her higher level of inputs (bookkeeping, closing the store, and going to the bank).

Similarly, under conditions of equity, if you receive more outcomes than a referent, then your inputs are perceived to be proportionally higher. Continuing with our example, when Sanchez compares her outcome–input ratio to King's (her referent's) ratio, she perceives them to be equitable because her higher level of pay is proportional to her higher level of inputs.

When equity exists, people are motivated to continue contributing their current levels of inputs to their organizations to receive their current levels of outcomes. If people wish to increase their outcomes under conditions of equity, they are motivated to increase their inputs.

Inequity

inequity Lack of fairness.

Inequity, lack of fairness, exists when a person's outcome–input ratio is not perceived to be equal to a referent's. Inequity creates pressure or tension inside people and motivates them to restore equity by bringing the two ratios back into balance.

Table 9.2
Equity Theory

Condition	Person		Referent	Example
Equity	$\frac{\text{Outcomes}}{\text{Inputs}}$	=	$\frac{\text{Outcomes}}{\text{Inputs}}$	An engineer perceives that he contributes more inputs (time and effort) and receives proportionally more outcomes (a higher salary and choice job assignments) than his referent.
Underpayment inequity	$\frac{\text{Outcomes}}{\text{Inputs}}$	< (less than)	$\frac{\text{Outcomes}}{\text{Inputs}}$	An engineer perceives that he contributes more inputs but receives the same outcomes as his referent.
Overpayment inequity	$\frac{\text{Outcomes}}{\text{Inputs}}$	> (greater than)	$\frac{\text{Outcomes}}{\text{Inputs}}$	An engineer perceives that he contributes the same inputs but receives more outcomes than his referent.

There are two types of inequity: underpayment inequity and overpayment inequity (see Table 9.2). **Underpayment inequity** exists when a person's own outcome–input ratio is perceived to be *less* than that of a referent. In comparing yourself to a referent, you think that you are *not* receiving the outcomes you should be, given your inputs. **Overpayment inequity** exists when a person perceives that his or her own outcome–xinput ratio is *greater* than that of a referent. In comparing yourself to a referent, you think that you are receiving *more* outcomes than you should be, given your inputs.

underpayment inequity The inequity that exists when a person perceives that his or her own outcome–input ratio is less than the ratio of a referent.

overpayment inequity The inequity that exists when a person perceives that his or her own outcome–input ratio is greater than the ratio of a referent.

Ways to Restore Equity

According to equity theory, both underpayment inequity and overpayment inequity create tension that motivates most people to restore equity by bringing the ratios back into balance.[60] When people experience *underpayment* inequity, they may be motivated to lower their inputs by reducing their working hours, putting forth less effort on the job, or being absent or they may be motivated to increase their outcomes by asking for a raise or a promotion. Susan Richie, a financial analyst at a large corporation, noticed that she was working longer hours and getting more work accomplished than a coworker who had the same position, yet they both received the exact same pay and other outcomes. To restore equity, Richie decided to stop coming in early and staying late. Alternatively, she could have tried to restore equity by trying to increase her outcomes, say, by asking her boss for a raise.

When people experience *underpayment* inequity and other means of equity restoration fail, they can change their perceptions of their own or the referent's inputs or outcomes. For example, they may realize that their referent is really working on more difficult projects than they are or that they really take more time off from work than their referent does. Alternatively, if people who feel that they are underpaid have other employment options, they may leave the organization. As an example, John Steinberg, an assistant principal in a high school, experienced underpayment inequity when he realized that all of the other assistant principals of high schools in his school district had received promotions to the position of principal even though they had been in their jobs for a shorter time than he had been. Steinberg's performance had always been appraised as being high, so after his repeated requests for a promotion went unheeded, he found a job as a principal in a different school district.

When people experience *overpayment* inequity, they may try to restore equity by changing their perceptions of their own or their referent's inputs or outcomes. Equity can be restored when people realize that they are contributing more inputs than they originally thought. Equity also can be restored by perceiving the referent's inputs to be lower or the referent's outcomes to be higher than one originally thought. When equity is restored in this way, actual inputs and outcomes are unchanged and the person being overpaid takes no real action. What is changed is how people think about or view their or the referent's inputs and outcomes. For instance, Mary McMann experienced overpayment inequity when she realized that she was being paid $2 an hour more than a coworker who had the same job as she did in a record store and who contributed the same amount of inputs. McMann restored equity by changing her perceptions of her inputs. She realized that she worked harder than her coworker and solved more problems that came up in the store.

Experiencing either overpayment or underpayment inequity, you might decide that your referent is not appropriate because, for example, the referent is too different from yourself. Choosing a more appropriate referent may bring the ratios back into balance. Angela Martinez, a middle manager in the engineering department of a chemical company, experienced overpayment inequity when she realized that she was being paid quite a bit more than her friend, who was a middle manager in the marketing department of the same company. After thinking about the discrepancy for a while, Martinez decided that engineering and marketing were so different that she should not be comparing her job to her friend's job even though they were both middle managers. Martinez restored equity by changing her referent; she picked a middle manager in the engineering department as a new referent.

Motivation is highest when as many people as possible in an organization perceive that they are being equitably treated–their outcomes and inputs are in balance. Top contributors and performers are motivated to continue contributing a high level of inputs because they are receiving the outcomes they deserve. Mediocre contributors and performers realize that if they want to increase their outcomes, they have to increase their inputs. Managers of effective organizations, like Jack and Andrew Taylor at Enterprise Rent-A-Car, realize the importance of equity for motivation and performance and continually strive to ensure that employees believe they are being equitably treated.

Tough economic times and increased global competition have resulted in some workers' putting in longer and longer working hours (i.e., increasing their inputs) without any kind of increase in their outcomes. For those whose referents are not experiencing a similar change, perceptions of inequity are likely. According to Jill Andresky Fraser, author of *White Collar Sweatshop,* over 25 million U.S. workers work more than 49 hours per week in the office, almost 11 million work more than 60 hours per week in the office, and many also put in additional work hours at home. Moreover, advances in information technology, such as e-mail and cell phones, have resulted in work intruding on home time, vacation time, and even special occasions.[61]

Goal-Setting Theory

Goal-setting theory focuses on motivating workers to contribute their inputs to their jobs and organizations; in this way it is similar to expectancy theory and equity theory. But goal-setting theory takes this focus a step further by considering as well how managers can ensure that organizational members focus their inputs in the direction of high performance and the achievement of organizational goals.

LO3 Explain how goals and needs motivate people and what kinds of goals are especially likely to result in high performance.

goal-setting theory A theory that focuses on identifying the types of goals that are most effective in producing high levels of motivation and performance and explaining why goals have these effects.

Ed Locke and Gary Latham, the leading researchers on goal-setting theory, suggest that the goals that organizational members strive to attain are prime determinants of their motivation and subsequent performance. A *goal* is what a person is trying to accomplish through his or her efforts and behaviors.[62] Just as you may have a goal to get a good grade in this course, so do members of an organization have goals that they strive to meet. For example, salespeople at Neiman Marcus strive to meet sales goals, while top managers pursue market share and profitability goals.

Goal-setting theory suggests that to stimulate high motivation and performance, goals must be *specific* and *difficult*.[63] Specific goals are often quantitative–a salesperson's goal to sell $200 worth of merchandise per day, a scientist's goal to finish a project in one year, a CEO's goal to reduce debt by 40% and increase revenues by 20%, a restaurant manager's goal to serve 150 customers per evening. In contrast to specific goals, vague goals such as "doing your best" or "selling as much as you can" do not have much motivational impact.

Specific, difficult goals can encourage people to exert high levels of effort and to focus efforts in the right direction.

Difficult goals are hard but not impossible to attain. In contrast to difficult goals, easy goals are those that practically everyone can attain, and moderate goals are goals that about one-half of the people can attain. Both easy and moderate goals have less motivational power than difficult goals.

Regardless of whether specific, difficult goals are set by managers, workers, or teams of managers and workers, they lead to high levels of motivation and performance. When managers set goals for their subordinates, their subordinates must accept the goals or agree to work toward them; also, they should be committed to them or really want to attain them. Some managers find that having subordinates participate in the actual setting of goals boosts their acceptance of and commitment to the goals. In addition, organizational members need to receive *feedback* about how they are doing; feedback can often be provided by the performance appraisal and feedback component of an organization's human resource management system (see Chapter 12).

Specific, difficult goals affect motivation in two ways. First, they motivate people to contribute more inputs to their jobs. Specific, difficult goals cause people to put forth high levels of effort, for example. Just as you would study harder if you were trying to get an A in a course instead of a C, so too will a salesperson work harder to reach a $200 sales goal instead of a $100 sales goal. Specific, difficult goals also cause people to be more persistent than easy, moderate, or vague goals when they run into difficulties. Salespeople who are told to sell as much as possible might stop trying on a slow day, whereas having a specific, difficult goal to reach causes them to keep trying.

A second way in which specific, difficult goals affect motivation is by helping people focus their inputs in the right direction. These goals let people know what they should be focusing their attention on, be it increasing the quality of customer service or sales or lowering new product development times. The fact that the goals are specific and difficult also frequently causes people to develop *action plans* for reaching them.[64] Action plans can include the strategies to attain the goals and timetables or schedules for the completion of different activities crucial to goal attainment. Like the goals themselves, action plans also help ensure that efforts are focused in the right direction and that people do not get sidetracked along the way.

Although specific, difficult goals have been found to increase motivation and performance in a wide variety of jobs and organizations both in the United States and abroad, recent research suggests that they may detract from performance under certain conditions. When people are performing complicated and very challenging tasks that require them to focus on a considerable amount of learning, specific, difficult goals may actually impair performance.[65] Striving to reach such goals may direct some of a person's attention away from learning about the task and toward trying to figure out how to achieve the goal. Once a person has learned the task and it no longer seems complicated or difficult, then the assignment of specific, difficult goals is likely to have its usual effects. Additionally, for work that is very creative and uncertain, specific, difficult goals may be detrimental.

Learning Theories

learning theories Theories that focus on increasing employee motivation and performance by linking the outcomes that employees receive to the performance of desired behaviors and the attainment of goals.

learning A relatively permanent change in knowledge or behavior that results from practice or experience.

The basic premise of **learning theories** as applied to organizations is that managers can increase employee motivation and performance by the ways they link the outcomes that employees receive to the performance of desired behaviors and the attainment of goals. Thus, learning theory focuses on the linkage between performance and outcomes in the motivation equation (refer back to Figure 9.1).

Learning can be defined as a relatively permanent change in a person's knowledge or behavior that results from practice or experience.[66] Learning takes place in organizations when people learn to perform certain behaviors to receive certain outcomes. For example, a person learns to perform at a higher level than in the past or to come to work earlier because he or she is motivated to obtain the outcomes that result from these behaviors, such as a pay raise or praise from a supervisor. In the "Management Snapshot," Enterprise Rent-A-Car's emphasis on training ensures that new hires learn how to provide excellent customer service and perform all the tasks necessary for successful branch operations.

Of the different learning theories, operant conditioning theory and social learning theory provide the most guidance to managers in their efforts to have a highly motivated workforce.

LO4 Identify the motivation lessons that managers can learn from operant conditioning theory and social learning theory.

Operant Conditioning Theory

operant conditioning theory The theory that people learn to perform behaviors that lead to desired consequences and learn not to perform behaviors that lead to undesired consequences.

According to **operant conditioning theory**, developed by psychologist B. F. Skinner, people learn to perform behaviors that lead to desired consequences and learn not to perform behaviors that lead to undesired consequences.[67] Translated into motivation terms, Skinner's theory means that people will be motivated to perform at a high level and attain their work goals to the extent that high performance and goal attainment allow them to obtain outcomes they desire. Similarly, people avoid performing behaviors that lead to outcomes they do not desire. By linking the performance of *specific behaviors* to the attainment of *specific outcomes,* managers can motivate organizational members to perform in ways that help an organization achieve its goals.

Operant conditioning theory provides four tools that managers can use to motivate high performance and prevent workers from engaging in absenteeism and other behaviors that detract from organizational effectiveness. These tools are positive reinforcement, negative reinforcement, extinction, and punishment.[68]

positive reinforcement Giving people outcomes they desire when they perform organizationally functional behaviors.

POSITIVE REINFORCEMENT **Positive reinforcement** gives people outcomes they desire when they perform organizationally functional behaviors. These desired outcomes, called *positive reinforcers,* include any outcomes that a person desires, such as pay, praise, or a promotion. Organizationally functional behaviors are behaviors that contribute to organizational effectiveness; they can include producing high-quality goods and services, providing high-quality customer service, and meeting deadlines. By linking positive reinforcers to the performance of functional behaviors, managers motivate people to perform the desired behaviors.

negative reinforcement Eliminating or removing undesired outcomes when people perform organizationally functional behaviors.

NEGATIVE REINFORCEMENT **Negative reinforcement** also can encourage members of an organization to perform desired or organizationally functional behaviors. Managers using negative reinforcement actually eliminate or remove undesired outcomes once the functional behavior is performed. These undesired outcomes, called *negative reinforcers,* can range from a manager's constant nagging or criticism to unpleasant assignments or the ever-present threat of losing one's job. When negative reinforcement is used, people are motivated to perform behaviors because they want to stop receiving or avoid undesired outcomes. Managers who try to encourage salespeople to sell more by threatening them with being fired are using negative reinforcement. In this case, the negative reinforcer is the threat of job loss, which is removed once the functional behavior is performed.

Whenever possible, managers should try to use positive reinforcement. Negative reinforcement can create a very unpleasant work environment and even a negative culture in an organization. No one likes to be nagged, threatened, or exposed to other kinds of negative outcomes. The use of negative reinforcement sometimes causes subordinates to resent managers and try to get back at them.

IDENTIFYING THE RIGHT BEHAVIORS FOR REINFORCEMENT Even managers who use positive reinforcement (and refrain from using negative reinforcement) can get into trouble if they are not careful to identify the right behaviors to reinforce–behaviors that are truly functional for the organization. Doing this is not always as straightforward as it might seem. First, it is crucial for managers to choose behaviors over which subordinates have control; in other words, subordinates must have the freedom and opportunity to perform the behaviors that are being reinforced. Second, it is crucial that these behaviors contribute to organizational effectiveness.

EXTINCTION Sometimes members of an organization are motivated to perform behaviors that actually detract from organizational effectiveness. According to operant conditioning theory, all behavior is controlled or determined by its consequences; one way for managers to curtail the performance of dysfunctional behaviors is to eliminate whatever is reinforcing the behaviors. This process is called **extinction.**

extinction Curtailing the performance of dysfunctional behaviors by eliminating whatever is reinforcing them.

Suppose a manager has a subordinate who frequently stops by his office to chat–sometimes about work-related matters but at other times about various topics ranging from politics to last night's football game. The manager and the subordinate share certain interests and views, so these conversations can get quite involved, and both seem to enjoy them. The manager, however, realizes that these frequent and sometimes lengthy conversations are actually causing him to stay at work later in the evenings to make up for the time he loses during the day. The manager also realizes that he is actually reinforcing his subordinate's behavior by acting interested in the topics the subordinate brings up and responding at length to them. To extinguish this behavior, the manager stops acting interested in these non-work-related conversations and keeps his responses polite and friendly but brief. No longer being reinforced with a pleasurable conversation, the subordinate eventually ceases to be motivated to interrupt the manager during working hours to discuss non-work-related issues.

PUNISHMENT Sometimes managers cannot rely on extinction to eliminate dysfunctional behaviors because they do not have control over whatever is reinforcing the behavior or because they cannot afford the time needed for extinction to work. When employees are performing dangerous behaviors or behaviors that are illegal or unethical, the behavior needs to be eliminated immediately. Sexual harassment, for example, is an organizationally dysfunctional behavior that cannot be tolerated. In such cases managers often rely on **punishment,** administering an undesired or negative consequence to subordinates when they perform the dysfunctional behavior. Punishments used by organizations range from verbal reprimands to pay cuts, temporary suspensions, demotions, and firings. Punishment, however, can have some unintended side effects–resentment, loss of self-respect, a desire for retaliation–and should be used only when necessary.

punishment Administering an undesired or negative consequence when dysfunctional behavior occurs.

To avoid the unintended side effects of punishment, managers should keep in mind these guidelines:

- Downplay the emotional element involved in punishment. Make it clear that you are punishing a person's performance of a dysfunctional behavior, not the person himself or herself.
- Try to punish dysfunctional behaviors as soon after they occur as possible, and make sure the negative consequence is a source of punishment for the individuals involved. Be certain that organizational members know exactly why they are being punished.
- Try to avoid punishing someone in front of others, for this can hurt a person's self-respect and lower esteem in the eyes of coworkers as well as make coworkers feel uncomfortable.[69] Even so, making organizational members aware that an individual who has committed a serious infraction has been punished can sometimes be effective in preventing future infractions and teaching all members of the organization that certain behaviors are unacceptable. For example, when organizational members are informed that a manager who has sexually harassed subordinates has been punished, they learn or are reminded of the fact that sexual harassment is not tolerated in the organization.

Managers and students alike often confuse negative reinforcement and punishment. To avoid such confusion, keep in mind the two major differences between them. First, negative reinforcement is used to promote the performance of functional behaviors in organizations; punishment is used to stop the performance of dysfunctional behaviors. Second, negative reinforcement entails the *removal* of a negative consequence when functional behaviors are performed; punishment entails the *administration* of negative consequences when dysfunctional behaviors are performed.

Social Learning Theory

social learning theory A theory that takes into account how learning and motivation are influenced by people's thoughts and beliefs and their observations of other people's behavior.

Social learning theory proposes that motivation results not only from direct experience of rewards and punishments but also from a person's thoughts and beliefs. Social learning theory extends operant conditioning's contribution to managers' understanding of motivation by explaining (1) how people can be motivated by observing other people perform a behavior and be reinforced for doing so *(vicarious learning),* (2) how people can be motivated to control their behavior themselves *(self-reinforcement),* and (3) how people's beliefs about their ability to successfully perform a behavior affect motivation *(self-efficacy).*[70] We look briefly at each of these motivators.

vicarious learning Learning that occurs when the learner becomes motivated to perform a behavior by watching another person perform it and be reinforced for doing so; also called *observational learning.*

VICARIOUS LEARNING **Vicarious learning**, often called *observational learning,* occurs when a person (the learner) becomes motivated to perform a behavior by watching another person (the model) perform the behavior and be positively reinforced for doing so. Vicarious learning is a powerful source of motivation on many jobs in which people learn to perform functional behaviors by watching others. Salespeople learn how to be helpful to customers, medical school students learn how to treat patients, law clerks learn how to practice law, and nonmanagers learn how to be managers, in part, by observing experienced members of an organization perform these behaviors properly and be reinforced for them. In general, people are more likely to be motivated to imitate the behavior of models who are highly competent, are (to some extent) experts in the behavior, have high status, receive attractive reinforcers, and are friendly or approachable.[71]

One of the ways in which aspiring physicians learn is by watching skilled physicians treat patients.

To promote vicarious learning, managers should strive to have the learner meet the following conditions:

- The learner observes the model performing the behavior.
- The learner accurately perceives the model's behavior.
- The learner remembers the behavior.
- The learner has the skills and abilities needed to perform the behavior.
- The learner sees or knows that the model is positively reinforced for the behavior.[72]

self-reinforcer Any desired or attractive outcome or reward that a person gives to himself or herself for good performance.

SELF-REINFORCEMENT Although managers are often the providers of reinforcement in organizations, sometimes people motivate themselves through self-reinforcement. People can control their own behavior by setting goals for themselves and then reinforcing themselves when they achieve the goals.[73] **Self-reinforcers** are any desired or attractive outcomes or rewards that people can give to themselves for good performance, such as a feeling of accomplishment, going to a movie, having dinner out, buying a new CD, or taking time out for a golf game. When members of an organization control their own behavior through self-reinforcement, managers do not need to spend as much time as they ordinarily would trying to motivate and control behavior through the administration of consequences because subordinates are controlling and motivating themselves. In fact, this self-control is often referred to as the *self-management of behavior.*

When employees are highly skilled and are responsible for creating new goods and services, managers typically rely on self-control and self-management of behavior, as is the case at Google. Employees at Google are given the flexibility and autonomy to experiment, take risks, and sometimes fail as they work on new projects. They are encouraged to learn from their failures and apply what they learn to subsequent projects.[74] Google's engineers are given one day a week to work on their own projects that they are highly involved with, and new products such as Google News often emerge from these projects.[75]

self-efficacy A person's belief about his or her ability to perform a behavior successfully.

SELF-EFFICACY **Self-efficacy** is a person's belief about his or her ability to perform a behavior successfully.[76] Even with all the most attractive consequences or reinforcers hinging on high performance, people are not going to be motivated if they do not think that they can actually perform at a high level. Similarly, when people control their own behavior, they are likely to set for themselves difficult goals that will lead to outstanding accomplishments only if they think that they have the capability to reach those goals. Thus, self-efficacy influences motivation both when managers provide reinforcement and when workers themselves provide it.[77] The greater the self-efficacy, the greater is the motivation and performance. In the "Management Snapshot," managers at Enterprise Rent-A-Car boost self-efficacy by providing employees with training, increasing their levels of autonomy and responsibility as they gain experience with the company, and expressing confidence in their ability to manage their own units. Such verbal persuasion, as well as a person's own past performance and accomplishments and the accomplishments of other people, plays a role in determining a person's self-efficacy.

Pay and Motivation

In Chapter 12, we discuss how managers establish a pay level and structure for an organization as a whole. Here we focus on how, once a pay level and structure are in place, managers can use pay to motivate employees to perform at a high level and attain their work goals. Pay is used to motivate entry-level workers, first-line and middle managers, and even top managers such as CEOs. Pay can be used to motivate people to perform behaviors that help an organization achieve its goals, and it can be used to motivate people to join and remain with an organization.

LO5 Explain why and how managers can use pay as a major motivation tool.

Each of the theories described in this chapter alludes to the importance of pay and suggests that pay should be based on performance:

- *Expectancy theory:* Instrumentality, the association between performance and outcomes such as pay, must be high for motivation to be high. In addition, pay is an outcome that has high valence for many people.
- *Need theories:* People should be able to satisfy their needs by performing at a high level; pay can be used to satisfy several different kinds of needs.
- *Equity theory:* Outcomes such as pay should be distributed in proportion to inputs (including performance levels).
- *Goal-setting theory:* Outcomes such as pay should be linked to the attainment of goals.
- *Learning theories:* The distribution of outcomes such as pay should be contingent on the performance of organizationally functional behaviors.

As these theories suggest, to promote high motivation, managers should base the distribution of pay to organizational members on performance levels so that high performers receive more pay than low performers (other things being equal).[78] At General Mills, for example, the pay of all employees, ranging from mailroom clerks to senior managers, is based, at least in part, on performance.[79] A compensation plan basing pay on performance is often called a **merit pay plan.** Once managers have decided to use a merit pay plan, they face two important choices: whether to base pay on individual, group, or organizational performance or to use salary increases or bonuses.

merit pay plan A compensation plan that bases pay on performance.

Basing Merit Pay on Individual, Group, or Organizational Performance

Managers can base merit pay on individual, group, or organizational performance. When individual performance (such as the dollar value of merchandise a salesperson sells, the number of loudspeakers a factory worker assembles, and a lawyer's billable hours) can be accurately determined, individual motivation is likely to be highest when pay is based on individual performance.[80] When members of an organization work closely together and individual performance cannot be accurately determined (as in a team of computer programmers developing a single software package), pay cannot be based on individual performance, and a group- or organization-based plan must be used. When the attainment of organizational goals hinges on members' working closely together and cooperating with each other (as in a small construction company that builds custom homes), group- or organization-based plans may be more appropriate than individual-based plans.[81]

It is possible to combine elements of an individual-based plan with a group- or organization-based plan to motivate each individual to perform highly and, at the same time, motivate all individuals to work well together, cooperate with one another, and help one another as needed. Lincoln Electric, a very successful company and a leading manufacturer of welding machines, uses a combination individual- and organization-based plan.[82] Pay is based on individual performance. In addition, each year the size of a bonus fund depends on organizational performance. Money from the bonus fund is distributed to people on the basis of their contributions to the organization, attendance, levels of cooperation, and other indications of performance. Employees of Lincoln Electric are motivated to cooperate and help one another because when the firm as a whole performs well, everybody benefits by having a larger bonus fund. Employees also are motivated to contribute their inputs to the organization because their contributions determine their share of the bonus fund.

Salary Increase or Bonus?

Managers can distribute merit pay to people in the form of a salary increase or a bonus on top of regular salaries. Although the dollar amount of a salary increase or bonus might be identical, bonuses tend to have more motivational impact for at least three reasons. First, salary levels are typically based on performance levels, cost-of-living increases, and so forth, from the day people start working in an organization, which means that the absolute level of the salary is based largely on factors unrelated to *current* performance. A 5% merit increase in salary, for example, may seem relatively small in comparison to one's total salary. Second, a current salary increase may be affected by other factors in addition to performance, such as cost-of-living increases or across-the-board market adjustments. Third, because organizations rarely reduce salaries, salary levels tend to vary less than performance levels do. Related to this point is the fact that bonuses give managers more flexibility in distributing outcomes. If an organization is doing well, bonuses can be relatively high to reward employees for their contributions. However, unlike salary increases, bonus levels can be reduced when an organization's performance lags. All in all, bonus plans have more motivational impact than salary increases because the amount of the bonus can be directly and exclusively based on performance.[83]

employee stock option A financial instrument that entitles the bearer to buy shares of an organization's stock at a certain price during a certain period of time or under certain conditions.

Consistent with the lessons from motivation theories, bonuses can be linked directly to performance and vary from year to year and employee to employee, as at Gradient Corporation, a Cambridge, Massachusetts, environmental consulting firm.[84] Another organization that successfully uses bonuses is Nucor Corporation. Steelworkers at Nucor tend to be much more productive than steelworkers in other companies–probably because they can receive bonuses tied to performance and quality that are from 130% to 150% of their regular or base pay.[85]

A steelworker at Nucor burns impurities from a tube used to pour molten steel in Decatur, Alabama. Nucor steelworkers can receive bonuses tied to performance and quality that are from 130 to 150 percent of their regular pay.

In addition to receiving pay raises and bonuses, high-level managers and executives are sometimes granted employee stock options. **Employee stock options** are financial instruments that entitle the bearer to buy shares of an organization's stock at a certain price during a certain period of time or under certain conditions.[86] For example, in addition to salaries, stock options are sometimes used to attract high-level managers. The exercise price is the stock price at which the bearer can buy the stock, and the vesting conditions specify when the bearer can actually buy the stock at the exercise price. The option's exercise price is generally set equal to the market price of the stock on the date it is granted, and the vesting conditions might specify that the manager has to have worked at the organization for 12 months or perhaps met some performance target (increase in profits) before being able to exercise the option. In high-technology firms and start-ups, options are sometimes used in a similar fashion for employees at various levels in the organization.[87]

From a motivation standpoint, stock options are used not so much to reward past individual performance but, rather, to motivate employees to work in the future for the good of the company as a whole. This is true because stock options issued at current stock prices have value in the future only if an organization does well and its stock price appreciates; thus, giving employees stock options should encourage them to help the organization improve its performance over time.[88] At high-technology start-ups and dot-coms, stock options have often motivated potential employees to leave promising jobs in larger companies and work for the start-ups. In the late 1990s and early 2000s, many dot-commers were devastated to learn not only that their stock options were worthless, because their companies went out of business or were doing poorly, but also that they were unemployed. Unfortunately, stock options have also lead to unethical behavior; for example, sometimes individuals seek to artificially inflate the value of a company's stock to increase the value of stock options.

Examples of Merit Pay Plans

Managers can choose among several merit pay plans, depending on the work that employees perform and other considerations. Using *piece-rate pay,* an individual-based merit plan, managers base employees' pay on the number of units each employee produces, whether televisions, computer components, or welded auto parts. Managers at Lincoln Electric use piece-rate pay to determine individual pay levels. Advances in information technology are currently simplifying the administration of piece-rate pay in a variety of industries. For example, farmers typically allocated piece-rate pay to farmworkers through a laborious, time-consuming process. Now, they can rely on metal buttons the size of a dime that farmworkers clip to their shirts or put in their pockets. Made by Dallas Semiconductor Corporation, these buttons are customized for use in farming by Agricultural Data Systems, based in Laguna Niguel, California.[89] Each button contains a semiconductor linked to payroll computers by a wandlike probe in the field.[90] The wand relays the number of boxes of fruit or vegetables that each worker picks as well as the type and quality of the produce picked, the location it was picked in, and the time and the date. The buttons are activated by touching them with the probe; hence, they are called Touch Memory Buttons. Managers generally find that the buttons save time, improve accuracy, and provide valuable information about their crops and yields.[91]

Using *commission pay,* another individual-based merit pay plan, managers base pay on a percentage of sales. Managers at the successful real-estate company Re/Max International Inc. use commission pay for their agents, who are paid a percentage of their sales. Some department stores, such as Neiman Marcus, use commission pay for their salespeople.

Examples of organizational-based merit pay plans include the Scanlon plan and profit sharing. The *Scanlon plan* (developed by Joseph Scanlon, a union leader in a steel and tin plant in the 1920s) focuses on reducing expenses or cutting costs; members of an organization are motivated to come up with and implement cost-cutting strategies because a percentage of the cost savings achieved during a specified time is distributed to the employees.[92] Under *profit sharing,* employees receive a share of an organization's profits. Approximately 16% of the employees in medium or large firms receive profit sharing, and about 25% of small firms give their employees a share of the profits.[93] Regardless of the specific kind of plan that is used, managers should always strive to link pay to the performance of behaviors that help an organization achieve its goals.

Japanese managers in large corporations have long shunned merit pay plans in favor of plans that reward seniority. However, more and more Japanese companies are adopting merit-based pay due to its motivational benefits; among such companies are SiteDesign,[94] Tokio Marine and Fire Insurance, and Hissho Iwai, a trading organization.[95]

Summary and Review

THE NATURE OF MOTIVATION Motivation encompasses the psychological forces within a person that determine the direction of the person's behavior in an organization, the person's level of effort, and the person's level of persistence in the face of obstacles. Managers strive to motivate people to contribute their inputs to an organization, to focus these inputs in the direction of high performance, and to ensure that people receive the outcomes they desire when they perform at a high level. **[LO1]**

EXPECTANCY THEORY According to expectancy theory, managers can promote high levels of motivation in their organizations by taking steps to ensure that expectancy is high (people think that if they try, they can perform at a high level), instrumentality is high (people think that if they perform at a high level, they will receive certain outcomes), and valence is high (people desire these outcomes). **[LO2]**

NEED THEORIES Need theories suggest that to motivate their workforces, managers should determine what needs people are trying to satisfy in organizations and then ensure that people receive outcomes that satisfy these needs when they perform at a high level and contribute to organizational effectiveness. **[LO3]**

EQUITY THEORY According to equity theory, managers can promote high levels of motivation by ensuring that people perceive that there is equity in the organization or that outcomes are distributed in proportion to inputs. Equity exists when a person perceives that his or her own outcome–input ratio equals the outcome–input ratio of a referent. Inequity motivates people to try to restore equity. **[LO2]**

GOAL-SETTING THEORY Goal-setting theory suggests that managers can promote high motivation and performance by ensuring that people are striving to achieve specific, difficult goals. It is important for people to accept the goals, be committed to them, and receive feedback about how they are doing. **[LO3]**

LEARNING THEORIES Operant conditioning theory suggests that managers can motivate people to perform highly by using positive reinforcement or negative reinforcement (positive reinforcement being the preferred strategy). Managers can motivate people to avoid performing dysfunctional behaviors by using extinction or punishment. Social learning theory suggests that people can also be motivated by observing how others perform behaviors and receive rewards, by engaging in self-reinforcement, and by having high levels of self-efficacy. **[LO4]**

PAY AND MOTIVATION Each of the motivation theories discussed in this chapter alludes to the importance of pay and suggests that pay should be based on performance. Merit pay plans can be individual-, group-, or organization-based and can entail the use of salary increases or bonuses. **[LO5]**

Management in Action

Topics for Discussion and Action

Discussion

1. Discuss why two people with similar abilities may have very different expectancies for performing at a high level. [LO2]
2. Describe why some people have low instrumentalities even when their managers distribute outcomes based on performance. [LO2]
3. Analyze how professors try to promote equity to motivate students. [LO2]
4. Describe three techniques or procedures that managers can use to determine whether a goal is difficult. [LO3]
5. Discuss why managers should always try to use positive reinforcement instead of negative reinforcement. [LO4]

Action

6. Interview three people who have the same kind of job (such as salesperson, waiter/waitress, or teacher), and determine what kinds of needs each is trying to satisfy at work. [LO3]
7. Interview a manager in an organization in your community to determine the extent to which the manager takes advantage of vicarious learning to promote high motivation among subordinates. [LO3]

Building Management Skills

Diagnosing Motivation [LO1, 2, 3, 4]

Think about the ideal job that you would like to obtain upon graduation. Describe this job, the kind of manager you would like to report to, and the kind of organization you would be working in. Then answer the following questions:

1. What would be your levels of expectancy and instrumentality on this job? Which outcomes would have high valence for you on this job? What steps could your manager take to influence your levels of expectancy, instrumentality, and valence?
2. Whom would you choose as a referent on this job? What steps could your manager take to make you feel that you were being equitably treated? What would you do if, after a year on the job, you experienced underpayment inequity?
3. What goals would you strive to achieve on this job? Why? What role would your manager play in determining your goals?
4. What needs would you strive to satisfy on this job? Why? What role would your manager play in helping you satisfy these needs?
5. What behaviors would your manager positively reinforce on this job? Why? What positive reinforcers would your manager use?
6. Would there be any vicarious learning on this job? Why or why not?
7. To what extent would you be motivated by self-control on this job? Why?
8. What would be your level of self-efficacy on this job? Why would your self-efficacy be at this level? Should your manager take steps to boost your self-efficacy? If not, why not? If so, what would these steps be?

Managing Ethically [LO5]

Sometimes pay is so contingent upon performance that it creates stress for employees. Imagine a salesperson who knows that if sales targets are not met, she or he will not be able to make a house mortgage payment or pay the rent.

Questions

1. Either individually or in a group, think about the ethical implications of closely linking pay to performance.
2. Under what conditions might contingent pay be most stressful, and what steps can managers take to try to help their subordinates perform effectively and not experience excessive amounts of stress?

Small Group Breakout Exercise

Increasing Motivation [LO1, 2, 3, 4, 5]

Form groups of three or four people, and appoint one member as the spokesperson who will communicate your findings to the class when called on by the instructor. Then discuss the following scenario:

You and your partners own a chain of 15 dry-cleaning stores in a medium-size town. All of you are concerned about a problem in customer service that has surfaced recently. When any one of you spends the day, or even part of the day, in a particular store, clerks seem to provide excellent customer service, spotters are making sure all stains are removed from garments, and pressers are doing a good job of pressing difficult items such as silk blouses. Yet during those same visits customers complain to you about such things as stains not being removed and items being poorly pressed in some of their previous orders; indeed, several customers have brought garments in to be redone. Customers also sometimes comment on having waited too long for service on previous visits. You and your partners are meeting today to address this problem.

1. Discuss the extent to which you believe that you have a motivation problem in your stores.
2. Given what you have learned in this chapter, design a plan to increase the motivation of clerks to provide prompt service to customers even when they are not being watched by a partner.
3. Design a plan to increase the motivation of spotters to remove as many stains as possible even when they are not being watched by a partner.
4. Design a plan to increase the motivation of pressers to do a top-notch job on all clothes they press, no matter how difficult.

Be the Manager [LO1, 2, 3, 4, 5]

You supervise a team of marketing analysts who work on different snack products in a large food products company. The marketing analysts have recently received undergraduate degrees in business or liberal arts and have been on the job between one and three years. Their responsibilities include analyzing the market for their respective products, including competitors; tracking current marketing initiatives; and planning future marketing campaigns. They also need to prepare quarterly sales and expense reports for their products and estimated budgets for the next three quarters; to prepare these reports, they need to obtain data from financial and accounting analysts assigned to their products.

When they first started on the job, you took each marketing analyst through the reporting cycle, explaining what needs to be done and how to accomplish it and emphasizing the need for timely reports. While preparing the reports can be tedious, you think the task is pretty straightforward and easily accomplished if the analysts plan ahead and allocate sufficient time for it. When reporting time approaches, you remind the analysts through e-mails and emphasize the need for accurate and timely reports in team meetings.

You believe that this element of the analysts' jobs couldn't be more straightforward. However, at the end of each quarter, the majority of the analysts turn their reports in a day or two late, and, worse yet, your own supervisor (whom the reports are eventually turned in to) has indicated that information is often missing and sometimes the reports contain errors. Once you started getting flak from your supervisor about this problem, you decided you had better fix things, and quickly. You met with the marketing analysts, explained the problem, told them to turn the reports in to you a day or two early so that you could look them over, and more generally emphasized that they really needed to get their act together. Unfortunately, things have not improved much, and you are spending more and more of your own time doing the reports. What are you going to do?

BusinessWeek Case in the News [LO1, 2, 3]

The Chore Goes Offshore

David Cain loves his job. Well, most of it anyway. As an executive director for global engineering at Pfizer, Cain finds real satisfaction in assessing environmental real estate risks, managing facilities, and overseeing a multimillion-dollar budget for the pharmaceutical giant. What he doesn't love so much: creating PowerPoint slides and riffling through spreadsheets.

Lucky for Cain, Pfizer now lets him punt those tedious and time-consuming tasks to India with the click of a button. PfizerWorks, launched early last year, permits some 4,000 employees to pass off parts of their jobs to outsiders. You might call it personal outsourcing. With workers in India handling everything from basic market research projects to presentations, professionals such as Cain can focus on higher-value work. "It has really been a godsend," says Cain. "I can send them something in the evening, and the next morning it's waiting for me when I get to the office."

This novel twist on outsourcing comes at a time when other resources are dwindling. As companies cull people by the thousands—Pfizer itself announced some 8,000 job cuts in January—those who stay behind are being asked to do more. In a down economy, though, it's especially critical that executives direct their energies to motivating teams, creating new products, and thinking strategically about their next move. "The stakes go up even higher," says David Kreutter, Pfizer's vice president for U.S. commercial operations.

Originally dubbed the Office of the Future, PfizerWorks is partly the by-product of a cost-cutting push that began several years ago. Jordan Cohen, the architect and head of the program, came up with the idea after reading Thomas L. Friedman's book *The World Is Flat* and observing how his own team worked. Cohen recalls seeing one of his recruits from the consulting firm McKinsey & Co., a new father, stay late at the office one night to crunch numbers and search for information on the Web. To Cohen, it didn't seem like time best spent.

Instead of shifting jobs overseas, as companies have done for years, Cohen wanted to find a way to shift tasks. He also felt the program should let employees do one-stop shopping. Instead of setting up a few specialized services, Pfizer employees click a single button on their computer desktop that sends them to the PfizerWorks site. They write up what they need on an online form, which is sent to one of two Indian service-outsourcing firms: Genpact, in Gurgaon, and a unit of Chicago's R.R. Donnelley.

Once a request is received, a team member such as R.R. Donnelley's Biju Kurian in India sets up a call with the Pfizer employee to clarify what's needed and when. The costs involved in each project are charged to the employee's department. Says Shantanu Ghosh, a senior vice president at Genpact, "The way Pfizer's model is constructed is really pretty unique."

Pfizer is now looking to expand the program to more employees and to a wider array of tasks. While he was introducing a group of Pfizer scientists to the service last year, Cohen says, one of them immediately pointed out its limitations. "I got it, Jordan, we can use this," the researcher said. "But what I really need is a smart guy for a day." He had a point. Some tasks can't easily be broken down into instructions on an online form, Cohen admits, and sometimes employees need an assistant working in the same time zone.

Local Help

As a result, Pfizer is testing an arrangement with a small Columbus (Ohio)-based firm called Pearl Interactive Network. Pearl employs mostly people with physical disabilities who help with such administrative tasks as organizing a marketing team's research documents on a shared server or scheduling meetings. While the partnership is modest and isn't meant to supplant arrangements in India or administrative jobs, Cohen hopes it will make Pfizer staff even more productive.

Although Pfizer Works hasn't quite reached its first anniversary, Cohen estimates that it has already freed up 66,500 hours for employees. Pfizer finds employees are now spending less money on other providers, such as graphic design shops or market research firms. Employees are asked to rate their satisfaction with the finished product. If the score isn't high enough, a department can refuse to pay, which has happened only a handful of times.

Cain, for one, relishes working with what he prefers to call his "personal consulting organization." After getting such good results with basic spreadsheets and PowerPoints, he has asked teams in India to help him with more complex projects. One was to mine archived company "playbooks" on past acquisitions and pull together any lessons on what worked and what didn't when it came to consolidating facilities. That prep work should benefit the pharma giant now that it has announced a $68 billion acquisition of Wyeth.

The facilities report came together in a month, says Cain, versus the six months it would have taken him to do it alone. "Pfizer pays me not to work tactically," he says, "but to work strategically."

Questions

1. Is David Cain intrinsically motivated on his job? Why or why not?
2. How might being able to outsource certain tasks contribute to employee motivation?
3. How might being able to outsource tasks increase job holders' levels of expectancy? Does it have the potential to decrease expectancy? Why or why not?
4. When managers outsource certain tasks, what potential motivational implications are there for their subordinates?

Source: Jena McGregor, "The Chore Goes Offshore." Reprinted from March 23 and 30, 2009 issue of *BusinessWeek* by special permission, copyright © 2009 by The McGraw-Hill Companies, Inc.

BusinessWeek Case in the News [LO1, 2, 4, 5]

The Case For Unequal Perks

A cabal of HR renegades is taking advantage of the economic downturn to push an unorthodox notion: that the current vogue of slashing perks and pay is managerial insanity. Officeland may be burning, but Richard W. Beatty, who teaches human resources strategy at Rutgers University, says the tendency to treat everyone the same is "misguided and absolutely the wrong approach. It's strategic suicide."

Beatty and like-minded thinkers argue that the prevailing attitude is equivalent to an airline sticking its platinum passengers in coach with scratchy blankets and shrink-wrapped food. Once the good times reappear, or so the argument goes, disenchanted top players will bolt for better treatment and more pay. Companies that hew to the status quo will "pay dearly," says Beatty, who, with Brian Becker and Mark Huselid, coauthored the upcoming *The Differentiated Workforce* and consults for Sony, GlaxoSmithKline, Lockheed Martin, and others.

The Beatty approach has attracted a growing number of adherents. HR czars at companies as varied as Sony and metal manufacturer Precision Castparts are engaging in nothing less than a compensation revolution: steerage treatment for mediocre players—and business-class benefits for superstars. At these organizations, HR departments are morphing into what amounts to a concierge service dedicated to the care and feeding of the people whose positions and performance are making their companies the most money.

HR types tend to believe in an egalitarian approach, so the idea that people in the same position would be treated differently is counterintuitive. Traditionalists also argue that one-size-fits-all cuts help prevent layoffs and protect companies from being understaffed when the economy rebounds. The credo could be summed up as, Everybody is in this together. "There are a lot of HR people who don't think [preferential treatment] is right, who think it's really unfair," says Beatty. "They want to save everybody and be the St. Bernards."

Not Craig E. Schneier. The HR boss at pharma giant Biogen Idec is more like a terrier. Schneier is maniacal about fine-tuning Biogen's employee measurement and performance appraisal systems. "A lot of companies talk about this," says Schneier. "But if you look at their outcomes in regard to pay, you will see they don't necessarily differentiate at the end of the day." Sure, there's a percentage or two difference in the raise or bonus. But most employees in similar positions languish in the same pay bands and are shuttled off to the same conferences as the slackers and substellar.

Schneier doesn't believe all people—or positions—are equal. At Biotec Idec, it's common for one vice president to get double what the guy in the next office doing a similar job gets. "Twice as big a merit increase, twice as big a bonus, and twice as big an equity grant," says Schneier. Performance metrics at Biogen are so exacting that employees essentially must re-earn their standard of living every year.

Micromeasuring Performance

In this new world, thicker paychecks come with training and development par excellence, more lunches with top leaders, and personal attention lavished on the A player's every whim. Where there are two classes of workers, even the office events can be different. The American Heart Association, for example, has swankier events for über-achievers. Last year the Association took 13 of them to the World Business Forum in New York City.

How does one pay for rewards for top performers at a time when budgets are under siege? Beatty and Huselid say they have clients who are starting to stealthily freeze or cut pay for some so as to be able to reward others. "They are robbing Peter to pay Paul," Beatty says. "Look, there are an awful lot of long-term employees who are poor performers who have locked-in high salaries through cost-of-living increases."

Companies are getting better at deploying their techno-brawn to monitor, measure, and analyze their workforces—from those who placed which call that landed what deal to those who are infamous for talking up their work only to underdeliver. These granular measures of performance are making it far easier to tailor rewards, doling out different deals to different employees. This will lead to a more Darwinian workplace.

Federal rules currently prohibit companies from sculpting benefits like health care, 401(k) matches, or maternity leaves to fit individuals. The regulations enforce one-size-fits-all and prevent a cafeteria-style approach. But experts believe the rules will get a performance-era update within five years. You can already hear HR luminaries like Microsoft's Lisa Brummel and IBM's Randall MacDonald fantasize about it: customizing benefits and compensation to life stages, performance levels, and work styles. The day may not be far off when the childless Gen Yer will be able to pick more vacation over adoption benefits or the graying boomer will be able to opt out of tuition assistance in favor of better elder care. As MacDonald says, "Why can't I make my 401(k) performance-based?"

Questions

1. What are the motivational implications of treating top performers the same as average or below-average performers?
2. What are the motivational implications of treating top performers better than average or below-average performers?
3. In tough economic times when jobs are scarce, why do managers still need to pay attention to employee motivation?
4. Are there any potential downsides to trying to "micromeasure" performance?

Source: Michelle Conlin, "The Case for Unequal Perks." Reprinted from March 23 and 30, 2009 issue of *BusinessWeek* by special permission, copyright © 2009 by The McGraw-Hill Companies, Inc.

Leaders and Leadership

CHAPTER 10

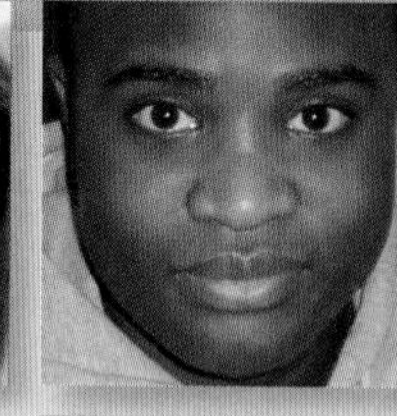

Learning Objectives

After studying this chapter, you should be able to

1. Explain what leadership is, when leaders are effective and ineffective, and the sources of power that enable managers to be effective leaders. **[LO1]**
2. Identify the traits that show the strongest relationship to leadership, the behaviors leaders engage in, and the limitations of the trait and behavior models of leadership. **[LO2]**
3. Explain how contingency models of leadership enhance our understanding of effective leadership and management in organizations. **[LO3]**
4. Describe what transformational leadership is, and explain how managers can engage in it. **[LO4]**
5. Characterize the relationship between gender and leadership and explain how emotional intelligence may contribute to leadership effectiveness. **[LO5]**

Chairperson and CEO Judy McGrath successfully leads the complex organization that is MTV Networks.

MANAGEMENT SNAPSHOT

Judy McGrath and MTV Networks

How Can a Manager Continuously Transform a Hip Company in a Rapidly Changing Environment?

As chairperson and CEO of MTV Networks, Judy McGrath has one of the most challenging and encompassing leadership positions in the media industry.[1] MTV Networks, a unit of Viacom, is home to the original MTV as well as Nickelodeon, VH1, Comedy Central, LOGO, MTV2, Nick at Nite, NOGGIN, TV Land, CMT, mtvU, the N, and Spike TV.[2] Operating in an industry and markets whose rate of change is parallel to none, keeping MTV Networks hip and maintaining its appeal in an ever-changing digital landscape is a daunting task.[3]

McGrath certainly seems up to the challenge; in 2006, she received the Vanguard Award for Distinguished Leadership, and she was ranked 18th in *Fortune* magazine's list of the "50 Most Powerful Women" in 2008.[4] Interestingly enough, McGrath, who was born in Scranton, Pennsylvania, first came to New York City in the late 1970s with hopes of combining her love of rock music with her college degree in English literature to write for *Rolling Stone* magazine. Instead, McGrath started writing for *Mademoiselle* magazine and later for *Glamour.* In 1981, friends told her about the newly launched MTV, and she took a job there writing promotional pieces. And the rest has been history. With MTV from its earliest days, McGrath is now in the top post.[5]

McGrath is far from what comes to some people's minds when they think of a traditional CEO. Widely read, she is very attuned to pop culture, is nurturing of employees and talent alike, and is a creative leader who encourages the same in others; she has been credited with creating a very inclusive culture at MTV, where all employees are listened to and heard. She is down to earth, as comfortable planning strategies with top managers as she is interacting with hip-hoppers or seeing live indie music acts. McGrath's confidence and high energy are matched by her knowledge of the industry, creativity, and integrity.[6]

Her personal leadership style emphasizes empowering all members of the MTV organization as well as its viewers. According to McGrath, creativity and innovation stem from employees at all ranks, leaders and managers should listen to employees' ideas, and change must be the rule of the day in a dynamic environment.[7] She has also strived to empower the MTV viewing audience and raise viewers' awareness about important social concerns with award-winning programming such as the *Fight For Your Rights series.*[8]

McGrath networks with wide-ranging contacts on a daily basis, keeping up with the latest developments in the industry and pop culture and always on the lookout for new ideas and opportunities. She is visionary and can see possibilities and opportunities where others might see just risks or potential downsides. She works hard, perseveres, and believes that anything is possible. Under her leadership, MTV has launched scores of successful new programs, all of which were risky and could have failed. As she puts it, "Falling flat on your face is a great motivator. The smartest thing we can do when confronted by something truly creative is to get out of the way."[9]

McGrath faces new challenges as she leads MTV forward. MTV's programming is now part of the media establishment, and in an era of broadband, iPods, and online everything, she realizes that MTV cannot rest on its laurels: It must continually transform itself to maintain its hip and edgy focus and continue to appeal to its audience. Thus, McGrath is pushing MTV to deliver services from multiple digital platforms ranging from cell phones to new broadband channels to video games.[10]

Clearly, challenging times lie ahead for McGrath as she seeks to transform MTV in the digital era. Her vision and decisiveness, combined with her style of empowering employees, encouraging risk taking and creativity, and making sure that all enjoy the ride suggest that MTV is in good hands.[11]

Overview

Judy McGrath exemplifies the many facets of effective leadership. In Chapter 1 we explained that one of the four primary tasks of managers is leading. Thus, it should come as no surprise that leadership is a key ingredient in effective management. When leaders are effective, their subordinates or followers are highly motivated, committed, and high-performing. When leaders are ineffective, chances are good that their subordinates do not perform up to their capabilities, are demotivated, and may be dissatisfied as well. CEO Judy McGrath is a leader at the very top of an organization, but leadership is an important ingredient for managerial success at all levels of organizations: top management, middle management, and first-line management. Moreover, leadership is a key ingredient for managerial success for organizations large and small.

LO1 Explain what leadership is, when leaders are effective and ineffective, and the sources of power that enable managers to be effective leaders.

In this chapter we describe what leadership is and examine the major leadership models that shed light on the factors that contribute to a manager's being an effective leader. We look at trait and behavior models, which focus on what leaders are like and what they do, and contingency models–Fiedler's contingency model, path-goal theory, and the leader substitutes model–each of which takes into account the complexity surrounding leadership and the role of the situation in leader effectiveness. We also describe how managers can use transformational leadership to dramatically affect their organizations. By the end of this chapter, you will have a good appreciation of the many factors and issues that managers face in their quest to be effective leaders.

The Nature of Leadership

Leadership is the process by which a person exerts influence over other people and inspires, motivates, and directs their activities to help achieve group or organizational goals.[12] The person who exerts such influence is a **leader.** When leaders are effective, the influence they exert over others helps

leadership The process by which an individual exerts influence over other people and inspires, motivates, and directs their activities to help achieve group or organizational goals.

leader An individual who is able to exert influence over other people to help achieve group or organizational goals.

a group or organization achieve its performance goals. When leaders are ineffective, their influence does not contribute to, and often detracts from, goal attainment. As the "Management Snapshot" makes clear, Judy McGrath is taking multiple steps to inspire and motivate MTV's employees so that they help MTV achieve its goals.

Beyond facilitating the attainment of performance goals, effective leadership increases an organization's ability to meet all the contemporary challenges discussed throughout this book, including the need to obtain a competitive advantage, the need to foster ethical behavior, and the need to manage a diverse workforce fairly and equitably. Leaders who exert influence over organizational members to help meet these goals increase their organizations' chances of success.

In considering the nature of leadership, we first look at leadership styles and how they affect managerial tasks and at the influence of culture on leadership styles. We then focus on the key to leadership, *power,* which can come from a variety of sources. Finally, we consider the contemporary dynamic of empowerment and how it relates to effective leadership.

Personal Leadership Style and Managerial Tasks

A manager's *personal leadership style*–that is, the specific ways in which a manager chooses to influence other people–shapes the way that manager approaches planning, organizing, and controlling (the other principal tasks of managing). Consider Judy McGrath's personal leadership style in the "Management Snapshot": She is down to earth, nurturing of employees and talent, and at the same time decisive and visionary. She empowers employees, encourages them to be creative and take risks, and fosters an inclusive culture at MTV Networks.[13]

Managers at all levels and in all kinds of organizations have their own personal leadership styles that determine not only how they lead their subordinates but also how they perform the other management tasks. Michael Kraus, owner and manager of a dry-cleaning store in the northeastern United States, for example, takes a hands-on approach to leadership. He has the sole authority for determining work schedules and job assignments for the 15 employees in his store (an organizing task), makes all important decisions by himself (a planning task), and closely monitors his employees' performance and rewards top performers with pay increases (a control task). Kraus's personal leadership style is effective in his organization. His employees are generally motivated, perform highly, and are satisfied, and his store is highly profitable.

Developing an effective personal leadership style often is a challenge for managers at all levels in an organization. This challenge is often exacerbated when times are tough, due, for example, to an economic downturn or a decline in customer demand. The dot-com bust and the slowing economy in the early 2000s provided many leaders with just such a challenge.

While leading is one of the four principal tasks of managing, a distinction is often made between managers and leaders. When this distinction is made, managers are thought of as those organizational members who establish and implement procedures and processes to ensure smooth functioning and who are accountable for goal accomplishment.[14] Leaders look to the future, chart the course for the organization, and attract, retain, motivate, inspire, and develop relationships with employees based on trust and mutual respect.[15] Leaders provide meaning and purpose, seek innovation rather than stability, and impassion employees to work together to achieve the leaders' vision.[16]

servant leader A leader who has a strong desire to serve and work for the benefit of others.

As part of their personal leadership style, some leaders strive to truly serve others. Robert Greenleaf, who was director of management research at AT&T and upon his retirement in 1964 embarked on a second career focused on writing, speaking, and consulting, came up with the term *servant leadership* to describe these leaders.[17] **Servant leaders,** above all else, have a strong desire to serve and work for the benefit of others.[18] Servant leaders share power with followers; strive to ensure that followers' most important needs are met, they are able to develop as individuals, and their well-being is enhanced; and seek to focus attention on those who are least well-off in a society.[19] Greenleaf founded a nonprofit organization called the Greenleaf Center for Servant-Leadership (formerly called the Center for Applied Ethics) to foster leadership focused on service to others, power sharing, and a sense of community between organizations and their multiple stakeholders.[20] Some entrepreneurs strive to incorporate servant leadership into their personal leadership styles, as profiled in the following "Ethics in Action."

ETHICS IN ACTION

Servant Leadership at Zingerman's

Ari Weinzweig and Paul Saginaw founded Zingerman's Delicatessen in Ann Arbor, Michigan, in 1982.[21] Food lovers at heart, Weinzweig and Saginaw delighted in finding both traditional and exotic foods from around the world, making delicious sandwiches to order, and having extensive selections of food items ranging from olives, oils, and vinegars to cheeses, smoked fish, and salami. As their business grew, and in order

Paul Saginaw (left) and Ari Weinzweig have incorporated servant leadership into their personal leadership styles at Zingerman's.

to maintain an intimate atmosphere with excellent customer service, Weinzweig and Saginaw expanded from their original deli into a community of related businesses called Zingerman's Community of Businesses. In addition to the original deli, Zingerman's Community of Businesses now includes a mail-order business, a bakery, a catering business, a creamery, a restaurant, a wholesale coffee business, and a training business and has combined annual revenues of about $30 million.[22] From the start, Weinzweig and Saginaw have been committed to excellent customer service, great food, and a commitment to people and community.[23]

As part of their commitment to people and community, Weinzweig and Saginaw have incorporated servant leadership into their personal leadership styles. As their business has grown and prospered, they have realized that increasing success means increasing responsibility to serve others. They strive to treat their employees as well as they treat their customers and give their employees opportunities for growth and development on the job. They have also realized that when their own needs or desires differ from what is best for their company, they should do what is best for the company.[24]

To this day, the cofounders encourage their employees to let them know how they can help them and what they can do for them. And given Zingerman's culture of mutual respect and trust, employees do not hesitate to communicate how their leaders can serve them in many and varied ways. For example, when Weinzweig visits the Zingerman's Roadhouse restaurant and the staff is very busy, they may ask him to help out by serving customers or cleaning off tables. As he indicates, "People give me assignments all the time. Sometimes I'm the note-taker. Sometimes I'm the cleaner-upper. . . . Sometimes I'm on my hands and knees wiping up what people spilled."[25]

Weinzweig and Saginaw also have a strong sense of commitment to serving the local community; Zingerman's founded the nonprofit organization Food Gatherers to eliminate hunger and distribute food to the needy, and Food Gatherers is now an independent nonprofit responsible for the Washtenaw County Food Bank with over 3,900 volunteers and a 15-member staff.[26] On Zingerman's 20th anniversary, 13 nonprofit community organizations in Ann Arbor erected a plaque next to Zingerman's Delicatessen with a dedication that read, "Thank you for feeding, sheltering, educating, uplifting, and inspiring an entire community."[27] Clearly, for Weinzweig and Saginaw, leadership does entail being of service to others.[28]

Leadership Styles across Cultures

Some evidence suggests that leadership styles vary not only among individuals but also among countries or cultures. Some research indicates that European managers tend to be more humanistic or people-oriented than both Japanese and American managers. The collectivistic culture in Japan places prime emphasis on the group rather than the individual, so the importance of individuals' own personalities, needs, and desires is minimized. Organizations in the United States tend to be very profit-oriented and thus tend to downplay the importance of individual employees' needs and desires. Many countries in Europe have a more individualistic perspective than Japan and a more humanistic perspective than the United States, and this may result in some European managers being more people-oriented than their Japanese or American counterparts. European managers, for example, tend to be reluctant to lay off employees, and when a layoff is absolutely necessary, they take careful steps to make it as painless as possible.[29]

Another cross-cultural difference occurs in time horizons. While managers in any one country often differ in their time horizons, there are also national differences. For example, U.S. organizations tend to have a short-run profit orientation, and thus U.S. managers' personal leadership styles emphasize short-run performance. Japanese organizations tend to have a long-run growth orientation, so Japanese managers' personal leadership styles emphasize long-run performance. Justus Mische, a personnel manager at the European organization Hoechst, suggests that "Europe, at least the big international firms in Europe, have a philosophy between the Japanese, long term, and the United States, short term."[30] Research on these and other global aspects of leadership is in its infancy; as it continues, more cultural differences in managers' personal leadership styles may be discovered.

Power: The Key to Leadership

No matter what one's leadership style, a key component of effective leadership is found in the *power* the leader has to affect other people's behavior and get them to act in certain ways.[31] There are several types of power: legitimate, reward, coercive, expert, and referent power (see Figure 10.1).[32] Effective leaders take steps to ensure that they have sufficient levels of each type and that they use the power they have in beneficial ways.

legitimate power The authority that a manager has by virtue of his or her position in an organization's hierarchy.

LEGITIMATE POWER Legitimate power is the authority a manager has by virtue of his or her position in an organization's hierarchy. Personal leadership style often influences how a manager exercises legitimate power. Take the case of Carol Loray, who is a first-line manager in a greeting card company and leads a group of 15 artists and designers. Loray has the legitimate power to hire new employees, assign projects to the artists and designers, monitor their work, and appraise their performance. She uses this power effectively. She always makes sure that her project assignments match the interests of her subordinates as much as possible so that they will enjoy their work.

Figure 10.1
Sources of Managerial Power

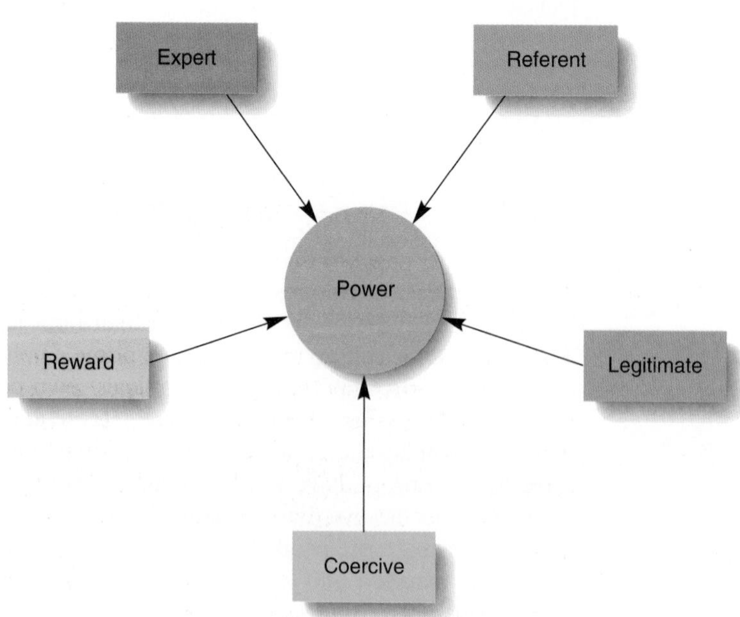

She monitors their work to make sure they are on track but does not engage in close supervision, which can hamper creativity. She makes sure her performance appraisals are developmental, providing concrete advice for areas where improvements could be made. Recently, Loray negotiated with her manager to increase her legitimate power so that now she can initiate and develop proposals for new card lines.

reward power The ability of a manager to give or withhold tangible and intangible rewards.

REWARD POWER Reward power is the ability of a manager to give or withhold tangible rewards (pay raises, bonuses, choice job assignments) and intangible rewards (verbal praise, a pat on the back, respect). As you learned in Chapter 9, members of an organization are motivated to perform at a high level by a variety of rewards. Being able to give or withhold rewards based on performance is a major source of power that allows managers to have a highly motivated workforce. Managers of salespeople in retail organizations like Neiman Marcus and Dillard's Department Stores, in car dealerships like General Motors and Ford, and in travel agencies like Liberty Travel and the Travel Company often use their reward power to motivate their subordinates. Subordinates in organizations such as these often receive commissions on whatever they sell and rewards for the quality of their customer service, which motivate them to do the best they can.

Effective managers use their reward power in such a way that subordinates feel that their rewards signal that they are doing a good job and their efforts are appreciated. Ineffective managers use rewards in a more controlling manner (wielding the "stick" instead of offering the "carrot") that signals to subordinates that the manager has the upper hand. Managers also can take steps to increase their reward power.

coercive power The ability of a manager to punish others.

COERCIVE POWER Coercive power is the ability of a manager to punish others. Punishment can range from verbal reprimands to reductions in pay or working hours to actual dismissal. In the previous chapter, we discussed how punishment can have negative side effects such as resentment and retaliation and should be used only when necessary (for example, to curtail a dangerous behavior). Managers who rely heavily on coercive power tend to be ineffective as leaders and sometimes even get fired themselves. William J. Fife is one example; he was fired from his position as CEO of Giddings and Lewis Inc., a manufacturer of factory equipment, because of his overreliance on coercive power. In meetings, Fife often verbally criticized, attacked, and embarrassed top managers. Realizing how destructive Fife's use of punishment was for them and the company, these managers complained to the board of directors, who, after a careful consideration of the issues, asked Fife to resign.[33]

Excessive use of coercive power seldom produces high performance and is questionable ethically. Sometimes it amounts to a form of mental abuse, robbing workers of their dignity and causing excessive levels of stress. Overuse of coercive power can even result in dangerous working conditions. Better results and, importantly, an ethical workplace that respects employee dignity can be obtained by using reward power.

expert power Power that is based on the special knowledge, skills, and expertise that a leader possesses.

EXPERT POWER Expert power is based on the special knowledge, skills, and expertise that a leader possesses. The nature of expert power varies, depending on the leader's level in the hierarchy. First-level and middle managers often have technical expertise relevant to the tasks that their subordinates perform. Their expert power gives them considerable influence over subordinates. Carol Loray has expert power: She is an artist herself and has drawn and designed some of her company's top-selling greeting cards. Judy McGrath, in the "Management Snapshot," has expert power from over 25 years' experience in the media industry, as well as from her efforts to stay attuned to pop culture through extensive networking, reading, and ever-ready openness for the new and the quirky.

Some top managers derive expert power from their technical expertise. Craig Barrett, chairman of the board of directors of Intel, has a PhD in materials science from Stanford University and is very knowledgeable about the ins and outs of Intel's business–producing semiconductors and microprocessors.[34] Similarly, Bill Gates, chairman of Microsoft, and CEO Steve Ballmer have expertise in software design; and Tachi Yamada, president of the Bill and Melinda Gates Foundation's Global Health Program, has an MD and was previously chairman of research and development at GlaxoSmithKline.[35] Many top-level managers, however, lack technical expertise and derive their expert power from their abilities as decision makers, planners, and strategists. Jack Welch, the former, well-known leader and CEO of General Electric, summed it up this way: "The basic thing that we at the top of the company know is that we don't know the business. What we have, I hope, is the ability to allocate resources, people, and dollars."[36]

Effective leaders take steps to ensure that they have an adequate amount of expert power to perform their leadership roles. They may obtain additional training or education in their fields, make sure they keep up to date with the latest developments and changes in technology, stay abreast of changes in their fields through involvement in professional associations, and read widely to be aware of momentous changes in the organization's task and general environments. Expert power tends to be best used in a guiding or coaching manner rather than in an arrogant, high-handed manner.

referent power Power that comes from subordinates' and coworkers' respect, admiration, and loyalty.

REFERENT POWER Referent power is more informal than the other kinds of power. Referent power is a function of the personal characteristics of a leader; it is the power that comes from subordinates' and coworkers' respect, admiration, and loyalty. Leaders who are likable and whom subordinates wish to use as a role model are especially likely to possess referent power, as is true of Judy McGrath in the "Management Snapshot."

In addition to being a valuable asset for top managers like McGrath, referent power can help first-line and middle managers be effective leaders as well. Sally Carruthers, for example, is the first-level manager of a group of secretaries in the finance department of a large state university. Carruthers's secretaries are known to be among the best in the university. Much of their willingness to go above and beyond the call of duty has been attributed to Carruthers's warm and caring nature, which makes each of them feel important and valued. Managers can take steps to increase their referent power, such as taking time to get to know their subordinates and showing interest in and concern for them.

Empowerment: An Ingredient in Modern Management

empowerment The expansion of employees' knowledge, tasks, and decision-making responsibilities.

More and more managers today are incorporating into their personal leadership styles an aspect that at first glance seems to be the opposite of being a leader. In Chapter 1, we described how empowerment–the process of giving employees at all levels the authority to make decisions, be responsible for their outcomes, improve quality, and cut costs–is becoming increasingly popular in organizations. When leaders empower their subordinates, the subordinates typically take over some of the responsibilities and authority that used to reside with the leader or manager, such as the right to reject parts that do not meet quality standards, the right to check one's own work, and the right to schedule work activities. Empowered subordinates are given the power to make some of the decisions that their leaders or supervisors used to make.

Empowerment might seem to be the opposite of effective leadership because managers are allowing subordinates to take a more active role in leading themselves. In actuality, however, empowerment can contribute to effective leadership for several reasons:

- Empowerment increases a manager's ability to get things done because the manager has the support and help of subordinates who may have special knowledge of work tasks.
- Empowerment often increases workers' involvement, motivation, and commitment, and this helps ensure that they are working toward organizational goals.
- Empowerment gives managers more time to concentrate on their pressing concerns because they spend less time on day-to-day supervisory activities.

Effective managers like Judy McGrath realize the benefits of empowerment. The personal leadership style of managers who empower subordinates often entails developing subordinates' ability to make good decisions as well as being their guide, coach, and source of inspiration. Empowerment is a popular trend in the United States at companies as diverse as United Parcel Service (a package delivery company) and Coram Healthcare Corporation (a provider of medical equipment and services) and is a part of servant leadership. Empowerment is also taking off around the world.[37] For instance, companies in South Korea (such as Samsung, Hyundai, and Daewoo), in which decision making typically was centralized with the founding families, are now empowering managers at lower levels to make decisions.[38]

Trait and Behavior Models of Leadership

Leading is such an important process in all organizations–nonprofit organizations, government agencies, and schools, as well as for-profit corporations–that it has been researched for decades. Early approaches to leadership, called the *trait model* and the *behavior model,* sought to determine what effective leaders are like as people and what they do that makes them so effective.

LO2 Identify the traits that show the strongest relationship to leadership, the behaviors leaders engage in, and the limitations of the trait and behavior models of leadership.

The Trait Model

The trait model of leadership focused on identifying the personal characteristics that cause effective leadership. Researchers thought effective leaders must have certain personal qualities that set them apart from ineffective leaders and from people who never become leaders. Decades of research (beginning in the 1930s) and hundreds of studies indicate that certain personal characteristics do appear to be associated with effective leadership. (See Table 10.1 for a list of these.)[39] Notice that although this model is called the "trait" model, some of the personal characteristics that it identifies are not personality traits per se but, rather, are concerned with a leader's skills, abilities, knowledge, and expertise. As the "Management Snapshot" shows, Judy McGrath certainly appears to possess many of these characteristics (such as intelligence, knowledge and expertise, self-confidence, high energy, and integrity and honesty). Leaders who do not possess these traits may be ineffective.

Traits alone are not the key to understanding leader effectiveness, however. Some effective leaders do not possess all of these traits, and some leaders who do possess them are not effective in their leadership roles. This lack of a consistent relationship between leader traits and leader effectiveness led researchers to shift their attention away from traits and to search for new explanations for effective leadership. Rather

Table 10.1
Traits and Personal Characteristics Related to Effective Leadership

Trait	Description
Intelligence	Helps managers understand complex issues and solve problems
Knowledge and expertise	Helps managers make good decisions and discover ways to increase efficiency and effectiveness
Dominance	Helps managers influence their subordinates to achieve organizational goals
Self-confidence	Contributes to managers' effectively influencing subordinates and persisting when faced with obstacles or difficulties
High energy	Helps managers deal with the many demands they face
Tolerance for stress	Helps managers deal with uncertainty and make difficult decisions
Integrity and honesty	Helps managers behave ethically and earn their subordinates' trust and confidence
Maturity	Helps managers avoid acting selfishly, control their feelings, and admit when they have made a mistake

than focusing on what leaders are like (the traits they possess), researchers began looking at what effective leaders actually do–in other words, at the behaviors that allow effective leaders to influence their subordinates to achieve group and organizational goals.

The Behavior Model

After extensive study in the 1940s and 1950s, researchers at The Ohio State University identified two basic kinds of leader behaviors that many leaders in the United States, Germany, and other countries engaged in to influence their subordinates: *consideration* and *initiating structure*.[40]

consideration Behavior indicating that a manager trusts, respects, and cares about subordinates.

CONSIDERATION Leaders engage in **consideration** when they show their subordinates that they trust, respect, and care about them. Managers who truly look out for the well-being of their subordinates, and do what they can to help subordinates feel good and enjoy their work, perform consideration behaviors. In the "Management Snapshot," Judy McGrath engages in consideration when she listens to employees and fosters an inclusive, nurturing culture at MTV Networks.

initiating structure Behavior that managers engage in to ensure that work gets done, subordinates perform their jobs acceptably, and the organization is efficient and effective.

INITIATING STRUCTURE Leaders engage in **initiating structure** when they take steps to make sure that work gets done, subordinates perform their jobs acceptably, and the organization is efficient and effective. Assigning tasks to individuals or work groups, letting subordinates know what is expected of them, deciding how work should be done, making schedules, encouraging adherence to rules and regulations, and motivating subordinates to do a good job are all examples of initiating structure.[41] Michael Teckel, the manager of an upscale store selling imported men's and women's shoes in a midwestern city, engages in initiating structure when he establishes weekly work, lunch, and break schedules to ensure that the store has enough salespeople on the floor. Teckel also initiates structure when he discusses the latest shoe designs with his subordinates so that they are knowledgeable with customers, when he encourages adherence to the store's refund and exchange policies, and when he encourages his staff to provide high-quality customer service and to avoid a hard-sell approach.

You might expect that effective leaders and managers would perform both kinds of behaviors, but research has found that this is not necessarily the case. The relationship between performance of consideration and initiating-structure behaviors and leader effectiveness is not clear-cut. Some leaders are effective even when they do not perform consideration or initiating-structure behaviors, and some leaders are ineffective even when they do perform both kinds of behaviors. Like the trait model of leadership, the behavior model alone cannot explain leader effectiveness. Realizing this, researchers began building more complicated models of leadership, models focused not only on the leader and what he or she does but also on the situation or context in which leadership occurs.

Contingency Models of Leadership

LO3 Explain how contingency models of leadership enhance our understanding of effective leadership and management in organizations.

Simply possessing certain traits or performing certain behaviors does not ensure that a manager will be an effective leader in all situations calling for leadership. Some managers who seem to possess the "right" traits and perform the "right" behaviors turn out to be ineffective leaders. Managers lead in a wide variety of situations and organizations and have various kinds of subordinates performing diverse tasks in a multiplicity of environmental contexts. Given the wide variety of situations in which leadership occurs, what makes a manager an effective leader in one situation (such as certain traits or behaviors) is not necessarily what that manager needs to be equally effective in a different situation. An effective army general might not be an effective university president; an effective manager of a restaurant might not be an effective manager of a clothing store; an effective coach of a football team might not be an effective manager of a fitness center; and an effective first-line manager in a manufacturing company might not be an effective middle manager. The traits or behaviors that may contribute to a manager's being an effective leader in one situation might actually result in the same manager's being an ineffective leader in another situation.

Contingency models of leadership take into account the situation or context within which leadership occurs. According to contingency models, whether or not a manager is an effective leader is the result of the interplay between what the manager is like, what he or she does, and the situation in which leadership takes place. Contingency models propose that whether a leader who possesses certain traits or performs certain behaviors is effective depends on, or is contingent on, the situation or context. In this section, we discuss three prominent contingency models developed to shed light on what makes managers effective leaders: Fred Fiedler's contingency model, Robert House's path-goal theory, and the leader substitutes model. As you will see, these leadership models are complementary; each focuses on a somewhat different aspect of effective leadership in organizations.

Fiedler's Contingency Model

Fred E. Fiedler was among the first leadership researchers to acknowledge that effective leadership is contingent on, or depends on, the characteristics of the leader *and* of the situation. Fiedler's contingency model helps explain why a manager may be an effective leader in one situation and ineffective in another; it also suggests which kinds of managers are likely to be most effective in which situations.[42]

LEADER STYLE As with the trait approach, Fiedler hypothesized that personal characteristics can influence leader effectiveness. He used the term *leader style* to refer to a manager's characteristic approach to leadership and identified two basic leader styles: *relationship-oriented* and *task-oriented.* All managers can be described as having one style or the other.

relationship-oriented leaders Leaders whose primary concern is to develop good relationships with their subordinates and to be liked by them.

Relationship-oriented leaders are primarily concerned with developing good relationships with their subordinates and being liked by them. Relationship-oriented managers focus on having high-quality interpersonal relationships with subordinates. This does not mean, however, that the job does not get done when such leaders are at the helm. But it does mean that the quality of interpersonal relationships with subordinates is a prime concern for relationship-oriented leaders. Lawrence Fish, for example, is the chairman of Citizens Financial Group Inc. of Providence, Rhode Island, which has tripled its assets in the last three years. As the top manager who helped to engineer this rapid growth, Fish has never lost sight of the importance of good relationships and personally writes a thank-you note to at least one of his subordinates each day.[43]

task-oriented leaders Leaders whose primary concern is to ensure that subordinates perform at a high level.

Task-oriented leaders are primarily concerned with ensuring that subordinates perform at a high level and focus on task accomplishment. Some task-oriented leaders, like the top managers of the family-owned C. R. England Refrigerated Trucking Company based in Salt Lake City, Utah, go so far as to closely measure and evaluate performance on a weekly basis to ensure subordinates are performing as well as they can.[44]

leader–member relations The extent to which followers like, trust, and are loyal to their leader; a determinant of how favorable a situation is for leading.

task structure The extent to which the work to be performed is clear-cut so that a leader's subordinates know what needs to be accomplished and how to go about doing it; a determinant of how favorable a situation is for leading.

SITUATIONAL CHARACTERISTICS According to Fiedler, leadership style is an enduring characteristic; managers cannot change their style, nor can they adopt different styles in different kinds of situations. With this in mind, Fiedler identified three situational characteristics that are important determinants of how favorable a situation is for leading: leader–member relations, task structure, and position power. When a situation is favorable for leading, it is relatively easy for a manager to influence subordinates so that they perform at a high level and contribute to organizational efficiency and effectiveness. In a situation unfavorable for leading, it is much more difficult for a manager to exert influence.

LEADER–MEMBER RELATIONS The first situational characteristic that Fiedler described, **leader–member relations,** is the extent to which followers like, trust, and are loyal to their leader. Situations are more favorable for leading when leader–member relations are good.

Developing good relations with employees can make the "situation" more favorable for leading.

TASK STRUCTURE The second situational characteristic that Fiedler described, **task structure,** is the extent to which the work to be performed is clear-cut so that a leader's subordinates know what needs to be accomplished and how to go about doing it. When task structure is high, the situation is favorable for leading. When task structure is low, goals may be vague, subordinates may be unsure of what they should be doing or how they should do it, and the situation is unfavorable for leading.

Task structure was low for Geraldine Laybourne when she was a top manager at Nickelodeon, the children's television network. It was never precisely clear what would appeal to her young viewers, whose tastes can change dramatically, or how to motivate her subordinates to come up with creative and novel ideas.[45] In contrast, Herman Mashaba, founder of Black Like Me, a hair care products company based in South Africa, seemed to have relatively high task structure when he started his company. His company's goals were to produce and sell inexpensive hair care products to native Africans, and managers accomplish these goals by using simple yet appealing packaging and distributing the products through neighborhood beauty salons.[46]

position power The amount of legitimate, reward, and coercive power that a leader has by virtue of his or her position in an organization; a determinant of how favorable a situation is for leading.

POSITION POWER The third situational characteristic that Fiedler described, **position power**, is the amount of legitimate, reward, and coercive power a leader has by virtue of his or her position in an organization. Leadership situations are more favorable for leading when position power is strong.

COMBINING LEADER STYLE AND THE SITUATION By taking all possible combinations of good and poor leader–member relations, high and low task structure, and strong and weak position power, Fiedler identified eight leadership situations, which vary in their favorability for leading (see Figure 10.2). After extensive research, he determined that relationship-oriented leaders are most effective in moderately favorable situations (IV, V, VI, and VII in Figure 10.2) and task-oriented leaders are most effective in situations that are either very favorable (I, II, and III) or very unfavorable (VIII).

PUTTING THE CONTINGENCY MODEL INTO PRACTICE Recall that, according to Fiedler, leader style is an enduring characteristic that managers cannot change. This suggests that to be effective, either managers need to be placed in leadership situations that fit their style or situations need to be changed to suit the managers. Situations can be changed, for example, by giving a manager more position power or taking steps to increase task structure, such as by clarifying goals.

Take the case of Mark Compton, a relationship-oriented leader employed by a small construction company, who was in a very unfavorable situation and having a rough time leading his construction crew. His subordinates did not trust him to look out for their well-being (poor leader–member relations); the construction jobs he supervised tended to be novel and complex (low task structure); and he had no control over

Figure 10.2
Fielder's Contingency Theory of Leadership

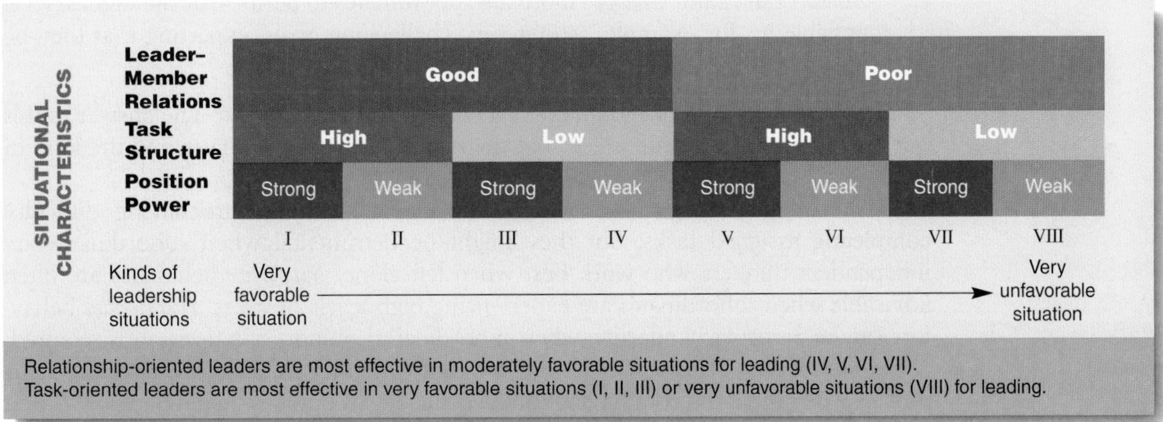

Relationship-oriented leaders are most effective in moderately favorable situations for leading (IV, V, VI, VII).
Task-oriented leaders are most effective in very favorable situations (I, II, III) or very unfavorable situations (VIII) for leading.

the rewards and disciplinary actions his subordinates received (weak position power). Recognizing the need to improve matters, Compton's supervisor gave him the power to reward crew members with bonuses and overtime work as he saw fit and to discipline crew members for poor-quality work and unsafe on-the-job behavior. As his leadership situation improved to moderately favorable, so too did Compton's effectiveness as a leader and the performance of his crew.

Research studies tend to support some aspects of Fiedler's model but also suggest that, like most theories, it needs some modifications.[47] Some researchers have questioned what the least-preferred coworker scale (used to measure leader style) really measures. Others find fault with the model's premise that leaders cannot alter their styles. That is, it is likely that at least some leaders can diagnose the situation they are in and, when their style is inappropriate for the situation, modify their style so that it is more in line with what the leadership situation calls for.

House's Path-Goal Theory

path-goal theory A contingency model of leadership proposing that leaders can motivate subordinates by identifying their desired outcomes, rewarding them for high performance and the attainment of work goals with these desired outcomes, and clarifying for them the paths leading to the attainment of work goals.

In what he called **path-goal theory,** leadership researcher Robert House focused on what leaders can do to motivate their subordinates to achieve group and organizational goals.[48] The premise of path-goal theory is that effective leaders motivate subordinates to achieve goals by (1) clearly identifying the outcomes that subordinates are trying to obtain from the workplace, (2) rewarding subordinates with these outcomes for high performance and the attainment of work goals, and (3) clarifying for subordinates the *paths* leading to the attainment of work *goals*. Path-goal theory is a contingency model because it proposes that the steps managers should take to motivate subordinates depend on both the nature of the subordinates and the type of work they do.

Path-goal theory identifies four kinds of leadership behaviors that motivate subordinates:

- *Directive behaviors* are similar to initiating structure and include setting goals, assigning tasks, showing subordinates how to complete tasks, and taking concrete steps to improve performance.
- *Supportive behaviors* are similar to consideration and include expressing concern for subordinates and looking out for their best interests.
- *Participative behaviors* give subordinates a say in matters and decisions that affect them.
- *Achievement-oriented behaviors* motivate subordinates to perform at the highest level possible by, for example, setting very challenging goals, expecting that they be met, and believing in subordinates' capabilities.

Which of these behaviors should managers use to lead effectively? The answer to this question depends, or is contingent on, the nature of the subordinates and the kind of work they do.

Directive behaviors may be beneficial when subordinates are having difficulty completing assigned tasks, but they might be detrimental when subordinates are independent thinkers who work best when left alone. *Supportive* behaviors are often advisable when subordinates are experiencing high levels of stress. *Participative* behaviors can be particularly effective when subordinates' support of a decision is required. *Achievement-oriented* behaviors may increase motivation levels of highly capable subordinates who are bored from having too few challenges, but they might backfire if used with subordinates who are already pushed to their limit.

The Leader Substitutes Model

leadership substitute A characteristic of a subordinate or of a situation or context that acts in place of the influence of a leader and makes leadership unnecessary.

The leader substitutes model suggests that leadership is sometimes unnecessary because substitutes for leadership are present. A **leadership substitute** is something that acts in place of the influence of a leader and makes leadership unnecessary. This model suggests that under certain conditions managers do not have to play a leadership role–that members of an organization sometimes can perform at a high level without a manager exerting influence over them.[49] The leader substitutes model is a contingency model because it suggests that in some situations leadership is unnecessary.

Take the case of David Cotsonas, who teaches English at a foreign-language school in Cyprus, an island in the Mediterranean Sea. Cotsonas is fluent in Greek, English, and French; is an excellent teacher; and is highly motivated. Many of his students are businesspeople who have some rudimentary English skills and wish to increase their fluency to be able to conduct more of their business in English. He enjoys not only teaching them English but also learning about the work they do, and he often keeps in touch with his students after they finish his classes. Cotsonas meets with the director of the school twice a year to discuss semiannual class schedules and enrollments.

With practically no influence from a leader, Cotsonas is a highly motivated top performer at the school. In his situation, leadership is unnecessary because substitutes for leadership are present. Cotsonas's teaching expertise, his motivation, and his enjoyment of his work all are substitutes for the influence of a leader–in this case, the school's director. If the school's director were to try to exert influence over the way Cotsonas goes about performing his job, Cotsonas would probably resent this infringement on his autonomy, and it is unlikely that his performance would improve because he is already one of the school's best teachers.

As in Cotsonas's case, *characteristics of subordinates*–such as their skills, abilities, experience, knowledge, and motivation–can be substitutes for leadership.[50] *Characteristics of the situation or context*–such as the extent to which the work is interesting and enjoyable–also can be substitutes. When work is interesting and enjoyable, as it is for Cotsonas, jobholders do not need to be coaxed into performing because performing is rewarding in its own right. Similarly, when managers *empower* their subordinates or use *self-managed work teams,* (discussed in Chapter 11), the need for leadership influence from a manager is decreased because team members manage themselves.

Substitutes for leadership can increase organizational efficiency and effectiveness because they free up some of managers' valuable time and allow managers to focus their efforts on discovering new ways to improve organizational effectiveness. The director of the language school, for example, was able to spend much of his time making arrangements to open a second school in Rhodes, an island in the Aegean Sea, because of the presence of leadership substitutes, not only in the case of Cotsonas but in that of most of the other teachers at the school as well.

Bringing It All Together

Effective leadership in organizations occurs when managers take steps to lead in a way that is appropriate for the situation or context in which leadership occurs and for the subordinates who are being led. The three contingency models of leadership just discussed help managers focus on the necessary ingredients for effective leadership. They are complementary in that each one looks at the leadership question from a different angle. Fiedler's contingency model explores how a manager's leadership style needs to be matched to that person's leadership situation for maximum effectiveness. House's path-goal theory focuses on how managers should motivate subordinates and

Table 10.2
Contingency Models of Leadership

Model	Focus	Key Contingencies
Fiedler's contingency model	Describes two leader styles, relationship-oriented and task-oriented, and the kinds of situations in which each kind of leader will be most effective	Whether or not a relationship-oriented or a task-oriented leader is effective is contingent on the situation
House's path-goal theory	Describes how effective leaders motivate their followers	The behaviors that managers should engage in to be effective leaders are contingent on the nature of the subordinates and the work they do
Leader substitutes model	Describes when leadership is unnecessary	Whether or not leadership is necessary for subordinates to perform highly is contingent on characteristics of the subordinates and the situation

describes the specific kinds of behaviors that managers can engage in to have a highly motivated workforce. The leadership substitutes model alerts managers to the fact that sometimes they do not need to exert influence over subordinates and thus can free up their time for other important activities. Table 10.2 recaps these three contingency models of leadership.

Transformational Leadership

LO4 Describe what transformational leadership is, and explain how managers can engage in it.

Time and time again, throughout business history, certain leaders seem to literally transform their organizations, making sweeping changes to revitalize and renew operations. For example, when Sue Nokes became senior vice president of sales and customer service at T-Mobile USA in 2002, the quality of T-Mobile's customer service was lower than that of its major competitors, on average; 12% of employees were absent on any day; and annual employee turnover was over 100%.[51] T-Mobile USA is a subsidiary of Deutsche Telekom, has 36,000 employees, and provides wireless voice, messaging, and data services.[52] When Nokes arrived at T-Mobile, valuable employees were quitting their jobs and customers weren't receiving high-quality service; neither employees nor customers were satisfied with their experience with the company.[53] By the late 2000s, T-Mobile was regularly receiving highest rankings for customer care and satisfaction in the wireless category by J. D. Power and Associates, absence and turnover rates substantially declined, and around 80% of employees indicated that they were satisfied with their jobs.[54] In fact, when Nokes visits call centers, it is not uncommon for employees to greet her with cheers and accolades.[55]

transformational leadership Leadership that makes subordinates aware of the importance of their jobs and performance to the organization and aware of their own needs for personal growth and that motivates subordinates to work for the good of the organization.

Nokes literally transformed T-Mobile into a company in which satisfied employees provide excellent service to customers.[56] When managers have such dramatic effects on their subordinates and on an organization as a whole, they are engaging in transformational leadership. **Transformational leadership** occurs when managers change (or transform) their subordinates in three important ways:[57]

1. *Transformational managers make subordinates aware of how important their jobs are for the organization and how necessary it is for them to perform those jobs as best they can so that the organization*

Sue Nokes transformed T-Mobile into a company in which satisfied employees provide excellent service to customers.

can attain its goals. At T-Mobile, Nokes visited call centers, conducted focus groups, and had town hall meetings to find out what employees and customers were unhappy with and the steps she could take to improve matters.[58] Her philosophy is that when employees are satisfied with their jobs and view their work as important, they are much more likely to provide high-quality customer service. She made employees aware of how important their jobs were by the many steps she took to improve their working conditions, ranging from providing them with their own workspaces to substantially raising their salaries.[59] She emphasized the importance of providing excellent customer service by periodically asking employees what is working well and what is not working well, asking them what steps can be taken to improve problem areas, and taking actions to ensure that employees are able to provide excellent customer service. Nokes also instituted a performance measurement system to track performance in key areas such as quality of service and speed of problem resolution.[60] She sincerely tells employees that "You are No. 1, and the customer is why."[61]

2. *Transformational managers make their subordinates aware of the subordinates' own needs for personal growth, development, and accomplishment.* Nokes made T-Mobile's employees aware of their own needs in this regard by transforming training and development at T-Mobile and increasing opportunities for promotions to more responsible positions. Employees now spend over 130 hours per year in training and development programs and team meetings. Nokes also instituted a promote-from-within policy, and around 80% of promotions are given to current employees.[62]
3. *Transformational managers motivate their subordinates to work for the good of the organization as a whole, not just for their own personal gain or benefit.* Nokes emphasizes that employees should be focused on what matters to customers, coworkers, and T-Mobile as a whole. She lets employees know that when they are unnecessarily absent from their jobs, they are not doing right by their coworkers. And she emphasizes the need to try to resolve customer problems in a single phone call so customers can get on with their busy lives.[63]

When managers transform their subordinates in these three ways, subordinates trust the managers, are highly motivated, and help the organization achieve its goals. How do managers such as Nokes transform subordinates and produce dramatic effects in their organizations? There are at least three ways in which transformational leaders can influence their followers: by being a charismatic leader, by intellectually stimulating subordinates, and by engaging in developmental consideration (see Table 10.3).

charismatic leader An enthusiastic, self-confident leader who is able to clearly communicate his or her vision of how good things could be.

Being a Charismatic Leader

Transformational managers such as Nokes are **charismatic leaders.** They have a vision of how good things could be in their work groups and organizations that is in contrast with the status quo. Their vision usually entails dramatic improvements in group and organizational performance as a result of changes in the organization's structure,

Table 10.3
Transformational Leadership

Transformational managers
- Are charismatic.
- Intellectually stimulate subordinates.
- Engage in developmental consideration.

Subordinates of transformational managers
- Have increased awareness of the importance of their jobs and high performance.
- Are aware of their own needs for growth, development, and accomplishment.
- Work for the good of the organization and not just their own personal benefit.

culture, strategy, decision making, and other critical processes and factors. This vision paves the way for gaining a competitive advantage. From the "Management Snapshot," it is clear that part of Judy McGrath's vision for MTV Networks is increasing its digital offerings and transforming MTV into a truly digital company.

Charismatic leaders are excited and enthusiastic about their vision and clearly communicate it to their subordinates, as does Judy McGrath. The excitement, enthusiasm, and self-confidence of a charismatic leader contribute to the leader's being able to inspire followers to enthusiastically support his or her vision.[64] People often think of charismatic leaders or managers as being "larger than life." The essence of charisma, however, is having a vision and enthusiastically communicating it to others. Thus, managers who appear to be quiet and earnest can also be charismatic.

Stimulating Subordinates Intellectually

Transformational managers openly share information with their subordinates so that they are aware of problems and the need for change. The manager causes subordinates to view problems in their groups and throughout the organization from a different perspective, consistent with the manager's vision. Whereas in the past subordinates might not have been aware of some problems, may have viewed problems as a "management issue" beyond their concern, or may have viewed problems as insurmountable, the transformational manager's **intellectual stimulation** leads subordinates to view problems as challenges that they can and will meet and conquer. The manager engages and empowers subordinates to take personal responsibility for helping solve problems, as does Nokes at T-Mobile.[65]

intellectual stimulation Behavior a leader engages in to make followers be aware of problems and view these problems in new ways, consistent with the leader's vision.

Engaging in Developmental Consideration

When managers engage in **developmental consideration,** they not only perform the consideration behaviors described earlier, such as demonstrating true concern for the well-being of subordinates, but go one step further. The manager goes out of his or her way to support and encourage subordinates, giving them opportunities to enhance their skills and capabilities and to grow and excel on the job.[66] As mentioned earlier, Nokes does this in numerous ways. In fact, after she had first met with employees in a call center in Albuquerque, New Mexico, Karen Viola, the manager of the call center, said, "Everyone came out crying. The people said that they had never felt so inspired in their lives, and that they had never met with any leader at that level who [they felt] cared."[67]

developmental consideration Behavior a leader engages in to support and encourage followers and help them develop and grow on the job.

All organizations, no matter how large or small, successful or unsuccessful, can benefit when their managers engage in transformational leadership. Moreover, while the benefits of transformational leadership are often most apparent when an organization is in trouble, transformational leadership can be an enduring approach to leadership, leading to long-run organizational effectiveness.

The Distinction between Transformational and Transactional Leadership

transactional leadership Leadership that motivates subordinates by rewarding them for high performance and reprimanding them for low performance.

Transformational leadership is often contrasted with transactional leadership. In **transactional leadership,** managers use their reward and coercive powers to encourage high performance. When managers reward high performers, reprimand or otherwise punish low performers, and motivate subordinates by reinforcing desired behaviors and extinguishing or punishing undesired ones, they are engaging in transactional leadership.[68] Managers who effectively influence their subordinates to achieve goals, yet do not seem to be making the kind of dramatic changes that are part of transformational leadership, are engaging in transactional leadership.

Many transformational leaders engage in transactional leadership. They reward subordinates for a job well done and notice and respond to substandard performance. But they also have their eyes on the bigger picture of how much better things could be in their organizations, how much more their subordinates are capable of achieving, and how important it is to treat their subordinates with respect and to help them reach their full potential.

Research has found that when leaders engage in transformational leadership, their subordinates tend to have higher levels of job satisfaction and performance.[69] Additionally, subordinates of transformational leaders may be more likely to trust their leaders and their organizations and feel that they are being fairly treated, and this, in turn, may positively influence their work motivation (see Chapter 9).[70]

Gender and Leadership

LO5 Characterize the relationship between gender and leadership and explain how emotional intelligence may contribute to leadership effectiveness.

The increasing number of women entering the ranks of management, as well as the problems some women face in their efforts to be hired as managers or promoted into management positions, has prompted researchers to explore the relationship between gender and leadership. Although there are relatively more women in management positions today than there were 10 years ago, there are still relatively few women in top management and, in some organizations, even in middle management.

When women do advance to top-management positions, special attention often is focused on them and the fact that they are women. For example, women CEOs of large companies are still very rare; those who make it to the very top post, such as Meg Whitman, former CEO of eBay, Judy McGrath of MTV Networks, and Andrea Jung of Avon, are very salient. As business writer Linda Tischler puts it, "In a workplace where women CEOs of major companies are so scarce . . . they can be identified, like rock stars, by first name only."[71] While women have certainly made inroads into leadership positions in organizations, they continue to be very underrepresented in top leadership posts. For example, as was indicated in Chapter 3, while around 50.5% of the employees in managerial and professional jobs in the United States are women, only about 15.4% of corporate officers in the *Fortune* 500 are women, and only 6.7% of the top earners are women.[72]

A widespread stereotype of women is that they are nurturing, supportive, and concerned with interpersonal relations. Men are stereotypically viewed as being directive and focused on task accomplishment. Such stereotypes suggest that women tend to be more relationship-oriented as managers and engage in more consideration behaviors, whereas men are more task-oriented and engage in more initiating-structure behaviors. Does the behavior of actual male and female managers bear out these stereotypes? Do women managers lead in different ways than men do? Are male or female managers more effective as leaders?

Research suggests that male and female managers who have leadership positions in organizations behave in similar ways.[73] Women do not engage in more consideration than men, and men do not engage in more initiating structure than women. Research does suggest, however, that leadership style may vary between women and men. Women tend to be somewhat more participative as leaders than are men, involving subordinates in decision making and seeking their input.[74] Male managers tend to be less participative than are female managers, making more decisions on their own and wanting to do things their own way. Moreover, research suggests that men tend to be harsher when they punish their subordinates than do women.[75]

There are at least two reasons why female managers may be more participative as leaders than are male managers.[76] First, subordinates may try to resist the influence of female managers more than they do the influence of male managers. Some subordinates may never have reported to a woman before; some may incorrectly see a management role as being more appropriate for a man than for a woman; and some may just resist being led by a woman. To overcome this resistance and encourage subordinates' trust and respect, women managers may adopt a participative approach.

A second reason why female managers may be more participative is that they sometimes have better interpersonal skills than male managers.[77] A participative approach to leadership requires high levels of interaction and involvement between a manager and his or her subordinates, sensitivity to subordinates' feelings, and the ability to make decisions that may be unpopular with subordinates but necessary for goal attainment. Good interpersonal skills may help female managers have the effective interactions with their subordinates that are crucial to a participative approach.[78] To the extent that male managers have more difficulty managing interpersonal relationships, they may shy away from the high levels of interaction with subordinates necessary for true participation.

The key finding from research on leader behaviors, however, is that male and female managers do *not* differ significantly in their propensities to perform different leader behaviors. Even though they may be more participative, female managers do not engage in more consideration or less initiating structure than male managers.

Perhaps a question even more important than whether male and female managers differ in the leadership behaviors they perform is whether they differ in effectiveness. Consistent with the findings for leader behaviors, research suggests that across different kinds of organizational settings, male and female managers tend to be *equally effective* as leaders.[79] Thus, there is no logical basis for stereotypes favoring male managers and leaders or for the existence of the "glass ceiling" (an invisible barrier that seems to prevent women from advancing as far as they should in some organizations). Because women and men are equally effective as leaders, the increasing number of women in the workforce should result in a larger pool of highly qualified candidates for management positions in organizations, ultimately enhancing organizational effectiveness.[80]

Emotional Intelligence and Leadership

Do the moods and emotions leaders experience on the job influence their behavior and effectiveness as leaders? Research suggests that this is likely to be the case. For example, one study found that when store managers experienced positive moods at work, salespeople in their stores provided high-quality customer service and were less likely to quit.[81] Another study found that groups whose leaders experienced positive moods had better coordination, while groups whose leaders experienced negative moods exerted more effort; members of groups with leaders in positive moods also tended to experience more positive moods themselves; and members of groups with leaders in negative moods tended to experience more negative moods.[82]

Moreover, a leader's level of emotional intelligence (see Chapter 2) may play a particularly important role in leadership effectiveness.[83] For example, emotional intelligence may help leaders develop a vision for their organizations, motivate their subordinates to commit to this vision, and energize them to enthusiastically work to achieve this vision. Moreover, emotional intelligence may enable leaders to develop a significant identity for their organization and instill high levels of trust and cooperation throughout the organization, while maintaining the flexibility needed to respond to changing conditions.[84]

Emotional intelligence also plays a crucial role in how leaders relate to and deal with their followers, particularly when it comes to encouraging followers to be creative.[85] Creativity in organizations is an emotion-laden process, as it often entails challenging the status quo, being willing to take risks and accept and learn from failures, and doing much hard work to bring creative ideas to fruition in terms of new products, services, or procedures and processes when uncertainty is bound to be high.[86] Leaders who are high on emotional intelligence are more likely to understand all the emotions surrounding creative endeavors, to be able to awaken and support the creative pursuits of their followers, and to provide the kind of support that enables creativity to flourish in organizations.[87]

Leaders, like people everywhere, sometimes make mistakes. Emotional intelligence may also help leaders respond appropriately when they realize that they have made a mistake. Recognizing, admitting, and learning from mistakes can be especially important for entrepreneurs who start their own businesses, as profiled in the following "Focus on Diversity."

FOCUS ON DIVERSITY

Admitting a Mistake Helps a Small-Business Leader

Things seemed to be going well for Maureen Borzacchiello, CEO of Creative Display Solutions, located in Garden City, New York.[88] She founded her small business in 2001; it provides displays, graphics, and exhibits for use in trade shows and at events for companies ranging from American Express, FedEx, and General Electric to JetBlue Airways, AIG, and The Weather Channel.[89] Her company was growing, and she had received an award from the nonprofit organization Count Me In for Women's Economic Independence.[90]

Small Business

However, in 2006 she realized that she had overextended her business financially. A large investment in inventory coupled with a sizable lease commitment, the need for office space renovations, the purchase of new furniture, and the addition of three new employees brought her to the point where she lacked the cash on hand to pay her employees their regular salaries. When she had made these decisions, she thought she and her husband (who also works in the company) would be able to generate the revenues to cover the expenditures. But her brother-in-law unexpectedly passed away, and their involvement in family matters meant that they weren't able to get new accounts as quickly as she had thought they would.[91]

By being honest and open with her employees, Maureen Borzacchiello has gained their commitment and support.

Still confident that if she could get through this tough period, she would be able to get her business back on track, Borzacchiello decided to be honest with her employees about the company's current financial problems, why they occurred, and how she would strive to prevent such problems in the future. She met with her employees and told them, "All I can tell you is that I apologize. . . . We were so focused on accelerating growth that I didn't see it coming."[92] She also admitted that she needed to have a better understanding of her company's financial situation and cash flow on a day-to-day basis, reassured employees that the company would be back on square footing in two to three months, and promised that she would pay much more attention to ongoing financial performance and cash flow in the future.[93]

Borzacchiello also told employees that she and her husband would take no money out of the business for their own salaries until the financial problems were resolved. By being honest and open with employees, Borzacchiello gained their commitment and support. All employees decided to work shorter hours, and two employees were willing to have their hourly pay rates cut.[94] True to her promise, within two months, all employees were able to return to their regular work hours; and by the beginning of 2007, Creative Display Solutions had over $1 million in revenues (which was more than double its revenues at the time of the financial problems).[95] To this day, Creative Display Solutions remains a profitable business; and by 2008, its list of clients included more than 500 companies.[96] Clearly, Borzacchiello effectively handled the temporary crisis her company faced by admitting and apologizing for her mistake and being open and honest with employees about her company's future prospects.[97]

Summary and Review

THE NATURE OF LEADERSHIP Leadership is the process by which a person exerts influence over other people and inspires, motivates, and directs their activities to help achieve group or organizational goals. Leaders are able to influence others because they possess power. The five types of power available to managers are legitimate power, reward power, coercive power, expert power, and referent power. Many managers are using empowerment as a tool to increase their effectiveness as leaders. **[LO1]**

TRAIT AND BEHAVIOR MODELS OF LEADERSHIP The trait model of leadership describes personal characteristics or traits that contribute to effective leadership. However, some managers who possess these traits are not effective leaders, and some managers who do not possess all the traits are nevertheless effective leaders. The behavior model of leadership describes two kinds of behavior that most leaders engage in: consideration and initiating structure. **[LO2]**

CONTINGENCY MODELS OF LEADERSHIP Contingency models take into account the complexity surrounding leadership and the role of the situation in determining whether a manager is an effective or ineffective leader. Fiedler's contingency model explains why managers may be effective leaders in one situation and ineffective in another. According to Fiedler's model, relationship-oriented leaders are most effective in situations that are moderately favorable for leading, and task-oriented leaders are most effective in situations that are very favorable or very unfavorable for leading. House's path-goal theory describes how effective managers motivate their subordinates by determining what outcomes their subordinates want, rewarding subordinates with these outcomes when they achieve their goals and perform at a high level, and clarifying the paths to goal attainment. Managers can engage in four different kinds of behaviors to motivate subordinates: directive behaviors, supportive behaviors, participative behaviors, or achievement-oriented behaviors. The leader substitutes model suggests that sometimes managers do not have to play a leadership role because their subordinates perform at a high level without the manager having to exert influence over them. **[LO3]**

TRANSFORMATIONAL LEADERSHIP Transformational leadership occurs when managers have dramatic effects on their subordinates and on the organization as a whole, and inspire and energize subordinates to solve problems and improve performance. These effects include making subordinates aware of the importance of their own jobs and high performance; making subordinates aware of their own needs for personal growth, development, and accomplishment; and motivating subordinates to work for the good of the organization and not just their own personal gain. Managers can engage in transformational leadership by being charismatic leaders, by intellectually stimulating subordinates, and by engaging in developmental consideration. Transformational managers also often engage in transactional leadership by using their reward and coercive powers to encourage high performance. **[LO4]**

GENDER AND LEADERSHIP Female and male managers do not differ in the leadership behaviors that they perform, contrary to stereotypes suggesting that women are more relationship-oriented and men more task-oriented. Female managers sometimes are more participative than male managers, however. Research has found that women and men are equally effective as managers and leaders. **[LO5]**

EMOTIONAL INTELLIGENCE AND LEADERSHIP The moods and emotions leaders experience on the job, and their ability to effectively manage these feelings, can influence their effectiveness as leaders. Moreover, emotional intelligence has the potential to contribute to leadership effectiveness in multiple ways, including encouraging and supporting creativity among followers. **[LO5]**

Management in Action

Topics for Discussion and Action

Discussion

1. Describe the steps managers can take to increase their power and ability to be effective leaders. **[LO1]**
2. Think of specific situations in which it might be especially important for a manager to engage in consideration and in initiating structure. **[LO2]**
3. Discuss why managers might want to change the behaviors they engage in, given their situation, their subordinates, and the nature of the work being done. Do you think managers are able to readily change their leadership behaviors? Why or why not? **[LO3]**
4. Discuss why substitutes for leadership can contribute to organizational effectiveness. **[LO3]**
5. Describe what transformational leadership is, and explain how managers can engage in it. **[LO4]**
6. Imagine that you are working in an organization in an entry-level position after graduation and have come up with what you think is a great idea for improving a critical process in the organization that relates to your job. In what ways might your supervisor encourage you to actually implement your idea? How might your supervisor discourage you from even sharing your idea with others? **[LO4, 5]**

Action

7. Interview a manager to find out how the three situational characteristics that Fiedler identified are affecting his or her ability to provide leadership. **[LO3]**
8. Find a company that has dramatically turned around its fortunes and improved its performance. Determine whether a transformational manager was behind the turnaround and, if one was, what this manager did. **[LO4]**

Building Management Skills

Analyzing Failures of Leadership [LO1, 2, 3, 4]

Think about a situation you are familiar with in which a leader was very ineffective. Then answer the following questions:

1. What sources of power did this leader have? Did the leader have enough power to influence his or her followers?
2. What kinds of behaviors did this leader engage in? Were they appropriate for the situation? Why or why not?
3. From what you know, do you think this leader was a task-oriented leader or a relationship-oriented leader? How favorable was this leader's situation for leading?
4. What steps did this leader take to motivate his or her followers? Were these steps appropriate or inappropriate? Why?
5. What signs, if any, did this leader show of being a transformational leader?

Managing Ethically [LO1]

Managers who verbally criticize their subordinates, put them down in front of their coworkers, or use the threat of job loss to influence behavior are exercising coercive power. Some employees subject to coercive power believe that using it is unethical.

Questions

1. Either alone or in a group, think about the ethical implications of the use of coercive power.
2. To what extent do managers and organizations have an ethical obligation to put limits on the amount of coercive power that is exercised?

Small Group Breakout Exercise

Improving Leadership Effectiveness [LO1, 2, 3, 4]

Form groups of three to five people, and appoint one member as the spokesperson who will communicate your findings and conclusions to the class when called on by the instructor. Then discuss the following scenario:

You are a team of human resource consultants who have been hired by Carla Caruso, an entrepreneur who has started her own interior decorating business. A highly competent and creative interior decorator, Caruso established a working relationship with most of the major home builders in her community. At first, she worked on her own as an independent contractor. Then because of a dramatic increase in the number of new homes being built, she became swamped with requests for her services and decided to start her own company.

She hired a secretary-bookkeeper and four interior decorators, all of whom are highly competent. Caruso still does decorating jobs herself and has adopted a hands-off approach to leading the four decorators who report to her because she feels that interior design is a very personal, creative endeavor. Rather than pay the decorators on some kind of commission basis (such as a percentage of their customers' total billings), she pays them a premium salary, higher than average, so that they are motivated to do what's best for a customer's needs and not what will result in higher billings and commissions.

Caruso thought everything was going smoothly until customer complaints started coming in. The complaints ranged from the decorators' being hard to get hold of, promising unrealistic delivery times, and being late for or failing to keep appointments to their being impatient and rude when customers had trouble making up their minds. Caruso knows that her decorators are very competent and is concerned that she is not effectively leading and managing them. She wonders, in particular, if her hands-off approach is to blame and if she should change the manner in which she rewards or pays her decorators. She has asked for your advice.

1. Analyze the sources of power that Caruso has available to her to influence the decorators. What advice can you give her to either increase her power base or use her existing power more effectively?
2. Given what you have learned in this chapter (for example, from the behavior model and path-goal theory), does Caruso seem to be performing appropriate leader behaviors in this situation? What advice can you give her about the kinds of behaviors she should perform?
3. What steps would you advise Caruso to take to increase the decorators' motivation to deliver high-quality customer service?
4. Would you advise Caruso to try to engage in transformational leadership in this situation? If not, why not? If so, what steps would you advise her to take?

Be the Manager [LO1, 2, 3, 4, 5]

You are the CEO of a medium-size company that makes window coverings such as Hunter Douglas blinds and Duettes. Your company has a real cost advantage in terms of being able to make custom window coverings at costs that are relatively low in the industry. However, the performance of your company has been lackluster. In order to make needed changes and improve performance, you met with the eight other top managers in your company and charged them with identifying problems and missed opportunities in each of their areas and coming up with an action plan to address the problems and take advantage of opportunities.

Once you gave the managers the okay, they were charged with implementing their action plans in a timely fashion and monitoring the effects of their initiatives on a monthly basis for the next 8 to 12 months.

You approved each of the manager's action plans, and a year later most of the managers were reporting that their initiatives had been successful in addressing the problems and opportunities they had identified a year ago. However, overall company performance continues to be lackluster and shows no signs of improvement. You are confused and starting to question your leadership capabilities and approach to change. What are you going to do to improve the performance and effectiveness of your company?

BusinessWeek Case in the News [LO1, 2, 3, 5]

Are People in Your Office Acting Oddly?

Bosses are witnessing a lot of bizarre behavior in Officeland these days. The lumpy and rumpled are showing up all spiffy and dry-cleaned. Mouthy iconoclasts are newly docile. Clock-watching slackers are suddenly the last to leave. People, it seems, are performing transplants on themselves—like the senior vice president at a pharmaceutical company known as a terrible flirt who says she recently forced herself to go oh-so-straitlaced.

The desperation hustle may seem like a giant productivity boost for companies. Bosses can extract the work of two or three people out of a single body. But are employees really working harder? Or are they simply kissing up? And if they are working harder, how do managers tap into these paranoid spirits without turning workplaces into sweatshops? "Everybody is weirding out all over the place," says Stanford University management professor Robert I. Sutton. "I am surrounded by people who are just hysterical." The danger, says Sutton, is that fear in the workplace can be contagious. "Bosses need to be patient, understanding, and forgiving. These insecurities aren't irrational."

Damaging Diligence

For some bosses, managing the fear and loathing has become a job in itself. Trevor Traina, a Silicon Valley entrepreneur who has sold start-ups to Microsoft and Intuit, now heads DriverSide.com, a Web site that provides drivers with everything they need to know to manage car ownership. Since the downturn, the offices of the San Francisco company have become a tableau of Boy Scout–like diligence. "I'm getting e-mails all day long that say 'I'm doing this and I'm doing that,' and it makes my job harder," says Traina. "Every time I turn around, there is someone sticking their head in my office reminding me what they are doing for me." Traina has taken to informing his staff on a daily basis that the company just secured another round of funding and that they should lighten up on the oversharing.

At law firm Skadden, Arps, Slate, Meagher & Flom, one senior associate is being bombarded by junior associates hitting her up for new work. But she is also contending with the opposite problem: the recent law school grads, coddled and clueless, who are "sort of psyched there isn't that much to do." Every day is a managerial juggling act: keeping hope alive for some while trying to provide a reality check for others. "It's a giant time suck," she says.

For some leaders, the paranoia is a kind of blessing. "The world's best innovation comes from the greatest desperation," says Tom Szaky, CEO of TerraCycle, a

Trenton (New Jersey) company that makes organic fertilizer and other planet-friendly products. Times are tough for TerraCycle, as they are for a lot of companies that supply hard-pressed retailers. "We have no money to hire anyone," says Szaky. He put the challenge out to his charges: Do more with less. Amp up sales without spending any money.

So the TerraCyclers decided to become their own marketing machines, hitting the road and visiting stores in person. Normally, when TerraCycle staffers visit far-flung Wal-Marts and Home Depots to check on displays and chat up customers, they take a plane, stay in a hotel, and expense their meals. But last month three members of the marketing department drove their cars more than 1,000 miles each instead. As if that weren't *Grapes of Wrath* enough: They also slept in their back seats.

Szaky says he has already seen a revenue jump. "Money is easy," he says. "It's good to starve companies sometimes. That's where innovation comes from."

Questions

1. Why do some employees try to make themselves seem irreplaceable during tough economic times?
2. What type(s) of leader power may be causing employees to act in this manner?
3. What kinds of behaviors do you think leaders should engage in when they think that employees are trying to impress them during tough economic times?
4. How might emotional intelligence help leaders deal with employees who are trying hard to be, or look like, model employees in tough economic times?

Source: Michelle Conlin, "Are People in Your Office Acting Oddly?" Reprinted from April 13, 2009 issue of *BusinessWeek* by special permission, copyright © 2009 by The McGraw-Hill Companies, Inc.

BusinessWeek Case in the News [LO1, 2, 4]

Taking the Ted Out of Turner Broadcasting

You may not have heard of Phil Kent. After all, the CEO of Turner Broadcasting is a whole lot quieter than Ted Turner, the so-called Mouth of the South who remained front and center long after selling his cable empire to Time Warner in the 1990s. But Kent has emerged from Turner's shadow and is fast becoming one of Time Warner's most important executives. If the media giant spins off its long-troubled AOL division as expected, the collection of channels that Kent oversees—including TNT, TBS, TCM, and CNN—will contribute nearly half of Time Warner's earnings.

In the past six years, Kent has taken on the broadcast networks with a smorgasbord of programming matched by few other cable outfits. As more ad dollars flow from broadcast to cable networks, he is on a mission to get advertisers to pay as much for time on Turner as they do the Big Four broadcasters. It's a campaign Kent plans to press in the coming weeks as advertisers gather in New York for the annual ad-buying ritual known as the upfronts.

Kent, 54, is the first person to run Turner without the looming presence of its mercurial founder, who stepped away from Time Warner in 2006. As such, Turner is a much changed place. "Under Ted," says Time Warner CEO Jeffrey L. Bewkes, "the top management was always Ted." Whereas Turner reveled in making his own news, Kent is the antithesis of the media executive. Although he learned the business working for legendary Hollywood power broker Michael Ovitz at Creative Artists Agency in the late 1980s, he finds Tinseltown self-promotion repellent and abhors the cult of the CEO. "He's definitely not a rock star chief executive," says Steven R. Koonin, one of Kent's top lieutenants.

At two key junctures of his career, Kent took himself out of the fray—both times when he wasn't having fun anymore. After working for Ovitz for six years, he bailed and embarked on an around-the-world trip, ignoring the blandishments of headhunters, who tracked him to a rooftop café in Marrakesh. In the 1990s, Kent worked at Turner, but he quit in 2001 after the AOL–Time Warner merger. "Not until you leave a job do you appreciate that the sun really will rise and fall without you," he explains. "This does make you more fearless in making tough decisions. After all, if you've fired yourself, you're much less afraid of being fired."

Pump Up The Brands

Bewkes was looking for someone to make tough decisions when he lured Kent back to run Turner in 2003. At the time, the cable network was in a lull, and Bewkes, who turned HBO into a pop culture sensation, wanted Kent to pump up Turner's brands and create buzz around its channels.

Kent has invested heavily to broaden Turner's offerings in news, scripted shows, cartoons, and sports. To lure young, professional viewers, a coveted cohort, Kent pushed TNT and TBS into original programming with marquee names. TNT's *The Closer,* starring Kyra Sedgwick as a sugar-addicted police chief, has become one of cable's top-rated shows. Ditto for *Saving Grace,* which features Holly Hunter as an Oklahoma cop with a dark past and a guardian angel.

Kent backed Adult Swim, a comedy channel that appears on Turner's Cartoon Network in the evenings. This network-within-a-network has allowed Turner to reel in two key demographics: teenage and early-twentysomething males, who watch the racy fare on Adult Swim at night, and kids and their parents, who watch the cartoons during the rest of the day. This year, TNT and TBS will air 13 original shows, versus none in 2003.

Kent's strategy is attracting a range of blue–chip advertisers, among them T-Mobile, DirecTV, Hewlett-Packard, and Procter & Gamble. Under Kent, Turner revenues, a mix of ad dollars and distribution fees, have nearly doubled, to $7 billion, according to people familiar with the numbers. So has cash flow, to $2.3 billion. (Time Warner does not break them out.)

By many accounts, Turner has become a far more inclusive place since Kent took the reins. Kent says his sabbaticals taught him that the CEO mania for scheduling every moment of the day is counterproductive. Splitting his weeks between Turner's headquarters in Atlanta and New York, he leaves time for colleagues, walking the halls and popping into people's offices. Koonin says it was during one of those office visits that he and Kent talked about focusing more on underserved audiences. That chat led eventually to offering comedian George Lopez his own late-night talk show on TBS to compete with Conan and Dave and bring in Hispanic viewers.

Kent's tenure hasn't been seamless. In 2007 he was forced to apologize for an Adult Swim guerrilla marketing stunt in Boston involving cartoonish devices that passersby mistook for bombs. This month, TNT canceled the advertising comedy *Trust Me* after just one season. Now, as Turner emerges as a more important part of a leaner Time Warner, Kent will have to morph into a role that makes him uneasy: the high-profile CEO.

Investors will be watching closely to see if he can, in fact, get advertisers to pay more for commercial airtime on Turner channels. Cable networks typically get a third or so less in advertising rates versus the broadcast networks. Kent acknowledges changing that dynamic won't be easy but says, "We can do a much better job of selling [the Turner] story."

Questions

1. How would you describe Phil Kent's personal leadership style?
2. What traits do you think he is high on?
3. What behaviors do you think he is likely to engage in?
4. Do you think Phil Kent is a transformational leader? Why or why not?

Source: Tom Lowry, "Taking the Ted Out of Turner Broadcasting." Reprinted from May 4, 2009 issue of *BusinessWeek* by special permission,

Effective Team Management

CHAPTER 11

Learning Objectives

After studying this chapter, you should be able to

1. Explain why groups and teams are key contributors to organizational effectiveness. **[LO1]**
2. Identify the different types of groups and teams that help managers and organizations achieve their goals. **[LO2]**
3. Explain how different elements of group dynamics influence the functioning and effectiveness of groups and teams. **[LO3]**
4. Explain why it is important for groups and teams to have a balance of conformity and deviance and a moderate level of cohesiveness. **[LO4]**
5. Describe how managers can motivate group members to achieve organizational goals and reduce social loafing in groups and teams. **[LO5]**

George Lopez empowers ICU Medical employees to form teams to address problems and seize opportunities.

MANAGEMENT SNAPSHOT

Teams at ICU Medical

How Can an Entrepreneur Use Teams to Help Manage a Rapidly Growing Organization?

Dr. George Lopez, an internal medicine physician, founded ICU Medical in San Clemente, California, in 1984 after a patient of his accidentally died when an intravenous (IV) line became inadvertently disconnected.[1] Lopez thought that there must be a better way to design components of IV lines so that these kinds of tragic accidents didn't happen. He developed a product called the Click Lock, which has both a locking mechanism for IV systems and also a protected needle so that health care workers are protected from accidental needle pricks.[2] Today, ICU Medical has approximately 1,829 employees and net revenues over $214 million.[3] Lopez is CEO of the company, which is now publicly traded on the NASDAQ stock exchange.[4] ICU Medical continues to focus on the development and manufacture of products that improve the functioning of IV lines and systems while protecting health care workers from accidental needle pricks.[5] For example, the CLAVE NeedleFree Connector for IV lines is one of ICU Medical's top-selling products.[6]

In the early 1990s, Lopez experienced something not uncommon to successful entrepreneurs as their businesses grow. As the entrepreneur–CEO, he continued to make the majority of important decisions himself; yet, he had close to 100 employees, demand for the CLAVE was very high, and he was starting to feel overloaded to the point where he would often sleep at nights in the office.[7] After watching one of his son's hockey games, he realized that a well-functioning team could work wonders. Lopez decided to empower employees to form teams to work on a pressing goal for ICU Medical, increasing production.[8] While employees did form teams and spent a lot of time engaged in team interactions, the teams did not seem to come up with any really tangible results, perhaps because there were no team leaders in place and the teams had no guidelines or rules for behavior to follow to help them accomplish their goals.[9]

In an effort to improve team effectiveness, Lopez told employees that teams should elect team leaders. And together with Jim Reitz, who is currently ICU

Medical's director of human resources, Lopez came up with rules or guidelines teams should follow such as "challenge the issue, not the person" and "stand up for your position, but never argue against the facts."[10] ICU Medical also started to reward team members for their team's contributions to organizational effectiveness. With these changes, Reitz and Lopez were striving to ensure that teams had leaders, had some guidelines for team member behavior, and were rewarded for their contributions to organizational effectiveness but, at the same time, were not bogged down by unnecessary constraints and structures and were truly self-managing.[11]

With these changes in place, teams at ICU Medical really did start to live up to their promise. Today, any ICU Medical employee can create a team to address a problem, seize an opportunity, or work on a project ranging from developing a new product to making improvements in the physical work environment.[12] The teams are self-managing, and team members divide up the work among themselves, assign roles and responsibilities, schedule meetings, and determine their own deadlines. Regardless of the extent of their involvement in teams, employees are still expected to perform all of the regular tasks and responsibilities that make up their individual jobs. On average, teams tend to have between five and seven members and meet once a week; and at the end of each quarter, around 12 to 15 teams have completed their projects. On a quarterly basis, ICU Medical makes available $75,000 to reward teams that successfully complete their projects.[13] Rewards to teams are based on the salaries of their members and the success and importance of their projects.[14]

Recognizing that self-managed teams still need rules, guidelines, leadership, and structure, a team of employees developed a 25-page guidebook for effective team functioning. And in order to ensure that teams learn from each other as well as get feedback, teams are required to put up notes from each of their meetings on ICU Medical's intranet, and any employee can provide feedback to any of the teams.[15]

All in all, self-managed teams have helped Lopez manage his rapidly growing business and have substantially contributed to ICU Medical's overall effectiveness.[16]

Overview

ICU Medical is not alone in using groups and teams to improve organizational effectiveness. Managers in companies large and small are using groups and teams to enhance performance, increase responsiveness to customers, spur innovation, and motivate employees. In this chapter we look in detail at how groups and teams can contribute to organizational effectiveness and the types of groups and teams used in organizations. We discuss how different elements of group dynamics influence the functioning and effectiveness of groups, and we describe how managers can motivate group members to achieve organizational goals and reduce social loafing in groups and teams. By the end of this chapter, you will appreciate why the effective management of groups and teams is a key ingredient for organizational performance and effectiveness.

Groups, Teams, and Organizational Effectiveness

A **group** may be defined as two or more people who interact with each other to accomplish certain goals or meet certain needs.[17] A **team** is a group whose members work *intensely* with one another to achieve a specific common goal or objective. As these definitions imply, all teams are groups but not all groups are teams. The two characteristics that distinguish teams from groups are the *intensity* with which team members work together and the presence of a *specific, overriding team goal or objective*.

LO1 Explain why groups and teams are key contributors to organizational effectiveness.

At ICU Medical (see the "Management Snapshot"), Don Ramstead, who was responsible for production schedules, formed a team that worked intensively to achieve the goal of improving the production process for the CLAVE; within six months, the team had reduced the number of steps in the production process from 27 to 9 for annual cost savings of around $500,000.[18] In contrast, the accountants who work in a small CPA firm are a group: They may interact with one another to achieve goals such as keeping up to date on the latest changes in accounting rules and regulations, maintaining a smoothly functioning office, satisfying clients, and attracting new clients. But they are not a team because they do not work intensely with one another. Each accountant concentrates on serving the needs of his or her own clients.

group Two or more people who interact with each other to accomplish certain goals or meet certain needs.

team A group whose members work intensely with one another to achieve a specific common goal or objective.

Because all teams are also groups, whenever we use the term *group* in this chapter, we are referring to both groups *and* teams. As you might imagine, because members of teams work intensely together, teams can sometimes be difficult to form and it may take time for members to learn how to effectively work together. Groups and teams can help an organization gain a competitive advantage because they can (1) enhance its performance, (2) increase its responsiveness to customers, (3) increase innovation, and (4) increase employees' motivation and satisfaction (see Figure 11.1). In this section, we look at each of these contributions in turn.

Groups and Teams as Performance Enhancers

synergy Performance gains that result when individuals and departments coordinate their actions.

One of the main advantages of using groups is the opportunity to obtain a type of synergy: People working in a group are able to produce more or higher-quality outputs than would have been produced if each person had worked separately and all their individual efforts were later combined. The essence of synergy is captured in the saying "The whole is more than the sum of its parts." Factors that can contribute to synergy in groups include the ability of group members to bounce ideas off one another, to correct one another's mistakes, to solve problems immediately as they arise, to bring a diverse knowledge base to bear on a problem or goal, and to accomplish work that is too vast or all-encompassing for any one individual to achieve on his or her own.

To take advantage of the potential for synergy in groups, managers need to make sure that groups are composed of members who have complementary skills and knowledge relevant to the group's work. For example, at Hallmark Cards, synergies are created by bringing together all the different functions needed to create and

Figure 11.1
Groups' and Teams' Contributions to Organizational Effectiveness

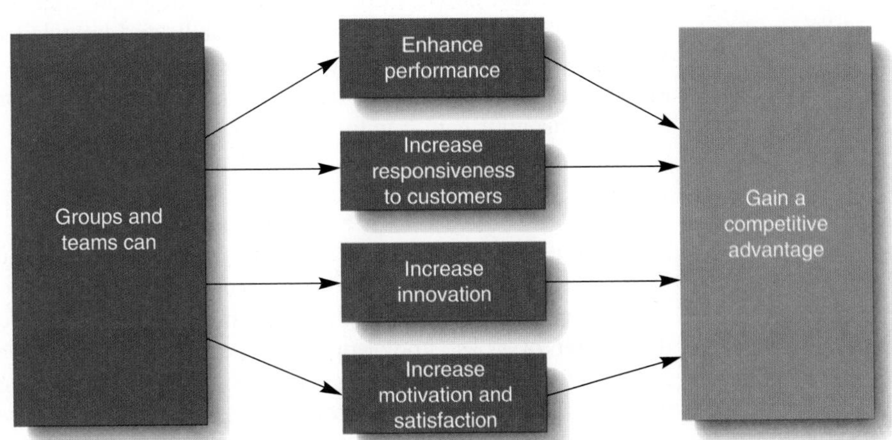

produce a greeting card in a cross-functional team (a team composed of members from different departments or functions). For instance, artists, writers, designers, and marketing experts work together as members of a team to develop new cards.[19]

At Hallmark, the skills and expertise of the artists complement the contributions of the writers and vice versa. Managers also need to give groups enough autonomy so that the groups, rather than the manager, are solving problems and determining how to achieve goals and objectives, as is true in the cross-functional teams at Hallmark and the teams employees form at ICU Medical in the "Management Snapshot." To promote synergy, managers need to empower their subordinates and be coaches, guides, and resources for groups while refraining from playing a more directive or supervisory role. The potential for synergy in groups may be the reason why more and more managers are incorporating empowerment into their personal leadership styles (see Chapter 10).

Groups, Teams, and Responsiveness to Customers

Being responsive to customers is not always easy. In manufacturing organizations, for example, customers' needs and desires for new and improved products have to be balanced against engineering constraints, production costs and feasibilities, government safety regulations, and marketing challenges. In service organizations such as health maintenance organizations (HMOs), being responsive to patients' needs and desires for prompt, high-quality medical care and treatment has to be balanced against meeting physicians' needs and desires and keeping health care costs under control. Being responsive to customers often requires the wide variety of skills and expertise found in different departments and at different levels in an organization's hierarchy. Sometimes, for example, employees at lower levels in an organization's hierarchy, such as sales representatives for a computer company, are closest to its customers and the most attuned to their needs. However, lower-level employees like salespeople often lack the technical expertise needed to come up with new product ideas; such expertise is found in the research and development department. Bringing salespeople, research and development experts, and members of other departments together in a group or cross-functional team can enhance responsiveness to customers. Consequently, when managers form a team, they need to make sure that the diversity of expertise and knowledge needed to be responsive to customers exists within the team; this is why cross-functional teams are so popular.

In a cross-functional team, the expertise and knowledge in different organizational departments are brought together in the skills and knowledge of the team members. Managers of high-performing organizations are careful to determine which types of expertise and knowledge are required for teams to be responsive to customers, and they use this information in forming teams.

Teams and Innovation

Innovation–the implementation of creative ideas for new products, new technologies, new services, or even new organizational structures–is essential for organizational effectiveness. Often, an individual working alone does not possess the extensive and diverse set of skills, knowledge, and expertise required for successful innovation. Managers can better encourage innovation by creating teams of diverse individuals who together have the knowledge relevant to a particular type of innovation rather than by relying on individuals working alone.

Using teams to innovate has other advantages as well. First, team members can often uncover one another's errors or false assumptions; an individual acting alone would not be able to do this. Second, team members can critique one another's approaches when need be and build off one another's strengths while compensating for weaknesses, one of the advantages of devil's advocacy, discussed in Chapter 5.

To further promote innovation, managers are well advised to empower teams and make their members fully responsible and accountable for the innovation process. The manager's role is to provide guidance, assistance, coaching, and the resources team members need and *not* to closely direct or supervise their activities. To speed innovation, managers also need to form teams in which each member brings some unique resource to the team, such as engineering prowess, knowledge of production, marketing expertise, or financial savvy. Successful innovation sometimes requires that managers form teams with members from different countries and cultures.

Amazon uses teams to spur innovation, and many of the unique features on its Web site that enable it to be responsive to customers and meet their needs have been developed by teams, as indicated in the following "Information Technology Byte."

INFORMATION TECHNOLOGY BYTE

Pizza Teams Innovate at Amazon

Jeff Bezos, founder, CEO, and chairman of the board of Amazon, is a firm believer in the power of teams to spur innovation.[20] At Amazon, teams have considerable autonomy to develop their ideas and experiment without interference from managers or other groups. And teams are kept deliberately small. According to Bezos, no team should need more than two pizzas to feed its members. If more than two pizzas are needed to nourish a team, the team is too large. Thus, teams at Amazon typically have no more than about five to seven members.[21]

At Amazon, teams adhere to the two-pizza rule; that is, no team should need more than two pizzas to feed its members.

"Pizza teams" have come up with unique and popular innovations that individuals working alone might never have thought of. A team developed the "Gold Box" icon that customers can click on to receive special offers that expire within an hour of opening the treasure chest. Another team developed "Search Inside the Book," which that allows customers to search and read content from over 100,000 books.[22] And a team developed the Amazon Kindle, a wireless reader that weighs 10.3 ounces, can hold over 200 titles, can receive automatic delivery of major newspapers and blogs, and has a high-resolution screen that appears like and can be read like paper.[23]

While Bezos gives teams autonomy to develop and run with their ideas, he also believes in the careful analysis and testing of ideas. A great advocate of the power of facts, data, and analysis, Bezos feels that whenever an idea can be tested through analysis, analysis should rule the day. When an undertaking is just too large or too uncertain or when data are lacking and hard to come by, Bezos and other experienced top managers make the final call.[24] But in order to make such judgment calls about implementing new ideas (either by data analysis or expert judgment), what really is needed are truly creative ideas. To date, teams have played a very important role in generating ideas that have helped Amazon be responsive to its customers, have a widely known Internet brand name, and be the highly successful and innovative company it is today.[25]

Groups and Teams as Motivators

Managers often decide to form groups and teams to accomplish organizational goals and then find that using groups and teams brings additional benefits. Members of groups, and especially members of teams (because of the higher intensity of interaction in teams), are likely to be more satisfied than they would have been if they were working on their own. The experience of working alongside other highly charged and motivated people can be very stimulating. In addition, working on a team can be very motivating: Team members more readily see how their efforts and expertise directly contribute to the achievement of team and organizational goals, and they feel personally responsible for the outcomes or results of their work. This has been the case at Hallmark Cards.

The increased motivation and satisfaction that can accompany the use of teams can also lead to other outcomes, such as lower turnover. This has been Frank B. Day's experience as founder and chairman of the board of Rock Bottom Restaurants Inc.[26] To provide high-quality customer service, Day has organized the restaurants' employees into wait staff teams, whose members work together to refill beers, take orders, bring hot chicken enchiladas to the tables, or clear off the tables. Team members share the burden of undesirable activities and unpopular shift times, and customers no longer have to wait until a particular waitress or waiter is available. Motivation and satisfaction levels in Rock Bottom restaurants seem to be higher than in other restaurants, and turnover is about one-half of that experienced in other U.S. restaurant chains.[27]

Working in a group or team can also satisfy organizational members' needs for engaging in social interaction and feeling connected to other people. For workers who perform highly stressful jobs, such as hospital emergency and operating room staff, group membership can be an important source of social support and motivation. Family members or friends may not be able to fully understand or appreciate some sources of work stress that these group members experience firsthand. Moreover, group members may cope better with work stressors when they are able to share them with other members of their group. In addition, groups often devise techniques to relieve stress, such as the telling of jokes among hospital operating room staff.

Why do managers in all kinds of organizations rely so heavily on groups and teams? Effectively managed groups and teams can help managers in their quest for high performance, responsiveness to customers, and employee motivation. Before explaining how managers can effectively manage groups, however, we will describe the types of groups that are formed in organizations.

Types of Groups and Teams

To achieve their goals of high performance, responsiveness to customers, innovation, and employee motivation, managers can form various types of groups and teams (see Figure 11.2). **Formal groups** are those managers establish to achieve organizational goals. The formal work groups are *cross-functional* teams composed of members from different departments, such as those at Hallmark Cards, and *cross-cultural* teams composed of members from different cultures or countries, such as the teams at global carmakers. As you will see, some of the groups discussed in this section also can be considered to be cross-functional (if they are composed of members from different departments) or cross-cultural (if they are composed of members from different countries or cultures).

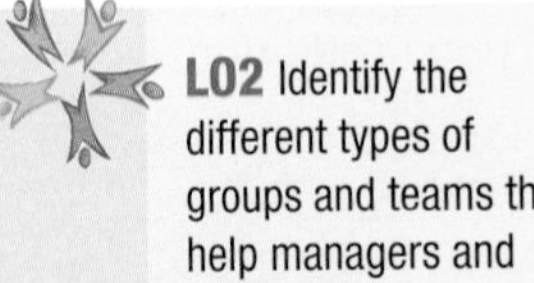

LO2 Identify the different types of groups and teams that help managers and organizations achieve their goals.

formal group A group that managers establish to achieve organizational goals.

informal group A group that managers or nonmanagerial employees form to help achieve their own goals or meet their own needs.

top-management team A group composed of the CEO, the president, and the heads of the most important departments.

Sometimes organizational members, managers or nonmanagers, form groups because they feel that groups will help them achieve their own goals or meet their own needs (for example, the need for social interaction). Groups formed in this way are **informal groups.** Four nurses who work in a hospital and have lunch together twice a week constitute an informal group.

The Top-Management Team

A central concern of the CEO and president of a company is to form a **top-management team** to help the organization achieve its mission and goals. Top-management teams are responsible for developing the strategies that result in an organization's competitive advantage; most have between five and seven members. In forming their top-management teams, CEOs are well advised to stress diversity–diversity in expertise, skills, knowledge, and experience. Thus, many top-management teams are also cross-functional teams: They are composed of members from different departments, such as finance, marketing, production, and engineering. Diversity helps ensure that the top-management team will have all the background and resources it needs to make good decisions. Diversity also helps guard against *groupthink,* faulty group decision making that results when group members strive for agreement at the expense of an accurate assessment of the situation (see Chapter 5).

Figure 11.2
Types of Groups and Teams in Organizations

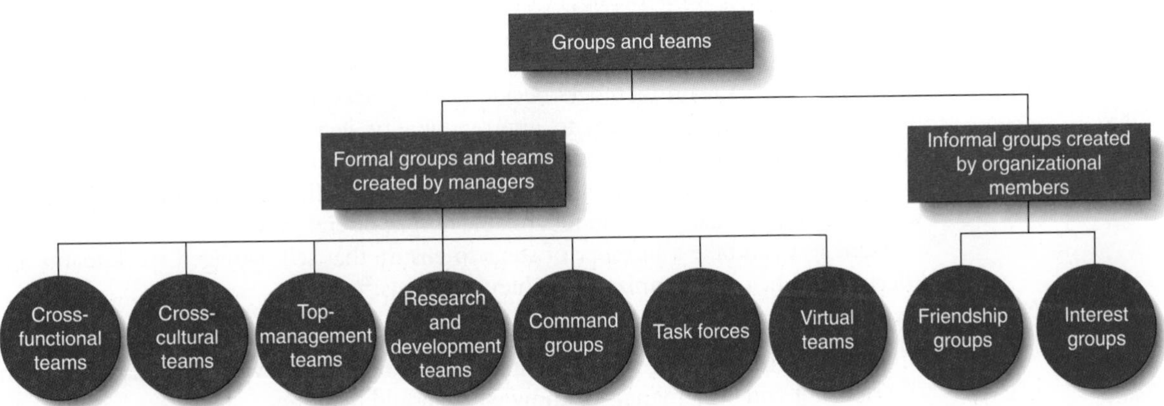

Research and Development Teams

research and development team A team whose members have the expertise and experience needed to develop new products.

Managers in pharmaceuticals, computers, electronics, electronic imaging, and other high-tech industries often create **research and development teams** to develop new products. Managers select R&D team members on the basis of their expertise and experience in a certain area. Sometimes R&D teams are cross-functional teams with members from departments such as engineering, marketing, and production in addition to members from the research and development department.

Command Groups

command group A group composed of subordinates who report to the same supervisor; also called *department* or *unit.*

Subordinates who report to the same supervisor compose a **command group.** When top managers design an organization's structure and establish reporting relationships and a chain of command, they are essentially creating command groups. Command groups, often called *departments* or *units,* perform a significant amount of the work in many organizations. In order to have command groups that help an organization gain a competitive advantage, managers not only need to motivate group members to perform at a high level but also need to be effective leaders.

Task Forces

task force A committee of managers or nonmanagerial employees from various departments or divisions who meet to solve a specific, mutual problem; also called *ad hoc committee.*

Managers form **task forces** to accomplish specific goals or solve problems in a certain time period; task forces are sometimes called *ad hoc committees.* For example, Michael Rider, owner and top manager of a chain of six gyms and fitness centers in the Midwest, created a task force composed of the general managers of the six gyms to determine whether the fitness centers should institute a separate fee schedule for customers who wanted to use the centers only for aerobics classes (and not use other facilities such as weights, steps, tracks, and swimming pools). The task force was given three months to prepare a report summarizing the pros and cons of the proposed change in fee schedules. Once the task force completed its report and reached the conclusion that the change in fee structure probably would reduce revenues rather than increase them and thus should not be implemented, it was disbanded. As in Rider's case, task forces can be a valuable tool for busy managers who do not have the time to personally explore an important issue in depth.

Self-Managed Work Teams

self-managed work team A group of employees who supervise their own activities and monitor the quality of the goods and services they provide.

Self-managed work teams are teams in which team members are empowered and have the responsibility and autonomy to complete identifiable pieces of work. On a day-to-day basis, team members decide what the team will do, how it will do it, and which team members will perform which specific tasks.[28] Managers provide self-managed work teams with their overall goals (such as assembling defect-free computer keyboards) but let team members decide how to meet those goals. Managers usually form self-managed work teams to improve quality, increase motivation and satisfaction, and lower costs. Often, by creating self-managed work teams, they combine tasks that individuals working separately used to perform, so the team is responsible for the whole set of tasks that yields an identifiable output or end product.

Managers can take a number of steps to ensure that self-managed work teams are effective and help an organization achieve its goals:[29]

- Give teams enough responsibility and autonomy to be truly self-managing. Refrain from telling team members what to do or solving problems for them even if you (as a manager) know what should be done.

- Make sure that a team's work is sufficiently complex so that it entails a number of different steps or procedures that must be performed and results in some kind of finished end product.
- Carefully select members of self-managed work teams. Team members should have the diversity of skills needed to complete the team's work, have the ability to work with others, and want to be part of a team.
- As a manager, realize that your role vis-à-vis self-managed work teams calls for guidance, coaching, and supporting, not supervising. You are a resource for teams to turn to when needed.
- Analyze what type of training team members need, and provide it. Working in a self-managed work team often requires that employees have more extensive technical and interpersonal skills.

Managers in a wide variety of organizations have found that self-managed work teams help the organization achieve its goals,[30] as profiled in the following "Management Insight."

MANAGEMENT INSIGHT

Self-Managed Teams at Louis Vuitton and Nucor Corporation

Managers at Louis Vuitton, the most profitable luxury brand in the world, and managers at Nucor Corporation, the largest producer of steel and biggest recycler in the United States, have succeeded in effectively using self-managed teams to produce luxury accessories and steel, respectively. Self-managed teams at both companies not only are effective but truly excel and have helped to make the companies leaders in their respective industries.[31]

Teams with between 20 and 30 members make Vuitton handbags and accessories. The teams work on only one particular product at a time; a team with 24 members might produce about 120 handbags per day. Team members are empowered to take ownership for the goods they produce, are encouraged to suggest improvements, and are kept up to date on key facts such as products' selling prices and popularity. As Thierry Nogues, a team leader at a Vuitton factory in Ducey, France, puts it, "Our goal is to make everyone as multiskilled and autonomous as possible."[32]

A team member assembles classic Louis Vuitton bags at the company's fine leather goods factory in the Normandy town of Ducey in France.

Production workers at Nucor are organized into teams ranging in size from 8 to 40 members based on the kind of work the team is responsible for, such as rolling steel or operating a furnace. Team members have considerable autonomy to make decisions and creatively respond to problems and opportunities, and there are relatively few layers in the corporate hierarchy, supporting the empowerment of teams.[33] Teams develop their own informal rules for behavior and make their own decisions. As long as team members follow organizational rules and policies (e.g., for safety) and meet quality standards, they are free to govern themselves. Managers act as coaches or advisers rather than supervisors, helping teams out when they need some additional outside assistance.[34]

To ensure that production teams are motivated to help Nucor achieve its goals, team members are eligible for weekly bonuses based on the team's performance. Essentially, these production workers receive base pay that does not vary and are eligible to receive weekly bonus pay.[35] The bonus rate is predetermined by the work a team performs and the capabilities of the machinery they use. Given the immediacy of the bonus and its potential magnitude, team members are highly motivated to perform at a high level, develop informal rules that support high performance, and strive to help Nucor reach its goals. Moreover, because all members of a team receive the same amount of weekly bonus money, they are motivated to do their best for the team, cooperate, and help one another out.[36]

Crafting a luxury handbag and making steel joists couldn't be more different from each other in certain ways. Yet the highly effective self-managed teams at Louis Vuitton and Nucor share some fundamental qualities. These teams really do take ownership of their work and are highly motivated to perform effectively. Team members have the skills and knowledge they need to be effective, they are empowered to make decisions about their work, and they know that their teams are making vital contributions to their organizations.[37]

Sometimes employees have their own individual jobs but also are part of a self-managed team that is formed to accomplish a specific goal or work on an important project. Employees need to perform their own individual job tasks and also actively contribute to the self-managed team that they are a member of so the team achieves its goal. Recall from the "Management Snapshot" how employees at ICU Medical form their own self-managed teams to work on projects; at ICU Medical, employees have their own individual jobs and assigned responsibilities and also work in self-managed teams the employees form themselves to achieve specific goals such as reducing inefficiencies in a production process or developing a new product.[38]

Like all groups, self-managed work teams can sometimes run into trouble. Members may be reluctant to discipline one another by withholding bonuses from members who are not performing up to par or by firing members.[39] Buster Jarrell, a manager who oversaw self-managed work teams in AES Corporation's Houston plant, found that although the self-managed work teams were highly effective, they had a very difficult time firing team members who were performing poorly.[40]

virtual team A team whose members rarely or never meet face-to-face but, rather, interact by using various forms of information technology such as e-mail, computer networks, telephone, fax, and videoconferences.

Virtual Teams

Virtual teams are teams whose members rarely or never meet face-to-face but, rather, interact by using various forms of information technology such as e-mail, text messaging, computer networks, telephone, fax, and videoconferences. As organizations become increasingly global, and as the need for specialized knowledge increases due to advances in technology, managers can create virtual teams to solve problems or explore opportunities without being limited by team members' needing to work in the same geographic location.[41]

Take the case of an organization that has manufacturing facilities in Australia, Canada, the United States, and Mexico and is encountering a quality problem in a complex manufacturing process. Each of its facilities has a quality control team headed by a quality control manager. The vice president for production does not try to solve the problem by forming and leading a team at one of the four manufacturing facilities; instead, she forms and leads a virtual team composed of the quality control managers of the four plants and the plants' general managers. When these team members communicate via e-mail, the company's networking site, and videoconferencing, a wide array of knowledge and experience is brought to bear to solve the problem.

The principal advantage of virtual teams is that they enable managers to disregard geographic distances and form teams whose members have the knowledge, expertise, and experience to tackle a particular problem or take advantage of a specific opportunity.[42] Virtual teams also can include members who are not actually employees of the organization itself; a virtual team might include members of a company that is used for outsourcing. More and more companies, including BP PLC, Nokia Corporation, and Ogilvy & Mather, are using virtual teams.[43]

There are two forms of information technologies that members of virtual teams rely on, synchronous technologies and asynchronous technologies.[44] *Synchronous technologies* enable virtual team members to communicate and interact with one another in real time simultaneously and include videoconferencing, teleconferencing, and electronic meetings. *Asynchronous technologies* delay communication and include e-mail, electronic bulletin boards, and Internet Web sites. Many virtual teams use both kinds of technology depending on what projects they are working on.

Increasing globalization is likely to result in more organizations relying on virtual teams to a greater extent.[45] One of the major challenges members of virtual teams face is building a sense of camaraderie and trust among team members who rarely, if ever, meet face-to-face. To address this challenge, some organizations schedule recreational activities, such as ski trips, so that virtual team members can get together. Other organizations make sure that virtual team members have a chance to meet in person soon after the team is formed and then schedule periodic face-to-face meetings to promote trust, understanding, and cooperation in the teams.[46] The need for such meetings is underscored by research that suggests that while some virtual teams can be as effective as teams that meet face-to-face, virtual team members might be less satisfied with teamwork efforts and have fewer feelings of camaraderie or cohesion. (Group cohesiveness is discussed in more detail later in the chapter.)[47]

Some virtual teams periodically meet face-to-face to promote trust, understanding, and cooperation in the team.

Research also suggests that it is important for managers to keep track of virtual teams and intervene when necessary by, for example, encouraging members of teams who do not communicate often enough to monitor their team's progress and make sure that team members actually have the time, and are recognized for, their virtual teamwork.[48] Additionally, when virtual teams are experiencing downtime or rough spots, managers might try to schedule face-to-face team time to bring team members together and help them focus on their goals.[49]

Researchers at the London Business School, including Professor Lynda Gratton, recently studied global virtual teams to try to identify factors that might help such teams be effective.[50] Based on their research, Gratton suggests that when forming virtual teams, it is helpful to include a few members who already know each other, other members who are very well connected to people outside of the team, and when possible, members who have volunteered to be a part of the team.[51] It is also advantageous for companies to have some kind of online site where team members can learn more about each other and the kinds of work they are engaged in, and in particular, a shared online workspace that team members can access around the clock.[52] Frequent communication is beneficial. Additionally, virtual team projects should be perceived as meaningful, interesting, and important by their members to promote and sustain their motivation.[53]

Friendship Groups

friendship group An informal group composed of employees who enjoy one another's company and socialize with one another.

The groups described so far are formal groups created by managers. **Friendship groups** are informal groups composed of employees who enjoy one another's company and socialize with one another. Members of friendship groups may have lunch together, take breaks together, or meet after work for meals, sports, or other activities. Friendship groups help satisfy employees' needs for interpersonal interaction, can provide needed social support in times of stress, and can contribute to people's feeling good at work and being satisfied with their jobs. Managers themselves often form friendship groups. The informal relationships that managers build in friendship groups can often help them solve work-related problems because members of these groups typically discuss work-related matters and offer advice.

Interest Groups

interest group An informal group composed of employees seeking to achieve a common goal related to their membership in an organization.

Employees form informal **interest groups** when they seek to achieve a common goal related to their membership in an organization. Employees may form interest groups, for example, to encourage managers to consider instituting flexible working hours, providing on-site child care, improving working conditions, or more proactively supporting environmental protection. Interest groups can provide managers with valuable insights into the issues and concerns that are foremost in employees' minds. They also can signal the need for change.

Group Dynamics

The ways in which groups function and, ultimately, their effectiveness hinge on group characteristics and processes known collectively as *group dynamics*. In this section, we discuss five key elements of group dynamics: group size and roles; group leadership; group development; group norms; and group cohesiveness.

Group Size and Roles

Managers need to take group size and group roles into account as they create and maintain high-performing groups and teams.

LO3 Explain how different elements of group dynamics influence the functioning and effectiveness of groups and teams.

GROUP SIZE The number of members in a group can be an important determinant of members' motivation and commitment and group performance. There are several advantages to keeping a group relatively small–between two and nine members. Recall how the average size of self-managed teams at ICU Medical is around five to seven members.[54] Compared with members of large groups, members of small groups tend to (1) interact more with each other and find it easier to coordinate their efforts, (2) be more motivated, satisfied, and committed, (3) find it easier to share information, and (4) be better able to see the importance of their personal contributions for group success. A disadvantage of small rather than large groups is that members of small groups have fewer resources available to accomplish their goals.

Large groups–with 10 or more members–also offer some advantages. They have more resources at their disposal to achieve group goals than small groups do. These resources include the knowledge, experience, skills, and abilities of group members as well as their actual time and effort. Large groups also enable managers to obtain the advantages stemming from the **division of labor**–splitting the work to be performed into particular tasks and assigning tasks to individual workers. Workers who specialize in particular tasks are likely to become skilled at performing those tasks and contribute significantly to high group performance.

division of labor Splitting the work to be performed into particular tasks and assigning tasks to individual workers.

The disadvantages of large groups include the problems of communication and coordination and the lower levels of motivation, satisfaction, and commitment that members of large groups sometimes experience. It is clearly more difficult to share information with, and coordinate the activities of, 16 people rather than 8 people. Moreover, members of large groups might not think that their efforts are really needed and sometimes might not even feel a part of the group.

In deciding on the appropriate size for any group, managers attempt to gain the advantages of small-group size and, at the same time, form groups with sufficient resources to accomplish their goals and have a well-developed division of labor. As a general rule of thumb, groups should have no more members than necessary to achieve a division of labor and provide the resources needed to achieve group goals. In R&D teams, for example, group size is too large when (1) members spend more time communicating what they know to others than applying what they know to solve problems and create new products, (2) individual productivity decreases, and (3) group performance suffers.[55]

group role A set of behaviors and tasks that a member of a group is expected to perform because of his or her position in the group.

GROUP ROLES A **group role** is a set of behaviors and tasks that a member of a group is expected to perform because of his or her position in the group. Members of cross-functional teams, for example, are expected to perform roles relevant to their special areas of expertise. In our earlier example of cross-functional teams at Hallmark Cards, it is the role of writers on the teams to create verses for new cards, the role of artists to draw illustrations, and the role of designers to put verse and artwork together in an attractive and appealing card design. The roles of members of top-management teams are shaped primarily by their areas of expertise–production, marketing, finance, research and development–but members of top-management teams also typically draw on their broad-based expertise as planners and strategists.

In forming groups and teams, managers need to clearly communicate to group members the expectations for their roles in the group, what is required of them, and how the different roles in the group fit together to accomplish group goals. Managers also need to realize that group roles often change and evolve as a group's tasks and goals change and as group members gain experience and knowledge. Thus, to get the performance gains that come from experience or "learning by doing," managers should

role making Taking the initiative to modify an assigned role by assuming additional responsibilities.

encourage group members to take the initiative to assume additional responsibilities as they see fit and modify their assigned roles. This process, called **role making**, can enhance individual and group performance.

In self-managed work teams and some other groups, group members themselves are responsible for creating and assigning roles. Many self-managed work teams also pick their own team leaders. When group members create their own roles, managers should be available to group members in an advisory capacity, helping them effectively settle conflicts and disagreements. At Johnsonville Foods, for example, the position titles of first-line managers have been changed to "advisory coach" to reflect the managers' new role vis-à-vis the self-managed work teams they oversee.[56]

Group Leadership

All groups and teams need leadership, as George Lopez learned at ICU Medical in the "Management Snapshot."[57] Indeed, as we discussed in detail in Chapter 10, effective leadership is a key ingredient for high-performing groups, teams, and organizations. Sometimes managers assume the leadership role in groups and teams, as is the case in many command groups and top-management teams. Or a manager may appoint a member of a group who is not a manager to be group leader or chairperson, as is the case in a task force or standing committee. In other cases, group or team members may choose their own leaders, or a leader may emerge naturally as group members work together to achieve group goals. When managers empower members of self-managed work teams, they often let group members choose their own leaders. Some self-managed work teams find it effective to rotate the leadership role among their members. Whether leaders of groups and teams are managers or not, and whether they are appointed by managers (often referred to as *formal leaders*) or emerge naturally in a group (often referred to as *informal leaders*), they play an important role in ensuring that groups and teams perform up to their potential.

Group Development over Time

As many managers overseeing self-managed teams have learned, it sometimes takes a self-managed work team two or three years to perform up to its true capabilities.[58] As their experience suggests, what a group is capable of achieving depends in part on its stage of development. Knowing that it takes considerable time for self-managed work teams to get up and running has helped managers have realistic expectations for new teams and know that they need to provide new team members with considerable training and guidance.

Although every group's development over time is somewhat unique, researchers have identified five stages of group development that many groups seem to pass through (see Figure 11.3).[59] In the first stage, *forming,* members try to get to know one another and reach a common understanding of what the group is trying to accomplish and how group members should behave. During this stage, managers should strive to make each member feel that he or she is a valued part of the group.

In the second stage, *storming,* group members experience conflict and disagreements because some members do not wish to submit to the demands of other group members. Disputes may arise over who should lead the group. Self-managed work teams can be particularly vulnerable during the storming stage. Managers need to keep an eye on groups at this stage to make sure that conflict does not get out of hand.

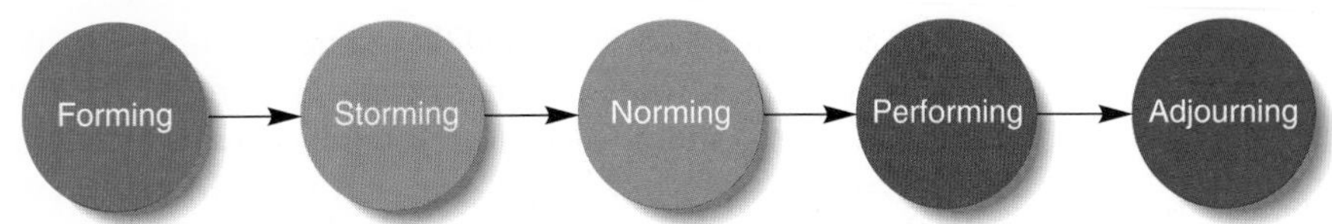

Figure 11.3
Five Stages of Group Development

During the third stage, *norming,* close ties between group members develop, and feelings of friendship and camaraderie emerge. Group members arrive at a consensus about what goals they should be seeking to achieve and how group members should behave toward one another. In the fourth stage, *performing,* the real work of the group gets accomplished. Depending on the type of group in question, managers need to take different steps at this stage to help ensure that groups are effective. Managers of command groups need to make sure that group members are motivated and that they are effectively leading group members. Managers overseeing self-managed work teams have to empower team members and make sure that teams are given enough responsibility and autonomy at the performing stage.

The last stage, *adjourning,* applies only to groups that eventually are disbanded, such as task forces. During adjourning a group is dispersed. Sometimes, adjourning takes place when a group completes a finished product, such as when a task force evaluating the pros and cons of providing on-site child care produces a report supporting its recommendation.

Managers should have a flexible approach to group development and should keep attuned to the different needs and requirements of groups at the various stages.[60] Above all else, and regardless of the stage of development, managers need to think of themselves as *resources* for groups. Thus, managers always should be striving to find ways to help groups and teams function more effectively.

Group Norms

LO4 Explain why it is important for groups and teams to have a balance of conformity and deviance and a moderate level of cohesiveness.

All groups, whether top-management teams, self-managed work teams, or command groups, need to control their members' behaviors to ensure that the group performs at a high level and meets its goals. Assigning roles to each group member is one way to control behavior in groups. Another important way in which groups influence members' behavior is through the development and enforcement of group norms.[61] **Group norms** are shared guidelines or rules for behavior that most group members follow. Groups develop norms concerning a wide variety of behaviors, including working hours, the sharing of information among group members, how certain group tasks should be performed, and even how members of a group should dress.

group norms Shared guidelines or rules for behavior that most group members follow.

Managers should encourage members of a group to develop norms that contribute to group performance and the attainment of group goals. For example, group norms dictating that each member of a cross-functional team should always be available for the rest of the team when his or her input is needed, return phone calls as soon as possible, inform other team members of travel plans, and give team members a phone number at which he or she can be reached when traveling on business help to ensure that the team is efficient, performs at a high level, and achieves its goals. A norm in a command group of secretaries that dictates that secretaries who happen to have a light workload in any given week should help out secretaries with heavier workloads helps to ensure that the group completes all assignments in a timely and efficient manner. And a norm in a top-management team that dictates that team members should always consult with one another before making major decisions helps to ensure that good decisions are made with a minimum of errors.

CONFORMITY AND DEVIANCE Group members conform to norms for three reasons: (1) They want to obtain rewards and avoid punishments. (2) They want to imitate group members whom they like and admire. (3) They have internalized the norm and believe it is the right and proper way to behave.[62] Consider the case of Robert King, who conformed to his department's norm of attending a fund-raiser for a community food bank. King's conformity could be due to (1) his desire to be a member of the group in good standing and to have friendly relationships with other group members (rewards), (2) his copying the behavior of other members of the department whom he respects and who always attend the fund-raiser (imitating other group members), or (3) his belief in the merits of supporting the activities of the food bank (believing that is the right and proper way to behave).

Failure to conform, or deviance, occurs when a member of a group violates a group norm. Deviance signals that a group is not controlling one of its member's behaviors. Groups generally respond to members who behave defiantly in one of three ways:[63]

1. The group might try to get the member to change his or her deviant ways and conform to the norm. Group members might try to convince the member of the need to conform, or they might ignore or even punish the deviant. For example, in a Jacksonville Foods plant, Liz Senkbiel, a member of a self-managed work team responsible for weighing sausages, failed to conform to a group norm dictating that group members should periodically clean up an untidy interview room. Because Senkbiel refused to take part in the team's cleanup efforts, team members reduced her monthly bonus by about $225 for a two-month period.[64] Senkbiel clearly learned the costs of deviant behavior in her team.
2. The group might expel the member.
3. The group might change the norm to be consistent with the member's behavior.

That last alternative suggests that some deviant behavior can be functional for groups. Deviance is functional for a group when it causes group members to evaluate norms that may be dysfunctional but are taken for granted by the group. Often, group members do not think about why they behave in a certain way or why they follow certain norms. Deviance can cause group members to reflect on their norms and change them when appropriate.

Take the case of a group of receptionists in a beauty salon who followed the norm that all appointments would be handwritten in an appointment book and, at the end of each day, the receptionist on duty would enter the appointments into the salon's computer system, which printed out the hairdressers' daily schedules. One day, a receptionist decided to enter appointments directly into the computer system at the time they were being made, bypassing the appointment book. This deviant behavior caused the other receptionists to think about why they were using the appointment book in the first place, since all appointments could be entered into the computer directly. After consulting with the owner of the salon, the group changed its norm. Now appointments are entered directly into the computer, which saves time and cuts down on scheduling errors.

ENCOURAGING A BALANCE OF CONFORMITY AND DEVIANCE To effectively help an organization gain a competitive advantage, groups and teams need to have the right balance of conformity and deviance (see Figure 11.4). A group needs a certain level of conformity to ensure that it can control members' behavior and channel it in the direction of high performance and group goal accomplishment. A group also

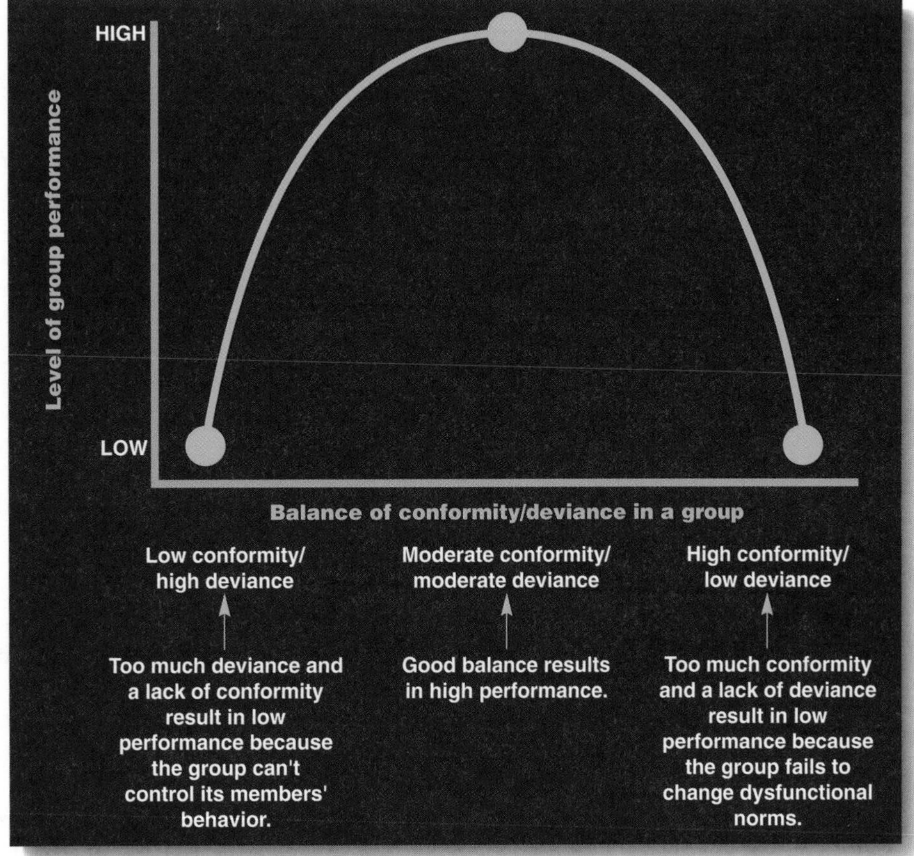

Figure 11.4
Balancing Conformity and Deviance in Groups

needs a certain level of deviance to ensure that dysfunctional norms are discarded and replaced with functional ones. Balancing conformity and deviance is a pressing concern for all groups, whether they are top-management teams, R&D teams, command groups, or self-managed work teams.

The extent of conformity and reactions to deviance within groups are determined by group members themselves. The three bases for conformity just described are powerful forces that more often than not result in group members' conforming to norms. Sometimes these forces are so strong that deviance rarely occurs in groups, and when it does, it is stamped out.

Managers can take several steps to ensure that there is enough tolerance of deviance in groups so that group members are willing to deviate from dysfunctional norms and, when deviance occurs in their group, reflect on the appropriateness of the violated norm and change the norm if necessary. First, managers can be role models for the groups and teams they oversee. When managers encourage and accept employees' suggestions for changes in procedures, do not rigidly insist that tasks be accomplished in a certain way, and admit when a norm that they once supported is no longer functional, they signal to group members that conformity should not come at the expense of needed changes and improvements. Second, managers should let employees know that there are always ways to improve group processes and performance levels and thus opportunities to replace existing norms with norms that will better enable a group to achieve its goals and perform at a high level. Third, managers should encourage members of groups and teams to periodically assess the appropriateness of their existing norms.

Group Cohesiveness

group cohesiveness The degree to which members are attracted to or loyal to their group.

Another important element of group dynamics that affects group performance and effectiveness is **group cohesiveness**, the degree to which members are attracted to or loyal to their group or team.[65] When group cohesiveness is high, individuals strongly value their group membership, find the group very appealing, and have strong desires to remain a part of the group. When group cohesiveness is low, group members do not find their group particularly appealing and have little desire to retain their group membership. Research suggests that managers should strive to have a moderate level of cohesiveness in the groups and teams they manage because that is most likely to contribute to an organization's competitive advantage.

CONSEQUENCES OF GROUP COHESIVENESS There are three major consequences of group cohesiveness: level of participation within a group, level of conformity to group norms, and emphasis on group goal accomplishment (see Figure 11.5).[66]

LEVEL OF PARTICIPATION WITHIN A GROUP As group cohesiveness increases, the extent of group members' participation within the group increases. Participation contributes to group effectiveness because group members are actively involved in the group, ensure that group tasks get accomplished, readily share information with each other, and have frequent and open communication (the important topic of communication is covered in depth in Chapter 13).

A moderate level of group cohesiveness helps to ensure that group members actively participate in the group and communicate effectively with one another. The reason managers may not want to encourage high levels of cohesiveness is illustrated by the example of two cross-functional teams responsible for developing new toys. Members of the highly cohesive Team Alpha often have lengthy meetings that usually start with non-work-related conversations and jokes, meet more often than most of the other cross-functional teams in the company, and spend a good portion of their time

Figure 11.5
Sources and Consequences of Group Cohesiveness

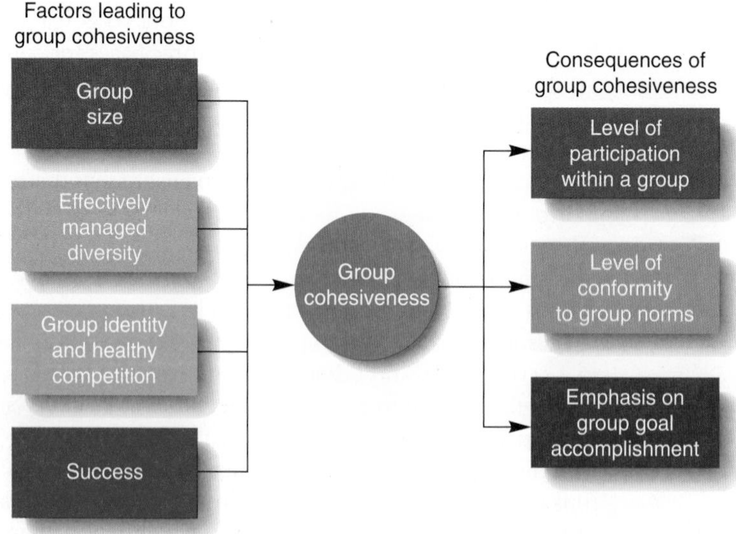

communicating the ins and outs of their department's contribution to toy development to other team members. Members of the moderately cohesive Team Beta generally have efficient meetings in which ideas are communicated and discussed as needed, do not meet more often than necessary, and share the ins and outs of their expertise with one another to the extent needed for the development process. Teams Alpha and Beta have both developed some top-selling toys. However, it generally takes Team Alpha 30% longer to do so than Team Beta. This is why too much cohesiveness can be too much of a good thing.

LEVEL OF CONFORMITY TO GROUP NORMS Increasing levels of group cohesiveness result in increasing levels of conformity to group norms, and when cohesiveness becomes high, there may be so little deviance in groups that group members conform to norms even when they are dysfunctional. In contrast, low cohesiveness can result in too much deviance and undermine the ability of a group to control its members' behaviors to get things done.

Teams Alpha and Beta in the toy company both had the same norm for toy development. It dictated that members of each team would discuss potential ideas for new toys, decide on a line of toys to pursue, and then have the team member from R&D design a prototype. Recently, a new animated movie featuring a family of rabbits produced by a small film company was an unexpected hit, and major toy companies were scrambling to reach licensing agreements to produce toy lines featuring the rabbits. The top-management team in the toy company assigned Teams Alpha and Beta to develop the new toy lines and to do so quickly to beat the competition.

Members of Team Alpha followed their usual toy development norm even though the marketing expert on the team believed that the process could have been streamlined to save time. The marketing expert on Team Beta urged the team to deviate from its toy development norm. She suggested that the team not have R&D develop prototypes but, instead, modify top-selling toys the company already made to feature rabbits and then reach a licensing agreement with the film company based on the high sales potential (given the company's prior success). Once the licensing agreement was signed, the company could take the time needed to develop innovative and unique rabbit toys with more input from R&D.

As a result of the willingness of the marketing expert on Team Beta to deviate from the norm for toy development, the toy company obtained an exclusive licensing agreement with the film company and had its first rabbit toys on the shelves of stores in a record three months. Groups need a balance of conformity and deviance, so a moderate level of cohesiveness often yields the best outcome, as it did in the case of Team Beta.

EMPHASIS ON GROUP GOAL ACCOMPLISHMENT As group cohesiveness increases, the emphasis placed on group goal accomplishment also increases within a group. A very strong emphasis on group goal accomplishment, however, does not always lead to organizational effectiveness. For an organization to be effective and gain a competitive advantage, the different groups and teams in the organization must cooperate with one another and be motivated to achieve *organizational goals,* even if doing so sometimes comes at the expense of the achievement of group goals. A moderate level of cohesiveness motivates group members to accomplish both group and organizational goals. High levels of cohesiveness can cause group members to be so focused on group goal accomplishment that they may strive to achieve group goals no matter what—even when doing so jeopardizes organizational performance.

At the toy company, the major goal of the cross-functional teams was to develop new toy lines that were truly innovative, utilized the latest in technology, and were in some way fundamentally distinct from other toys on the market. When it came to the rabbit project, Team Alpha's high level of cohesiveness contributed to its continued emphasis on its group goal of developing an innovative line of toys; thus, the team stuck with its usual design process. Team Beta, in contrast, realized that developing the new line of toys quickly was an important organizational goal that should take precedence over the group's goal of developing groundbreaking new toys, at least in the short run. Team Beta's moderate level of cohesiveness contributed to team members' doing what was best for the toy company in this case.

FACTORS LEADING TO GROUP COHESIVENESS Four factors contribute to the level of group cohesiveness (see Figure 11.5).[67] By influencing these *determinants of group cohesiveness,* managers can raise or lower the level of cohesiveness to promote moderate levels of cohesiveness in groups and teams.

GROUP SIZE As we mentioned earlier, members of small groups tend to be more motivated and committed than members of large groups. Thus, to promote cohesiveness in groups, when feasible, managers should form groups that are small to medium in size (about 2 to 15 members). If a group is low in cohesiveness and large in size, managers might want to consider the feasibility of dividing the group in two and assigning different tasks and goals to the two newly formed groups.

EFFECTIVELY MANAGED DIVERSITY In general, people tend to like and get along with others who are similar to themselves. It is easier to communicate with someone, for example, who shares your values, has a similar background, and has had similar experiences. However, as discussed in Chapter 3, diversity in groups, teams, and organizations can help an organization gain a competitive advantage. Diverse groups often come up with more innovative and creative ideas. One reason cross-functional teams are so popular in organizations like Hallmark Cards is that the diversity in expertise represented in the teams results in higher levels of team performance.

In forming groups and teams, managers need to make sure that the diversity in knowledge, experience, expertise, and other characteristics necessary for group goal accomplishment is represented in the new groups. Managers then have to make sure that this diversity in group membership is effectively managed so that groups will be cohesive (see Chapter 3).

GROUP IDENTITY AND HEALTHY COMPETITION When group cohesiveness is low, managers can often increase it by encouraging groups to develop their own identities or personalities and to engage in healthy competition. This is precisely what managers at Eaton Corporation's manufacturing facility in Lincoln, Illinois, did. Eaton's employees manufacture products such as engine valves, gears, truck axles, and circuit breakers. Managers at Eaton created self-managed work teams to cut costs and improve performance. They realized, however, that the teams would have to be cohesive to ensure that they would strive to achieve their goals. Managers promoted group identity by having the teams give themselves names such as "The Hoods," "The Worms," and "Scrap Attack" (a team striving to reduce costly scrap-metal waste by 50%). Healthy competition among groups was promoted by displaying measures of each team's performance and the extent to which teams met their goals on a large TV screen in the cafeteria and by rewarding team members for team performance.[68]

If groups are too cohesive, managers can try to decrease cohesiveness by promoting organizational (rather than group) identity and making the organization as a whole the focus of the group's efforts. Organizational identity can be promoted by making group members feel that they are valued members of the organization and by stressing cooperation across groups to promote the achievement of organizational goals. Excessive levels of cohesiveness also can be reduced by reducing or eliminating competition among groups and rewarding cooperation.

SUCCESS When it comes to promoting group cohesiveness, there is more than a grain of truth to the saying "Nothing succeeds like success." As groups become more successful, they become increasingly attractive to their members, and their cohesiveness tends to increase. When cohesiveness is low, managers can increase cohesiveness by making sure that a group can achieve some noticeable and visible successes.

Take the case of a group of salespeople in the housewares department of a medium-size department store. The housewares department was recently moved to a corner of the store's basement. Its remote location resulted in low sales because of infrequent customer traffic in that part of the store. The salespeople, who were generally evaluated favorably by their supervisors and were valued members of the store, tried various initiatives to boost sales, but to no avail. As a result of this lack of success and the poor performance of their department, their cohesiveness started to plummet. To increase and preserve the cohesiveness of the group, the store manager implemented a group-based incentive across the store. In any month, members of the group with the best attendance and punctuality records would have their names and pictures posted on a bulletin board in the cafeteria and would each receive a $50 gift certificate. The housewares group frequently had the best records, and their success on this dimension helped to build and maintain their cohesiveness. Moreover, this initiative boosted attendance and discouraged lateness throughout the store.

Managing Groups and Teams for High Performance

Now that you have a good understanding of why groups and teams are so important for organizations, the types of groups that managers create, and group dynamics, we consider some additional steps that managers can take to make sure groups and teams perform at a high level and contribute to organizational effectiveness. Managers striving to have top-performing groups and teams need to motivate group members to work toward the achievement of organizational goals and reduce social loafing.

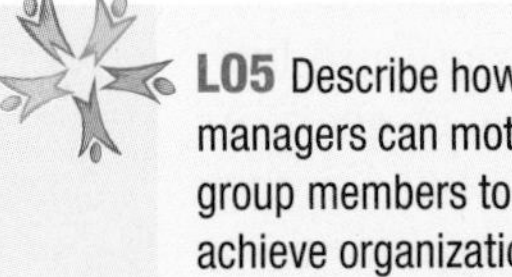

LO5 Describe how managers can motivate group members to achieve organizational goals and reduce social loafing in groups and teams.

Motivating Group Members to Achieve Organizational Goals

When work is difficult, tedious, or requires a high level of commitment and energy, managers cannot assume that group members will always be motivated to work toward the achievement of organizational goals. Consider the case of a group of house painters who paint the interiors and exteriors of new homes for a construction company and are paid on an hourly basis. Why should they strive to complete painting jobs quickly and efficiently if doing so will just make them feel more tired at the end of the day and they will not receive any tangible benefits? It makes more sense for the painters to adopt a more relaxed approach, to take frequent breaks, and to work at a leisurely pace. This relaxed approach, however, impairs the construction company's ability to gain a competitive advantage because it raises costs and increases the time needed to complete a new home.

Managers can motivate members of groups and teams to achieve organizational goals by making sure that the members themselves benefit when the group or team performs highly. For example, if members of a self-managed work team know that they will receive a weekly bonus based on team performance, they will be highly motivated to perform at a high level. Recall from the "Management Snapshot" how teams of employees formed at ICU Medical are rewarded when they successfully complete their projects.[69]

Managers often rely on some combination of individual and group-based incentives to motivate members of groups and teams to work toward the achievement of organizational goals. When individual performance within a group can be assessed, pay is often determined by individual performance or by both individual and group performance. When individual performance within a group cannot be accurately assessed, then group performance should be the key determinant of pay levels. Many companies that use self-managed work teams base team members' pay in part on team performance.[70] A major challenge for managers is to develop a fair pay system that will lead to both high individual motivation and high group or team performance.

Other benefits that managers can make available to high-performance group members–in addition to monetary rewards–include extra resources such as equipment and computer software, awards and other forms of recognition, and choice of future work assignments. For example, members of self-managed work teams that develop new software at companies such as Microsoft often value working on interesting and important projects; members of teams that have performed at a high level are rewarded by being assigned to interesting and important new projects.

At IDEO, the innovative design firm based in Palo Alto, California, managers motivate team members by making them feel important. As Tom Kelley, IDEO's general manager, puts it, "When people feel special, they'll perform beyond your wildest dreams."[71] To make IDEO team members feel special, IDEO managers plan unique and fun year-end parties, give teams the opportunity to take time off if they feel they need or want to, encourage teams to take field trips, and see pranks as a way to incorporate fun into the workplace.[72]

Valero Energy Corp. helped workers, like Ronald Lewis, get back on their feet in the wake of Hurricane Katrina, which damaged many homes and communities in Louisiana.

Valero Energy motivates groups and teams to achieve organizational goals by valuing its employees, looking out for their well-being, and standing by them in crisis situations.[73] For example, employees with medical emergencies can use Valero's corporate jet if they need to, and Valero covers the complete cost of employee's health insurance premiums.[74] In turn, group members put forth high levels of effort to help Valero achieve its goals. As former Valero CEO and chairman Bill Greehey put it, "The more you do for your employees, the more they do for shareholders and the more they do for the community."[75]

When Hurricane Katrina hit the Louisiana coastline in 2005, the way Valero stood by employees in its St. Charles oil refinery near New Orleans and the way employees stood by each other and the company brought plant manager

Jonathan Stuart to tears as he was briefing Greehey and other top managers a few days after the hurricane hit.[76] Stuart led a 50-person crew that rode out the hurricane in the shut-down refinery. The day before the storm hit, a supervisor used his personal credit card to buy supplies and stayed up all night preparing meals for the crew. Crew members worked round the clock, putting up new power poles, repairing power lines, and replacing motors. The refinery was up and running within eight days (while a Shell refinery close by was still shut down), and the crew had located all of the plant's 570 employees.[77]

Valero's headquarters had supplies delivered to employees whose homes were damaged; trucks brought in food, water, generators, chain saws, refrigerators, shovels, and Nextel phones (the only cell phone system that was still working). Sixty mobile homes were brought in for employees whose houses were unlivable. Employees and law enforcement personnel were provided with free fuel, and employees were given up to $10,000 in aide from Valero's SAFE fund. Valero continued issuing paychecks to its employees, while other affected refineries did not.[78]

Reducing Social Loafing in Groups

We have been focusing on the steps that managers can take to encourage high levels of performance in groups. Managers, however, need to be aware of an important downside to group and team work: the potential for social loafing, which reduces group performance. **Social loafing** is the tendency of individuals to put forth less effort when they work in groups than when they work alone.[79] Have you ever worked on a group project in which one or two group members never seemed to be pulling their weight? Have you ever worked in a student club or committee in which some members always seemed to be missing meetings and never volunteered for activities? Have you ever had a job in which one or two of your coworkers seemed to be slacking off because they knew that you or other members of your work group would make up for their low levels of effort? If you have, you have witnessed social loafing in action.

social loafing The tendency of individuals to put forth less effort when they work in groups than when they work alone.

Social loafing can occur in all kinds of groups and teams and in all kinds of organizations. It can result in lower group performance and may even prevent a group from attaining its goals. Fortunately, there are steps managers can take to reduce social loafing and sometimes completely eliminate it; we will look at three (see Figure 11.6).

Figure 11.6
Three Ways to Reduce Social Loafing

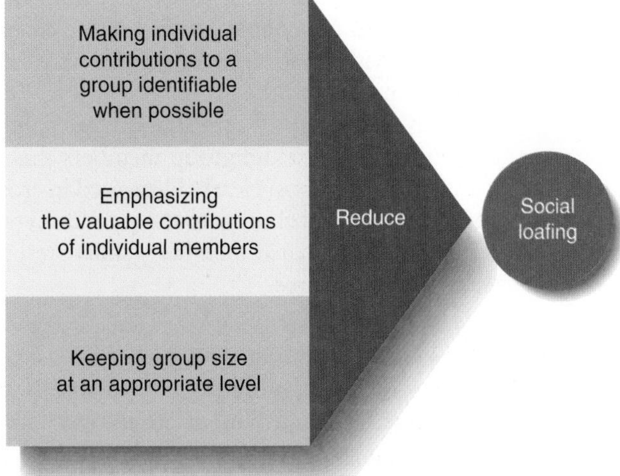

1. *Make individual contributions to a group identifiable.* Some people may engage in social loafing when they work in groups because they think that they can hide in the crowd–that no one will notice if they put forth less effort than they should. Other people may think that if they put forth high levels of effort and make substantial contributions to the group, their contributions will not be noticed and they will receive no rewards for their work–so why bother?[80]

One way in which managers can effectively eliminate social loafing is by making individual contributions to a group identifiable so that group members perceive that low and high levels of effort will be noticed and individual contributions evaluated.[81] Managers can accomplish this by assigning specific tasks to group members and holding them accountable for their completion. Take the case of a group of eight employees responsible for reshelving returned books in a large public library in New York. The head librarian was concerned that there was always a backlog of seven or eight carts of books to be reshelved, even though the employees never seemed to be particularly busy and some even found time to sit down and read newspapers and magazines. The librarian decided to try to eliminate the apparent social loafing by assigning each employee sole responsibility for reshelving a particular section of the library. Because the library's front-desk employees sorted the books by section on the carts as they were returned, holding the shelvers responsible for particular sections was easily accomplished. Once the shelvers knew that the librarian could identify their effort or lack of effort, there were rarely any backlogs of books to be reshelved.

Sometimes the members of a group can cooperate to eliminate social loafing by making individual contributions identifiable. For example, in a small security company, members of a self-managed work team who assemble control boxes for home alarm systems start each day by deciding who will perform which tasks that day and how much work each member and the group as a whole should strive to accomplish. Each team member knows that, at the end of the day, the other team members will know exactly how much he or she has accomplished. With this system in place, social loafing never occurs in the team. Remember, however, that in some teams, individual contributions cannot be made identifiable.

2. *Emphasize the valuable contributions of individual members.* Another reason why social loafing may occur is that people sometimes think that their efforts are unnecessary or unimportant when they work in a group. They feel the group will accomplish its goals and perform at an acceptable level whether or not they personally perform at a high level. To counteract this belief, when managers form groups, they should assign individuals to a group on the basis of the valuable contributions that *each* person can make to the group as a whole. Clearly communicating to group members why each person's contributions are valuable to the group is an effective means by which managers and group members themselves can reduce or eliminate social loafing.[82] This is most clearly illustrated in cross-functional teams, where each member's valuable contribution to the team derives from a personal area of expertise. By emphasizing why each member's skills are important, managers can reduce social loafing in such teams.

3. *Keep group size at an appropriate level.* Group size is related to the causes of social loafing we just described. As size increases, identifying individual contributions becomes increasingly difficult and members are increasingly likely to think that their individual contributions are not very important. To overcome this, managers should form groups with no more members than are needed to accomplish group goals and perform at a high level.[83]

Summary and Review

GROUPS, TEAMS, AND ORGANIZATIONAL EFFECTIVENESS A group is two or more people who interact with each other to accomplish certain goals or meet certain needs. A team is a group whose members work intensely with one another to achieve a specific common goal or objective. Groups and teams can contribute to organizational effectiveness by enhancing performance, increasing responsiveness to customers, increasing innovation, and being a source of motivation for their members. **[LO1]**

TYPES OF GROUPS AND TEAMS Formal groups are groups that managers establish to achieve organizational goals; they include cross-functional teams, cross-cultural teams, top-management teams, research and development teams, command groups, task forces, self-managed work teams, and virtual teams. Informal groups are groups that employees form because they believe that the groups will help them achieve their own goals or meet their needs; they include friendship groups and interest groups. **[LO2]**

GROUP DYNAMICS Key elements of group dynamics are group size, tasks, and roles; group leadership; group development; group norms; and group cohesiveness. The advantages and disadvantages of large and small groups suggest that managers should form groups with no more members than are needed to provide the group with the human resources it needs to achieve its goals and use a division of labor. A group role is a set of behaviors and tasks that a member of a group is expected to perform because of his or her position in the group. All groups and teams need leadership. **[LO3]**

Five stages of development that many groups pass through are forming, storming, norming, performing, and adjourning. Group norms are shared rules for behavior that most group members follow. To be effective, groups need a balance of conformity and deviance. Conformity allows a group to control its members' behavior to achieve group goals; deviance provides the impetus for needed change. **[LO3, 4]**

Group cohesiveness is the attractiveness of a group or team to its members. As group cohesiveness increases, so, too, does the level of participation and communication within a group, the level of conformity to group norms, and the emphasis on group goal accomplishment. Managers should strive to achieve a moderate level of group cohesiveness in the groups and teams they manage. **[LO4]**

MANAGING GROUPS AND TEAMS FOR HIGH PERFORMANCE To make sure that groups and teams perform at a high level, managers need to motivate group members to work toward the achievement of organizational goals and reduce social loafing. Managers can motivate members of groups and teams to work toward the achievement of organizational goals by making sure that members personally benefit when the group or team performs at a high level. **[LO5]**

Management in Action

Topics for Discussion and Action

Discussion

1. Why do all organizations need to rely on groups and teams to achieve their goals and gain a competitive advantage? [LO1]
2. What kinds of employees would prefer to work in a virtual team? What kinds of employees would prefer to work in a team that meets face-to-face? [LO2]
3. Think about a group that you are a member of, and describe that group's current stage of development. Does the development of this group seem to be following the forming, storming, norming, performing, and adjourning stages described in the chapter? [LO3]
4. Discuss the reasons why too much conformity can hurt groups and their organizations. [LO4]
5. Why do some groups have very low levels of cohesiveness? [LO4]
6. Imagine that you are the manager of a hotel. What steps will you take to reduce social loafing by members of the cleaning staff who are responsible for keeping all common areas and guest rooms spotless? [LO5]

Action

7. Interview one or more managers in an organization in your local community to identify the types of groups and teams that the organization uses to achieve its goals. What challenges do these groups and teams face? [LO2]

Building Management Skills

Diagnosing Group Failures [LO1, 2, 3, 4, 5]

Think about the last dissatisfying or discouraging experience you had as a member of a group or team. Perhaps the group did not accomplish its goals, perhaps group members could agree about nothing, or perhaps there was too much social loafing. Now answer the following questions:

1. What type of group was this?
2. Were group members motivated to achieve group goals? Why or why not?
3. How large was the group, and what group roles did members play?
4. What were the group's norms? How much conformity and deviance existed in the group?
5. How cohesive was the group? Why do you think the group's cohesiveness was at this level? What consequences did this level of group cohesiveness have for the group and its members?
6. Was social loafing a problem in this group? Why or why not?
7. What could the group's leader or manager have done differently to increase group effectiveness?
8. What could group members have done differently to increase group effectiveness?

Managing Ethically [LO1, 2, 3, 4, 5]

Some self-managed teams encounter a vexing problem: One or more members engage in social loafing, and other members are reluctant to try to rectify the situation. Social loafing can be especially troubling if team members' pay is based on team performance and social loafing reduces the team's performance and thus the pay of all members (even the highest performers). Even if managers are aware of the problem, they may be reluctant to take action because the team is supposedly self-managing.

Questions

1. Either individually or in a group, think about the ethical implications of social loafing in a self-managed team.
2. Do managers have an ethical obligation to step in when they are aware of social loafing in a self-managed team? Why or why not? Do other team members have an obligation to try to curtail the social loafing? Why or why not?

Small Group Breakout Exercise

Creating a Cross-Functional Team [LO1, 2, 3, 4, 5]

Form groups of three or four people, and appoint one member as the spokesperson who will communicate your findings to the class when called on by the instructor. Then discuss the following scenario:

You are a group of managers in charge of food services for a large state university in the Midwest. Recently a survey of students, faculty, and staff was conducted to evaluate customer satisfaction with the food services provided by the university's eight cafeterias. The results were disappointing, to put it mildly. Complaints ranged from dissatisfaction with the type and range of meals and snacks provided, operating hours, and food temperature to frustration about unresponsiveness to current concerns about low-carbohydrate diets and the needs of vegetarians. You have decided to form a cross-functional team that will further evaluate reactions to the food services and will develop a proposal for changes to be made to increase customer satisfaction.

1. Indicate who should be on this important cross-functional team, and explain why.
2. Describe the goals the team should be striving to achieve.
3. Describe the different roles that will need to be performed on this team.
4. Describe the steps you will take to help ensure that the team has a good balance between conformity and deviance and has a moderate level of cohesiveness.

Be the Manager [LO1, 2, 3, 4, 5]

You were recently hired in a boundary-spanning role for the global unit of an educational and professional publishing company. The company is headquartered in New York (where you work) and has divisions in multiple countries. Each division is responsible for translating, manufacturing, marketing, and selling a set of books in its country. Your responsibilities include interfacing with managers in each of the divisions in your region (Central and South America), overseeing their budgeting and financial reporting to headquarters, and leading a virtual team consisting of the top managers in charge of each of the divisions in your region. The virtual team's mission is to promote global learning, explore new potential opportunities and markets, and address ongoing problems. You communicate directly with division managers via telephone and e-mail, as well as written reports, memos, and faxes. When virtual team meetings are convened, videoconferencing is often used.

After your first few virtual team meetings, you noticed that the managers seemed to be reticent about speaking up. Interestingly enough, when each manager communicates with you individually, primarily in telephone conversations and e-mails, she or he tends to be very forthcoming and frank and you feel you have a good rapport with each of them. However, getting the managers to communicate with one another as a virtual team has been a real challenge. At the last meeting, you tried to prompt some of the managers to raise issues relevant to the agenda that you knew were on their minds from your individual conversations with them. Surprisingly, the managers skillfully avoided informing their teammates about the heart of the issues in question. You are confused and troubled. While you feel your other responsibilities are going well, you know that your virtual team is not operating like a team at all and, no matter what you try, discussions in virtual team meetings are forced and generally unproductive. What are you going to do to address this problem?

BusinessWeek Case in the News [LO1, 2, 3, 4, 5]

The Globe Is IBM's Classroom

When 10 IBM management trainees piled into a minibus in the Philippines for a weekend tour last October, the last thing they expected was to wind up local heroes. Yet that's what happened in the tiny village of Carmen. After passing a water well project, they learned the effort had stalled because of engineering mistakes and a lack of money. The IBMers decided to do something about it. They organized a meeting of the key people involved in the project and volunteered to pay $250 out of their own pockets for additional building materials. Two weeks later the well was completed. Locals would no longer have to walk four miles for drinkable water. And the trainees learned a lesson in collaborative problem-solving. "You motivate people to take the extra step, you create a shared vision, you divide the labor, and the impact can be big," says Erwin van Overbeek, 40, who runs environmental sustainability projects for IBM clients.

While saving a village well wasn't part of the group agenda for that trip, it's the kind of experience the architects of IBM's Corporate Service Corps had in mind when they launched the initiative last year. Modeled on the U.S. Peace Corps, the program aims to turn IBM employees into global citizens. Last year, IBM selected 300 top management prospects out of 5,400 applicants. It then trained and dispatched them to emerging markets for a month in groups of 8 to 10 to help solve economic and social problems. The goal, says IBM's human resources chief, J. Randall MacDonald, is to help future leaders "understand how the world works, show them how to network, and show them how to work collaboratively with people who are far away."

Like most corporations, IBM trains managers in classrooms, so this represents a dramatic departure. And while other companies encourage employees to volunteer for social service, IBM is the first to use such programs for management training, says Rosabeth Moss Kanter, a professor at Harvard Business School. "This is a big innovation. This kind of active service is a good way to train managers."

The program is growing rapidly. This year some 500 people will participate, and the list of countries will expand from five to nine, including Brazil, India, Malaysia, and South Africa. The teams spend three months before going overseas reading about their host countries, studying the problems they're assigned to work on, and getting to know their teammates via teleconferences and social networking Web sites. On location, they work with local governments, universities, and business groups to do anything from upgrading technology for a government agency to improving public water quality.

Malaria and Wild Dogs

Participating in the program is not without its risks. Charlie Ung, a new-media producer from IBM Canada, got malaria while working in Ghana and spent a week in the hospital. Other participants report encounters with wild dogs in Romania. IBM planners deliberately choose out-of-the-way places and bunk the teams in guest houses that lack such amenities as Western food and CNN. "We want them to have a transformative experience, so they're shaken up and walk away feeling they're better equipped to confront the challenges of the 21st century," says Kevin Thompson, the IBMer who conceived of the CSC program and now manages it.

IBM concedes that one month overseas is a short stint, but it believes participants can pick up valuable lessons. Debbie Maconnel, a 45-year-old IT project manager in Lexington, Kentucky, says the trip prompted her to change her management style. She coordinates the activities of 13 people in the United States and 12 in India, Mexico, and China. She used to give assignments to the overseas employees and then leave them on their own. Now she spends more time trying to build a global team.

Harvard Business School assistant professor Christopher Marquis, who's writing a Harvard case study on the program, recommends that others build similar teams. "As the world gets flatter, cultural differences and the ability to manage across them is going to be much more important."

Questions

1. Why does IBM use teams in its Corporate Services Corps?
2. What type of team(s) does IBM use in its Corporate Services Corps?
3. What factors likely contribute to the cohesiveness of these teams?
4. What factors do you think motivate team members to work toward the Corporate Services Corps' goals?

Source: Steve Hamm, "The Globe Is IBM's Classroom." Reprinted from March 23 and 30, 2009 issues of *BusinessWeek*, by special permission. copyright © 2009 by The McGraw-Hill Companies, Inc.

BusinessWeek Case in the News [LO1, 2, 3, 4, 5]

Managing at a Distance

Managing virtually offers many benefits: It's easy to accommodate differing schedules, schedule meetings on short notice, reduce travel expenses, be more ecologically friendly, and decrease unproductive travel time. It also allows for the creation of more diverse teams that bring together broader experience and knowledge. But the most important thing for managers to remember is that the success of any team, virtual or not, depends on the people. Technology can bring you together, but it's the manager who must make sure the relationships stay vital, each team member is valued, and productivity is high.

A lot of companies are now looking at having people work virtually. The younger generation expects flexibility. You have to be visible in your activities, especially in this environment, but visibility doesn't have to be face-to-face. Those who can demonstrate how to do more with less money are the leaders of tomorrow. Insisting on more face time makes you look out of touch.

Technology matters, so understand the latest innovations and make an effort to incorporate them into your work life. Simply having access to e-mail and the company intranet isn't enough. Think about setting up a community home space featuring pictures and profiles of team members, a discussion board, a team calendar, or a chat room. That will help team members connect with each other outside of meetings and create a closer bond as a group.

Also, listen carefully to every team member on phone calls. You don't have the benefit of face-to-face interactions (although videoconferencing can help). I focus on how the person is speaking. Is the person excited? Bored? Is the choice of words overly careful? Is there a quality in the speaker's voice that would make a private conversation advisable?

It's important to listen to everything, particularly any silences. Silence can mean consent, or it can mean the person you're not hearing from disagrees with the team's strategy or is disengaged. You need to hear from everyone to make sure the team is moving forward together. If I sense that a team member is lacking engagement—not responding, not participating, or missing deadlines—I call as soon as possible after the meeting to find out what's going on. And I always send an e-mail after each meeting to document and confirm discussions, conclusions, and next steps.

Managing a global team brings another set of challenges. You have to be sensitive to language differences, business protocols, and time zones. When managing a team that serves a multicountry client or one in which many of the team members speak English as a second language, it's vital to determine that everyone understands what has been said. "I heard you say . . ." is something I often say when I have a sense that a point may need clarification.

A virtual manager also shows respect by making sure the burden of holding international conference calls is shared. Scheduling regular calls at convenient times for everyone may not be possible. In this case, I shift the start time so that people take turns participating in the calls during their early morning or late evening. Don't simply assume that everyone should adapt to your time zone.

"Virtual" also should not mean you never meet. With international teams, I visit each country's team once a year. With Ernst & Young's Americas Inclusiveness team, which has members in a number of locations, we all get together annually. In the current economy, it might not be possible to meet as often as you would like. But you need to step up the frequency of communication. Check in more often, and make sure people understand what's going on.

Questions

1. What are the advantages of using virtual teams in place of teams that meet face-to-face?
2. What factors are important for ensuring the effectiveness of virtual teams?
3. Why is listening so important in virtual teamwork?
4. Why is it important to follow up with team members who are silent?

Source: Billie Williamson, "Managing at a Distance." Reprinted from July 27, 2009 issue of *BusinessWeek*, by special permission, copyright © 2009 by The McGraw-Hill Companies, Inc.

The Four Seasons treats its employees well, and in turn they treat customers well.

MANAGEMENT SNAPSHOT

Effectively Managing Human Resources at the Four Seasons

How Can Managers Promote High Levels of Personalized Customer Service in an Industry Known for High Employee Turnover?

Four Seasons Hotels and Resorts is one of only about 14 companies to be ranked one of the "100 Best Companies to Work For" every year since *Fortune* magazine started this annual ranking of companies over 10 years ago.[1] And the Four Seasons often receives other awards and recognition based on customers' responses.[2] In an industry in which annual turnover rates are over 35%, the Four Seasons' is around 18%.[3] Evidently, employees and customers alike are very satisfied with the way they are treated at the Four Seasons. Understanding that the two are causally linked is perhaps the key to the Four Seasons' success. As the Four Seasons' founder, chairman of the board, and CEO Isadore Sharp suggests, "How you treat your employees is how you expect them to treat the customer."[4]

The Four Seasons was founded by Sharp in 1961. After opening and running both small and large hotels, Sharp decided that he could provide customers with a very different kind of hotel experience by trying to combine the best features of both kinds of hotel experiences—the sense of closeness and personal attention that a small hotel brings with the amenities of a big hotel to suit the needs of business travelers.[5]

Sharp sought to provide the kind of personal service that would really help business travelers on the road—providing them with the amenities they have at home and in the office and miss when traveling on business. Thus, the Four Seasons was the first hotel chain to provide many amenities such as bathrobes and shampoo.[6] While these are relatively concrete ways of personalizing the hotel experience, Sharp realized that the ways in which employees treat customers are just as, or perhaps even more, important. When employees view each customer as an individual with his or her own needs and desires, and empathetically try to meet these needs and desires and help customers both overcome any problems or challenges they face and truly enjoy their hotel experience, customers are likely to be both loyal and highly satisfied.[7]

Sharp has always realized that in order for employees to treat customers well, the Four Seasons needs to treat its employees well. Salaries are relatively high at the Four Seasons, by industry standards (i.e., between the 75th and 90th percentiles), employees participate in a profit-sharing plan, and the company contributes to their 401(k) plans. All employees are provided with free meals in the hotel cafeteria, have access to staff showers and a locker room, and are provided with an additional, highly attractive benefit. Once a new employee has worked for the Four Seasons for six months, he or she can stay for three nights free at any Four Seasons hotel or resort in the world. After a year of employment, this benefit increases to six free nights and it continues to increase as tenure with the company increases.[8]

All aspects of human resource management at the Four Seasons are oriented around ensuring that the guiding principle behind all Four Seasons operations is upheld. As Sharp indicates, all employees and managers should ". . . deal with others—partners, customers, coworkers, everyone—as we would want them to deal with us."[9]

All job applicants to the Four Seasons, regardless of level or area, have a minimum of four interviews, one of which is with the general manager of the property.[10] The Four Seasons devotes so much attention to hiring the right people because of the importance of each and every employee providing a consistently high level of empathetic and responsive customer service.[11]

New hires participate in a three-month training program that includes improvisation activities to help new hires learn how to anticipate guests' needs, requirements, and actions and appropriately respond to them.[12] The aim of training is to help ensure that all employees, regardless of area or function, provide consistently high-quality and highly responsive customer service. Since customer service is everyone's responsibility, the Four Seasons has no separate customer service department per se. Training is an ongoing activity at the Four Seasons and never really stops.[13]

The Four Seasons also tends to promote from within.[14] For example, while recent college graduates may start out as assistant managers, those who do well and have high aspirations could potentially become general managers in less than 15 years. This helps to ensure that managers have empathy and respect for those in lower-level positions as well as the ingrained ethos of treating others (employees, subordinates, coworkers, and customers) the way they would like to be treated themselves. All in all, the ways in which the Four Seasons manages its human resources helps to ensure that customers are treated very well indeed.[15]

Overview

Managers are responsible for acquiring, developing, protecting, and utilizing the resources that an organization needs to be efficient and effective. One of the most important resources in all organizations is human resources–the people involved in the production and distribution of goods and services. Human resources include all members of an organization, ranging from top managers to entry-level employees. Effective managers like Isadore Sharp in the "Management Snapshot" realize how valuable human resources are and take active steps to make sure that their organizations build and fully utilize their human resources to gain a competitive advantage.

LO1 Explain why strategic human resource management can help an organization gain a competitive advantage.

This chapter examines how managers can tailor their human resource management system to their organization's strategy and structure. We discuss in particular the major components of human resource management: recruitment and selection, training and development, performance appraisal, pay and benefits, and labor relations. By the end of this chapter, you will understand the central role human resource management plays in creating a high-performing organization.

Strategic Human Resource Management

human resource management (HRM) Activities that managers engage in to attract and retain employees and to ensure that they perform at a high level and contribute to the accomplishment of organizational goals.

strategic human resource management The process by which managers design the components of an HRM system to be consistent with each other, with other elements of organizational architecture, and with the organization's strategy and goals.

Human resource management (HRM) includes all the activities managers engage in to attract and retain employees and to ensure that they perform at a high level and contribute to the accomplishment of organizational goals. These activities make up an organization's human resource management system, which has five major components: recruitment and selection, training and development, performance appraisal and feedback, pay and benefits, and labor relations (see Figure 12.1).

Strategic human resource management is the process by which managers design the components of an HRM system to be consistent with each other, with other elements of organizational architecture, and with the organization's strategy and goals.[16] The objective of strategic HRM is the development of an HRM system that enhances an organization's efficiency, quality, innovation, and responsiveness to customers–the four building blocks of competitive advantage. At the Four Seasons in the "Management Snapshot," HRM practices ensure that all employees provide excellent customer service.

As part of strategic human resource management, some managers have adopted "Six Sigma" quality improvement plans. These plans ensure that an organization's products and services are as free of error or defects as possible through a variety of human resource–related initiatives. Jack Welch, former CEO of General Electric Company, has indicated that these initiatives have saved his company millions of dollars, and other companies, such as Whirlpool and Motorola, also have implemented Six Sigma initiatives. In order for such initiatives to be effective, however, top managers have to

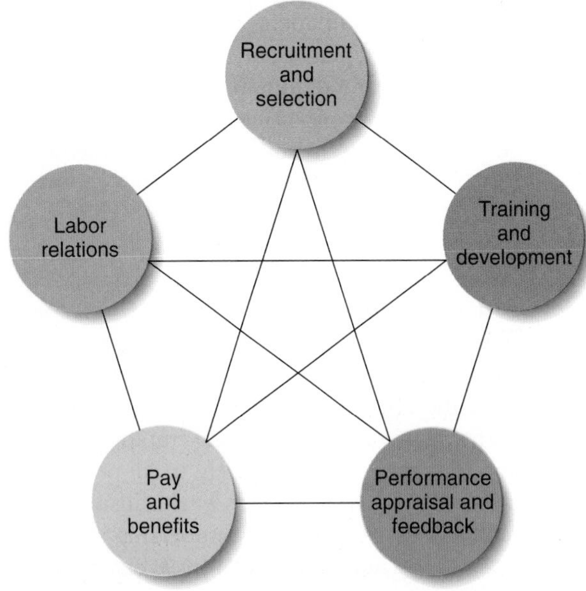

Each component of an HRM system influences the others, and all five must fit together

Figure 12.1
Components of a Human Resource Management System

be committed to Six Sigma, employees must be motivated, and there must be demand for the products or services of the organization in the first place. David Fitzpatrick, head of Deloitte Consulting's Lean Enterprise Practice, estimates that most Six Sigma plans are not effective because the conditions for effective Six Sigma are not in place. For example, if top managers are not committed to the quality initiative, they may not devote the necessary time and resources to make it work and may lose interest in it prematurely.[17]

Overview of the Components of HRM

Managers use *recruitment and selection,* the first component of an HRM system, to attract and hire new employees who have the abilities, skills, and experiences that will help an organization achieve its goals. Microsoft Corporation, for example, has the goal of remaining the premier computer software company in the world. To achieve this goal, managers at Microsoft realize the importance of hiring only the best software designers: hundreds of highly qualified candidates are interviewed and rigorously tested. This careful attention to selection has contributed to Microsoft's competitive advantage. Microsoft has little trouble recruiting top programmers because candidates know they will be at the forefront of the industry if they work for Microsoft.[18]

After recruiting and selecting employees, managers use the second component, *training and development,* to ensure that organizational members develop the skills and abilities that will enable them to perform their jobs effectively in the present and the future. Training and development are an ongoing process; changes in technology and the environment, as well as in an organization's goals and strategies, often require that organizational members learn new techniques and ways of working. At Microsoft Corporation, newly hired program designers receive on-the-job training by joining small teams that include experienced employees who serve as mentors or advisers. New recruits learn firsthand from team members how to go about developing computer systems that are responsive to customers' programming needs.[19]

The third component, *performance appraisal and feedback,* serves two different purposes in HRM. First, performance appraisal can provide managers with the information they need to make good human resources decisions–decisions about how to train, motivate, and reward organizational members.[20] Second, feedback from performance appraisal serves a developmental purpose for members of an organization. When managers regularly evaluate their subordinates' performance, they can provide employees with valuable information about their strengths and weaknesses and the areas in which they need to concentrate.

On the basis of performance appraisals, managers distribute *pay* to employees, part of the fourth component of an HRM system. By rewarding high-performing organizational members with pay raises, bonuses, and the like, managers increase the likelihood that an organization's most valued human resources are motivated to continue their high levels of contribution to the organization. Moreover, if pay is linked to performance, high-performing employees are more likely to stay with the organization, and managers are more likely to fill positions that become open with highly talented individuals. *Benefits* such as health insurance are important outcomes that employees receive by virtue of their membership in an organization.

Last, but not least, *labor relations* encompass the steps that managers take to develop and maintain good working relationships with the labor unions that may represent their employees' interests. For example, an organization's labor relations component can help managers establish safe working conditions and fair labor practices in their offices and plants.

Managers must ensure that all five of these components fit together and complement their company's structure and control systems.[21] For example, if managers decide to decentralize authority and empower employees, they need to invest in training and development to ensure that lower-level employees have the knowledge and expertise they need to make the decisions that top managers would make in a more centralized structure.

Each of the five components of HRM influences the others (see Figure 12.1).[22] The kinds of people that the organization attracts and hires through recruitment and selection, for example, determine (1) the kinds of training and development that are necessary, (2) the way performance is appraised, and (3) the appropriate levels of pay and benefits. Managers at Microsoft ensure that their organization has highly qualified program designers by (1) recruiting and selecting the best candidates, (2) providing new hires with the guidance of experienced team members, (3) appraising program designers' performance in terms of their individual contributions and their team's performance, and (4) basing programmers' pay on individual and team performance.

The Legal Environment of HRM

In the rest of this chapter we focus in detail on the choices managers must make in strategically managing human resources to attain organizational goals and gain a competitive advantage. Effectively managing human resources is a complex undertaking for managers, and we provide an overview of some of the major issues they face. First, however, we need to look at how the legal environment affects human resource management.

The local, state, and national laws and regulations that managers and organizations must abide by add to the complexity of HRM. For example, the U.S. government's commitment to **equal employment opportunity (EEO)** has resulted in the creation and enforcement of a number of laws that managers must abide by. The goal of EEO is to ensure that all citizens have an equal opportunity to obtain employment regardless of their gender, race, country of origin, religion, age, or disabilities. Table 12.1 summarizes some of the major EEO laws affecting HRM. Other laws, such as the Occupational Safety and Health Act of 1970, require that managers ensure that employees are protected from workplace hazards and safety standards are met.

equal employment opportunity (EEO) The equal right of all citizens to the opportunity to obtain employment regardless of their gender, age, race, country of origin, religion, or disabilities.

In Chapter 3, we explained how effectively managing diversity is an ethical and business imperative, and we discussed the many issues surrounding diversity. EEO laws and their enforcement make the effective management of diversity a legal imperative as well. The Equal Employment Opportunity Commission (EEOC) is the division of the Department of Justice that enforces most of the EEO laws and handles discrimination complaints. In addition, the EEOC issues guidelines for managers to follow to ensure that they are abiding by EEO laws. For example, the Uniform Guidelines on Employee Selection Procedures issued by the EEOC (in conjunction with the Departments of Labor and Justice and the Civil Service Commission) provide managers with guidance on how to ensure that the recruitment and selection component of human resource management complies with Title VII of the Civil Rights Act (which prohibits discrimination based on gender, race, color, religion, and national origin).[23]

Table 12.1
Major Equal Employment Opportunity Laws Affecting HRM

Year	Law	Description
1963	Equal Pay Act	Requires that men and women be paid equally if they are performing equal work
1964	Title VII of the Civil Rights Act	Prohibits discrimination in employment decisions on the basis of race, religion, sex, color, or national origin; covers a wide range of employment decisions, including hiring, firing, pay, promotion, and working conditions
1967	Age Discrimination in Employment Act	Prohibits discrimination against workers over the age of 40 and restricts mandatory retirement
1978	Pregnancy Discrimination Act	Prohibits discrimination against women in employment decisions on the basis of pregnancy, childbirth, and related medical decisions
1990	Americans with Disabilities Act	Prohibits discrimination against individuals with disabilities in employment decisions and requires that employers make accommodations for such workers to enable them to perform their jobs
1991	Civil Rights Act	Prohibits discrimination (as does Title VII) and allows for the awarding of punitive and compensatory damages, in addition to back pay, in cases of intentional discrimination
1993	Family and Medical Leave Act	Requires that employers provide 12 weeks of unpaid leave for medical and family reasons including paternity and illness of a family member

Contemporary challenges that managers face related to the legal environment include how to eliminate sexual harassment (see Chapter 3 for an in-depth discussion of sexual harassment), how to make accommodations for employees with disabilities, how to deal with employees who have substance abuse problems, and how to manage HIV-positive employees and employees with AIDS.[24] HIV-positive employees are infected with the virus that causes AIDS but may show no AIDS symptoms and may not develop AIDS in the near future. Often, such employees are able to perform their jobs effectively, and managers must take steps to ensure that they are allowed to do so and are not discriminated against in the workplace.[25] Employees with AIDS may or may not be able to perform their jobs effectively, and, once again, managers need to ensure that they are not unfairly discriminated against.[26] Many organizations have instituted AIDS awareness training programs to educate organizational members about HIV and AIDS, dispel unfounded myths about how HIV is spread, and ensure that individuals infected with the HIV virus are treated fairly and are able to be productive as long as they can be while not putting others at risk.[27]

Recruitment and Selection

Recruitment includes all the activities managers engage in to develop a pool of qualified candidates for open positions.[28] **Selection** is the process by which managers determine the relative qualifications of job applicants and their potential for performing well in a particular job. Prior to actually recruiting and selecting employees, managers need to engage in two important activities: human resource planning and job analysis (Figure 12.2).

Figure 12.2
The Recruitment and Selection System

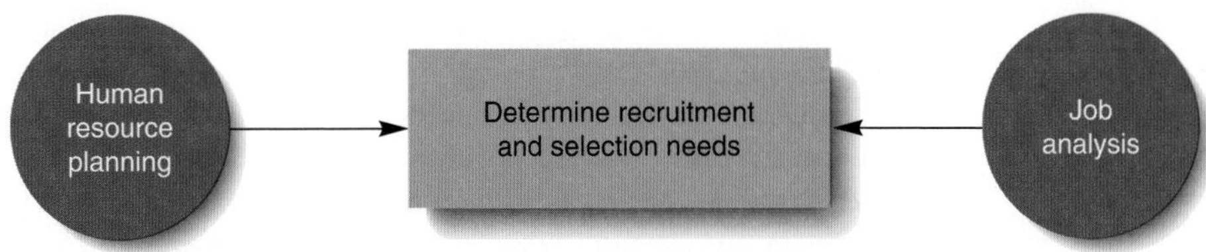

LO2 Describe the steps managers take to recruit and select organizational members.

recruitment Activities that managers engage in to develop a pool of qualified candidates for open positions.

selection The process that managers use to determine the relative qualifications of job applicants and their potential for performing well in a particular job.

human resource planning Activities that managers engage in to forecast their current and future needs for human resources.

outsource To use outside suppliers and manufacturers to produce good and services.

Human Resource Planning

Human resource planning includes all the activities managers engage in to forecast their current and future human resource needs. Current human resources are the employees an organization needs today to provide high-quality goods and services to customers. Future human resource needs are the employees the organization will need at some later date to achieve its longer-term goals.

As part of human resource planning, managers must make both demand forecasts and supply forecasts. *Demand forecasts* estimate the qualifications and numbers of employees an organization will need given its goals and strategies. *Supply forecasts* estimate the availability and qualifications of current employees now and in the future, as well as the supply of qualified workers in the external labor market.

As a result of their human resource planning, managers sometimes decide to **outsource** to fill some of their human resource needs. Instead of recruiting and selecting employees to produce goods and services, managers contract with people who are not members of their organization to produce goods and services. Managers in publishing companies, for example, frequently contract with freelance editors to copyedit books that they intend to publish. Kelly Services is an organization that provides temporary typing, clerical, and secretarial workers to managers who want to use outsourcing to fill some of their human resource requirements in these areas.

Two reasons why human resource planning sometimes leads managers to outsource are flexibility and cost. First, outsourcing can give managers increased *flexibility,* especially when accurately forecasting human resource needs is difficult, human resource needs fluctuate over time, or finding skilled workers in a particular area is difficult. Second, outsourcing can sometimes allow managers to make use of human resources at a lower *cost.* When work is outsourced, costs can be lower for a number of reasons: The organization does not have to provide benefits to workers; managers are able to contract for work only when the work is needed; and managers do not have to invest in training. Outsourcing can be used for functional activities such as after-sales service on appliances and equipment, legal work, and the management of information systems.

Outsourcing does have its disadvantages, however.[29] When work is outsourced, managers may lose some control over the quality of goods and services. Also, individuals performing outsourced work may have less knowledge of organizational practices, procedures, and goals and less commitment to an organization than regular employees. In addition, unions resist outsourcing because it has the potential to eliminate some of their members. To gain some of the flexibility and cost savings of outsourcing and avoid some of its disadvantages, a number of organizations, such as Microsoft and IBM, rely on a pool of temporary employees to, for example, debug programs.

A major trend reflecting the increasing globalization of business is the outsourcing of office work, computer programming, and technical jobs from the United States and countries in Western Europe, with high labor costs, to countries like India and China, with low labor costs.[30] For example, computer programmers in India and China earn a fraction of what their U.S. counterparts earn. According to estimates by Gartner Inc., outsourcing (or *offshoring,* as it is also called when work is outsourced to other countries) of information technology and business process work is valued at over $34 billion per year.

As companies gain experience in outsourcing software and technological services, managers are learning what kinds of work can be effectively outsourced and what work should probably not be outsourced. In India, for example, the workforce is highly trained and motivated, and cities like Bangalore are bustling with high-tech jobs and companies like Infosys Technologies, providing software services to companies abroad. Managers who have outsourcing experience have found that outsourcing works best for tasks that can be rule-based, do not require closeness/familiarity with customers and/or the customs and culture of the country in which the company is based, and do not require creativity.[31] When the work requires the recognition and solution of problems rather than the application of preexisting algorithms, creativity in developing solutions, and independent thinking and judgment without the guidance of standard operating procedures, performance might suffer from outsourcing. Essentially, the more complex and uncertain the work and the more it depends on being close to customers and the company itself, the less advantageous outsourcing tends to be.[32]

Nonetheless, there are many kinds of tasks that can be effectively outsourced, and the cost savings for these tasks can be considerable.[33] And some managers believe that many tasks can be effectively outsourced, even those requiring creativity.

General Electric (GE) and McKinsey & Co. are two companies at the forefront of offshoring, seeing it as a way not only to cut costs but to grow (while boosting efficiency).[34] GE Capital first started off with an office in Delhi, India, because the company was having a difficult time filling positions in its growing business of mortgage refinancing. Called GE Capital Investment Services, the office had around 300 employees in the late 1990s. Today, Genpact (a company owned by GE and two private equity firms) has over 20,000 employees, offices in Mexico, Romania, Hungary, India, China, and the United States, and over $490 million in revenues.[35]

McKinsey and GE have such a legacy in offshoring that many current top managers of outsourcing companies were former McKinsey and GE employees. For example, the current president and CEO of Genpact, Pramod Bhasin, was a former GE employee.[36] As another example, Rizwan Koita, a former employee of McKinsey in London and New Delhi, has gone on to found two outsourcing companies, TransWork Information Services Ltd. (recently purchased by AV Birla Group) and Citius Tech. Inc.[37] Additionally, other former employees of GE and McKinsey have used their knowledge and experience of outsourcing in subsequent positions in other organizations.[38]

Job Analysis

job analysis Identifying the tasks, duties, and responsibilities that make up a job and the knowledge, skills, and abilities needed to perform the job.

Job analysis is a second important activity that managers need to undertake prior to recruitment and selection.[39] **Job analysis** is the process of identifying (1) the tasks, duties, and responsibilities that make up a job (the *job description*) and (2) the knowledge, skills, and abilities needed to perform the job (the *job specifications*).[40] For each job in an organization, a job analysis needs to be done.

A job analysis can be done in a number of ways, including observing current employees as they perform the job or interviewing them. Often, managers rely on questionnaires compiled by jobholders and their managers. The questionnaires ask about the skills and abilities needed to perform the job, job tasks and the amount of time spent on them, responsibilities, supervisory activities, equipment used, reports prepared, and decisions made.[41] A trend, in some organizations, is toward more flexible jobs in which tasks and responsibilities change and cannot be clearly specified in advance. For these kinds of jobs, job analysis focuses more on determining the skills and knowledge workers need to be effective and less on specific duties.

After managers have completed human resource planning and job analyses for all jobs in an organization, they will know their human resource needs and the jobs they need to fill. They will also know the knowledge, skills, and abilities that potential employees need to perform those jobs. At this point, recruitment and selection can begin.

External and Internal Recruitment

As noted earlier, recruitment is what managers do to develop a pool of qualified candidates for open positions.[42] They traditionally have used two main types of recruiting: external and internal, which are now supplemented by recruiting over the Internet.

EXTERNAL RECRUITING When managers recruit externally to fill open positions, they look outside the organization for people who have not worked for the organization previously. There are multiple means through which managers can recruit externally: advertisements in newspapers and magazines, open houses for students and career counselors at high schools and colleges or on-site at the organization, career fairs at colleges, and recruitment meetings with groups in the local community.

Many colleges and universities hold job fairs to connect employers with students looking for jobs.

Many large organizations send teams of interviewers to college campuses to recruit new employees. External recruitment can also take place through informal networks, as occurs when current employees inform friends about open positions in their companies or recommend people they know to fill vacant spots. Some organizations use employment agencies for external recruitment, and some external recruitment takes place simply through walk-ins–job hunters coming to an organization and inquiring about employment possibilities.

With all the downsizings and corporate layoffs that have taken place in recent years, you might think that external recruiting would be a relatively easy task for managers. However, it often is not, because even though many people may be looking for jobs, many of the jobs that are opening up require skills and abilities that these job hunters do not have. Managers needing to fill vacant positions and job hunters seeking employment opportunities are increasingly relying on the Internet to make connections with each other through employment Web sites such as Monster.com[43] and Jobline International. Jobline is Europe's largest electronic recruiting site, with operations in 12 countries.[44] Major corporations such as Coca-Cola, Cisco, Ernst & Young, Canon, and Telia have relied on Jobline to fill global positions.[45]

External recruiting has both advantages and disadvantages for managers. Advantages include having access to a potentially large applicant pool, being able to attract people who have the skills, knowledge, and abilities that an organization needs to achieve its goals, and being able to bring in newcomers who may have a fresh approach to problems and be up to date on the latest technology. These advantages have to be weighed against the disadvantages, including the relatively high costs of external recruitment. Employees recruited externally also lack knowledge about the inner workings of the organization and may need to receive more training than those recruited internally. Finally, when employees are recruited externally, there is always uncertainty concerning whether they will actually be good performers. Nonetheless, there are steps managers can take to reduce some of the uncertainty surrounding external recruitment, as profiled in the following "Information Technology Byte."

INFORMATION TECHNOLOGY BYTE

Fog Creek Software's Approach to Recruiting

Fog Creek Software is a small, privately owned software company founded in 2000 by Joel Spolsky and Michael Pryor in a renovated loft in the Fashion District of New York City.[46] Fog Creek has earned a profit and doubled in size each year since its founding.[47] Hiring great computer software developers is essential for a company like Fog Creek; according to Spolsky, the top 1% of software developers outperform average developers by a ratio of around 10:1. And the top 1% are the inventive types who can successfully develop new products while also being highly efficient.[48]

Small Business

Finding, never mind recruiting, the top 1% is a real challenge for a small company like Fog Creek since many of these people already have great jobs and are not looking to switch employers. Because the top 1% of developers might rarely apply for positions with Fog Creek (or any other company), over 50% of Fog Creek's developers were first recruited for a paid summer internship while still in college and then hired on full-time upon graduation.[49]

In the fall of every year, Spolsky sends personalized letters to computer science majors across the country who have the potential to be top developers in the future, contacts professors at leading computer science programs for recommendations, and also seeks applications through his blog.[50] This process yields hundreds of applicants for internships, the best of whom are then given phone interviews. During the interviews, the candidates describe themselves and their classes, are asked how they would go about solving a software development problem or challenge, and then can ask Spolsky anything they want about the company or living in New York City.[51]

Those who do well in the phone interview are then flown to New York for an all-expense-paid visit to Fog Creek–they are met at the airport in a limousine, stay in a hip hotel, receive welcoming gifts in their rooms, have a full day of interviews at Fog Creek, and then are given the option of staying two extra nights (at no cost to themselves) to get a feel for New York City. Typically, only one out of every three recruits who have on-site visits receives an internship offer.[52]

Interns perform real software development work–several summers ago, a team of four interns developed a new successful technology support product called

Fog Creek Software uses paid summer internships to help identify and attract promising software developers.

Fog Creek Copilot.[53] This both is motivating for the interns and also helps managers decide which interns they would like to offer full-time jobs to upon graduation. The interns are also treated very well–in addition to being paid, they receive free housing and are invited to outings, parties, and cultural events in New York City. At the conclusion of the internship, managers have a good sense of which interns are great programmers. These top programmers are offered jobs upon graduation with generous salaries, excellent working conditions, and great benefits. While Fog Creek's approach to external recruitment is somewhat lengthy and expensive, it more than pays for itself in terms of identifying and attracting top programmers. As Spolsky indicates, "An internship program creates a pipeline for great employees. It's a pretty long pipeline, so you need to have a long-term perspective, but it pays off in spades."[54]

lateral move A job change that entails no major changes in responsibility or authority levels.

INTERNAL RECRUITING When recruiting is internal, managers turn to existing employees to fill open positions. Employees recruited internally are either seeking **lateral moves** (job changes that entail no major changes in responsibility or authority levels) or promotions. Internal recruiting has several advantages. First, internal applicants are already familiar with the organization (including its goals, structure, culture, rules, and norms). Second, managers already know the candidates; they have considerable information about their skills and abilities and actual behavior on the job. Third, internal recruiting can help boost levels of employee motivation and morale, both for the employee who gets the job and for other workers. Those who are not seeking a promotion or who may not be ready for one can see that promotion is a possibility in the future; or a lateral move can alleviate boredom once a job has been fully mastered and can also be a useful way to learn new skills. Finally, internal recruiting is normally less time-consuming and expensive than external recruiting.

Given the advantages of internal recruiting, why do managers rely on external recruiting as much as they do? The answer lies in the disadvantages of internal recruiting–among them, a limited pool of candidates and a tendency among those candidates to be set in the organization's ways. Often, the organization simply does not have suitable internal candidates. Sometimes, even when suitable internal applicants are available, managers may rely on external recruiting to find the very best candidate or to help bring new ideas and approaches into their organization. When organizations are in trouble and performing poorly, external recruiting is often relied on to bring in managerial talent with a fresh approach.

The Selection Process

Once managers develop a pool of applicants for open positions through the recruitment process, they need to find out whether each applicant is qualified for the position and likely to be a good performer. If more than one applicant meets these two conditions, managers must further determine which applicants are likely to be better performers than others. They have several selection tools to help them sort out the relative

Figure 12.3
Selection Tools

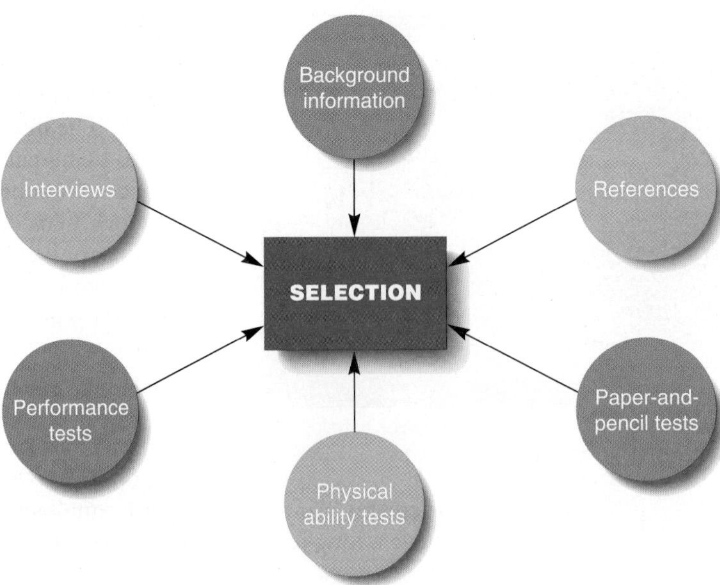

qualifications of job applicants and appraise their potential for being good performers in a particular job. These tools include background information, interviews, paper-and-pencil tests, physical ability tests, performance tests, and references (see Figure 12.3).[55]

BACKGROUND INFORMATION To aid in the selection process, managers obtain background information from job applications and from résumés. Such information might include the highest levels of education obtained, college majors and minors, type of college or university attended, years and type of work experience, and mastery of foreign languages. Background information can be helpful both to screen out applicants who are lacking key qualifications (such as a college degree) and to determine which qualified applicants are more promising than others. For example, applicants with a BS may be acceptable, but those who also have an MBA are preferable.

Increasing numbers of organizations are performing background checks to verify that the background information prospective employees provide is accurate (and also to uncover any negative information such as crime convictions).[56] According to ADP Employer Services, an outsourcing company that performs payroll and human resource functions for organizations, more and more companies are performing background checks on prospective employees and are uncovering inaccuracies, inconsistencies, and negative information such as prior convictions or driving violations.[57] According to a recent survey ADP conducted, about half of all background checks turn up an inconsistency between the education and credentials applicants list and the information other sources provide (e.g., universities or prior employers). And in some cases, background checks reveal convictions and driving violations.[58]

INTERVIEWS Virtually all organizations use interviews during the selection process, as is true at the Four Seasons in the "Management Snapshot." Interviews may be structured or unstructured. In a *structured interview,* managers ask each applicant the same standard questions (e.g., "What are your unique qualifications for this position?" and "What characteristics of a job are most important to you?"). Particularly informative questions may be those that prompt an interviewee to demonstrate skills and abilities

Practically all organizations use some kind of interview during the selection process.

needed for the job by answering the question. Sometimes called *situational interview questions,* these often present interviewees with a scenario that they would likely encounter on the job and ask them to indicate how they would handle it.[59] For example, applicants for a sales job may be asked to indicate how they would respond to a customer who complains about waiting too long for service, a customer who is indecisive, and a customer whose order is lost.

An *unstructured interview* proceeds more like an ordinary conversation. The interviewer feels free to ask probing questions to discover what the applicant is like and does not ask a fixed set of questions determined in advance. In general, structured interviews are superior to unstructured interviews because they are more likely to yield information that will help identify qualified candidates, are less subjective, and may be less influenced by the interviewer's biases.

When conducting interviews, managers cannot ask questions that are irrelevant to the job in question; otherwise, their organizations run the risk of costly lawsuits. It is inappropriate and illegal, for example, to inquire about an interviewee's spouse or to ask questions about whether an interviewee plans to have children. Because questions such as these are irrelevant to job performance, they are discriminatory and violate EEO laws (see again Table 12.1). Thus, interviewers need to be instructed in EEO laws and informed about questions that may violate those laws.

PAPER-AND-PENCIL TESTS The two main kinds of paper-and-pencil tests used for selection purposes are ability tests and personality tests. *Ability tests* assess the extent to which applicants possess the skills necessary for job performance, such as verbal comprehension or numerical skills. Autoworkers hired by General Motors, Chrysler, and Ford, for example, are typically tested for their ability to read and to do mathematics.[60]

Personality tests measure personality traits and characteristics relevant to job performance. Some retail organizations, for example, give job applicants honesty tests to determine how trustworthy they are. The use of personality tests (including honesty tests) for hiring purposes is controversial. Some critics maintain that honesty tests do not really measure honesty (that is, they are not valid) and can be faked by job applicants. Before using any paper-and-pencil tests for selection purposes, managers must have sound evidence that the tests are actually good predictors of performance on the job in question. Managers who use tests without such evidence may be subject to costly discrimination lawsuits.

PHYSICAL ABILITY TESTS For jobs requiring physical abilities, such as firefighting, garbage collecting, and package delivery, managers use physical ability tests that measure physical strength and stamina as selection tools. Autoworkers are typically tested for mechanical dexterity because this physical ability is an important skill for high job performance in many auto plants.[61]

PERFORMANCE TESTS *Performance tests* measure job applicants' performance on actual job tasks. Applicants for secretarial positions, for example, typically are required to complete a keyboarding test that measures how quickly and accurately they type. Applicants for middle- and top-management positions are sometimes given short-term projects to complete–projects that mirror the kinds of situations that arise in the job being filled–to assess their knowledge and problem-solving capabilities.[62]

Assessment centers, first used by AT&T, take performance tests one step further. In a typical assessment center, about 10 to 15 candidates for managerial positions participate in a variety of activities over a few days. During this time they are assessed for the skills an effective manager needs–problem-solving, organizational, communication, and conflict resolution skills. Some of the activities are performed individually; others are performed in groups. Throughout the process, current managers observe the candidates' behavior and measure performance. Summary evaluations are then used as a selection tool.

REFERENCES Applicants for many jobs are required to provide references from former employers or other knowledgeable sources (such as a college instructor or adviser) who know the applicants' skills, abilities, and other personal characteristics. These individuals are asked to provide candid information about the applicant. References are often used at the end of the selection process to confirm a decision to hire. Yet the fact that many former employers are reluctant to provide negative information in references sometimes makes it difficult to interpret what a reference is really saying about an applicant.

In fact, several recent lawsuits filed by applicants who felt that they were unfairly denigrated or had their privacy invaded by unfavorable references from former employers have caused managers to be increasingly wary of providing any negative information in a reference, even if it is accurate. For jobs in which the jobholder is responsible for the safety and lives of other people, however, failing to provide accurate negative information in a reference does not just mean that the wrong person might get hired; it may also mean that other people's lives will be at stake.

THE IMPORTANCE OF RELIABILITY AND VALIDITY Whatever selection tools a manager uses, these tools need to be both reliable and valid. **Reliability** is the degree to which a tool or test measures the same thing each time it is administered. Scores on a selection test should be very similar if the same person is assessed with the same tool on two different days; if there is quite a bit of variability, the tool is unreliable. For interviews, determining reliability is more complex because the dynamic is personal interpretation. That is why the reliability of interviews can be increased if two or more different qualified interviewers interview the same candidate. If the interviews are reliable, the interviewers should come to similar conclusions about the interviewee's qualifications.

reliability The degree to which a tool or test measures the same thing each time it is used.

Validity is the degree to which a tool measures what it purports to measure–for selection tools, it is the degree to which the test predicts performance on the tasks or job in question. Does a physical ability test used to select firefighters, for example, actually predict on-the-job performance? Do assessment center ratings actually predict managerial performance? Do keyboarding tests predict secretarial performance? These are all questions of validity. Honesty tests, for example, are controversial because it is not clear that they validly predict honesty in such jobs as retailing and banking.

validity The degree to which a tool or test measures what it purports to measure.

Managers have an ethical and legal obligation to use reliable and valid selection tools. Yet reliability and validity are matters of degree rather than all-or-nothing characteristics. Thus, managers should strive to use selection tools in such a way that they can achieve the greatest degree of reliability and validity. For ability tests of a particular skill, managers should keep up to date on the latest advances in the development of valid paper-and-pencil tests and use the test with the highest reliability and validity ratings for their purposes. Regarding interviews, managers can improve reliability by having more than one person interview job candidates.

Training and Development

Training and development help to ensure that organizational members have the knowledge and skills needed to perform jobs effectively, take on new responsibilities, and adapt to changing conditions. **Training** primarily focuses on teaching organizational members how to perform their current jobs and helping them acquire the knowledge and skills they need to be effective performers. **Development** focuses on building the knowledge and skills of organizational members so that they are prepared to take on new responsibilities and challenges. Training tends to be used more frequently at lower levels of an organization; development tends to be used more frequently with professionals and managers.

LO3 Discuss the training and development options that ensure organizational members can effectively perform their jobs.

Before creating training and development programs, managers should perform a **needs assessment** to determine which employees need training or development and what type of skills or knowledge they need to acquire (see Figure 12.4).[63]

Types of Training

There are two types of training: classroom instruction and on-the-job training.

training Teaching organizational members how to perform their current jobs and helping them acquire the knowledge and skills they need to be effective performers.

CLASSROOM INSTRUCTION Through classroom instruction, employees acquire knowledge and skills in a classroom setting. This instruction may take place within the organization or outside it, such as courses at local colleges and universities. Many organizations actually establish their own formal instructional divisions–some are even called "colleges"–to provide needed classroom instruction.

Classroom instruction frequently includes the use of videos and role playing in addition to traditional written materials, lectures, and group discussions. *Videos* can

Figure 12.4
Training and Development

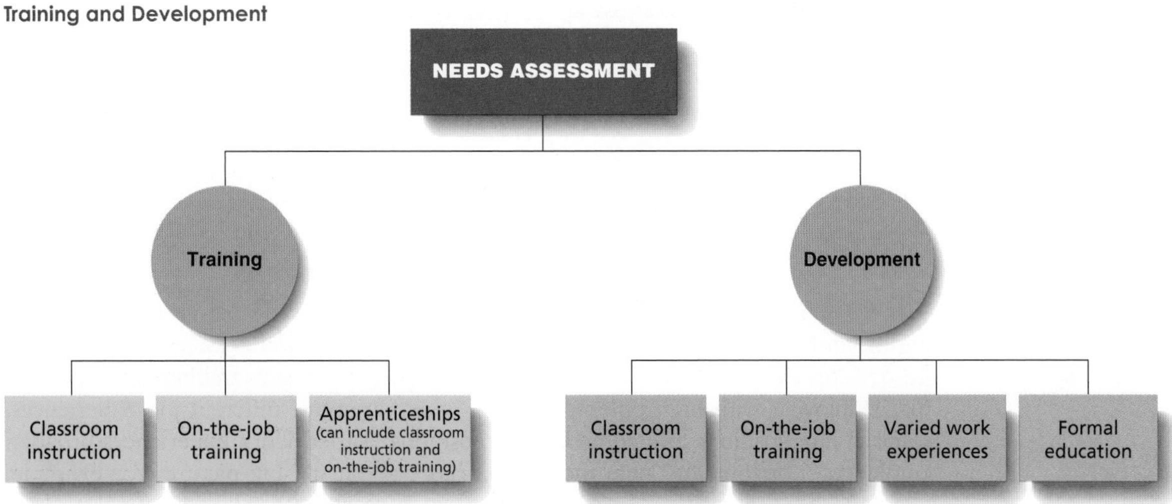

development Building the knowledge and skills of organizational members so that they are prepared to take on new responsibilities and challenges.

needs assessment An assessment of which employees need training or development and what type of skills or knowledge they need to acquire.

on-the-job training Training that takes place in the work setting as employees perform their job tasks.

be used to demonstrate appropriate and inappropriate job behaviors. For example, by watching an experienced salesperson effectively deal with a loud and angry customer in a video clip, inexperienced salespeople can develop skills in handling similar situations. During *role playing,* trainees either directly participate in or watch others perform actual job activities in a simulated setting. At McDonald's Hamburger University, for example, role playing helps franchisees acquire the knowledge and skills they need to manage their restaurants.

Simulations also can be part of classroom instruction, particularly for complicated jobs that require an extensive amount of learning and in which errors carry a high cost. In a simulation, key aspects of the work situation and job tasks are duplicated as closely as possible in an artificial setting. For example, air traffic controllers are trained by simulations because of the complicated nature of the work, the extensive amount of learning involved, and the very high costs of air traffic control errors.

ON-THE-JOB TRAINING In on-the-job training, learning occurs in the work setting as employees perform their job tasks. On-the-job training can be provided by coworkers or supervisors or can occur simply as jobholders gain experience and knowledge from doing the work. Newly hired waiters and waitresses in chains such as Red Lobster or the Olive Garden often receive on-the-job training from experienced employees. The supervisor of a new bus driver for a campus bus system may ride the bus for a week to ensure that the driver has learned the routes and follows safety procedures. For all on-the-job training, employees learn by doing.

At many restaurants, new employees receive on-the-job training by shadowing more experienced waiters and waitresses as they go about their work.

Managers often use on-the-job training on a continuing basis to ensure that their subordinates keep up to date with changes in goals, technology, products, or customer needs and desires. For example, sales representatives at Mary Kay Cosmetics Inc. receive ongoing training so that they not only are knowledgeable about new cosmetic products and currently popular colors but also are reminded of Mary Kay's guiding principles. Mary Kay's expansion into Russia has been very successful, in part because of the ongoing training that Mary Kay's Russian salespeople receive.[64]

Types of Development

Although both classroom instruction and on-the-job training can be used for development purposes as well as training, development often includes additional activities such as varied work experiences and formal education.

VARIED WORK EXPERIENCES Top managers need to develop an understanding of, and expertise in, a variety of functions, products and services, and markets. To develop executives who will have this expertise, managers frequently make sure that employees with high potential have a wide variety of different job experiences, some in line positions and some in staff positions. Varied work experiences broaden employees' horizons and help them think more about the big picture. For example, one- to three-year stints overseas are being used increasingly to provide managers with international work experiences. With organizations becoming more global, managers need to develop an understanding of the different values, beliefs, cultures, regions, and ways of doing business in different countries.

Another development approach is mentoring. A *mentor* is an experienced member of an organization who provides advice and guidance to a less experienced member, called a *protégé*. Having a mentor can help managers seek out work experiences and assignments that will contribute to their development and can enable them to gain the most possible from varied work experiences.[65] While some mentors and protégés hook up informally, organizations have found that formal mentorship programs can be valuable ways to contribute to the development of managers and all employees.

Formal mentoring programs ensure that mentoring takes place in an organization, structure the process, and make sure that diverse organizational members have equal access to mentors. Participants receive training, efforts are focused on matching up mentors and protégés so that meaningful developmental relationships ensue, and organizations can track reactions and assess the potential benefits of mentoring. Formal mentoring programs can also ensure that diverse members of an organization receive the benefits of mentoring. A study conducted by David A. Thomas, a professor at the Harvard Business School, found that members of racial minority groups at three large corporations who were very successful in their careers had the benefit of mentors. Formal mentorship programs help organizations make this valuable development tool available to all employees.[66]

When diverse members of an organization lack mentors, their progress in the organization and advancement to high-level positions can be hampered. Ida Abott, a lawyer and consultant on work-related issues, recently presented a paper to the Minority Corporate Counsel Association in which she concluded, "The lack of adequate mentoring has held women and minority lawyers back from achieving professional success and has led to high rates of career dissatisfaction and attrition."[67]

Mentoring can benefit all kinds of employees in all kinds of work.[68] John Washko, a manager at the Four Seasons hotel chain, benefited from the mentoring he received from Stan Bromley on interpersonal relations and how to deal with employees; mentor Bromley, in turn, found that participating in the Four Seasons' mentoring program helped him develop his own management style.[69] More generally, development is an ongoing process for all managers, and mentors often find that mentoring contributes to their own personal development.

FORMAL EDUCATION Many large corporations reimburse employees for tuition expenses they incur while taking college courses and obtaining advanced degrees. This is not just benevolence on the part of the employer or even a simple reward given to the employee; it is an effective way to develop employees who are able to take on new responsibilities and more challenging positions. For similar reasons, corporations spend thousands of dollars sending managers to executive development programs such as executive MBA programs. In these programs, experts teach managers the latest in business and management techniques and practices.

To save time and travel costs, managers are increasingly relying on *long-distance learning* to formally educate and develop employees. Using videoconferencing technologies, business schools such as the Harvard Business School, the University of Michigan, and Babson College are teaching courses on video screens in corporate conference rooms. Business schools are also customizing courses and degrees to fit the development needs of employees in a particular company.

Transfer of Training and Development

Whenever training and development take place off the job or in a classroom setting, it is vital for managers to promote the transfer of the knowledge and skills acquired *to the actual work situation.* Trainees should be encouraged and expected to use their newfound expertise on the job.

Performance Appraisal and Feedback

The recruitment/selection and training/development components of a human resource management system ensure that employees have the knowledge and skills needed to be effective now and in the future. Performance appraisal and feedback complement recruitment, selection, training, and development. **Performance appraisal** is the evaluation of employees' job performance and contributions to the organization. **Performance feedback** is the process through which managers share performance appraisal information with their subordinates, give subordinates an opportunity to reflect on their own performance, and develop, with subordinates, plans for the future. Before performance feedback, performance appraisal must take place. Performance appraisal could take place without providing performance feedback, but wise managers are careful to provide feedback because it can contribute to employee motivation and performance.

LO4 Explain why performance appraisal and feedback are such crucial activities, and list the choices managers must make in designing effective performance appraisal and feedback procedures.

performance appraisal The evaluation of employees' job performance and contributions to their organization.

performance feedback The process through which managers share performance appraisal information with subordinates, give subordinates an opportunity to reflect on their own performance, and develop, with subordinates, plans for the future.

Performance appraisal and feedback contribute to the effective management of human resources in several ways. Performance appraisal gives managers important information on which to base human resource decisions.[70] Decisions about pay raises, bonuses, promotions, and job moves all hinge on the accurate appraisal of performance. Performance appraisal can also help managers determine which workers are candidates for training and development and in what areas. Performance feedback encourages high levels of employee motivation and performance. It lets good performers know that their efforts are valued and appreciated. It also lets poor performers know that their lackluster performance needs improvement. Performance feedback can provide both good and poor performers with insight on their strengths and weaknesses and ways in which they can improve their performance in the future.

Types of Performance Appraisal

Performance appraisal focuses on the evaluation of traits, behaviors, and results.[71]

TRAIT APPRAISALS When trait appraisals are used, managers assess subordinates on personal characteristics that are relevant to job performance, such as skills, abilities, or personality. A factory worker, for example, may be evaluated based on her ability to use computerized equipment and perform numerical calculations. A social worker may be appraised based on his empathy and communication skills.

Three disadvantages of trait appraisals often lead managers to rely on other appraisal methods. First, possessing a certain personal characteristic does not ensure that the personal characteristic will actually be used on the job and result in high performance. For example, a factory worker may possess superior computer and numerical skills but be a poor performer due to low motivation. The second disadvantage of trait appraisals is linked to the first. Because traits do not always show a direct association with performance, workers and courts of law may view them as unfair and potentially discriminatory. The third disadvantage of trait appraisals is that they often do not enable managers to provide employees with feedback that they can use to improve performance. Because trait appraisals focus on relatively enduring human characteristics that change only over the long term, employees can do little to change their behavior in response to performance feedback from a trait appraisal. Telling a social worker that he lacks empathy provides him with little guidance about how to improve his interactions with clients, for example. These disadvantages suggest that managers should use trait appraisals only when they can demonstrate that the assessed traits are accurate and important indicators of job performance.

BEHAVIOR APPRAISALS Through behavior appraisals, managers assess how workers perform their jobs–the actual actions and behaviors that workers exhibit on the job. Whereas trait appraisals assess what workers are *like,* behavior appraisals assess what workers *do*. For example, with a behavior appraisal, a manager might evaluate a social worker on the extent to which he looks clients in the eye when talking with them, expresses sympathy when they are upset, and refers them to community counseling and support groups geared toward the specific problem they are encountering. Behavior appraisals are especially useful when *how* workers perform their jobs is important. In educational organizations such as high schools, for example, the number of classes and students taught is important, but also important are how they are taught and the methods teachers use to ensure that learning takes place.

Behavior appraisals have the advantage of providing employees with clear information about what they are doing right and wrong and how they can improve their performance. And because behaviors are much easier for employees to change than traits, performance feedback from behavior appraisals is more likely to lead to performance improvements.

RESULT APPRAISALS For some jobs, *how* people perform the job is not as important as *what* they accomplish or the results they obtain. With result appraisals, managers appraise performance by the results or the actual outcomes of work behaviors. Take the case of two new-car salespersons. One salesperson strives to develop personal relationships with her customers. She spends hours talking to them and frequently calls them up to see how their decision-making process is going. The other salesperson has a much more hands-off approach. He is very knowledgeable, answers customers' questions, and then waits for them to come to him. Both salespersons sell, on average, the same number of cars, and the customers of both are satisfied with the service they receive, according to postcards that the dealership mails to customers asking for an assessment of their satisfaction. The manager of the dealership appropriately uses result appraisals (sales and customer satisfaction) to evaluate the salespeople's performance because it does not matter which behavior salespeople use to sell cars as long as they sell the desired number and satisfy customers. If one salesperson sells too few cars, however, the manager can give that person performance feedback about his or her low sales.

OBJECTIVE AND SUBJECTIVE APPRAISALS Whether managers appraise performance in terms of traits, behaviors, or results, the information they assess is either *objective* or *subjective*. **Objective appraisals** are based on facts and are likely to be numerical–the number of cars sold, the number of meals prepared, the number of times late, the number of audits completed. Managers often use objective appraisals when results are being appraised because results tend to be easier to quantify than traits or behaviors. When *how* workers perform their jobs is important, however, subjective behavior appraisals are more appropriate than result appraisals.

objective appraisal An appraisal that is based on facts and is likely to be numerical.

subjective appraisal An appraisal that is based on perceptions of traits, behaviors, or results.

Subjective appraisals are based on managers' perceptions of traits, behaviors, or results. Because subjective appraisals rest on managers' perceptions, there is always the chance that they are inaccurate. This is why both researchers and managers have spent considerable time and effort on determining the best way to develop reliable and valid subjective measures of performance.

Who Appraises Performance?

We have been assuming that managers or the supervisors of employees evaluate performance. This is a pretty reasonable assumption, for supervisors are the most common appraisers of performance; indeed, each year 70 million U.S. citizens have their job performance appraised by their managers or supervisors.[72] Performance appraisal is an important part of most managers' job duties. Managers are responsible for not only motivating their subordinates to perform at a high level but also making many decisions hinging on performance appraisals, such as pay raises or promotions. Appraisals by managers can be usefully augmented by appraisals from other sources (see Figure 12.5).

SELF, PEERS, SUBORDINATES, AND CLIENTS When self-appraisals are used, managers supplement their evaluations with an employee's assessment of his or her own performance. Peer appraisals are provided by an employee's coworkers. Especially when subordinates work in groups or teams, feedback from peer appraisals can motivate team members while providing managers with important information for decision making. A growing number of companies are having subordinates appraise their managers' performance and leadership as well. And sometimes customers or clients provide assessments of employee performance in terms of responsiveness to customers and quality of service. Although appraisals from each of these sources can be useful, managers need to be aware of potential issues that may arise when they are used. Subordinates sometimes may be inclined to inflate self-appraisals, especially if organizations are downsizing and they are worried about their job security. Managers who are appraised by their subordinates may fail to take needed but unpopular

Figure 12.5
Who Appraises Performance?

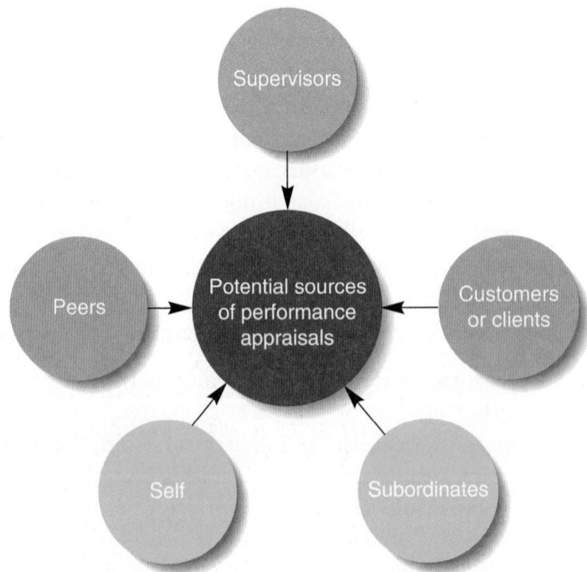

actions out of fear that their subordinates will appraise them negatively. Some of these potential issues can be mitigated to the extent that there are high levels of trust in an organization.

360-degree appraisal A performance appraisal by peers, subordinates, superiors, and sometimes clients who are in a position to evaluate a manager's performance.

360-DEGREE PERFORMANCE APPRAISALS To improve motivation and performance, some organizations include 360-degree appraisals and feedback in their performance appraisal systems, especially for managers. In a 360-degree appraisal, a variety of people, beginning with the manager and including peers or coworkers, subordinates, superiors, and sometimes even customers or clients, appraise a manager's performance. The manager receives feedback based on evaluations from these multiple sources.

The growing number of companies using 360-degree appraisals and feedback include AT&T Corp., Allied Signal Inc., Eastman Chemical Co., and Baxter International Inc.[73] For 360-degree appraisals and feedback to be effective, there has to be trust throughout an organization. More generally, trust is a critical ingredient in any performance appraisal and feedback procedure. In addition, research suggests that 360-degree appraisals should focus on behaviors rather than traits or results and that managers need to carefully select appropriate raters. Moreover, appraisals tend to be more honest when made anonymously and when raters have been trained in how to use 360-degree appraisal forms.[74] Additionally, managers need to think carefully about the extent to which 360-degree appraisals are appropriate for certain jobs and be willing to modify any appraisal system they implement if they become aware of unintended problems it creates.[75]

Even when 360-degree appraisals are used, it is sometimes difficult to design an effective process by which subordinates' feedback can be communicated to their managers. Advances in information technology provide organizations with a potential solution to this problem. For example, ImproveNow.com has online questionnaires that subordinates fill out to evaluate the performance of their managers and provide the managers with feedback. Each subordinate of a particular manager completes the questionnaire independently, all responses are tabulated, and the manager is given specific feedback on behaviors in a variety of areas, such as rewarding good performance, looking out for subordinates' best interest and being supportive, and having a vision for the future.[76]

Effective Performance Feedback

formal appraisal An appraisal conducted at a set time during the year and based on performance dimensions and measures that were specified in advance.

For the appraisal and feedback component of a human resource management system to encourage and motivate high performance, managers must provide their subordinates with feedback. To generate useful information to feed back to their subordinates, managers can use both formal and informal appraisals. Formal appraisals are conducted at set times during the year and are based on performance dimensions and measures that have been specified in advance.

Managers in most large organizations use formal performance appraisals on a fixed schedule dictated by company policy, such as every six months or every year. An integral part of a formal appraisal is a meeting between the manager and the subordinate in which the subordinate is given feedback on performance. Performance feedback lets subordinates know which areas they are excelling in and which areas need improvement; it also should provide them with guidance for improving performance.

Formal performance appraisals supply both managers and subordinates with valuable information; but subordinates often want feedback on a more frequent

informal appraisal An unscheduled appraisal of ongoing progress and areas for improvement.

basis, and managers often want to motivate subordinates as the need arises. For these reasons, many companies supplement formal performance appraisal with frequent **informal appraisals,** for which managers and their subordinates meet as the need arises to discuss ongoing progress and areas for improvement. Moreover, when job duties, assignments, or goals change, informal appraisals can provide workers with timely feedback concerning how they are handling their new responsibilities.

Managers often dislike providing performance feedback, especially when the feedback is negative, but doing so is an important managerial activity.[77] Here are some guidelines for giving effective performance feedback that contributes to employee motivation and performance:

- *Be specific and focus on behaviors or outcomes that are correctable and within a worker's ability to improve.* Example: Telling a salesperson that he is too shy when interacting with customers is likely to do nothing more than lower his self-confidence and prompt the salesperson to become defensive. A more effective approach would be to give the salesperson feedback about specific behaviors to engage in–greeting customers as soon as they enter the department, asking customers whether they need help, and volunteering to help customers find items.
- *Approach performance appraisal as an exercise in problem solving and solution finding, not criticizing.* Example: Rather than criticizing a financial analyst for turning in reports late, the manager helps the analyst determine why the reports are late and identify ways to better manage her time.
- *Express confidence in a subordinate's ability to improve.* Example: Instead of being skeptical, a first-level manager tells a subordinate that he is confident that the subordinate can increase quality levels.
- *Provide performance feedback both formally and informally.* Example: The staff of a preschool receives feedback from formal performance appraisals twice a year. The director of the school also provides frequent informal feedback such as complimenting staff members on creative ideas for special projects, noticing when they do a particularly good job handling a difficult child, and pointing out when they provide inadequate supervision.
- *Praise instances of high performance and areas of a job in which a worker excels.* Example: Rather than focusing on just the negative, a manager discusses the areas her subordinate excels in as well as the areas in need of improvement.
- *Avoid personal criticisms and treat subordinates with respect.* Example: An engineering manager acknowledges her subordinates' expertise and treats them as professionals. Even when the manager points out performance problems to subordinates, she refrains from criticizing them personally.
- *Agree to a timetable for performance improvements.* Example: A first-level manager and his subordinate decide to meet again in one month to determine whether quality levels have improved.

In following these guidelines, managers need to remember *why* they are giving performance feedback: to encourage high levels of motivation and performance. Moreover, the information that managers gather through performance appraisal and feedback helps them determine how to distribute pay raises and bonuses.

Pay and Benefits

LO5 Explain the issues managers face in determining levels of pay and benefits.

Pay includes employees' base salaries, pay raises, and bonuses and is determined by a number of factors such as characteristics of the organization and the job and levels of performance. Employee *benefits* are based on membership in an organization (and not necessarily on the particular job held) and include sick days, vacation days, and medical and life insurance. In Chapter 9, we discussed the ways in which pay can motivate organizational members to perform at a high level, as well as the different kinds of pay plans managers can use to help an organization achieve its goals and gain a competitive advantage. It is important for pay to be linked to behaviors or results that contribute to organizational effectiveness. Next, we focus on establishing an organization's pay level and pay structure.

Pay Level

pay level The relative position of an organization's pay incentives in comparison with those of other organizations in the same industry employing similar kinds of workers.

Pay level is a broad comparative concept that refers to how an organization's pay incentives compare, in general, to those of other organizations in the same industry employing similar kinds of workers. Managers must decide if they want to offer relatively high wages, average wages, or relatively low wages. High wages help ensure that an organization is going to be able to recruit, select, and retain high performers, but high wages also raise costs. Low wages give an organization a cost advantage but may undermine the organization's ability to select and recruit high performers and to motivate current employees to perform at a high level. Either of these situations may lead to inferior quality or inadequate customer service.

In determining pay levels, managers should take into account their organization's strategy. A high pay level may prohibit managers from effectively pursuing a low-cost strategy. But a high pay level may be well worth the added costs in an organization whose competitive advantage lies in superior quality and excellent customer service. As one might expect, hotel and motel chains with a low-cost strategy, such as Days Inn and Hampton Inns, have lower pay levels than chains striving to provide high-quality rooms and services, such as Four Seasons and Hyatt Regency.

Pay Structure

pay structure The arrangement of jobs into categories reflecting their relative importance to the organization and its goals, levels of skill required, and other characteristics.

After deciding on a pay level, managers have to establish a pay structure for the different jobs in the organization. A **pay structure** clusters jobs into categories reflecting their relative importance to the organization and its goals, levels of skill required, and other characteristics managers consider to be important. Pay ranges are established for each job category. Individual jobholders' pay within job categories is then determined by factors such as performance, seniority, and skill levels.

There are some interesting global differences in pay structures. Large corporations based in the United States tend to pay their CEOs and top managers higher salaries than do their European or Japanese counterparts. Also, the pay differential between employees at the bottom of the corporate hierarchy and those higher up is much greater in U.S. companies than in European or Japanese companies.[78]

Concerns have been raised over whether it is equitable or fair for CEOs of large companies in the United States to be making millions of dollars in years when their companies are restructuring and laying off a large portion of their workforces.[79] Additionally, the average CEO in the United States typically earns over 430 times what the average hourly worker earns.[80] Is a pay structure with such a huge pay differential ethical? Shareholders and the public are increasingly asking this very question and asking large corporations to rethink their pay structures.[81] Also troubling are the millions of dollars in severance packages that some CEOs receive when they leave their organizations. In an era in which many workers are struggling to find and keep jobs and make ends meet, more and more people are questioning whether it is ethical for some top managers to be making so much money.[82]

Benefits

Organizations are legally required to provide certain benefits to their employees, including workers' compensation, Social Security, and unemployment insurance. Workers' compensation provides employees with financial assistance if they become unable to work due to a work-related injury or illness. Social Security provides financial assistance to retirees and disabled former employees. Unemployment insurance provides financial assistance to workers who lose their jobs due to no fault of their own. The legal system in the United States views these three benefits as ethical requirements for organizations and thus mandates that they be provided.

Other benefits such as health insurance, dental insurance, vacation time, pension plans, life insurance, flexible working hours, company-provided day care, and employee assistance and wellness programs are provided at the option of employers. Recall how a very attractive benefit at the Four Seasons in the "Management Snapshot" is being able to stay for free in any of the company's hotels and resorts. Benefits enabling workers to simultaneously balance the demands of their jobs and of their lives away from the office or factory are of growing importance for many workers who have competing demands on their all-too-scarce time and energy.

In some organizations, top managers determine which benefits might best suit the employees and organization and offer the same benefit package to all employees. Other organizations, realizing that employees' needs and desires might differ, offer **cafeteria-style benefit plans** that let employees themselves choose the benefits they want. Cafeteria-style benefit plans sometimes assist managers in dealing with employees who feel unfairly treated because they are unable to take advantage of certain benefits available to other employees who, for example, have children. Some organizations have success with cafeteria-style benefit plans; others find them difficult to manage.

cafeteria-style benefit plan A plan from which employees can choose the benefits that they want.

Some organizations seek to promote employee wellness by providing on-site fitness centers.

As health care costs are escalating and overstretched employees are finding it hard to take time out to exercise and take care of their health, more companies are providing benefits and incentives to promote employee wellness. AstraZeneca International offers its employees on-site counseling with a nutritionist and pays employees $125 for voluntarily taking a health risk assessment that covers wellness-related factors such as weight and nutrition.[83] Dole Food Company rewards employees with points toward gift certificates for participating in wellness activities provided on-site, such as yoga classes.[84]

For working parents and single mothers and fathers, family-friendly benefits are especially attractive, as profiled in the following "Focus on Diversity."

FOCUS ON DIVERSITY

Family-Friendly Benefits at Guerra DeBerry Coody

Small Business

Guerra DeBerry Coody is a small public relations and advertising firm based in San Antonio, Texas.[85] Founded in 1995, the firm has 61 employees and over $50 million in annual revenues. Recently, Guerra DeBerry Coody was named a "Top Small Workplace" by *The Wall Street Journal* and Winning Workplaces, a nonprofit organization. Employees at Guerra DeBerry Coody nominated their employer for this award, and given the family-friendly benefits this firm provides, it is easy to understand why.[86]

Guerra DeBerry Coody provides its employees with on-site child care until employees' children enter kindergarten with the firm covering 85% of the cost and employees paying $20 per day per child.[87] Employees are able to spend time with their children during the workday–employees often eat with their children, play with them, and settle them down for naps. The on-site child care center has a ratio of 1 child care worker for every 2 children enrolled, and around 11 children are currently enrolled. Employees with older children are able to bring their children to work after school if they wish. Senior account supervisor Patti Tanner sometimes has her two young teenage children come to the office after school. She indicates that "I don't even have any angst about having them here because I know it's completely and totally accepted."[88]

Guerra DeBerry Coody provides other benefits that help employees deal with the multiple demands and obligations in their lives. For example, employees who are having a major financial problem can apply for interest-free loans from the company. Employees also have the option of working from home and telecommuting and flexible work schedules. Guerra DeBerry Coody provides free health insurance for all its employees, and those with dependents needing coverage can purchase it for around $125–$200 per month. The company also contributes to a 401(k) retirement plan for its employees.[89] As Frank Guerra, one of the founding partners of Guerra DeBerry Coody and its current CEO, indicated upon the firm being named a "Top Small Workplace," "With or without this recognition we are so proud that we have the ability to offer our employees a family-friendly work environment where everyone has a vested interest in each other and in the business, caring for one another like family."[90]

Guerra DeBerry Coody offers family-friendly benefits such as child care.

Same-sex domestic-partner benefits are also being used to attract and retain valued employees. Gay and lesbian workers are more and more reluctant to work for companies that do not provide them with the same kinds of benefits for their partners as those provided for partners of the opposite sex.[91]

Labor Relations

Labor relations are the activities that managers engage in to ensure that they have effective working relationships with the labor unions that represent their employees' interests. Although the U.S. government has responded to the potential for unethical and unfair treatment of workers by creating and enforcing laws regulating employment (including the EEO laws listed in Table 12.1), some workers believe that a union will ensure that their interests are fairly represented in their organizations.

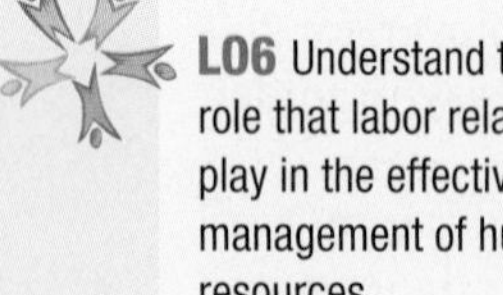

LO6 Understand the role that labor relations play in the effective management of human resources.

Before we describe unions in more detail, let's take a look at some examples of important employment legislation. In 1938 the government passed the Fair Labor Standards Act, which prohibited child labor and made provisions for minimum wages, overtime pay, and maximum working hours to protect workers' rights. In 1963 the Equal Pay Act mandated that men and women performing equal work (work requiring the same levels of skill, responsibility, and effort performed in the same kind of working conditions) receive equal pay (see Table 12.1). In 1970 the Occupational Safety and Health Act mandated procedures for managers to follow to ensure workplace safety. These are just a few of the U.S. government's efforts to protect workers' rights. State legislatures also have been active in promoting safe, ethical, and fair workplaces.

labor relations The activities that managers engage in to ensure that they have effective working relationships with the labor unions that represent their employees' interests.

Unions

Unions exist to represent workers' interests in organizations. Given that managers have more power than rank-and-file workers and that organizations have multiple stakeholders, there is always the potential that managers might take steps that benefit one set of stakeholders such as shareholders while hurting another such as employees. For example, managers may decide to speed up a production line to lower costs and increase production in the hopes of increasing returns to shareholders. Speeding up the line, however, could hurt employees forced to work at a rapid pace and may increase the risk of injuries. Also, employees receive no additional pay for the extra work they are performing. Unions would represent workers' interests in a scenario such as this one.

Congress acknowledged the role that unions could play in ensuring safe and fair workplaces when it passed the National Labor Relations Act of 1935. This act made it legal for workers to organize into unions to protect their rights and interests and declared certain unfair or unethical organizational practices to be illegal. The act also established the National Labor Relations Board (NLRB) to oversee union activity. Currently, the NLRB conducts certification elections, which are held among the employees of an organization to determine whether they want a union to represent their interests. The NLRB also makes judgments concerning unfair labor practices and specifies practices that managers must refrain from.

Employees might vote to have a union represent them for any number of reasons.[92] They may think that their wages and working conditions are in need of improvement. They may believe that managers are not treating them with respect. They may think that their working hours are unfair or that they need more job security or a safer work environment. Or they may be dissatisfied with management and find it difficult to communicate their concerns to their bosses. Regardless of the specific reason, one overriding reason is power: A united group inevitably wields more power than an

The 2007–2008 Writer's Guild of America strike lasted for 100 days.

individual, and this type of power may be especially helpful to employees in some organizations.

Although these would seem to be potent forces for unionization, some workers are reluctant to join unions. Sometimes this reluctance is due to the perception that union leaders are corrupt. Some workers may simply believe that belonging to a union might not do them much good or may actually cause more harm than good while costing them money in membership dues. Employees also might not want to be forced into doing something they do not want to, such as striking because the union thinks it is in their best interest. Moreover, although unions can be a positive force in organizations, sometimes they also can be a negative force, impairing organizational effectiveness. For example, when union leaders resist needed changes in an organization or are corrupt, organizational performance can suffer.

The percentage of U.S. workers represented by unions today is smaller than it was in the 1950s, an era when unions were especially strong.[93] The American Federation of Labor and Congress of Industrial Organizations (AFL-CIO) includes 56 national and international unions representing 11 million workers.[94] Union influence in manufacturing and heavy industries has been on the decline. Recently, however, unions have made inroads in other segments of the workforce, particularly the low-wage end. Garbage collectors in New Jersey, poultry plant workers in North Carolina, and janitors in Baltimore are among the growing numbers of low-paid workers who are currently finding union membership attractive. North Carolina poultry workers voted in a union in part because they thought it was unfair that they had to buy their own gloves and hairnets used on the job and had to ask their supervisors' permission to go to the restroom.[95]

collective bargaining Negotiations between labor unions and managers to resolve conflicts and disputes about issues such as working hours, wages, benefits, working conditions, and job security.

Collective Bargaining

Collective bargaining is negotiation between labor unions and managers to resolve conflicts and disputes about important issues such as working hours, wages, working conditions, and job security. Before sitting down with management to negotiate, union members sometimes go on strike to drive home their concerns to managers. Once an agreement that union members support has been reached (sometimes with the help of a neutral third party called a *mediator*), union leaders and managers sign a contract spelling out the terms of the collective bargaining agreement.

Summary and Review

STRATEGIC HUMAN RESOURCE MANAGEMENT Human resource management (HRM) includes all the activities that managers engage in to ensure that their organizations are able to attract, retain, and effectively utilize human resources. Strategic HRM is the process by which managers design the components of a human resource management system to be consistent with each other, with other elements of organizational architecture, and with the organization's strategies and goals. **[LO1]**

RECRUITMENT AND SELECTION Before recruiting and selecting employees, managers must engage in human resource planning and job analysis. Human resource planning includes all the activities managers engage in to forecast their current and future needs for human resources. Job analysis is the process of identifying (1) the tasks, duties, and responsibilities that make up a job and (2) the knowledge, skills, and abilities needed to perform the job. Recruitment includes all the activities that managers engage in to develop a pool of qualified applicants for open positions. Selection is the process by which managers determine the relative qualifications of job applicants and their potential for performing well in a particular job. **[LO2]**

TRAINING AND DEVELOPMENT Training focuses on teaching organizational members how to perform effectively in their current jobs. Development focuses on broadening organizational members' knowledge and skills so that they will be prepared to take on new responsibilities and challenges. **[LO3]**

PERFORMANCE APPRAISAL AND FEEDBACK Performance appraisal is the evaluation of employees' job performance and contributions to the organization. Performance feedback is the process through which managers share performance appraisal information with their subordinates, give them an opportunity to reflect on their own performance, and develop with them plans for the future. Performance appraisal provides managers with useful information for decision-making purposes. Performance feedback can encourage high levels of motivation and performance. **[LO4]**

PAY AND BENEFITS Pay level is the relative position of an organization's pay incentives in comparison with those of other organizations in the same industry employing similar workers. A pay structure clusters jobs into categories according to their relative importance to the organization and its goals, the levels of skill required, and other characteristics. Pay ranges are then established for each job category. Organizations are legally required to provide certain benefits to their employees; other benefits are provided at the discretion of employers. **[LO5]**

LABOR RELATIONS Labor relations include all the activities managers engage in to ensure that they have effective working relationships with the labor unions that represent their employees' interests. The National Labor Relations Board oversees union activity. Collective bargaining is the process through which labor unions and managers resolve conflicts and disputes and negotiate agreements. **[LO6]**

Management in Action

Topics for Discussion and Action

Discussion

1. Discuss why it is important for human resource management systems to be in sync with an organization's strategy and goals and with each other. [LO1]
2. Discuss why training and development are ongoing activities for all organizations. [LO3]
3. Describe the type of development activities you think middle managers are most in need of. [LO3]
4. Evaluate the pros and cons of 360-degree performance appraisals and feedback. Would you like your performance to be appraised in this manner? Why or why not? [LO4]
5. Discuss why two restaurants in the same community might have different pay levels. [LO5]

Action

6. Interview a manager in a local organization to determine how that organization recruits and selects employees. [LO6]

Building Management Skills [LO1, 2, 3, 4, 5]

Analyzing Human Resource Systems

Think about your current job or a job that you have had in the past. If you have never had a job, then interview a friend or family member who is currently working. Answer the following questions about the job you have chosen:

1. How are people recruited and selected for this job? Are the recruitment and selection procedures that the organization uses effective or ineffective? Why?
2. What training and development do people who hold this job receive? Is it appropriate? Why or why not?
3. How is performance of this job appraised? Does performance feedback contribute to motivation and high performance on this job?
4. What levels of pay and benefits are provided on this job? Are these levels appropriate? Why or why not?

Managing Ethically [LO4, 5]

Some managers do not want to become overly friendly with their subordinates because they are afraid that if they do so, their objectivity when conducting performance appraisals and making decisions about pay raises and promotions will be impaired. Some subordinates resent it when they see one or more of their coworkers being very friendly with the boss; they are concerned about the potential for favoritism. Their reasoning runs something like this: If two subordinates are equally qualified for a promotion and one is a good friend of the boss and the other is a mere acquaintance, who is more likely to receive the promotion?

Questions

1. Either individually or in a group, think about the ethical

implications of managers' becoming friendly with their subordinates.

2. Do you think that managers should feel free to socialize and become good friends with their subordinates outside the workplace if they so desire? Why or why not?

Small Group Breakout Exercise [LO1, 2, 3, 4, 5]

Building a Human Resource Management System

Form groups of three or four people, and appoint one group member as the spokesperson who will communicate your findings to the class when called on by the instructor. Then discuss the following scenario:

You and your three partners are engineers who minored in business at college and have decided to start a consulting business. Your goal is to provide manufacturing-process engineering and other engineering services to large and small organizations. You forecast that there will be an increased use of outsourcing for these activities. You discussed with managers in several large organizations the services you plan to offer, and they expressed considerable interest. You have secured funding to start your business and now are building the HRM system. Your human resource planning suggests that you need to hire between five and eight experienced engineers with good communication skills, two clerical/secretarial workers, and two MBAs who between them have financial, accounting, and human resource skills. You are striving to develop your human resources in a way that will enable your new business to prosper.

1. Describe the steps you will take to recruit and select (a) the engineers, (b) the clerical/secretarial workers, and (c) the MBAs.
2. Describe the training and development the engineers, the clerical/secretarial workers, and the MBAs will receive.
3. Describe how you will appraise the performance of each group of employees and how you will provide feedback.
4. Describe the pay level and pay structure of your consulting firm.

Be the Manager [LO4]

You are Walter Michaels and have just received some disturbing feedback. You are the director of human resources for Maxi Vision Inc., a medium-size window and glass-door manufacturer. You recently initiated a 360-degree performance appraisal system for all middle and upper managers at Maxi Vision, including yourself but excluding the most senior executives and the top-management team.

You were eagerly awaiting the feedback you would receive from the managers who report to you; you had recently implemented several important initiatives that affected them and their subordinates, including a complete overhaul of the organization's performance appraisal system. While the managers who report to you were evaluated based on 360-degree appraisals, their own subordinates were evaluated based on behavior appraisals you recently created. Conducted annually, appraisals are an important input into pay raise and bonus decisions.

You were so convinced that the new performance appraisal procedures were highly effective that you hoped your own subordinates would mention them in their feedback to you. And boy did they! You were amazed to learn that the managers *and* their subordinates thought the new behavior appraisals were unfair, inappropriate, and a waste of time. In fact, the managers' feedback to you was that their own performance was suffering, based on the 360-degree appraisals they received, because their subordinates hated the new appraisal system and partially blamed their bosses, who were part of management. Some managers even admitted giving all their subordinates approximately the same scores on the scales so that their pay raises and bonuses would not be affected by their performance appraisals.

You couldn't believe your eyes when you read these comments. You had spent so much time developing what you thought was the ideal rating scale for this group of employees. Evidently, for some unknown reason, they were being very closed-minded and wouldn't give it a chance. Your own supervisor was aware of these complaints and said that it was a top priority for you to fix "this mess" (with the implication that you were responsible for creating it). What are you going to do?

BusinessWeek Case in the News [LO1, 2, 3]

How P&G Finds—and Keeps—a Prized Workforce

Few employers spend as much time cultivating their workforce as Procter & Gamble. The consumer-products company expects to get 400,000 applications for entry-level management positions this year. It will hire less than one-half of 1% of them, selecting only those most likely to fit the P&G culture. "We actually recruit for values," says Chief Operating Officer Robert McDonald. "If you are not inspired to improve lives, this isn't the company you want to work for."

The careful vetting, training, and career development pay off. P&G boasts 23 brands with at least $1 billion in annual sales and is the market leader in everything from detergent to diapers to razors. True, the company's renowned marketing skills and deep pockets help. But another important edge is personnel management—bringing in and promoting creative thinkers.

Intense Internal Training

The P&G strategy starts on college campuses. The Cincinnati company dispatches line managers rather than human resource staffers to do much of its recruiting. They home in on schools whose earlier graduates have moved up at P&G, such as Harvard and Stanford. Interviewers look for what they call a candidate's "power," including leadership ability and empathy. Innovation skills and values are measured in an online assessment. "Our managers are skilled at probing for the right fit," says William Reina, director for global talent. "The people they identify score well on the assessment."

For the few who get hired, their work life becomes a career-long development process. At every level, P&G has a different "college" to train individuals, and every department has its own "university." The general manager's college, which McDonald leads, holds a week-long school term once a year when there are a handful of newly promoted managers. Further training—there are nearly 50 courses—helps managers with technical writing or financial analysis.

Career education takes place outside the classroom, too. P&G pushes every general manager to log at least one foreign assignment of three to five years. Even high-ranking employees visit the homes of consumers to watch how they cook, clean, and generally live, in a practice dubbed "live it, work it." Managers also visit retail stores, occasionally even scanning and bagging items at checkout lanes, to learn more about customers. Rosabeth Moss Kanter, a professor of business administration at Harvard Business School, says this level of involvement by executives is rare. But that's what separates P&G from the pack.

Source: R. O. Crockett, "How P&G Finds—and Keeps—a Prized Workforce." Reprinted from April 20, 2009 issue of *BusinessWeek* by special permission, copyright © 2009 by The McGraw-Hill Companies, Inc.

Questions

1. How does P&G recruit and select new employees? Why do they recruit and select new employees in this manner?
2. How do training and development take place at P&G?
3. Why are general managers at P&G encouraged to have at least one international assignment?
4. Why do P&G employees visit and observe consumers in their homes?

BusinessWeek **Case in the News** [LO4]

Job Review In 140 Keystrokes

In the world of Facebook or Twitter, people love to hear feedback about what they're up to. But sit them down for a performance review, and suddenly the experience becomes traumatic.

Now companies are taking a page from social networking sites to make the performance evaluation process more fun and useful. Accenture has developed a Facebook-style program called Performance Multiplier in which, among other things, employees post status updates, photos, and two or three weekly goals that can be viewed by fellow staffers. Even more immediate: new software from a Toronto start-up called Rypple that lets people post Twitter-length questions about their performance in exchange for anonymous feedback. Companies ranging from sandwich chain Great Harvest Bread Co. to Firefox developer Mozilla have signed on as clients.

Such initiatives upend the dreaded rite of annual reviews by making performance feedback a much more real-time and ongoing process. Stanford University management professor Robert Sutton argues that performance reviews "mostly suck" because they're conceived from the top rather than designed with employees' needs in mind. "If you have regular conversations with people, and they know where they stand, then the performance evaluation is maybe unnecessary," says Sutton.

What Rypple's and Accenture's tools do is create a process in which evaluations become dynamic—and more democratic. Rypple, for example, gives employees the chance to post brief, 140-character questions, such as "What did you think of my presentation?" or "How can I run meetings better?" The queries are e-mailed to managers, peers, or anyone else the user selects. Short anonymous responses are then aggregated and sent back, providing a quick-and-dirty 360-degree review. The basic service is free. But corporate clients can pay for a premium version that includes tech support, extra security, and analysis of which topics figure highest in employee posts. Rypple's cofounders have also launched software called TouchBase that's meant to replace the standard annual review with quick monthly surveys and discussions.

Galvanizing Goals

Accenture's software, which it's using internally and hoping to sell to outside clients, is more about motivating employees than it is about measuring them. With help from management guru Marcus Buckingham, the consultancy's product has a similar look and feel to other corporate social networks. The major difference is that users are expected to post brief goals for the week on their profile page, as well as a couple for each quarter. If they don't, the lack of goals is visible to their managers, who are also alerted of the omission by e-mail. By prompting people to document and adjust their goals constantly, Accenture hopes the formal discussions will improve. "You don't have to desperately recreate examples of what you've done," says Buckingham. Typically, "managers and employees are scrambling to fill [evaluation forms] out in the 24 hours before HR calls saying 'where's yours?' "

If having your performance goals posted for the world to see sounds a bit Orwellian, consider this: Rypple reports that some two-thirds of the questions posted on its service come from managers wanting feedback about business questions or their own performance. The biggest payoff of these social network–style tools may prove to be better performance by the boss.

Questions

1. Why are some organizations using social networking–style systems for performance appraisals?
2. How might the feedback generated from these kinds of systems differ from feedback generated from more traditional performance appraisals?
3. How might use of these kinds of systems influence employee motivation and performance?
4. Are there any potential drawbacks or disadvantages of these kinds of systems?

Communication and Information Technology Management

CHAPTER 13

Learning Objectives

After studying this chapter, you should be able to

1. Differentiate between data and information, list the attributes of useful information, and describe three reasons why managers must have access to information to perform their tasks and roles effectively. **[LO1]**
2. Explain why effective communication—the sharing of information—helps an organization gain a competitive advantage, and describe the communication process. **[LO2]**
3. Define information richness, and describe the information richness of communication media available to managers. **[LO3]**
4. Differentiate among four kinds of management information systems. **[LO4]**

Herman Miller's custom-made ergonomic office furniture arrives on time due to the company's use of IT that links its dealers with its manufacturing hub.

MANAGEMENT SNAPSHOT

Herman Miller's Office of the Future

How Can Managers Create Competitive Advantage by Using IT to Improve Communication?

Managers at Herman Miller have been finding countless ways to use IT and the Internet to give their company a competitive advantage over rival office furniture makers (OFMs) such as Steelcase and Hon.[1] Early on, Miller's managers saw the potential of the Internet for selling its furniture to business customers. Other furniture companies' Web sites were online advertisements for their products, services, and other marketing information. However, Miller's managers quickly realized the true potential of using both the company's intranet and the Internet to reach customers.

First, Miller's managers developed IT that linked all the company's dealers and salespeople to its manufacturing hub so that sales orders could be coordinated with the custom design department and with manufacturing, enabling customers to receive pricing and scheduling information promptly. Then, with this customer delivery system in place, Miller developed IT to link its manufacturing operations with its network of suppliers so that its input supply chain would be coordinated with its customer needs.

When Miller's managers noticed that competitors were quickly imitating its IT, they began to search for new ways to use it to gain a competitive advantage. Soon they realized that IT could transform the office furniture business itself. When they began to define Herman Miller as a "digital" enterprise infused with e-business, they realized IT could not only improve efficiency but also change the way the customer experienced "Herman Miller" and increase value for the customer. A major Web initiative was the establishment of an e-learning tool, Uknowit.com, which became Herman Miller's online university. Via the Web thousands of Miller's employees and dealers are currently enrolled in Uknowit.com, where they choose from 85 courses covering technology, products and services, product applications, consultative/selling skills, and industry competitive knowledge. The benefits to Miller, its dealers, and its customers from this IT initiative are improved speed to market and better ability to respond to competitors' tactics. That is, salespeople and dealers now have the information and tools they need to better compete for and keep customers.

Moreover, the office furniture business offers highly customized solutions to its customers. A main source of competitive advantage is the ability to give customers exactly what they want and at the right price. Using its new IT, Miller's salespeople are giving design and manufacturing more accurate and timely information, which has reduced the incidence of sales and specification errors during the selling process. Also, with the new systems time to market has been reduced, and Miller is committed to being able to offer customers highly customized furniture in 10 business days or less.

Of course, all these IT initiatives have been costly to Herman Miller. Thousands of hours of management time have been spent developing the IT and providing content, such as information on competitors for the company's online classes. Herman Miller's managers are looking at the long term; they believe they have created a real source of competitive advantage for their company that will sustain it in the years ahead.

Overview

As Herman Miller's initiatives suggest, developing new IT to improve communication and decision making is a vital managerial task. In this chapter we survey information systems and information technology in general, looking at the relationship between information and the manager's job. Then we describe the nature of communication and explain why it is so important for all managers and their subordinates to be effective communicators. We describe the communication media available to managers and the factors they need to consider when selecting a communication medium for each message they send. We consider the communication networks that organizational members rely on, and we explore how advances in information technology have expanded managers' communication options.

Finally, we discuss several types of information systems that managers can use to help themselves perform their jobs, and we examine the impact that rapidly evolving information systems and technologies may have on managers' jobs and on an organization's competitive advantage. By the end of this chapter, you will understand the profound ways in which new developments in information systems and technology are shaping the way managers communicate and their functions and roles.

Information and the Manager's Job

Managers cannot plan, organize, lead, and control effectively unless they have access to information. Information is the source of the knowledge and intelligence that they need to make the right decisions. Information, however, is not the same as data.[2] **Data** are raw, unsummarized, and unanalyzed facts such as volume of sales, level of costs, or number of customers. **Information** is data that are organized in a meaningful fashion, such as in a graph showing changes in sales volume or costs over time. Alone, data do not tell managers anything; information, in contrast, can communicate a great deal of useful knowledge to the person who receives it–such as a manager who sees sales falling or costs rising. The distinction between data and information is important because one of the uses of information technology is to help managers transform data into information in order to make better managerial decisions.

data Raw, unsummarized, and unanalyzed facts.

information Data that are organized in a meaningful fashion.

LO1 Differentiate between data and information, list the attributes of useful information, and describe three reasons why managers must have access to information to perform their tasks and roles effectively.

Consider the case of a manager in a supermarket who must decide how much shelf space to allocate to two breakfast cereal brands for children: Dentist's Delight and Sugar Supreme. Most supermarkets use checkout scanners to record individual sales and store the data on a computer. Accessing this computer, the manager might find that Dentist's Delight sells 50 boxes per day and Sugar Supreme sells 25 boxes per day. These raw data, however, are of little help in assisting the manager to decide how to allocate shelf space. The manager also needs to know how much shelf space each cereal currently occupies and how much profit each cereal generates for the supermarket.

Suppose the manager discovers that Dentist's Delight occupies 10 feet of shelf space and Sugar Supreme occupies 4 feet and that Dentist's Delight generates 20 cents of profit a box while Sugar Supreme generates 40 cents of profit a box. By putting these three bits of data together (number of boxes sold, amount of shelf space, and profit per box), the manager gets some useful information on which to base a decision: Dentist's Delight generates $1 of profit per foot of shelf space per day [(50 boxes @ $.20)/10 feet], and Sugar Supreme generates $2.50 of profit per foot of shelf space per day [(25 boxes @ $.40)/4 feet]. Armed with this information, the manager might decide to allocate less shelf space to Dentist's Delight and more to Sugar Supreme.

Attributes of Useful Information

Four factors determine the usefulness of information to a manager: quality, timeliness, completeness, and relevance (see Figure 13.1).

QUALITY Accuracy and reliability determine the quality of information.[3] The greater accuracy and reliability are, the higher is the quality of information. For an information system to work well, the information that it provides must be of high quality. If managers conclude that the quality of information provided by their information system is low, they are likely to lose confidence in the system and stop using it. Alternatively, if managers base decisions on low-quality information, poor and even disastrous decision making can result. For example, the partial meltdown of the nuclear reactor at Three Mile Island in Pennsylvania in 1979 was the result of poor information caused by an information system malfunction. The information system indicated to engineers

Figure 13.1
Factors Affecting the Usefulness of Information

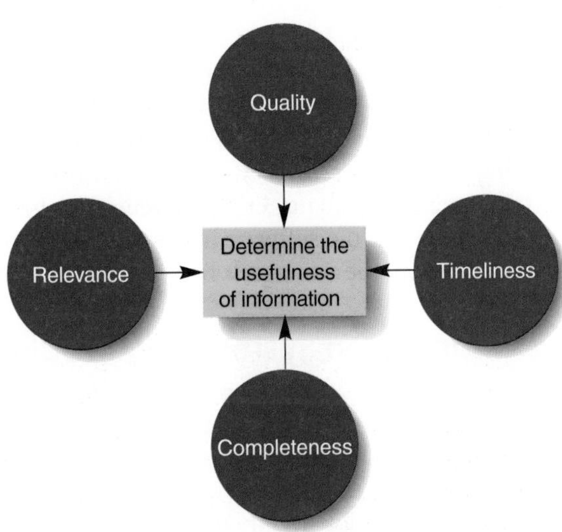

controlling the reactor that there was enough water in the reactor core to cool the nuclear pile, although this was in fact not the case. The consequences included the partial meltdown of the reactor and the release of radioactive gas into the atmosphere.

TIMELINESS Information that is timely is available when it is needed for managerial action, not after the decision has been made. In today's rapidly changing world, the need for timely information often means that information must be available on a real-time basis.[4] **Real-time information** is information that reflects current conditions. In an industry that experiences rapid changes, real-time information may need to be updated frequently.

real-time information Frequently updated information that reflects current conditions.

Airlines use real-time information about the number of flight bookings and about competitors' prices to adjust their prices on an hour-to-hour basis to maximize their revenues. Thus, for example, the fare for flights from New York to Seattle might change from one hour to the next as fares are reduced to fill empty seats and raised when most seats have been sold. Airlines use real-time information about reservations to adjust fares at the last possible moment to fill planes and maximize revenues. U.S. airlines make more than 80,000 fare changes each day.[5] Obviously, the managers who make such pricing decisions need real-time information about the current state of demand in the marketplace.

COMPLETENESS Information that is complete gives managers all the information they need to exercise control, achieve coordination, or make an effective decision. Recall from Chapter 5, however, that managers rarely have access to complete information. Instead, because of uncertainty, ambiguity, and bounded rationality, they have to make do with incomplete information.[6] One of the functions of information systems is to increase the completeness of the information that managers have at their disposal.

RELEVANCE Information that is relevant is useful and suits a manager's particular needs and circumstances. Irrelevant information is useless and may actually hurt the performance of a busy manager who has to spend valuable time determining whether information is relevant. Given the massive amounts of information that managers are now exposed to and humans' limited information-processing capabilities, the people who design information systems need to make sure that managers receive only relevant information.

Today, software agents are increasingly being used by managers to scan and sort incoming e-mail and prioritize it. A software agent is a software program that can be used to perform simple tasks such as scanning incoming information for relevance, taking some of the burden away from managers. Moreover, by recording and analyzing a manager's own efforts to prioritize incoming information, the software agent can mimic the manager's preferences and thus perform such tasks more effectively. For example, the software agent can automatically reprogram itself to place incoming e-mail from the manager's boss at the top of the pile.[7]

information system A system for acquiring, organizing, storing, manipulating, and transmitting information.

management information system An information system that managers plan and design to provide themselves with the specific information they need.

Information Systems and Technology

An **information system** is a system for acquiring, organizing, storing, manipulating, and transmitting information.[8] A **management information system** (MIS) is an information system that managers plan and design to provide themselves with the specific information they need to perform their roles effectively. Information systems have existed for as long as there have been organizations—a long time indeed. Before the computer age, most information systems were paper based: Clerks recorded important information on documents (often in duplicate or triplicate) in the form of words and numbers, sent a copy of the document to superiors, customers, or suppliers, as the case might be, and stored other copies in files for future reference.

information technology The means by which information is acquired, organized, stored, manipulated, and transmitted.

Information technology is the means by which information is acquired, organized, stored, manipulated, and transmitted. Rapid advances in the power of information technology–specifically, through the use of computers–are having a fundamental impact on information systems and on managers, their organizations, and their suppliers and customers.[9] So important are these advances in information technology that organizations that do not adopt new information technology, or adopt it ineffectively, will become uncompetitive with those that put it to good use.[10]

Managers need information for three reasons: to make effective decisions; to control the activities of the organization; and to coordinate the activities of the organization.[11] We now examine these uses of information in detail.

Information and Decision Making

Much of management (planning, organizing, leading, and controlling) is about making decisions. The marketing manager must decide what price to charge for a product, what distribution channels to use, and what promotional messages to emphasize. The manufacturing manager must decide how much of a product to make and how to make it. The purchasing manager must decide from whom to purchase inputs and what inventory of inputs to hold. The human relations manager must decide how much employees should be paid, how they should be trained, and what benefits they should be given. The engineering manager must make decisions about new product design. Top managers must decide how to allocate scarce financial resources among competing projects, how best to structure and control the organization, and what business-level strategy the organization should be pursuing. And, regardless of their functional orientation, all managers have to make decisions about matters such as what performance evaluation to give to a subordinate.

Decision making cannot be effective in an information vacuum. To make effective decisions, managers need information, both from inside the organization and from external stakeholders. When deciding how to price a product, for example, the marketing manager needs information about how consumers will react to different prices. She needs information about unit costs because she does not want to set the price below the costs of production. And she needs information about competitive strategy, since pricing strategy should be consistent with an organization's competitive strategy. Some of this information will come from outside the organization (for example, from consumer surveys) and some from inside the organization (information about unit production costs comes from manufacturing). As this example suggests, managers' ability to make effective decisions rests on their ability to acquire and process information.

Information and Control

As discussed in Chapter 8, controlling is the process whereby managers regulate how efficiently and effectively an organization and its members are performing the activities necessary to achieve organizational goals.[12] Managers achieve control over organizational activities by taking four steps (see Figure 8.2): (1) They establish measurable standards of performance or goals. (2) They measure actual performance. (3) They compare actual performance against established goals. (4) They evaluate the result and take corrective action if necessary.[13] FedEx, for example, has a delivery goal: to deliver by noon tomorrow 100% of the packages it picks up today. Throughout the United States, FedEx has thousands of ground stations that are responsible for the physical pickup and delivery of packages. FedEx managers monitor the delivery performance of these stations on a regular basis; if they find that the 100% goal is not being attained, they determine why and take corrective action if necessary.[14]

To achieve control over any organizational activity, managers must have information. To control a ground station, a manager at FedEx needs to know how many of that station's packages are being delivered by noon. To get this information, the manager needs to make sure that an information system is in place. Packages to be shipped by FedEx are scanned with a handheld scanner by the FedEx driver who first picks them up. The pickup information is sent by a wireless link to a central computer at FedEx's headquarters. The packages are scanned again by the truck driver when they are delivered. The delivery information is also transmitted to FedEx's central computer. So managers can quickly find out what percentage of packages are delivered by noon of the day after they were picked up.[15]

Management information systems, discussed later in the chapter, are used to control a variety of operations within organizations. In accounting, for example, information systems can be used to monitor expenditures and compare them against budgets.[16] To track expenditures against budgets, managers need information on current expenditures broken down by relevant organizational units. Accounting information systems are designed to provide managers with such information. Another example of an information system used to monitor and control the daily activities of employees is the online MBO information system used by T. J. Rodgers at Cypress Semiconductor, discussed in Chapter 8. Rodgers implemented a computer-based information system that allows him to review the goals of all his employees in about four hours.[17]

FedEx's nationwide computer tracking system ensures that each package is routed most efficiently and cost-effectively to its specific location.

Information and Coordination

Coordinating department and divisional activities to achieve organizational goals is another basic task of management. As an extreme example of the size of the coordination task that managers face, consider the coordination effort involved in building Boeing's commercial jet aircraft, the 777. The 777 is composed of 3 million individual parts and thousands of major components. Managers at Boeing have to coordinate the production and delivery of these parts so that they all arrive at Boeing's Everett, Washington, facility exactly when they are needed (for example, they want the wings to arrive before the engines). Boeing managers jokingly refer to this task as "coordinating 3 million parts in flying formation." To achieve this high level of coordination, managers need information about which supplier is producing what, when it is to be produced, and when it is to be delivered. Managers also need this information so that they are able to track the delivery performance of suppliers against expectations and receive advance warning of any likely problems. To meet these needs, managers at Boeing established a computer-based information system that links Boeing to all its suppliers and can track the flow of 3 million component parts through the production process–an immense task.

As noted in previous chapters, the coordination problems that managers face in managing their global supply chains to take advantage of national differences in the costs of production are increasing. To deal with global coordination problems, managers have been adopting sophisticated computer-based information systems that help them coordinate the flow of materials, semifinished goods, and finished products around the world.

Communication, Information, and Management

Communication is the sharing of information between two or more people or groups to reach a common understanding.[18] The "Management Snapshot" that opens this chapter highlights some important aspects of this definition. First and foremost, communication, no matter how electronically based, is a human endeavor and involves individuals and groups. Second, communication does not take place unless a common understanding is reached. Thus, if you try to call a business to speak to a person in customer service or billing and you are bounced back and forth between endless automated messages and menu options and eventually hang up in frustration, communication has not taken place.

communication The sharing of information between two or more individuals or groups to reach a common understanding.

The Importance of Good Communication

LO2 Explain why effective communication—the sharing of information—helps an organization gain a competitive advantage, and describe the communication process.

In Chapter 1, we described how in order for an organization to gain a competitive advantage, managers must strive to increase efficiency, quality, responsiveness to customers, and innovation. Good communication is essential for attaining each of these four goals and thus is a necessity for gaining a competitive advantage.

Managers can *increase efficiency* by updating the production process to take advantage of new and more efficient technologies and by training workers to operate the new technologies and expand their skills. Good communication is necessary for managers to learn about new technologies, implement them in their organizations, and train workers in how to use them. Similarly, *improving quality* hinges on effective communication. Managers need to communicate to all members of an organization the meaning and importance of high quality and the routes to attaining it. Subordinates need to communicate quality problems and suggestions for increasing quality to their superiors, and members of self-managed work teams need to share their ideas for improving quality with each other.

Good communication can also help to increase *responsiveness to customers*. When the organizational members who are closest to customers, such as salespeople in department stores and tellers in banks, are empowered to communicate customers' needs and desires to managers, managers are better able to respond to these needs. Managers, in turn, must communicate with other organizational members to determine how best to respond to changing customer preferences.

Innovation, which often takes place in cross-functional teams, also requires effective communication. Members of a cross-functional team developing a new kind of compact disc player, for example, must communicate effectively with each other to develop a disc player that customers will want, that will be of high quality, and that can be produced efficiently. Members of the team also must communicate with managers to secure the resources they need to develop the disc player and keep the managers informed of progress on the project.

Effective communication is necessary for managers and all members of an organization to increase efficiency, quality, responsiveness to customers, and innovation and thus gain a competitive advantage for their organization. Managers therefore must have a good understanding of the communication process if they are to perform effectively. Collaboration software is IT that aims to promote highly interdependent interactions among members of a team and provide the team with an electronic meeting site for communication.[19] For work that is truly team-based, entails a number of highly interdependent yet distinct components, and involves team members with distinct areas of expertise who need to closely coordinate their efforts, collaboration software can be a powerful communication tool, as profiled in the following "Information Technology Byte."

INFORMATION TECHNOLOGY BYTE

Collaboration Software Facilitates Communication in Teams

Collaboration software provides members of a team with an online work site where they can post, share, and save data, reports, sketches, and other documents; keep calendars; have team-based online conferences; and send and receive messages. The software can also keep and update progress reports, survey team members about different issues, forward documents to managers, and let users know which of their team members are also online and at the site.[20] Having an integrated online work area can help to organize and centralize the work of a team, help to ensure that information is readily available as needed, and also help team members to make sure that important information is not overlooked. Collaboration software can be much more efficient than e-mail or instant messaging for managing ongoing team collaboration and interaction that is not face-to-face. Moreover, when a team does meet face-to-face, all documents the team might need in the course of the meeting are just a click away.[21]

The New York–based public relations company Ketchum Inc. uses collaboration software for some of its projects. For example, Ketchum is managing public relations, marketing, and advertising for a new charitable program that Fireman's Fund Insurance Co. has undertaken. By using the eRoom software provided by Documentum (a part of EMC Corporation), Ketchum employees working on the project at six different locations, employee representatives from Fireman's, and a graphics company that is designing a Web site for the program can share plans, documents, graphic designs, and calendars at an online work site.[22] Members of the Ketchum–Fireman team get e-mail alerts when something has been modified or added to the site. As Ketchum's chief information officer Andy Roach puts it, "The fact that everyone has access to the same document means Ketchum isn't going to waste time on the logistics and can focus on the creative side."[23]

Another company taking advantage of collaboration software is Honeywell International Inc. Managers at Honeywell decided to use the SharePoint collaboration software provided by Microsoft, in part because it can be integrated with other Microsoft software such as Outlook. So, for example, if a team using SharePoint makes a change to the team's calendar, that change will be automatically made in team members' Outlook calendars.[24] Clearly, collaboration software has the potential to enhance communication efficiency and effectiveness in teams.

sender The person or group wishing to share information.

message The information that a sender wants to share.

encoding Translating a message into understandable symbols or language.

noise Anything that hampers any stage of the communication process.

receiver The person or group for which a message is intended.

medium The pathway through which an encoded message is transmitted to a receiver.

decoding Interpreting and trying to make sense of a message.

verbal communication The encoding of messages into words, either written or spoken.

The Communication Process

The communication process consists of two phases. In the *transmission phase,* information is shared between two or more individuals or groups. In the *feedback phase,* a common understanding is assured. In both phases, a number of distinct stages must occur for communication to take place (see Figure 13.2).[25]

Starting the transmission phase, the **sender**, the person or group wishing to share information with some other person or group, decides on the **message**, what information to communicate. Then the sender translates the message into symbols or language, a process called **encoding**; often messages are encoded into words. **Noise** is a general term that refers to anything that hampers any stage of the communication process.

Once encoded, a message is transmitted through a medium to the **receiver**, the person or group for which the message is intended. A **medium** is simply the pathway, such as a phone call, a letter, a memo, or face-to-face communication in a meeting, through which an encoded message is transmitted to a receiver. At the next stage, the receiver interprets and tries to make sense of the message, a process called **decoding**. This is a critical point in communication.

The feedback phase is initiated by the receiver (who becomes a sender). The receiver decides what message to send to the original sender (who becomes a receiver), encodes it, and transmits it through a chosen medium (see Figure 13.2). The message might contain a confirmation that the original message was received and understood or a restatement of the original message to make sure that it has been correctly interpreted; or it might include a request for more information. The original sender decodes the message and makes sure that a common understanding has been reached. If the original sender determines that a common understanding has not been reached, sender and receiver cycle through the whole process as many times as are needed to reach a common understanding.

The encoding of messages into words, written or spoken, is **verbal communication**. We also encode messages without using written or spoken language.

Figure 13.2
The Communication Process

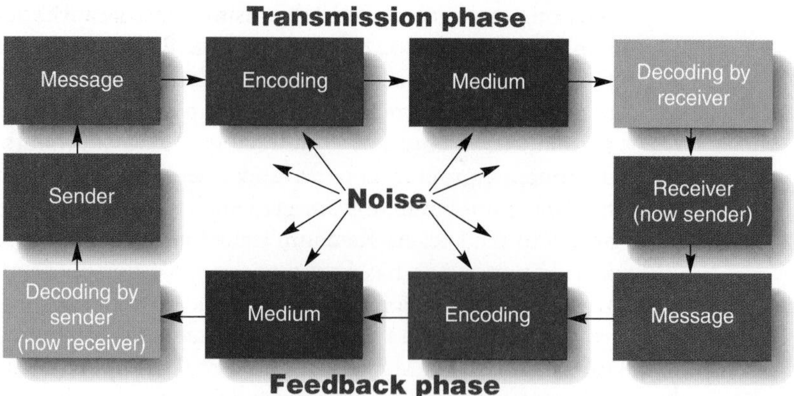

nonverbal communication The encoding of messages by means of facial expressions, body language, and styles of dress.

Nonverbal communication shares information by means of facial expressions (smiling, raising an eyebrow, frowning, dropping one's jaw), body language (posture, gestures, nods, shrugs), and even style of dress (casual, formal, conservative, trendy). For example, to communicate or signal that General Motors' old bureaucracy has been dismantled and the company is decentralized and more informal than it used to be, top managers at GM wear slacks and sport jackets rather than business suits when they walk around GM plants.[26] The trend toward increasing empowerment of the workforce has led GM and other managers to dress informally to communicate that all employees of an organization are team members, working together to create value for customers.

Nonverbal communication can be used to back up or reinforce verbal communication. Just as a warm and genuine smile can back up words of appreciation for a job

Nonverbal cues, such as the intense look being exchanged by these people, can provide managers and employees with vital information that helps them make better decisions.

well done, a concerned facial expression can back up words of sympathy for a personal problem. In such cases, the congruence between verbal and nonverbal communication helps to ensure that a common understanding is reached.

Sometimes when members of an organization decide not to express a message verbally, they inadvertently do so nonverbally. People tend to have less control over nonverbal communication, and often a verbal message that is withheld gets expressed through body language or facial expressions. A manager who agrees to a proposal that she or he actually is not in favor of may unintentionally communicate disfavor by grimacing.

Sometimes nonverbal communication is used to send messages that cannot be sent through verbal channels. Many lawyers are well aware of this communication tactic. Lawyers are often schooled in techniques of nonverbal communication such as choosing where to stand in the courtroom for maximum effect and using eye contact during different stages of a trial. Lawyers sometimes get into trouble for using inappropriate nonverbal communication in an attempt to influence juries. In a Louisiana court, prosecuting attorney Thomas Pirtle was admonished and fined $2,500 by Judge Yada Magee for shaking his head in an expression of doubt, waving his arms indicating disfavor, and chuckling when attorneys for the defense were stating their case.[27]

The Dangers of Ineffective Communication

Because managers must communicate with others to perform their various roles and tasks, managers spend most of their time communicating, whether in meetings, in telephone conversations, through e-mail, or in face-to-face interactions. Indeed, some experts estimate that managers spend approximately 85% of their time engaged in some form of communication.[28] Effective communication is so important that managers cannot just be concerned that they themselves are effective communicators; they also have to help their subordinates be effective communicators. When all members of an organization are able to communicate effectively with each other and with people outside the organization, the organization is much more likely to perform highly and gain a competitive advantage.

When managers and other members of an organization are ineffective communicators, organizational performance suffers, and any competitive advantage the organization might have is likely to be lost. Moreover, poor communication sometimes can be downright dangerous and even lead to tragic and unnecessary loss of human life. For example, researchers from Harvard University studied the causes of mistakes, such as a patient receiving the wrong medication, in two large hospitals in the Boston area. They discovered that some mistakes in hospitals occur because of communication problems–physicians not having the information they need to correctly order medications for their patients or nurses not having the information they need to correctly administer medications. The researchers concluded that some of the responsibility for these mistakes lies with hospital management, which has not taken active steps to improve communication.[29] Indeed, in 2008 over 400,000 recorded events of mistakes were documented. The following "Management Insight" shows how some managers are trying to promote effective communication.

MANAGEMENT INSIGHT

Managers Need Feedback from Employees

www.fatwire.com

As managers advance in the corporate hierarchy and assume positions with increased responsibility, they often become removed from the day-to-day operations of their organizations. Thus, they are less likely to notice or become aware of problems with existing processes and procedures and sources of inefficiencies as well as how customers and clients are reacting to the goods and services the organization provides. Moreover, ideas for ways to improve goods and services sometimes occur to those who are most closely and immediately linked to producing and delivering products and services. Some of these ideas may rarely occur to upper-level managers who are not engaged in these activities on a day-to-day basis.[30]

Thus, it is crucial that managers receive and listen to feedback from employees. While this might seem pretty straightforward and easily accomplished, managers are sometimes the last ones to know about problems for a number of reasons. Employees sometimes fear that they will be blamed for problems that they make their bosses aware of, that they will be seen as "troublemakers," or that managers will perceive their well-intentioned feedback as a personal criticism or attack.[31] Moreover, if employees feel that their feedback, even suggestions for improvements or ways to seize new opportunities, will fall on deaf ears and be ignored, they will be reluctant to speak up.

Effective managers recognize the importance of receiving feedback from employees and take active steps to ensure that this happens. When Yogesh Gupta recently accepted the position of president and CEO of FatWire Software, one of his priorities was to ensure that his employees provided him with feedback on an ongoing basis.[32] FatWire Software, headquartered in Mineola, New York, has 200 employees, offices in over 10 countries, and over 450 customers such as 3M, *The New York Times,* and Best Buy. In his career, Gupta had often witnessed managers inadvertently discouraging employees from providing them with feedback, even when the managers desired it.[33] As he indicates, "I've heard so many executives tell employees to be candid and then jump down their throats if they bring up a problem or ask a critical question."[34]

Gupta spends a lot of time talking with FatWire employees and managers to get their perspectives and feedback. He holds individual meetings with managers so they feel more comfortable providing him with frank and honest feedback. And he explicitly asks them if he is doing anything wrong, if there is a better way for him to do things. As a result of listening to the feedback he has received, Gupta realized that FatWire might benefit from having more employees focused on product development and marketing and that customer support services and processes could be enhanced.[35]

When Gupta receives valuable feedback, he makes it a point to positively reinforce the manager or employee who provided it in a public fashion, so other employees realize he really wants their feedback. As he indicates, "I know I have to say 'You did the right thing to speak up' again and again, because employees fear they'll get blamed if they say anything negative."[36]

At Intuit Inc., a major provider of accounting and financial software, managers receive valuable feedback from employees in a number of ways. An annual employee survey is used to find out what employees they think about Intuit's practices and procedures.[37] Managers are advised to have what are called "skip level" meetings throughout the year whereby they meet with the subordinates of the managers who report to them to get their feedback on how things are going.[38] Jim Grenier, vice president for human resources at Intuit, suggests that obtaining employee feedback through this process leads to improved decision making.[39] As he puts it, "You're looking for more input so you can make a better decision. Employees know that we are serious about asking for their feedback, and we listen and we do something about it."[40]

Information Richness and Communication Media

To be effective communicators, managers (and other members of an organization) need to select an appropriate communication medium for *each* message they send. Should a change in procedures be communicated to subordinates in a memo sent through e-mail? Should a congratulatory message about a major accomplishment be communicated in a letter, in a phone call, or over lunch? Should a layoff announcement be made in a memo or at a plant meeting? Should the members of a purchasing team travel to Europe to cement a major agreement with a new supplier, or should they do so through faxes? Managers deal with these questions day in and day out.

LO3 Define information richness, and describe the information richness of communication media available to managers.

There is no one best communication medium for managers to rely on. In choosing a communication medium for any message, managers need to consider three factors. The first and most important is the level of information richness that is needed. **Information richness** is the amount of information a communication medium can carry and the extent to which the medium enables the sender and receiver to reach a common understanding.[41] The communication media that managers use vary in their information richness (see Figure 13.3).[42] Media high in information richness are able to carry an extensive amount of information and generally enable receivers and senders to come to a common understanding.

Figure 13.3
The Information Richness of Communication Media

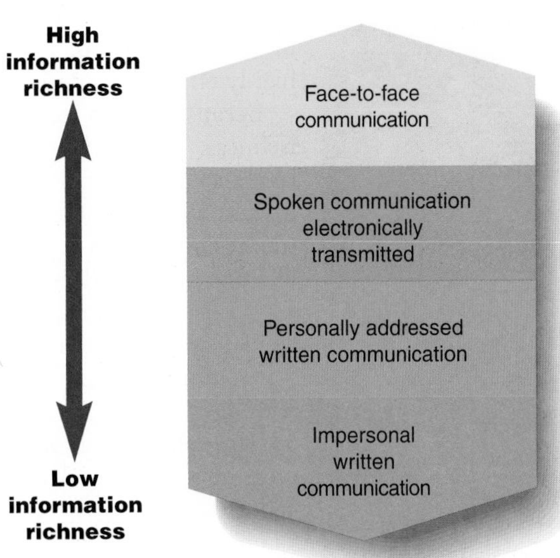

information richness The amount of information that a communication medium can carry and the extent to which the medium enables the sender and receiver to reach a common understanding.

The second factor that managers need to take into account in selecting a communication medium is the *time* needed for communication, because managers' and other organizational members' time is valuable. Managers at United Parcel Service, for example, dramatically reduced the amount of time they spent by using videoconferences instead of face-to-face communication, which required managers to travel overseas.[43]

The third factor that affects the choice of a communication medium is the *need for a paper or electronic trail* or some kind of written documentation that a message was sent and received. A manager may wish to document in writing, for example, that a subordinate was given a formal warning about excessive lateness.

In the remainder of this section we examine four types of communication media that vary along the three dimensions of information richness, time, and the availability of a paper or electronic trail.[44]

Face-to-Face Communication

Face-to-face communication is the medium that is highest in information richness. When managers communicate face-to-face, they not only can take advantage of verbal communication but they also can interpret each other's nonverbal signals such as facial expressions and body language. A look of concern or puzzlement can sometimes tell more than a thousand words, and managers can respond to these nonverbal signals on the spot. Face-to-face communication also enables managers to receive instant feedback. Points of confusion, ambiguity, or misunderstanding can be resolved, and managers can cycle through the communication process as many times as they need to, to reach a common understanding.

management by wandering around A face-to-face communication technique in which a manager walks around a work area and talks informally with employees about issues and concerns.

Management by wandering around is a face-to-face communication technique that is effective for many managers at all levels in an organization.[45] Rather than scheduling formal meetings with subordinates, managers walk around work areas and talk informally with employees about issues and concerns that both employees and managers may have. These informal conversations provide managers and subordinates with important information and at the same time foster the development of positive relationships. William Hewlett and David Packard, founders and former top managers of Hewlett-Packard, found management by wandering around a highly effective way to communicate with their employees.

In spite of the popularity of electronic communication, face-to-face communication is still the medium that is highest in information richness.

Because face-to-face communication is highest in information richness, you might think that it should always be the medium of choice for managers. This is not the case, however, because of the amount of time it takes and the lack of a paper or electronic trail resulting from it. For messages that are important, personal, or likely to be misunderstood, it is often well worth managers' time to use face-to-face communication and, if need be, supplement it with some form of written communication documenting the message.

Advances in information technology are providing managers with new and close alternative communication media for face-to-face communication. Many organizations such as American Greetings Corp. and Hewlett-Packard are using *videoconferences* to capture some of the advantages of face-to-face communication (such as access to facial expressions) while saving time and money because managers in different locations do not have to travel to meet with one another. During a videoconference, managers in two or more locations communicate with each other over large TV or video screens; they not only hear each other but also see each other throughout the meeting.

In addition to saving travel costs, videoconferences sometimes have other advantages. Managers at American Greetings have found that decisions get made more quickly when videoconferences are used, because more managers can be involved in the decision-making process and therefore fewer managers have to be consulted outside the meeting itself. Managers at Hewlett-Packard have found that videoconferences have shortened new product development time by 30% for similar reasons. Videoconferences also seem to lead to more efficient meetings. Some managers have found that their meetings are 20% to 30% shorter when videoconferences are used instead of face-to-face meetings.[46]

Taking videoconferences a leap forward, Cisco Systems has developed its TelePresence line of products, which enables individuals and teams in different locations to communicate live and in real time over the Internet with high-definition and life-size video and excellent-quality audio that makes it feel like all the people taking part, no matter where they are, are in the same room.[47] One morning, Cisco CEO John Chambers was able to participate in meetings with employees and teams in India, Japan, Cleveland, and London in less than four hours by using TelePresence.[48] Other companies, such as HP, have developed similar products. What distinguishes these products from older videoconferencing systems is the fact that there are no delays in transmission and the video quality is sharp, clear, lifelike, and life-size.[49]

Spoken Communication Electronically Transmitted

After face-to-face communication, spoken communication electronically transmitted over phone lines is second highest in information richness (see Figure 13.2). Although managers communicating over the telephone do not have access to body language

Cisco Systems conducts a press conference with Yao Ming using TelePresence's videoconferencing system with life-size imaging.

and facial expressions, they do have access to the tone of voice in which a message is delivered, the parts of the message the sender emphasizes, and the general manner in which the message is spoken, in addition to the actual words themselves. Thus, telephone conversations have the capacity to convey extensive amounts of information. Managers also can ensure that mutual understanding is reached because they can get quick feedback over the phone and answer questions.

Voice mail systems and answering machines also allow managers to send and receive verbal electronic messages over telephone lines. Voice mail systems are companywide systems that enable senders to record messages for members of an organization who are away from their desks and allow receivers to access their messages when hundreds of miles away from the office. Such systems are obviously a necessity when managers are frequently out of the office, and managers on the road are well advised to periodically check their voice mail.

Personally Addressed Written Communication

Lower than electronically transmitted verbal communication in information richness is personally addressed written communication (see Figure 13.2). One of the advantages of face-to-face communication and verbal communication electronically transmitted is that they both tend to demand attention, which helps ensure that receivers pay attention. Personally addressed written communications such as memos and letters also have this advantage. Because they are addressed to a particular person, the chances are good that the person will actually pay attention to (and read) them. Moreover, the sender can write the message in a way that the receiver is most likely to understand. Like voice mail, written communication does not enable a receiver to have his or her questions answered immediately, but when messages are clearly written and feedback is provided, common understandings can still be reached.

Even if managers use face-to-face communication, a follow-up in writing is often needed for messages that are important or complicated and need to be referred to later. This is precisely what Karen Stracker, a hospital administrator, did when she needed to tell one of her subordinates about an important change in the way the hospital would be handling denials of insurance benefits. Stracker met with the subordinate and described the changes face-to-face. Once she was sure that the subordinate understood them, she handed her a sheet of instructions to follow, which essentially summarized the information they had discussed.

E-mail also fits into this category of communication media because senders and receivers are communicating through personally addressed written words. The words, however, are appearing on their personal computer screens rather than on pieces of paper. E-mail is becoming so widespread in the business world that managers are even developing their own e-mail etiquette. To save time, Andrew Giangola, a manager at Simon & Schuster, a book publisher, used to type all his e-mail messages in capital letters. He was surprised when a receiver of one of his messages responded, "Why are you screaming at me?" Messages in capital letters are often perceived as being shouted or screamed, and thus Giangola's routine use of capital letters was bad e-mail etiquette. Here are some other guidelines from polite e-mailers: Always punctuate messages; do not ramble on or say more than you need to; do not act as though you do not understand something when in fact you do understand it; and pay attention to spelling and format (put a memo in memo form). To avoid embarrassments like Giangola's, managers at Simon & Schuster created a task force to develop guidelines for e-mail etiquette.[50]

The growing popularity of e-mail has also enabled many workers and managers to become telecommuters, people who are employed by organizations and work out of offices in their own homes. There are approximately 8.4 million telecommuters in the United States. Many telecommuters indicate that the flexibility of working at home enables them to be more productive while giving them a chance to be closer to their families and not waste time traveling to and from the office.[51] A study conducted by Georgetown University found that 75% of the telecommuters surveyed said their productivity increased and 83% said their home life improved once they started telecommuting.[52]

Unfortunately, the growing use of e-mail has been accompanied by growing abuse of e-mail. Some employees sexually harass coworkers through e-mail, and divorcing spouses who work together sometimes sign their spouse's name to e-mail and send insulting or derogatory messages to the spouse's boss. Robert Mirguet, information systems manager at Eastman Kodak, has indicated that some Kodak employees have used Kodak's e-mail system to try to start their own businesses during working hours. Kodak managers monitor employees' e-mail messages when they suspect some form of abuse. Top managers also complain that sometimes their e-mail is clogged with junk mail. In a recent survey over half of the organizations contacted acknowledged some problems with their e-mail systems.[53]

To avoid these and other costly forms of e-mail abuse, managers need to develop a clear policy specifying what company e-mail can and should be used for and what is out of bounds. Managers also should clearly communicate this policy to all members of an organization, as well as the procedures that will be used when e-mail abuse is suspected and the consequences that will result when e-mail abuse is confirmed.

Impersonal Written Communication

Impersonal written communication is lowest in information richness and is well suited for messages that need to reach a large number of receivers. Because such messages are not addressed to particular receivers, feedback is unlikely, so managers must make sure that messages sent by this medium are written clearly in language that all receivers will understand.

Managers often find company newsletters useful vehicles for reaching large numbers of employees. Many managers give their newsletters catchy names to spark employee interest and also to inject a bit of humor into the workplace. Managers at the pork-sausage maker Bob Evans Farms Inc. called their newsletter "The Squealer" for many years but recently changed the title to "The Homesteader" to reflect the company's broadened line of products. Managers at American Greetings Corp., at Yokohama Tire Corp., and at Eastman Kodak call their newsletters "Expressions," "TreadLines," and "Kodakery," respectively. Managers at Quaker State Corp. held a contest to rename their newsletter. Among the 1,000 submitted names were "The Big Q Review," "The Pipeline," and "Q. S. Oil Press"; the winner was "On Q."[54]

Managers can use impersonal written communication for various types of messages, including rules, regulations, policies, newsworthy information, and announcements of changes in procedures or the arrival of new organizational members. Impersonal written communication also can be used to communicate instructions about how to use machinery or how to process work orders or customer requests. For these kinds of messages, the paper or electronic trail left by this communication medium can be invaluable for employees.

Like personal written communication, impersonal written communication can be delivered and retrieved electronically, and this is increasingly being done in companies large and small. Unfortunately, the ease with which electronic messages can be spread has led to their proliferation. The electronic inboxes of many managers and workers are backlogged, and they rarely have time to read all the electronic work-related information available to them. The problem with such **information overload**—a superabundance of information—is the potential for important information to be ignored or overlooked while tangential information receives attention. Moreover, information overload can result in thousands of hours and millions in dollars in lost productivity.

information overload A superabundance of information that increases the likelihood that important information is ignored or overlooked and tangential information receives attention.

Realizing the hazards of overload, Nathan Zeldes, computing productivity manager for Intel's division in Israel, decided to tackle this problem head-on.[55] In Zeldes's division, some 3 million e-mails are sent or received each day, and some employees receive more than 300 messages a day. On average, employees spend around two and a half hours a day dealing with this barrage of information. To combat this problem, Zeldes developed a training program to educate employees about how e-mail can improve productivity and how it can be used in ways that limit overload.[56] Reactions to the training program have been positive, and it is now used in Intel divisions around the globe.[57]

Advances in Information Technology

Computer-based information technology can greatly facilitate and improve the communication process. It has allowed managers to develop computer-based management information systems that provide timely, complete, relevant, and high-quality information. As we have discussed, IT allows companies to improve their responsiveness to customers, minimize costs, and thus improve their competitive position. The link between information systems, communication, and competitive position is an important one that may determine the success or failure of organizations in an increasingly competitive global environment. To better explain the current revolution in information technology, in this section we examine several key aspects of computer-based information technology.

The Tumbling Price of Information

The information technology revolution began with the development of the first computers—the hardware of computer-based information technology—in the 1950s. The language of computers is a digital language of zeros and ones. Words, numbers, images, and sounds can all be expressed in zeros and ones. Each letter in the alphabet has its own unique code of zeros and ones, as does each number, each color, and each sound. For example, the digital code for the number 20 is 10100. In the language of computers it takes a lot of zeros and ones to express even a simple sentence, to say nothing of complex color graphics or moving video images. Nevertheless, modern computers can read, process, and store millions of instructions per second (an instruction is a line of software code) and thus vast amounts of zeros and ones. It is this awesome power that forms the foundation of the current information technology revolution.

The brains of modern computers are microprocessors (Intel's Pentium chips and its newest chip, the Itanium chip, are microprocessors). Between 1991 and 2001, the relative cost of computer processing fell so dramatically that Gordon Moore, a computer guru, noted that "If the auto industry advanced as rapidly as the semiconductor

In 2003, McDonald's launched a major wireless Internet rollout in New York City and in three major U.S. markets. Now there are more than 15,000 Wi-Fi enabled restaurants around the world.

industry, a Rolls Royce would get a half a million miles per gallon, and it would be cheaper to throw it away than to park it."[58] As the costs of acquiring, organizing, storing, and transmitting information have tumbled, computers have become almost as common as wireless phones and microwaves.[59] In addition, advances in microprocessor technology have led to dramatic reductions in the cost of communication between computers, which also have contributed to the falling price of information and information systems.

Wireless Communications

Another trend of considerable significance for information systems has been the rapid growth of wireless communication technologies, particularly digital communications. Wireless communication is significant for the information technology revolution because it facilitates linking together people and computers, which greatly increases their decision-making ability. An engineer or salesperson working in the field can send information to, and receive information from, the home office by using the wireless capability built into smartphones, laptops, and netbooks.

Computer Networks

networking The exchange of information through a group or network of interlinked computers.

The tumbling price of computing power and information and the use of wireless communication channels have facilitated **networking**, the exchange of information through a group or network of interlinked computers. The most common arrangement now emerging is a three-tier network consisting of clients, servers, and a mainframe (see Figure 13.4). At the outer nodes of a typical three-tier network are the personal computers (PCs) that sit on the desks of individual users. These personal computers, referred to as *clients,* are linked to a local *server,* a high-powered midrange computer that "serves" the client personal computers. Servers often store power-hungry software programs that can be run more effectively on a server than on individuals' personal computers. Servers may also manage several printers that can be used by hundreds of clients; servers also store data files and handle e-mail communications between clients. The client computers linked directly to a server constitute a *local area network (LAN)*. Within any organization there may be several LANs–for example, one in every division and function.

At the hub of a three-tier system are *mainframe computers,* large and powerful computers that can be used to store and process vast amounts of information. The mainframe can also be used to handle electronic communications between personal computers situated in different LANs. In addition, the mainframe may be connected to mainframes in other organizations and, through them, to LANs in other organizations. Increasingly, the Internet, a worldwide network of interlinked computers, is used as the conduit for connecting the computer systems of different organizations.

A manager with a personal computer hooked into a three-tier system can access data and software stored in the local server, in the mainframe, or through the Internet

Figure 13.4
A Typical Three-Tier Information System

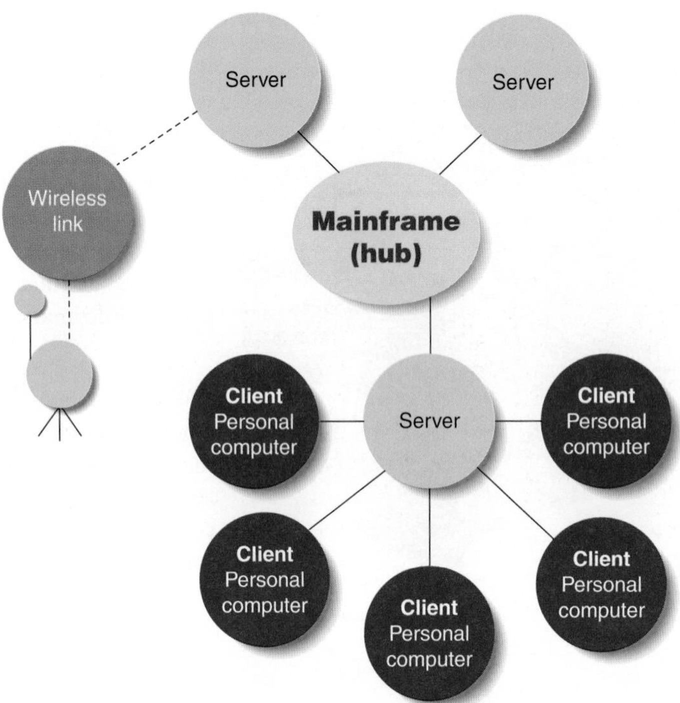

in computers based in another organization. A manager can therefore communicate electronically with other individuals hooked into the system, whether they are in the manager's LAN, in another LAN within the manager's organization, or in another organization altogether. Moreover, because of the growth of wireless communications, an individual with the proper equipment can hook into the system from any location–at home, on a boat, on the beach, in the air–anywhere a wireless communications link can be established.

Software Developments

operating system software Software that tells computer hardware how to run.

applications software Software designed for a specific task or use.

If computer hardware has been developing rapidly, so has computer software. **Operating system software** tells the computer hardware how to run. **Applications software**, such as programs for word processing, spreadsheets, graphics, and database management, is software developed for a specific task or use. The increase in the power of computer hardware has allowed software developers to write increasingly powerful programs that are, at the same time, increasingly user-friendly. By harnessing the rapidly growing power of microprocessors, applications software has vastly increased the ability of managers to acquire, organize, manipulate, and transmit information. In doing so, it also has increased the ability of managers to coordinate and control the activities of their organization and to make decisions, as discussed earlier.

artificial intelligence Behavior performed by a machine that would be called intelligent if performed by a human being.

Artificial intelligence is another interesting and potentially fruitful software development. **Artificial intelligence** has been defined as behavior by a machine that would be called intelligent if performed by a human being.[60] Artificial intelligence has already made it possible to write programs that can solve problems and perform simple tasks. For example, software programs variously called "software agents," "softbots," or "knowbots" can be used to perform simple managerial tasks such as sorting through

"Well, being single and a robot, I'm able to put in a lot of overtime."

reams of data or incoming e-mail messages to look for important data and messages. The interesting feature of these programs is that from "watching" a manager sort through such data they can "learn" what his or her preferences are. Having done this, they then can take over some of this work from the manager, freeing up more time for work on other tasks. Most of these programs are in the development stage, but they may be commonplace within a decade.[61]

Another software development that is starting to have an impact on the manager's job is speech recognition software. Currently speech recognition software must be "trained" to recognize and understand each individual's voice, and it requires the speaker to pause after each word. The increasing power of microprocessors, however, has enabled the development of faster speech recognition programs that can handle more variables and much greater complexity. Now a manager driving down the road may be able to communicate with a computer through a wireless link and give that computer complex voice instructions.[62]

Types of Management Information Systems

LO4 Differentiate among four kinds of management information systems.

Four types of computer-based management information systems can be particularly helpful in providing managers with the information they need to make decisions and to coordinate and control organizational resources: transaction-processing systems, operations information systems, decision support systems, and expert systems. In Figure 13.5, these systems are arranged along a continuum according to their increasing usefulness in providing managers with the information they need to make nonprogrammed decisions. (Recall from Chapter 5 that nonprogrammed decision making occurs in response to unusual, unpredictable opportunities and threats.) We examine each of these systems after focusing on the management information system that preceded them all: the organizational hierarchy.

The Organizational Hierarchy: The Traditional Information System

Traditionally, managers have used the organizational hierarchy as a system for gathering the information they need to achieve coordination and control and make decisions (see Chapter 7 for a discussion of organizational structure and hierarchy). According to

Figure 13.5

Four Computer-Based Management Information Systems

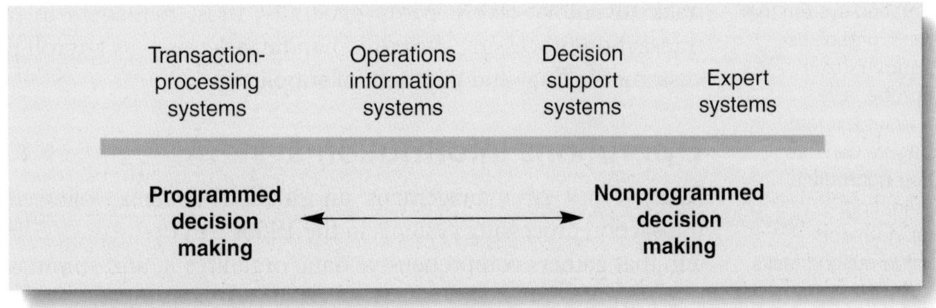

business historian Alfred Chandler, the use of the hierarchy as an information network was perfected by railroad companies in the United States during the 1850s.[63] At that time, the railroads were the largest industrial organizations in the United States. By virtue of their size and geographical spread, they faced unique problems of coordination and control. In the 1850s, they started to solve these problems by designing hierarchical management structures that provided senior managers with the information they needed to achieve coordination and control and to make decisions about running the railroads.

Daniel McCallum, superintendent of the Erie Railroad in the 1850s, realized that the lines of authority and responsibility defining the Erie's management hierarchy also represented channels of communication along which information traveled. McCallum established what was perhaps the first modern management information system. Regular daily and monthly reports were fed up the management chain so that top managers could make decisions about, for example, controlling costs and setting freight rates. Decisions were then relayed back down the hierarchy so they could be carried out. Imitating the railroads, most other organizations used their hierarchies as systems for collecting and channeling information. This practice began to change only when electronic information technologies became more reasonably priced in the 1960s.

Although the organizational hierarchy is a useful information system, several drawbacks are associated with it. First, in organizations with many layers of managers, it can take a long time for information to travel up the hierarchy and for decisions to travel back down. This slow pace can reduce the timeliness and usefulness of information and prevent an organization from responding quickly to changing market conditions.[64] Second, information can be distorted as it moves from one layer of management to another. **Information distortion**, changes in meaning that occur as information passes through a series of senders and receivers, reduces the quality of information.[65] Third, because managers have only a limited span of control, as an organization grows larger, its hierarchy lengthens and this tall structure can make the hierarchy a very expensive information system. The popular idea that companies with tall management hierarchies are bureaucratic and unresponsive to the needs of their customers arises from the inability of tall hierarchies to effectively process data and provide managers with timely, complete, relevant, and high-quality information. Until modern computer-based information systems came along, however, the management hierarchy was the best information system available.

information distortion Changes in meaning that occur as information passes through a series of senders and receivers.

Transaction-Processing Systems

A **transaction-processing system** is a system designed to handle large volumes of routine, recurring transactions. Transaction-processing systems began to appear in the early 1960s with the advent of commercially available mainframe computers. They were the first type of computer-based management information system adopted by many organizations, and today they are commonplace. Bank managers use a transaction-processing system to record deposits into, and payments out of, bank accounts. Supermarket managers use a transaction-processing system to record the sale of items and to track inventory levels. More generally, most managers in large organizations use a transaction-processing system to handle tasks such as payroll preparation and payment, customer billing, and payment of suppliers.

transaction-processing system A management information system designed to handle large volumes of routine, recurring transactions.

operations information system A management information system that gathers, organizes, and summarizes comprehensive data in a form that managers can use in their nonroutine coordinating, controlling, and decision-making tasks.

Operations Information Systems

Many types of management information systems followed hard on the heels of transaction-processing systems in the 1960s. An **operations information system** is a system that gathers comprehensive data, organizes it, and summarizes it in a form that is of value to managers. Whereas a transaction-processing system processes routine transactions, an operations information system provides managers with information that they can use in their nonroutine coordinating, controlling, and decision-making tasks. Most operations information systems are coupled with a transaction-processing system. An operations information system typically accesses data gathered by a transaction-processing system, processes those data into useful information, and organizes that information into a form accessible to managers. Managers often use an operations information system to obtain sales, inventory, accounting, and other performance-related information. For example, the information that T. J. Rodgers at Cypress Semiconductor gets on individual employee goals and performance is provided by an operations information system.

FedEx uses an operations information system to track the performance of its 1,500 or so ground stations. Each ground station is evaluated according to four criteria: delivery (the goal is to deliver 100% of all packages by noon the day after they were picked up), productivity (measured by the number of packages shipped per employee-hour), controllable cost, and station profitability. Each ground station also has specific delivery, efficiency, cost, and profitability targets that it must attain. Every month FedEx's operations information system is used to gather information on these four criteria and summarize it for top managers, who are then able to compare the performance of each station against its previously established targets. The system quickly alerts senior managers to underperforming ground stations, so they can intervene selectively to help solve any problems that may have given rise to the poor performance.[66]

Decision Support Systems

decision support system An interactive computer-based management information system with model-building capability that managers can use when they must make nonroutine decisions.

A **decision support system** is an interactive computer-based system that provides models that help managers make better nonprogrammed decisions.[67] Recall from Chapter 5 that nonprogrammed decisions are decisions that are relatively unusual or novel, such as decisions to invest in new productive capacity, develop a new product, launch a new promotional campaign, enter a new market, or expand internationally. Although an operations information system organizes important information for managers, a decision support system gives managers a model-building capability and so provides them with the ability to manipulate information in a variety of ways. Managers might use a decision support system to help them decide whether to cut prices for a product. The decision support system might contain models of how customers and competitors would respond to a price cut. Managers could run these models and use the results as an *aid* to decision making.

The stress on the word *aid* is important, for in the final analysis a decision support system is not meant to make decisions for managers. Rather, its function is to provide valuable information that managers can use to improve the quality of their decision making. A good example of a sophisticated decision support system, developed by Judy Lewent, chief financial officer of the U.S. pharmaceutical company Merck, is given in the next "Manager as a Person."

Expert Systems and Artificial Intelligence

expert system A management information system that employs human knowledge captured in a computer to solve problems that ordinarily require human expertise.

Expert systems are the most advanced management information systems available. An **expert system** is a system that employs human knowledge captured in a computer to solve problems that ordinarily require human expertise.[68] Expert systems are a variant of artificial intelligence.[69] Mimicking human expertise (and intelligence) requires a computer that can at a minimum (1) recognize, formulate, and solve a problem; (2) explain the solution; and (3) learn from experience.

MANAGER AS A PERSON

How Judy Lewent Became One of the Most Powerful Women in Corporate America

With annual sales of over $45 billion, Merck is one of the largest developers and marketers of advanced pharmaceuticals. In 2000, the company spent more than $3 billion on R&D to develop new drugs–an expensive and difficult process fraught with risk. Most new drug ideas fail to emerge from development. It takes an average of $300 million and 10 years to bring a new drug to market, and 7 out of 10 new drugs fail to make a profit for the developing company.

Given the costs, risks, and uncertainties of new drug development, Judy Lewent, then director of capital analysis at Merck, decided to develop a decision support system that could help managers make more effective R&D investment decisions. Her aim was to give Merck's top managers the information they needed to evaluate proposed R&D projects on a case-by-case basis. The system that Lewent and her staff developed is referred to in Merck as the "Research Planning Model."[70] At the heart of this decision support system is a sophisticated model. The input variables include data on R&D spending, manufacturing costs, selling costs, and demand conditions. The relationships between the input variables are modeled by means of several equations that factor in the probability of a drug's making it through development and to market. The outputs of this modeling process are the revenues, cash flows, and profits that a project might generate.

The Merck model does not use a single value for an input variable, nor does it compute a single value for each output. Rather, a range is specified for each input variable (such as high, medium, and low R&D spending). The computer repeatedly samples at random from the range of values for each input variable and produces a probability distribution of values for each output. So, for example, instead of stating categorically that a proposed R&D project will yield a profit of $500 million, the decision support system produces a probability distribution. It might state that although $500 million is the most likely profit, there is a 25% chance that the profit will be less than $300 million and a 25% chance that it will be greater than $700 million.

Judy Lewent, chief financial officer of Merck, consults with managers of Sweden's Astra Pharmaceuticals as they work out the details of their global venture.

Merck now uses Lewent's decision support system to evaluate all proposed R&D investment decisions. In addition, Lewent has developed other decision support system models that Merck's managers can use to help them decide, for example, whether to enter into joint ventures with other companies or how best to hedge foreign exchange risk. As for Lewent, her reward was promotion to the position of chief financial officer of Merck. She became one of the most powerful women in corporate America.

Recent developments in artificial intelligence that go by names such as "fuzzy logic" and "neural networks" have resulted in computer programs that, in a primitive way, try to mimic human thought processes. Although artificial intelligence is still at a fairly early stage of development, an increasing number of business applications are beginning to emerge in the form of expert systems. General Electric, for example, has developed an expert system to help troubleshoot problems in the diesel locomotive engines it manufactures. The expert system was originally based on knowledge collected from David Smith, GE's top locomotive troubleshooter, who retired in the 1980s after 40 years of service at GE. A novice engineer or technician can use the system to uncover a fault by spending only a few minutes at a computer terminal. The system can explain to the user the logic of its advice, thereby serving as a teacher as well as a problem solver. The system is based on a flexible, humanlike thought process, and it can be updated to incorporate new knowledge as it becomes available. GE has installed the system in every railroad repair shop that it serves, thus eliminating delays and boosting maintenance productivity.[71]

Limitations of Information Systems

Despite their usefulness, information systems have some limitations. A serious potential problem is the one noted at the beginning of this chapter. In all of the enthusiasm for management information systems, electronic communication by means of a computer network, and the like, a vital human element of communication may be lost. Some kinds of information cannot be aggregated and summarized on an MIS report because of issues surrounding information richness. Very rich information is often required to coordinate and control an enterprise and to make informed decisions, far beyond that which can be quantified and aggregated.

The importance of information richness is a strong argument in favor of using electronic communication to *support* face-to-face communication, not to replace it. For example, it would be wrong to make a judgment about an individual's performance merely by "reading the numbers" provided by a management information system. Instead, the numbers should be used to alert managers to individuals who may have a performance problem. The nature of this performance problem should then be explored in a face-to-face meeting, during which rich information can be gathered. As a top Boeing manager noted, "In our company, the use of e-mail and videoconferencing has not reduced the need to visit people at other sites; it has increased it. E-mail has facilitated the establishment of communications channels between people who previously would not communicate, which is good, but direct visits are still required to cement any working relationships that evolve out of these electronic meetings."

Summary and Review

INFORMATION AND THE MANAGER'S JOB Computer-based information systems are central to the operation of most organizations. By providing managers with high-quality, timely, relevant, and relatively complete information, properly implemented information systems can improve managers' ability to coordinate and control the operations of an organization and to make effective decisions. Moreover, information systems can help the organization to attain a competitive advantage through their beneficial impact on productivity, quality, innovation, and responsiveness to customers. **[LO1]**

COMMUNICATION AND MANAGEMENT Communication is the sharing of information between two or more individuals or groups to reach a common understanding. Good communication is necessary for an organization to gain a competitive advantage. Communication occurs in a cyclical process that entails two phases, transmission and feedback. **[LO2]**

INFORMATION RICHNESS AND COMMUNICATION MEDIA Information richness is the amount of information a communication medium can carry and the extent to which the medium enables the sender and receiver to reach a common understanding. Four categories of communication media in descending order of information richness are face-to-face communication (includes videoconferences), spoken communication electronically transmitted (includes voice mail), personally addressed written communication (includes e-mail), and impersonal written communication (includes newsletters). **[LO3]**

THE INFORMATION TECHNOLOGY REVOLUTION Over the last 30 years there have been rapid advances in the power, and rapid declines in the cost, of information technology. Falling prices, wireless communication, computer networks, and software developments have all radically improved the power and efficacy of computer-based information systems. **[LO4]**

TYPES OF MANAGEMENT INFORMATION SYSTEMS Traditionally managers used the organizational hierarchy as the main system for gathering the information they needed to coordinate and control the organization and to make effective decisions. Today, managers use four types of computer-based information systems. Listed in ascending order of sophistication, they are transaction-processing systems, operations information systems, decision support systems, and expert systems. **[LO4]**

Management in Action

Topics for Discussion and Action

Discussion

1. What is the relationship between information systems and competitive advantage? [LO2]
2. Which medium (or media) do you think would be appropriate for each of the following kinds of messages that a subordinate could receive from his or her boss: (a) a raise, (b) not receiving a promotion, (c) an error in a report prepared by the subordinate, (d) additional job responsibilities, and (e) the schedule for company holidays for the upcoming year? Explain your choices. [LO3]
3. Ask a manager to describe the main kinds of information systems that he or she uses on a routine basis at work. [LO1, 2]
4. Because of the growth of high-powered low-cost computing, wireless communications, and technologies such as videoconferencing, many managers soon may not need to come into the office; they will be able to work at home. What are the pros and cons of such an arrangement? [LO3]
5. Many companies have reported that it is difficult to implement advanced management information and decision support systems. Why do you think this is so? How might the roadblocks to implementation be removed? [LO4]
6. Why is face-to-face communication between managers still important in an organization? [LO2, 3]

Building Management Skills [LO2, 3]

Diagnosing Ineffective Communication

Think about the last time you experienced very ineffective communication with another person—someone you work with, a classmate, a friend, a member of your family. Describe the incident. Then answer these questions:

1. Why was your communication ineffective in this incident?
2. What stages of the communication process were particularly problematic and why?
3. Describe any filtering or information distortion that occurred.
4. How could you have handled this situation differently so that communication would have been effective?

Managing Ethically [LO2, 3]

In organizations today, employees often take advantage of their company's information systems. E-mail abuse is increasing, and so is the amount of time employees spend surfing the Internet on company time. Indeed, statistics suggest that approximately 70% of the total amount of time spent surfing the Internet is company time.

Questions

1. Either by yourself or in a group, explore the ethics of using IT for personal uses at work. Should employees have some rights to use these resources? When does their behavior become unethical?
2. Some companies keep track of the way their employees use IT and the Internet. Is it ethical for managers to read employees' private e-mail or to record the sites that employees visit on the World Wide Web?

Small Group Breakout Exercise [LO2, 4]

Using New Information Systems

Form groups of three or four people, and appoint one member as the spokesperson who will communicate your findings to the whole class when called upon by the instructor. Then discuss the following scenario:

You are a team of managing partners of a large firm of accountants. You are responsible for auditing your firm's information systems to determine whether they are appropriate and up-to-date. To your surprise, you find that although your organization does have an e-mail system in place and accountants are connected into a powerful local area network (LAN), most of the accountants (including partners) are not using this technology. You also find that the organizational hierarchy is still the preferred information system of the managing partners.

Given this situation, you are concerned that your organization is not exploiting the opportunities offered by new information systems to obtain a competitive advantage. You have discussed this issue and are meeting to develop an action plan to get accountants to appreciate the need to learn, and to take advantage of, the potential of the new information technology.

1. What advantages can you tell accountants they will obtain when they use the new information technology?
2. What problems do you think you may encounter in convincing accountants to use the new information technology?
3. Discuss how you might make it easy for accountants to learn to use the new technology.

Be the Manager [LO2, 3]

A Problem in Communication

Mark Chen supervises support staff for an Internet merchandising organization that sells furniture over the Internet. Chen has always thought that he should expand his staff. When he was about to approach his boss with such a request, the economy slowed, and other areas of the company experienced layoffs. Thus, Chen's plans for trying to add to his staff are on indefinite hold.

Chen has noticed a troubling pattern of communication with his staff. Ordinarily, when he wants one of his staff members to work on a task, he e-mails the pertinent information to that person. For the last few months, his e-mail requests have gone unheeded, and his subordinates comply with his requests only after he visits with them in person and gives them a specific deadline. Each time, they apologize for the delay but say that they are so overloaded with requests that they sometimes stop answering their phones. Unless someone asks for something more than once, they feel a request is not particularly urgent and can be put on hold.

Chen thinks this state of affairs is deplorable. He realizes, however, that his subordinates have no way of prioritizing tasks and that is why some very important projects were put on hold until he inquired about them. Knowing that he cannot add to his staff in the short term, Chen has come to you for advice. He wants to develop a system whereby his staff will provide some kind of response to requests within 24 hours, will be able to prioritize tasks, identifying their relative importance, and will not feel so overloaded that they ignore their boss's requests and don't answer their phones. As an expert in communication, advise Chen.

BusinessWeek Case in the News [LO3, 4]

IBM's Big Push into Business Consulting

When Riswan Khalfan, chief information officer at TD Securities, set out to improve the performance of the bank's options-trading system last year, he couldn't find ready-to-use technology suitable for the job. So he agreed to let his company become a test subject for a research project at IBM called "stream" computing. The technology, developed over half a decade by a team of 70 scientists and engineers at IBM Research, allows companies to analyze data as they are being received—rather than having to place them first in a database.

In TD Securities' case, stream computing lets it handle 5 million pieces of options trading data per second, analyze them on the fly, and make automated trading decisions. That compares with the 1 to 2 million per second rate the bank typically handles with its current trading system. "In this business, quicker decisions are better decisions," says Khalfan. "If you fall behind, you're dealing with stale data and that puts you at a disadvantage." The bank is now considering switching its entire trading system to the new technology.

Stream computing is just one part of IBM's biggest foray into business consulting since it acquired PricewaterhouseCoopers Consulting seven years ago. The company is creating a new unit, IBM Business Analytics & Optimization Services, that will advise corporations on how to better analyze data and make smarter decisions. The group's staff of 4,000 consultants will mine IBM's research and software divisions for algorithms, applications, and other innovations to do the job.

IBM's most direct rival in business analytics consulting may be Hewlett-Packard. The Silicon Valley giant formed a business unit two years ago and fields nearly 3,000 consultants. "We respect what they're doing in this space, but we're not afraid to go head-to-head with them," says Giuliano Di Vitantonio, global marketing chief for HP's business intelligence solutions group.

IBM also faces stiff competition in the software end of the business from Oracle and SAP. All three companies bought business intelligence software players during the past two years and have roughly comparable capabilities. An even tougher contender for IBM is SAS Institute, a specialist in data mining. IBM can't match SAS's ability to analyze huge storehouses of corporate information. Still, IBM's consulting arm installs a large amount of SAS software for clients—so the two companies are partners as well as competitors.

Bright Spot

Competition is heating up because analytics is one of the few bright spots in an otherwise subdued technology market. Overall demand for corporate technology is expected to shrink this year, but the market research firm IDC forecasts 3.45% growth for the $23 billion market for business analytics software in 2009. The firm expects 2% growth in the $45 billion analytics consulting business.

Analytics revenues are rising because it's one of the most strategically important fields in corporate computing. Executives analyze their sales patterns so they can do a better job of targeting customers with specific products and advertising. They pick apart and modify operations to make them ever more efficient. Increasingly, they want to slice and dice data as quickly as they come into their computing systems to make more accurate forecasts of future sales and shifting market conditions. "Now more than ever, leaders need to know what's really going on in their businesses," says IDC analyst Dan Vesset.

Creation of the new IBM unit is the first major move by Frank Kern since he took over IBM's Global Business Services division in January. He sees rich opportunity for the company to profit if it can help improve productivity in sectors such as transportation, electric utilities, and health care. "We're at the beginning of a new wave," says Kern. "We've begun to instrument the world [with sensors and other devices that collect information], but now we have to take those data and analyze them."

Questions

1. What is business analytics consulting?
2. In what different ways can it help improve a company's performance?
3. Why is competition so fierce in the business analytics business?

Operations Management: Managing Vital Operations and Processes

CHAPTER 14

Learning Objectives

After studying this chapter, you should be able to

1. Explain the role of operations management in achieving superior quality, efficiency, and responsiveness to customers. **[LO1]**

2. Describe what customers want, and explain why it is so important for managers to be responsive to their needs. **[LO2]**

3. Explain why achieving superior quality is so important. **[LO3]**

4. Explain why achieving superior efficiency is so important. **[LO4]**

Assembly-line workers for Japanese auto giant Toyota put tires onto Toyota's vehicle "Wish" at the company's Tsutsumi plant in Toyota, central Japan. Toyota is widely credited with pioneering a number of critical innovations in the way cars are built that have helped it achieve superior productivity and quality—the basis of Toyota's competitive advantage.

MANAGEMENT SNAPSHOT

Why Toyota Is a Leader in Operations Management

How Can Managers Work to Increase Operating Performance?

Toyota has long been known as a company that constantly works to modify and change its production systems to improve efficiency, quality, and customer responsiveness. Toyota pioneered the system of lean production, the continuous incremental improvement of work procedures that results in dramatic improvements in vehicle quality. In lean production, employees become responsible for improving work procedures to drive down costs and drive up quality. Individually, and in quality groups or circles, employees suggest ways to improve how a particular Toyota car model is made. Over time, their thousands of suggestions result in major improvements to the final product. Employees receive cash bonuses and rewards for finding ways to improve work procedures, and the result has been a continuous increase in car quality and reduced manufacturing costs.

In the 2000s, under the leadership of its then president, Jujio Cho, Toyota strived to increase further its efficiency and quality. Toyota wanted to maintain competitive advantage over global competitors such as General Motors, Ford, and DaimlerChrysler, car companies that also utilized lean production. So Toyota began a series of programs with the goal of improving selected aspects of its operations.

One of the programs, called "pokayoke" or mistake-proofing, concentrates on the stages of the assembly process that previously have led to the most quality problems; employees are required to double- and triple-check a particular stage to discover any defective parts or to fix improper assembly operations that may lead to subsequent customer complaints. Another program is CCC21, in which Toyota is working continually with its suppliers to find ways to reduce the costs of the cars' components. By 2005, these costs were reduced by 30% and Toyota saved billions of dollars a year in operating costs.

Another change Toyota made introduced a new manufacturing process called GBL, which uses a sophisticated new assembly process to hold a car body firmly in place during production so that all welding and assembly operations can be performed more accurately—and also results in a better-quality vehicle. GBL has also allowed Toyota to build factories that can assemble several different kinds of cars along the same production line with no loss in efficiency or quality. This initiative is a major source of competitive advantage because Toyota's global network of car plants can now move quickly to alter the cars they are making to respond to increasing or decreasing customer demand for a certain type of vehicle.

Toyota's mastery of production operations and processes has made it by far the most profitable global carmaker. With all its new operations initiatives proceeding at full speed, Toyota replaced Ford as the world's second largest carmaker in 2004 and replaced GM as the world's biggest carmaker in 2008.

Overview

Toyota constantly searches for ways to improve its vehicle assembly operations and processes to reduce costs and improve quality, allowing the company to be more responsive to customers who purchase a high-quality vehicle for a reasonable price.

operations management The management of any aspect of the production system that transforms inputs into finished goods and services.

In this chapter we focus on operations management techniques that managers can use to increase the quality of an organization's products, the efficiency of production, and the organization's responsiveness to customers. By the end of this chapter, you will understand the vital role operations management plays in building competitive advantage and creating a high-performing organization.

Operations Management and Competitive Advantage

Operations management is the management of any aspect of the production system that transforms inputs into finished goods and services. A **production system** is the system that an organization uses to acquire inputs, convert inputs into outputs, and dispose of the outputs (goods or services). **Operations managers** are managers who are responsible for managing an organization's production system. They do whatever it takes to transform inputs into outputs. Their job is to manage the three stages of production–acquisition of inputs, control of conversion processes, and disposal of goods and services–and to determine where operating improvements might be made in order to increase quality, efficiency, and responsiveness to customers and so give an organization a competitive advantage (see Figure 14.1).

production system The system that an organization uses to acquire inputs, convert the inputs into outputs, and dispose of the outputs.

operations manager A manager who is responsible for managing an organization's production system and for determining where operating improvements might be made.

Quality refers to goods and services that are reliable, dependable, or psychologically satisfying: They do the job they were designed for and do it well, or they possess some attribute that gives their users something they value.[1] *Efficiency* refers to the amount of inputs required to produce a given output. *Responsiveness to customers* refers to actions taken to meet the demands and needs of customers. Operations managers are responsible for ensuring that an organization has sufficient supplies of high-quality, low-cost inputs, and they are responsible for designing a production system that creates high-quality, low-cost products that customers are willing to buy.

Figure 14.1
The Purpose of Operations Management

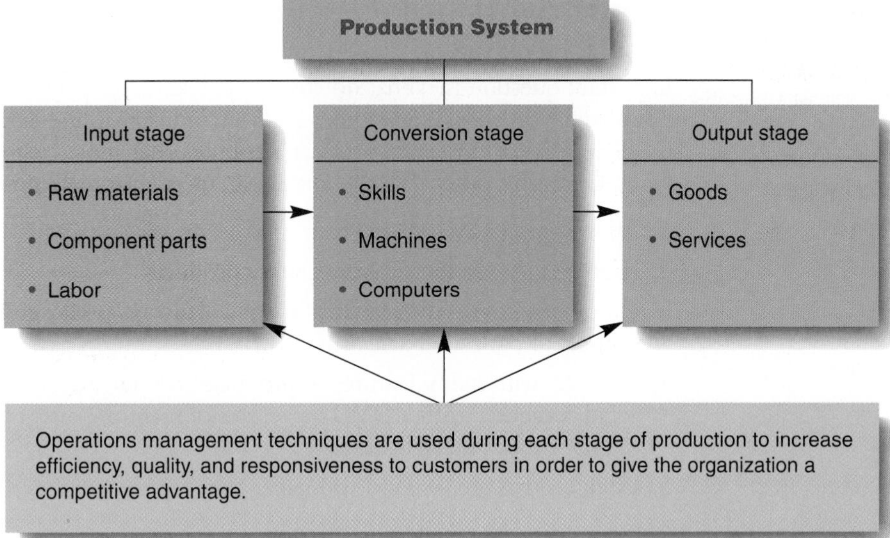

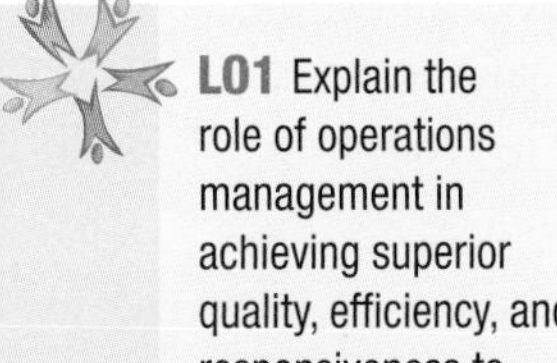

LO1 Explain the role of operations management in achieving superior quality, efficiency, and responsiveness to customers.

Notice that achieving superior efficiency and quality is part of attaining superior responsiveness to customers. Customers want value for their money, and an organization whose efficient production system creates high-quality, low-cost products is best able to deliver this value. For this reason, we begin by discussing how operations managers can design the production system to increase responsiveness to customers.

Improving Responsiveness to Customers

Organizations produce outputs–goods or services–that are consumed by customers. All organizations, profit seeking or not-for-profit, have customers. Without customers, most organizations would cease to exist. Because customers are vital to the survival of most organizations, managers must correctly identify customers and promote organizational strategies that respond to their needs. This is why management writers recommend that organizations define their business in terms of the customer needs they are satisfying, not the type of products they are producing.[2] The credo of pharmaceutical company Johnson & Johnson, for example, begins, "We believe our first responsibility is to the doctors, nurses and patients, to mothers and fathers and all others who use our products and services."[3] Through the credo Johnson & Johnson's managers emphasize their commitment to exemplary customer service. In contrast, in the early 2000s, Lucent Technologies decided that, given its expertise in transistor technology, it would focus on producing transistor-based Internet routers that could handle vast quantities of information. When it became clear that customers were choosing optical Internet routers because these routers could transfer information extremely quickly, Lucent lost a large part of its business.

LO2 Describe what customers want, and explain why it is so important for managers to be responsive to their needs.

What Do Customers Want?

Given that satisfying customer demands is central to the survival of an organization, an important question is, What do customers want? To specify exactly what they want is not possible because their wants vary from industry to industry. However, it is possible to identify some universal product attributes that most customers in most industries want. Generally, other things being equal, most customers prefer

1. A lower price to a higher price.
2. High-quality products to low-quality products.
3. Quick service to slow service. (They will always prefer good after-sales service and support to poor after-sales support.)
4. Products with many features to products with few features. (They will prefer a personal computer with a DVD drive, lots of memory, and a powerful microprocessor to one without these features.)
5. Products that are, as far as possible, customized or tailored to their unique needs.

Of course, the problem is that other things are not equal. For example, providing high quality, quick service, and after-sales service and support, products with many features, and products that are customized raises costs and thus the price that must be charged to cover costs.[4] So customers' demands for these attributes typically conflict with their demands for low prices. Accordingly, customers must make a trade-off between price and preferred attributes, and so must managers.

Designing Production Systems to Be Responsive to Customers

Because satisfying customers is so important, managers try to design production systems that can produce the outputs that have the attributes customers desire. The attributes of an organization's outputs–their quality, cost, and features–are determined by the organization's production system.[5] Since the ability of an organization to satisfy the demands of its customers derives from its production system, managers need to devote considerable attention to constantly improving production systems. Managers' desire to attract customers with improved products explains their adoption of many new operations management techniques in recent years. These include flexible manufacturing systems, just-in-time inventory, and, of course, the new information systems and technologies discussed in Chapter 13.

A Southwest ticket agent assists a customer. Southwest's operating system is geared toward satisfying customer demands for low-priced, reliable, and convenient air travel, making it one of the most consistently successful airlines in recent years. To help keep flights on schedule, Southwest's workforce has been cross-trained to perform multiple tasks. For example, the person who checks tickets might also help with baggage loading.

As an example of the link between responsiveness to customers and an organization's production system, consider the success of Southwest Airlines. One of the most consistently successful airlines in the United States, Southwest Airlines has been expanding rapidly. One reason for Southwest's success is that its managers created a production system uniquely tailored to satisfy the demands of its customers for low-priced, reliable (on-time), and convenient air travel. Southwest commands high customer loyalty precisely because its production system delivers products, such as flights from Houston to Dallas, that have all the desired attributes: reliability, convenience, and low price.

Southwest's low-cost production system focuses not only on improving the maintenance of aircraft but also on the company's ticket reservation system, route structure, flight frequency, baggage-handling system, and in-flight services. Each of these elements of Southwest's production system is geared toward satisfying customer demands for low-priced, reliable, and convenient air travel. For example, Southwest offers a no-frills approach to in-flight customer service. No meals are served on board, and there are no first-class seats. Southwest does not subscribe to the big reservation computers used by travel agents because the booking fees are too costly. Also, the airline flies only one aircraft, the fuel-efficient Boeing 737, which keeps training and maintenance costs down. All this translates into low prices for customers.

Southwest's reliability derives from the fact that it has the quickest aircraft turnaround time in the industry. A Southwest ground crew needs only 15 minutes to turn around an incoming aircraft and prepare it for departure. This speedy operation helps to keep flights on time. Southwest has such quick turnaround because it has a flexible workforce that has been cross-trained to perform multiple tasks. Thus, the person who checks tickets might also help with baggage loading if time is short.

Southwest's convenience comes from its scheduling multiple flights every day between its popular locations, such as Dallas and Houston, and its use of airports that are close to downtown (Hobby at Houston and Love Field at Dallas) instead of more distant major airports.[6]

Customer Relationship Management

customer relationship management (CRM) A technique that uses IT to develop an ongoing relationship with customers to maximize the value an organization can deliver to them over time.

One strategy managers can use to get close to customers and understand their needs is **customer relationship management (CRM)**. CRM is a technique that uses IT to develop an ongoing relationship with customers to maximize the value an organization can deliver to them over time. In the 2000s, most large companies have installed sophisticated CRM IT to track customers' changing demands for a company's products; it has become a vital tool used to maximize responsiveness to customers. CRM IT monitors, controls, and links each of the functional activities involved in marketing, selling, and delivering products to customers, such as monitoring the delivery of products through the distribution channel, monitoring salespeople's selling activities, setting product pricing, and coordinating after-sales service. CRM systems have three interconnected components, sales and selling, after-sales service and support, and marketing.

Suppose that a sales manager has access only to sales data that show the total sales revenue each salesperson had generated in the last 30 days. This information does not break down how much revenue came from sales to existing customers versus sales to new customers. What important knowledge is being lost? First, if most revenues are earned from sales to existing customers, this suggests that the money being spent by a company to advertise and promote its products is not attracting new customers and so is being wasted. Second, important dimensions involved in sales are pricing, financing, and order processing. In many companies, to close a deal, a salesperson has to send the paperwork to a central sales office that handles matters such as approving the customer for special financing and determining specific shipping and delivery dates. In some companies, different departments handle these activities, and it can take a long time to get a response from them; this keeps customers waiting–something that often leads to lost sales. Until CRM systems were introduced, these kinds of problems were widespread and resulted in missed sales and higher operating costs. Today, the sales and selling CRM software contains *best sales practices* that analyze this information and then recommend ways to improve the way the sales process operates. One company that has improved its sales, and after-sales, practices by implementing CRM is discussed in the following "Information Technology Byte."

When a company implements after-sales service and support CRM software, salespeople are required to input detailed information about their follow-up visits to customers. Because the system is now tracking and documenting every customer's case history, salespeople have instant access to a record of everything that occurred during previous phone calls or visits. They are now in a much better position to be responsive to customers' needs and build customer loyalty, so a company's after-sales service improves. Telephone providers like Sprint and MCI, for example, require that telephone sales reps collect information about all customers' inquiries, complaints, and requests, and this is recorded electronically in customer logs. The CRM module can analyze the information in these logs to evaluate whether the customer service reps are meeting or exceeding the company's required service standards.

The CRM system also identifies the top 10 reasons why customer complaints are arising. Sales managers can then work to eliminate the sources of these problems and improve after-sales support procedures. The CRM system also identifies the top 10 best service and support practices, which can then be taught to all sales reps.

Finally, as a CRM system processes information about changing customer needs, this improves the way marketing operates in many ways. Marketing managers, for example, now have access to detailed customer profiles, including data on purchases and the reasons why individuals were or were not attracted to a company's products. Armed with this knowledge, marketing can better identify customers and the specific

INFORMATION TECHNOLOGY BYTE

How CRM Helped Empire HealthChoice

Empire HealthChoice Inc., the largest health insurance provider in New York, sells its policies through 1,800 sales agents. For years, these agents were responsible for collecting all of the customer-specific information needed to determine the price of each policy. Once they had collected the necessary information, the agents called Empire to get their price quotes. After waiting days to get these quotes, the agents relayed them back to customers, who often then modified their requests to reduce the cost of their policies. When this occurred, the agent had to telephone Empire again to get a revised price quote. Because this frequently happened several times with each transaction, it often took more than 20 days to close a sale and another 10 days for customers to get their insurance cards.[7]

Recognizing that these delays were resulting in lost sales, Empire decided to examine how a CRM system could help improve the sales process. Its managers chose a Web-based system so that agents themselves could calculate the insurance quotes online. Once an agent has entered a customer's data, a quote is generated in just a few seconds. The agent can continually modify a policy while sitting face-to-face with the customer until the policy and price are agreed upon. As a result, the sales process can now be completed in a few hours, and customers receive their insurance cards in 2 to 3 days rather than 10.[8]

product attributes they desire. It may become clear, for example, that a customer group that marketing had targeted has a specific need that is not being satisfied by a product–such as a need for a cell phone containing a 5-megapixel digital camera and an MP3 player. With real-time information, marketing can work with product development to redesign the product to better meet customer needs. In sum, a CRM system is a comprehensive method of gathering crucial information about the way customers respond to a company's products. It is a powerful functional strategy used to better align a company's products with customer needs.

Improving Quality

As noted earlier, high-quality products possess attributes such as superior design, features, reliability, and after-sales support; these products are designed to better meet customer requirements.[9] Quality is a concept that can be applied to the products of both manufacturing and service organizations–goods such as a Toyota car or services such as Southwest Airlines flight service or customer service in a Citibank branch. Why do managers seek to control and improve the quality of their organizations' products?[10] There are two reasons (see Figure 14.2).

LO3 Explain why achieving superior quality is so important.

First, customers usually prefer a higher-quality product to a lower-quality product. So an organization able to provide, *for the same price,* a product of higher quality than a competitor's product is serving its customers better–it is being more responsive to its customers. Often, providing high-quality products creates a brand-name reputation for an organization's products. In turn, this enhanced reputation may allow the organization to charge more for its products than its competitors are able to charge, and thus it makes even greater profits. In 2007 Lexus was ranked number one, as it has been for over a decade, on the J. D. Power list of the 10 most reliable carmakers, and Toyota was close behind.[11] The high quality of Toyota/Lexus vehicles enables the company to charge higher prices for its cars than the prices charged by rival carmakers.

The second reason for trying to boost product quality is that higher product quality can increase efficiency and thereby lower operating costs and boost profits. Achieving high product quality lowers operating costs because of the effect of quality on employee productivity: Higher product quality means less employee time is wasted in making defective products that must be discarded or in providing substandard services, and thus less time has to be spent fixing mistakes. This translates into higher employee productivity, which means lower costs.

To increase quality, managers need to develop strategic plans that state goals exactly and spell out how they will be achieved. Managers should embrace the philosophy that mistakes, defects, and poor-quality materials are not acceptable and should be

Figure 14.2
The Impact of Increased Quality on Organizational Performance

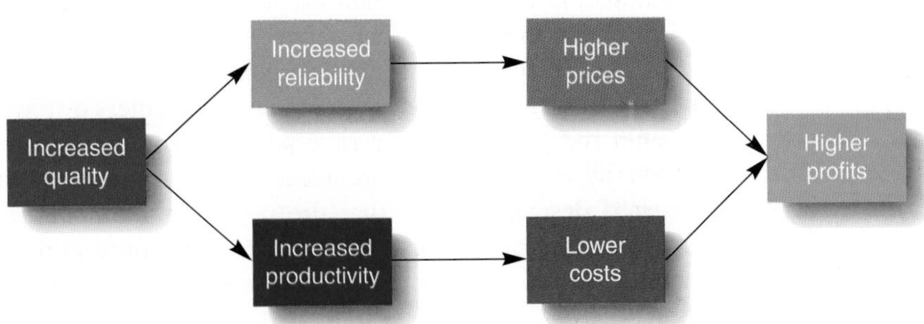

eliminated. First-line managers should spend more time working with nonmanagerial employees and providing them with the tools they need to do the job. Managers should create an environment in which subordinates will not be afraid to report problems or recommend improvements. Output goals and targets need to include not only numbers or quotas but also some notion of quality to promote the production of defect-free output. Managers also need to train employees in new skills to keep pace with changes in the workplace. Finally, achieving better quality requires managers to develop organizational values and norms centered on improving quality.

Improving Efficiency

The third goal of operations management is to increase the efficiency of an organization's production system. The fewer the inputs required to produce a given output, the higher will be the efficiency of the production system. Managers can measure efficiency at the organization level in two ways. The measure, known as *total factor productivity*, looks at how well an organization utilizes all of its resources—such as labor, capital, materials, or energy—to produce its outputs. It is expressed in the following equation:

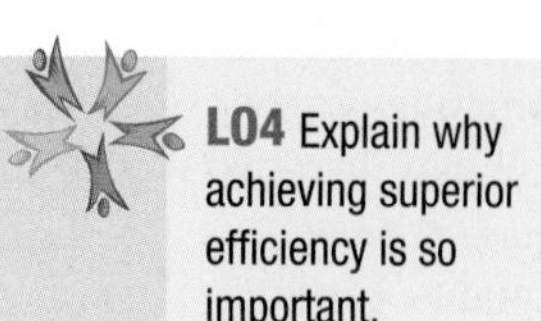

LO4 Explain why achieving superior efficiency is so important.

$$\text{Total factor productivity} = \frac{\text{Outputs}}{\text{All inputs}}$$

The problem with total factor productivity is that each input is typically measured in different units: Labor's contribution to producing an output is measured by hours worked; the contribution of materials is measured by the amount consumed (for example, tons of iron ore required to make a ton of steel); the contribution of energy is measured by the units of energy consumed (for example, kilowatt-hours); and so on. To compute total factor productivity, managers must convert all the inputs to a common unit, such as dollars, before they can work the equation.

Though sometimes a useful measure of efficiency overall, total factor productivity obscures the exact contribution of an individual input—such as labor—to the production of a given output. Consequently, most organizations focus on specific measures of efficiency, known as *partial productivity,* that measure the efficiency of an individual unit. For example, the efficiency of labor inputs is expressed as

$$\text{Labor productivity} = \frac{\text{Outputs}}{\text{Direct labor}}$$

Labor productivity is most commonly used to draw efficiency comparisons between different organizations. For example, one study found that in 1994 it took the average Japanese automobile components supplier half as many labor hours to produce a part, such as a car seat or exhaust system, as the average British company.[12] Thus, the study concluded, Japanese companies use labor more efficiently than British companies.

The management of efficiency is an extremely important issue in most organizations, because increased efficiency lowers production costs, thereby allowing the organization to make a greater profit or to attract more customers by lowering its price. For example, in 1990 the price of the average personal computer sold in the United States was $3,000, by 1995 the price was around $1,800, and in 2005 it was $550. This decrease occurred despite the fact that the power and capabilities of the average personal computer increased dramatically during this time period (microprocessors became more powerful, memory increased, modems were built in, and multimedia capability was added).

Why was the decrease in price possible? Manufacturers of personal computers such as Compaq and Dell focused on quality and boosted their efficiency by improving the quality of their components and making PCs easier to assemble. This allowed them to lower their costs and prices yet still make a profit.[13]

Facilities Layout, Flexible Manufacturing, and Efficiency

Another factor that influences efficiency is the way managers decide to lay out or design an organization's physical work facilities. This is important for two reasons. First, the way in which machines and workers are organized or grouped together into workstations affects the efficiency of the production system. Second, a major determinant of efficiency is the cost associated with setting up the equipment needed to make a particular product. **Facilities layout** is the operations management technique whose goal is to design the machine–worker interface to increase production system efficiency. **Flexible manufacturing** is the set of operations management techniques that attempt to reduce the setup costs associated with a production system.

facilities layout The operations management technique whose goal is to design the machine–worker interface to increase production system efficiency.

flexible manufacturing Operations management techniques that attempt to reduce the setup costs associated with a production system.

FACILITIES LAYOUT The way in which machines, robots, and people are grouped together affects how productive they can be. Figure 14.3 shows three basic ways of arranging workstations: product layout, process layout, and fixed-position layout.

In a *product layout,* machines are organized so that each operation needed to manufacture a product is performed at workstations arranged in a fixed sequence. Typically, workers are stationary in this arrangement, and a moving conveyor belt takes the product being worked on to the next workstation so that it is progressively assembled. Mass production is the familiar name for this layout; car assembly lines are probably the best-known example. Formerly product layout was efficient only when products were created in large quantities; however, the introduction of modular assembly lines controlled by computers makes it efficient to make products in small batches.

Figure 14.3 Three Facilities Layouts

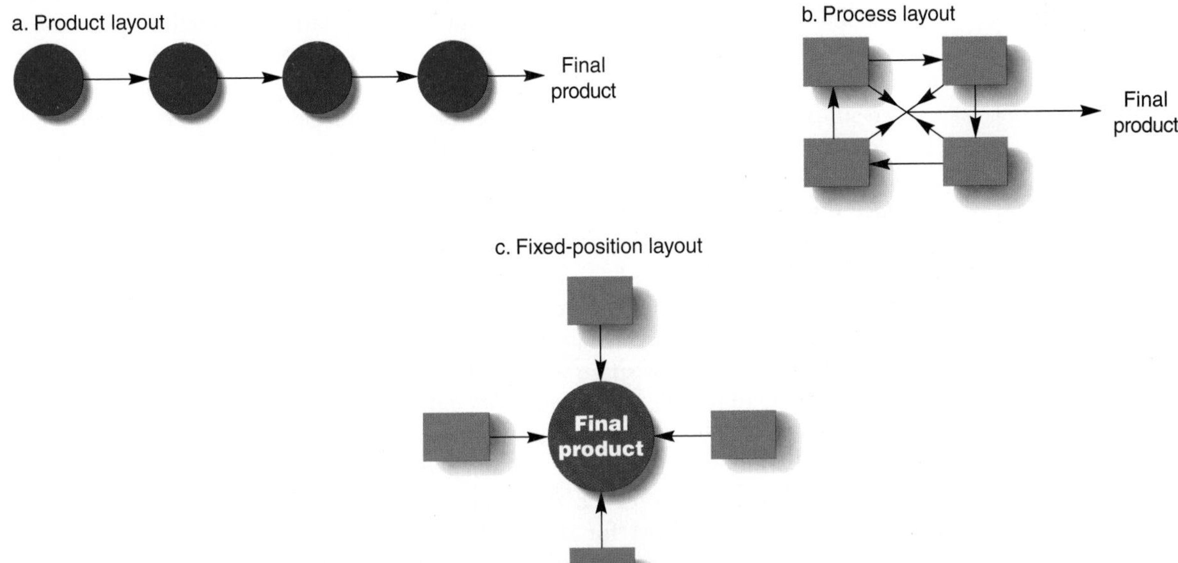

In a *process layout,* workstations are not organized in a fixed sequence. Rather, each workstation is relatively self-contained, and a product goes to whichever workstation is needed to perform the next operation to complete the product. Process layout is often suited to manufacturing settings that produce a variety of custom-made products, each tailored to the needs of a different kind of customer. For example, a custom furniture manufacturer might use a process layout so that different teams of workers can produce different styles of chairs or tables made from different kinds of woods and finishes. A process layout provides the flexibility needed to change the product. Such flexibility, however, often reduces efficiency because it is expensive.

In a *fixed-position layout,* the product stays in a fixed position. Its component parts are produced in remote workstations and brought to the production area for final assembly. Increasingly, self-managed teams are using fixed-position layouts. Different teams assemble each component part and then send these parts to the final assembly team, which makes the final product. A fixed-position layout is commonly used for products such as jet airlines, mainframe computers, and gas turbines–products that are complex and difficult to assemble or so large that moving them from one workstation to another would be difficult. The effects of moving from one facilities layout to another can be dramatic, as the following "Manager as a Person" suggests.

MANAGER AS A PERSON

How to Improve Facilities Layout

Paddy Hopkirk established his car accessories business in Bedfordshire, England, shortly after he had shot to motor car racing fame by winning the Monte Carlo Rally. Sales of Hopkirk's accessories, such as bicycle racks and axle stands, were always brisk, but Hopkirk was the first to admit that his production system left a lot to be desired, so he invited consultants to help reorganize his production system.

After analyzing his factory's production system, the consultants realized that the source of the problem was the facilities layout Hopkirk had established. Over time, as sales grew, Hopkirk simply added new workstations to the production system as they were needed. The result was a process layout in which the product being assembled moved in the irregular sequences shown in the "Before Change" half of Figure 14.4. The consultants suggested that to save time and effort, the workstations should be reorganized into the sequential product layout shown in the "After Change" illustration.

Once this change was made, the results were dramatic. One morning the factory was an untidy sprawl of workstations surrounded by piles of crates holding semifinished components. Two days later, when the 170-person workforce came back to work, the machines had been brought together into tightly grouped workstations arranged in the fixed sequence shown in the illustration. The piles of components had disappeared, and the newly cleared floor space was neatly marked with color-coded lines mapping out the new flow of materials between workstations.

In the first full day of production, efficiency increased by as much as 30%. The space needed for some operations had been cut in half, and work-in-progress had been cut considerably. Moreover, the improved layout allowed for some jobs to be combined, freeing operators for deployment elsewhere in the factory. An amazed Hopkirk exclaimed, "I was expecting a change but nothing as dramatic as this . . . it is fantastic."[14]

Figure 14.4 Changing a Facilities Layout

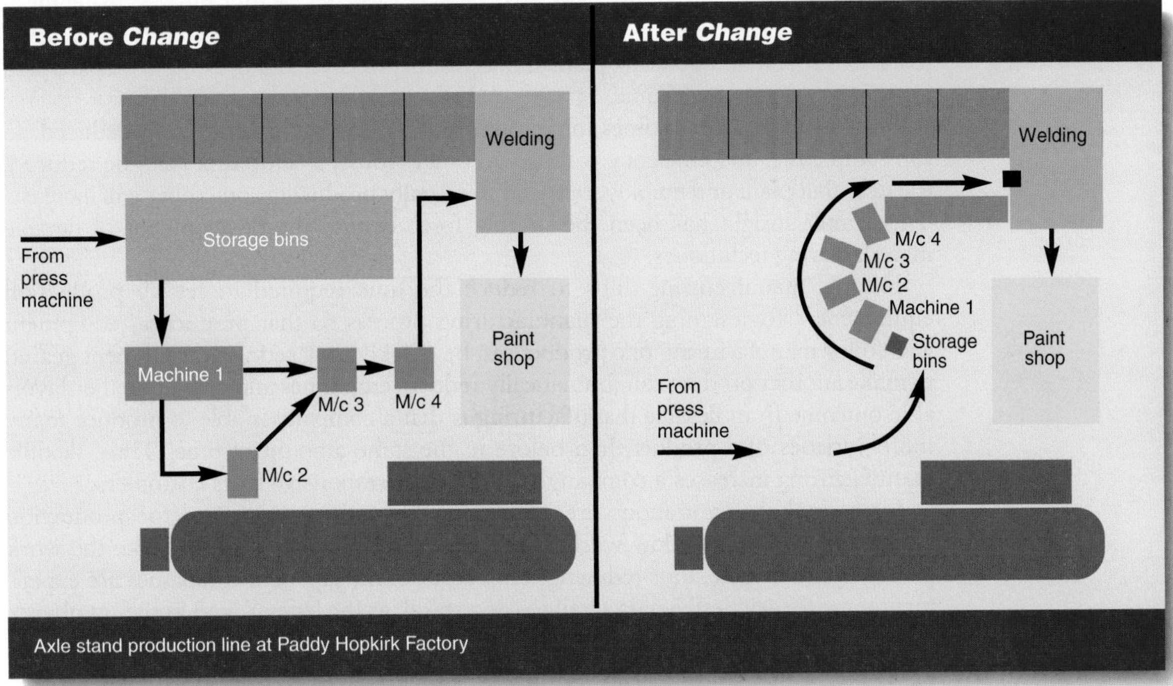

Source: Reprinted from *Financial Times* of January 4, 1994, by permission of Financial Times Syndication, London.

FLEXIBLE MANUFACTURING In a manufacturing company, a major source of costs is the costs associated with setting up the equipment needed to make a particular product. One of these costs is the cost of production that is forgone because nothing is produced while the equipment is being set up. For example, components manufacturers often

Assisted by Web-based online work instructions, an operator at Dell Computer determines the sequence in which Dell's custom-built computers are to be assembled by its computer-controlled flexible manufacturing system. This flexible system makes possible Dell's low-cost strategy.

need as much as half a day to set up automated production equipment when switching from production of one component part (such as a washer ring for the steering column of a car) to another (such as a washer ring for the steering column of a truck). During this half-day, a manufacturing plant is not producing anything, but employees are paid for this "nonproductive" time.

It follows that if setup times for complex production equipment can be reduced, so can setup costs, and efficiency will rise. In other words, if setup times can be reduced, the time that plant and employees spend in actually producing something will increase. This simple insight has been the driving force behind the development of flexible manufacturing techniques.

Flexible manufacturing aims to reduce the time required to set up production equipment.[15] Redesigning the manufacturing process so that production equipment geared for manufacturing one product can be quickly replaced with equipment geared to make another product can dramatically reduce setup times and costs. Another favorable outcome from flexible manufacturing is that a company is able to produce many more varieties of a product than before in the same amount of time. Thus, flexible manufacturing increases a company's ability to be responsive to its customers.

Increasingly, organizations are experimenting with new designs for production systems that not only allow workers to be more productive but also make the work process more flexible, thus reducing setup costs. Some Japanese companies are experimenting with facilities layouts arranged as a spiral, as the letter Y, and as the number 6, to see how these various configurations affect setup costs and worker productivity. At a camcorder plant in Kohda, Japan, for example, Sony changed from a fixed-position layout in which 50 workers sequentially built a camcorder to a flexible spiral process design in which four workers perform all the operations necessary to produce the camcorder. This new layout allows the most efficient workers to work at the highest pace, and it reduces setup costs because workers can easily switch from one model to another, increasing efficiency by 10%.[16]

MANAGING GLOBALLY

Igus's Factory of the Future

Igus Inc., headquartered in Cologne, Germany, makes over 28,000 polymer bearings and energy supply cable products used in applications the world over. In the 1990s, the company's managers realized they needed to build a new factory that could handle the company's rapidly growing product line.[17]

Igus's product line changes constantly as new products are developed and old ones become obsolete. At Igus new products are often introduced on a daily basis, so the need for flexibility is great. Moreover, because many of its products are highly customized, the specific and changing needs of customers drive new product development.

Igus's new factory–as big as three football fields–was designed with the need for flexibility in mind. Nothing in the factory is tied down or bolted to the floor. All the machines, computers, and equipment can be moved and repositioned to suit changing product requirements. Moreover, all Igus employees are trained to be flexible and can perform many different production tasks. For example, when one new product line proved popular with customers, employees and production operations were relocated four times into increasingly larger spaces. Igus can change its production system at a moment's notice and with minimal disruption, and because the company operates seven days a week, 24 hours a day, these changes are occurring constantly.

To facilitate these changes, workers are equipped with power scooters so they can move around the plant quickly to reconfigure operations. The scooters also allow them to move quickly to wherever in the factory their skills are most needed. Employees also carry mobile phones so they are always on call.

Igus's decision to create a flexible factory has paid off. In the last five years its sales have increased from $10 million to $100 million, and its global staff has tripled.

Just-in-Time Inventory and Efficiency

inventory The stock of raw materials, inputs, and component parts that an organization has on hand at a particular time.

just-in-time inventory system A system in which parts or supplies arrive at an organization when they are needed, not before.

Inventory is the stock of raw materials, inputs, and component parts that an organization has on hand at a particular time. Just-in-time (JIT) inventory systems play a major role in the process of identifying and finding the source of defects in inputs. When an organization has a **just-in-time inventory system,** parts or supplies arrive at the organization when they are needed, not before. Under a JIT inventory system, defective parts enter an organization's production system immediately; they are not warehoused for months before use. This means that defective inputs can be quickly spotted. Managers can then trace a problem to the supply source and fix it before more defective parts are produced.

JIT systems, such as Toyota's *kanban* system, were originally developed as part of the effort to improve product quality; they have major implications for efficiency. Toyota's system is based on the delivery of components to the production line just as they are needed. This leads to major cost savings from increasing inventory turnover and reducing inventory holding costs, such as warehousing and storage costs and the cost of capital tied up in inventory. Although companies that manufacture and assemble products can obviously use JIT to great advantage, so can service organizations. Wal-Mart, the biggest retailer in the United States, uses JIT systems to replenish the stock in its stores at least twice a week. Many Wal-Mart stores receive daily deliveries. Wal-Mart's main competitors, Kmart and Sears, typically replenish their stock every two weeks. Wal-Mart can maintain the same service levels as these competitors but at one-fourth the inventory-holding cost, a major source of cost savings. Faster inventory turnover has helped Wal-Mart achieve an efficiency-based competitive advantage in the retailing industry.[18]

One drawback of JIT systems is that they leave an organization without a buffer stock of inventory.[19] Although buffer stocks of inventory can be expensive to store, they can help an organization when it is affected by shortages of inputs brought about by a disruption among suppliers (such as a labor dispute in a key supplier). Moreover, buffer stocks can help an organization respond quickly to increases in customer demand–that is, they can increase an organization's responsiveness to customers.

Even a small company can benefit from a kanban, as the experience of United Electric suggests. United Electric Controls, headquartered in Watertown, Massachusetts, is the market leader in the application of threshold detection and switching technology. Once the company simply warehoused its inputs and dispensed them as needed. Then it decided to reduce costs by storing these inputs at their point of use in the production system. However, this practice caused problems because inventories of some inputs actually started to increase while other inputs were used up without anyone knowing which input caused a stoppage in production. Thus, managers decided to experiment with a supplier kanban system even though United Electric had fewer than 40 suppliers who were totally up-to-date with the company's input requirements.

Managers decided to store a three-week supply of parts in a central storeroom, a supply large enough to avoid unexpected shortages.[20] They began by asking their casting supplier to deliver inputs in kanbans and bins. Once a week, this supplier checks up on the bins to determine how much stock needs to be delivered the following week. Other suppliers were then asked to participate in this system, and now more than 35 of United Electric's major suppliers operate some form of the kanban system. By all measures of performance, the results have been successful. Inventory-holding costs have fallen sharply. Products are delivered to all customers on time. And even new products' design-to-production cycles have dropped by 50% because suppliers are now involved much earlier in the design process, so they can supply new inputs as needed.

Self-Managed Work Teams and Efficiency

Another efficiency-boosting technique is the use of self-managed work teams (see Chapter 11).[21] The typical team consists of from 5 to 15 employees who produce an entire product instead of only parts of it.[22] Team members learn all team tasks and move from job to job. The result is a flexible workforce because team members can fill in for absent coworkers. The members of each team also assume responsibility for work and vacation scheduling, ordering materials, and hiring new members–previously all responsibilities of first-line managers. Because people often respond well to being given greater autonomy and responsibility, the use of empowered self-managed teams can increase productivity and efficiency. Moreover, cost savings arise from eliminating supervisors and creating a flatter organizational hierarchy, which further increases efficiency.

The effect of introducing self-managed teams is often an increase in efficiency of 30% or more, sometimes much more. After the introduction of flexible manufacturing technology and self-managed teams, a GE plant in Salisbury, North Carolina, increased efficiency by 250% compared with other GE plants producing the same products.[23]

Process Reengineering and Efficiency

process reengineering The fundamental rethinking and radical redesign of business processes to achieve dramatic improvements in critical measures of performance such as cost, quality, service, and speed.

Think of the major activities of businesses as processes that take one or more kinds of inputs and create an output that is of value to the customer.[24] **Process reengineering** is the fundamental rethinking and radical redesign of business processes to achieve dramatic improvements in critical measures of performance such as cost, quality, service, and speed.[25] Customer relationship management can be thought of as a business process: Once a customer's order is received (the input), all the activities necessary to process the order are performed, and the ordered goods are delivered to the customer (the output). Process reengineering can boost efficiency because it eliminates the time devoted to activities that do not add value.

As an example of process reengineering in practice, consider how Ford Motor Company used it. One day a manager from Ford was working at its Japanese partner Mazda and discovered quite by accident that Mazda had only five people in its accounts payable department. The Ford manager was shocked, for Ford's U.S. operation had 500 employees in accounts payable. He reported his discovery to Ford's U.S. managers, who decided to form a task force to figure out why the difference existed.

Ford managers discovered that procurement began when the purchasing department sent a purchase order to a supplier and sent a copy of the purchase order to Ford's accounts payable department. When the supplier shipped the goods and they arrived at Ford, a clerk at the receiving dock completed a form describing the goods and sent the form to accounts payable. The supplier, meanwhile, sent accounts payable an invoice. Thus, accounts payable received three documents relating to these goods: a copy of the original purchase order, the receiving document, and the invoice. If the information in all three was in agreement (most of the time it was), a clerk in accounts payable issued payment. Occasionally, however, all three documents did not agree. Ford discovered that accounts payable clerks spent most of their time straightening out the 1% of instances in which the purchase order, receiving document, and invoice contained conflicting information.[26]

Ford managers decided to reengineer the procurement process to simplify it. Now when a buyer in the purchasing department issues a purchase order to a supplier, that buyer also enters the order into an online database. As before, suppliers send goods to the receiving dock. When the goods arrive, the clerk at the receiving dock checks a computer terminal to see whether the received shipment matches the description on the purchase order. If it does, the clerk accepts the goods and pushes a button on the terminal keyboard that tells the database the goods have arrived. Receipt of the goods is recorded in the database, and a computer automatically issues and sends a check to the supplier. If the goods do not correspond to the description on the purchase order in the database, the clerk at the dock refuses the shipment and sends it back to the supplier.

Managers at Ford Motor Company used process reengineering to improve the efficiency of their procurement process by simplifying it. Now, when one of Ford's dealers issues a purchase order to buy a collection of Ford vehicles for delivery to its lot, the dealer also enters the order into an online database. When the vehicles ordered arrive at the receiving dock for shipment by train, a clerk checks on a computer terminal to ensure that the specific shipment matches the purchase order and checks online with the dealer that the order is still correct. If it is, the vehicles are shipped. The use of process engineering has significantly cut down on the time accounts payable clerks spend to rectify complex vehicle orders that contain conflicting information.

Payment authorization, which used to be performed by accounts payable, is now accomplished at the receiving dock. The new process has come close to eliminating the need for an accounts payable department. In some parts of Ford, the size of the accounts payable department has been cut by 95%. By reducing the head count in accounts payable, the reengineering effort reduced the amount of time wasted on unproductive activities, thereby increasing the efficiency of the total organization.

In sum, managers at all levels have important roles to play in a company's effort to boost efficiency. Top management's role is to encourage efficiency improvements by, for example, emphasizing the need for continuous improvement or reengineering. Top management also must ensure that managers from different functional departments work together to find ways to increase efficiency. However, while top managers might recognize the need for such actions, functional-level managers are in the best position to identify opportunities for making efficiency-enhancing improvements to an organization's production systems. They are the managers who are involved in an organization's production system on a day-to-day basis. Improving efficiency, like quality, is an ongoing, never-ending process.

Operations Management: Some Remaining Issues

Achieving superior responsiveness to customers through quality and efficiency often requires a profound shift in management operations and in the culture of an organization. Many reports have appeared in the popular press about widespread disillusionment with JIT, flexible manufacturing, and reengineering. It is possible that many of the disillusioned organizations are those that failed to understand that implementing these systems requires a marked shift in organizational culture.[27] None of these systems is a panacea that can be taken once, like a pill, to cure industrial ills. Making these techniques work within an organization can pose a significant challenge that calls for hard work and years of persistence by the sponsoring managers.

Managers also need to understand the ethical implications of the adoption of many of the production techniques discussed here. JIT, flexible manufacturing, and reengineering can all increase quality, efficiency, and responsiveness to customers, but they may do so at great cost to employees. Employees may see the demands of their job increase, or, worse, they may see themselves reengineered out of a job. For example, Toyota is the most efficient car manufacturer in the world, but some of its gains have been achieved at a significant cost to its employees, as discussed in the following "Ethics in Action."

ETHICS IN ACTION

The Human Cost of Improving Productivity

Hisashi Tomiki is the leader of a four-man self-managed team in a Toyota production plant, 200 miles south of Tokyo, Japan. Tomiki and his team work at a grueling pace to build cowls (steel chambers onto which windshields and steering columns are attached). Consider this description of Tomiki at work:

> *In two minutes Tomiki fits 24 metal pieces into designated slots on three welding machines; runs two large metal sheets through each of the machines, which weld on the parts; and fuses*

the two sheets together with two spot welds. There is little room for error. Once or twice an hour a mistake is made or a machine sticks, causing the next machine in line to stop. A yellow light flashes. Tomiki runs over. The squad must fix the part and work faster to catch up. A red button halts the production line if the problems are severe, but there is an unspoken rule against pushing it. Only once this day does Tomiki call in a special maintenance worker.[28]

The experience of workers like Tomiki has become increasingly common. Workers are heard to complain that constant attempts to increase quality and reduce costs really mean continuous speedup and added job stress from the increased pressure on employees to perform. Although some pressure is good, past a certain point it can seriously harm employees. Moreover, consider the following comment by Jerry Miller, a former employee of US West, whose team of billing clerks reengineered themselves out of a job: "When we first formed our teams, the company came in talking teams and empowerment and promised that we wouldn't lose any jobs. It turns out all this was a big cover. The company had us all set up for reengineering. We showed them how to streamline the work, and now 9,000 people are gone. It was cut-your-own-throat. It makes you feel used."[29]

Is it ethical to continually increase the demands placed on employees, regardless of the human cost in terms of job stress? Obviously, the answer is no. Employee support is vital if an organization is to function effectively. What kinds of work pressures are legitimate, and what pressures are excessive? There is no clear answer to this question. Ultimately the issue comes down to the judgment of responsible managers seeking to act ethically.

Summary and Review

OPERATIONS MANAGEMENT AND COMPETITIVE ADVANTAGE To achieve high performance, managers try to improve their responsiveness to customers, the quality of their products, and the efficiency of their organization. To achieve these goals, managers can use a number of operations management techniques to improve the way an organization's production system operates. **[LO1]**

IMPROVING RESPONSIVENESS TO CUSTOMERS To achieve high performance in a competitive environment, it is imperative that the production system of an organization responds to customer demands. Managers try to design production systems that produce outputs that have the attributes customers desire. One of the central tasks of operations management is to develop new and improved production systems that enhance the ability of the organization to deliver economically more of the product attributes that customers desire for the same price. Techniques such as JIT, flexible manufacturing, and process reengineering are popular because they promise to do this. Managers should analyze carefully the links between responsiveness to customers and the production system of an organization. The ability of an organization to satisfy the demands of its customers for lower prices, acceptable quality, better features, and so on depends critically on the nature of the organization's production system. As important as responsiveness to customers is, however, managers need to recognize that there are limits to how responsive an organization can be and still cover its costs. **[LO2]**

IMPROVING QUALITY Managers seek to improve the quality of their organization's output because it enables them to better serve customers, to raise prices, and to lower production costs. The attempt to improve quality requires an organizationwide commitment; managers emphasize a strong customer focus, find ways to measure quality, set quality improvement goals, solicit input from employees about how to improve product quality, and design products for ease of manufacture. **[LO3]**

IMPROVING EFFICIENCY Improving efficiency requires one or more of the following: improve quality, adopt flexible manufacturing technologies, introduce just-in-time inventory systems, establish self-managed work teams, and use process reengineering. Top management is responsible for setting the context within which efficiency improvements can take place by, for example, emphasizing the need for continuous improvement. Functional-level managers bear prime responsibility for identifying and implementing efficiency-enhancing improvements in production systems. **[LO4]**

Management in Action

Topics for Discussion and Action

Action

1. Ask a manager how quality, efficiency, and responsiveness to customers are defined and measured in his or her organization. [LO2, 3, 4]
2. Go into a local store, restaurant, or supermarket, and list the ways in which you think the organization is being responsive or unresponsive to the needs of its customers. How could this business's responsiveness to customers be improved? [LO2]

Discussion

3. What is efficiency, and what are some of the techniques that managers can use to increase it? [LO4]
4. Why is it important for managers to pay close attention to their organization's production system if they wish to be responsive to their customers? [LO1]
5. "Total customer service is the goal toward which most organizations should strive." To what degree is this statement correct? [LO2]

Building Management Skills [LO1]

Managing a Production System

Choose an organization with which you are familiar—one that you have worked in or patronized or one that has received extensive coverage in the popular press. The organization should be involved in only one industry or business. Answer these questions about the organization:

1. What is the output of the organization?
2. Describe the production system that the organization uses to produce this output.
3. What product attributes do customers of the organization desire?
4. Does its production system allow the organization to deliver the desired product attributes?
5. Try to identify improvements that might be made to the organization's production system to boost the organization's responsiveness to customers, quality, and efficiency.

Managing Ethically [LO1]

Review "Ethics in Action: The Human Cost of Improving Productivity." After the implementing of many operations management techniques, layoffs occur in many companies, and, frequently, employees must perform more tasks more quickly, which can generate employee stress and other work-related problems.

Questions

1. Either by yourself or in a group, discuss how to think through the ethical implications of using a new operations management technique to improve organizational performance.
2. What criteria would you use to decide what kind of technique is ethical to adopt and how far to push employees to raise the level of their performance?
3. How big a layoff, if any, would be acceptable? If layoffs are acceptable, what could be done to reduce their harm to employees?

Small Group Breakout Exercise [LO1, 2, 3, 4]

How to Compete in the Sandwich Business

Form groups of three or four people, and appoint one member as the spokesperson who will communicate your findings to the whole class when called on by the instructor. Then discuss the following scenario:

You and your partners are thinking about opening a new kind of sandwich shop that will compete head-to-head with Subway and Thundercloud Subs. Because these chains have good brand-name recognition, it is vital that you find some source of competitive advantage for your new sandwich shop, and you are meeting to brainstorm ways of obtaining one.

1. Identify the product attributes that a typical sandwich shop customer most wants.
2. In what ways do you think you will be able to improve on the operations and processes of existing sandwich shops and achieve a competitive advantage through better (a) product quality, (b) efficiency, or (c) responsiveness to customers?

Be the Manager [LO1, 3]

How to Build Flat-Panel Displays

You are an operations management consultant who has been called in by the management team of a start-up company that will produce flat-screen displays for personal computer manufacturers like Dell and Compaq. The flat-screen display market is highly competitive; there is considerable pressure to reduce costs because prices fall rapidly due to competition. Also, personal computer makers are demanding ever higher quality and better features to please customers, and they demand delivery of your product to meet their production schedules. Managers want your advice on how to best meet these requirements. They are in the process of recruiting new workers and building a production facility.

Questions

1. What kinds of techniques discussed in the chapter can help these managers to increase efficiency?
2. In what ways can these managers go about developing a program to increase quality?
3. What critical lessons can these managers learn from operations management?

BusinessWeek Case in the News [LO1, 3, 4]

How Kiva Robots Help Zappos and Walgreens

In a warehouse at the headquarters of Kiva Systems in Woburn, Massachusetts, an ottoman-shaped robot slides beneath a four-shelf storage unit holding an assortment of consumer goods, lifts it, and navigates back to Mick Mountz, the start-up's founder and chief executive. Mountz grabs a box of Kellogg's Frosted Mini-Wheats off of the shelf and turns to put it in a shipping box. By the time he has turned back again, the robot is carrying the 8-foot-tall shelving unit away, and he is facing another stack of goods carried by a different robot.

This is Kiva's demo space, where Mountz shows potential customers what his wireless robotic fulfillment system can do. It's also where Kiva handles manufacturing, turning out 200 squat, orange robots—one model can hoist 1,000 pounds, while the other is strong enough for 3,000-pound pallets—every month. But you don't have to go to this Boston suburb to see Kiva's bots and pods, as the company calls the shelving units: They're already fast at work in warehouses run by Staples, Walgreens, Gap.com, and online retailer Zappos.

"It's exceeded all of our expectations, doubling the productivity of our pickers and cutting our energy costs in half," says Craig Adkins, vice president for fulfillment operations at Zappos, which began using Kiva nine months ago. Adkins won't say how much Zappos paid for its little helpers, but the average Kiva installation costs $5 million, with setups ranging from $1 million to $25 million now in the works.

Integrated Technologies

Mountz, now 43, first grappled with the challenge of efficient fulfillment as an executive at Webvan, the ill-fated online grocer that went under in 2001. Deciding robotics held the answer, he moved back to Boston, where he had studied mechanical engineering at Massachusetts Institute of Technology and earned his MBA at Harvard. To date, after two rounds of funding led by Bain Capital Ventures, Mountz's six-year-old company has raised more than $18 million, with annual sales topping $50 million.

Robots have been around a long time, of course. The newness of Kiva, which has 4 patents, with another 14 pending, is the way in which Mountz's team has integrated three technologies: WiFi, digital cameras, and low-cost servers capable of parallel processing. The servers work in real time, receiving orders, immediately dispatching robots to bring the required pods to the worker fulfilling the order, and then returning the pods to their storage locations. The robots receive their orders wirelessly, while using cameras to read navigational barcode stickers on the warehouse floor.

In combining these technologies, the 125-employee company is bringing a potentially breakthrough innovation to warehousing and distribution, which supply-chain research firm Armstrong & Associates estimates is a $37.5 billion-a-year business. "Kiva represents the first really 'new' technology in order fulfillment in years," wrote analysts at Aberdeen Group after touring the Zappos warehouse last year.

With plans for 1,000 bots in its distribution centers by summer, Walgreens will be Kiva's biggest customer. "I don't need to tell my competitors how much more productive it makes us," says Randy Lewis, senior vice president for supply chain and logistics at the Deerfield, Illinois, drugstore chain. "It's been a good investment."

Beyond the Conveyor Belt

Most of the 8,000 commercial warehouses in the United States depend on humans to stock the shelves with incoming goods and then retrieve them for outbound shipments. Those workers might use tow racks and forklifts, but the basic tasks haven't changed much in decades. Roughly 20% of U.S. warehouses are automated, meaning that after workers pull goods off of the shelves, they are put on conveyer belts, carousels, and/or other automatic sorting systems that move the products through the warehouse more efficiently.

That's the kind of system that Amazon.com employs—its distribution center in Fernley, Nevada, boasts nine miles of conveyer belts. And that's what Zappos installed in its Shepherdsville, Kentucky, distribution center in 2006. "We have static shelves, four stories high, 128 carousels, and 20,000 feet of conveyer belts," says Adkins. This loud, Rube Goldberg-like setup, which was state-of-the-art when Zappos bought it, covers 86 acres and enables workers to fulfill orders in anywhere from 48 minutes to three-and-a-half hours.

Off to the side in the Shepherdsville warehouse, 72 Kiva bots are in constant, quiet motion, carrying one of Zappos's 3,000 storage pods to or fro. Every six seconds, a worker takes an item from its pod and puts it into a shipping box, packing some 600 items an hour. While the initial cost of a Kiva system is roughly 10% to 20% more than a conveyer belt system, orders to the Kiva side of the warehouse are fulfilled within 12 minutes, at least four times faster.

But higher productivity isn't the only advantage, according to Adkins. Because the bots don't care about air conditioning or lighting, Zappos, based in Henderson, Nevada, has cut in half its utility costs per square foot. And although the company didn't lay off any workers, Adkins says that because of Kiva's efficiency, "as we continue to grow, we won't hire as many as we would have."

The fact that fulfillment is so critical to a company's business makes some resistant to try a new technology. "No one really likes revolutionary changes, especially in an industry like warehousing and distribution where people have been doing things a certain way for years," says Bruce Welty, CEO of Quiet Logistics in Andover, Massachusetts, a new third-party distribution and fulfillment service based entirely on the Kiva system. "But once they understand Kiva, it's a revelation."

Questions

1. How does Kiva Systems' robotic warehousing system affect a company's operations management process?
2. In what ways can the use of Kiva's robots improve a company's operating performance?

Source: Jessie Scanlon, "How Kiva Robots Help Zappos and Walgreens." Reprinted from *BusinessWeek* online, April 15, 2009, by special permission, copyright © 2009 by The McGraw-Hill Companies, Inc.

APPENDIX B Career Development

career The sum total of work-related experiences throughout a person's life.

Managers face several challenges both in the course of their own careers and in facilitating effective career management for their subordinates. A **career** is the sum total of work-related experiences throughout a person's life.[1] Careers encompass all of the different jobs people hold and the different organizations they work for. Careers are important to most people for at least two reasons. First, a career is a means to support oneself and one's loved ones, providing basic necessities and opportunities to pursue outside interests. Second, a career can be a source of personal fulfillment and meaning. Many managers find that making a difference in an organization and helping improve organizational efficiency and effectiveness are personally as well as financially rewarding.

Career development is a concern for managers both in terms of how their own careers unfold over time and how careers are managed in their organizations. In the development of their own careers, managers seek out challenging and interesting jobs that will develop their skills, lead to future opportunities, and allow them the opportunity to do the kind of work that will be personally meaningful. Similarly, in motivating and leading subordinates, managers need to be attuned to subordinates' career development. When careers (of both managers and rank-and-file employees) are effectively managed in an organization, the organization makes the best use of its human resources and employees tend to be motivated by, and satisfied with, their jobs.

Both employees and managers play an important role in effectively managing careers. For example, employees need to understand themselves, the kind of work they find motivating and fulfilling, and their own future aspirations for their careers. Employees then need to proactively seek the education, training, and kinds of work experiences that will help them to have the careers they want. Managers can motivate employees to make meaningful contributions to organizations by providing them with work assignments, experiences, training, and opportunities that contribute to employees' career development.[2]

Former eBay CEO Margaret (Meg) Whitman served in different posts for an array of companies, such as Stride Rite, FTD, Procter & Gamble, Disney, and Hasbro, before leading eBay from 1998 to 2008.

Types of Careers

While every person's career is unique, the different types of careers that people have fall into four general categories: steady-state careers, linear careers, spiral careers, and transitory careers.[3]

steady-state career A career consisting of the same kind of job during a large part of an individual's work life.

STEADY-STATE CAREERS A person with a steady-state career makes a one-time commitment to a certain kind of job that he or she maintains throughout his or her working life.[4] People with steady-state careers can become very skilled and expert at their work. A playwright who starts writing plays upon graduation from college and continues to write plays until retiring at age 70 has a steady-state career. So too does a dentist who maintains a steady dental practice upon graduation from dental school until retirement.

Some managers choose to have a steady-state career, holding the same kind of job during a large part of their work life, often becoming highly skilled and expert in what they do. A talented and creative graphic artist at a magazine publishing company, for example, may turn down promotions and other "opportunities" so that he can continue to work on designing attractive magazine spreads and covers, what he really likes to do. Similarly, some managers at Dillard's have steady-state careers as area sales managers because they enjoy the direct supervision of salespeople and the opportunity to "stay close to" customers.

linear career A career consisting of a sequence of jobs in which each new job entails additional responsibility, a greater impact on an organization, new skills, and upward movement in an organization's hierarchy.

LINEAR CAREERS A person who has a linear career moves through a sequence of jobs in which each new job entails additional responsibility, a greater impact on an organization, new skills, and upward movement in an organization's hierarchy.[5] The careers of many managers are linear, whether they stay with the same company or frequently switch organizations. A linear career traces a line of upward progress in the positions held.

Top managers in large corporations have moved through a series of lower-level positions in a variety of organizations before they became CEOs. Similarly, the assistant manager at the Red Lobster in College Station, Texas, started out in an entry-level position as a cashier. A linear career at Dillard's department stores may include the following sequencing of positions: executive trainee, area sales manager, assistant buyer, buyer, assistant store manager of merchandising, store manager, and divisional merchandise manager.[6] Managers' subordinates also may have linear careers, although some subordinates may have other types of careers.

spiral career A career consisting of a series of jobs that build on each other but tend to be fundamentally different.

SPIRAL CAREERS A person who has a spiral career tends to hold jobs that, while building off of each other, tend to be fundamentally different.[7] An associate professor of chemical engineering who leaves university teaching and research to head up the R&D department of a chemical company for 10 years and then leaves that position to found her own consulting firm has a spiral career. Similarly, a marketing manager in a large corporation who transfers to a job in public relations and then, after several years in that position, takes a job in an advertising firm has a spiral career. Those three jobs tend to be quite different from each other and do not necessarily entail increases in levels of responsibility.

transitory career A career in which a person changes jobs frequently and in which each job is different from the one that precedes it.

TRANSITORY CAREERS Some people change jobs frequently and each job is different from the one that precedes it; this kind of career is a transitory career.[8] A middle school teacher who leaves teaching after two years to work as an administrative assistant in a consumer products company for a year and then moves on to do carpentry work has a transitory career.

Career Stages

Every person's career is unique, but there are certain career stages that at least some people appear to progress through. Even if a person does not progress through all the stages, typically some of the stages are experienced. Each stage is associated with certain kinds of activities, hurdles, and potential opportunities. Regardless of the extent to which a person experiences each stage, and regardless of the exact number of the stages, about which there is some disagreement among researchers, here we discuss five stages (see Exhibit A) that are useful to understand and manage careers.[9]

These career stages apply to managers and nonmanagers alike. Thus, understanding the stages is important for managers both in terms of their own career development and in terms of the career development of their subordinates. Importantly, and increasingly, these career stages are experienced by most people in a variety of organizations. That is, while in the past, at least some people might have spent most of their careers in a single organization (or in just a few organizations), this is becoming increasingly rare. Rapid changes in technology, increased global competition, environmental uncertainty, outsourcing, and the layoffs many organizations resort to at one point or another to reduce costs are just some of the factors responsible for people's careers unfolding in a series of positions in a number of different organizations. Thus, a **boundaryless career,** or a career that is not attached or bound to a single organization, is becoming increasingly common, and most people have a variety of work experiences in multiple organizations throughout their careers.[10]

boundaryless career A career that is not attached to or bound to a single organization and consists of a variety of work experiences in multiple organizations.

PREPARATION FOR WORK During this stage, people decide what kind of career they desire and learn what qualifications and experiences they will need in order to pursue their chosen career.[11] Deciding on a career is no easy task and requires a certain degree of self-awareness and reflection. Sometimes people turn to professional career counselors to help them discover the kinds of careers in which they are most likely to be happy. A person's personality, values, attitudes, and moods impact the initial choice of a career.[12]

After choosing a career area, a person must gain the knowledge, skills, and education necessary to get a good starting position. A person may need an undergraduate or graduate degree or may be able to acquire on-the-job training through an apprenticeship program (common in Germany and some other countries).

ORGANIZATIONAL ENTRY At this stage, people are trying to find a good first job. The search entails identifying potential opportunities in a variety of ways (such as reading advertisements, attending career/job fairs, and mining personal contacts), finding out as much as possible about alternative positions, and making oneself an attractive candidate for prospective employers. Organizational entry is a more challenging stage for some kinds of careers than for others. An accounting major who knows she wants to work for an accounting firm already has a good idea of her opportunities and of how to make herself attractive to such firms. An English major who wants a career as an editor for a book publisher may find entry-level positions that seem a "good"

Exhibit A
Career Stages

start to such a career few and far between and may decide her best bet is to take a position as a sales representative for a well-respected publisher. More often than not, managers do not start out in management positions but rather begin their careers in an entry-level position in a department such as finance, marketing, or engineering.

EARLY CAREER The early-career stage begins after a person obtains a first job in his or her chosen career. At this stage there are two important steps: establishment and achievement. *Establishment* means learning the ropes of one's new job and organization–learning, for example, specific job responsibilities and duties, expected and desired behaviors, and important values of other organizational members such as the boss.[13] A person who has acquired the basic know-how to perform a job and function in the wider organization is ready to take the second step. *Achievement* means making one's mark, accomplishing something noteworthy, or making an important contribution to the job or organization.[14]

The achievement step can be crucial for future career progression. It is a means of demonstrating one's potential and standing out from others who are aspiring to become managers and are competing for desired positions. Downsizing and restructuring have reduced the number of management positions at many large companies, making it very important for individuals to manage the early-career stage effectively and thus increase their chances of advancement. By identifying where and how you can make a truly significant contribution to an organization, you can enhance your career prospects both inside and outside the organization.

mentor An experienced member of an organization who provides advice and guidance to a less experienced worker.

Some people find that seeking out and gaining the assistance of a mentor can be a valuable asset for the early-career and subsequent stages. A **mentor** is an experienced member of an organization who provides advice and guidance to a less experienced worker (the protégé, or mentee). The help that a mentor provides can range from advice about handling a tricky job assignment, dealing with a disagreement with a supervisor, and what kind of subsequent positions to strive for, to information about appropriate behavior and what to wear in various situations. Mentors often seek out protégés, but individuals also can be proactive and try to enlist the help of a potential mentor. Generally, especially good potential mentors are successful managers who have had a variety of experiences, genuinely desire to help junior colleagues, and are interpersonally compatible with the would-be protégé. Research has found that receiving help from a mentor is associated with an increase in pay, pay satisfaction, promotion, and feeling good about one's accomplishments.[15]

MIDCAREER The midcareer stage generally occurs when people have been in the workforce between 20 and 35 years. Different managers experience this stage in quite different ways. For some managers, the midcareer stage is a high point–a time of major accomplishment and success. For other managers, the midcareer stage is a letdown because their careers plateau.

career plateau A position from which the chances of being promoted or obtaining a more responsible job are slight.

Managers reach a **career plateau** when their chances of being promoted into a higher position in their current organizations or of obtaining a more responsible position in another organization dwindle.[16] Some managers inevitably will experience a career plateau because fewer and fewer managerial positions are available as one moves up an organization's hierarchy. In some organizations upper-level positions are especially scarce because of downsizing and restructuring.

Plateaued managers who are able to come to terms with their situation can continue to enjoy their work and make important contributions to their organization. Some plateaued managers, for example, welcome lateral moves, which give them the chance to learn new things and contribute in different ways to the organization. Some find being a mentor especially appealing and a chance to share their wisdom and make a difference for someone starting out in their field.

LATE CAREER This stage lasts as long as a person continues to work and has an active career. Many managers remain productive at this stage and show no signs of slowing down.

Effective Career Management

Managers face the challenge of ensuring not only that they have the kind of career they personally desire but also that effective career management exists for all employees in their organization. **Effective career management** means that at all levels in the organization there are well-qualified workers who can assume more responsible positions as needed and that as many members of the organization as possible are highly motivated and satisfied with their jobs and careers. As you might imagine, effectively managing careers in a whole organization is no easy task. At this point, however, it is useful to discuss two important foundations of effective career management in any organization: a commitment to ethical career practices and accommodations for workers' multidimensional lives.

effective career management Ensuring that at all levels in the organization there are well-qualified workers who can assume more responsible positions as needed.

COMMITMENT TO ETHICAL CAREER PRACTICES Ethical career practices are among the most important ingredients in effective career management and, at a basic level, rest on honesty, trust, and open communication among organizational members. Ethical career practices include basing promotions on performance, not on irrelevant considerations such as personal friendships and ties, and ensuring that diverse members of an organization receive the career opportunities they deserve. Supervisors must never abuse their power to make career decisions affecting others and must never behave unethically to advance their own careers. Managers at all levels must abide by and be committed to ethical career practices and actively demonstrate this commitment; they must communicate that violation of these practices will not be tolerated; and they must make sure that organizational members who feel that they were not ethically treated can communicate their concerns without fear of retaliation.

ACCOMMODATIONS FOR WORKERS' MULTIDIMENSIONAL LIVES Effectively managing careers also means being sensitive to and providing accommodations for the multiple demands that many organizational members face in their lives. The dual-career couple is now the norm rather than the exception, the number of single parents is at an all-time high, and more and more midcareer workers need to care for their elderly and infirm parents. By limiting unnecessary moves and travel, adopting flexible work arrangements and schedules, providing on-site day care, and allowing workers to take time off to care for children or elderly parents, managers make it possible for workers to have satisfying and productive careers while fulfilling their other commitments.

Careers are as important for managers' subordinates as they are for managers themselves. Understanding the many issues involved in effectively managing careers helps ensure that both managers and their subordinates will have the kinds of careers they want while helping an organization achieve its goals.

Glossary

A

ACHIEVEMENT ORIENTATION A worldview that values assertiveness, performance, success, and competition.

ADMINISTRATIVE MANAGEMENT The study of how to create an organizational structure and control system that leads to high efficiency and effectiveness.

ADMINISTRATIVE MODEL An approach to decision making that explains why decision making is inherently uncertain and risky and why managers usually make satisfactory rather than optimum decisions.

AGREEABLENESS The tendency to get along well with other people.

AMBIGUOUS INFORMATION Information that can be interpreted in multiple and often conflicting ways.

APPLICATIONS SOFTWARE Software designed for a specific task or use.

ARBITRATOR A third-party negotiator who can impose what he or she thinks is a fair solution to a conflict that both parties are obligated to abide by.

ARTIFICIAL INTELLIGENCE Behavior performed by a machine that, if performed by a human being, would be called "intelligent."

ATTITUDE A collection of feelings and beliefs.

ATTRACTION-SELECTION-ATTRITION (ASA) FRAMEWORK A model that explains how personality may influence organizational culture.

AUTHORITY The power to hold people accountable for their actions and to make decisions concerning the use of organizational resources.

B

B2B MARKETPLACE An Internet-based trading platform set up to connect buyers and sellers in an industry.

B2B NETWORK STRUCTURE A series of global strategic alliances that an organization creates with suppliers, manufacturers, and/or distributors to produce and market a product.

BARRIERS TO ENTRY Factors that make it difficult and costly for an organization to enter a particular task environment or industry.

BEHAVIORAL MANAGEMENT The study of how managers should behave to motivate employees and encourage them to perform at high levels and be committed to the achievement of organizational goals.

BENCHMARKING The process of comparing one company's performance on specific dimensions with the performance of other, high-performing organizations.

BOTTOM-UP CHANGE A gradual or evolutionary approach to change in which managers at all levels work together to develop a detailed plan for change.

BOUNDARY SPANNING Interacting with individuals and groups outside the organization to obtain valuable information from the environment.

BOUNDARYLESS CAREER A career that is not attached to or bound to a single organization and consists of a variety of work experiences in multiple organizations.

BOUNDARYLESS ORGANIZATION An organization whose members are linked by computers, faxes, computer-aided design systems, and video teleconferencing and who rarely, if ever, see one another face-to-face.

BOUNDED RATIONALITY Cognitive limitations that constrain one's ability to interpret, process, and act on information.

BRAND LOYALTY Customers' preference for the products of organizations currently existing in the task environment.

BUREAUCRACY A formal system of organization and administration designed to ensure efficiency and effectiveness.

BUREAUCRATIC CONTROL Control of behavior by means of a comprehensive system of rules and standard operating procedures.

BUSINESS-LEVEL PLAN Divisional managers' decisions pertaining to divisions' long-term goals, overall strategy, and structure.

BUSINESS-LEVEL STRATEGY A plan that indicates how a division intends to compete against its rivals in an industry.

BUSINESS-TO-BUSINESS (B2B) COMMERCE Trade that takes place between companies using IT and the Internet to link and coordinate the value chains of different companies.

BUSINESS-TO-CUSTOMER (B2C) COMMERCE Trade that takes place between a company and individual customers using IT and the Internet.

C

CAFETERIA-STYLE BENEFIT PLAN A plan from which employees can choose the benefits that they want.

CAREER The sum total of work-related experiences throughout a person's life.

CAREER PLATEAU A position from which the chances of being promoted or obtaining a more responsible job are slight.

CENTRALIZATION The concentration of authority at the top of the managerial hierarchy.

CHARISMATIC LEADER An enthusiastic, self-confident leader who is able to clearly communicate his or her vision of how good things could be.

CLAN CONTROL The control exerted on individuals and groups in an organization by shared values, norms, standards of behavior, and expectations.

CLASSICAL DECISION-MAKING MODEL A prescriptive approach to decision making based on the assumption that the decision maker can identify and evaluate all possible alternatives and their consequences and rationally choose the most appropriate course of action.

COERCIVE POWER The ability of a manager to punish others.

COLLECTIVE BARGAINING Negotiations between labor unions and managers to resolve conflicts and disputes about issues such as working hours, wages, benefits, working conditions, and job security.

COLLECTIVISM A worldview that values subordination of the individual to the goals of the group and adherence to the principle that people should be judged by their contribution to the group.

COMMAND GROUP A group composed of subordinates who report to the same supervisor; also called department or unit.

COMMUNICATION The sharing of information between two or more individuals or groups to reach a common understanding.

COMMUNICATION NETWORKS The pathways along which information flows in groups and teams and throughout the organization.

COMPETITIVE ADVANTAGE The ability of one organization to outperform other organizations because it produces desired goods or services more efficiently and effectively than they do.

COMPETITORS Organizations that produce goods and services that are similar to a particular organization's goods and services.

CONCENTRATION ON A SINGLE INDUSTRY Reinvesting a company's profits to strengthen its competitive position in its current industry.

CONCEPTUAL SKILLS The ability to analyze and diagnose a situation and to distinguish between cause and effect.

CONCURRENT CONTROL Control that gives managers immediate feedback on how efficiently inputs are being transformed into outputs so that managers can correct problems as they arise.

CONSCIENTIOUSNESS The tendency to be careful, scrupulous, and persevering.

CONSIDERATION Behavior indicating that a manager trusts, respects, and cares about subordinates.

CONTINGENCY THEORY The idea that the organizational structures and control systems managers choose depend on–are contingent on–characteristics of the external environment in which the organization operates.

CONTROL SYSTEMS Formal target-setting, monitoring, evaluation, and feedback systems that provide managers with information about how well the organization's strategy and structure are working.

CONTROLLING Evaluating how well an organization is achieving its goals and taking action to maintain or improve performance; one of the four principal tasks of management.

CORE COMPETENCY The specific set of departmental skills, knowledge, and experience that allows one organization to outperform another.

CORE MEMBERS The members of a team who bear primary responsibility for the success of a project and who stay with a project from inception to completion.

CORPORATE-LEVEL PLAN Top management's decisions pertaining to the organization's mission, overall strategy, and structure.

CORPORATE-LEVEL STRATEGY A plan that indicates in which industries and national markets an organization intends to compete.

CREATIVITY A decision maker's ability to discover original and novel ideas that lead to feasible alternative courses of action.

CROSS-FUNCTIONAL TEAM A group of managers brought together from different departments to perform organizational tasks.

CUSTOMER RELATIONSHIP MANAGEMENT (CRM) A technique that uses IT to develop an ongoing relationship with customers to maximize the value an organization can deliver to them over time.

CUSTOMERS Individuals and groups that buy the goods and services that an organization produces.

D

DATA Raw, unsummarized, and unanalyzed facts.

DECENTRALIZING AUTHORITY Giving lower-level managers and nonmanagerial employees the right to make important decisions about how to use organizational resources.

DECISION MAKING The process by which managers respond to opportunities and threats by analyzing options and making determinations about specific organizational goals and courses of action.

DECISION SUPPORT SYSTEM An interactive computer-based management information system that managers can use to make nonroutine decisions.

DECODING Interpreting and trying to make sense of a message.

DEFENSIVE APPROACH Companies and their managers behave ethically to the degree that they stay within the law and abide strictly with legal requirements.

DELPHI TECHNIQUE A decision-making technique in which group members do not meet face-to-face but respond in writing to questions posed by the group leader.

DEMOGRAPHIC FORCES Outcomes of changes in, or changing attitudes toward, the characteristics of a population, such as age, gender, ethnic origin, race, sexual orientation, and social class.

DEPARTMENT A group of people who work together and possess similar skills or use the same knowledge, tools, or techniques to perform their jobs.

DEVELOPMENT Building the knowledge and skills of organizational members so that they are prepared to take on new responsibilities and challenges.

DEVELOPMENTAL CONSIDERATION Behavior a leader engages in to support and encourage followers and help them develop and grow on the job.

DEVIL'S ADVOCACY Critical analysis of a preferred alternative, made in response to challenges raised by a group member who, playing the role of devil's advocate, defends unpopular or opposing alternatives for the sake of argument.

DIFFERENTIATION STRATEGY Distinguishing an organization's products from the products of competitors on dimensions such as product design, quality, or after-sales service.

DISTRIBUTIVE JUSTICE A moral principle calling for the distribution of pay raises, promotions, and other organizational resources to be based on meaningful contributions that individuals have made and not on personal characteristics over which they have no control.

DISTRIBUTORS Organizations that help other organizations sell their goods or services to customers.

DIVERSIFICATION Expanding a company's business operations into a new industry in order to produce new kinds of valuable goods or services.

DIVERSITY Differences among people in age, gender, race, ethnicity, religion, sexual orientation, socioeconomic background, and capabilities/disabilities.

DIVISIONAL STRUCTURE An organizational structure composed of separate business units within which are the functions that work together to produce a specific product for a specific customer.

DIVISION OF LABOR Splitting the work to be performed into particular tasks and assigning tasks to individual workers.

E

E-COMMERCE Trade that takes place between companies, and between companies and individual customers, using IT and the Internet.

ECONOMIC FORCES Interest rates, inflation, unemployment, economic growth, and other factors that affect the general health and well-being of a nation or the regional economy of an organization.

ECONOMIES OF SCALE Cost advantages associated with large operations.

EFFECTIVE CAREER MANAGEMENT Ensuring that at all levels in the organization there are well-qualified workers who can assume more responsible positions as needed.

EFFECTIVENESS A measure of the appropriateness of the goals an organization is pursuing and of the degree to which the organization achieves those goals.

EFFICIENCY A measure of how well or how productively resources are used to achieve a goal.

EMOTIONAL INTELLIGENCE The ability to understand and manage one's own moods and emotions and the moods and emotions of other people.

EMOTIONS Intense, relatively short-lived feelings.

EMPLOYEE STOCK OPTION A financial instrument that entitles the bearer to buy shares of an organization's stock at a certain price during a certain period of time or under certain conditions.

EMPOWERMENT The expansion of employees' knowledge, tasks, and decision-making responsibilities.

ENCODING Translating a message into understandable symbols or language.

ENTERPRISE RESOURCE PLANNING (ERP) SYSTEMS Multimodule application software packages that coordinate the functional activities necessary to move products from the product design stage to the final customer stage.

ENTREPRENEUR An individual who notices opportunities and decides how to mobilize the resources necessary to produce new and improved goods and services.

ENTREPRENEURSHIP The mobilization of resources to take advantage of an opportunity to provide customers with new or improved goods and services.

EQUAL EMPLOYMENT OPPORTUNITY (EEO) The equal right of all citizens to the opportunity to obtain employment regardless of their gender, age, race, country of origin, religion, or disabilities.

EQUITY The justice, impartiality, and fairness to which all organizational members are entitled.

EQUITY THEORY A theory of motivation that focuses on people's perceptions of the fairness of their work outcomes relative to their work inputs.

ETHICAL DILEMMA The quandary people find themselves in when they have to decide if they should act in a way that might help another person or group even though doing so might go against their own self-interest.

ETHICS The inner guiding moral principles, values, and beliefs that people use to analyze or interpret a situation and then decide what is the "right" or appropriate way to behave.

ETHICS OMBUDSMAN A manager responsible for communicating and teaching ethical standards to all employees and monitoring their conformity to those standards.

EXECUTIVE SUPPORT SYSTEM A sophisticated version of a decision support system that is designed to meet the needs of top managers.

EXPECTANCY In expectancy theory, a perception about the extent to which effort results in a certain level of performance.

EXPECTANCY THEORY The theory that motivation will be high when workers believe that high levels of effort lead to high performance and high performance leads to the attainment of desired outcomes.

EXPERT POWER Power that is based on the special knowledge, skills, and expertise that a leader possesses.

EXPERT SYSTEM A management information system that employs human knowledge, embedded in a computer, to solve problems that ordinarily require human expertise.

EXPORTING Making products at home and selling them abroad.

EXTERNAL LOCUS OF CONTROL The tendency to locate responsibility for one's fate in outside forces and to believe that one's own behavior has little impact on outcomes.

EXTINCTION Curtailing the performance of dysfunctional behaviors by eliminating whatever is reinforcing them.

EXTRAVERSION The tendency to experience positive emotions and moods and to feel good about oneself and the rest of the world.

EXTRINSICALLY MOTIVATED BEHAVIOR Behavior that is performed to acquire material or social rewards or to avoid punishment.

F

FACILITIES LAYOUT The strategy of designing the machine–worker interface to increase operating system efficiency.

FEEDBACK CONTROL Control that gives managers information about customers' reactions to goods and services so that corrective action can be taken if necessary.

FEEDFORWARD CONTROL Control that allows managers to anticipate problems before they arise.

FILTERING Withholding part of a message because of the mistaken belief that the receiver does not need or will not want the information.

FIRST-LINE MANAGER A manager who is responsible for the daily supervision of nonmanagerial employees.

FLEXIBLE MANUFACTURING The set of techniques that attempt to reduce the costs associated with the product assembly process or the way services are delivered to customers.

FOCUSED DIFFERENTIATION STRATEGY Serving only one segment of the overall market and trying to be the most differentiated organization serving that segment.

FOCUSED LOW-COST STRATEGY Serving only one segment of the overall market and trying to be the lowest-cost organization serving that segment.

FOLKWAYS The routine social conventions of everyday life.

FORMAL APPRAISAL An appraisal conducted at a set time during the year and based on performance dimensions and measures that were specified in advance.

FORMAL GROUP A group that managers establish to achieve organizational goals.

FRANCHISING Selling to a foreign organization the rights to use a brand name and operating know-how in return for a lump-sum payment and a share of the profits.

FREE-TRADE DOCTRINE The idea that if each country specializes in the production of the goods and services that it can produce most efficiently, this will make the best use of global resources.

FRIENDSHIP GROUP An informal group composed of employees who enjoy one another's company and socialize with one another.

FUNCTIONAL STRUCTURE An organizational structure composed of all the departments that an organization requires to produce its goods or services.

FUNCTIONAL-LEVEL PLAN Functional managers' decisions pertaining to the goals that they propose to pursue to help the division attain its business-level goals.

FUNCTIONAL-LEVEL STRATEGY A plan of action to improve the ability of each of an organization's functions to perform its task-specific activities in ways that add value to an organization's goods and services.

G

GATEKEEPING Deciding what information to allow into the organization and what information to keep out.

GENERAL ENVIRONMENT The wide-ranging global, economic, technological, sociocultural, demographic, political, and legal forces that affect an organization and its task environment.

GEOGRAPHIC STRUCTURE An organizational structure in which each region of a country or area of the world is served by a self-contained division.

GLASS CEILING A metaphor alluding to the invisible barriers that prevent minorities and women from being promoted to top corporate positions.

GLOBAL ENVIRONMENT The set of global forces and conditions that operate beyond an organization's boundaries but affect a manager's ability to acquire and utilize resources.

GLOBAL ORGANIZATION An organization that operates and competes in more than one country.

GLOBAL OUTSOURCING The purchase of inputs from overseas suppliers or the production of inputs abroad to lower production costs and improve product quality or design.

GLOBAL STRATEGY Selling the same standardized product and using the same basic marketing approach in each national market.

GLOBALIZATION The set of specific and general forces that work together to integrate and connect economic, political, and social systems *across* countries, cultures, or geographical regions so that nations become increasingly interdependent and similar.

GOAL-SETTING THEORY A theory that focuses on identifying the types of goals that are most effective in producing high levels of motivation and performance and explaining why goals have these effects.

GROUP Two or more people who interact with each other to accomplish certain goals or meet certain needs.

GROUP COHESIVENESS The degree to which members are attracted to or loyal to their group.

GROUP DECISION SUPPORT SYSTEM An executive support system that links top managers so that they can function as a team.

GROUP NORMS Shared guidelines or rules for behavior that most group members follow.

GROUP ROLE A set of behaviors and tasks that a member of a group is expected to perform because of his or her position in the group.

GROUPTHINK A pattern of faulty and biased decision making that occurs in groups whose members strive for agreement among themselves at the expense of accurately assessing information relevant to a decision.

GROUPWARE Computer software that enables members of groups and teams to share information with one another.

H

HAWTHORNE EFFECT The finding that a manager's behavior or leadership approach can affect workers' level of performance.

HERZBERG'S MOTIVATOR-HYGIENE THEORY A need theory that distinguishes between motivator needs (related to the nature of the work itself) and hygiene needs (related to the physical and psychological context in which the work is performed) and proposes that motivator needs must be met for motivation and job satisfaction to be high.

HIERARCHY OF AUTHORITY An organization's chain of command, specifying the relative authority of each manager.

HOSTILE WORK ENVIRONMENT SEXUAL HARASSMENT Telling lewd jokes, displaying pornography, making sexually oriented remarks about someone's personal appearance, and other sex-related actions that make the work environment unpleasant.

HUMAN RELATIONS MOVEMENT A management approach that advocates the idea that supervisors should receive behavioral training to manage subordinates in ways that elicit their cooperation and increase their productivity.

HUMAN RESOURCE MANAGEMENT (HRM) Activities that managers engage in to attract and retain employees and to ensure that they perform at a high level and contribute to the accomplishment of organizational goals.

HUMAN RESOURCE PLANNING Activities that managers engage in to forecast their current and future needs for human resources.

HUMAN SKILLS The ability to understand, alter, lead, and control the behavior of other individuals and groups.

HYBRID STRUCTURE The structure of a large organization that has many divisions and simultaneously uses many different organizational structures.

HYPERCOMPETITION Permanent, ongoing, intense competition brought about in an industry by advancing technology or changing customer tastes.

I

ILLUSION OF CONTROL A source of cognitive bias resulting from the tendency to overestimate one's own ability to control activities and events.

IMPORTING Selling products at home that are made abroad.

INCREMENTAL PRODUCT INNOVATION The gradual improvement and refinement to existing products that occurs over time as existing technologies are perfected.

INDIVIDUAL ETHICS Personal standards and values that determine how people view their responsibilities to others and how they should act in situations when their own self-interests are at stake.

INDIVIDUALISM A worldview that values individual freedom and self-expression and adherence to the principle that people should be judged by their individual achievements rather than by their social background.

INEQUITY Lack of fairness.

INFORMAL APPRAISAL An unscheduled appraisal of ongoing progress and areas for improvement.

INFORMAL GROUP A group that managers or nonmanagerial employees form to help achieve their own goals or meet their own needs.

INFORMAL ORGANIZATION The system of behavioral rules and norms that emerge in a group.

INFORMATION Data that are organized in a meaningful fashion.

INFORMATION DISTORTION Changes in the meaning of a message as the message passes through a series of senders and receivers.

INFORMATION OVERLOAD The potential for important information to be ignored or overlooked while tangential information receives attention.

INFORMATION RICHNESS The amount of information that a communication medium can carry and the extent to which the medium enables the sender and receiver to reach a common understanding.

INFORMATION SYSTEM A system for acquiring, organizing, storing, manipulating, and transmitting information.

INFORMATION TECHNOLOGY The set of methods or techniques for acquiring, organizing, storing, manipulating, and transmitting information.

INITIATING STRUCTURE Behavior that managers engage in to ensure that work gets done, subordinates perform their jobs acceptably, and the organization is efficient and effective.

INITIATIVE The ability to act on one's own, without direction from a superior.

INNOVATION The process of creating new or improved goods and services or developing better ways to produce or provide them.

INPUT Anything a person contributes to his or her job or organization.

INSTRUMENTAL VALUE A mode of conduct that an individual seeks to follow.

INSTRUMENTALITY In expectancy theory, a perception about the extent to which performance results in the attainment of outcomes.

INTEGRATING MECHANISMS Organizing tools that managers can use to increase communication and coordination among functions and divisions.

INTELLECTUAL STIMULATION Behavior a leader engages in to make followers be aware of problems and view these problems in new ways, consistent with the leader's vision.

INTEREST GROUP An informal group composed of employees seeking to achieve a common goal related to their membership in an organization.

INTERNAL LOCUS OF CONTROL The tendency to locate responsibility for one's fate within oneself.

INTERNET A global system of computer networks.

INTRANET A companywide system of computer networks.

INTRAPRENEUR A manager, scientist, or researcher who works inside an organization and notices opportunities to develop new or improved products and better ways to make them.

INTRINSICALLY MOTIVATED BEHAVIOR Behavior that is performed for its own sake.

INTUITION Feelings, beliefs, and hunches that come readily to mind, require little effort and information gathering, and result in on-the-spot decisions.

INVENTORY The stock of raw materials, inputs, and component parts that an organization has on hand at a particular time.

J

JARGON Specialized language that members of an occupation, group, or organization develop to facilitate communication among themselves.

JOB ANALYSIS Identifying the tasks, duties, and responsibilities that make up a job and the knowledge, skills, and abilities needed to perform the job.

JOB DESIGN The process by which managers decide how to divide tasks into specific jobs.

JOB ENLARGEMENT Increasing the number of different tasks in a given job by changing the division of labor.

JOB ENRICHMENT Increasing the degree of responsibility a worker has over his or her job.

JOB SATISFACTION The collection of feelings and beliefs that managers have about their current jobs.

JOB SIMPLIFICATION The process of reducing the number of tasks that each worker performs.

JOB SPECIALIZATION The process by which a division of labor occurs as different workers specialize in different tasks over time.

JOINT VENTURE A strategic alliance among two or more companies that agree to jointly establish and share the ownership of a new business.

JUST-IN-TIME (JIT) INVENTORY SYSTEM A system in which parts or supplies arrive at an organization when they are needed, not before.

JUSTICE RULE An ethical decision is a decision that distributes benefits and harms among people and groups in a fair, equitable, or impartial way.

K

KNOWLEDGE MANAGEMENT SYSTEM A company-specific virtual information system that systematizes the knowledge of its employees and facilitates the sharing and integrating of their expertise.

L

LABOR RELATIONS The activities that managers engage in to ensure that they have effective working relationships with the labor unions that represent their employees' interests.

LATERAL MOVE A job change that entails no major changes in responsibility or authority levels.

LEADER An individual who is able to exert influence over other people to help achieve group or organizational goals.

LEADER–MEMBER RELATIONS The extent to which followers like, trust, and are loyal to their leader; a determinant of how favorable a situation is for leading.

LEADERSHIP The process by which an individual exerts influence over other people and inspires, motivates, and directs their activities to help achieve group or organizational goals.

LEADERSHIP SUBSTITUTE A characteristic of a subordinate or of a situation or context that acts in place of the influence of a leader and makes leadership unnecessary.

LEADING Articulating a clear vision and energizing and enabling organizational members so that they understand the part they play in achieving organizational goals; one of the four principal tasks of management.

LEARNING A relatively permanent change in knowledge or behavior that results from practice or experience.

LEARNING ORGANIZATION An organization in which managers try to maximize the ability of individuals and groups to think and behave creatively and thus maximize the potential for organizational learning to take place.

LEARNING THEORIES Theories that focus on increasing employee motivation and performance by linking the outcomes that employees receive to the performance of desired behaviors and the attainment of goals.

LEGITIMATE POWER The authority that a manager has by virtue of his or her position in an organization's hierarchy.

LICENSING Allowing a foreign organization to take charge of manufacturing and distributing a product in its country or world region in return for a negotiated fee.

LINEAR CAREER A career consisting of a sequence of jobs in which each new job entails additional responsibility, a greater impact on an organization, new skills, and upward movement in an organization's hierarchy.

LINE MANAGER Someone in the direct line or chain of command who has formal authority over people and resources at lower levels.

LINE OF AUTHORITY The chain of command extending from the top to the bottom of an organization.

LONG-TERM ORIENTATION A worldview that values thrift and persistence in achieving goals.

LOW-COST STRATEGY Driving the organization's costs down below the costs of its rivals.

M

MANAGEMENT The planning, organizing, leading, and controlling of human and other resources to achieve organizational goals efficiently and effectively.

MANAGEMENT BY OBJECTIVES (MBO) A goal-setting process in which a manager and each of his or her subordinates negotiate specific goals and objectives for the subordinate to achieve and then periodically evaluate the extent to which the subordinate is achieving those goals.

MANAGEMENT BY WANDERING AROUND A face-to-face communication technique in which a manager walks around a work area and talks informally with employees about issues and concerns.

MANAGEMENT INFORMATION SYSTEM (MIS) A specific form of IT that managers utilize to generate the specific, detailed information they need to perform their roles effectively.

MARKET STRUCTURE An organizational structure in which each kind of customer is served by a self-contained division; also called *customer structure.*

MASLOW'S HIERARCHY OF NEEDS An arrangement of five basic needs that, according to Maslow, motivate behavior. Maslow proposed that the lowest level of unmet needs is the prime motivator and that only one level of needs is motivational at a time.

MATRIX STRUCTURE An organizational structure that simultaneously groups people and resources by function and by product.

MECHANISTIC STRUCTURE An organizational structure in which authority is centralized, tasks and rules are clearly specified, and employees are closely supervised.

MEDIUM The pathway through which an encoded message is transmitted to a receiver.

MENTORING A process by which an experienced member of an organization (the mentor) provides advice and guidance to a less experienced member (the protégé) and helps the less experienced member learn how to advance in the organization and in his or her career.

MERIT PAY PLAN A compensation plan that bases pay on performance.

MESSAGE The information that a sender wants to share.

MIDDLE MANAGER A manager who supervises first-line managers and is responsible for finding the best way to use resources to achieve organizational goals.

MISSION STATEMENT A broad declaration of an organization's purpose that identifies the organization's products and customers and distinguishes the organization from its competitors.

MOOD A feeling or state of mind.

MORAL RIGHTS RULE An ethical decision is one that best maintains and protects the fundamental or inalienable rights and privileges of the people affected by it.

MORES Norms that are considered to be central to the functioning of society and to social life.

MOTIVATION Psychological forces that determine the direction of a person's behavior in an organization, a person's level of effort, and a person's level of persistence.

MULTIDOMESTIC STRATEGY Customizing products and marketing strategies to specific national conditions.

N

NATIONAL CULTURE The set of values that a society considers important and the norms of behavior that are approved or sanctioned in that society.

NEED A requirement or necessity for survival and well-being.

NEED FOR ACHIEVEMENT The extent to which an individual has a strong desire to perform challenging tasks well and to meet personal standards for excellence.

NEED FOR AFFILIATION The extent to which an individual is concerned about establishing and maintaining good interpersonal relations, being liked, and having other people get along.

NEED FOR POWER The extent to which an individual desires to control or influence others.

NEED THEORIES Theories of motivation that focus on what needs people are trying to satisfy at work and what outcomes will satisfy those needs.

NEEDS ASSESSMENT An assessment of which employees need training or development and what type of skills or knowledge they need to acquire.

NEGATIVE AFFECTIVITY The tendency to experience negative emotions and moods, to feel distressed, and to be critical of oneself and others.

NEGATIVE REINFORCEMENT Eliminating or removing undesired outcomes when people perform organizationally functional behaviors.

NETWORKING The exchange of information through a group or network of interlinked computers.

NETWORK STRUCTURE A series of strategic alliances that an organization creates with suppliers, manufacturers, and distributors to produce and market a product.

NOISE Anything that hampers any stage of the communication process.

NOMINAL GROUP TECHNIQUE A decision-making technique in which group members write down ideas and solutions, read their suggestions to the whole group, and discuss and then rank the alternatives.

NONPROGRAMMED DECISION MAKING Nonroutine decision making that occurs in response to unusual, unpredictable opportunities and threats.

NONVERBAL COMMUNICATION The encoding of messages by means of facial expressions, body language, and styles of dress.

NORMS Unwritten, informal codes of conduct that prescribe how people should act in particular situations and are considered important by most members of a group or organization.

NURTURING ORIENTATION A worldview that values the quality of life, warm personal friendships, and services and care for the weak.

OBJECTIVE APPRAISAL An appraisal that is based on facts and is likely to be numerical.

OCCUPATIONAL ETHICS Standards that govern how members of a profession, trade, or craft should conduct themselves when performing work-related activities.

ON-THE-JOB TRAINING Training that takes place in the work setting as employees perform their job tasks.

OPENNESS TO EXPERIENCE The tendency to be original, have broad interests, be open to a wide range of stimuli, be daring, and take risks.

OPERANT CONDITIONING THEORY The theory that people learn to perform behaviors that lead to desired consequences and learn not to perform behaviors that lead to undesired consequences.

OPERATING BUDGET A budget that states how managers intend to use organizational resources to achieve organizational goals.

OPERATING SYSTEM SOFTWARE Software that tells computer hardware how to run.

OPERATIONS INFORMATION SYSTEM A management information system that gathers, organizes, and summarizes comprehensive data in a form that managers can use in their nonroutine coordinating, controlling, and decision-making tasks.

OPERATIONS MANAGEMENT The management of any aspect of the production system that transforms inputs into finished goods and services.

OPERATIONS MANAGER A manager who is responsible for managing an organization's production system and for determining where operating improvements might be made.

OPTIMUM DECISION The most appropriate decision in light of what managers believe to be the most desirable future consequences for the organization.

ORDER The methodical arrangement of positions to provide the organization with the greatest benefit and to provide employees with career opportunities.

ORGANIC STRUCTURE An organizational structure in which authority is decentralized to middle and first-line managers and tasks and roles are left ambiguous to encourage employees to cooperate and respond quickly to the unexpected.

ORGANIZATION A collection of people who work together and coordinate their actions to achieve a wide variety of goals or desired future outcomes.

ORGANIZATION CHANGE The movement of an organization away from its present state and toward some desired future state to increase its efficiency and effectiveness.

ORGANIZATIONAL BEHAVIOR The study of factors that affect how individuals and groups respond to and act in organizations.

ORGANIZATIONAL BEHAVIOR MODIFICATION (OB MOD) The systematic application of operant conditioning techniques to promote the performance of organizationally functional behaviors and discourage the performance of dysfunctional behaviors.

ORGANIZATIONAL CITIZENSHIP BEHAVIORS (OCBs) Behaviors that are not required of organizational members but that contribute to and are necessary for organizational efficiency, effectiveness, and competitive advantage.

ORGANIZATIONAL COMMITMENT The collection of feelings and beliefs that managers have about their organization as a whole.

ORGANIZATIONAL CULTURE The shared set of beliefs, expectations, values, norms, and work routines that influence the ways in which individuals, groups, and teams interact with one another and cooperate to achieve organizational goals.

ORGANIZATIONAL DESIGN The process by which managers make specific organizing choices that result in a particular kind of organizational structure.

ORGANIZATIONAL ENVIRONMENT The set of forces and conditions that operate beyond an organization's boundaries but affect a manager's ability to acquire and utilize resources.

ORGANIZATIONAL ETHICS The guiding practices and beliefs through which a particular company and its managers view their responsibility toward their stakeholders.

ORGANIZATIONAL LEARNING The process through which managers seek to improve employees' desire and ability to understand and manage the organization and its task environment.

ORGANIZATIONAL PERFORMANCE A measure of how efficiently and effectively a manager uses resources to satisfy customers and achieve organizational goals.

ORGANIZATIONAL SOCIALIZATION The process by which newcomers learn an organization's values and norms and acquire the work behaviors necessary to perform jobs effectively.

ORGANIZATIONAL STRUCTURE A formal system of task and reporting relationships that coordinates and motivates organizational members so that they work together to achieve organizational goals.

ORGANIZING Structuring working relationships in a way that allows organizational members to work together to achieve organizational goals; one of the four principal tasks of management.

OUTCOME Anything a person gets from a job or organization.

OUTSOURCE To use outside suppliers and manufacturers to produce goods and services.

OUTSOURCING Contracting with another company, usually abroad, to have it perform an activity the organization previously performed itself.

OVERPAYMENT INEQUITY The inequity that exists when a person perceives that his or her own outcome–input ratio is greater than the ratio of a referent.

P

PATH–GOAL THEORY A contingency model of leadership proposing that leaders can motivate subordinates by identifying their desired outcomes, rewarding them for high performance and the attainment of work goals with these desired outcomes, and clarifying for them the paths leading to the attainment of work goals.

PAY LEVEL The relative position of an organization's pay incentives in comparison with those of other organizations in the same industry employing similar kinds of workers.

PAY STRUCTURE The arrangement of jobs into categories reflecting their relative importance to the organization and its goals, levels of skill required, and other characteristics.

PERCEPTION The process through which people select, organize, and interpret what they see, hear, touch, smell, and taste to give meaning and order to the world around them.

PERFORMANCE APPRAISAL The evaluation of employees' job performance and contributions to their organization.

PERFORMANCE FEEDBACK The process through which managers share performance appraisal information with subordinates, give subordinates an opportunity to reflect on their own performance, and develop, with subordinates, plans for the future.

PERSONALITY TRAITS Enduring tendencies to feel, think, and act in certain ways.

PLANNING Identifying and selecting appropriate goals and courses of action; one of the four principal tasks of management.

POLITICAL AND LEGAL FORCES Outcomes of changes in laws and regulations, such as the deregulation of industries, the privatization of organizations, and the increased emphasis on environmental protection.

POOLED TASK INTERDEPENDENCE The task interdependence that exists when group members make separate and independent contributions to group performance.

POSITION POWER The amount of legitimate, reward, and coercive power that a leader has by virtue of his or her position in an organization; a determinant of how favorable a situation is for leading.

POSITIVE REINFORCEMENT Giving people outcomes they desire when they perform organizationally functional behaviors.

POTENTIAL COMPETITORS Organizations that presently are not in a task environment but could enter if they so choose.

POWER DISTANCE The degree to which societies accept the idea that inequalities in the power and well-being of their citizens are due to differences in individuals' physical and intellectual capabilities and heritage.

PRACTICAL RULE An ethical decision is one that a manager has no reluctance about communicating to people outside the company because the typical person in a society would think it is acceptable.

PROACTIVE APPROACH Companies and their managers actively embrace socially responsible behavior, going out of their way to learn about the needs of different stakeholder groups and utilizing organizational resources to promote the interests of all stakeholders.

PROCEDURAL JUSTICE A moral principle calling for the use of fair procedures to determine how to distribute outcomes to organizational members.

PROCESS REENGINEERING The fundamental rethinking and radical redesign of business processes to achieve dramatic improvement in critical measures of performance such as cost, quality, service, and speed.

PRODUCT CHAMPION A manager who takes "ownership" of a project and provides the leadership and vision that take a product from the idea stage to the final customer.

PRODUCT DEVELOPMENT The management of the value chain activities involved in bringing new or improved goods and services to the market.

PRODUCT LIFE CYCLE The way demand for a product changes in a predictable pattern over time.

PRODUCT STRUCTURE An organizational structure in which each product line or business is handled by a self-contained division.

PRODUCT TEAM STRUCTURE An organizational structure in which employees are permanently assigned to a cross-functional team and report only to the product team manager or to one of his or her direct subordinates.

PRODUCTION BLOCKING A loss of productivity in brainstorming sessions due to the unstructured nature of brainstorming.

PRODUCTION SYSTEM The system that an organization uses to acquire inputs, convert the inputs into outputs, and dispose of the outputs.

PROFESSIONAL ETHICS Standards that govern how members of a profession are to make decisions when the way they should behave is not clear-cut.

PROGRAMMED DECISION MAKING Routine, virtually automatic decision making that follows established rules or guidelines.

PROSOCIALLY MOTIVATED BEHAVIOR Behavior that is performed to benefit or help others.

PUNISHMENT Administering an undesired or negative consequence when dysfunctional behavior occurs.

Q

QUID PRO QUO SEXUAL HARASSMENT Asking for or forcing an employee to perform sexual favors in exchange for receiving some reward or avoiding negative consequences.

R

REAL-TIME INFORMATION Frequently updated information that reflects current conditions.

REALISTIC JOB PREVIEW (RJP) An honest assessment of the advantages and disadvantages of a job and organization.

REASONED JUDGMENT A decision that takes time and effort to make and results from careful information gathering, generation of alternatives, and evaluation of alternatives.

RECEIVER The person or group for which a message is intended.

RECIPROCAL TASK INTERDEPENDENCE The task interdependence that exists when the work performed by each group member is fully dependent on the work performed by other group members.

RECRUITMENT Activities that managers engage in to develop a pool of qualified candidates for open positions.

REFERENT POWER Power that comes from subordinates' and coworkers' respect, admiration, and loyalty.

RELATED DIVERSIFICATION Entering a new business or industry to create a competitive advantage in one or more of an organization's existing divisions or businesses.

RELATIONSHIP-ORIENTED LEADERS Leaders whose primary concern is to develop good relationships with their subordinates and to be liked by them.

RELIABILITY The degree to which a tool or test measures the same thing each time it is used.

REPUTATION The esteem or high repute that individuals or organizations gain when they behave ethically.

RESEARCH AND DEVELOPMENT TEAM A team whose members have the expertise and experience needed to develop new products.

RESTRUCTURING Downsizing an organization by eliminating the jobs of large numbers of top, middle, and first-line managers and nonmanagerial employees.

REWARD POWER The ability of a manager to give or withhold tangible and intangible rewards.

RISK The degree of probability that the possible outcomes of a particular course of action will occur.

ROLE MAKING Taking the initiative to modify an assigned role by assuming additional responsibilities.

RULES Formal written instructions that specify actions to be taken under different circumstances to achieve specific goals.

S

SATISFICING Searching for and choosing an acceptable, or satisfactory, response to problems and opportunities, rather than trying to make the best decision.

SCIENTIFIC MANAGEMENT The systematic study of relationships between people and tasks for the purpose of redesigning the work process to increase efficiency.

SELECTION The process that managers use to determine the relative qualifications of job applicants and their potential for performing well in a particular job.

SELF-EFFICACY A person's belief about his or her ability to perform a behavior successfully.

SELF-ESTEEM The degree to which individuals feel good about themselves and their capabilities.

SELF-MANAGED TEAM A group of employees who assume responsibility for organizing, controlling, and supervising their own activities and monitoring the quality of the goods and services they provide.

SELF-MANAGED WORK TEAM A group of employees who supervise their own activities and monitor the quality of the goods and services they provide.

SELF-REINFORCER Any desired or attractive outcome or reward that a person gives to himself or herself for good performance.

SENDER The person or group wishing to share information.

SEQUENTIAL TASK INTERDEPENDENCE The task interdependence that exists when group members must perform specific tasks in a predetermined order.

SERVANT LEADER A leader who has a strong desire to serve and work for the benefit of others.

SHORT-TERM ORIENTATION A worldview that values personal stability or happiness and living for the present.

SKUNKWORKS A group of intrapreneurs who are deliberately separated from the normal operation of an organization to encourage them to devote all their attention to developing new products.

SOCIAL ENTREPRENEUR An individual who pursues initiatives and opportunities and mobilizes resources to address social problems and needs in order to improve society and well-being through creative solutions.

SOCIAL LEARNING THEORY A theory that takes into account how learning and motivation are influenced by people's thoughts and beliefs and their observations of other people's behavior.

SOCIAL LOAFING The tendency of individuals to put forth less effort when they work in groups than when they work alone.

SOCIAL RESPONSIBILITY The way a company's managers and employees view their duty or obligation to make decisions that protect, enhance, and promote the welfare and well-being of stakeholders and society as a whole.

SOCIAL STRUCTURE The arrangement of relationships between individuals and groups in a society.

SOCIETAL ETHICS Standards that govern how members of a society should deal with one another in matters involving issues such as fairness, justice, poverty, and the rights of the individual.

SOCIOCULTURAL FORCES Pressures emanating from the social structure of a country or society or from the national culture.

SPAN OF CONTROL The number of subordinates who report directly to a manager.

SPIRAL CAREER A career consisting of a series of jobs that build on each other but tend to be fundamentally different.

STAFF MANAGER Someone responsible for managing a specialist function, such as finance or marketing.

STAKEHOLDERS The people and groups that supply a company with its productive resources and so have a claim on and stake in the company.

STANDARD OPERATING PROCEDURES (SOPs) Specific sets of written instructions about how to perform a certain aspect of a task.

STEADY-STATE CAREER A career consisting of the same kind of job during a large part of an individual's work life.

STEREOTYPE Simplistic and often inaccurate beliefs about the typical characteristics of particular groups of people.

STRATEGIC ALLIANCE An agreement in which managers pool or share their organization's resources and know-how with a foreign company, and the two organizations share the rewards and risks of starting a new venture.

STRATEGIC HUMAN RESOURCE MANAGEMENT The process by which managers design the components of an HRM system to be consistent with each other, with other elements of organizational architecture, and with the organization's strategy and goals.

STRATEGIC LEADERSHIP The ability of the CEO and top managers to convey a compelling vision of what they want the organization to achieve to their subordinates.

STRATEGY A cluster of decisions about what goals to pursue, what actions to take, and how to use resources to achieve goals.

STRATEGY FORMULATION The development of a set of corporate-, business-, and functional-level strategies that allow an organization to accomplish its mission and achieve its goals.

SUBJECTIVE APPRAISAL An appraisal that is based on perceptions of traits, behaviors, or results.

SUPPLIERS Individuals and organizations that provide an organization with the input resources that it needs to produce goods and services.

SWOT ANALYSIS A planning exercise in which managers identify organizational strengths (S) and weaknesses (W) and environmental opportunities (O) and threats (T).

SYNERGY Performance gains that result when individuals and departments coordinate their actions.

T

TARIFF A tax that a government imposes on imported or, occasionally, exported goods.

TASK ENVIRONMENT The set of forces and conditions that originate with suppliers, distributors, customers, and competitors and affect an organization's ability to obtain inputs and dispose of its outputs because they influence managers on a daily basis.

TASK FORCE A committee of managers or nonmanagerial employees from various departments or divisions who meet to solve a specific, mutual problem; also called *ad hoc committee.*

TASK INTERDEPENDENCE The degree to which the work performed by one member of a group influences the work performed by other members.

TASK STRUCTURE The extent to which the work to be performed is clear-cut so that a leader's subordinates know what needs to be accomplished and how to go about doing it; a determinant of how favorable a situation is for leading.

TASK-ORIENTED LEADERS Leaders whose primary concern is to ensure that subordinates perform at a high level.

TEAM A group whose members work intensely with one another to achieve a specific common goal or objective.

TECHNICAL SKILLS The job-specific knowledge and techniques required to perform an organizational role.

TECHNOLOGICAL FORCES Outcomes of changes in the technology that managers use to design, produce, or distribute goods and services.

TECHNOLOGY The combination of skills and equipment that managers use in the design, production, and distribution of goods and services.

TERMINAL VALUE A lifelong goal or objective that an individual seeks to achieve.

THEORY X A set of negative assumptions about workers that lead to the conclusion that a manager's task is to supervise workers closely and control their behavior.

THEORY Y A set of positive assumptions about workers that lead to the conclusion that a manager's task is to create a work setting that encourages commitment to organizational goals and provides opportunities for workers to be imaginative and to exercise initiative and self-direction.

360-DEGREE APPRAISAL A performance appraisal by peers, subordinates, superiors, and sometimes clients who are in a position to evaluate a manager's performance.

TIME HORIZON The intended duration of a plan.

TOP MANAGER A manager who establishes organizational goals, decides how departments should interact, and monitors the performance of middle managers.

TOP-DOWN CHANGE A fast, revolutionary approach to change in which top managers identify what needs to be changed and then move quickly to implement the changes throughout the organization.

TOP-MANAGEMENT TEAM A group composed of the CEO, the COO, the president, and the heads of the most important departments.

TRAINING Teaching organizational members how to perform their current jobs and helping them acquire the knowledge and skills they need to be effective performers.

TRANSACTION-PROCESSING SYSTEM A management information system designed to handle large volumes of routine, recurring transactions.

TRANSACTIONAL LEADERSHIP Leadership that motivates subordinates by rewarding them for high performance and reprimanding them for low performance.

TRANSFORMATIONAL LEADERSHIP Leadership that makes subordinates aware of the importance of their jobs and performance to the organization and aware of their own needs for personal growth and that motivates subordinates to work for the good of the organization.

TRANSITORY CAREER A career in which a person changes jobs frequently and in which each job is different from the one that precedes it.

TRUST The willingness of one person or group to have faith or confidence in the goodwill of another person, even though this puts them at risk.

TURNAROUND MANAGEMENT The creation of a new vision for a struggling company based on a new approach to planning and organizing to make better use of a company's resources to allow it to survive and prosper.

U

UNCERTAINTY Unpredictability.

UNCERTAINTY AVOIDANCE The degree to which societies are willing to tolerate uncertainty and risk.

UNDERPAYMENT INEQUITY The inequity that exists when a person perceives that his or her own outcome–input ratio is less than the ratio of a referent.

UNRELATED DIVERSIFICATION Entering a new industry or buying a company in a new industry that is not related in any way to an organization's current businesses or industries.

UTILITARIAN RULE An ethical decision is a decision that produces the greatest good for the greatest number of people.

VALENCE In expectancy theory, how desirable each of the outcomes available from a job or organization is to a person.

VALIDITY The degree to which a tool or test measures what it purports to measure.

VALUE CHAIN The coordinated series or sequence of functional activities necessary to transform inputs such as new product concepts, raw materials, component parts, or professional skills into the finished goods or services customers value and want to buy.

VALUE SYSTEM The terminal and instrumental values that are guiding principles in an individual's life.

VALUES Ideas about what a society believes to be good, right, desirable, or beautiful.

VERBAL COMMUNICATION The encoding of messages into words, either written or spoken.

VERTICAL INTEGRATION Expanding a company's operations either backward into an industry that produces inputs for its products or forward into an industry that uses, distributes, or sells its products.

VICARIOUS LEARNING Learning that occurs when the learner becomes motivated to perform a behavior by watching another person perform it and be reinforced for doing so; also called *observational learning.*

VIRTUAL TEAM A team whose members rarely or never meet face-to-face but, rather, interact by using various forms of information technology such as e-mail, computer networks, telephone, fax, and videoconferences.

W

WHOLLY OWNED FOREIGN SUBSIDIARY Production operations established in a foreign country independent of any local direct involvement.

Credits

Notes

Chapter 1

1. G. R. Jones, *Organizational Theory, Design, and Change* (Upper Saddle River, NJ: Pearson, 2007).

2. J. P. Campbell, "On the Nature of Organizational Effectiveness," in P. S. Goodman, J. M. Pennings, et al., *New Perspectives on Organizational Effectiveness* (San Francisco: Jossey-Bass, 1977).

3. M. J. Provitera, "What Management Is: How It Works and Why It's Everyone's Business," *Academy of Management Executive* 17 (August 2003), 152–54.

4. J. McGuire and E. Matta, "CEO Stock Options: The Silent Dimension of Ownership," *Academy of Management Journal* 46 (April 2003), 255–66.

5. www.apple.com, press releases, 2000, 2001, 2003, 2006, 2008.

6. J. G. Combs and M. S. Skill, "Managerialist and Human Capital Explanations for Key Executive Pay Premium: A Contingency Perspective," *Academy of Management Journal* 46 (February 2003), 63–74.

7. H. Fayol, *General and Industrial Management* (New York: IEEE Press, 1984). Fayol actually identified five different managerial tasks, but most scholars today believe these four capture the essence of Fayol's ideas.

8. P. F. Drucker, *Management Tasks, Responsibilities, and Practices* (New York: Harper & Row, 1974).

9. www.dell.com, 2008.

10. www.apple.com, press release, 2003.

11. G. McWilliams, "Lean Machine–How Dell Fine-Tunes Its PC Pricing to Gain Edge in a Slow Market," *The Wall Street Journal*, June 8, 2001, A1.

12. J. Kotter, *The General Managers* (New York: Free Press, 1992).

13. C. P. Hales, "What Do Managers Do? A Critical Review of the Evidence," *Journal of Management Studies*, January 1986, 88–115; A. I. Kraul, P. R. Pedigo, D. D. McKenna, and M. D. Dunnette, "The Role of the Manager: What's Really Important in Different Management Jobs," *Academy of Management Executive*, November 1989, 286–93.

14. A. K. Gupta, "Contingency Perspectives on Strategic Leadership," in D. C. Hambrick, ed., *The Executive Effect: Concepts and Methods for Studying Top Managers* (Greenwich, CT: JAI Press, 1988), 147–78.

15. D. G. Ancona, "Top Management Teams: Preparing for the Revolution," in J. S. Carroll, ed., *Applied Social Psychology and Organizational Settings* (Hillsdale, NJ: Erlbaum, 1990); D. C. Hambrick and P. A. Mason, "Upper Echelons: The Organization as a Reflection of Its Top Managers," *Academy of Management Journal* 9 (1984), 193–206.

16. T. A. Mahony, T. H. Jerdee, and S. J. Carroll, "The Jobs of Management," *Industrial Relations* 4 (1965), 97–110; L.Gomez-Mejia, J. McCann, and R. C. Page, "The Structure of Managerial Behaviors and Rewards," *Industrial Relations* 24 (1985), 147–54.

17. W. R. Nord and M. J. Waller, "The Human Organization of Time: Temporal Realities and Experiences," *Academy of Management Review* 29 (January 2004), 137–40.

18. R. L. Katz, "Skills of an Effective Administrator," *Harvard Business Review*, September–October 1974, 90–102.

19. Ibid.

20. P. Tharenou, "Going Up? Do Traits and Informal Social Processes Predict Advancing in Management?" *Academy of Management Journal* 44 (October 2001), 1005–18.

21. C. J. Collins and K. D. Clark, "Strategic Human Resource Practices, Top Management Team Social Networks, and Firm Performance: The Role of Human Resource Practices in Creating Organizational Competitive Advantage," *Academy of Management Journal* 46 (December 2003), 740–52.

22. R. Stewart, "Middle Managers: Their Jobs and Behaviors," in J. W. Lorsch, ed., *Handbook of Organizational Behavior* (Englewood Cliffs, NJ: Prentice-Hall, 1987), 385–91.

23. S. C. de Janasz, S. E. Sullivan, and V. Whiting, "Mentor Networks and Career Success: Lessons for Turbulent Times," *Academy of Management Executive* 17 (November 2003), 78–92.

24. K. Labich, "Making Over Middle Managers," *Fortune*, May 8, 1989, 58–64.

25. B. Wysocki, "Some Companies Cut Costs Too Far, Suffer from Corporate Anorexia," *The Wall Street Journal*, July 5, 1995, A1.

26. www.dell.com, 2008.

27. V. U. Druskat and J. V. Wheeler, "Managing from the Boundary: The Effective Leadership of Self-Managing Work Teams," *Academy of Management Journal* 46 (August 2003), 435–58.

28. S. R. Parker, T. D. Wall, and P. R. Jackson, "That's Not My Job: Developing Flexible Work Orientations," *Academy of Management Journal* 40 (1997), 899–929.

29. B. Dumaine, "The New Non-Manager," *Fortune*, February 22, 1993, 80–84.

30. H. G. Baum, A. C. Joel, and E. A. Mannix, "Management Challenges in a New Time," *Academy of Management Journal* 45 (October 2002), 916–31.

31. A. Shama, "Management under Fire: The Transformation of Management in the Soviet Union and Eastern Europe," *Academy of Management Executive* 10 (1993), 22–35.

32. www.apple.com, 2006; www.nike.com, 2006.

33. K. Seiders and L. L. Berry, "Service Fairness: What It Is and Why It Matters," *Academy of Management Executive* 12 (1998), 8–20.

34. T. Donaldson, "Editor's Comments: Taking Ethics Seriously–A Mission Now More Possible," *Academy of Management Review* 28 (July 2003), 363–67.

35. C. Anderson, "Values-Based Management," *Academy of Management Executive* 11 (1997), 25–46.

36. W. H. Shaw and V. Barry, *Moral Issues in Business,* 6th ed. (Belmont, CA: Wadsworth, 1995); T. Donaldson, *Corporations and Morality* (Englewood Cliffs, NJ: Prentice-Hall, 1982).

37. www.consumerreports.com, 2003.

38. www.fda.com, 2004.

39. www.fda.org, press releases, 2004.

40. E. Werner, "Slaughterhouse Owner Acknowledges Abuse," www.pasadenastarnews.com, March 13, 2008.

41. D. Bunis and N. Luna, "Sick Cows Never Made Food Supply, Meat Plant Owner Says," www.ocregister.com, March 12, 2008.

42. "Worker Sentenced in Slaughterhouse Abuse," www.yahoo.com, March 22, 2008.

43. S. Jackson et al., *Diversity in the Workplace: Human Resource Initiatives* (New York: Guilford Press, 1992).

44. G. Robinson and C. S. Daus, "Building a Case for Diversity," *Academy of Management Executive* 3 (1997), 21–31; S. J. Bunderson and K. M. Sutcliffe, "Comparing Alternative Conceptualizations of Functional Diversity in Management Teams: Process and Performance Effects," *Academy of Management Journal* 45 (October 2002), 875–94.

45. D. Jamieson and J. O'Mara, *Managing Workforce 2000: Gaining a Diversity Advantage* (San Francisco: Jossey-Bass, 1991).

46. www.uboc.com, 2008.

47. J. Hickman, C. Tkaczyk, E. Florian, and J. Stemple, "The 50 Best Companies for Minorities to Work For," *Fortune,* July 7, 2003, 55–58.

48. A. R. Randel and K. S. Jaussi, "Functional Background Identity, Diversity, and Individual Performance in Cross-Functional Teams," *Academy of Management Journal* 46 (December 2003), 763–75.

49. "Union Bank of California Honored by U.S. Labor Department for Employment Practices," press release, September 11, 2000.

50. Ibid.

51. D. R. Tobin, *The Knowledge Enabled Organization* (New York: AMACOM, 1998).

Appendix A

1. F. W. Taylor, *Shop Management* (New York: Harper, 1903); F. W. Taylor, *The Principles of Scientific Management* (New York: Harper, 1911).

2. L. W. Fry, "The Maligned F. W. Taylor: A Reply to His Many Critics," *Academy of Management Review* 1 (1976), 124–29.

3. J. A. Litterer, *The Emergence of Systematic Management as Shown by the Literature from 1870–1900* (New York: Garland, 1986).

4. D. Wren, *The Evolution of Management Thought* (New York: Wiley, 1994), 134.

5. C. Perrow, *Complex Organizations,* 2nd ed. (Glenview, IL: Scott, Foresman, 1979).

6. M. Weber, *From Max Weber: Essays in Sociology,* ed. H. H. Gerth and C. W. Mills (New York: Oxford University Press, 1946), 331.

7. See Perrow, *Complex Organizations,* Ch. 1, for a detailed discussion of these issues.

8. L. D. Parker, "Control in Organizational Life: The Contribution of Mary Parker Follett," *Academy of Management Review* 9 (1984), 736–45.

9. P. Graham, *M. P. Follett–Prophet of Management: A Celebration of Writings from the 1920s* (Boston: Harvard Business School Press, 1995).

10. M. P. Follett, *Creative Experience* (London: Longmans, 1924).

11. E. Mayo, *The Human Problems of Industrial Civilization* (New York: Macmillan, 1933); F. J. Roethlisberger and W. J. Dickson, *Management and the Worker* (Cambridge, MA: Harvard University Press, 1947).

12. D. W. Organ, "Review of *Management and the Worker,* by F. J. Roethlisberger and W. J. Dickson," *Academy of Management Review* 13 (1986), 460–64.

13. D. Roy, "Banana Time: Job Satisfaction and Informal Interaction," *Human Organization* 18 (1960), 158–61.

14. For an analysis of the problems in distinguishing cause from effect in the Hawthorne studies and in social settings in general, see A. Carey, "The Hawthorne Studies: A Radical Criticism," *American Sociological Review* 33 (1967), 403–16.

15. D. McGregor, *The Human Side of Enterprise* (New York: McGraw-Hill, 1960).

16. Ibid., 48.

Chapter 2

1. S. Covel, "Telemarketer Bucks High Turnover Trend," *The Wall Street Journal,* November 19, 2007, B4; "Ryla History & Culture!" www.rylateleservices.com/print.asp?level=2&id=166, January 24, 2008.

2. L. Hall, "Call Center Bucks Overseas Outsourcing Trend," *Atlanta Business Chronicle,* http://atlanta.bizjournals.com/atlanta/stories/2005/12/12/smallb4.html?t=printable, January 24, 2008.

3. Covel, "Telemarketer Bucks High Turnover Trend."

4. A. Field, "Capital for Companies That Aid Communities, *The New York Times,* October 16, 2003.

5. Covel, "Telemarketer Bucks High Turnover Trend"; "Ryla History & Culture!"

6. "Company Culture," www.rylateleservices.com/print.asp?level=2&id=98, January 24, 2008.

7. Covel, "Telemarketer Bucks High Turnover Trend."

8. "A Great Career Is Waiting for You at Ryla," www.rylateleservices.com/print.asp?level=1&id=13, January 25, 2008.

9. Covel, "Telemarketer Bucks High Turnover Trend."

10. Ibid.

11. "Ryla Launches Call Center Services for Crisis Response, Seasonal Retail and Political Solutions," Tuesday, November 20, 2007, www.rylateleservices.com/print.asp?level=2&id=171, January 24, 2008.

12. Ibid.; www.ryla.com, April 14, 2009.

13. "Ryla Named by *The Wall Street Journal* and Winning Workplaces as a Top Small Workplace in US," October 1, 2007, www.rylateleservices.com/print.asp?level=2&id=168, January 24, 2008.

14. Covel, "Telemarketer Bucks High Turnover Trend."

15. S. Carpenter, "Different Dispositions, Different Brains," *Monitor on Psychology,* February 2001, 66–68.

16. J. M. Digman, "Personality Structure: Emergence of the Five-Factor Model," *Annual Review of Psychology* 41 (1990), 417–40; R. R. McCrae and P. T. Costa, "Validation of the Five-Factor Model of Personality across Instruments and Observers," *Journal of Personality and Social Psychology* 52 (1987), 81–90; R. R. McCrae and P. T. Costa, "Discriminant Validity of NEO-PIR Facet Scales," *Educational and Psychological Measurement* 52 (1992), 229–37.

17. Digman, "Personality Structure"; McCrae and Costa, "Validation of the Five-Factor Model"; McCrae and Costa, "Discriminant Validity"; R. P. Tett and D. D. Burnett, "A Personality Trait-Based Interactionist Model of Job Performance," *Journal of Applied Psychology* 88, no. 3 (2003), 500–17; J. M. George, "Personality, Five-Factor Model," in S. Clegg and J. R. Bailey, eds., *International Encyclopedia of Organization Studies* (Thousand Oaks, CA: Sage, 2007).

18. L. A. Witt and G. R. Ferris, "Social Skills as Moderator of Conscientiousness-Performance Relationship: Convergent Results across Four Studies," *Journal of Applied Psychology* 88, no. 5 (2003), 809–20; M. J. Simmering, J. A. Colquitte, R. A. Noe, and C. O. L. H. Porter, "Conscientiousness, Autonomy Fit, and Development: A Longitudinal Study," *Journal of Applied Psychology* 88, no. 5 (2003), 954–63.

19. M. R. Barrick and M. K. Mount, "The Big Five Personality Dimensions and Job Performance: A Meta-Analysis," *Personnel Psychology* 44 (1991), 1–26; S. Komar, D. J. Brown, J. A. Komar, and C. Robie, "Faking and the Validity of Conscientiousness: A Monte Carlo Investigation," *Journal of Applied Psychology* 93 (2008), 140–54.

20. Digman, "Personality Structure"; McCrae and Costa, "Validation of the Five-Factor Model"; McCrae and Costa, "Discriminant Validity."

21. E. McGirt, "The Dirtiest Mind in Business: How Filth Met Opportunity and Created a Franchise," *Fast Company* 122 (February 2008), 64, www.fastcompany.com/magazine/122/the-dirtiest-mind-in-business_Printer_Friendl. . ., January 23, 2008.

22. "Mike Rowe's World: Mike's Bio: Discovery Channel," http://dsc.discovery.com/fansites/dirtyjobs/bio/bio-print.html, January 23, 2008.

23. McGirt, "The Dirtiest Mind in Business."

24. "Dirty Jobs: Season 1 DVD Set–Discovery Channel Store–754317," http://shopping.discovery.com/product-60948.html?jzid=40588004-66-0, January 25, 2008; "Mike Rowe's World: Mike's Bio: Discovery Channel."

25. McGirt, "The Dirtiest Mind in Business."

26. Ibid.

27. Ibid.

28. McGirt, "The Dirtiest Mind in Business"; M. Rowe, "Seven Dirty Habits of Highly Effluent People: Mike Rose's Seven Rules for Job Satisfaction," *Fast Company* 122 (February 2008), 69, www.fastcompany.com/magazine/122/seven-dirty-habits-of-highly-effluent-people_. . ., January 23, 2008.

29. J. B. Rotter, "Generalized Expectancies for Internal versus External Control of Reinforcement," *Psychological Monographs* 80 (1966), 1–28; P. Spector, "Behaviors in Organizations as a Function of Employees' Locus of Control," *Psychological Bulletin* 91 (1982), 482–97.

30. J. Brockner, *Self-Esteem at Work* (Lexington, MA: Lexington Books, 1988).

31. D. C. McClelland, *Human Motivation* (Glenview, IL: Scott, Foresman, 1985); D. C. McClelland, "How Motives, Skills, and Values Determine What People Do," *American Psychologist* 40 (1985), 812–25; D. C. McClelland, "Managing Motivation to Expand Human Freedom," *American Psychologist* 33 (1978), 201–10.

32. D. G. Winter, *The Power Motive* (New York: Free Press 1973).

33. M. J. Stahl, "Achievement, Power, and Managerial Motivation: Selecting Managerial Talent with the Job Choice Exercise," *Personnel Psychology* 36 (1983), 775–89; D. C. McClelland and D. H. Burnham, "Power Is the Great Motivator," *Harvard Business Review* 54 (1976), 100–10.

34. R. J. House, W. D. Spangler, and J. Woycke, "Personality and Charisma in the U.S. Presidency: A Psychological Theory of Leader Effectiveness," *Administrative Science Quarterly* 36 (1991), 364–96.

35. G. H. Hines, "Achievement, Motivation, Occupations and Labor Turnover in New Zealand," *Journal of Applied Psychology* 58 (1973), 313–17; P. S. Hundal, "A Study of Entrepreneurial Motivation: Comparison of Fast- and Slow-Progressing Small Scale Industrial Entrepreneurs in Punjab, India," *Journal of Applied Psychology* 55 (1971), 317–23.

36. M. Rokeach, *The Nature of Human Values* (New York: Free Press 1973).

37. Ibid.

38. Ibid.

39. K. K. Spors, "Top Small Workplaces 2007: Gentle Giant Moving," *The Wall Street Journal,* October 1, 2007, R4–R5; "Gentle Giant Sees Revenue Boost," *Boston Business Journal,* January 15, 2008, www.gentlegiant.com/news-011508-1.htm, February 5, 2008.

40. Spors, "Top Small Workplaces 2007: Gentle Giant Moving."

41. Ibid.

42. Ibid.

43. Spors, "Top Small Workplaces 2007: Gentle Giant Moving."; "Gentle Giant Receives Top Small Workplace Award," www.gentlegiant.com/topsmallworkplace.htm, January 5, 2008.

44. Spors, "Top Small Workplaces 2007: Gentle Giant Moving."

45. Ibid.

46. A. P. Brief, *Attitudes In and Around Organizations* (Thousand Oaks, CA: Sage, 1998).

47. D. Stafford, "Job Satisfaction Takes a Tumble," *Houston Chronicle,* February 25, 2007, D6.

48. Ibid.

49. D. W. Organ, *Organizational Citizenship Behavior: The Good Soldier*

Syndrome (Lexington, MA: Lexington Books, 1988).

50. J. M. George and A. P. Brief, "Feeling Good–Doing Good: A Conceptual Analysis of the Mood at Work–Organizational Spontaneity Relationship," *Psychological Bulletin* 112 (1992), 310–29.

51. W. H. Mobley, "Intermediate Linkages in the Relationship between Job Satisfaction and Employee Turnover," *Journal of Applied Psychology* 62 (1977), 237–40.

52. C. Hymowitz, "Though Now Routine, Bosses Still Stumble during Layoff Process," *The Wall Street Journal,* June 25, 2007, B1; J. Brockner, "The Effects of Work Layoffs on Survivors: Research, Theory and Practice," in B. M. Staw and L. L. Cummings, eds., *Research in Organizational Behavior,* vol. 10 (Greenwich, CT: JAI Press, 1988), 213–55.

53. Hymowitz, "Though Now Routine, Bosses Still Stumble during Layoff Process."

54. Ibid.

55. Ibid.

56. N. Solinger, W. van Olffen, and R. A. Roe, "Beyond the Three-Component Model of Organizational Commitment," *Journal of Applied Psychology* 93 (2008), 70–83.

57. J. E. Mathieu and D. M. Zajac, "A Review and Meta-Analysis of the Antecedents, Correlates, and Consequences of Organizational Commitment," *Psychological Bulletin* 108 (1990), 171–94.

58. E. Slate, "Tips for Negotiations in Germany and France," *HR Focus,* July 1994, 18.

59. D. Watson and A. Tellegen, "Toward a Consensual Structure of Mood," *Psychological Bulletin* 98 (1985), 219–35.

60. Ibid.

61. J. M. George, "The Role of Personality in Organizational Life: Issues and Evidence," *Journal of Management* 18 (1992), 185–213.

62. H. A. Elfenbein, "Emotion in Organizations: A Review and Theoretical Integration," in J. P. Walsh and A. P. Brief, eds., *The Academy of Management Annals,* vol. 1 (New York: Lawrence Erlbaum Associates, 2008), 315–86.

63. J. P. Forgas, "Affect in Social Judgments and Decisions: A Multi-Process Model," in M. Zanna, ed., *Advances in Experimental and Social Psychology,* vol. 25 (San Diego, CA: Academic Press, 1992), 227–75; J. P. Forgas and J. M. George, "Affective Influences on Judgments and Behavior in Organizations: An Information Processing Perspective," *Organizational Behavior and Human Decision Processes* 86 (2001), 3–34; J. M. George, "Emotions and Leadership: The Role of Emotional Intelligence," *Human Relations* 53 (2000), 1027–55; W. N. Morris, *Mood: The Frame of Mind* (New York: Springer-Verlag, 1989).

64. George, "Emotions and Leadership."

65. J. M. George and K. Bettenhausen, "Understanding Prosocial Behavior, Sales Performance, and Turnover: A Group Level Analysis in a Service Context," *Journal of Applied Psychology* 75 (1990), 698–709.

66. George and Brief, "Feeling Good–Doing Good"; J. M. George and J. Zhou, "Understanding When Bad Moods Foster Creativity and Good Ones Don't: The Role of Context and Clarity of Feelings," paper presented at the Academy of Management Annual Meeting, 2001; A. M. Isen and R. A. Baron, "Positive Affect as a Factor in Organizational Behavior," in B. M. Staw and L. L. Cummings, eds., *Research in Organizational Behavior,* vol. 13 (Greenwich, CT: JAI Press, 1991), 1–53.

67. J. M. George and J. Zhou, "Dual Tuning in a Supportive Context: Joint Contributions of Positive Mood, Negative Mood, and Supervisory Behaviors to Employee Creativity," *Academy of Management Journal* 50 (2007), 605–622; J. M. George, "Creativity in Organizations," in J. P. Walsh and A. P. Brief, eds., *The Academy of Management Annals,* vol. 1 (New York: Lawrence-Erlbaum Associates, 2008), 439–77.

68. J. D. Greene, R. B. Sommerville, L. E. Nystrom, J. M. Darley, and J. D. Cohen, "An FMRI Investigation of Emotional Engagement in Moral Judgment," *Science,* September 14, 2001, 2105–08; L. Neergaard, "Brain Scans Show Emotions Key to Resolving Ethical Dilemmas," *Houston Chronicle,* September 14, 2001, 13A.

69. www.thethinkers.com/homemain.cfm, February 5, 2008.

70. L. Berton, "It's Audit Time! Send in the Clowns," *The Wall Street Journal,* January 18, 1995, B1, B6.

71. R. C. Sinclair, "Mood, Categorization Breadth, and Performance Appraisal: The Effects of Order of Information Acquisition and Affective State on Halo, Accuracy, Informational Retrieval, and Evaluations," *Organizational Behavior and Human Decision Processes* 42 (1988), 22–46.

72. D. Goleman, *Emotional Intelligence* (New York: Bantam Books, 1994); J. D. Mayer and P. Salovey, "The Intelligence of Emotional Intelligence," *Intelligence* 17 (1993), 433–42; J. D. Mayer and P. Salovey, "What Is Emotional Intelligence?" in P. Salovey and D. Sluyter, eds., *Emotional Development and Emotional Intelligence: Implications for Education* (New York: Basic Books, 1997); P. Salovey and J. D. Mayer, "Emotional Intelligence," *Imagination, Cognition, and Personality* 9 (1989–1990), 185–211.

73. S. Epstein, *Constructive Thinking* (Westport, CT: Praeger, 1998).

74. "Leading by Feel," *Inside the Mind of the Leader,* January 2004, 27–37.

75. P. C. Early and R. S. Peterson, "The Elusive Cultural Chameleon: Cultural Intelligence as a New Approach to Intercultural Training for the Global Manger," *Academy of Management Learning and Education* 3, no. 1 (2004), 100–15.

76. George, "Emotions and Leadership"; S. Begley, "The Boss Feels Your Pain," *Newsweek,* October 12, 1998, 74; D. Goleman, *Working with Emotional Intelligence* (New York: Bantam Books, 1998).

77. "Leading by Feel," *Inside the Mind of the Leader,* January 2004, 27–37.

78. George, "Emotions and Leadership."

79. J. Zhou and J. M. George, "Awakening Employee Creativity: The Role of Leader Emotional Intelligence," *Leadership Quarterly* 14 (2003), 545–68.

80. A. Jung, "Leading by Feel: Seek Frank Feedback," *Inside the Mind of the Leader,* January 2004, 31.

81. H. M. Trice and J. M. Beyer, *The Cultures of Work Organizations* (Englewood Cliffs, NJ: Prentice-Hall, 1993).

82. J. B. Sørensen, "The Strength of Corporate Culture and the Reliability of Firm Performance," *Administrative Science Quarterly* 47, (2002), 70–91.

83. "Personality and Organizational Culture," in B. Schneider and D. B. Smith, eds., *Personality and Organizations* (Mahway, NJ: Lawrence Erlbaum, 2004), 347–69; J. E. Slaughter, M. J. Zickar, S. Highhouse, and D. C. Mohr, "Personality Trait Inferences about Organizations: Development of a Measure and Assessment of Construct Validity," *Journal of Applied Psychology* 89, no. 1 (2004), 85–103.

84. T. Kelley, *The Art of Innovation: Lessons in Creativity from IDEO, America's Leading Design Firm* (New York: Random House, 2001).

85. "Personality and Organizational Culture."

86. B. Schneider, "The People Make the Place," *Personnel Psychology* 40 (1987), 437–53.

87. "Personality and Organizational Culture."

88. Ibid.

89. B. Schneider, H. B. Goldstein, and D. B. Smith, "The ASA Framework: An Update," *Personnel Psychology* 48 (1995), 747–73; J. Schaubroeck, D. C. Ganster, and J. R. Jones, "Organizational and Occupational Influences in the Attraction–Selection–Attrition Process," *Journal of Applied Psychology* 83 (1998), 869–91.

90. Kelley, *The Art of Innovation.*

91. www.ideo.com, February 5, 2008.

92. Kelley, *The Art of Innovation.*

93. "Personality and Organizational Culture."

94. Kelley, *The Art of Innovation.*

95. George, "Emotions and Leadership."

96. Kelley, *The Art of Innovation.*

97. Ibid.

98. D. C. Feldman, "The Development and Enforcement of Group Norms," *Academy of Management Review* 9 (1984), 47–53.

99. G. R. Jones, *Organizational Theory, Design, and Change* (Upper Saddle River, NJ: Prentice-Hall, 2003).

100. J. M. George, "Personality, Affect, and Behavior in Groups," *Journal of Applied Psychology* 75 (1990), 107–16.

101. J. Van Maanen, "Police Socialization: A Longitudinal Examination of Job Attitudes in an Urban Police Department," *Administrative Science Quarterly* 20 (1975), 207–28.

102. www.intercotwest.com/Disney; M. N. Martinez, "Disney Training Works Magic," *HRMagazine,* May 1992, 53–57.

103. P. L. Berger and T. Luckman, *The Social Construction of Reality* (Garden City, NY: Anchor Books, 1967).

104. H. M. Trice and J. M. Beyer, "Studying Organizational Culture through Rites and Ceremonials," *Academy of Management Review* 9 (1984), 653–69.

105. Kelley, *The Art of Innovation.*

106. H. M. Trice and J. M. Beyer, *The Cultures of Work Organizations* (Englewood Cliffs, NJ: Prentice-Hall, 1993).

107. B. Ortega, "Wal-Mart's Meeting Is a Reason to Party," *The Wall Street Journal,* June 3, 1994, A1.

108. Trice and Beyer, "Studying Organizational Culture."

109. Kelley, *The Art of Innovation.*

110. www.ibm.com.

111. S. McGee, "Garish Jackets Add to Clamor of Chicago Pits," *The Wall Street Journal,* July 31, 1995, C1.

112. K. E. Weick, *The Social Psychology of Organization* (Reading, MA: Addison–Wesley, 1979).

113. B. McLean and P. Elkind, *The Smartest Guys in the Room: The Amazing Rise and Scandalous Fall of Enron* (New York: Penguin Books, 2003); R. Smith and J. R. Emshwiller, *24 Days: How Two Wall Street Journal Reporters Uncovered the Lies That Destroyed Faith in Corporate America* (New York: HarperCollins, 2003); M. Swartz and S. Watkins, *Power Failure: The Inside Story of the Collapse of ENRON* (New York: Doubleday, 2003).

Chapter 3

1. S. Greenhouse, "How Costco Became the Anti-Wal-Mart," *The New York Times,* July 17, 2005, BU1, BU8; Associated Press, "Costco to Shut Down Its 2 Home Furnishing Stores," April 2, 2009; *BusinessWeek Online,* http://www.businessweek.com/ap/financialnews/D97AAEMO0.htm, April 15, 2009.

2. "Corporate Governance," *Costco Wholesale Investor Relations,* April 28, 2006, http://phx.corporate-ir.net/phoenix. zhtml?c=83830&p=irol-govhighlights; "Code of Ethics," *Costco Wholesale Investor Relations,* http://phx.corporate-ir.net/phoenix. zhtml?c=83830&p=irol-govhighlights, April 15, 2009.

3. Greenhouse, "How Costco Became the Anti-Wal-Mart."

4. Ibid.

5. Ibid.; S. Clifford, "Because Who Knew a Big-Box Chain Could Have a Generous Soul," *Inc.* magazine, April 2005, 88.

6. S. Holmes and W. Zellner, "Commentary: The Costco Way," *BusinessWeek Online,* April 12, 2004, www.businessweek.com/ print/ magazine/content/04_15/b3878084_ mz021.htm?chan . . .; M. Herbst, "The Costco Challenge: An Alternative to Wal-Martization?" *LRA Online,* July 5, 2005, www.laborresearch.org/print. php?id=391.

7. Greenhouse, "How Costco Became the Anti-Wal-Mart."

8. Ibid.; "Company Profile," *Costco Wholesale, Investor Relations,* http://phx.corporate-ir.net/phoenix. zhtml?c=83830&p=irol-homeprofile, April 8, 2008; "Company Profile, *Costco Wholesale Investor Relations,* http://phx.corporate-ir.net/phoenix. zhtml?c=83830&p=irol-homeprofile, April 15, 2009.

9. M. Kimes, "Why Costco Investors Are Smiling," *CNNMoney.com,* January 30, 2009, http://cnnmoney.printthis. clickability.com/pt/cpt?action=cpt&title =Why+are+Costco+inve. . ., April 15, 2009.

10. Associated Press, "Costco to Shut Down Its 2 Home Furnishing Stores."

11. J. Aversa, "Some Business Make Layoffs the Last Option," April 6, 2009, *BusinessWeek Online,* http://www. businessweek.com/ap/financialnews/ D97D79SG3.htm, April 15, 2009; J. Aversa, "Layoffs Not an Option for Some US Businesses," April 7, 2009, *BusinessWeek Online,* http:// www.business.com/ap/financialnews/ D97DDDI00.htm, April 15, 2009.

12. "Code of Ethics," *Costco Wholesale Investor Relations.*

13. A. E. Tenbrunsel, "Misrepresentation and Expectations

of Misrepresentation in an Ethical Dilemma: The Role of Incentives and Temptation," *Academy of Management Journal* 41 (June 1998), 330–40.

14. D. Kravets, "Supreme Court to Hear Case on Medical Pot," www.yahoo.com, June 29, 2004; C. Lane "A Defeat for Users of Medical Marijuana," www.washingtonpost.com, June 7, 2005.

15. www.yahoo.com, 2003; www.mci.com, 2004.

16. J. Child, "The International Crisis of Confidence in Corporations," *Academy of Management Executive* 16 (August 2002), 145–48.

17. T. Donaldson, "Editor's Comments: Taking Ethics Seriously–A Mission Now More Possible," *Academy of Management Review* 28 (July 2003), 463–67.

18. R. E. Freeman, *Strategic Management: A Stakeholder Approach* (Marshfield, MA: Pitman, 1984).

19. J. A. Pearce, "The Company Mission as a Strategic Tool," *Sloan Management Review,* Spring 1982, 15–24.

20. J. Robertson, "Ex-Brocade CEO Sentenced to 21 Months, www.yahoo.com, January 16, 2008.

21. C. I. Barnard, *The Functions of the Executive* (Cambridge, MA: Harvard University Press, 1948).

22. Freeman, *Strategic Management.*

23. http://data.bls.gov/cgi-bin/-surveymost, 2006.

24. G. Brown, "How to Embrace Change," *Newsweek,* June 12, 2006, 69.

25. P. S. Adler, "Corporate Scandals: It's Time for Reflection in Business Schools," *Academy of Management Executive* 16 (August 2002), 148–50.

26. W. G. Sanders, and D. C. Hambrick, "Swinging for the Fences: The Effects of CEO Stock Options on Company Risk-Taking and Performance," *Academy of Management Journal* 53, no. 5 (2007), 1055–78.

27. House Oversight and Government Reform Committee Proceedings, February 2008, http://oversight.house.gov.

28. J. Abrams, "CEOs Involved in Mortgage Crisis Defend Their High Pay before Congressional Panel," www.yahoo.com, March 7, 2008.

29. T. L. Beauchamp and N. E. Bowie, eds., *Ethical Theory and Business* (Englewood Cliffs, NJ: Prentice-Hall, 1979); A. MacIntyre, *After Virtue* (South Bend, IN: University of Notre Dame Press, 1981).

30. R. E. Goodin, "How to Determine Who Should Get What," *Ethics,* July 1975, 310–21.

31. E. P. Kelly, "A Better Way to Think about Business" (book review), *Academy of Management Executive* 14 (May 2000), 127–29.

32. T. M. Jones, "Ethical Decision Making by Individuals in Organizations: An Issue Contingent Model," *Academy of Management Journal* 16 (1991), 366–95; G. F. Cavanaugh, D. J. Moberg, and M. Velasquez, "The Ethics of Organizational Politics," *Academy of Management Review* 6 (1981), 363–74.

33. L. K. Trevino, "Ethical Decision Making in Organizations: A Person-Situation Interactionist Model," *Academy of Management Review* 11 (1986), 601–17; W. H. Shaw and V. Barry, *Moral Issues in Business,* 6th ed. (Belmont, CA: Wadsworth, 1995).

34. T. M. Jones, "Instrumental Stakeholder Theory: A Synthesis of Ethics and Economics," *Academy of Management Review* 20 (1995), 404–37.

35. B. Victor and J. B. Cullen, "The Organizational Bases of Ethical Work Climates," *Administrative Science Quarterly* 33 (1988), 101–25.

36. D. Collins, "Organizational Harm, Legal Consequences and Stakeholder Retaliation," *Journal of Business Ethics* 8 (1988), 1–13.

37. R. C. Soloman, *Ethics and Excellence* (New York: Oxford University Press, 1992).

38. T. E. Becker, "Integrity in Organizations: Beyond Honesty and Conscientiousness," *Academy of Management Review* 23 (January 1998), 154–62.

39. S. W. Gellerman, "Why Good Managers Make Bad Decisions," in K. R. Andrews, ed., *Ethics in Practice: Managing the Moral Corporation* (Boston: Harvard Business School Press, 1989).

40. J. Dobson, "Corporate Reputation: A Free Market Solution to Unethical Behavior," *Business and Society* 28 (1989), 1–5.

41. M. S. Baucus and J. P. Near, "Can Illegal Corporate Behavior Be Predicted? An Event History Analysis," *Academy of Management Journal* 34 (1991), 9–36.

42. Trevino, "Ethical Decision Making in Organizations."

43. A. S. Waterman, "On the Uses of Psychological Theory and Research in the Process of Ethical Inquiry," *Psychological Bulletin* 103, no. 3 (1988): 283–98.

44. M. S. Frankel, "Professional Codes: Why, How, and with What Impact?" *Ethics* 8 (1989): 109–15.

45. J. Van Maanen and S. R. Barley, "Occupational Communities: Culture and Control in Organizations," in B. Staw and L. Cummings, eds., *Research in Organizational Behavior,* vol. 6 (Greenwich, CT: JAI Press, 1984), 287–365.

46. Jones, "Ethical Decision Making by Individuals in Organizations."

47. M. Conlin, "Where Layoffs Are a Last Resort," *BusinessWeek,* October 8, 2001, *BusinessWeek* Archives; *Southwest Airlines Fact Sheet,* June 19, 2001, www.swabiz.com.

48. G. R. Jones, *Organizational Theory: Text and Cases* (Reading, MA: Addison-Wesley, 1997).

49. P. E. Murphy, "Creating Ethical Corporate Structure," *Sloan Management Review* (Winter 1989), 81–87.

50. C. Stavraka, "Strong Corporate Reputation at J&J Boosts Diversity Recruiting Efforts," DiversityInc.com, February 16, 2001.

51. "Our Credo," www.jj.com, 2008.

52. Ibid.

53. L. L. Nash, *Good Intentions Aside* (Boston: Harvard Business School Press, 1993).

54. Ibid.; L. L. Nash, "Johnson & Johnson's Credo," in *Corporate Ethics: A Prime Business Asset* (New York: Business Roundtable, February 1988).

55. Nash, *Good Intentions Aside.*

56. Stavraka, "Strong Corporate Reputation."

57. Nash, *Good Intentions Aside.*

58. W. B. Swann, Jr., J. T. Polzer, D. C. Seyle, and S. J. Ko, "Finding Value in Diversity: Verification of Personal and Social Self-Views in Diverse Groups," *Academy of Management Review* 29, no. 1 (2004), 9–27.

59. "Usual Weekly Earnings Summary," *News: Bureau of Labor Statistics,* April 16, 2004, www.bls.gov/news.release/whyeng.nr0.htm; "Facts on Affirmative Action in Employment and Contracting," *Americans for a Fair Chance,* January, 28, 2004, fairchance.civilrights.org/research_center/details.cfm?id=18076; "Household Data Annual Averages," www.bls.gov, April 28, 2004.

60. "Prejudice: Still on the Menu," *BusinessWeek,* April 3, 1995, 42.

61. "She's a Woman, Offer Her Less," *BusinessWeek,* May 7, 2001, 34.

62. "Glass Ceiling Is a Heavy Barrier for Minorities, Blocking Them from Top Jobs," *The Wall Street Journal,* March 14, 1995, A1.

63. "Catalyst Report Outlines Unique Challenges Faced by African-American Women in Business," *Catalyst news release,* February 18, 2004.

64. C. Gibson, "Nation's Median Age Highest Ever, but 65-and-Over Population's Growth Lags, Census 2000 Shows," *U.S. Census Bureau News,* May 30, 2001, www.census.gov; "U.S. Census Press Releases: Nation's Population One-Third Minority," *U.S. Census Bureau News,* May 10, 2006, www.census.gov/Press-Release/www/releases/archives/population/006808.html.

65. "Table 2: United States Population Projections by Age and Sex: 2000–2050," *U.S. Census Board, International Data Base, 94,* April 28, 2004, www.census.gov/ipc/www.idbprint.html.

66. U.S. Equal Employment Opportunity Commission, "Federal Laws Prohibiting Job Discrimination–Questions and Answers," www.eeoc.gov, June 20, 2001.

67. "Sex by Industry by Class of Worker for the Employed Civilian Population 16 Years and Over," *American FactFinder,* October 15, 2001, factfinder.census.gov; "2002 Catalyst Census of Women Corporate Officers and Top Earners in the *Fortune* 500," www.catalystwomen.org, August 17, 2004.

68. "Profile of Selected Economic Characteristics: 2000," *American FactFinder,* October 15, 2001, factfinder.census.gov; "Usual Weekly Earnings Summary," www.bls.gov/news.release, August 17, 2004.

69. "2000 Catalyst Census of Women Corporate Officers and Top Earners of the *Fortune* 500," www.catalystwomen.org, October 21, 2001; S. Wellington, M. Brumit Kropf, and P. R. Gerkovich, "What's Holding Women Back?" *Harvard Business Review,* June 2003, 18–19; D. Jones, "The Gender Factor," *USA Today.com,* December 30, 2003; "2002 Catalyst Census of Women Corporate Officers and Top Earners in the *Fortune* 500," www.catalystwomen.org, August 17, 2004; "2007 Catalyst Census of Women Corporate Officers and Top Earners of the *Fortune* 500," www.catalyst.org/knowledge/titles/title.php?page=cen_COTE_07, February 8, 2008.

70. T. Gutner, "Wanted: More Diverse Directors," *BusinessWeek,* April 30, 2001, 134; "2003 Catalyst Census of Women Board Directors," www.catalystwomen.org, August 17, 2004; "2007 Catalyst Census of Women Board Directors of the *Fortune* 500," www.catalyst.org/knowledge/titles/title.php?page+cen_WBD_07, February 8, 2008.

71. Gutner, "Wanted: More Diverse Directors"; "2003 Catalyst Census of Women Board Directors."

72. R. Sharpe, "As Leaders, Women Rule," *BusinessWeek,* November 20, 2000, 75–84.

73. Ibid.

74. "New Catalyst Study Reveals Financial Performance Is Higher for Companies with More Women at the Top," *Catalyst news release,* January 26, 2004.

75. P. Sellers, "Women on Boards (NOT!)," *Fortune,* October 15, 2007, 105.

76. B. Guzman, "The Hispanic Population," U.S. Census Bureau, May 2001; U.S. Census Bureau, "Profiles of General Demographic Characteristics," May 2001; U.S. Census Bureau, "Revisions to the Standards for the Classification of Federal Data on Race and Ethnicity," November 2, 2000, 1–19.

77. L. Chavez, "Just Another Ethnic Group," *The Wall Street Journal,* May 14, 2001, A22.

78. Bureau of Labor Statistics, "Civilian Labor Force 16 and Older by Sex, Age, Race, and Hispanic Origin, 1978, 1988, 1998, and Projected 2008," stats.bls.gov/emp, October 16, 2001.

79. U.S. Census Bureau, "Profile of General Demographic Characteristics: 2000," *Census 2000,* www.census.gov; "U.S. Census Press Releases: Nation's Population One-Third Minority," *U.S. Census Bureau News,* May 10, 2006, www.census.gov/Press-Release/www/releases/archives/population/006808.html.

80. U.S. Census Bureau, "Census Bureau Projects Tripling of Hispanic and Asian Populations in 50 Years; Non-Hispanic Whites May Drop to Half of Total Populations," www.census.gov/Press-Release/www/releases/archives/population/001720.html, March 18, 2004; "Asians Projected to Lead Next Population Growth Surge," *Houston Chronicle,* May 1, 2004, 3A.

81. "Report Says Disparities Abound between Blacks, Whites," *Houston Chronicle,* March 24, 2004, 7A.

82. Ibid.

83. J. Flint, "NBC to Hire More Minorities on TV Shows," *The Wall Street Journal,* January 6, 2000, B13.

84. J. Poniewozik, "What's Wrong with This Picture?" *Time,* June 1, 2001, www.Time.com.

85. Ibid.

86. National Association of Realtors, "Real Estate Industry Adapting to Increasing Cultural Diversity," *PR Newswire,* May 16, 2001.

87. "Toyota Apologizes to African Americans over Controversial Ad," *Kyodo News Service,* Japan, May 23, 2001.

88. J. H. Coplan, "Putting a Little Faith in Diversity," *BusinessWeek Online,* December 21, 2000.

89. Ibid.

90. Ibid.

91. K. Holland, "When Religious Needs Test Company," *The New York Times,* February 25, 2007, BU17.

92. J. N. Cleveland, J. Barnes-Farrell, and J. M. Ratz, "Accommodation in the Workplace," *Human Resource Management Review* 7 (1997), 77–108; A. Colella, "Coworker Distributive Fairness Judgments of the Workplace Accommodations of Employees with Disabilities," *Academy of Management Review* 26 (2001), 100–16.

93. Colella, "Coworker Distributive Fairness Judgments"; D. Stamps, "Just

How Scary Is the ADA?" *Training* 32 (1995), 93–101; M. S. West and R. L. Cardy, "Accommodating Claims of Disability: The Potential Impact of Abuses," *Human Resource Management Review* 7 (1997), 233–46.

94. G. Koretz, "How to Enable the Disabled," *BusinessWeek,* November 6, 2000 (BusinessWeek Archives).

95. Colella, "Coworker Distributive Fairness Judgments."

96. "Notre Dame Disability Awareness Week 2004 Events," www.nd.edu/~bbuddies/daw.html, April 30, 2004.

97. P. Hewitt, "UH Highlights Abilities, Issues of the Disabled," *Houston Chronicle,* October 22, 2001, 24A.

98. "Notre Dame Disability Awareness Week 2004 Events"; Hewitt, "UH Highlights Abilities, Issues of the Disabled."

99. J. M. George, "AIDS/AIDS-Related Complex," in L. H. Peters, C. R. Greer, and S. A. Youngblood, eds., *The Blackwell Encyclopedic Dictionary of Human Resource Management* (Oxford, UK: Blackwell, 1997), 6–7.

100. Ibid., 6.

101. S. Armour, "Firms Juggle Stigma, Needs of More Workers with HIV," *USA Today,* September 7, 2000, B1.

102. Ibid.

103. Ibid.; S. Vaughn, "Career Challenge; Companies' Work Not Over in HIV and AIDS Education," *Los Angeles Times,* July 8, 2001.

104. R. Brownstein, "Honoring Work Is Key to Ending Poverty," *Detroit News,* October 2, 2001, 9; G. Koretz, "How Welfare to Work Worked," *BusinessWeek,* September 24, 2001 (*BusinessWeek* Archives).

105. "As Ex-Welfare Recipients Lose Jobs, Offer Safety Net," *The Atlanta Constitution,* October 10, 2001, A18.

106. "Profile of Selected Economic Characteristics: 2000," *American FactFinder,* factfinder.census.gov.

107. U.S. Census Bureau, "Poverty–How the Census Bureau Measures Poverty," *Census 2000,* September 25, 2001.

108. U.S. Census Bureau, "Poverty 2000," www.census.gov, October 26, 2001.

109. I. Lelchuk, "Families Fear Hard Times Getting Worse/$30,000 in the Bay Area Won't Buy Necessities, Survey Says," *San Francisco Chronicle,* September 26, 2001, A13; S. R. Wheeler, "Activists: Welfare-to-Work Changes Needed," *Denver Post,* October 10, 2001, B6.

110. B. Carton, "Bedtime Stories: In 24-Hour Workplace, Day Care Is Moving to the Night Shift," *The Wall Street Journal,* July 6, 2001, A1, A4.

111. Ibid.

112. Ibid.

113. Ibid.

114. "Google View Question: Q: Homosexual Statistics," answers.google.com/answers/threadview?id=271269, April 30, 2004; D. M. Smith and G. Gates, "Gay and Lesbian Families in the United States," *Urban Institute,* May 28, 2006, www.urban.org/publications/1000491.html.

115. S. E. Needleman, "More Programs Move to Halt Bias against Gays," *The Wall Street Journal,* November 26, 2007, B3.

116. K. Fahim, "United Parcel Service Agrees to Benefits in Civil Unions," *The New York Times,* July 31, 2007, A19.

117. J. Hempel, "Coming Out in Corporate America," *BusinessWeek,* December 15, 2003, 64–72.

118. Ibid.

119. J. Files, "Study Says Discharges Continue under 'Don't Ask, Don't Tell,'" *The New York Times,* March 24, 2004, A14; J. Files, "Gay Ex-Officers Say 'Don't Ask' Doesn't Work," *The New York Times,* December 10, 2003, A14.

120. Hempel, "Coming Out in Corporate America"; "DreamWorks Animation SKG Company History," www.dreamworksanimation.com/dwa/opencms/company/history/index.html, May 29, 2006; J. Chng, "Allan Gilmour: Former Vice-Chairman of Ford Speaks on Diversity," www.harbus.org/media/storage/paper343/news/2006/04/18/News/Allan.Gilmour.Former.ViceChairman.Of.Ford.Speaks.On.Diversity-1859600.shtml?nore write200606021800&sourcedomain=www.harbus.org, April 18, 2006.

121. Needleman, "More Programs Move to Halt Bias against Gays."

122. Hempel, "Coming Out in Corporate America."

123. Needleman, "More Programs Move to Halt Bias against Gays."

124. Ibid.

125. "For Women, Weight May Affect Pay," *Houston Chronicle,* March 4, 2004, 12A.

126. V. Valian, *Why So Slow? The Advancement of Women* (Cambridge, MA: MIT Press, 2000).

127. S. T. Fiske and S. E. Taylor, *Social Cognition,* 2d ed. (New York: McGraw-Hill, 1991); Valian, *Why So Slow?*

128. Valian, *Why So Slow?*

129. S. Rynes and B. Rosen, "A Field Survey of Factors Affecting the Adoption and Perceived Success of Diversity Training," *Personnel Psychology* 48 (1995), 247–70; Valian, *Why So Slow?*

130. V. Brown and F. L. Geis, "Turning Lead into Gold: Leadership by Men and Women and the Alchemy of Social Consensus," *Journal of Personality and Social Psychology* 46 (1984), 811–24; Valian, *Why So Slow?*

131. Valian, *Why So Slow?*

132. J. Cole and B. Singer, "A Theory of Limited Differences: Explaining the Productivity Puzzle in Science," in H. Zuckerman, J. R. Cole, and J. T. Bruer, eds., *The Outer Circle: Women in the Scientific Community* (New York: Norton, 1991), 277–310; M. F. Fox, "Sex, Salary, and Achievement: Reward-Dualism in Academia," *Sociology of Education* 54 (1981), 71–84; J. S. Long, "The Origins of Sex Differences in Science," *Social Forces* 68 (1990), 1297–1315; R. F. Martell, D. M. Lane, and C. Emrich, "Male-Female Differences: A Computer Simulation," *American Psychologist* 51 (1996), 157–58; Valian, *Why So Slow?*

133. Cole and Singer, "A Theory of Limited Differences"; M. F. Fox, "Sex, Salary, and Achievement: Reward Dualism in Academia," *Sociology of Education* 54 (1981), 71–84; Long, "The Origins of Sex Differences in Science"; R. F. Martell, D. M. Lane, and C. Emrich, "Male-Female Differences: A Computer Simulation," *American Psychologist* 51 (1996), 157–58; Valian, *Why So Slow?*

134. G. Robinson and K. Dechant, "Building a Case for Business Diversity," *Academy of Management Executive* 3 (1997), 32–47.

135. A. Patterson, "Target 'Micromarkets' Its Way to Success; No 2 Stores Are Alike," *The Wall Street Journal,* May 31, 1995, A1, A9.

136. "The Business Case for Diversity: Experts Tell What Counts, What Works," *DiversityInc.com,* October 23, 2001.

137. B. Hetzer, "Find a Niche–and Start Scratching," *BusinessWeek,* September 14, 1998 (*BusinessWeek* Archives).

138. K. Aaron, "Woman Laments Lack of Diversity on Boards of Major Companies," *The Times Union,* May 16, 2001, www.timesunion.com.

139. "The Business Case for Diversity."

140. B. Frankel, "Measuring Diversity Is One Sure Way of Convincing CEOs of Its Value," *DiversityInc.com,* October 5, 2001.

141. A. Stevens, "Lawyers and Clients," *The Wall Street Journal,* June 19, 1995, B7.

142. J. Kahn, "Diversity Trumps the Downturn," *Fortune,* July 9, 2001, 114–16.

143. "Chevron Settles Claims of 4 Women at Unit as Part of Sex Bias Suit," *The Wall Street Journal,* January 22, 1995, B12.

144. D. K. Berman, "TWA Settles Harassment Claims at JFK Airport for $2.6 Million," *The Wall Street Journal,* June 25, 2001, B6.

145. A. Lambert, "Insurers Help Clients Take Steps to Reduce Sexual Harassment," *Houston Business Journal,* March 19, 2004, Houston.bizjournals.com/Houston/stories/2004/03/22/focus4.html.

146. T. Segal, "Getting Serious about Sexual Harassment," *BusinessWeek,* November 9, 1992, 78–82.

147. U.S. Equal Employment Opportunity Commission, "Facts about Sexual Harassment," www.eeoc.gov/facts/fs-sex.html, May 1, 2004.

148. B. Carton, "Muscled Out? At Jenny Craig, Men Are Ones Who Claim Sex Discrimination," *The Wall Street Journal,* November 29, 1994, A1, A7.

149. R. L. Paetzold and A. M. O'Leary-Kelly, "Organizational Communication and the Legal Dimensions of Hostile Work Environment Sexual Harassment," in G. L. Kreps, ed., *Sexual Harassment: Communication Implications* (Cresskill, NJ: Hampton Press, 1993).

150. M. Galen, J. Weber, and A. Z. Cuneo, "Sexual Harassment: Out of the Shadows," *Fortune,* October 28, 1991, 30–31.

151. A. M. O'Leary-Kelly, R. L. Paetzold, and R. W. Griffin, "Sexual Harassment as Aggressive Action: A Framework for Understanding Sexual Harassment," paper presented at the annual meeting of the Academy of Management, Vancouver, August 1995.

152. B. S. Roberts and R. A. Mann, "Sexual Harassment in the Workplace: A Primer," www3.uakron.edu/lawrev/robert1.html, May 1, 2004.

153. "Former FedEx Driver Wins EEOC Lawsuit," *Houston Chronicle,* February 26, 2004, 9B.

154. Ibid.

155. J. Robertson, "California Jury Awards $61M for Harassment," http://news.Yahoo.com, June 4, 2006.

156. "2 FedEx Drivers Win Slur Lawsuit," *Houston Chronicle,* June 4, 2006, A9.

157. S. J. Bresler and R. Thacker, "Four-Point Plan Helps Solve Harassment Problems," *HR Magazine,* May 1993, 117–24.

158. "Du Pont's Solution," *Training,* March 1992, 29.

159. Ibid.

160. Ibid.

Chapter 4

1. L. J. Bourgeois, "Strategy and Environment: A Conceptual Integration," *Academy of Management Review* 5 (1985), 25–39.

2. M. E. Porter, *Competitive Strategy* (New York: Free Press, 1980).

3. "Coca-Cola versus Pepsi-Cola and the Soft Drink Industry," Harvard Business School Case 9-391-179.

4. www.splenda.com, 2008.

5. A. K. Gupta and V. Govindarajan, "Cultivating a Global Mind-Set," *Academy of Management Executive* 16 (February 2002), 116–27.

6. "Boeing's Worldwide Supplier Network," *Seattle Post-Intelligencer,* April 9, 1994, 13.

7. I. Metthee, "Playing a Large Part," *Seattle Post-Intelligencer,* April 9, 1994, 13.

8. R. J. Trent and R. M. Monczke, "Pursuing Competitive Advantage through Integrated Global Sourcing," *Academy of Management Executive* 16 (May 2002), 66–81.

9. R. B. Reich, *The Work of Nations* (New York: Knopf, 1991).

10. "Business: Link in the Global Chain," *The Economist,* June 2, 2001, 62–63.

11. M. E. Porter, *Competitive Advantage* (New York: Free Press, 1985).

12. www.walmart.com, 2008.

13. "The Tech Slump Doesn't Scare Michael Dell," *BusinessWeek,* April 16, 2001, 48.

14. T. Levitt, "The Globalization of Markets," *Harvard Business Review,* May–June 1983, 92–102.

15. "Dell CEO Would Like 40 Percent PC Market Share," www.dailynews.yahoo.com, June 20, 2001.

16. "Dell Expanding China Presence via Large Retailers," www.yahoo.com, April 17, 2008.

17. For views on barriers to entry from an economics perspective, see Porter, *Competitive Strategy.* For the sociological perspective, see J. Pfeffer and G. R. Salancik, *The External Control of Organization: A Resource Dependence Perspective* (New York: Harper & Row, 1978).

18. Porter, *Competitive Strategy;* J. E. Bain, *Barriers to New Competition* (Cambridge, MA: Harvard University Press, 1956); R. J. Gilbert, "Mobility Barriers and the Value of Incumbency," in R. Schmalensee and R. D. Willig, eds., *Handbook of Industrial Organization,* vol. 1 (Amsterdam: North Holland, 1989).

19. Press release, www.amazon.com, May 2001.

20. C. W. L. Hill, "The Computer Industry: The New Industry of Industries," in Hill and Jones, *Strategic Management: An Integrated Approach* (Boston: Houghton Mifflin, 2003).

21. J. Bhagwati, *Protectionism* (Cambridge, MA: MIT Press, 1988).

22. www.yahoo.com, July 18, 2004.

23. J. Schumpeter, *Capitalism, Socialism and Democracy* (London: Macmillan, 1950), 68. Also see R. R. Winter and

S. G. Winter, *An Evolutionary Theory of Economic Change* (Cambridge, MA: Harvard University Press, 1982).

24. "The Coming Clash of Logic," *The Economist*, July 3, 1993, 21–23.

25. S. Sherman, "The New Computer Revolution," *Fortune*, June 14, 1993, 56–84; www.amd.com, 2006.

26. N. Goodman, *An Introduction to Sociology* (New York: HarperCollins, 1991); C. Nakane, *Japanese Society* (Berkeley: University of California Press, 1970).

27. The Economist, *The Economist Book of Vital World Statistics* (New York: Random House, 1990).

28. For a detailed discussion of the importance of the structure of law as a factor explaining economic change and growth, see D. C. North, *Institutions, Institutional Change and Economic Performance* (Cambridge: Cambridge University Press, 1990).

29. Reich, *The Work of Nations.*

30. Bhagwati, *Protectionism.*

31. www.cnn.com, 2004.

32. M. A. Carpenter and J. W. Fredrickson, "Top Management Teams, Global Strategic Posture, and the Moderating Role of Uncertainty," *Academy of Management Journal* 44 (June 2001), 533–46.

33. Bhagwati, *Protectionism.*

34. For a summary of these theories, see P. Krugman and M. Obstfeld, *International Economics: Theory and Policy* (New York: HarperCollins, 1991). Also see C. W. L. Hill, *International Business* (New York: McGraw-Hill, 1997), chap. 4.

35. A. M. Rugman, "The Quest for Global Dominance," *Academy of Management Executive* 16 (August 2002), 157–60.

36. www.wto.org.com, 2004.

37. www.wto.org.com, 2001.

38. C. A. Bartlett and S. Ghoshal, *Managing across Borders* (Boston: Harvard Business School Press, 1989).

39. C. Arnst and G. Edmondson, "The Global Free-for-All," *Business Week*, September 26, 1994, 118–26.

40. W. Konrads, "Why Leslie Wexner Shops Overseas," *Business Week*, February 3, 1992, 30.

41. E. B. Tylor, *Primitive Culture* (London: Murray, 1971).

42. For details on the forces that shape culture, see Hill, *International Business*, chap. 2.

43. G. Hofstede, B. Neuijen, D. D. Ohayv, and G. Sanders, "Measuring Organizational Cultures: A Qualitative and Quantitative Study across Twenty Cases," *Administrative Science Quarterly* 35 (1990), 286–316.

44. M. H. Hoppe, "Introduction: Geert Hofstede's Culture's Consequences: International Differences in Work-Related Values," *Academy of Management Executive* 18 (February 2004), 73–75.

45. R. Bellah, *Habits of the Heart: Individualism and Commitment in American Life* (Berkeley: University of California Press, 1985).

46. R. Bellah, *The Tokugawa Religion* (New York: Free Press, 1957).

47. C. Nakane, *Japanese Society* (Berkeley: University of California Press, 1970).

48. Ibid.

49. G. Hofstede, "The Cultural Relativity of Organizational Practices and Theories," *Journal of International Business Studies*, Fall 1983, 75–89.

50. Hofstede et al., "Measuring Organizational Cultures."

51. J. Perlez, "GE Finds Tough Going in Hungary," *The New York Times*, July 25, 1994, C1, C3.

52. www.ge.com, 2004.

53. J. P. Fernandez and M. Barr, *The Diversity Advantage* (New York: Lexington Books, 1994).

Chapter 5

1. D. Sacks, "The Catalyst," *Fast Company*, October 2006, 59–61.

2. About PUMA, http://about.puma.com/EN/1/, February 13, 2008.

3. Sacks, "The Catalyst."

4. Ibid.

5. "Puma Expects 2008 Sales, Profits to Rise–PPR CFO," January 24, 2008, www.reuters.com/articlePrint?articleId=USL2491288920080124, February 13, 2008.

6. Sacks, "The Catalyst."

7. Ibid.

8. Ibid.

9. Ibid.; "Fashion in Motion Africa 2005, Zuly Bet," www.vam.ac.uk/collections/fashion/fashion_motion/africa_05/index.html, February 14, 2008.

10. www.puma.com, April 18, 2009.

11. Sacks, "The Catalyst."

12. Company Structure, http://about.puma.com/EN/1/9/9/, February 13, 2008

13. Sacks, "The Catalyst."

14. G. P. Huber, *Managerial Decision Making* (Glenview, IL: Scott, Foresman, 1993).

15. Sacks, "The Catalyst."

16. H. A. Simon, *The New Science of Management* (Englewood Cliffs, NJ: Prentice Hall, 1977).

17. N. A. Hira, "The Making of a UPS Driver," *Fortune*, November 12, 2007, 118–29.

18. Ibid.; J. Lovell, "Left-Hand-Turn Elimination," *The New York Times, nytimes.com*, December 9, 2007, www.nytimes.com/2007/12/09/magazine/09left-handturn.html?_r=2&oref=slogin&r, February 20, 2008.

19. Hira, "The Making of a UPS Driver."

20. L. Osburn, "Expecting the World on a Silver Platter," *Houston Chronicle*, September 17, 2007, D1, D6.

21. Hira, "The Making of a UPS Driver."

22. Ibid.; "Welcome to UPS Careers," https://ups.managehr.com/Home.htm, February 20, 2008.

23. Hira, "The Making of a UPS Driver."

24. Ibid.

25. Ibid.

26. Ibid.

27. Ibid.

28. D. Kahneman, "Maps of Bounded Rationality: A Perspective on Intuitive Judgment and Choice," Prize Lecture, December 8, 2002; E. Jaffe, "What Was I Thinking? Kahneman Explains How Intuition Leads Us Astray," *American Psychological Society* 17, no. 5 (May 2004), 23–26; E. Dane and M. Pratt, "Exploring Intuition and Its Role in Managerial Decision-Making," *Academy of Management Review* 32 (2007), 33–54.

29. One should be careful not to generalize too much here, however; for as Peter Senge has shown, programmed decisions rely on the implicit assumption that the environment is in a steady state. If environmental conditions change, then sticking to a routine decision rule can produce disastrous results. See P. Senge, *The Fifth Discipline: The Art and Practice of the Learning Organization* (New York: Doubleday, 1990).

30. Kahneman, "Maps of Bounded Rationality"; Jaffe, "What Was I Thinking?"

31. H. A. Simon, *Administrative Behavior* (New York: Macmillan, 1947), 79.

32. H. A. Simon, *Models of Man* (New York: Wiley, 1957).

33. K. J. Arrow, *Aspects of the Theory of Risk Bearing* (Helsinki: Yrjo Johnssonis Saatio, 1965).

34. Ibid.

35. R. L. Daft and R. H. Lengel, "Organizational Information Requirements, Media Richness and Structural Design," *Management Science* 32 (1986), 554–71.

36. R. Cyert and J. March, *Behavioral Theory of the Firm* (Englewood Cliffs, NJ: Prentice Hall, 1963).

37. J. G. March and H. A. Simon, *Organizations* (New York: Wiley, 1958).

38. H. A. Simon, "Making Management Decisions: The Role of Intuition and Emotion," *Academy of Management Executive* 1 (1987), 57–64.

39. M. H. Bazerman, *Judgment in Managerial Decision Making* (New York: Wiley, 1986). Also see Simon, *Administrative Behavior.*

40. "Sun Microsystems–Investor Relations: Officers and Directors," www.sun.com/aboutsun/investor/sun_facts/officers_ directors.html, June 1, 2004; "How Sun Delivers Value to Customers," *Sun Microsytems–Investor Relations: Support & Training,* June 1, 2004, www.sun.com/aboutsun/investor/sun_facts/core_strategies.html; "Sun at a Glance," *Sun Microsystems–Investor Relations: Sun Facts,* June 1, 2004, www.sun.com/aboutsun/ investor/sun_facts/index.html; "Plug in the System, and Everything Just Works," *Sun Microsystems–Investor Relations: Product Portfolio,* June 1, 2004, www.sun.com/aboutsun/investor/sun_facts/portfolio/html.

41. N. J. Langowitz and S. C. Wheelright, "Sun Microsystems, Inc. (A)," Harvard Business School Case 686–133.

42. R. D. Hof, "How to Kick the Mainframe Habit," *BusinessWeek,* June 26, 1995, 102–4.

43. Bazerman, *Judgment in Managerial Decision Making;* J. E. Russo and P. J. Schoemaker, *Decision Traps* (New York: Simon & Schuster, 1989).

44. M. D. Cohen, J. G. March, and J. P. Olsen, "A Garbage Can Model of Organizational Choice," *Administrative Science Quarterly* 17 (1972), 1–25.

45. Ibid.

46. Bazerman, *Judgment in Managerial Decision Making.*

47. Senge, *The Fifth Discipline.*

48. E. de Bono, *Lateral Thinking* (London: Penguin, 1968); Senge, *The Fifth Discipline.*

49. Russo and Schoemaker, *Decision Traps.*

50. Bazerman, *Judgment in Managerial Decision Making.*

51. B. Berger, "NASA: One Year after *Columbia*–Bush's New Vision Changes Agency's Course Midstream," *Space News Business Report,* January 26, 2004, www.space.com/spacenews/businessmonday_040126. html.

52. J. Glanz and J. Schwartz, "Dogged Engineer's Effort to Assess Shuttle Damage," *The New York Times,* September 26, 2003, A1.

53. M. L. Wald and J. Schwartz, "NASA Chief Promises a Shift in Attitude," *The New York Times,* August 28, 2003, A23.

54. S. Clifford, "Marc Shuman Was Determined to Expand Fast," *Inc.,* March 2006, 44–50

55. Russo and Schoemaker, *Decision Traps.*

56. I. L. Janis, *Groupthink: Psychological Studies of Policy Decisions and Disasters,* 2d ed. (Boston: Houghton Mifflin, 1982).

57. C. R. Schwenk, *The Essence of Strategic Decision Making* (Lexington, MA: Lexington Books, 1988).

58. See R. O. Mason, "A Dialectic Approach to Strategic Planning," *Management Science* 13 (1969), 403–14; R. A. Cosier and J. C. Aplin, "A Critical View of Dialectic Inquiry in Strategic Planning," *Strategic Management Journal* 1 (1980), 343–56; I. I. Mitroff and R. O. Mason, "Structuring III–Structured Policy Issues: Further Explorations in a Methodology for Messy Problems," *Strategic Management Journal* 1 (1980), 331–42.

59. D. M. Schweiger and P. A. Finger, "The Comparative Effectiveness of Dialectic Inquiry and Devil's Advocacy," *Strategic Management Journal* 5 (1984), 335–50.

60. Mary C. Gentile, *Differences That Work: Organizational Excellence through Diversity* (Boston: Harvard Business School Press, 1994); F. Rice, "How to Make Diversity Pay," *Fortune,* August 8, 1994, 78–86.

61. B. Hedberg, "How Organizations Learn and Unlearn," in W. H. Starbuck and P. C. Nystrom, eds., *Handbook of Organizational Design,* vol. 1 (New York: Oxford University Press, 1981), 1–27.

62. Senge, *The Fifth Discipline.*

63. Ibid.

64. P. M. Senge, "The Leader's New Work: Building Learning Organizations," *Sloan Management Review,* Fall 1990, 7–23.

65. W. Zellner, K. A. Schmidt, M. Ihlwan, and H. Dawley, "How Well Does Wal-Mart Travel?" *BusinessWeek,* September 3, 2001, 82–84.

66. J. M. George, "Creativity in Organizations," in J. P. Walsh and A. P. Brief, eds., *The Academy of Management Annals,* vol. 1 (New York: Erlbaum), 2008, 439–77.

67. Ibid.

68. C. Salter, "FAST 50: The World's Most Innovative Companies," *Fast Company,* March 2008, 73–117.

69. R. W. Woodman, J. E. Sawyer, and R. W. Griffin, "Toward a Theory of Organizational Creativity," *Academy of Management Review* 18 (1993), 293–321.

70. T. J. Bouchard, Jr., J. Barsaloux, and G. Drauden, "Brainstorming Procedure, Group Size, and Sex as Determinants of Problem Solving Effectiveness of Individuals and Groups," *Journal of Applied Psychology* 59 (1974), 135–38.

71. M. Diehl and W. Stroebe, "Productivity Loss in Brainstorming Groups: Toward the Solution of a Riddle," *Journal of Personality and Social Psychology* 53 (1987), 497–509.

72. D. H. Gustafson, R. K. Shulka, A. Delbecq, and W. G. Walster, "A Comparative Study of Differences in Subjective Likelihood Estimates Made by Individuals, Interacting Groups, Delphi Groups, and Nominal Groups," *Organizational Behavior and Human Performance* 9 (1973), 280–91.

73. N. Dalkey, *The Delphi Method: An Experimental Study of Group Decision Making* (Santa Monica, CA: Rand Corp., 1989).

74. T. Lonier, "Some Insights and Statistics on Working Solo," www.workingsolo.com.

75. I. N. Katsikis and L. P. Kyrgidou, "The Concept of Sustainable Entrepreneurship: A Conceptual Framework and Empirical Analysis," *Academy of Management Proceedings,* 2007, 1–6, 6p, web.ebscohost.com/ehost/delivery?vid=7&hid=102&sid=434afdf5-5ed9-45d4-993b-, January 24, 2008; "What Is a Social Entrepreneur?" http://ashoka.org/social_entrepreneur, February 20, 2008; C. Hsu, "Entrepreneur for Social Change," October 31, 2005, *U.S.News.com,* www.usnews.com/usnews/news/articles/051031/31drayton.htm; D. M. Sullivan, "Stimulating Social Entrepreneurship: Can Support From Cities Make a Difference? *Academy of Management Perspectives,* February 2007, 78.

76. Ibid.

77. N. Tiku, "Do-Gooder Finance: How a New Crop of Investors is Helping Social Entrepreneurs," *Inc.* Magazine, February 2008.

78. Ibid.; "About World of Good," *World of Good, Inc.,* www.worldofgoodinc.com/about/, February 20, 2008; "What Is Fair Trade?" *World of Good,* "Original Good," www.originalgood.com/FT/, February 20, 2008.

79. Tiku, "Do-Gooder Finance."

80. Ibid.

81. Ibid.

82. Ibid.

83. Ibid.

Chapter 6

1. A. Chandler, *Strategy and Structure: Chapters in the History of the American Enterprise* (Cambridge, MA: MIT Press, 1962).

2. Ibid.

3. H. Fayol, *General and Industrial Management* (1884; New York: IEEE Press, 1984).

4. Ibid., 18.

5. F. J. Aguilar, "General Electric: Reg Jones and Jack Welch," in *General Managers in Action* (Oxford: Oxford University Press, 1992).

6. Ibid.

7. www.ge.com, 2008.

8. C. W. Hofer and D. Schendel, *Strategy Formulation: Analytical Concepts* (St. Paul, MN: West, 1978).

9. P. Wack, "Scenarios: Shooting the Rapids," *Harvard Business Review,* November–December 1985, 139–50.

10. R. Phelps, C. Chan, and S. C. Kapsalis, "Does Scenario Planning Affect Firm Performance?" *Journal of Business Research,* March 2001, 223–32.

11. J. A. Pearce, "The Company Mission as a Strategic Tool," *Sloan Management Review,* Spring 1992, 15–24.

12. D. F. Abell, *Defining the Business: The Starting Point of Strategic Planning* (Englewood Cliffs, NJ: Prentice Hall, 1980).

13. G. Hamel and C. K. Prahalad, "Strategic Intent," *Harvard Business Review,* May–June 1989, 63–73.

14. D. I. Jung and B. J. Avolio, "Opening the Black Box: An Experimental Investigation of the Mediating Effects of Trust and Value Congruence on Transformational and Transactional Leadership," *Journal of Organizational Behavior,* December 2000, 949–64; B. M. Bass and B. J. Avolio, "Transformational and Transactional Leadership: 1992 and Beyond," *Journal of European Industrial Training,* January 1990, 20–35.

15. J. Porras and J. Collins, *Built to Last: Successful Habits of Visionary Companies* (New York: HarperCollins, 1994).

16. E. A. Locke, G. P. Latham, and M. Erez, "The Determinants of Goal Commitment," *Academy of Management Review* 13 (1988), 23–39.

17. K. R. Andrews, *The Concept of Corporate Strategy* (Homewood, IL: Irwin, 1971).

18. G. Mulvihill, "Campbell Is Really Cooking," *San Diego Tribune.com,* August 5, 2004.

19. W. D. Crotty, "Campbell Soup Is Not So Hot," www.MotleyFool.com, May 24, 2004.

20. A. Halperin, "Chicken Soup for the Investor's Soul," *BusinessWeek Online,* May 25, 2006, www.businessweek.com.

21. A. Carter, "Lighting a Fire under Campbell, www.businessweek.com, December 4, 2006.

22. www.campbellsoupcompany.com, 2008.

23. "Campbell Completes $850M Godiva Sale," www.yahoo.com, March 18, 2008.

24. R. D. Aveni, *Hypercompetition* (New York: Free Press, 1994).

25. M. E. Porter, *Competitive Strategy* (New York: Free Press, 1980).

26. C. W. L. Hill, "Differentiation versus Low Cost or Differentiation and Low Cost: A Contingency Framework," *Academy of Management Review* 13 (1988), 401–12.

27. For details, see J. P. Womack, D. T. Jones, and D. Roos, *The Machine That Changed the World* (New York: Rawson Associates, 1990).

28. Porter, *Competitive Strategy.*

29. www.cott.com, 2008.

30. www.zara.com, 2008.

31. C. Vitzthum, "Just-in-Time-Fashion," *The Wall Street Journal,* May 18, 2001, B1, B4.

32. www.zara.com, 2008.

33. www.hitachi.com, 2008.

34. M. K. Perry, "Vertical Integration: Determinants and Effects," in R. Schmalensee and R. D. Willig, *Handbook of Industrial Organization,* vol. 1 (New York: Elsevier Science, 1989).

35. "Matsushita Electric Industrial (MEI) in 1987," Harvard Business School Case 388-144.

36. P. Ghemawat, *Commitment: The Dynamic of Strategy* (New York: Free Press, 1991).

37. www.ibm.com, 2008.

38. E. Penrose, *The Theory of the Growth of the Firm* (Oxford: Oxford University Press, 1959).

39. M. E. Porter, "From Competitive Advantage to Corporate Strategy," *Harvard Business Review* 65 (1987), 43–59.

40. D. J. Teece, "Economies of Scope and the Scope of the Enterprise," *Journal of Economic Behavior and Organization* 3 (1980), 223–47.

41. M. E. Porter, *Competitive Advantage: Creating and Sustaining Superior Performance* (New York: Free Press, 1985).

42. www.3M.com, 2008.

43. Ibid.

44. C. Wyant, "Minnesota Companies Make *BusinessWeek*'s 'Most Innovative' List," *Minneapolis/St. Paul Business Journal,* April 18, 2008.

45. For a review of the evidence, see C. W. L. Hill and G. R. Jones, *Strategic Management: An Integrated Approach,* 5th ed. (Boston: Houghton Mifflin, 2003), chap. 10.

46. C. R. Christensen et al., *Business Policy Text and Cases* (Homewood, IL: Irwin, 1987), 778.

47. C. W. L. Hill, "Conglomerate Performance over the Economic Cycle," *Journal of Industrial Economics* 32 (1983), 197–213.

48. V. Ramanujam and P. Varadarajan, "Research on Corporate Diversification: A Synthesis," *Strategic Management Journal* 10 (1989), 523–51. Also see A. Shleifer and R. W. Vishny, "Takeovers in the 1960s and 1980s: Evidence and Implications," in R. P. Rumelt, D. E. Schendel, and D. J. Teece, eds., *Fundamental Issues in Strategy* (Boston: Harvard Business School Press, 1994).

49. J. R. Williams, B. L. Paez, and L. Sanders, "Conglomerates Revisited," *Strategic Management Journal* 9 (1988), 403–14.

50. G. Marcial, "As Tyco Splits into Three," www.businessweek.com, March 12, 2007.

51. www.tyco.com, 2008.

52. C. A. Bartlett and S. Ghoshal, *Managing across Borders* (Boston: Harvard Business School Press, 1989).

53. C. K. Prahalad and Y. L. Doz, *The Multinational Mission* (New York: Free Press, 1987).

54. "Gillette Co.'s New $40 Million Razor Blade Factory in St. Petersburg Russia," *Boston Globe,* June 7, 2000, C6.

55. D. Sewell, "P&G Replaces Ex-Gillette CEO at Operations," www.yahoo.com, May 24, 2006.

56. www.pg.com, 2005, 2008.

57. R. E. Caves, *Multinational Enterprise and Economic Analysis* (Cambridge: Cambridge University Press, 1982).

58. B. Kogut, "Joint Ventures: Theoretical and Empirical Perspectives," *Strategic Management Journal* 9 (1988), 319–33.

59. "Venture with Nestlé SA Is Slated for Expansion," *The Wall Street Journal,* April 15, 2001, B2.

60. B. Bahree, "BP Amoco, Italy's ENI Plan $2.5 Billion Gas Plant," *The Wall Street Journal,* March 6, 2001, A16.

61. N. Hood and S. Young, *The Economics of the Multinational Enterprise* (London: Longman, 1979).

Chapter 7

1. www.avon.com, 2008.

2. N. Byrnes, "Avon: More Than Just Cosmetic Changes," www.businessweek.com, March 12, 2007.

3. www.avon.com, 2008.

4. G. R. Jones, *Organizational Theory, Design and Change: Text and Cases* (Upper Saddle River: Prentice Hall, 2003).

5. J. Child, *Organization: A Guide for Managers and Administrators* (New York: Harper & Row, 1977).

6. P. R. Lawrence and J. W. Lorsch, *Organization and Environment* (Boston: Graduate School of Business Administration, Harvard University, 1967).

7. R. Duncan, "What Is the Right Organizational Design?" *Organizational Dynamics,* Winter 1979, 59–80.

8. T. Burns and G. R. Stalker, *The Management of Innovation* (London: Tavistock, 1966).

9. D. Miller, "Strategy Making and Structure: Analysis and Implications for Performance," *Academy of Management Journal* 30 (1987), 7–32.

10. A. D. Chandler, *Strategy and Structure* (Cambridge, MA: MIT Press, 1962).

11. J. Stopford and L. Wells, *Managing the Multinational Enterprise* (London: Longman, 1972).

12. C. Perrow, *Organizational Analysis: A Sociological View* (Belmont, CA: Wadsworth, 1970).

13. F. W. Taylor, *The Principles of Scientific Management* (New York: Harper, 1911).

14. R. W. Griffin, *Task Design: An Integrative Approach* (Glenview, IL: Scott, Foresman, 1982).

15. Ibid.

16. J. R. Hackman and G. R. Oldham, *Work Redesign* (Reading, MA: Addison-Wesley, 1980).

17. J. R. Galbraith and R. K. Kazanjian, *Strategy Implementation: Structure, System, and Process,* 2d ed. (St. Paul, MN: West, 1986).

18. Lawrence and Lorsch, *Organization and Environment.*

19. Jones, *Organizational Theory.*

20. Lawrence and Lorsch, *Organization and Environment.*

21. R. H. Hall, *Organizations: Structure and Process* (Englewood Cliffs, NJ: Prentice Hall, 1972); R. Miles, *Macro Organizational Behavior* (Santa Monica, CA: Goodyear, 1980).

22. Chandler, *Strategy and Structure.*

23. G. R. Jones and C. W. L. Hill, "Transaction Cost Analysis of Strategy-Structure Choice," *Strategic Management Journal* 9 (1988), 159–72.

24. www.gsk.com, 2006.

25. Ibid.

26. www.nokia.com, 2008.

27. N. Lakshman, "Nokia's Global Design Sense," www.businessweek.com, August 10, 2007.

28. www.nokia.com, 2008.

29. S. M. Davis and P. R. Lawrence, *Matrix* (Reading, MA: Addison-Wesley, 1977); J. R. Galbraith, "Matrix Organization Designs: How to Combine Functional and Project Forms," *Business Horizons* 14 (1971), 29–40.

30. L. R. Burns, "Matrix Management in Hospitals: Testing Theories of Matrix Structure and Development," *Administrative Science Quarterly* 34 (1989), 349–68.

31. C. W. L. Hill, *International Business* (Homewood, IL: Irwin, 2003).

32. Jones, *Organizational Theory.*

33. A. Farnham, "America's Most Admired Company," *Fortune,* February 7, 1994, 50–54.

34. P. Blau, "A Formal Theory of Differentiation in Organizations,"

American Sociological Review 35 (1970), 684–95.

35. S. Grey, "McDonald's CEO Announces Shifts of Top Executives," *The Wall Street Journal,* July 16, 2004, A11.

36. www.mcdonalds.com, 2008.

37. Child, *Organization.*

38. S. McCartney, "Airline Industry's Top-Ranked Woman Keeps Southwest's Small-Fry Spirit Alive," *The Wall Street Journal,* November 30, 1995, B1.

39. www.plexus.com, 2006.

40. W. M. Bulkeley, "Plexus Strategy: Smaller Runs of More Things," *The Wall Street Journal,* October 8, 2003, B1, B12.

41. P. M. Blau and R. A. Schoenherr, *The Structure of Organizations* (New York: Basic Books, 1971).

42. Jones, *Organizational Theory.*

43. Lawrence and Lorsch, *Organization and Environment,* 50–55.

44. J. R. Galbraith, *Designing Complex Organizations* (Reading, MA: Addison-Wesley, 1977), chap. 1; Galbraith and Kazanjian, *Strategy Implementation,* chap. 7.

45. Lawrence and Lorsch, *Organization and Environment,* 55.

46. B. Kogut, "Joint Ventures: Theoretical and Empirical Perspectives," *Strategic Management Journal* 9 (1988), 319–32.

47. G. S. Capowski, "Designing a Corporate Identity," *Management Review,* June 1993, 37–38.

48. J. Marcia, "Just Doing It," *Distribution,* January 1995, 36–40.

49. "Nike Battles Backlash from Overseas Sweatshops," *Marketing News,* November 9, 1998, 14.

50. J. Laabs, "Mike Gives Indonesian Workers a Raise," *Workforce,* December 1998, 15–16.

51. W. Echikson, "It's Europe's Turn to Sweat about Sweatshops," *BusinessWeek,* July 19, 1999, 96.

52. Copyright © 2006, Gareth R. Jones.

Chapter 8

1. www.ford.com, 2008.

2. D. Kiley, "The New Heat on Ford," www.businessweek.com, June 4, 2007.

3. Ibid.

4. www.ford.com, 2008.

5. W. G. Ouchi, "Markets, Bureaucracies, and Clans," *Administrative Science Quarterly* 25 (1980), 129–41.

6. P. Lorange, M. Morton, and S. Ghoshal, *Strategic Control* (St. Paul, MN: West, 1986).

7. H. Koontz and R. W. Bradspies, "Managing through Feedforward Control," *Business Horizons,* June 1972, 25–36.

8. E. E. Lawler III and J. G. Rhode, *Information and Control in Organizations* (Pacific Palisades, CA: Goodyear, 1976).

9. C. W. L. Hill and G. R. Jones, *Strategic Management: An Integrated Approach,* 6th ed. (Boston: Houghton Mifflin, 2003).

10. W. M. Bulkeley and J. S. Lublin, "Xerox Appoints Insider Mulcahy to Execute Turnaround as CEO," *The Wall Street Journal,* July 27, 2001, A2.

11. E. Flamholtz, "Organizational Control Systems as a Management Tool," *California Management Review,* Winter 1979, 50–58.

12. W. G. Ouchi, "The Transmission of Control through Organizational Hierarchy," *Academy of Management Journal* 21 (1978), 173–92.

13. W. G. Ouchi, "The Relationship between Organizational Structure and Organizational Control," *Administrative Science Quarterly* 22 (1977), 95–113.

14. Ouchi, "Markets, Bureaucracies, and Clans."

15. W. H. Newman, *Constructive Control* (Englewood Cliffs, NJ: Prentice Hall, 1975).

16. J. D. Thompson, *Organizations in Action* (New York: McGraw-Hill, 1967).

17. R. N. Anthony, *The Management Control Function* (Boston: Harvard Business School Press, 1988).

18. Ouchi, "Markets, Bureaucracies, and Clans."

19. Hill and Jones, *Strategic Management.*

20. R. Simons, "Strategic Orientation and Top Management Attention to Control Systems," *Strategic Management Journal* 12 (1991), 49–62.

21. G. Schreyogg and H. Steinmann, "Strategic Control: A New Perspective," *Academy of Management Review* 12 (1987), 91–103.

22. B. Woolridge and S. W. Floyd, "The Strategy Process, Middle Management Involvement, and Organizational Performance," *Strategic Management Journal* 11 (1990), 231–41.

23. J. A. Alexander, "Adaptive Changes in Corporate Control Practices," *Academy of Management Journal* 34 (1991), 162–93.

24. www.gillette.com, 2004.

25. Hill and Jones, *Strategic Management.*

26. G. H. B. Ross, "Revolution in Management Control," *Management Accounting* 72 (1992), 23–27.

27. P. F. Drucker, *The Practice of Management* (New York: Harper & Row, 1954).

28. S. J. Carroll and H. L. Tosi, *Management by Objectives: Applications and Research* (New York: Macmillan, 1973).

29. R. Rodgers and J. E. Hunter, "Impact of Management by Objectives on Organizational Productivity," *Journal of Applied Psychology* 76 (1991), 322–26.

30. M. B. Gavin, S. G. Green, and G. T. Fairhurst, "Managerial Control Strategies for Poor Performance over Time and the Impact on Subordinate Reactions," *Organizational Behavior and Human Decision Processes* 63 (1995), 207–21.

31. www.cypress.com, 2001.

32. B. Dumaine, "The Bureaucracy Busters," *Fortune,* June 17, 1991, 46.

33. D. S. Pugh, D. J. Hickson, C. R. Hinings, and C. Turner, "Dimensions of Organizational Structure," *Administrative Science Quarterly* 13 (1968), 65–91.

34. B. Elgin, "Running the Tightest Ships on the Net," *BusinessWeek,* January 29, 2001, 125–26.

35. P. M. Blau, *The Dynamics of Bureaucracy* (Chicago: University of Chicago Press, 1955).

36. www.ups.com, 2004.

37. J. Van Maanen, "Police Socialization: A Longitudinal Examination of Job Attitudes in an Urban Police Department," *Administrative Science Quarterly* 20 (1975), 207–28.

38. www.nokia.com, 2001.

39. P. de Bendern, "Quirky Culture Paves Nokia's Road to Fortune," www.yahoo.com, 2000.

40. K. E. Weick, *The Social Psychology of Organization* (Reading, MA: Addison-Wesley, 1979).

41. J. W. Schulz, L. C. Hauck, and R. M. Hauck, "Using the Power of Corporate Culture to Achieve Results: A Case Study of Sunflower Electric Power Corporation," *Management Quarterly* 2 (2001), 2–19.

42. L. Brown, "Research Action: Organizational Feedback, Understanding and Change," *Journal of Applied Behavioral Research* 8 (1972), 697–711; P. A. Clark, *Action Research and Organizational Change* (New York: Harper & Row, 1972); N. Margulies and A. P. Raia, eds., *Conceptual Foundations of Organizational Development* (New York: McGraw-Hill, 1978).

43. W. L. French and C. H. Bell, *Organizational Development* (Englewood Cliffs, NJ: Prentice-Hall, 1990).

44. J. McGregor, "The World's Most Innovative Companies," www.businessweek.com, May 4, 2007.

45. R. Nakashima, "Iger: Disney to Reap $1 Billion Online," www.yahoo.com, March 11, 2008.

46. W. L. French, "A Checklist for Organizing and Implementing an OD Effort," in W. L. French, C. H. Bell, and R. A. Zawacki, eds., *Organizational Development and Transformation* (Homewood, IL: Irwin, 1994), 484–95.

Chapter 9

1. C. J. Loomis, *Fortune* editor at large, "The Big Surprise Is Enterprise: Quietly beating out rivals Hertz and Avis, this privately held outfit reigns as the No. 1 car-rental company in America, and the Taylor family aims to keep it on top," *Fortune*, July 14, 2006, http://cnnmoney.printthis.clickability.com/pt/cpt?action=cpt&title=Fortune%3A+The+big . . . , March 31, 2008; http://aboutus.enterprise.com/who we are.html, April 21, 2009.

2. "Overview," *Enterprise Rent-A-Car Careers–Overview*, www.erac.com/recruit/about_enterprise.asp?navID=overview, March 27, 2008.

3. A. Fisher, *Fortune* senior writer, "Who's Hiring New College Grads Now," *CNNMoney.com*, http://cnnmoney.printthis.clickability.com/pt/cpt?action=cpt&title=Who%27s+hiring+coll. . . , March 31, 2008; Francesca Di Meglio, "A Transcript for Soft Skills,: Wisconsin is considering a dual transcript–one for grades and one to assess critical areas such as leadership and communication," www.businessweek.com/print/bschools/content/feb2008/bs20080221_706663.htm, March 28, 2008.

4. "Enterprise Ranked in Top 10 of BusinessWeek's 'Customer Service Champs,' " February 22, 2007, *Enterprise Rent-A-Car Careers–Enterprise in the News*, www.erac.com/recruit/news_detail.asp?navID=frontpage&RID=211, March 27, 2008; L. Gerdes, "The Best Places to Launch a Career," *BusinessWeek*, September 24, 2007, 49–60; P. Lehman, "A Clear Road to the Top," *Business Week*, September 18, 2006, 72–82.

5. Loomis, "The Big Surprise Is Enterprise."

6. "Enterprise Rent-A-Car's Pam Nicholson Named to *Fortune's* 50 Most Powerful Women in Business 2007," October 1, 2007, www.erac.com/recruit/news_details.asp?navID=frontpage&RID=234, March 27, 2008.

7. "Enterprise Ranked in Top 10 of *BusinessWeek's* 'Customer Service Champs' "; Gerdes, "The Best Places to Launch a Career."

8. "It's Running a Business . . . Not Doing a Job," *Enterprise Rent-A-Car Careers–Opportunities*, www.erac.com/recruit/opportunities.asp, March 27, 2008.

9. Loomis, "The Big Surprise Is Enterprise"; Lehman, "A Clear Road to the Top."

10. Ibid.

11. Lehman, "A Clear Road to the Top."

12. Loomis, "The Big Surprise Is Enterprise."

13. Ibid.; Lehman, "A Clear Road to the Top."

14. J. A. Taylor Kindle, "Enterprise: Why We Give Where We Give: For Enterprise Rent-A-Car, giving back is linked to the primary business. That means planting 50 million trees over 50 years, for starters," www.businessweek.com/print/investor/content/jun2007/pi20070628_339711.htm, March 28, 2008.

15. Ibid.

16. M. Gunther, senior writer, "Renting 'Green'? Not So Easy, Enterprise-Rent-A-Car Goes Green, with Limits," *CNNMoney.com*, January 17, 2008, http://cnnmoney.printthis.clickability.com/pt/cpt?action=cpt&title=Enterprise-Rent-A-Car. . . , March 3, 2008; "Enterprise Rent-A-Car Announces Most Comprehensive Environmental Platform in Its Industry, Wednesday, June 6, 2007, *Enterprise Rent-A-Car Careers–Enterprise In The News*, www.erac.com/ recruit/news_detail.asp?navID=front page&RID=221, March 27, 2008.

17. Loomis, "The Big Surprise Is Enterprise"; Lehman, "A Clear Road to the Top."

18. R. Kanfer, "Motivation Theory and Industrial and Organizational Psychology," in M. D. Dunnette and L. M. Hough, eds., *Handbook of Industrial and Organizational Psychology*, 2d ed., vol. 1 (Palo Alto, CA: Consulting Psychologists Press, 1990), 75–170.

19. G. P. Latham and M. H. Budworth, "The Study of Work Motivation in the 20th Century," in L. L. Koppes, ed., *Historical Perspectives in Industrial and Organizational Psychology* (Hillsdale, NJ: Laurence Erlbaum, 2006).

20. N. Nicholson, "How to Motivate Your Problem People," *Harvard Business Review*, January 2003, 57–65.

21. A. M. Grant, "Does Intrinsic Motivation Fuel the Prosocial Fire? Motivational Synergy in Predicting Persistence, Performance, and Productivity," *Journal of Applied Psychology* 93, no. 1 (2008), 48–58.

22. Ibid.; C. D. Batson, "Prosocial Motiviation: Is It Ever Truly Altruistic?" in L. Berkowitz, ed., *Advances in Experimental Social Psychology*, vol. 20 (New York: Academic Press, 1987), 65–122.

23. Grant, "Does Intrinsic Motivation Fuel the Prosocial Fire?"

24. J. P. Campbell and R. D. Pritchard, "Motivation Theory in Industrial and Organizational Psychology," in M. D. Dunnette, ed., *Handbook of Industrial and Organizational Psychology* (Chicago: Rand McNally, 1976), 63–130; T. R. Mitchell, "Expectancy Value Models in Organizational Psychology," in N. T. Feather, ed., *Expectations and Actions:*

Expectancy Value Models in Psychology (Hillsdale, NJ: Erlbaum, 1982), 293–312; V. H. Vroom, *Work and Motivation* (New York: Wiley, 1964).

25. N. Shope Griffin, "Personalize Your Management Development," *Harvard Business Review* 8, no. 10 (2003), 113–119.

26. T. A. Stewart, "Just Think: No Permission Needed," *Fortune,* January 8, 2001, www.fortune.com, June 26, 2001.

27. M. Copeland, "Best Buy's Selling Machine," *Business 2.0,* July 2004, 91–102; L. Heller, "Best Buy Still Turning on the Fun," *DSN Retailing Today* 43, no. 13 (July 5, 2004), 3; S. Pounds, "Big-Box Retailers Cash In on South Florida Demand for Home Computer Repair," *Knight Ridder Tribune Business News,* July 5, 2004 (gateway.proquest.com); J. Bloom, "Best Buy Reaps the Rewards of Risking Marketing Failure," *Adveristing Age* 75, no. 25 (June 21, 2004), 16; L. Heller, "Discount Turns Up the Volume: PC Comeback, iPod Popularity Add Edge," *DSN Retailing Today* 43, no. 13 (July 5, 2004), 45; www.bestbuy.com, June 8, 2006.

28. T. J. Maurer, E. M. Weiss, and F. G. Barbeite, "A Model of Involvement in Work-Related Learning and Development Activity: The Effects of Individual, Situational, Motivational, and Age Variables," *Journal of Applied Psychology* 88, no. 4 (2003), 707–24.

29. "Learn About Us," *The Container Store,* www.containerstore.com/learn/index.jhtml, April 1, 2008; www.containerstore.com, April 24, 2009.

30. M. Duff, "Top-Shelf Employees Keep Container Store on Track," www.looksmart.com, www.findarticles.com, March 8, 2004; M. K. Ammenheuser, "The Container Store Helps People Think Inside the Box," www.icsc.org, May 2004; "The Container Store: Store Location," www.containerstore.com/find/index/jhtml, June 5, 2006; "Store Locations," *The Container Store,* www.containerstore.com/find/index.jhtml, April 1, 2008.

31. "Learn About Us," www.containerstore.com, June 26, 2001.

32. Ibid.

33. J. Schlosser and J. Sung, "The 100 Best Companies to Work For," *Fortune,* January 8, 2001, 148–68; "*Fortune* 100 Best Companies to Work For 2006," *cnn.com,* June 5, 2006, http://money.cnn.com/magazines/fortune/bestcompanies/snapshots/359.html; "Learn About Us," *The Container Store,* www. containerstore.com/learn/index.jhtml, April 1, 2008.

34. "The Container Store," www.careerbuilder.com, July 13, 2004; "Tom Takes Re-imagine to PBS," Case Studies, www.tompeters.com, March 15, 2004; "2004 Best Companies to Work For," www.fortune.com, July 12, 2004; "*Fortune* 100 Best Companies to Work For 2006," *cnn.com,* June 5, 2006, http://money.cnn.com/magazines/fortune/bestcompanies/snapshots/359.html; R. Levering and M. Moskowitz, "100 Best Companies to Work For: The Rankings," *Fortune,* February 4, 2008, 75–94; http://money.cnn.com/magazines/fortune/bestcompanies/2009/full_list/, April 23, 2009.

35. D. Roth, "My Job at the Container Store," *Fortune,* January 10, 2000, www.fortune.com, June 26, 2001; "*Fortune* 2004: 100 Best Companies to Work For," www.containerstore.com/careers/FortunePR_2004.jhtml?message=/repository/messages/fortuneCareer.jhtml, January 12, 2004; R. Levering, M. Moskowitz, and S. Adams, "The 100 Best Companies to Work For," *Fortune* 149, no. 1 (2004), 56–78; www. containerstore.com/careers/FortunePR_2004.jhtml?message=/repository/messages/fortuneCareer.jhtml, January 12, 2004.

36. Roth, "My Job at the Container Store."

37. "Learn About Us," *The Container Store,* http://www.containerstore.com/learn/index.jhtml, April 1, 2008.

38. R. Yu, "Some Texas Firms Start Wellness Programs to Encourage Healthier Workers," *Knight Ridder Tribune Business News,* July 7, 2004, gateway.proquest.com; Levering et al., "The 100 Best Companies to Work For."

39. Roth, "My Job at the Container Store"; "The Foundation Is Organization."

40. A. H. Maslow, *Motivation and Personality* (New York: Harper & Row, 1954); Campbell and Pritchard, "Motivation Theory in Industrial and Organizational Psychology."

41. Kanfer, "Motivation Theory and Industrial and Organizational Psychology."

42. S. Ronen, "An Underlying Structure of Motivational Need Taxonomies: A Cross-Cultural Confirmation," in H. C. Triandis, M. D. Dunnette, and L. M. Hough, eds., *Handbook of Industrial and Organizational Psychology,* vol. 4 (Palo Alto, CA: Consulting Psychologists Press, 1994), 241–69.

43. N. J. Adler, *International Dimensions of Organizational Behavior,* 2d ed. (Boston: P.W.S. Kent, 1991); G. Hofstede, "Motivation, Leadership and Organization: Do American Theories Apply Abroad?" *Organizational Dynamics,* Summer 1980, 42–63.

44. F. Herzberg, *Work and the Nature of Man* (Cleveland: World, 1966).

45. N. King, "Clarification and Evaluation of the Two-Factor Theory of Job Satisfaction," *Psychological Bulletin* 74 (1970), 18–31; E. A. Locke, "The Nature and Causes of Job Satisfaction," in Dunnette, *Handbook of Industrial and Organizational Psychology,* 1297–1349.

46. D. C. McClelland, *Human Motivation* (Glenview, IL: Scott, Foresman, 1985); D. C. McClelland, "How Motives, Skills, and Values Determine What People Do," *American Psychologist* 40 (1985), 812–25; D. C. McClelland, "Managing Motivation to Expand Human Freedom," *American Psychologist* 33 (1978), 201–10.

47. D. G. Winter, *The Power Motive* (New York: Free Press, 1973).

48. M. J. Stahl, "Achievement, Power, and Managerial Motivation: Selecting Managerial Talent with the Job Choice Exercise," *Personnel Psychology* 36 (1983), 775–89; D. C. McClelland and D. H. Burnham, "Power Is the Great Motivator," *Harvard Business Review* 54 (1976), 100–10.

49. R. J. House, W. D. Spangler, and J. Woycke, "Personality and Charisma in the U.S. Presidency: A Psychological Theory of Leader Effectiveness," *Administrative Science Quarterly* 36 (1991), 364–96.

50. G. H. Hines, "Achievement, Motivation, Occupations, and Labor Turnover in New Zealand," *Journal of Applied Psychology* 58 (1973), 313–17; P. S. Hundal, "A Study of Entrepreneurial Motivation: Comparison of Fast- and Slow-Progressing Small Scale Industrial Entrepreneurs in Punjab, India," *Journal of Applied Psychology* 55 (1971), 317–23.

51. R. A. Clay, "Green Is Good for You," *Monitor on Psychology,* April 2001, 40–42.

52. Schlosser and Sung, "The 100 Best Companies to Work For"; Levering et al., "The 100 Best Companies to Work For"; "*Fortune* 100 Best Companies to Work For 2006," CNNMoney.com, June 5, 2006, www.money.cnn.com/magazines/fortune/bestcompanies/snapshots/1181.html; "Awards," *SAS,* www.sas.com/awards/index.html, April 1, 2008; Levering and Moskowitz, "100 Best Companies to Work For"; http://money.cnn.com/magazines/fortune/bestcompanies/2009/full_list/.

53. E. P. Dalesio, "Quiet Giant Ready to Raise Its Profits," *Houston Chronicle,* May 6, 2001, 4D; Levering et al., "The 100 Best Companies to Work For"; J. Goodnight, "Welcome to SAS," www.sas.com/corporate/index.html, August 26, 2003; "SAS Press Center: SAS Corporate Statistics," www.sas.com/bin/pfp.pl?=fi, April 18, 2006; "SAS Continues Annual Revenue Growth Streak," www.sas.com/news/prelease/031003/newsl.html, August 28, 2003; Levering and Moskowitz, "100 Best Companies to Work For."

54. J. Pfeffer, "SAS Institute: A Different Approach to Incentives and People Management Practices in the Software Industry," Harvard Business School Case HR-6, January 1998; "Saluting the Global Awards Recipients of Arthur Andersen's Best Practices Awards 2000," www.fortune.com, September 6, 2000; N. Stein, "Winning the War to Keep Top Talent," www.fortune.com, September 6, 2000.

55. Ibid.

56. Ibid.

57. Goodnight, "Welcome to SAS"; "By Solution," www.sas.com/success/solution.html, August 26, 2003; www.sas.com, June 8, 2006.

58. S. H. Wildstrom, "Do Your Homework, Microsoft," *BusinessWeek Online,* August 8, 2005, www.businessweek.com/print/magazine/content/05-b3946033-mz006. htm?chan; www.sas.com, June 8, 2006.

59. J. S. Adams, "Toward an Understanding of Inequity," *Journal of Abnormal and Social Psychology* 67 (1963), 422–36.

60. Ibid.; J. Greenberg, "Approaching Equity and Avoiding Inequity in Groups and Organizations," in J. Greenberg and R. L. Cohen, eds., *Equity and Justice in Social Behavior* (New York: Academic Press, 1982), 389–435; J. Greenberg, "Equity and Workplace Status: A Field Experiment," *Journal of Applied Psychology* 73 (1988), 606–13; R. T. Mowday, "Equity Theory Predictions of Behavior in Organizations," in R. M. Steers and L. W. Porter, eds., *Motivation and Work Behavior* (New York: McGraw-Hill, 1987), 89–110.

61. A. Goldwasser, "Inhuman Resources," *Ecompany.com,* March 2001, 154–55.

62. E. A. Locke and G. P. Latham, *A Theory of Goal Setting and Task Performance* (Englewood Cliffs, NJ: Prentice Hall, 1990).

63. Ibid.; J. J. Donovan and D. J. Radosevich, "The Moderating Role of Goal Commitment on the Goal Difficulty-Performance Relationship: A Meta-Analytic Review and Critical Analysis," *Journal of Applied Psychology* 83 (1998), 308–15; M. E. Tubbs, "Goal Setting: A Meta Analytic Examination of the Empirical Evidence," *Journal of Applied Psychology* 71 (1986), 474–83.

64. E. A. Locke, K. N. Shaw, L. M. Saari, and G. P. Latham, "Goal Setting and Task Performance: 1969–1980," *Psychological Bulletin* 90 (1981), 125–52.

65. P. C. Earley, T. Connolly, and G. Ekegren, "Goals, Strategy Development, and Task Performance: Some Limits on the Efficacy of Goal Setting," *Journal of Applied Psychology* 74 (1989), 24–33; R. Kanfer and P. L. Ackerman, "Motivation and Cognitive Abilities: An Integrative/Aptitude-Treatment Interaction Approach to Skill Acquisition," *Journal of Applied Psychology* 74 (1989), 657–90.

66. W. C. Hamner, "Reinforcement Theory and Contingency Management in Organizational Settings," in H. Tosi and W. C. Hamner, eds., *Organizational Behavior and Management: A Contingency Approach* (Chicago: St. Clair Press, 1974).

67. B. F. Skinner, *Contingencies of Reinforcement* (New York: Appleton-Century-Crofts, 1969).

68. H. W. Weiss, "Learning Theory and Industrial and Organizational Psychology," in Dunnette and Hough, *Handbook of Industrial and Organizational Psychology,* 171–221.

69. Hamner, "Reinforcement Theory and Contingency Management."

70. A. Bandura, *Principles of Behavior Modification* (New York: Holt, Rinehart and Winston, 1969); A. Bandura, *Social Learning Theory* (Englewood Cliffs, NJ: Prentice Hall, 1977); T. R. V. Davis and F. Luthans, "A Social Learning Approach to Organizational Behavior," *Academy of Management Review* 5 (1980), 281–90.

71. A. P. Goldstein and M. Sorcher, *Changing Supervisor Behaviors* (New York: Pergamon Press, 1974); F. Luthans and R. Kreitner, *Organizational Behavior Modification and Beyond* (Glenview, IL: Scott, Foresman, 1985).

72. Bandura, *Social Learning Theory;* Davis and Luthans, "A Social Learning Approach to Organizational Behavior"; Luthans and Kreitner, *Organizational Behavior Modification and Beyond.*

73. A. Bandura, "Self-Reinforcement: Theoretical and Methodological Considerations," *Behaviorism* 4 (1976), 135–55.

74. Hammonds, "Growth Search."

75. B. Elgin, "Managing Google's Idea Factory," *BusinessWeek,* October 3, 2005, 88–90.

76. A. Bandura, *Self-Efficacy: The Exercise of Control* (New York: W.H. Freeman, 1997); J. B. Vancouver, K. M. More, and R. J. Yoder, "Self-Efficacy and Resource Allocation: Support for a Nonmonotonic, Discontinous Model," *Journal of Applied Psychology* 93, no. 1 (2008), 35–47.

77. A. Bandura, "Self-Efficacy Mechanism in Human Agency," *American Psychologist* 37 (1982), 122–27; M. E. Gist and T. R. Mitchell, "Self-Efficacy: A Theoretical Analysis of Its Determinants and Malleability," *Academy of Management Review* 17 (1992), 183–211.

78. E. E. Lawler III, *Pay and Organization Development* (Reading, MA: Addison-Wesley, 1981).

79. "The Risky New Bonuses," *Newsweek,* January 16, 1995, 42.

80. Lawler, *Pay and Organization Development.*

81. Ibid.

82. J. F. Lincoln, *Incentive Management* (Cleveland: Lincoln Electric Company, 1951); R. Zager, "Managing Guaranteed Employment," *Harvard Business Review* 56 (1978), 103–15.

83. Lawler, *Pay and Organization Development.*

84. M. Gendron, "Gradient Named 'Small Business of Year,'" *Boston Herald,* May 11, 1994, 35.

85. W. Zeller, R. D. Hof, R. Brandt, S. Baker, and D. Greising, "Go-Go Goliaths," *BusinessWeek,* February 13, 1995, 64–70.

86. "Stock Option," *Encarta World English Dictionary,* June 28, 2001, www.dictionary.msn.com; personal interview with Professor Bala Dharan, Jones Graduate School of Business, Rice University, June 28, 2001.

87. Personal interview with Professor Bala Dharan.

88. Ibid.

89. A. J. Michels, "Dallas Semiconductor," *Fortune,* May 16, 1994, 81.

90. M. Betts, "Big Things Come in Small Buttons," *Computerworld,* August 3, 1992, 30.

91. M. Boslet, "Metal Buttons Toted by Crop Pickers Act as Mini Databases," *The Wall Street Journal,* June 1, 1994, B3.

92. C. D. Fisher, L. F. Schoenfeldt, and J. B. Shaw, *Human Resource Management* (Boston: Houghton Mifflin, 1990); B. E. Graham-Moore and T. L. Ross, *Productivity Gainsharing* (Englewood Cliffs, NJ: Prentice Hall, 1983); A. J. Geare, "Productivity from Scanlon Type Plans," *Academy of Management Review* 1 (1976), 99–108.

93. J. Labate, "Deal Those Workers In," *Fortune,* April 19, 1993, 26.

94. K. Belson, "Japan's Net Generation," *BusinessWeek,* March 19, 2001 (*BusinessWeek* Archives, June 27, 2001).

95. K. Belson, "Taking a Hint from the Upstarts," *BusinessWeek,* March 19, 2001 (*BusinessWeek* Archives, June 27, 2001); "Going for the Gold," *BusinessWeek,* March 19, 2001 (*BusinessWeek* Archives, June 27, 2001); "What the Government Can Do to Promote a Flexible Workforce," *BusinessWeek,* March 19, 2001 (*BusinessWeek* Archives, June 27, 2001).

Chapter 10

1. T. Lowry, "Can MTV Stay Cool?" *Business Week,* February 20, 2006, 51–60; "Senior Management," *VIACOM,* www.viacom.com/aboutviacom/Pages/seniormanagement.aspx, April 2, 2008.

2. www.viacom.com/2006/pdf/Viacom_Fact_Sheet_4_5_06.pdf, June 9, 2006; M. Gunther, "Mr. MTV Grows Up," CNNMoney.com, April 13, 2006, http://money.cnn.com/magazines/fortune/fortune_archive/2006/04/17/8374305/index.htm; "Viacom Completes Separation into CBS Corporation and 'New' Viacom," Viacom.com, January 1, 2006, www.viacom.com/view_release.jhtml?inID=10000040&inReleaseID=126683.

3. Lowry, "Can MTV Stay Cool?"; "VIACOM," *PULSE,* February 28, 2008, Fourth Quarter, 1, www.viacom.com/investorrelations/investor_relations_docs/pulse%20Q42007%20Final.pdf, April 2, 2008; www.mtv.com, April 24, 2009.

4. J. H. Higgins, "A Rockin' Role: McGrath Keeps MTV Networks Plugged In and Focused," www.broadcastingcable.com, April 10, 2006, www.broadcastingcable.com/article/CA6323342.html?display=Search+Results&text=judy+mcgrath; "*Fortune* 50 Most Powerful Women in Business 2005," CNNMoney.com, November 14, 2005, http://money.cnn.com/magazines/fortune/mostpowerfulwomen/snapshots/10.html; E. Levenson, "Hall of Fame: Digging a Little Deeper into the List, We Salute the Highfliers and Share Some Facts to Inspire and Amuse," CNNMoney.com, November 14, 2005, http://money.cnn.com/magazines/fortune/fortune_ archive/2005/11/14/8360698/index.html; "50 Most Powerful Women 2007: The Power 50," *CNNMoney.com, Fortune,* The Power 50–Judy McGrath (18)–FORTUNE, http://money.cnn.com/galleries/2007/fortune/0709/gallery.women_mostpowerful.fortune/18. . . , April 2, 2008; "50 Most Powerful Women in Business," http://money.cnn.com/magazine, fortune/mostpowerfulwomen/2008/full_list/, April 24, 2009.

5. Lowry, "Can MTV Stay Cool?"; "Welcome to Viacom–Senior Management," www.viacom.com/management.html, June 9, 2006.

6. Lowry, "Can MTV Stay Cool?"

7. Ibid.

8. "The 2006 National Show Mobile E-dition–Judy McGrath," www.thenationalshoe.com/Mobile/SpeakerDetail.aspx?ID=199, June 9, 2006.

9. Lowry, "Can MTV Stay Cool?"

10. Lowry, "Can MTV Stay Cool?"; "Viacom's MTV Networks Completes Acquisition of Xfire, Inc.," www.viacom.com/view_release.jhtml?inID=10000040&inReleaseID=227008, June 9, 2006.

11. Lowry, "Can MTV Stay Cool?"

12. G. Yukl, *Leadership in Organizations,* 2d ed. (New York: Academic Press, 1989); R. M. Stogdill, *Handbook of Leadership: A Survey of the Literature* (New York: Free Press, 1974).

13. Lowry, "Can MTV Stay Cool?"

14. W. D. Spangler, R. J. House, and R. Palrecha, "Personality and Leadership," in B. Schneider and D. B. Smith, eds., *Personality and Organizations* (Mahwah, NJ: Lawrence Erlbaum, 2004), 251–90.

15. Ibid.; "Leaders vs. Managers: Leaders Master the Context of Their Mission, Managers Surrender to It," www.msue.msu.edu/msue/imp/modtd/visuals/tsld029.htm, July 28, 2004; *"Leadership,"* Leadership Center at Washington State University; M. Maccoby, "Understanding the Difference between Management and Leadership," *Research Technology Management* 43, no. 1 (January–February 2000), 57–59 (www.maccoby.com/articles/UtDBMaL.html); P. Coutts, "Leadership vs. Management," www.telusplanet.net/public/pdcoutts/leadership/LdrVsMgnt.htm, October 1, 2000; S. Robbins, "The Difference between Managing and Leading," www.Entrepreneur.com/article/0,4621,304743,00.html, November 18, 2002; W. Bennis, "The Leadership Advantage," *Leader to Leader* 12 (Spring 1999) (www.pfdf.org/leaderbooks/121/spring99/bennis/html).

16. Spangler et al., "Personality and Leadership"; "Leaders vs. Managers"; "Leadership"; Maccoby, "Understanding the Difference between Management and Leadership"; Coutts, "Leadership vs. Management"; Robbins, "The Difference between Managing and Leading"; Bennis, "The Leadership Advantage."

17. "Greenleaf: Center for Servant-Leadership: History," *Greenleaf Center for Servant-Leadership,* www.greenleaf.org/aboutus/history.html, April 7, 2008.

18. "What Is Servant Leadership?" *Greenleaf Center for Servant-Leadership,* http://www.greenleaf.org/whatissl/ index.html, April 2, 2008.

19. Ibid.; Review by F. Hamilton of L. Spears and M. Lawrence, *Practicing Servant Leadership: Succeeding through Trust, Bravery, and Forgiveness* (San Francisco: Jossey-Bass 2004), in *Academy of Management Review* 30 (October 2005), 875–87; R. R. Washington, "Empirical Relationships between Theories of Servant, Transformational, and Transactional Leadership," *Academy of Management,* Best Paper Proceedings 2007, 1–6.

20. "Greenleaf: Center for Servant-Leadership: History"; "What Is Servant Leadership?"; "Greenleaf: Center for Servant-Leadership: Our Mission," *Greenleaf Center for Servant-Leadership,* www.greenleaf.org/aboutus/mission.html, April 7, 2008.

21. B. Burlingham, "The Coolest Small Company in America," *Inc.* Magazine, January 2003, www.inc.com/magazine/20030101/25036_Printer_Friendly.html, April 7, 2008.

22. Ibid.; "Zingerman's Community of Businesses," *About Us,* www.-zingermans.com/AboutUs.aspx, April 7, 2008; L. Buchanan, "In Praise of Selflessness," *Inc.* Magazine, May 2007, 33–35.

23. Burlingham, "The Coolest Small Company in America"; "Zingerman's Community of Businesses"; Buchanan, "In Praise of Selflessness."

24. Buchanan, "In Praise of Selflessness."

25. Ibid.

26. Burlingham, "The Coolest Small Company in America"; "In a Nutshell," *food gatherers,* www.foodgatherers.org/about.htm, April 7, 2008.

27. "In a Nutshell."

28. Buchanan, "In Praise of Selflessness."

29. R. Calori and B. Dufour, "Management European Style," *Academy of Management Executive* 9, no. 3 (1995), 61–70.

30. Ibid.

31. H. Mintzberg, *Power In and Around Organizations* (Englewood Cliffs, NJ: Prentice Hall, 1983); J. Pfeffer, *Power in Organizations* (Marshfield, MA: Pitman, 1981).

32. R. P. French, Jr., and B. Raven, "The Bases of Social Power," in D. Cartwright and A. F. Zander, eds., *Group Dynamics* (Evanston, IL: Row, Peterson, 1960), 607–23.

33. R. L. Rose, "After Turning Around Giddings and Lewis, Fife Is Turned Out Himself," *The Wall Street Journal,* June 22, 1993, A1.

34. A. Grove, "How Intel Makes Spending Pay Off," *Fortune,* February 22, 1993, 56–61; "Craig R. Barrett, Chief Executive Officer: Intel Corporation," *Intel,* July 28, 2004, www.intel.com/pressroom/kits/bios/ barrett/bio.htm; "Corporate Officers," http://www.intel.com/pressroom/ExecBios.htm?id=SEARCH, May 5, 2009.

35. "Craig R. Barrett Bio," www.intel.com/pressroom/kits/bios/barrett.htm, April 8, 2008; "Microsoft Press Pass–Microsoft Board of Directors," www.microsoft.com/presspass/bod/default.mspx, April 8, 2008; "Tachi Yamada Selected to Lead Gates Foundation's Global Health Program," Announcements–Bill & Melinda Gates Foundation, February 6, 2006, www.gatesfoundation.org/GlobalHealth/Announcements/Announce-060106.htm, April 8, 2008; "Board of Directors," http://www.microsoft.com/presspass/bod/bod.aspx, May 5, 2009; "Co-Chairs, Trustees, and Management Committee," Bill and Melinda Gates Foundation, http://www.gatesfoundation.org/leadership/Pages/overview.aspx, May 5, 2009.

36. M. Loeb, "Jack Welch Lets Fly on Budgets, Bonuses, and Buddy Boards," *Fortune,* May 29, 1995, 146.

37. T. M. Burton, "Visionary's Reward: Combine 'Simple Ideas' and Some Failures; Result: Sweet Revenge," *The Wall Street Journal,* February 3, 1995, A1, A5.

38. L. Nakarmi, "A Flying Leap Toward the 21st Century? Pressure from Competitors and Seoul May Transform the Chaebol," *BusinessWeek,* March 20, 1995, 78–80.

39. B. M. Bass, *Bass and Stogdill's Handbook of Leadership: Theory, Research, and Managerial Applications,* 3d ed. (New York: Free Press, 1990); R. J. House and M. L. Baetz, "Leadership: Some Empirical Generalizations and New Research Directions," in B. M. Staw and L. L. Cummings, eds., *Research in Organizational Behavior,* vol. 1 (Greenwich, CT: JAI Press, 1979), 341–423; S. A. Kirpatrick and E. A. Locke, "Leadership: Do Traits Matter?" *Academy of Management Executive* 5, no. 2 (1991), 48–60; Yukl, *Leadership in Organizations;* G. Yukl and D. D. Van Fleet, "Theory and Research on Leadership in Organizations," in M. D. Dunnette and L. M. Hough, eds., *Handbook of Industrial and Organizational Psychology,* 2d ed., vol. 3 (Palo Alto, CA: Consulting Psychologists Press, 1992), 147–97.

40. E. A. Fleishman, "Performance Assessment Based on an Empirically Derived Task Taxonomy," *Human Factors* 9 (1967), 349–66; E. A. Fleishman, "The Description of Supervisory Behavior," *Personnel Psychology* 37 (1953), 1–6; A. W. Halpin and B. J. Winer, "A Factorial Study of the Leader Behavior Descriptions," in R. M. Stogdill and A. I. Coons, eds., *Leader Behavior: Its Description and Measurement* (Columbus Bureau of Business Research, Ohio State University, 1957); D. Tscheulin, "Leader Behavior Measurement in German Industry," *Journal of Applied Psychology* 56 (1971), 28–31.

41. E. A. Fleishman and E. F. Harris, "Patterns of Leadership Behavior Related to Employee Grievances and Turnover," *Personnel Psychology* 15 (1962), 43–56.

42. F. E. Fiedler, *A Theory of Leadership Effectiveness* (New York: McGraw-Hill, 1967); F. E. Fiedler, "The Contingency Model and the Dynamics of the Leadership Process," in L. Berkowitz, ed., *Advances in Experimental Social Psychology* (New York: Academic Press, 1978).

43. J. Rebello, "Radical Ways of Its CEO Are a Boon to Bank," *The Wall Street Journal,* March 20, 1995, B1, B3.

44. J. Fierman, "Winning Ideas from Maverick Managers," *Fortune,* February 6, 1995, 66–80.

45. Ibid.; "Laybourne, Geraldine, U.S. Media Executive," *Laybourne, Geraldine,* http://museum.tv/archives/etv/L/htmlL/laybournege/laybournege.htm, April 8, 2008.

46. M. Schuman, "Free to Be," *Forbes,* May 8, 1995, 78–80; "Profile–Herman

Mashaba," *SAIE–Herman Mashaba,* www.entrepreneurship.co.za/page/herman_mashaba, April 8, 2008.

47. House and Baetz, "Leadership"; L. H. Peters, D. D. Hartke, and J. T. Pohlmann, "Fiedler's Contingency Theory of Leadership: An Application of the Meta-Analysis Procedures of Schmidt and Hunter," *Psychological Bulletin* 97 (1985), 274–85; C. A. Schriesheim, B. J. Tepper, and L. A. Tetrault, "Least Preferred Co-Worker Score, Situational Control, and Leadership Effectiveness: A Meta-Analysis of Contingency Model Performance Predictions," *Journal of Applied Psychology* 79 (1994), 561–73.

48. M. G. Evans, "The Effects of Supervisory Behavior on the Path-Goal Relationship," *Organizational Behavior and Human Performance* 5 (1970), 277–98; R. J. House, "A Path-Goal Theory of Leader Effectiveness," *Administrative Science Quarterly* 16 (1971), 321–38; J. C. Wofford and L. Z. Liska, "Path-Goal Theories of Leadership: A Meta-Analysis," *Journal of Management* 19 (1993), 857–76.

49. S. Kerr and J. M. Jermier, "Substitutes for Leadership: Their Meaning and Measurement," *Organizational Behavior and Human Performance* 22 (1978), 375–403; P. M. Podsakoff, B. P. Niehoff, S. B. MacKenzie, and M. L. Williams, "Do Substitutes for Leadership Really Substitute for Leadership? An Empirical Examination of Kerr and Jermier's Situational Leadership Model," *Organizational Behavior and Human Decision Processes* 54 (1993), 1–44.

50. Kerr and Jermier, "Substitutes for Leadership"; Podsakoff et al., "Do Substitutes for Leadership Really Substitute for Leadership?"

51. J. Reingold, "You Got Served," *Fortune,* October 1, 2007, 55–58; "News on Women," *News On Women: Sue Nokes SVP at T-Mobile,* http://newsonwomen.typepad .com/news_on_women/2007/09/sue-nokes-svp-a.html, April 8, 2008.

52. "Company Information," *T-Mobile Cell Phone Carrier Quick Facts,* http://www.t-mobile/Company/CompanyInfo.aspx?tp=Abt_Tab_CompanyOverview, April 8, 2008.

53. Reingold, "You Got Served."

54. Ibid.; "Company Information," *Highest customer satisfaction & wireless call quality-J.D. Power Awards,* http://www.t-mobile.com/Company/CompanyInfo.aspx?tp=Abt_Tab_Awards, April 8, 2008.

55. Reingold, "You Got Served."

56. Ibid.

57. B. M. Bass, *Leadership and Performance beyond Expectations* (New York: Free Press, 1985); Bass, *Bass and Stogdill's Handbook of Leadership;* Yukl and Van Fleet, "Theory and Research on Leadership."

58. Reingold, "You Got Served."

59. Ibid.

60. Ibid.

61. Ibid.

62. Ibid.

63. Ibid.

64. J. A. Conger and R. N. Kanungo, "Behavioral Dimensions of Charismatic Leadership," in J. A. Conger, R. N. Kanungo, and Associates, *Charismatic Leadership* (San Francisco: Jossey-Bass, 1988).

65. Bass, *Leadership and Performance beyond Expectations;* Bass, *Bass and Stogdill's Handbook of Leadership;* Yukl and Van Fleet, "Theory and Research on Leadership"; Reingold, "You Got Served."

66. Bass, *Leadership and Performance beyond Expectations;* Bass, *Bass and Stogdill's Handbook of Leadership;* Yukl and Van Fleet, "Theory and Research on Leadership."

67. Reingold, "You Got Served."

68. Bass, *Leadership and Performance Beyond Expectations.*

69. Bass, *Bass and Stogdill's Handbook of Leadership;* B. M. Bass and B. J. Avolio, "Transformational Leadership: A Response to Critiques," in M. M. Chemers and R. Ayman, eds., *Leadership Theory and Research: Perspectives and Directions* (San Diego: Academic Press, 1993), 49–80; B. M. Bass, B. J. Avolio, and L. Goodheim, "Biography and the Assessment of Transformational Leadership at the World Class Level," *Journal of Management* 13 (1987), 7–20; J. J. Hater and B. M. Bass, "Supervisors' Evaluations and Subordinates' Perceptions of Transformational and Transactional Leadership," *Journal of Applied Psychology* 73, (1988), 695–702; R. Pillai, "Crisis and Emergence of Charismatic Leadership in Groups: An Experimental Investigation," *Journal of Applied Psychology* 26 (1996), 543–62; J. Seltzer and B. M. Bass, "Transformational Leadership: Beyond Initiation and Consideration," *Journal of Management* 16 (1990), 693–703; D. A. Waldman, B. M. Bass, and W. O. Einstein, "Effort, Performance, Transformational Leadership in Industrial and Military Service," *Journal of Occupation Psychology* 60 (1987), 1–10.

70. R. Pillai, C. A. Schriesheim, and E. S. Williams, "Fairness Perceptions and Trust as Mediators of Transformational and Transactional Leadership: A Two-Sample Study," *Journal of Management* 25 (1999), 897–933.

71. L. Tischler, "Where Are the Women?" *Fast Company,* February 2004, 52–60.

72. "2000 Catalyst Census of Women Corporate Officers and Top Earners of the *Fortune* 500," www.catalystwomen.org, October 21, 2001; S. Wellington, M. Brumit Kropf, and P. R. Gerkovich, "What's Holding Women Back?" *Harvard Business Review,* June 2003, 18–19; D. Jones, "The Gender Factor," *USA Today.com,* December 30, 2003; "2002 Catalyst Census of Women Corporate Officers and Top Earners in the *Fortune* 500," www.catalystwomen.org, August 17, 2004; "2007 Catalyst Census of Women Corporate Officers and Top Earners of the *Fortune* 500," www.catalyst.org/knowledge/titles/title/php?page=cen_COTE_07, February 8, 2008.

73. A. H. Eagly and B. T. Johnson, "Gender and Leadership Style: A Meta-Analysis," *Psychological Bulletin* 108 (1990), 233–56.

74. Ibid.

75. *The Economist,* "Workers Resent Scoldings from Female Bosses," *Houston Chronicle,* August 19, 2000, 1C.

76. Ibid.

77. Ibid.

78. Ibid.

79. A. H. Eagly, S. J. Karau, and M. G. Makhijani, "Gender and the Effectiveness of Leaders: A Meta-Analysis," *Psychological Bulletin* 117 (1995), 125–45.

80. Ibid.

81. J. M. George and K. Bettenhausen, "Understanding Prosocial Behavior, Sales Performance, and Turnover: A Group-Level Analysis in a Service Context," *Journal of Applied Psychology* 75 (1990), 698–709.

82. T. Sy, S. Cote, and R. Saavedra, "The Contagious Leader: Impact of the Leader's Mood on the Mood of Group Members, Group Affective Tone, and Group Processes," *Journal of Applied Psychology* 90, no. 2 (2005), 295–305.

83. J. M. George, "Emotions and Leadership: The Role of Emotional Intelligence," *Human Relations* 53 (2000), 1027–55.

84. Ibid.

85. J. Zhou and J. M. George, "Awakening Employee Creativity: The Role of Leader Emotional Intelligence," *The Leadership Quarterly* 14, no. 45 (August–October 2003), 545–68.

86. Ibid.

87. Ibid.

88. D. Fenn, "My Bad," *Inc.* Magazine, October 2007, 37–38; "About Us," *Creative Display Solutions: About Us,* www.creative displaysolutions.com/pages/about/about.html, April 4, 2008.

89. Ibid.

90. Fenn, "My Bad."

91. Ibid.

92. Ibid.

93. Ibid.

94. Ibid.

95. Ibid.; C. Mason-Draffen, "Inside Stories," "Feeling Like a Million," *Creative Display Solutions: CDS News,* www.creative displaysolutions.com/pages/about/news6.html, April 4, 2008.

96. D. Sonnenberg, "Mother Load: How to Balance Career and Family," July 30, 2007, *Creative Display Solutions: CDS News,* www.creativedisplaysolutions.com/pages/about/news8.html, April 4, 2008; C. Mason-Draffen, "Partnership at Work: Couples in Business Together Have Their Share of Sweet Rewards and Unique Challenges," February 13, 2007, *Creative Display Solutions, CDS News,* www.creative displaysolutions.com/pages/about/news7.html, April 4, 2008; "Client List," *Creative Display Solutions: About Us,* www.creative displaysolutions.com/pages/about/clients.html, April 8, 2008; Fenn, "My Bad."

97. Fenn, "My Bad."

Chapter 11

1. "About ICU Medical, Inc.," www.icumed.com/about.asp, April 11, 2008.

2. Ibid.

3. "ICU Medical, Inc.–Fundamentals," http://phx.corporate-ir.net/phoenix.zhtml?c=86695&p=irol-fundamentals, April 11, 2008; "ICU Medical Inc. (ICUI): Stock Quote & Company Profile–Business Week," *Business Week,* http://investing.businessweek.com/research/stocks/snapshot/snapshot_article.asp?symbol=..., April 11, 2008; "ICUI: Key Statistics for ICU Medical, Inc.–Yahoo! Finance," http://finance.yahoo.com/q/ks?s=ICUI, May 17, 2009; "ICUI: Profile for ICU Medical Inc.–Yahoo! Finance," http://finance.yahoo.com/q/pr?s=icui, May 17, 2009.

4. "ICU Medical, Inc.–Investor Relations Home," http://phx.corporate-ir.net/phoenix.zhtml?c=86695&p=irol-IRHome, April 11, 2008.

5. "About ICU Medical, Inc."

6. "Clave Connector," ICU Medical, Inc., www.icumend.com, April 11, 2008.

7. E. White, "How a Company Made Everyone a Team Player," *The Wall Street Journal,* August 13, 2007, B1, B7.

8. Ibid.

9. Ibid.

10. Ibid.

11. Ibid.

12. Ibid.

13. Ibid.

14. Ibid.

15. Ibid.

16. Ibid.

17. T. M. Mills, *The Sociology of Small Groups* (Englewood Cliffs, NJ: Prentice Hall, 1967); M. E. Shaw, *Group Dynamics* (New York: McGraw-Hill, 1981).

18. White, "How a Company Made Everyone a Team Player."

19. R. S. Buday, "Reengineering One Firm's Product Development and Another's Service Delivery," *Planning Review,* March–April 1993, 14–19; J. M. Burcke, "Hallmark's Quest for Quality Is a Job Never Done," *Business Insurance,* April 26, 1993, 122; M. Hammer and J. Champy, *Reengineering the Corporation* (New York: HarperBusiness, 1993); T. A. Stewart, "The Search for the Organization of Tomorrow," *Fortune,* May 18, 1992, 92–98.

20. "Amazon.com Investor Relations: Officers & Directors," http://phx.corporate-ir.net/phoenix.zhtml?c=97664&p=irol-gov Manage, June 19, 2006; "Amazon.com Investor Relations: Press Release," http://phx.corporate-ir.net/phoenix.zhtml? c=97664&p=irol-newsArticle&ID=1102342&hi..., April 17, 2008; "Amazon.com Investor Relations: Officers and Directors," http://phx.corporate-ir.net/Phoenix.2html?C=97664&p=irol-govmanage, May 19, 2009.

21. A. Deutschman, "Inside the Mind of Jeff Bezos," *Fast Company,* August 2004, 50–58.

22. Ibid.; "Amazon.com Digital Media Technology," http://media-server.amazon .com/jobs/jobs.html, June 19, 2006.

23. "Amazon.com: Kindle: Amazon's New Wireless Reading Device: Kindle Store," www.amazon.com/gp/product/B000F173MA/ref=amb_link_6369712_2? pf_rd_m=A..., April 17, 2008.

24. Deutschman, "Inside the Mind of Jeff Bezos."

25. "Online Extra: Jeff Bezos on Word-of-Mouth Power," *BusinessWeek Online,* August 2, 2004, www.businessweek.com; R. D. Hof, "Reprogramming Amazon," *BusinessWeek Online,* December 22, 2003, www.businessweek.com; "About Amazon.com: Company Information," www.amazon.com/exec/obidos/tg/browsw/-/574562/ 104-0138839-3693547, June 19, 2006; "Amazon.com Investor Relations: Press Release."

26. "RockBottom Restaurants," www.rockbottom.com/RockBottomWeb/RBR/index.aspx?PageName=/RockBottom..., April 15, 2008.

27. S. Dallas, "Rock Bottom Restaurants: Brewing Up Solid Profits," *BusinessWeek,* May 22, 1995, 74.

28. J. A. Pearce II and E. C. Ravlin, "The Design and Activation of Self-Regulating Work Groups," *Human Relations* 11 (1987), 751–82.

29. B. Dumaine, "Who Needs a Boss?" *Fortune,* May 7, 1990, 52–60; Pearce and Ravlin, "The Design and Activation of Self-Regulating Work Groups."

30. Dumaine, "Who Needs a Boss?"; A. R. Montebello and V. R. Buzzotta, "Work Teams That Work," *Training and Development,* March 1993, 59–64.

31. C. Matlack, R. Tiplady, D. Brady, R. Berner, and H. Tashiro, "The Vuitton Machine," *BusinessWeek,* March 22, 2004, 98–102; "America's Most Admired Companies," *Fortune.com,* August 18, 2004, www.fortune.com/fortune/mostadmired/snapshot/0,15020,383,00.html; "Art Samberg's Ode to Steel," *Big Money Weekly,* June 29, 2004, http://trading.sina/com/trading/rightside/bigmoney_weekly_040629.b5.shtml; "Nucor Reports Record Results for First Quarter of 2004," www.nucor.com/financials.asp?finpage=news releases, August 18, 2004; "Nucor Reports Results for First Half and Second Quarter of 2004," www.nucor.com/financials.asp?finpage=newsreleases; J. C. Cooper, "The Price of Efficiency," *BusinessWeek Online,* March 22, 2004, www.businessweek.com/magazine/content/04_12/b3875603.htm; "LVHM–Fashion & Leather Goods," www.lvmh.com, June 18, 2006; C. Matlack, "Rich Times for the Luxury Sector," *BusinessWeek Online,* March 6, 2006, www.businessweek.com/globalbiz/content/mar2006/gb20060306_296309.htm?-campaign_id=search; N. Byrnes, "The Art of Motivation," *BusinessWeek,* May 1, 2006, 56–62; "Nucor Steel," http://www.nucor.com/indexinner.aspx?finpage=aboutus, April 16, 2008; "Annual General Meetings–Group Investor Relations–Corporate Governance," http://www.lvmh.com/comfi/pg_home.asp?rub=6&srub=0, March 16, 2008.

32. C. Matlack et al., "The Vuitton Machine."

33. M. Arndt, "Out of the Forge and into the Fire," *BusinessWeek,* June 18, 2001 (*BusinessWeek* Archives); N. Byrnes, "The Art of Motivation," *BusinessWeek,* May 1, 2006, 56–62; N. Byrnes, "A Steely Resolve," *BusinessWeek,* April 16, 2009, p. 054.

34. S. Baker, "The Minimill That Acts Like a Biggie," *BusinessWeek,* September 30, 1996, 101–104; S. Baker, "Nucor," *BusinessWeek,* February 13, 1995, 70; S. Overman, "No-Frills at Nucor," *HRMagazine,* July 1994, 56–60.

35. www.nucor.com, November 21, 2001; "Nucor: About Us."

36. Baker, "The Minimill That Acts Like a Biggie"; Baker, "Nucor"; Overman, "No-Frills at Nucor"; www.nucor.com; Byrnes, "The Art of Motivation"; "Nucor: About Us."

37. Matlack et al., "The Vuitton Machine"; "About Nucor"; "America's Most Admired Companies"; "Art Samberg's Ode to Steel"; "Nucor Reports Record Results for First Quarter of 2004"; "Nucor Reports Results for First Half and Second Quarter of 2004"; Byrnes, "The Art of Motivation."

38. White, "How a Company Made Everyone a Team Player."

39. T. D. Wall, N. J. Kemp, P. R. Jackson, and C. W. Clegg, "Outcomes of Autonomous Work Groups: A Long-Term Field Experiment," *Academy of Management Journal* 29 (1986), 280–304.

40. A. Markels, "A Power Producer Is Intent on Giving Power to Its People," *The Wall Street Journal,* July 3, 1995, A1, A12; "AES Corporation / The Power of Being Global," www.aes.com/aes/index?page=home, April 15, 2008.

41. W. R. Pape, "Group Insurance," *Inc.* Magazine (Technology Supplement), June 17, 1997, 29–31; A. M. Townsend, S. M. DeMarie, and A. R. Hendrickson, "Are You Ready for Virtual Teams?" *HRMagazine,* September 1996, 122–126; A. M. Townsend, S. M. DeMarie, and A. M. Hendrickson, "Virtual Teams: Technology and the Workplace of the Future," *Academy of Management Executive* 12, no. 3 (1998), 17–29.

42. Townsend et al., "Virtual Teams."

43. Pape, "Group Insurance"; Townsend et al., "Are You Ready for Virtual Teams?"; L. Gratton, "Working Together . . . When Apart," *The Wall Street Journal,* June 16–17, 2007, R4.

44. D. L. Duarte and N. T. Snyder, *Mastering Virtual Teams* (San Francisco: Jossey-Bass, 1999); K. A. Karl, "Book Reviews: *Mastering Virtual Teams,*" *Academy of Management Executive,* August 1999, 118–19.

45. B. Geber, "Virtual Teams," *Training* 32, no. 4 (August 1995), 36–40; T. Finholt and L. S. Sproull, "Electronic Groups at Work," *Organization Science* 1 (1990), 41–64.

46. Geber, "Virtual Teams."

47. E. J. Hill, B. C. Miller, S. P. Weiner, and J. Colihan, "Influences of the Virtual Office on Aspects of Work and Work/Life Balance," *Personnel Psychology* 31 (1998), 667–83; S. G. Strauss, "Technology, Group Process, and Group Outcomes: Testing the Connections in Computer-Mediated and Face-to-Face Groups," *Human Computer Interaction* 12 (1997), 227–66; M. E. Warkentin, L. Sayeed, and R. Hightower, "Virtual Teams versus Face-to-Face Teams: An Exploratory Study of a Web-Based Conference System," *Decision Sciences* 28, no. 4 (Fall 1997), 975–96.

48. S. A. Furst, M. Reeves, B. Rosen, and R. S. Blackburn, "Managing the Life Cycle of Virtual Teams," *Academy of Management Executive* 18, no. 2 (May 2004), 6–20.

49. Ibid.

50. Gratton, "Working Together . . . When Apart."

51. Ibid.

52. Ibid.

53. Ibid.

54. White, "How a Company Made Everyone a Team Player."

55. A. Deutschman, "The Managing Wisdom of High-Tech Superstars," *Fortune,* October 17, 1994, 197–206.

56. J. S. Lublin, "My Colleague, My Boss," *The Wall Street Journal,* April 12, 1995, R4, R12.

57. White, "How a Company Made Everyone a Team Player."

58. R. G. LeFauve and A. C. Hax, "Managerial and Technological Innovations at Saturn Corporation," *MIT Management,* Spring 1992, 8–19.

59. B. W. Tuckman, "Developmental Sequences in Small Groups," *Psychological Bulletin* 63 (1965), 384–99; B. W. Tuckman and M. C. Jensen, "Stages of Small Group Development," *Group and Organizational Studies* 2 (1977), 419–27.

60. C. J. G. Gersick, "Time and Transition in Work Teams: Toward a New Model of Group Development," *Academy of Management Journal* 31 (1988),

9–41; C. J. G. Gersick, "Marking Time: Predictable Transitions in Task Groups," *Academy of Management Journal* 32 (1989), 274–309.

61. J. R. Hackman, "Group Influences on Individuals in Organizations," in M. D. Dunnette and L. M. Hough, eds., *Handbook of Industrial and Organizational Psychology,* 2d ed., vol. 3 (Palo Alto, CA: Consulting Psychologists Press, 1992), 199–267.

62. Ibid.

63. Ibid.

64. Lublin, "My Colleague, My Boss."

65. L. Festinger, "Informal Social Communication," *Psychological Review* 57 (1950), 271–82; Shaw, *Group Dynamics.*

66. Hackman, "Group Influences on Individuals in Organizations"; Shaw, *Group Dynamics.*

67. D. Cartwright, "The Nature of Group Cohesiveness," in D. Cartwright and A. Zander, eds., *Group Dynamics,* 3d ed. (New York: Harper & Row, 1968); L. Festinger, S. Schacter, and K. Black, *Social Pressures in Informal Groups* (New York: Harper & Row, 1950); Shaw, *Group Dynamics.*

68. T. F. O'Boyle, "A Manufacturer Grows Efficient by Soliciting Ideas from Employees," *The Wall Street Journal,* June 5, 1992, A1, A5.

69. White, "How a Company Made Everyone a Team Player."

70. Lublin, "My Colleague, My Boss."

71. T. Kelley and J. Littman, *The Art of Innovation* (New York: Doubleday, 2001), 93.

72. Kelley and Littman, *The Art of Innovation.*

73. "Shared Commitment," www.valero.com/Work/SharedCommitment.htm, April 18, 2008.

74. R. Levering and M. Moskowitz, "100 Best Companies to Work For: The Rankings," *Fortune,* February 4, 2008, 75–94.

75. J. Guyon, "The Soul of a Moneymaking Machine," *Fortune,* October 3, 2005, 113–20.

76. Ibid.

77. Ibid.

78. Ibid.

79. P. C. Earley, "Social Loafing and Collectivism: A Comparison of the United States and the People's Republic of China," *Administrative Science Quarterly* 34 (1989), 565–81; J. M. George, "Extrinsic and Intrinsic Origins of Perceived Social Loafing in Organizations," *Academy of Management Journal* 35 (1992), 191–202; S. G. Harkins, B. Latane, and K. Williams, "Social Loafing: Allocating Effort or Taking It Easy," *Journal of Experimental Social Psychology* 16 (1980), 457–65; B. Latane, K. D. Williams, and S. Harkins, "Many Hands Make Light the Work: The Causes and Consequences of Social Loafing," *Journal of Personality and Social Psychology* 37 (1979), 822–32; J. A. Shepperd, "Productivity Loss in Performance Groups: A Motivation Analysis," *Psychological Bulletin* 113 (1993), 67–81.

80. George, "Extrinsic and Intrinsic Origins"; G. R. Jones, "Task Visibility, Free Riding, and Shirking: Explaining the Effect of Structure and Technology on Employee Behavior," *Academy of Management Review* 9 (1984), 684–95; K. Williams, S. Harkins, and B. Latane, "Identifiability as a Deterrent to Social Loafing: Two Cheering Experiments," *Journal of Personality and Social Psychology* 40 (1981), 303–11.

81. S. Harkins and J. Jackson, "The Role of Evaluation in Eliminating Social Loafing," *Personality and Social Psychology Bulletin* 11 (1985), 457–65; N. L. Kerr and S. E. Bruun, "Ringelman Revisited: Alternative Explanations for the Social Loafing Effect," *Personality and Social Psychology Bulletin* 7 (1981), 224–231; Williams et al., "Identifiability as a Deterrent to Social Loafing."

82. M. A. Brickner, S. G. Harkins, and T. M. Ostrom, "Effects of Personal Involvement: Thought-Provoking Implications for Social Loafing," *Journal of Personality and Social Psychology* 51 (1986), 763–769; S. G. Harkins and R. E. Petty, "The Effects of Task Difficulty and Task Uniqueness on Social Loafing," *Journal of Personality and Social Psychology* 43 (1982), 1214–29.

83. B. Latane, "Responsibility and Effort in Organizations," in P. S. Goodman, ed., *Designing Effective Work Groups* (San Francisco: Jossey-Bass, 1986); Latane et al., "Many Hands Make Light the Work"; I. D. Steiner, *Group Process and Productivity* (New York: Academic Press, 1972).

Chapter 12

1. J. M. O'Brien, "100 Best Companies to Work For–A Perfect Season," *Fortune,* February 4, 2008, 64–66; "Four Seasons Employees Name Company to *Fortune* '100 Best Companies to Work For' List," www.fourseasons.com/about_us/press_release_280.html, February 22, 2008; "100 Best Companies to Work For 2009: Four Seasons Hotel," http://money.cnn.com/magazines/fortune/bestcompanies/2009/snapshots/92.html, May 20, 2009.

2. "Four Seasons Employees Name Company to *Fortune* '100 Best Companies to Work For' List."

3. O'Brien, "100 Best Companies to Work For–A Perfect Season."

4. Ibid.

5. Ibid; "Creating the Four Seasons Difference," www.businessweek.com/print/innovate/content/jan2008/id20080122_671354.htm, February 22, 2008.

6. O'Brien, "100 Best Companies to Work For–A Perfect Season"; "Creating the Four Seasons Difference."

7. Ibid.; "Four Seasons Employees Name Company to *Fortune* '100 Best Companies to Work For' List."

8. O'Brien, "100 Best Companies to Work For–A Perfect Season."

9. "Creating the Four Seasons Difference."

10. O'Brien, "100 Best Companies to Work For–A Perfect Season."

11. Ibid.

12. Ibid.

13. Ibid.

14. Ibid.

15. Ibid.; "Creating the Four Seasons Difference"; "Four Seasons Employees Name Company to *Fortune* '100 Best Companies to Work For' List."

16. J. E. Butler, G. R. Ferris, and N. K. Napier, *Strategy and Human Resource Management* (Cincinnati: Southwestern Publishing, 1991); P. M. Wright and G. C. McMahan, "Theoretical Perspectives for Strategic Human Resource Management," *Journal of Management* 18 (1992), 295–320.

17. L. Clifford, "Why You Can Safely Ignore Six Sigma," *Fortune,* January 22, 2001, 140.

18. J. B. Quinn, P. Anderson, and S. Finkelstein, "Managing Professional Intellect: Making the Most of the Best," *Harvard Business Review,* March–April 1996, 71–80.

19. Ibid.

20. C. D. Fisher, L. F. Schoenfeldt, and J. B. Shaw, *Human Resource Management* (Boston: Houghton Mifflin, 1990).

21. Wright and McMahan, "Theoretical Perspectives."

22. L. Baird and I. Meshoulam, "Managing Two Fits for Strategic Human Resource Management," *Academy of Management Review* 14, 116–28; J. Milliman, M. Von Glinow, and M. Nathan, "Organizational Life Cycles and Strategic International Human Resource Management in Multinational Companies: Implications for Congruence Theory," *Academy of Management Review* 16 (1991), 318–39; R. S. Schuler and S. E. Jackson, "Linking Competitive Strategies with Human Resource Management Practices," *Academy of Management Executive* 1 (1987), 207–19; P. M. Wright and S. A. Snell, "Toward an Integrative View of Strategic Human Resource Management," *Human Resource Management Review* 1 (1991), 203–225.

23. Equal Employment Opportunity Commission, "Uniform Guidelines on Employee Selection Procedures," *Federal Register* 43 (1978), 38290–315.

24. R. Stogdill II, R. Mitchell, K. Thurston, and C. Del Valle, "Why AIDS Policy Must Be a Special Policy," *BusinessWeek,* February 1, 1993, 53–54.

25. J. M. George, "AIDS/AIDS-Related Complex," in L. Peters, B. Greer, and S. Youngblood, eds., *The Blackwell Encyclopedic Dictionary of Human Resource Management* (Oxford, England: Blackwell Publishers, 1997).

26. Ibid.

27. Ibid.; Stogdill et al., "Why AIDS Policy Must Be a Special Policy"; K. Holland, "Out of Retirement and Into Uncertainty," *The New York Times,* May 27, 2007, BU17.

28. S. L. Rynes, "Recruitment, Job Choice, and Post-Hire Consequences: A Call for New Research Directions," in M. D. Dunnette and L. M. Hough, eds., *Handbook of Industrial and Organizational Psychology,* vol. 2 (Palo Alto, CA: Consulting Psychologists Press, 1991), 399–444.

29. E. Porter, "Send Jobs to India? U.S. Companies Say It's Not Always Best," *The New York Times,* April 28, 2004, A1, A7.

30. D. Wessel, "The Future of Jobs: New Ones Arise; Wage Gap Widens," *The Wall Street Journal,* April 2, 2004, A1, A5; "Relocating the Back Office," *The Economist,* December 13, 2003, 67–69.

31. Porter, "Send Jobs to India?"

32. Ibid.

33. "Learning to Live with Offshoring," *BusinessWeek,* January 30, 2006, 122.

34. "Offshoring: Spreading the Gospel," *BusinessWeek Online,* March 6, 2006 (www.businessweek.com/print/magazine/content/06_10/b3974074.htm?chan=gl).

35. Ibid.; "Genpact: Management Team," www.genpact.com/aboutus.asp?key=1&page=team.htm&submenu=0, April 25, 2006; "Genpact," www.genpact.com/genpact/aboutus?key=1, April 25, 2006; "Genpact: Growth History," www.genpact.com/genpact/aboutus.asp?key=1&page=growth.htm, April 25, 2006.

36. "Genpact: Management Team"; "Genpact."

37. "Offshoring: Spreading the Gospel."

38. Ibid.

39. R. J. Harvey, "Job Analysis," in Dunnette and Hough, *Handbook of Industrial and Organizational Psychology,* 71–163.

40. E. L. Levine, *Everything You Always Wanted to Know about Job Analysis: A Job Analysis Primer* (Tampa, FL: Mariner Publishing, 1983).

41. R. L. Mathis and J. H. Jackson, *Human Resource Management,* 7th ed. (Minneapolis: West, 1994).

42. Rynes, "Recruitment, Job Choice, and Post-Hire Consequences."

43. R. Sharpe, "The Life of the Party? Can Jeff Taylor Keep the Good Times Rolling at Monster.com?" *BusinessWeek,* June 4, 2001 (*BusinessWeek* Archives); D. H. Freedman, "The Monster Dilemma," *Inc.* Magazine, May 2007, 77–78; P. Korkki, "So Easy to Apply, So Hard to Be Noticed," *The New York Times,* July 1, 2007, BU16.

44. www.monster.com, June 2001.

45. www.jobline.org, Jobline press releases, May 8, 2001, accessed June 20, 2001.

46. J. Spolsky, "There Is a Better Way to Find and Hire the Very Best Employees," *Inc.* Magazine, May 2007, 81–82; "About the Company," www.fogcreek.com/, March 5, 2008; "Fog Creek Software," www.fogcreek.com/, March 5, 2008.

47. Spolsky, "There Is a Better Way to Find and Hire the Very Best Employees"; "Fog Creek Software."

48. Spolsky, "There Is a Better Way to Find and Hire the Very Best Employees."

49. Ibid.

50. Ibid.

51. Ibid.

52. Ibid.

53. Ibid.; "About the Company"; "Fog Creek Software."

54. Spolsky, "There Is a Better Way to Find and Hire the Very Best Employees."

55. R. M. Guion, "Personnel Assessment, Selection, and Placement," in Dunnette and Hough, *Handbook of Industrial and Organizational Psychology,* 327–97.

56. T. Joyner, "Job Background Checks Surge," *Houston Chronicle,* May 2, 2005, D6.

57. Ibid.; "ADP News Releases: Employer Services: ADP Hiring Index Reveals Background Checks Performed More Than Tripled Since 1997," Automatic Data Processing, Inc., June 3, 2006, www.investquest.com/iq/a/aud/ne/news/adp042505background.htm.

58. "ADP News Releases."

59. R. A. Noe, J. R. Hollenbeck, B. Gerhart, and P. M. Wright, *Human Resource Management: Gaining a Competitive Advantage* (Burr Ridge, IL: Irwin, 1994); J. A. Wheeler and J. A. Gier, "Reliability and Validity of the Situational Interview for a Sales Position," *Journal of Applied Psychology* 2 (1987), 484–87.

60. J. Flint, "Can You Tell Applesauce from Pickles?" *Forbes,* October 9, 1995, 106–8.

61. Ibid.

62. "Wanted: Middle Managers, Audition Required," *The Wall Street Journal,* December 28, 1995, A1.

63. I. L. Goldstein, "Training in Work Organizations," in Dunnette and Hough,

Handbook of Industrial and Organizational Psychology, 507–619.

64. N. Banerjee, "For Mary Kay Sales Reps in Russia, Hottest Shade Is the Color of Money," *The Wall Street Journal,* August 30, 1995, A8.

65. T. D. Allen, L. T. Eby, M. L. Poteet, E. Lentz, and L. Lima, "Career Benefits Associated with Mentoring for Protégés: A Meta-Analysis," *Journal of Applied Psychology* 89, no. 1 (2004), 127–36.

66. P. Garfinkel, "Putting a Formal Stamp on Mentoring," *The New York Times,* January 18, 2004, BU10.

67. Ibid.

68. Allen et al., "Career Benefits Associated with Mentoring"; L. Levin, "Lesson Learned: Know Your Limits; Get Outside Help Sooner Rather Than Later," *BusinessWeek Online,* July 5, 2004, www.businessweek.com; "Family, Inc.," *BusinessWeek Online,* November 10, 2003, www.businessweek.com; J. Salamon, "A Year with a Mentor; Now Comes the Test," *The New York Times,* September 30, 2003, B1, B5; E. White, "Making Mentorships Work," *The Wall Street Journal,* October 23, 2007, B11.

69. Garfinkel, "Putting a Formal Stamp on Mentoring."

70. Fisher et al., *Human Resource Management.*

71. Ibid.; G. P. Latham and K. N. Wexley, *Increasing Productivity through Performance Appraisal* (Reading, MA: Addison-Wesley, 1982).

72. J. S. Lublin, "It's Shape-Up Time for Performance Reviews," *The Wall Street Journal,* October 3, 1994, B1, B2.

73. J. S. Lublin, "Turning the Tables: Underlings Evaluate Bosses," *The Wall Street Journal,* October 4, 1994, B1, B14; S. Shellenbarger, "Reviews from Peers Instruct–and Sting," *The Wall Street Journal,* October 4, 1994, B1, B4.

74. C. Borman and D. W. Bracken, "360 Degree Appraisals," in C. L. Cooper and C. Argyris, eds., *The Concise Blackwell Encyclopedia of Management* (Oxford, England: Blackwell Publishers, 1998), 17; D. W. Bracken, "Straight Talk about Multi-Rater Feedback," *Training and Development* 48 (1994), 44–51; M. R. Edwards, W. C. Borman, and J. R. Sproul, "Solving the Double-Bind in Performance Appraisal: A Saga of Solves, Sloths, and Eagles," *Business Horizons* 85 (1985), 59–68.

75. M. A. Peiperl, "Getting 360 Degree Feedback Right," *Harvard Business Review,* January 2001, 142–47.

76. A. Harrington, "Workers of the World, Rate Your Boss!" *Fortune,* September 18, 2000, 340, 342; www.ImproveNow.com, June 2001.

77. S. E. Moss and J. I. Sanchez, "Are Your Employees Avoiding You? Managerial Strategies for Closing the Feedback Gap," *Academy of Management Executive* 18, no. 1 (2004), 32–46.

78. J. Flynn and F. Nayeri, "Continental Divide over Executive Pay," *BusinessWeek,* July 3, 1995, 40–41.

79. J. A. Byrne, "How High Can CEO Pay Go?" *BusinessWeek,* April 22, 1996, 100–6.

80. A. Borrus, "A Battle Royal against Regal Paychecks," *BusinessWeek,* February 24, 2003, 127; "Too Many Turkeys," *The Economist,* November 26, 2005, 75–76; G. Morgenson, "How to Slow Runaway Executive Pay," *The New York Times,* October 23, 2005, 1, 4.

81. "Executive Pay."

82. "Home Depot Chief's Pay in 2007 Could Reach $8.9m.," *The New York Times,* January 25, 2007, C7; E. Carr, "The Stockpot," *The Economist, A Special Report on Executive Pay,* January 20, 2007, 6–10; E. Porter, "More Than Ever, It Pays to Be the Top Executive," *The New York Times,* May 25, 2007, A1, C7.

83. E. Tahmincioglu, "Paths to Better Health (On the Boss's Nickel)," *The New York Times,* May 23, 2004, BU7.

84. Ibid.

85. K. K. Spors, "Top Small Workplaces 2007," *The Wall Street Journal,* October 1, 2007, R1–R6; K. K. Spors, "Guerra DeBerry Coody," *The Wall Street Journal,* October 1, 2007, R5; "Guerra DeBerry Coody Named One of the Nation's 15 Top Small Workplaces of 2007," *Business Wire,* http://findarticles.com/p/articles/mi_m0EIN/is_2007_Oct_1/ai_n20527510/print, March 6, 2008; "Guerra DeBerry Coody," www.gdc-co.com/, March 6, 2008; "Frank Guerra '83, Trish DeBerry-Mejia '87 and Tess Coody '93," *Trinity University, Alumni–Profiles,* www.trinity.edu/alumni/profiles/0503_guerra_deberry_coody.htm, March 6, 2008.

86. Spors, "Top Small Workplaces 2007"; Spors, "Guerra DeBerry Coody"; "Guerra DeBerry Coody Named One of the Nation's 15 Top Small Workplaces of 2007."

87. Spors, "Top Small Workplaces 2007"; Spors, "Guerra DeBerry Coody."

88. Ibid.

89. Ibid.

90. "Guerra DeBerry Coody Named One of the Nation's 15 Top Small Workplaces of 2007."

91. S. Shellenbarger, "Amid Gay Marriage Debate, Companies Offer More Benefits to Same-Sex Couples," *The Wall Street Journal,* March 18, 2004, D1.

92. S. Premack and J. E. Hunter, "Individual Unionization Decisions," *Psychological Bulletin* 103 (1988), 223–34.

93. M. B. Regan, "Shattering the AFL-CIO's Glass Ceiling," *BusinessWeek,* November 13, 1995, 46.

94. www.aflcio.org, June 2001; "AFL-CIO About Us," http://www.aflcio.org/aboutus/index.cfm?RenderForPrint=1, 5120/2009.

95. G. P. Zachary, "Some Unions Step Up Organizing Campaigns and Get New Members," *The Wall Street Journal,* September 1, 1995, A1, A2.

Chapter 13

1. www.hermanmiller.com, 2008.

2. N. B. Macintosh, *The Social Software of Accounting Information Systems* (New York: Wiley, 1995).

3. C. A. O'Reilly, "Variations in Decision Makers' Use of Information: The Impact of Quality and Accessibility," *Academy of Management Journal* 25 (1982), 756–71.

4. G. Stalk and T. H. Hout, *Competing Against Time* (New York: Free Press, 1990).

5. L. Uchitelle, "Airlines Off Course," *San Francisco Chronicle,* September 15, 1991, 7.

6. R. Cyert and J. March, *Behavioral Theory of the Firm* (Englewood Cliffs, NJ: Prentice Hall, 1963).

7. R. Brandt, "Agents and Artificial Life," *BusinessWeek: The Information Revolution,* special issue (1994), 64–68.

8. E. Turban, *Decision Support and Expert Systems* (New York: Macmillan, 1988).

9. R. I. Benjamin and J. Blunt, "Critical IT Issues: The Next Ten Years," *Sloan Management Review* (Summer 1992), 7–19; W. H. Davidow and M. S. Malone, *The Virtual Corporation* (New York: Harper Business, 1992).

10. Davidow and Malone, *The Virtual Corporation;* M. E. Porter, *Competitive Advantage* (New York: Free Press, 1984).

11. T. J. Mullaney, "This Race Isn't Even Close," *BusinessWeek,* December 18, 2000, 208–9.

12. S. M. Dornbusch and W. R. Scott, *Evaluation and the Exercise of Authority* (San Francisco: Jossey-Bass, 1975).

13. J. Child, *Organization: A Guide to Problems and Practice* (London: Harper and Row, 1984).

14. www.fedex.com, 2009.

15. Ibid.

16. Macintosh, *The Social Software of Accounting Information Systems.*

17. B. Dumaine, "The Bureaucracy Busters," *Fortune,* June 17, 1991, 46.

18. C. A. O'Reilly and L. R. Pondy, "Organizational Communication," in S. Kerr, ed., *Organizational Behavior* (Columbus, OH: Grid, 1979).

19. M. Totty, "The Path to Better Teamwork," *The Wall Street Journal,* May 20, 2004, R4; "Collaborative Software," *Wikipedia,* August 25, 2004, en.wikipedia.org/wiki/Collaborative_software; "Collaborative Groupware Software," www.svpal.org/grantbow/groupware.html, August 25, 2004.

20. Totty, "The Path to Better Teamwork"; "Collaborative Software."

21. Ibid.; "Collaborative Groupware Software."

22. Totty, "The Path to Better Teamwork"; "Collaborative Software."

23. Ibid.

24. Ibid.

25. E. M. Rogers and R. Agarwala-Rogers, *Communication in Organizations* (New York: Free Press, 1976).

26. W. Nabers, "The New Corporate Uniforms," *Fortune,* November 13, 1995, 132–56.

27. R. B. Schmitt, "Judges Try Curbing Lawyers' Body-Language Antics," *The Wall Street Journal,* September 11, 1997, B1, B7.

28. D. A. Adams, P. A. Todd, and R. R. Nelson, "A Comparative Evaluation of the Impact of Electronic and Voice Mail on Organizational Communication," *Information and Management* 24 (1993), 9–21.

29. R. Winslow, "Hospitals' Weak Systems Hurt Patients, Study Says," *The Wall Street Journal,* July 5, 1995, B1, B6.

30. C. Hymowitz, "Sometimes, Moving Up Makes It Harder to See What Goes On Below," *The Wall Street Journal,* October 15, 2007, B1.

31. Ibid.; J. Sandberg, "Shooting Messengers Makes Us Feel Better but Work Dumber," *The Wall Street Journal,* September 11, 2007, B1.

32. Hymowitz, "Sometimes, Moving Up Makes It Harder to See What Goes On Below"; "FatWire Software Appoints Former CA Executive Yogesh Gupta President and CEO," http://news.manta.com/press/description/200708070500230_66132700_ 1-0304, April 23, 2008.

33. "Management," *FatWire US: Company–Management,* www.fatwire.com/cs/ Satellite/ManagementPage_US.html, April 23, 2008; "Company Overview," *Company Overview–CA,* www.ca.com/us/ca.aspx, April 24, 2008.

34. Hymowitz, "Sometimes, Moving Up Makes It Harder to See What Goes On Below."

35. Ibid.

36. Ibid.

37. K. Holland, "The Silent May Have Something to Say," *The New York Times,* November 5, 2006, http://www.nytimes.com/2006/11/05/business/yourmoney/05mgmt.html, June 29, 2008.

38. Ibid.

39. Ibid.

40. Ibid.

41. R. L. Daft, R. H. Lengel, and L. K. Trevino, "Message Equivocality, Media Selection, and Manager Performance: Implications for Information Systems," *MIS Quarterly* 11 (1987), 355–66; R. L. Daft and R. H. Lengel, "Information Richness: A New Approach to Managerial Behavior and Organization Design," in B. M. Staw and L. L. Cummings, eds., *Research in Organizational Behavior* (Greenwich, CT: JAI Press, 1984).

42. R. L. Daft, *Organization Theory and Design* (St. Paul, MN: West, 1992).

43. "Lights, Camera, Meeting: Teleconferencing Becomes a Time-Saving Tool," *The Wall Street Journal,* February 21, 1995, A1.

44. Daft, *Organization Theory and Design.*

45. T. J. Peters and R. H. Waterman Jr., *In Search of Excellence* (New York: Harper and Row, 1982); T. Peters and N. Austin, *A Passion for Excellence: The Leadership Difference* (New York: Random House, 1985).

46. "Lights, Camera, Meeting."

47. R. Kirkland, "Cisco's Display of Strength," *Fortune,* November 12, 2007, 90–100; "Cisco TelePresence Overview," Overview *(TelePresence)–Cisco Systems,* www.cisco.com/en/US/solutions/ns669/networking_solutions_products_genericcont . . ., April 25, 2008.

48. R. Kirkland, "Cisco's Display of Strength."

49. Ibid.; "Cisco TelePresence Overview."

50. "E-Mail Etiquette Starts to Take Shape for Business Messaging," *The Wall Street Journal,* October 12, 1995, A1.

51. E. Baig, "Taking Care of Business–Without Leaving the House," *BusinessWeek,* April 17, 1995, 106–7.

52. "Life Is Good for Telecommuters, but Some Problems Persist," *The Wall Street Journal,* August 3, 1995, A1.

53. "E-Mail Abuse: Workers Discover High-Tech Ways to Cause Trouble in the Office," *The Wall Street Journal,* November 22, 1994, A1; "E-Mail Alert: Companies Lag in Devising Policies on How It Should Be Used," *The Wall Street Journal,* December 29, 1994, A1.

54. "Employee-Newsletter Names Include the Good, the Bad, and the Boring," *The Wall Street Journal,* July 18, 1995, A1.

55. A. Overholt, "Intel's Got [Too Much] Mail," *Fast Company,* March 2001, 56–58.

56. Ibid.

57. Ibid.

58. www.intel.com, 2001.

59. J. J. Donovan, *Business Re-Engineering with Information Technology* (Englewood Cliffs, NJ: Prentice Hall, 1994); C. W. L. Hill, "The Computer Industry: The New Industry of Industries," in C. W. L. Hill and G. R. Jones, *Strategic Management: An Integrated Approach,* 3d ed. (Boston: Houghton Mifflin, 1995).

60. E. Rich, *Artificial Intelligence* (New York: McGraw-Hill, 1983).

61. Brandt, "Agents and Artificial Life."

62. www.ibm.com, 2001.

63. A. D. Chandler, *The Visible Hand* (Cambridge, MA: Harvard University Press, 1977).

64. C. W. L. Hill and J. F. Pickering, "Divisionalization, Decentralization, and Performance of Large United Kingdom Companies," *Journal of Management Studies* 23 (1986), 26–50.

65. O. E. Williamson, *Markets and Hierarchies: Analysis and Anti-Trust Implications* (New York: Free Press, 1975).

66. www.fedex.com, 2009.

67. Turban, *Decision Support and Expert Systems.*

68. Ibid., 346.

69. Rich, *Artificial Intelligence.*

70. N. A. Nichols, "Scientific Management at Merck: An Interview with CFO Judy Lewent," *Harvard Business Review,* January–February 1994, 88–91.

71. P. P. Bonisson and H. E. Johnson, "Expert Systems for Diesel Electric Locomotive Repair," *Human Systems Management* 4 (1985), 1–25.

Chapter 14

1. The view of quality as including reliability goes back to the work of W. Edwards Deming and Joseph Juran. See A. Gabor, *The Man Who Discovered Quality* (New York: Times Books, 1990).

2. D. F. Abell, *Defining the Business: The Starting Point of Strategic Planning* (Englewood Cliffs, NJ: Prentice Hall, 1980).

3. For details, see "Johnson & Johnson (A)," *Harvard Business School Case* #384-053.

4. M. E. Porter, *Competitive Advantage* (New York: Free Press, 1985).

5. This is a central insight of the modern manufacturing literature. See R. H. Hayes and S. C. Wheelwright, "Link Manufacturing Process and Product Life Cycles," *Harvard Business Review* (January–February 1979), 127–36; R. H. Hayes and S. C. Wheelwright, "Competing through Manufacturing," *Harvard Business Review* (January–February 1985), 99–109.

6. B. O'Brian, "Flying on the Cheap," *The Wall Street Journal,* October 26, 1992, A1; B. O'Reilly, "Where Service Flies Right," *Fortune,* August 24, 1992, 116–17; A. Salpukas, "Hurt in Expansion, Airlines Cut Back and May Sell Hubs," *The Wall Street Journal,* April 1, 1993, A1, C8.

7. www.ciu.com, 2006.

8. www.crm.com, 2006.

9. The view of quality as reliability goes back to the work of Deming and Juran; see Gabor, *The Man Who Discovered Quality.*

10. See D. Garvin, "What Does Product Quality Really Mean?" *Sloan Management Review* 26 (Fall 1984), 25–44; P. B. Crosby, *Quality Is Free* (New York: Mentor Books, 1980); Gabor, *The Man Who Discovered Quality.*

11. www.jdpa.com, 2006.

12. J. Griffiths, "Europe's Manufacturing Quality and Productivity Still Lag Far behind Japan's," *Financial Times,* November 4, 1994, 11.

13. S. McCartney, "Compaq Borrows Wal-Mart's Idea to Boost Production," *The Wall Street Journal,* June 17, 1994, B4.

14. R. Gourlay, "Back to Basics on the Factory Floor," *Financial Times,* January 4, 1994, 12.

15. P. Nemetz and L. Fry, "Flexible Manufacturing Organizations: Implications for Strategy Formulation," *Academy of Management Review* 13 (1988), 627–38; N. Greenwood, *Implementing Flexible Manufacturing Systems* (New York: Halstead Press, 1986).

16. M. Williams, "Back to the Past," *The Wall Street Journal,* October 24, 1994, A1.

17. C. Salter, "This Is One Fast Factory," *Fast Company,* August 2001, 32–33.

18. G. Stalk and T. M. Hout, *Competing Against Time* (New York: Free Press, 1990).

19. For an interesting discussion of some other drawbacks of JIT and other "Japanese" manufacturing techniques, see S. M. Young, "A Framework for Successful Adoption and Performance of Japanese Manufacturing Practices in the United States," *Academy of Management Review* 17 (1992), 677–701.

20. T. Stundza, "Massachusetts Switch Maker Switches to Kanban," *Purchasing,* November 16, 2000, 103.

21. B. Dumaine, "The Trouble with Teams," *Fortune,* September 5, 1994, 86–92.

22. See C. W. L. Hill, "Transaction Cost Economizing, National Institutional Structures, and Competitive Advantage: The Case of Japan," *Organization Science* (1995), 119–31; M. Aoki, *Information, Incentives, and Bargaining in the Japanese Economy* (Cambridge: Cambridge University Press, 1989).

23. J. Hoerr, "The Payoff from Teamwork," *BusinessWeek,* July 10, 1989, 56–62.

24. M. Hammer and J. Champy, *Reengineering the Corporation* (New York: Harper Business, 1993), 35.

25. Ibid., 46.

26. Ibid.

27. For example, see V. Houlder, "Two Steps Forward, One Step Back," *Financial Times,* October 31, 1994, 8; Amal Kumar Naj, "Shifting Gears," *The Wall Street Journal,* May 7, 1993, A1; D. Greising, "Quality: How to Make It Pay," *BusinessWeek,* August 8, 1994, 54–59.

28. L. Helm and M. Edid, "Life on the Line: Two Auto Workers Who Are Worlds Apart," *BusinessWeek,* September 30, 1994, 76–78.

29. Dumaine, "The Trouble with Teams."

Appendix B

1. J. H. Greenhaus, *Career Management* (New York: Dryden Press, 1987).

2. L. Lovelle, "A Payday for Performance" *Business Week,* April 18, 2005, pp. 78–80.

3. M. J. Driver, "Careers: A Review of Personal and Organizational Research," in C. L. Cooper and I. Robertson (eds.), *International Review of Industrial and Organizational Psychology* (New York: Wiley, 1988).

4. Ibid.

5. M. J. Driver, "Careers: A Review of Personnel and Organizational Research," in C. L. Cooper and I. Robertson, eds., *International Review of Industrial and Organizational Psychology* (New York: Wiley, 1988).

6. *Career Path* (recruitment material provided by Dillard's, Inc., 1994).

7. J. H. Greenhaus, *Career Management* (New York: Dryden Press, 1987).

8. M. B. Arthur, "The Boundaryless Career: A New Perspective for Organizational Inquiry," *Journal of Organizational Behavior* 15 (1994), 295–306; M. B. Arthur and D. M. Rousseau, *The Boundaryless Career: A New Employment Principle for a New Organizational Era* (New York: Oxford University Press, 1996), 237–55; "Introduction: The Boundaryless Career as a New Employment Principle," in M. B. Arthur and D. M. Rousseau (eds.) *The Boundaryless Career: A New Employment Principle for a New Organizational Era* (New York: Oxford University Press, 1996), 3–20; L. T. Eby et al., "Predictors of Success in the Era of the Boundaryless Career," *Journal of Organizational Behavior* 24 (2003), 689–708; S. C. de Janasz, S. E. Sullivan and V. Whiting, "Mentor Networks and Career Success: Lessons for Turbulent Times," *Academy of Management Executive* 17, no. 4 (2003), 78–91.

9. N. Griffin, "Personalize Your Management Development," *Harvard Business Review,* March 2003, 113–19.

10. Driver, "Careers: A Review of Personal and Organizational Research."

11. Greenhaus, *Career Management.*

12. J. L. Holland, *Making Vocational Choices: A Theory of Careers* (Englewood Cliffs, NJ: Prentice Hall, 1973).

13. Greenhaus, *Career Management.*

14. Ibid.

15. G. Dreher and R. Ash, "A Comparative Study of Mentoring Among Men and Women in Managerial, Professional, and Technical Positions," *Journal of Applied Psychology* 75 (1990), 525–35; T. A. Scandura, "Mentorship and Career Mobility: An Empirical Investigation," *Journal of Organizational Behavior* 13 (1992), 169–74; D. B. Turban and T. W. Dougherty, "The Role of Protégé Personality in Receipt of Mentoring and Career Success," *Academy of Management Journal* 37 (1994), 688–702; W. Whitely, T. W. Dougherty, and G. F. Dreher, "Relationship of Career Mentoring and Socioeconomic Origin to Managers' and Professionals' Early Career Success," *Academy of Management Journal* 34 (1991), 331–51.

16. T. P. Ference, J. A. F. Stoner, and E. K. Warren, "Managing the Career Plateau," *Academy of Management Review* 2 (1977), 602–12.

Photo Credits

Chapter 1

page 2 Michael Nagle/Getty Images

page 8 Harry Cabluck/AP Images

page 10 Mark Peterson/Redux Pictures

page 18 Scott Olson/Getty Images

page 24 Chuck Kennedy/MCT/Landov

page 25 Bill Aron/Photoedit

Appendix A

page 36 Bettmann/Corbis

page 38 The Granger Collection, New York

page 39 With permission from Henley Management College

page 40 Fox Photos/Getty Images

Chapter 2

page 45 Ken Hawkins Photography

page 51 Paul Drinkwater/NBCU Photo Bank via AP Images

page 55 Courtesy Gentle Giant Moving Company

page 58 Corbis

page 64 Courtesy IDEO

page 67 Damian Dovarganes/AP Images

Chapter 3

page 79 Tim Boyle/Getty Images

page 82 The Granger Collection, New York

page 85 Susan Walsh/AP Images

page 100 Blend Images/Alamy

page 105 Ellen B. Senisi/The Image Works

page 106 Courtesy Chubb Group of Insurance Companies

Chapter 4

page 121 Guang Niu/Getty Images

page 125 The News Tribune/Lui Kit Wong/AP Images

page 132 AP Images

page 135 Pat Wellenbach/AP Images

page 138 © Reuters/Rupak De Chowdhari/Landov

page 143 Bob Daemmrich/The Image Works

page 146 © Kazuhiro Nogi/AFP/Getty Images

Chapter 5

page 157 Christof Stache/AP Images

page 160 Christopher Robbins/Getty Images/Digital Vision

page 171 © Corbis

page 175 Marc Romanelli/Getty Images/Workbook Stock

page 177 Courtesy World of Good, Inc.

page 178 © Image 100/Corbis

Chapter 6

page 187 Stephen Hird/Reuters/Corbis

page 190 Ryan McVay/Getty Images

page 199 Mel Evans/AP Photo

page 204 Courtesy Cott Corporation

page 205 Courtesy of Inditex

page 210 Bill Varie/Corbis

page 212 top Katsumi Kasahara/AP Images

page 212 bottom Pablo Bartholomew/Getty Images

Chapter 7

page 223 Jennifer Graylock/AP Images

page 228 Jeffery Allan Salter/Corbis

page 233 Tim Boyle/Getty Images

page 235 Kim Steele/Photodisc/Green/Getty Images

page 237 © Nokia

page 240 Orlin Wagner/AP Images

page 246 Tom Raymond/Getty Images

page 251 AP Images

Chapter 8

page 259 Fabrizio Costantini/The New York Times/Redux

page 262 Willie Hiu, Jr./The Image Works

page 263 Tomas dec Amo/Index Stock

page 270 Harry Cabluck/AP Images

page 273 Al Behrman/AP Images

page 278 David Frazier/The Image Works

page 280 AP Images

page 284 Felix Clay/Financial Times-REA/Redux

Chapter 9

page 295 Joe Raedle/Getty Images

page 302 Courtesy of The Container Store

page 305 Mick Tsikas/eps/Corbis

page 307 Copyright © 2008. SAS Institute Inc. All rights reserved. Reproduced with permission of SAS Institute Inc., Cary NC, USA.

page 311 Stockbyte/Punchstock Images

page 315 2005 Comstock Images, JupiterImages Corporation

page 317 The Decatur Daily/John Godbey/AP Images

Chapter 10

page 327 Frank Micelotta/Getty Images

page 330 Courtesy of Zingerman's

page 338 Royalty-Free/Corbis

page 343 Banana Stock, Ltd.

page 348 Courtesy of Creative Display Solutions, Inc.

Chapter 11

page 357 Courtesy ICU Medical, Inc. Eric Glover, photographer

page 361 Ryan McVay/Photodisc Blue/Getty Images

page 365 Alexandra Boulat VII/AP Images

page 367 Keith Brofsky/Getty Images/Photodisc

page 378 Haraz Ghanbari/AP Images

Chapter 12

page 389 Kevork Djansezian/AP Images

page 397 Amy Etra/Photoedit

page 399 Courtesy Fog Creek Software

page 401 Chabruken/Getty Images

page 404 Reza Estakhrian/Getty Images/Photographers Choice

page 412 Ann Heisenfelt/AP Images

page 413 Photo by Jess Haessler, Courtesy Guerra DeBerry Coody

page 415 Reed Saxon/AP Images

Chapter 13

page 423 Courtesy of Herman Miller, Inc.

page 428 Getty Images for DHL

page 432 Christopher Robbins/Digital Vision/Getty Images

page 436 Digital Vision/Getty Images

page 437 Copyright 2008 NBAE, Photo by Jennifer Pottheiser/NBAE via Getty Images

page 441 Justin Sullivan/Getty Images

page 446 Reuters/China News photo/Landov

Chapter 14

page 453 Toshifumi Kitamura/AFP/Getty Images

page 456 AP Images

page 463 Courtesy Dell Computer Corporation

page 467 Justin Sullivan/Getty Images

Appendix B

page 474 Al Behrman/AP Images

Index

Names

A

B

C

D

E

F

K

L

M

S

T

U

V

W

X

Y

Z

Subject

A

B

C

H

M

N

O

Q

R

S

T

U

V

W

Companies

A

C